T0216163

Lecture Notes in Computer Science

Vol. 60: Operating Systems, An Advanced Course. Edited by R. Bayer, R. M. Graham, and G. Seegmüller. X, 593 pages. 1978.

Vol. 61: The Vienna Development Method: The Meta-Language. Edited by D. Bjørner and C. B. Jones. XVIII, 382 pages. 1978.

Vol. 62: Automata, Languages and Programming. Proceedings 1978. Edited by G. Ausiello and C. Böhm. VIII, 508 pages. 1978.

Vol. 63: Natural Language Communication with Computers. Edited by Leonard Bolc. VI, 292 pages. 1978.

Vol. 64: Mathematical Foundations of Computer Science. Proceedings 1978. Edited by J. Winkowski. X, 551 pages. 1978.

Vol. 65: Information Systems Methodology, Proceedings, 1978. Edited by G. Bracchi and P. C. Lockemann. XII, 696 pages. 1978.

Vol. 66: N. D. Jones and S. S. Muchnick, TEMPO: A Unified Treatment of Binding Time and Parameter Passing Concepts in Programming Languages. IX, 118 pages. 1978.

Vol. 67: Theoretical Computer Science, 4th GI Conference, Aachen, March 1979. Edited by K. Weihrauch. VII, 324 pages. 1979.

Vol. 68: D. Harel, First-Order Dynamic Logic. X, 133 pages. 1979.

Vol. 69: Program Construction. International Summer School. Edited by F. L. Bauer and M. Broy. VII, 651 pages. 1979.

Vol. 70: Semantics of Concurrent Computation. Proceedings 1979. Edited by G. Kahn. VI, 368 pages. 1979.

Vol. 71: Automata, Languages and Programming. Proceedings 1979. Edited by H. A. Maurer. IX, 684 pages. 1979.

Vol. 72: Symbolic and Algebraic Computation. Proceedings 1979. Edited by E. W. Ng. XV, 557 pages. 1979.

Vol. 73: Graph-Grammars and Their Application to Computer Science and Biology. Proceedings 1978. Edited by V. Claus, H. Ehrig and G. Rozenberg. VII, 477 pages. 1979.

Vol. 74: Mathematical Foundations of Computer Science. Proceedings 1979. Edited by J. Bečvář. IX, 580 pages. 1979.

Vol. 75: Mathematical Studies of Information Processing. Proceedings 1978. Edited by E. K. Blum, M. Paul and S. Takasu. VIII, 629 pages. 1979.

Vol. 76: Codes for Boundary-Value Problems in Ordinary Differential Equations. Proceedings 1978. Edited by B. Childs et al. VIII, 388 pages. 1979.

Vol. 77: G. V. Bochmann, Architecture of Distributed Computer Systems. VIII, 238 pages. 1979.

Vol. 78: M. Gordon, R. Milner and C. Wadsworth, Edinburgh LCF. VIII, 159 pages. 1979.

Vol. 79: Language Design and Programming Methodology. Proceedings, 1979. Edited by J. Tobias. IX, 255 pages. 1980.

Vol. 80: Pictorial Information Systems. Edited by S. K. Chang and K. S. Fu. IX, 445 pages. 1980.

Vol. 81: Data Base Techniques for Pictorial Applications. Proceedings, 1979. Edited by A. Blaser. XI, 599 pages. 1980.

Vol. 82: J. G. Sanderson, A Relational Theory of Computing. VI, 147 pages. 1980.

Vol. 83: International Symposium Programming. Proceedings, 1980. Edited by B. Robinet. VII, 341 pages. 1980.

Vol. 84: Net Theory and Applications. Proceedings, 1979. Edited by W. Brauer. XIII, 537 Seiten. 1980.

Vol. 85: Automata, Languages and Programming. Proceedings, 1980. Edited by J. de Bakker and J. van Leeuwen. VIII, 671 pages. 1980.

Vol. 86: Abstract Software Specifications. Proceedings, 1979. Edited by D. Bjørner. XIII, 567 pages. 1980

Vol. 87: 5th Conference on Automated Deduction. Proceedings, 1980. Edited by W. Bibel and R. Kowalski. VII, 385 pages. 1980.

Vol. 88: Mathematical Foundations of Computer Science 1980. Proceedings, 1980. Edited by P. Dembiński. VIII, 723 pages. 1980.

Vol. 89: Computer Aided Design - Modelling, Systems Engineering, CAD-Systems. Proceedings, 1980. Edited by J. Encarnacao. XIV, 461 pages. 1980.

Vol. 90: D. M. Sandford, Using Sophisticated Models in Resolution Theorem Proving.
XI, 239 pages. 1980

Vol. 91: D. Wood, Grammar and L Forms: An Introduction. IX, 314 pages. 1980.

Vol. 92: R. Milner, A Calculus of Communication Systems. VI, 171 pages. 1980.

Vol. 93: A. Nijholt, Context-Free Grammars: Covers, Normal Forms, and Parsing. VII, 253 pages. 1980.

Vol. 94: Semantics-Directed Compiler Generation. Proceedings, 1980. Edited by N. D. Jones. V, 489 pages. 1980.

Vol. 95: Ch. D. Marlin, Coroutines. XII, 246 pages. 1980.

Vol. 96: J. L. Peterson, Computer Programs for Spelling Correction: VI, 213 pages. 1980.

Vol. 97: S. Osaki and T. Nishio, Reliability Evaluation of Some Fault-Tolerant Computer Architectures. VI, 129 pages. 1980.

Vol. 98: Towards a Formal Description of Ada. Edited by D. Bjørner and O. N. Oest. XIV, 630 pages. 1980.

Vol. 99: I. Guessarian, Algebraic Semantics. XI, 158 pages. 1981.

Vol. 100: Graphtheoretic Concepts in Computer Science. Edited by H. Noltemeier. X, 403 pages. 1981.

Vol. 101: A. Thayse, Boolean Calculus of Differences. VII, 144 pages. 1981.

Vol. 102: J. H. Davenport, On the Integration of Algebraic Functions. 1–197 pages. 1981.

Vol. 103: H. Ledgard, A. Singer, J. Whiteside, Directions in Human Factors of Interactive Systems. VI, 190 pages. 1981.

Vol. 104: Theoretical Computer Science. Ed. by P. Deussen. VII, 261 pages. 1981.

Vol. 105: B. W. Lampson, M. Paul, H. J. Siegert, Distributed Systems – Architecture and Implementation. XIII, 510 pages. 1981.

Vol. 106: The Programming Language Ada. Reference Manual. X, 243 pages. 1981.

Vol. 107: International Colloquium on Formalization of Programming Concepts. Proceedings. Edited by J. Diaz and I. Ramos. VII, 478 pages. 1981.

Vol. 108: Graph Theory and Algorithms. Edited by N. Saito and T. Nishizeki. VI, 216 pages. 1981.

Vol. 109: Digital Image Processing Systems. Edited by L. Bolc and Zenon Kulpa. V, 353 pages. 1981.

Vol. 110: W. Dehning, H. Essig, S. Maass, The Adaptation of Virtual Man-Computer Interfaces to User Requirements in Dialogs. X, 142 pages. 1981.

Vol. 111: CONPAR 81. Edited by W. Händler. XI, 508 pages. 1981.

Vol. 112: CAAP '81. Proceedings. Edited by G. Astesiano and C. Böhm. VI, 364 pages. 1981.

Vol. 113: E.-E. Doberkat, Stochastic Automata: Stability, Nondeterminism, and Prediction. IX, 135 pages. 1981.

Vol. 114: B. Liskov, CLU, Reference Manual. VIII, 190 pages. 1981.

Vol. 115: Automata, Languages and Programming. Edited by S. Even and O. Kariv. VIII, 552 pages. 1981.

Vol. 116: M. A. Casanova, The Concurrency Control Problem for Database Systems. VII, 175 pages. 1981.

Lecture Notes in Computer Science

Edited by G. Goos and J. Hartmanis

166

STACS 84

Symposium of Theoretical Aspects
of Computer Science
Paris, 11–13, 1984

Sponsored by AFCET (Association Francaise pour la
Cybernétique Economique et Technique) and
GI (Gesellschaft für Informatik)

Edited by M. Fontet and K. Mehlhorn

Springer-Verlag
Berlin Heidelberg New York Tokyo 1984

Editorial Board

D. Barstow W. Brauer P. Brinch Hansen D. Gries D. Luckham
C. Moler A. Pnueli G. Seegmüller J. Stoer N. Wirth

Editors

M. Fontet
Institut de Programmation
Laboratoire d'Informatique Théorique et de la Programmation
Université Pierre et Marie Curie
4, place Jussieu, F-75230 Paris Cedex 05

K. Mehlhorn
Fachbereich 10 der Universität Saarbrücken
Angewandte Mathematik und Informatik
D-6600 Saarbrücken

CR Subject Classifications (1982): F.1, F.2, F.3, F.4

ISBN 3-540-12920-0 Springer-Verlag Berlin Heidelberg New York Tokyo
ISBN 0-387-12920-0 Springer-Verlag New York Heidelberg Berlin Tokyo

Library of Congress Cataloging in Publication Data. Symposium of Theoretical Aspects of Computer Science (1984: Paris, France) STACS 84: Symposium of Theoretical Aspects of Computer Science, Paris, 11-13, 1984. (Lecture notes in computer science; 166) 1. Electronic data processing-Congresses. 2. Computers-Congresses. I. Fontet, M. (Max) II. Mehlhorn Von Kurt, 1949-. III. Association française pour la cybernétique économique et technique. IV. Gesellschaft für Informatik. V. Title. VI. Series.
QA75.5.S958 1984 001.64 84-5299
ISBN 0-387-12920-0 (U.S.)

This work is subject to copyright. All rights are reserved, whether the whole or part of the material is concerned, specifically those of translation, reprinting, re-use of illustrations, broadcasting, reproduction by photocopying machine or similar means, and storage in data banks. Under § 54 of the German Copyright Law where copies are made for other than private use, a fee is payable to "Verwertungsgesellschaft Wort", Munich.

© by Springer-Verlag Berlin Heidelberg 1984
Printed in Germany

Printing and binding: Beltz Offsetdruck, Hemsbach/Bergstr.
2145/3140-543210

REFEREES

The Program Committee for STACS Symposium 84 expresses its deep gratitude to the following referees who have collectively reviewed the papers submitted for consideration.

J. ALBERT
S. ANDERSON
K.R. APT
R.C. BACKHOUSE
P. BELLOT
P. BERGER
J. BERSTEL
F.J. BRANDENBURG
M. BROY
H.K. BÜNING
I. CASTELLANI
W.M. COLL
W. DAMM
W. DOSCH
Mr. FEHR
Mr. FILALI AMINE
M..P. FLE
G. GARDARIN
M.C. GAUDEL
U. GOLTZ
Mr. GONZINGER
P.M.D. GRAY
M. HENNESSY
R. HENNICKER
R. HENNIDEE
M. JERRUM
B. JOSKO
S. JUST
S. KAPLAN
W. KERSJES
H. KLAEREN
R. KLEIN
K.G. LARSEN`
R. LOAS
P. MARTHON
C. MASSOUTIE
M. MORCIETTE
A.. MYCROFT
F. NICKL
M. NORRIE
P. PADAWITZ
G. PADIOU
H. PARTSCH
P. PEPPER
D. PERRIN
A. PETTOROSSI
H. PETZSCH
T. PINEGGER
G. PUECH
J.C. RAOULT
A. REISER
E. SAINT JAMES
D. SANELLA
N. SCHAFER
D.A. SCHMIDT
M. SCHRAPP
R. STEINBRÜGGEN
H.W. SIX
E. SOISALON-SOININEN
J.P. SOUBRIER
C. STIRLING
A. STOUGHTON
A. TARLECKI
W. THOMAS
J.V. TUCKER
H. VOGEL
G. VOSSEN
S.S. WAINER
A.S. WIGHT
H.WOESSNER

FOREWORD

This volume contains the papers presented at the Symposium on Theoretical Aspects of Computer Science (STACS) held in Paris, April 11-13, 1984. This conference is organized jointly by the special interest group for theoretical computer science of the " Gesellschaft für Informatik" and the special interest group for applied mathematics of AFCET which is the " Association Française des Sciences et Techniques de l'Information, de l'Organisation et des Systèmes". It succeeds to the conferences on theoretical computer science organized every two years by G.I. and the symposium " Les Mathématiques de l'Informatique " sponsored by AFCET.

The programm committee has selected 27 papers from 78 ones submitted in response to the call for papers, which represent the leading research in theoretical computer science. In addition to these contributed papers, there are three invited papers which each survey a main topic of the conference.

It is a pleasure for the conference chairmen to thank here all those who submitted papers for consideration, those colleagues who helped in the evaluation of the papers (see next page), the programm committee who had to do the difficult selection task, the sponsoring organizations and all the secretariat of AFCET who did a beautiful job of organization.

Symposium Chairmen

M. FONTET - Université Pierre et Marie Curie,Paris .

K. MEHLHORN - Universität Saarbrücken, Saarbrücken.

Programm Committee

L. BOASSON - PARIS
G. COSTA - GENOA/ EDINBURG
P. VAN EMDE BOAS - AMSTERDAM
K. INDERMARK - AACHEN
B. MONIEN - PADERBORN
T. OTTMANN - KARLSRUHE
F. PREPARATA - URBANA
G. PLOTKIN - EDINBURGH
B. ROBINET - PARIS
F. RODRIGUEZ - TOULOUSE
G. ROUCAIROL - ORSAY
M. WIRSING - PASSAU

CONTENTS

INVITED LECTURES

CONTIBUTED PAPERS

KEY-PROBLEMS AND KEY-METHODS IN COMPUTATIONAL GEOMETRY

Herbert Edelsbrunner
Institutes for Information Processing
Technical University of Graz
Schießstattgasse 4a, A-8010 Graz, Austria.

ABSTRACT: Computational geometry, considered a subfield of computer science, is concerned with the computational aspects of geometric problems. The increasing activity in this rather young field made it split into several reasonably independent subareas. This paper presents several key-problems of the classical part of computational geometry which exhibit strong interrelations. A unified view of the problems is stressed, and the general ideas behind the methods that solve them are worked out.

INTRODUCTION

How can the field of computational geometry be defined and what are the characteristics of key-problems and key-methods in this area? Without attempting to answer these hardly defined questions, we believe that, from the present point of view, computational geometry can be described as the discipline that is concerned with the computational aspects of geometrical questions. So far, the overwhelming majority of problems dealt with in the field are low-dimensional, that is, defined in the plane or in three dimensions. We also believe, that key-problems and key-methods in the area are those that posses mathematical beauty and simplicity coupled with computational efficiency and broad influence.

Although few earlier publications exist, computational geometry was properly started by the doctoral thesis of Shamos [Sh]. He came up with the first and most influencing classification into problems around convex hulls, closest-point problems, and intersection problems. A period of flourishing activity on these issues, on rectangle problems, and on dynamization of data structures followed. Today, we are convinced to recognize three mainstreams, however classified according to a different type of criterium: (i) The investigation of underlying mathematical principles, (ii) considerable effort to work out implementation details which have been neglected in the early days, and (iii) a constant challenge of the field by renewing activity on the borderline between computational geometry and more practical areas of computer science such as pattern recognition, cluster analysis, computer graphics, linear programming, robotics, VLSI design, database theory, computer-aided design, and others.

The primary goal of this paper is to present a small collection of problems and methods of computational geometry that are considered central by the author. Part I exhibits problems that are related to each other in various ways. We believe that these relationships allow for a reasonably consistent treatment. Part II discusses the general methods that are exploited to efficiently solve the problems of Part I. Finally, conclusions are offered.

I. KEY-PROBLEMS

Eight problems from computational geometry are defined, discussed, and briefly treated. Four of these problems have a strong geometrical flavour as they require the construction of geometric structures: order-1 Voronoi diagrams, higher-order Voronoi diagrams, convex hulls, and arrangements. The beauty of the other four problems (post-office problem, point location search, linear programming, and halfplanar range search) stems from a mathematically clear and computationally efficient solution. Throughout, emphasis is laid on an intuitively appealing presentation of the problems and their interrelations.

1. The post-office problem.

Let S be a set of n points (or sites) in the Enclidean plane E^2. A site s that minimizes the distance to a query point q not necessarily in S is called the nearest neighbour of q. The post-office (or nearest neighbour) problem requires storing S such that queries of the following kind can be answered with little effort: Given a query point q, determine a nearest neighbour of q. In non-degenerate cases, q has a unique nearest neighbour. In Figure 1, the site b is the nearest neighbour of q.

This problem is motivated from database theory and cluster analysis. After being mentioned in [Kn] it became heavily examined in computational geometry. The first solution that answers a query in optimal, that is, O(logn) time was suggested in [ShH]: For each site s compute the locus of points q such that s is a nearest neighbour of q. This defines a subdivision of E^2, namely the so-called (order-1) Vo- ronoi diagram of S. A query can now be answered by locating a query point, that is, by determining the region of the subdivision that contains it. Anticipating results on constructing Voronoi diagrams and on point location, this leads to a solution with O(n) space, O(nlogn) preprocessing time, and O(logn) query time.

2. (Order-1) Voronoi diagrams.

For any two points s and t of S, let H(s,t) be the closed halfspace of points at least as close to s as to t. V(s)={q|q in H(s,t), t≠s in S} is called the Voronoi polygon of s. Being the intersection of n-1 halfplanes, V(s) is a convex polygon with at most n-1 edges. The

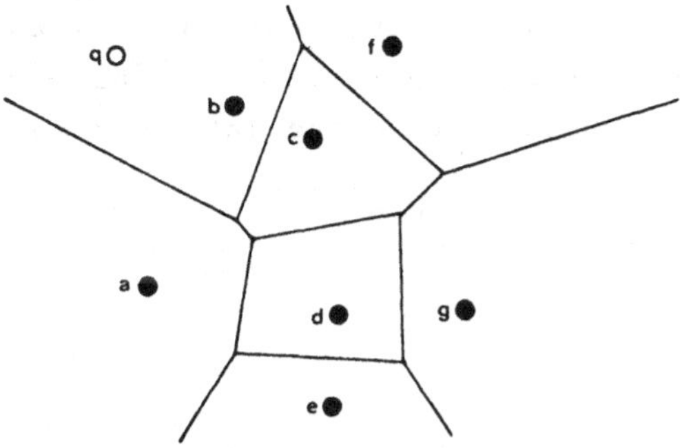

Figure 1: Order-1 Voronoi diagram.

totality of Voronoi polygons for all sites in S makes up the (order-1) Voronoi diagram 1-VOD(S) of S. Recall the equivalence of this definition to the one give in Section 1. 1-VOD(S) consists of regions, edges, and vertices (see Figure 1). Following from Euler's theorem on plane graphs, 1-VOD(S) has at most 3n-6 edges and 2n-4 vertices, for $n \geq 3$.

(Order-1) Voronoi diagrams are known in mathematics since [V]. Optimal algorithms for construction are given in [ShH] and [Br]. Borrowing from [Br] and [EOS], we propose the construction via the following geometric transform: Embed E^2 in the xy-plane of E^3 and associate each site $s=(s_x,x_y)$ with the halfspace h(s): $z \geq 2s_x x+2s_y y-(s_x{}^2+s_y{}^2)$. (The plane bounding h(s) is tangent to the paraboloid P: $z=x^2+y^2$ and touches P at the vertical projection of s onto P.) 1-VOD(S) can now be obtained by vertical projection of $\bigcap_{s \text{ in } S} h(s)$ onto the xy-plane.

3. Point location search.

Let G be a subdivision induced by a plane graph with m edges. G consists of regions, edges, and vertices. The point location search problem requires storing G in a data structure that supports efficient answering of the following kind of queries: For a query point q find the region (or edge or vertex) of G that contains q. An obvious application of such a data structure is to solve the post-office problem using the Voronoi diagram of the sites. Few of the numerous other applications can be found in [K] and [EGS].

The first optimal solution (that requires O(m) space and O(logm) query time) unfortunately without any practical significance was published in [LT]. Simpler yet optimal data structures well attractive for practical use were later suggested in [K] and [EGS]. Lack of space prevents us from describing the latter two substantially different approaches.

4. Higher-order Voronoi diagrams.

Such as the order-1 Voronoi diagram serves for nearest neighbour search, there is a generalization of the diagram to solve k-nearest neighbour search for fixed positive integer k: For a query point q report the k sites closest to q. For $T \subseteq S$, we call $V(T)=\{q|q$ in $H(t,s)$, t in T and s in $S-T\}$ the Voronoi polygon of T. The totality of non-empty Voronoi polygons of subsets T of S with $|T|=k$ is called the order-k Voronoi diagram k-VOD(S) of S. Figure 2 shows the order-3 Voronoi diagram for the point-set of Figure 1. Where space permits the regions are labelled with the three nearest sites. The three nearest neighbours of the query point q as depicted are a, b, and c.

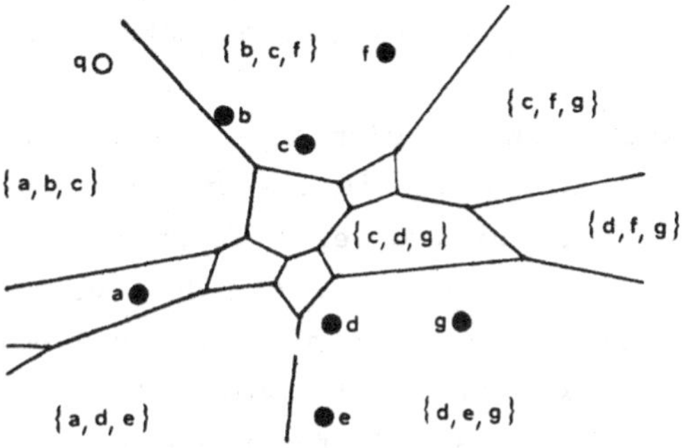

Figure 2: Order-3 Voronoi diagram.

To the best knowledge of the author, order-k Voronoi diagrams are invented by [ShH]. [L] shows that k-VOD(S) consists of $O(k(n-k))$ regions, edges, and vertices, and also gives an $O(k^2 n\log n)$ time algorithm to construct it. A different and intuitively more appealing method derives from using the geometric transform also outlined in Section 2: For each site $s=(s_x,s_y)$, the plane $p(s)$: $z=2s_x x+2s_y y-(s_x^2+s_y^2)$ touches the parapoloid $P: z=x^2+y^2$ in the vertical projection of s onto P. For each edge e in the arrangement A of planes obtained, we let a(e) denote the number of planes strictly above e. The vertical projection onto the xy-plane of the skeleton of edges e with $a(e)=k-1$ yields the order-k Voronoi diagram ([EOS]).

5. Convex hulls.

For S a set of n points in E^d, the smallest convex body that contains S is called the convex hull CH(S) of S ([G]). In E^2, CH(S) is a bounded and convex polygon with at most n edges, in E^3 it is a convex polytope with at most n vertices, 3n-6 edges, and 2n-4 faces, for $n \geq 3$. Several worst-case optimal (that is O(nlogn) time) algorithms are known in E^2 ([Gr], [PH], and others), while the divide-and-conquer approach described in [PH] yields the only O(nlogn) time method in E^3. On a rather coarse level, it reads as follows:

If $|S|=1$ then $CH(S)=p$ with $S=\{p\}$
  else DIVIDE: Let S_L contain the n/2 leftmost points of S and let $S_R=S-S_L$.
  RECURSION: Compute $CH(S_L)$ and $CH(S_R)$.
  MERGE: Derive CH(S) from $CH(S_L)$ and $CH(S_R)$ by "wrapping paper" around both polytopes.

Besides being an interesting problem for itself, constructing convex hulls can be exploited to compute intersections of halfspaces as e.g. required in Section 2 to build order-1 Voronoi diagrams: Each halfspace $h: z \geq ax+by+c$ is transformed into the dual vertical ray r(h) extending downwards from the point top(h)=(a/2,b/2,-c). Computing the lower half of the convex hull of all points top(h) is equivalent to constructing the forbidden space FS for the planes that intersect all rays r(h). Since these planes correspond to the points in the intersection of the halfspaces h, FS is dual to the required intersection of halfspaces. As a consequence, the O(nlogn) time algorithm for convex hulls implies an O(nlogn) time algorithm for FS and for order-1 Voronoi diagrams. Figure 3 illustrates the dual transform and the correspondence between FS and the intersection of halfplanes in E^2.

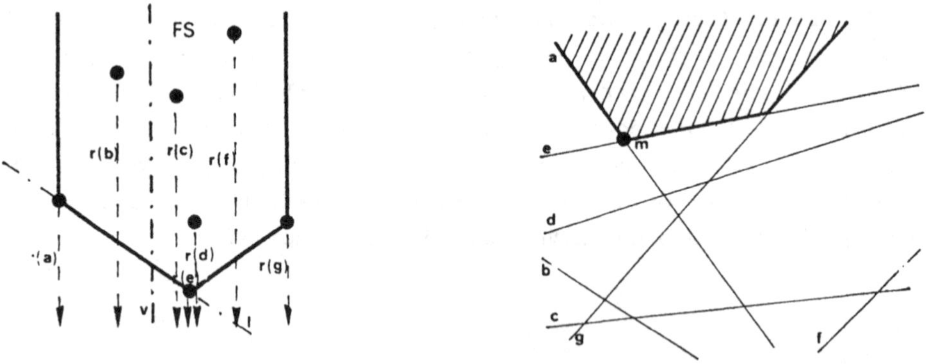

Figure 3: Lower convex hull and intersection of halfplanes in E^2.

6. Linear programming.

The linear programming problem involves a set H of n linear constraints in E^d and asks for finding the point m that maximizes a linear target function while satisfying all constraints in H. If d is considered to be a constant then O(n) time algorithms exist ([M]). For our presentation, we assume that d=2, all halfplanes in H are bounded below by a non-vertical line, and m is required to minimize the y-coordinate. Then the strategy of [M] is roughly as follows:

> If $|H| \leq 3$ then use a trivial algorithm
> else organize the halfplanes in pairs, and find the median x-coordinate x^* of the thus defined n/2 apices. Examining the slope of $f(x)=\min\{y|(x,y) \text{ in } h, h \text{ in } H\}$ at x^* allows us to decide whether m is to the left of, on, or to the right of $x=x^*$. Based on this decision, $m=(x^*,f(x^*))$ or n/4 of the halfplanes of H can be eliminated. In the latter case, the process is repeated recursively.

Although linear time is needed to carry out one level of the recursion, the geometric regression of |H| guarantees O(n) overall runtime.

Dualizing two-dimensional linear programming allows us to solve the following problem in O(n) time: For a set S of points in E^2 and a vertical line v, find the line l that has all points of S above or on it such that $l \cap v$ has maximal y-coordinate. Obviously l defines the lower edge of CH(S) that intersects v (see Figure 3). Building on these observations, [KS] developed an O(nlogV) time algorithm for constructing CH(S) if V is the number of its vertices.

7. Arrangements of hyperplanes.

If H denotes a set of n hyperplanes in E^d, then we call the cell complex A(H) induced by H the arrangement of H. Classical results in combinatorial geometry (see [G]) give exact upper bounds on the number of k-dimensional faces of A(H), for $0 \leq k \leq d$, which are in $\Theta(n^d)$. Thus, $\Omega(n^d)$ is a lower bound for the explicit construction of A(H), that is, of the incidence lattice that provides each k-face with pointers to the incident (k-1)-faces and (k+1)-faces. This lower bound matches the upper bound $O(n^d)$ which is achieved in [EOS] following an incremental strategy to build $A(H)$, $H=\{h_1,h_2,\ldots h_n\}$:

> <u>For</u> i=1 <u>to</u> n <u>do</u>
> construct $A(\{h_1,\ldots h_i\})$ by inserting h_i into
> $A(\{h_1,\ldots h_{i-1}\})$.

To insert a hyperplane h into an arrangement A of i hyperplanes needs only to check and update those faces of A that are incident with a face intersecting h. Figure 4 depicts an arrangement in E^2 with the solid edges to be checked at the insertion of a new line h shown as broken line.

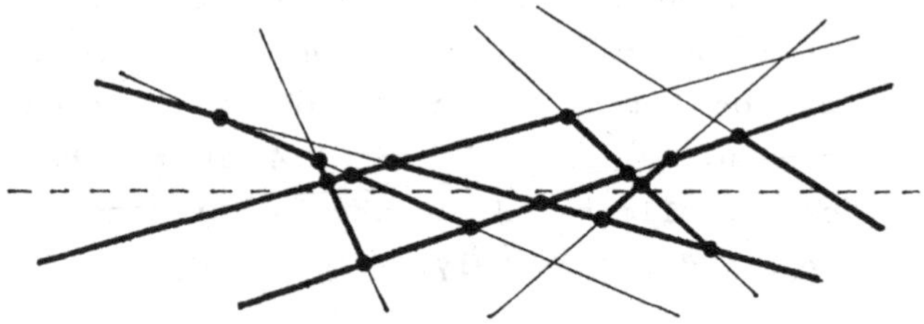

Figure 4: Two-dimensional arrangement.

As the number of such faces is in $O(i^{d-1})$ ([EOS]), h can be inserted in $O(i^{d-1})$ time implying the $O(n^d)$ time bound for the sketched construction of $A(H)$.

Arrangements in E^3 can be used to construct order-1 and higher-order Voronoi diagrams, convex hulls in E^3 (which is, however, quite a detour), and other structures. It also proves useful as a thinking paradigm for problems on finite sets of points.

8. <u>Halfplanar range search</u>.

Given a set S of n points in E^2, a <u>halfplanar range query</u> specifies a halfplane h and asks for the number $N(h)$ of points of S in h. The halfplanar range search problem requires storing S in a data structure that supports halfplanar range queries. The most efficient $O(n)$ space solution (give in [EW]) builds on the following geometric fact:

Let b be a <u>bisecting line of S</u>, that is, $2|S^+|\leq|S|$ and $2|S^-|)\leq|S|$, for S^+ (S^-) the set of points strictly above (below) b. Then there exists a <u>conjugate line</u> c, that is, c bisects S^+ and S^-.

Recursively dividing two sets separated by a line using a conjugate line defines a tree that stores S in O(n) space. Since the boundary of a query halfplane intersects at most three of four sectors defined by two crossing lines, the query time in this tree is governed by $Q(n)=Q(n/2)+Q(n/4)+O(1)=O(n^{0.695})$ (see [EW]).

The connection of this data structure to the material in Section 7 is provided by the requirement to find conjugate lines. By duality, conjugate lines that contain at least two points correspond to particular vertices in the two-dimensional arrangement dual to S. At the time, the most efficient strategy to find conjugate lines is given in [CSY] running in $O(n\log^2 n)$ time.

II. KEY-METHODS

Several rather general ideas and methods are used to solve the problems presented in Part I. It is the goal of this part to explicate these paradigms in a reasonably general way. The first two paradigms (locus approach and geometric transformation) are rather general ideas that turn out to be useful in approaching a large number of computational problems. Different in nature and closer to actually writing programs are the divide-and-conquer paradigm, the elimination method, and the incremental approach treated in the final three sections.

9. Locus approach.

The <u>locus approach</u> is the idea of subdividing some space into domains of constant answer ([O2]). A necessary assumption is therefore that the answer depends on a point in the same space; in other cases a geometric transform might be used to obtain this situation. This principle is responsible for the close relationship between nearest and k-nearest neighbour search and Voronoi diagrams (see Sections 1,

2, and 4). The importance of the locus approach can also be recognized by its independent development in other areas: e.g. [LP] calls the same principle the configuration approach to motion and location planning. The significance of the locus approach implies the importance of the point location search problem (see Section 3), since locating a point is the obvious operation one needs to perform in a subdivided space.

10. Geometric transformation.

Geometric construction gains surprisingly often from transforming the problem into some space and problem different from the originally given ones. The advantages that a suitable geometric transformation can provide are:

1. additional insight into the problem which might be well-obscured in the original setting, and
2. the possibility to use one program to solve several problems.

The transformations that turn out to be useful a good number of times are the dual transform and the inversion used to embed a d-dimensional problem in E^{d+1}. For both types of transformation, various different formulas exist that realize the desired properties. The motivation for using the particular dual mapping described in Sections 5 and 6 is based on its independence from the origin (as opposed to the classical formula [G]) and the fact that it is an involution (unlike the mapping most often used in computational geometry [Br]). Similar reasons lead is to use the particular embedding of two-dimensional problems in E^3 outlined in Sections 2, 4 and 7.

11. Divide-and-conquer.

The divide-and-conquer paradigm is applicable to problems that are, in some little understood sense, decomposable. If the principle applies then it implies a fairly large part of the algorithm's structure. We provide a loose outline of this invariant structure. S denotes a set of data and c a positive constant which can often be chosen equal to one.

<u>If</u> $|S| \leq c$ <u>then</u> solve the problem using a trivial algorithm
<u>else</u> DIVIDE: Split S into two roughly equally large sets S_1 and S_2.

RECURSION: Solve the problem recursively for S_1 and S_2.

MERGE: Combine the solutions for S_1 and S_2 to compute the solution for S.

Section 5 provides an example of this classical paradigm ([AHU]).

12. Elimination.

Equally concrete as the divide-and-conquer paradigm is the elimination method that implies the following kind of algorithm:

If $|S| \le c$ then solve the problem using a trivial algorithm
else ELIMINATE: Find a constant proportion of S that is irrelevant and eliminate it.
RECURSION: Solve the problem recursively for the reduced set S.

This method is applicable to problems whose solution is determined by at most c of the data-items, the other items being irrelevant or redundant. An example is provided in Section 6 where redundant or for the target function not significant constraints are eliminated. The key-step in the algorithm is the elimination part. To achieve efficiency in this step, computing some kind of a median [AHU] turns out to be extremely useful. The geometric regression of $|S|$ implies overall efficiency.

13. Incremental approach.

Geometric properties of certain problems favour a rather straightforward method called the incremental approach. Recently, it was shown to lead to optimal algorithms for constructing convex hulls in E^d (if d is even, [S]) and for constructing arrangements of hyperplanes in E^d ([EOS]). Let $S=\{d_1,\ldots d_n\}$ be a set of data and let C(S) denote the structure to be constructed. The incremental approach suggests the following strategy:

For i=1 to n do
construct $C(\{d_1,\ldots d_i\})$ by inserting d_i into $C(\{d_1,\ldots d_{i-1}\})$.

So the insertion of an item into an already existing structure is the crucial step which determines the efficiency of the algorithm. An example for this approach is given in Section 7.

DISCUSSION

Eight interrelated central problems from computational geometry are discussed, and the general ideas that lead to efficient solutions for these problems are explicated. By no means we claim any exhaustive treatment of computational geometry. In fact, large classes of problems like rectangle problems [E] or hidden line problems [Sch], and several design techniques like the plane-sweep technique [NP] or dynamization methods for static data structures [Ol], are not mentioned. Our primary goal thus remains to offer an introduction to an appealing part of where geometry and algorithms meet.

REFERENCES

[AHU] Aho,A.V., Hopcroft,J.E., and Ullman,J.D. The design and analysis of computer algorithms. Addison-Wesley, Reading, Mass., 1974.

[Br] Brown,K.Q. Geometric transforms for fast geometric algorithms. Ph.D.Thesis, Rep. CMU-CS-80-101, Dep.Comp.Sci., Carnegie-Mellon Univ., Pittsburgh, Penn., 1980.

[CSY] Cole,R., Sharir,M., and Yap,C.K. Convex k-hulls and related problems. Manuscript.

[E] Edelsbrunner,H. Intersection problems in computational geometry. Ph.D.Thesis, Rep.F93, Inst.Inf.Proc., TU Graz, Austria, 1982.

[EGS] Edelsbrunner,H., Guibas,L.J., and Stolfi,J. Optimal point location in a monotone subdivision. Manuscript.

[EOS] Edelsbrunner,H., O'Rourke,J., and Seidel,R. Constructing arrangements of lines and hyperplanes with applications. Proc. 24th Ann. Symp. Found. Comp. Sci. (1983), 83-91.

[EW] Edelsbrunner,H. and Welzl,E. Halfplanar range search in linear space and $O(n^{0.695})$ query time. Rep.F111, Inst.Inf. Proc., TU Graz, Austria, 1983.

[Gr] Graham,R.L. An efficient algorithm for determining the

convex hull of a finite planar set. Inf. Proc. Lett. (1972), 132-133.

[G] Gruenbaum,B. Convex polytopes. Pure and applied math. XVI, Interscience, London, 1967.

[K] Kirkpatrick,D.G. Optimal search in planar subdivisions. SIAM J. Comp. 12 (1983), 28-35.

[KS] Kirkpatrick,D.G. and Seidel,R. The ultimate planar convex hull algorithm? Proc. 20th Ann. Allerton Conf. Comm., Contr., Comp. (1982), 35-42.

[Kn] Knuth,D.E. Retrieval on secondary keys. Chapter 6.5 in Knuth, D.E.: Sorting and searching - the art of computer programming III. Addison-Wesley, Reading, Mass., 1973.

[L] Lee,D.T. On k-nearest neighbor Voronoi diagrams in the plane. IEEE Trans. Comp. C-31 (1982), 478-487.

[LT] Lipton,R.J. and Tarjan,R.E. Application of a planar separator theorem. Proc. 18th Ann. Symp. Found. Comp. Sci. (1977), 162-170.

[LP] Lozano-Perez,T. Spatial planning: a configuration space approach. IEEE Trans. Comp. C-32 (1983), 108-120.

[M] Megiddo,N. Linear-time algorithms for linear programming in R^3 and related problems. Proc. 23rd Ann. Symp. Found. Comp. Sci. (1982), 329-338.

[NP] Nievergelt,J. and Preparata,F.P. Plane-sweep algorithms for intersecting geometric figures. Comm. ACM 25 (1982), 739-747.

[O1] Overmars,M.H. The design of dynamic data structures. Lect. Notes Comp. Sci. 156, Springer, 1983.

[O2] Overmars,M.H. The locus approach. Rep. RUU-CS-83-12, Dep. Comp.Sci., Univ. Utrecht, the Netherlands, 1983.

[PH] Preparata,F.P. and Hong,S.J. Convex hulls of finite sets of points in two and three dimensions. Comm. ACM 20 (1977), 87-93.

[Sch] Schmitt,A. On the time and space complexity of certain exact hidden line algorithms. Rep. 24/81, Fak.Inf., Univ. Karlsruhe, Germany, 1981.

[S] Seidel,R. A convex hull algorithm optimal for point sets in even dimensions. Rep. 81-14, Dep.Comp.Sci., Univ. British Columbia, Vancouver, 1981.

[Sh] Shamos,M.I. Computational geometry. Ph.D.Thesis, Dep.Comp. Sci., Yale Univ., New Haven, Conn., 1978.

[ShH] Shamos,M.I. and Hoey,D. Closest-point problems. Proc. 16th Ann. Symp. Found. Comp. Sci. (1975), 151-162.

[V] Voronoi,G. Sur quelques proprietes des formes quadratiques positives parfaites. J. reine angew. Math. 133 (1907), 97-178.

Some recent results on squarefree words

by

Jean Berstel

Université Pierre et Marie Curie and L.I.T.P
Paris

> "Für die Entwicklung der logischen Wissenschaften wird es, ohne Rücksicht auf etwaige Anwendungen, von Bedeutung sein, ausgedehnte Felder für Spekulation über schwierige Probleme zu finden."
>
> Axel Thue, 1912.

1. Introduction.

When Axel Thue wrote these lines in the introduction to his 1912 paper on squarefree words, he certainly did not feel as a theoretical computer scientist. During the past seventy years, there was an increasing interest in squarefree words and more generally in repetitions in words. However, A. Thue's sentence seems still to hold : in some sense, he said that there is no reason to study squarefree words, excepted that it's a difficult question, and that it is of primary importance to investigate new domains. Seventy years later, these questions are no longer new, and one may ask if squarefree words served already.

First, we observe that infinite squarefree, overlap-free or cube-free words indeed served as examples or counter-examples in several, quite different domains. In symbolic dynamics, they were introduced by Morse in 1921 [36] . Another use is in group theory, where an infinite square-free word is one (of the numerous) steps in disproving the Burnside conjecture (see Adjan[2]). Closer to computer science is Morse and Hedlund's interpretation in relation with chess [37]. We also mention applications to formal language theory : Brzozowsky, K. Culik II and Gabriellian [7] use squarefree words in connection with noncounting languages, J. Goldstine uses the Morse sequence to show that a property of some family of languages [22]. See also Shyr [52], and Reutenauer [43]. All these are cases where repetition-free words served as explicit examples. In other cases, questions about these words led to new insights in other domains, such as for DOL languages and for context-free languages. At the present time, the set of results on repetitions constitutes a topic in combinatorics on words.

This paper gives a survey of some recent results concerning squarefree words and related topics. In the past years, the interest in this topic was indeed growing, and a number of results are now available. An account of basic results may be found in Salomaa [45,46] and in Lothaire [30]. For earlier work, see also Hedlund's paper [25]. The more general concept of unavoidable pattern is introduced in Bean, Ehrenfeucht, McNulty [4]. Part 2 deals with powers and repetitions, part 3 with language-theoretic results, part 4 gives the estimatations on growth, part 5 describes results on morphisms.

2. Powers and repetitions.

A <u>square</u> is a word of the form xx, with x a nonempty word. Cubes and k-th powers are defined accordingly. A word is squarefree if none of his factors (in the sense of Lothaire [30], or subwords) is a square. A word is <u>overlap-free</u> if it contains no factor of the form xuxux, with x nonempty. The concept of k-th power free words where k implicitly is a positive integer, can be extended to rational numbers as follows : If $r = n + s$ is a rational positive number with n positive integer and $0 < s < 1$, then an r-th power is a word of the form

$$u^n u'$$

with exactly n consecutive u's and one left factor u' of u satisfying $|u'|/|u| = s$.

The Thue-Morse sequence

$$m = 0110100110010110100101 10...$$

contains squares and is overlap-free (Thue [54], Morse [36]), the word

$$t = abcacbabcba...$$

derived from m by the inverse morphism a --> 011, b --> 01 , c --> 0 is square-free (Thue [55]). The Fibonacci word

$$f = abaababaabaababaabab...$$

contains cubes but is 4-th power free (see e.g. Karhumaki [27]). Many other special infinite words with some repetition property are known. Usually, they are constructed by iterating morphisms or by tag systems in the sense of Minsky [35]. (See also Pansiot's paper in the proceedings). Let us mention that some words may also be defined by an explicit description of the positions of the letters occurring in them. This holds for the Thue-Morse sequence, since the i-th letter can be shown to be 0 or 1 according to the number of "1" in the binary expansion of i being even or odd. A more systematic treatement of these descriptions is given in Christol, Kamae, Mendès-France, Rauzy [10]. One of the properties of these generalized sequences is given by Cerny [9]. He defines, for a given fixed word w over {0,1} an infinite word by setting the i-th letter to 0 or to 1 when the number of occurrences of w in the binary expansion of i is even or is odd. Thus the original

Thue-Morse sequence is the special case where w=1. Cerny shows that the infinite word that is obtained in this manner has no factors of the form

$$(xu)^k x$$

where $k=2^{|w|}$, and x is nonempty.

Squares are unavoidable over two letters, and they are avoidable over three letters. Here "unavoidable" means that every long enough word has a square. On the contrary, avoidable means that there are infinite square-free words. So one may ask for the minimal avoidable repetition or (almost) equivalently for the maximal unavoidable repetition over a fixed k letter alphabet. Denote the maximal unavoidable repetition over k letters by s(k). If s(k)=r, then every long enough word has a r-th power, and there is an infinite word with no factor of the form wa with w an r-th power and a the first letter of w. The Thue-Morse sequence shows that s(2)=2 (since squares are unavoidable over 2 letters). Over three letters, squares are avoidable. So s(3)<2. It has been shown by F. Dejean [15] that s(3)=7/4. (Indeed, every word over three letters of length 39 contains a 7/4th power!). For four letters, the lower bound $s(4) \geq 7/5$ has been verified by F. Dejean, and her conjecture that this bound is sharp has been proved by Pansiot [40]. For more than four letters, the precise value of s(k) is unknown. F. Dejean shows that $s(k) \geq k/(k-1)$ and conjectures that this is the right value.

The interesting question of constructing efficient algorithms for testing whether a word is squarefree was considered by several authors. The naive algorithm derived from the pattern matching algorithm is in time $O(n^2)$ for words of length n. The first significant improvement was made by Main, Lorentz [32] who proposed an O(nlog n) algorithm for testing squarefreeness. A linear algorithm, based on the suffix tree of Weiner [56] and McCreight [34] is given by Crochemore [13]. (See also Slisenko [53].)

Another related problem is to determine ALL repetitions in a word. Considering for instance the Fibonacci word (a finite left factor of it), one can see that there are "many" repetitions, even if one restricts to maximal repetitions, i.e. those which cannot be extended , neither to the left nor to the right: there are O(nlog n) in this left factor of lenght n.

THEOREM.- There is an algorithm to compute all powers in a word of length n in time O(n log n).

There are at least three different proofs of this result. By alphabetic order, Apostolico, Preparata [3] give an algorithm using suffix trees. Crochemore [11] uses partitioning in his algorithm. Main and Lorentz' paper [33] contains an extension of the divide-and-conquer method of their previous paper.

There still remain several open problems. First, to give linear algorithms for testing cubefreeness etc. Then, to give efficient algorithms (if they exist) for testing abelian squarefreeness.

3. The language of squarefree words.

The study of the language of squarefree words has produced new insights in formal language theory. Indeed, the special form of words of the complement of this language implies that standard techniques cannot be applied.

More precisely, it is a straightforward consequence of the pumping lemma that the set of squarefree words over a fixed alphabet is not context-free. Consider the complement of this set, that is the language of words containing a square. This set is not rational. However, the standard pumping technique obviously fails in this case, since any strict power of a word is in the language. The question whether the language of words containing powers is context-free was asked by Autebert, Beauquier, Boasson, Nivat [1]. The answer is no :

THEOREM .- The set of words containing a square is not context-free.

Two different proofs of this result exist, one by Ehrenfeucht, Rozenberg [20] (also [19]), and the other one by Ross and Winklmann [44] . The proofs are quite different, the first shows that there is no EOL-language separating squarefree words from the set of words containig squares, the second proof uses an argument on pushdown automata.

The second technique is more developed in the socalled Interchange Lemma for context-free languages of Ogden, Ross and Winklmann [38]. This lemma was used by Main in the proof of the following result

THEOREM (Main [31]).- The set of words over an alphabet of at least 16 letters containing an abelian square is not context-free.

An abelian square is a word uv, such that v is a permutation of u. It is known that there exist infinite words without abelian squares over a five letter alphabet (Pleasants [41]). It is easily seen by inspection that any word of length 8 over 3 letter contains an abelian square. It is open whether there is an infinite word without abelian square over a four letter alphabet.

OPEN PROBLEMS : There are several questions which seem still to be open, concerning the language of words containing squares. A conjecture by Ehrenfeucht, Haussler and Rozenberg [16] says that any context-free language which contains all square-containing words is cofinite. Another question concerns transformations that maintain the separation of squarefree and square-containing words : squarefree morphisms have this property, but also the reversal function. Are there other transformations of this kind ? The set of words containing cubes presumably is also noncontext-free. The same should hold for the set of words containing overlapping factors.

4. How many words are squarefree ?

There is an interesting question which remained open for some time and which was solved recently : are there "many" squarefree words ?

Consider a three letter alphabet. Since there is some difficulty involved with constructing squarefree words, one may suppose that there are only "few" such words. In other terms, the number c(n) of squarefree words of length n on three letters may grow as a polynomial. The following table gives the first values of c(n), they are token from Brandenburg[5] who gives values up to 24 :

n	1	2	3	4	5	6	7	8	9	10	11	12	13	14
c(n)	3	6	12	18	30	42	60	78	108	144	204	264	342	456

They seem to grow rather slowly. However, there is a surprising result due to Brandenburg showing that the number c(n) grows exponentially :

THEOREM (Brandenburg[5]).- Let c(n) be the number of squarefree words of length n on a three letter alphabet. Then

$$6 * c_1^n \leq c(n) \leq 6 * c_2^n$$

where $c_1 \geq 1.032$ and $c_2 \leq 1.38$.

The proof goes approximatively as follows. Take any squarefree word of length k over three letter a, b, c and replace any letter by itself and by a primed copy in all possible ways. This gives exactly 2^k squarefree words of length k over a six letter alphabet a, a', b, b', c, c'. Next map these words back into a three letter alphabet by a morphism that preserves squarefreeness. Such a morphism exists. Each of the six letters is mapped onto a word of length 22. Moreoever, the morphism is injective, and consequently there are at least 2^k squarefree words of length 22k over a three letter alphabet. Since

$$2^{(1/22)} = 1.032..$$

this gives the lower bound. The upper bound is obtained by observing that each squarefree word w can be extended to the right by at most c(n) words of length n. Thus $c(n+m) \leq c(n)+c(m)$, from which the conclusion follows by taking n=22.

There still remains a gap between the upper and the lower bounds, but the very precise value is not so important. There is also a similar proof of the result by Brinkhuis[6].

An analoguous proof shows that the number of cubefree words over a two letter alphabet also grows exponentially. In contrast, there is a very interesting polynomial bound on the number of overlap-free words :

THEOREM (Restivo, Salemi [42]).- There is a constant C such that the number p(n) of overlap-free words of length n over a two letter alphabet satifies

$$p(n) \leq C. n^{\log 15}$$

The proof is based on a clever factorization of overlap-free words into factors which are the initial factors of length 4^n of the two letter Thue-Morse sequence and those obtained by exchanging a and b. Each overlap-free word is shown to have a unique factorization of this kind. A computation of all possible factorizations for words of length n then gives the upper bound.

It remains to investigate the tree of squarefree words in more detail. This tree is obtained by assigning a node to each squarefree word and by connecting the node of a word to the node for each extension by a letter added on the right. Since there are infinitely many squarefree words, this tree is infinite. Therefore, there are infinite paths in it (Konig's lemma). But there are also finite branches in it, as for example abacaba. These correspond to maximal squarefree words which cannot be extended by any of the three letters. These right-maximal squarefree words were described by Li [29] : they have exactly the expected form, namely (over three letters) :

wvuabuacvuabua

provided they are squarefree. They are derived from the simplest of them, abacaba, by inserting a word u before the a's, a word v before the uabua's, and w in front.

It was shown by Kakutani (see [21]) that there are uncountably many infinite squarefree words over three letters. So one may ask "where" these words are in the tree : more precisely, is the tree uniform in some sense ? One could imagine indeed that there are infinite paths in the tree where all leaving paths are finite, yielding a "sparse" infinite branch. That this cannot happen was proved by Shelton and Soni.

THEOREM (Shelton, Soni [50,51]).- The set of infinite squarefree words over three letters is perfect.

This statement means that if there is an infinite word going through a node of the tree, then this infinte word will eventually split into two (and therefore into infinitely many) infinite squarefree words. There is a related result which says that one must not walk too much in the tree to find an infinite path.

THEOREM (Shelton, Soni [51]).- There is a constant K such that if u is a squarefree finite word on a three letter alphabet of length n and if u can be extended to a squarefree word uv of length $n + K*n^{3/2}$, then u can be extended to an infinite squarefree word.

5. Squarefree morphisms.

The first, and up to now the only technique to construct squarefree words which was systematically investigated are morphisms. The method goes as follows. First, a endomorphism is iterated, giving an infinite set of words (which can also be considered as an infinite word). Then a second morphism is applied to the set (infinite word). If everything is conveniently choosen, the result is squarefree.

This technique was used already by Axel Thue [55] to compute the first infinite squarefree word. Of course, there exist infinite squarefree words which cannot be constructed this way, since there are uncountably many of these words. However, the method still is very useful. The sets of words, squarefree or not, obtained by morphism, have interesting combinatorial properties. Among these, their "subword complexity". See Ehrenfeucht et al. [17, 18, 19].

One of the basic questions asked in this context is whether a given morphism

$$h : A^* \longrightarrow B^*$$

is squarefree. By definition, h is a squarefree morphism if h preserves squarefree words, i.e. if the image h(w) is a squarefree word whenever w is squarefree.

Examples : The morphism of Thue [55]

h(a)=abcab , h(b)=acabcb , h(c)=acbcacb

is squarefree. The following morphism (see Hall [23], Istrail[26])

h(a)=abc , h(b)=ac , h(c)=a

is not squarefree since h(abc)= abcacabc .

The last morphism is too "simple" to be squarefree. Indeed, A. Carpi [8] has shown that a squarefree morphism over three letters must have size at least 18. Here the size is the sum of the lengths of the images of the letters. Thue's morphism given above has size 18, so it is (already) optimal. The second morphism has only size 6.

Several people have investigated squarefreeness of morphisms, and have derived conditions that ensure that they are. The most precise description is that given by Crochemore :

THEOREM (Crochemore [12,13]).- Let $h : A^* \longrightarrow B^*$ be a morphism, with A having at least three letters. Then h is squarefree iff the two following conditions hold:

i) h(x) is squarefree for squarefree words x in A of length 3;

ii) No h(a), for a in A, contains a internal presquare.

Roughly speaking, a presquare is a factor u of h(a) such that h(ax) or h(xa) contains the square uu for some word x for which ax resp. xa is itself squarefree. Another condition is given in Ehrenfeucht, Rozenberg [19].

The theorem implies that it is decidable whether a morphism is squarefree : it suffices to test squarefreeness for long enough words. The following bound is derived by Crochemore from his theorem. For an nonerasing morphism $h : A^* \longrightarrow B^*$, define

$$m(h) = \min \{ |h(a)| : a \text{ in } A \}$$
$$M(h) = \max \{ |h(a)| : a \text{ in } A \}$$

PROPOSITION (Crochemore [ibid.]).- Let $h: A^* \longrightarrow B^*$ be a morphism. Then h is squarefree iff h(x) is squarefree for all squarefree words x of length $k = \max \{3, \lceil (M(h)-3)/m(h) \rceil + 1\}$.

Examples show that this bound is sharp. For uniform morphisms, i.e. when $M(h)=m(h)$, the bound is 3. The nicest corollary of Crochemore's theorem is perhaps the following

THEOREM (Crochemore [ibid.]).- Let $h : A^* \longrightarrow B^*$ be a morphism, with A a three letter alphabet. Then h is squarefree iff h(x) is squarefree for all words x of lengh 5.

Such an explicit bound which does not depend on the morphism cannot exist for bigger alphabets. Crochemore gives counterexamples. The results for higher powers than 2 are not yet so complete. I quote two of them which are particularly beautiful. The first concerns cube-free words generated by iterating a morphism over a two letter alphabet.

THEOREM (Karhumaki [27]).- Let $h : A^* \longrightarrow A^*$ be a morphism over a two letter alphabet, such that h(a) starts with an a. Then the infinite word $h^{\omega}(a)$ is cube-free iff the tenth power $h^{10}(a)$ is cube-free.

Another result concerns power-free morphisms. A morphism h is called power-free if for all $k \geq 2$, h(w) is k-th power free for all k-th power free words w.

THEOREM (Leconte [28]).- Let $h: A^* \longrightarrow B^*$ be a morphism. Then h is power-free iff h is squarefree and if h(aa) is cube-free for each letter a in A.

The situation for overlap-free morphisms is different : there are (essentially) only two such morphisms ! A more general result was proved by Seebold. Recall first that the socalled Morse morphism (rediscoverded independently by Morse [36] after Thue [54]) is defined by :

$$m(a)=ab \; ; \; m(b)=ba \; .$$

Pansiot [39] has observed that the only morphisms generating the Thue-Morse word are powers of m. This was extended by Seebold to :

THEOREM (Seebold [47,48,49]).- Let x be an infinite overlap-free word over the alphabet { a,b } that is generated by iterating some morphism h. Then h is a power of m .

The following is proved by Harju :

THEOREM (Harju [24]).- If $h : \{ a,b \}^* \longrightarrow \{ a,b \}^*$ is an overlap-free morphism, then either h is a power of m, of h is the product of the morphism that exchanges a and b and of a power of m.

This shows that there are only very few non overlapping morphisms over two letters. Harju characterizes also cyclically non overlapping words and morphisms and asks for a similar characterization of cyclically square-free words.

I gratefully acknowledge helpful discussions with M. Crochemore.

References.

[1] Autebert J., J. Beauquier, L. Boasson, M. Nivat, Quelques problèmes ouverts en théorie des langages algébriques, RAIRO Informatique théorique 13(1979), 363-379.

[2] Adjan S., "The Burnside problem and identities in groups", Ergeb. Math. Grenzgeb. vol 95, Springer 1979.

[3] Apostolico A., F. Preparata, Optimal off-line detection of repetitions in a string, Theor. Comp. Sci 22(1983), 297-315.

[4] Bean D., A. Ehrenfeucht, G. McNulty, Avoidable patterns in strings of symbols, Pacific J. Math. 85(1979), 261-294.

[5] Brandenburg F., Uniformly growing k-th power-free homomorphisms, Theor. Comput. Sci. 23(1983), 69-82.

[6] Brinkhuis J., Non-repetitive sequences on three symbols, Quart. J. Math. Oxford(2) 34(1983), 145-149.

[7] Brzozowski J., K. Culik II, A. Gabrielian, Classification of noncounting events, J. Comp. Syst, Sci. 5(1971), 41-53.

[8] Carpi A., On the size of a square-free morphism on a three letter alphabet, Inf. Proc. Letters 16(1983), 231-236.

[9] Cerny A., On generalized words of Thue-Morse, Techn. Report, Universite Paris VI, L.I.T.P. 83-44.

[10] Christol C., T. Kamae, M. Mendès-France, G. Rauzy, Suites algébriques, automates et substitutions, Bull. Soc. Math. France 108(1980), 401-419.

[11] Crochemore M. , An optimal algorithm for computing the repetitions in a word, Inf. Proc. Letters, 12(1981), 244-250.

[12] Crochemore M., Sharp characterizations of squarefree morphisms, Theor. Comp. Sci. 18(1982), 221-226.

[13] Crochemore M., Mots et morphismes sans carré, Annals of Discr. Math. 17(1983), 235-245.

[14] Crochemore M., Recherche linéaire d'un carré dans un mot, C. R. Acad. Sci. Paris, 296(1983), 781-784.

[15] Dejean F., Sur un théorème de Thue, J. Combinatorial Theory 13(1972), 90-99.

[16] Ehrenfeucht A., D. Haussler, G. Rozenberg, Conditions enforcing regularity of context-free languages, Techn. Report, Boulder University, 1982.

[17] Ehrenfeucht A., K. Lee, G. Rozenberg, Subword complexities of various classes of deterministic developmental languages without interaction, Theor. Comput. Sci. 1(1975), 59-75.

[18] Ehrenfeucht A., G. Rozenberg, On the subword complexity of square-free DOL languages, Theor. Comp. Sci. 16(1981), 25-32.

[19] Ehrenfeucht A., G. Rozenberg, Repetitions in homomorphisms and languages, 9th ICALP Symposium, Springer Lecture Notes in Computer Science 1982, 192-196.

[20] Ehrenfeucht A., G.Rozenberg, On the separating power of EOL systems, RAIRO Informatique 17(1983), 13-22.

[21] Gottschalk W. G.Hedlund, "Topological Dynamics", American Math. Soc. Colloq. Pub. Vol. 36, 1955.

[22] Goldstine J., Bounded AFLs, J. Comput. Syst. Sci. 12(1976), 399-419.

[23] Hall M., Generators and relations in groups - the Burnside problem, in: T.L. Saaty (ed.), "Lectures in Modern Mathematics", Vol. II, John Wiley & Sons, 1964, 42-92.

[24] Harju T., Morphisms that avoid overlapping, University of Turku, May 1983.

[25] Hedlund G., Remarks on the work of Axel Thue on sentences, Nord. Mat. Tidskr 16(1967), 148-1

[26] Istrail S., On irreductible languages and non rational numbers, Bull. Mat. Soc. Sci. Mat. R. S. Roumanie 21(1977), 301-308.

[27] Karhumäki J. , On cube-free ω-words generated by binary morphisms, Discr. Appl. Math 5(1983), 279-297 .

[28] Leconte M., A fine characterization of power-free morphisms, Techn. Report L.I.T.P. 1984.

[29] Li S. , Annihilators in nonrepetitive semigroups, Studies in Appl. Math. 55(1976), 83-85.

[30] Lothaire M., "Combinatorics on Words", Addison-Wesley 1983.

[31] Main M., Permutations are not context-free : an application of the 'Interchange Lemma', Inf. Proc. Letters 15(1982), 68-71.

[32] Main M., R. Lorentz, An O(n log n) algorithm for recognizing repetition, Washington State University, Techn. Report CS-79-056.

[33] Main M., R. Lorentz, An O(n log n) algorithm for finding all repetitions in a string, J. Algorithms, 1983, to appear.

[34] McCreight E., A space-economical suffix tree construction algorithm, J. Assoc. Mach. Comp. 23(1976), 262-272.

[35] Minsky S., "Computations : finite and infinite machines", Prentice-Hall 1967.

[36] Morse M. , Recurrent geodesics on a surface of negative curvature, Trans. Amer. Math. Soc. 22(1921), 84-100.

[37] Morse M., G. Hedlund, Unending chess, symbolic dynamics and a problem in semigroups, Duke Math. J. 11(1944), 1-7.

[38] Ogden W., R. Ross, K. Winklmann, An "Interchange lemma" for context-free languages, Washington State University, Techn. Report CS-81-080.

[39] Pansiot J., The Morse sequence and iterated morphisms, Inf. Proc. Letters 12(1981), 68-70.

[40] Pansiot J., A propos d'une conjecture de F. Dejean sur les répétitions dans les mots, Discrete Appl. Math.

[41] Pleasants P., Nonrepetitive sequences, Proc. Cambridge Phil. Soc. 68(1970), 267-274.

[42] Restivo A., S. Salemi, On weakly square free words, Inf. Proc. Letters, to appear.

[43] Reutenauer C., A new characterization of the regular languages, 8th ICALP, Springer Lecture Notes in Computer Science 115, 1981, 175-183.

[44] Ross R., K. Winklmann, Repetitive strings are not context-free, RAIRO Informatique théorique 16(1982), 191 - 199.

[45] Salomaa A., Morphisms on free monoids and language theory, in : R. Book (ed.) : "Formal language theory: perspectives and open problems", Academic Press 1098, 141-166.

[46] Salomaa A., "Jewels of Formal Language Theory", Pitman 1981.

[47] Seebold P., Morphismes itérés, mot de Morse et mot de Fibonacci, C. R. Acad. Sci. Paris, 295(1982), 439- 441.

[48] Seebold P. Sur les morphismes qui engendrent des mots infinis ayant des facteurs prescrits, 6. GI Tagung Theoretische Informatik, Lecture Notes Comp. Sci. 145, 1983, 301-311.

[49] Seebold P. , Sequences generated by infinitely iterated morphisms, Techn. Report Universite de Paris VII, L.I.T.P 83-13.

[50] Shelton R., Aperiodic words on three symbols, I, II, J. reine angew. Math. 321(1981), 195-209, 327(1981), 1-11.

[51] Shelton R., R. Soni, Aperiodic words on three symbols III, J. reine angew. Math. , 330(1982), 44-52.

[52] Shyr J., A strongly primitive word of arbitrary length and its applications, Int. J. Comp. Math A-6(19770, 165-170.

[53] Slisenko A., Determination in real time of all the periodicities in a word, Soviet Math. Dokl. 21(1980), 392-395.

[54] Thue A., Uber unendliche Zeichenreihen, Norske Vid. Selsk. Skr. I. Mat. Nat. Kl. Christiania (1906), 1-22.

[55] Thue A., Uber die gegenseitige Lage gleicher Teile gewisser Zeichenreihen, Norske Vid. Selsk. Skr. I. Mat. Nat. Kl. Christiania (1912), 1-67.

[56] Weiner P., Linear pattern matching algorithms, Proc. 14th Symp. switching automata theory, 1973, 1-11.

TRANSFORMATIONS REALIZING FAIRNESS ASSUMPTIONS FOR PARALLEL PROGRAMS

K.R. Apt

LITP
Université Paris VII
75251 Paris

E.-R. Olderog

Institut für Informatik
Universität Kiel
D-2300 Kiel 1

Abstract. Parallel programs with shared variables are studied under a semantics which assumes the fair execution of all parallel components. We present transformations which reduce this fair semantics to a simple interleaving semantics with help of random assignments z:=? . In fact, different notions of fairness are considered: impartiality, liveness, weak and strong fairness. All transformations preserve the structure of the original programs and are thus suitable as a basis for syntax-directed correctness proofs.

1. Introduction

This paper considers parallel programs $S = S_1 \| \ldots \| S_n$ where the components S_i of S are sequential programs which communicate with each other implicitly via shared variables. The correctness properties and (in-)formal reasoning about such programs depend on the semantical notion of execution of S.

The simplest way of modelling the execution of S is by arbitrary interleaving of the execution sequences of its components S_i /Br1,Br2,FS1,FS2/. But in general interleaving is not what we wish to express when writing $S = S_1 \| \ldots \| S_n$ since it models only the concept of multiprogramming where S runs on a single processor /MP/.

Here we investigate the more ambitious idea of a truly concurrent execution of S where every component S_i runs on its own processor. To formalize this idea we follow the proposal of /MP,OL/ to model concurrency of S by interleaving the execution sequences of its components, but with the additional assumption of fairness. Informally, fairness states that every component S_i of S which is sufficiently often enabled will eventually progress. Different interpretations of "sufficiently often enabled" give rise to different notions of fairness, viz. impartiality /LPS/, liveness /OL/, weak and strong fairness /AO/. For liveness e.g. "sufficiently often enabled" is interpreted as "not yet terminated".

So far semantics and proof theory for fairness assumptions have been studied mainly in the context of nondeterministic do-od-programs (see /Fr/ for an overview). For parallel programs $S = S_1 \| \ldots \| S_n$ the question of fairness has been dealt with only by translating the given program S back into a nondeterministic do-od-program /APS,LPS/ or by resorting to methods of temporal logic /OL/ which often requires a translation of the original program S into an equivalent formula in temporal logic /MP,Pn/.

In our paper we present a series of transformations T which reduce the concurrent or fair semantics of parallel programs to the simple interleaving semantics with help of random assignments z:=? /AP/, one transformation for each notion of fairness. All transformations preserve the parallel structure of the original programs. The approach represents a refinement of the transformation technique introduced in /AO/ for non-deterministic do-od-programs.

The interest in such transformations T is twofold:

(1) T can be considered as a sort of scheduler which guarantees that the resulting program T(S) realizes exactly all the fair executions of S.

(2) T can be used as a basis for syntax-directed correctness proofs. The idea is to apply an extension of the proof system of /OG/ dealing also with random assignments to T(S).

In this paper we concentrate on the first aspect. We state a number of results on the existence or non-existence of transformations with paricular properties. We hope that these results give a better insight into the structure of the various notions of fairness. Proofs will appear in the full version of this paper.

2. Parallel Programs

We assume sets Var of variables ranging over integers, Exp of expressions and Bex of Boolean expressions with typical elements $x,y,z \in Var$, $s,t \in Exp$ and $b,c \in Bex$. Sequential programs are defined by the following BNF-like syntax:

$$S ::= skip \mid x:=t \mid z:=? \mid S_1;S_2 \mid \underline{if}\ b\ \underline{then}\ S_1\ \underline{else}\ S_2\ \underline{fi} \mid$$
$$\underline{while}\ b\ \underline{do}\ S_1\ \underline{od} \mid \underline{await}\ b\ \underline{then}\ S_1\ \underline{end}$$

where for simplicity nested while's and await's are disallowed. Let if b then S_1 fi abbreviate if b then S_1 else skip fi.

Besides usual assignments of the form x:=t we consider random assignments z:=? which assign an arbitrary non-negative integer to z /AP/. Thus z:=? is an explicit form of unbounded nondeterminism in the sense that termination of z:=? is guaranteed but infinitely many final states are possible /Pa /.

Await-statements S = await b then S_1 end are used to achieve synchronization in the context of parallel composition. S is executed only if b is true. What makes it different from if b then S_1 fi is that the await guarantees that S_1 is executed as an indivisible action /OG/ (cf. Sec.3).

By a parallel program we mean a program of the form

$$S = S_o;(S_1 \| \dots \| S_n)$$

where S_o is a sequence of assignments and $S_1,\dots,S_n$ are sequential programs. S_o is the initial part of S and $S_1,\dots,S_n$ are the (parallel) components of S inside the parallel composition $S_1 \| \dots \| S_n$.

We distinguish four classes of programs: L(‖), L(‖,?), L(‖,<u>await</u>) and L(‖,<u>await</u>,?) depending on whether random assignments or/and await-statements are used. L(‖,<u>await</u>) is essentially the language studied in /OG/.

In our paper we will study certain (<u>program</u>) <u>transformations</u>, i.e. mappings

$$T: L(\|) \;[\text{or } L(\|,\underline{\text{await}})] \longrightarrow L(\|,\underline{\text{await}},?).$$

Sometimes it is more convenient to leave certain details of such a transformation open. To this end, we consider <u>transformation schemes</u>, i.e. mappings

$$\mathbb{T}: L(\|) \;[\text{or } L(\|,\text{await})] \longrightarrow \mathcal{P}(L(\|,\text{await},?))\setminus\{\emptyset\}$$

which assign to every program S a non-empty set of transformed programs $S' \in \mathbb{T}(S)$. ($\mathcal{P}(M)$ is the power set of a set M.) By selecting a particular $S' \in \mathbb{T}(S)$ for every program S we obtain a so-called <u>instance</u> T of $\mathbb{T}$. This is a transformation T as above.

3. Interleaving Semantics

We take an interpretation with integers as domain $\mathcal{D}$ assigning the standard meaning to all symbols of Peano arithmetic. The set of (<u>proper</u>) <u>states</u> is given by $\Sigma = Var \longrightarrow \mathcal{D}$ with typical elements σ, τ. Notations like $\sigma[d/x]$, $\sigma{\restriction}X$ and $\sigma(b)$ are as usual. We add two special states not present in Σ: $\perp$ reporting divergence and Δ reporting deadlock.

By a <u>configuration</u> we mean a pair $\langle S,\sigma\rangle$ consisting of a program $S \in L(\|,\underline{\text{await}},?)$ and a state σ. Following /HP,Pl/ we introduce a <u>transition relation</u> $\longrightarrow$ between configurations. $\langle S,\sigma\rangle \longrightarrow \langle S_1,\sigma_1\rangle$ means: executing S one step in σ can lead to σ_1 with S_1 being the remainder of S still to be executed. To express termination we allow the empty program E with E;S = S;E = E.

The relation $\longrightarrow$ is defined by structural induction on L(‖,<u>await</u>,?). Typical clauses are:

a) $\langle \text{skip},\sigma\rangle \longrightarrow \langle E,\sigma\rangle$

b) $\langle z:=?,\sigma\rangle \longrightarrow \langle E,\sigma[d/x]\rangle$ for every $0 \leq d \in \mathcal{D}$.

c) $\langle \underline{\text{while}}\ b\ \underline{\text{do}}\ S_1\ \underline{\text{od}},\sigma\rangle \longrightarrow \langle S_1;\underline{\text{while}}\ b\ \underline{\text{do}}\ S_1\ \underline{\text{od}},\sigma\rangle$ if $\sigma(b)$ = true.

d) $\langle \underline{\text{while}}\ b\ \underline{\text{do}}\ S_1\ \underline{\text{od}},\sigma\rangle \longrightarrow \langle E,\sigma\rangle$ if $\sigma(b)$ = false.

e) $\langle \underline{\text{await}}\ b\ \underline{\text{then}}\ S_1\ \underline{\text{end}},\sigma\rangle \longrightarrow \langle E,\tau\rangle$ if $\sigma(b)$ = true and $\langle S_1,\sigma\rangle \longrightarrow^* \langle E,\tau\rangle$ where $\longrightarrow^*$ denotes the reflexive, transitive closure of $\longrightarrow$.

f) If $\langle S_1,\sigma\rangle \longrightarrow \langle S_2,\tau\rangle$ then $\langle S_1;S,\sigma\rangle \longrightarrow \langle S_2;S,\tau\rangle$

g) If $\langle S_i,\sigma\rangle \longrightarrow \langle T_i,\tau\rangle$ then
$\langle S_1\|\ldots\|S_n,\sigma\rangle \longrightarrow \langle S_1\|\ldots\|S_{i-1}\|T_i\|S_{i+1}\|\ldots\|S_n,\tau\rangle$.

Note that assignments, evaluations of Boolean expressions, and await-statements are executed as atomic or indivisible actions. Therefore statements of the form skip, x:=t, z:=? and <u>await</u> b <u>then</u> S_1 <u>end</u> are called <u>atomic</u>. Parallel composition is modelled by <u>interleaving</u> the transitions of its components.

Based on $\rightarrow$ we introduce some further concepts. A configuration $\langle S,\sigma\rangle$ is <u>maximal</u> if it has no successor w.r.t. $\rightarrow$. A <u>terminal</u> configuration is a maximal configuration $\langle S,\sigma\rangle$ with $S = E \| \ldots \| E$. All other maximal configurations are called <u>deadlocked</u>. A <u>computation</u> of S (<u>starting in</u> σ) is a finite or infinite sequence

$$\xi : \langle S,\sigma\rangle \rightarrow \langle S_1,\sigma_1\rangle \rightarrow \ldots \rightarrow \langle S_k,\sigma_k\rangle \rightarrow \ldots$$

A computation of S is called <u>terminating</u> (<u>deadlocking</u>) if it is of the form

$$\xi : \langle S,\sigma\rangle \rightarrow \ldots \rightarrow \langle T,\tau\rangle$$

where $\langle T,\tau\rangle$ is terminal (deadlocked). Infinite computations of S are called <u>diverging</u>. We say that S <u>can diverge from</u> σ (<u>can deadlock from</u> σ) if there exists a diverging (deadlocking) computation of S starting in σ.

The <u>interleaving semantics</u> of programs $S \in L(\|, \underline{await}, ?)$ is

$$\mathcal{M}[\![S]\!] : \Sigma \rightarrow \mathcal{P}(\Sigma \cup \{\bot, \Delta\})$$

defined by

$$\begin{aligned}\mathcal{M}[\![S]\!](\sigma) = \; & \{\tau \mid \langle S,\sigma\rangle \rightarrow^* \langle E\|\ldots\|E,\tau\rangle\} \\ \cup\; & \{\bot \mid S \text{ can diverge from } \sigma\} \\ \cup\; & \{\Delta \mid S \text{ can deadlock from } \sigma\}\end{aligned}$$

We also consider a variant of $\mathcal{M}$ ignoring deadlocks:

$$\mathcal{M}_{-\Delta}[\![S]\!](\sigma) = \mathcal{M}[\![S]\!](\sigma) \setminus \{\Delta\} .$$

Some further notions. The component S_i has <u>terminated</u> in $\langle S_1\|\ldots\|S_n,\sigma\rangle$ if $S_i = E$. The component S_i is <u>disabled</u> in $\langle S_1\|\ldots\|S_n,\sigma\rangle$ if either $S_i = E$ or S_i = <u>await</u> b <u>then</u> S <u>end</u>; T with $\sigma(b)$ = false. The component S_i is <u>enabled</u> if it is not disabled, i.e. if S_i is not terminated and whenever S_i=<u>await</u> b <u>then</u> S <u>end</u>;T holds then $\sigma(b)$ = true. The component S_i is <u>active</u> in the step $\langle S_1\|\ldots\|S_n,\sigma\rangle \rightarrow \langle T_1\|\ldots\|T_n,\tau\rangle$ if $\langle S_i,\sigma\rangle \rightarrow \langle T_i,\tau\rangle$. A program S is <u>deadlock-free</u> if $\mathcal{M}[\![S]\!] = \mathcal{M}_{-\Delta}[\![S]\!]$.

4. Impartiality

Consider the program

$$S^* = \underbrace{\underline{\text{while}}\ b\ \underline{\text{do}}\ x:=x+1\ \underline{\text{od}}}_{S_1} \;\|\; \underbrace{b:=\text{false}}_{S_2}$$

Under the interleaving semantics S can diverge: $\bot \in \mathcal{M}[\![S^*]\!](\sigma)$ if $\sigma(b)$ = true. However, in every concurrent or "fair" computation of S^* the second component S_2 will eventually be executed causing termination of S_1 and hence S^* itself. The question is how to capture this intuitive notion of fairness.

In this section we define a first approximation to the concept of fairness, viz. <u>impartiality</u> /LPS/.

Definition 4.1 A computation $\xi: \langle S,\sigma\rangle = \langle T_1,\sigma_1\rangle \rightarrow \ldots \rightarrow \langle T_j,\sigma_j\rangle \rightarrow \ldots$ of an $L(\|,\underline{await})$-program $S = S_o;(S_1 \| \ldots \| S_n)$ is impartial if ξ is finite or for every $i \in \{1,\ldots,n\}$ there are infinitely many j such that component S_i is active in step $\langle T_j,\sigma_j\rangle \rightarrow \langle T_{j+1},\sigma_{j+1}\rangle$.

Thus in an infinite impartial computation every component will eventually progress. The concurrent semantics of programs $S \in L(\|,\underline{await})$, modelled here by interleaving and the assumption of impartiality, is now given by

$$\begin{aligned} \mathcal{M}_{imp}[\![S]\!](\sigma) = \; & \{\tau \mid \langle S,\sigma\rangle \longrightarrow^* \langle E\|\ldots\|E,\tau\rangle\} \\ & \cup \{\bot \mid \exists \text{ infinite } \underline{\text{impartial}} \text{ computation of } S \text{ starting in } \sigma\} \\ & \cup \{\Delta \mid S \text{ can deadlock from } \sigma\} \end{aligned}$$

To see the impact of this definition, let us look at the example S^* again. Under the assumption of impartiality S^* always terminates: $\bot \notin \mathcal{M}_{imp}[\![S^*]\!](\sigma)$ for every state σ.

5. Structure Preserving Transformations

In this section we restrict ourselves to programs in $L(\|)$. Our aim is to find a transformation T which reduces the concurrent semantics $\mathcal{M}_{imp}$ of $L(\|)$ to the ordinary interleaving semantics $\mathcal{M}$, i.e. with

$$\mathcal{M}_{imp}[\![S]\!] = \mathcal{M}[\![T(S)]\!] \quad .$$

Such transformations T are useful for two reasons: firstly, they describe a class of schedulers which implement true concurrency on a single processor machine, and secondly, they provide a systematic approach of refining existing proof methods for program correctness under interleaving semantics to methods for dealing directly with concurrent semantics. Of course, we cannot expect the transformed programs T(S) to be in $L(\|)$ because $\mathcal{M}_{imp}$ introduces unbounded nondeterminism (and thus discontinuous semantic operators /Di/) as opposed to $\mathcal{M}$. But we can control this unbounded nondeterminism by making it explicit via random assignments

z:=?

as analysed in /AP/.

First attempt

A simple way of reducing concurrency to interleaving is to combine two types of already existing transformations. Given a parallel program $S = S_o;(S_1 \| \ldots \| S_n)$ one first follows the approach of /FS1,FS2/ or /Br1,Br2/ and translates S into a big nondeterministic do-od-program $T_{nd}(S)$ which makes the interleaving semantics $\mathcal{M}[\![S]\!]$ syntactically visible. Then one can apply the transformations T_{fair} of /AO/ to $T_{nd}(S)$ which use random assignments to realize the assumption of fairness in the context of do-od-programs. The drawback of this solution is that the first translation T_{nd} destroys the syntactic structure of programs S.

Instead we are interested in transformations which preserve the parallel struture of programs.

Definition 5.1 A transformation $T:L(\|) \rightarrow L(\| ,\underline{await},?)$ is called $\|$-preserving if T satifies

$$T(\ S_0;(S_1 \| \dots \| S_n)\ ) = T^n_o(S_0);(\ T^n_1(S_1) \| \dots \| T^n_n(S_n)\ )$$

where T^n_i is a sub-transformation working on the i-th component of S. The notation implies that the only information T^n_i may use about the structure of S is the total number n of components in S and the index i of the currently transformed component. A transformation scheme $\mathbb{T}$ is $\|$-preserving if every instance T of $\mathbb{T}$ is $\|$-preserving.

Second attempt

In /AO/ we showed that in the context of Dijkstra's nondeterministic do-od-programs fairness assumptions can be realized by just adding random assignments z:=? and refining Boolean expressions in a certain "admissible" way. The question arises whether this is also possible for parallel programs $S \in L(\|)$.

Definition 5.2 A transformation $T:L(\|) \rightarrow L(\|,?)$ is admissible if it is $\|$-preserving and if for every $S \in L(\|)$ there is a set Z of new auxiliary variables $z \in Z$ used in T(S) for scheduling purposes in the following two ways:

(1) in additional assignments of the form z:=? and z:=t inside of S

(2) in Boolean conjuncts c used to strengthen Boolean expressions b of loops <u>while</u> b <u>do</u> S_1 <u>od</u> or conditionals <u>if</u> b <u>then</u> S_1 <u>else</u> S_2 <u>fi</u> in S. We require that this stregthening is done schematically, i.e. the conjunct c in independent of the actual form of b.

Again a transformation scheme $\mathbb{T}$ is admissible if every instance T of $\mathbb{T}$ is.

Note that because T(S) manipulates additional variables Z the best we can hope to prove is that $\mathcal{M}_{imp}[\![S]\!]$ agrees with $\mathcal{M}[\![T(S)]\!]$ "modulo Z". This notion is defined as follows: for states $\sigma \in \Sigma$ and sets $Z \subseteq Var$ of variables let

$$\sigma \setminus Z = \sigma \upharpoonright (Var \setminus Z).$$

This notation is extended to sets $M \subseteq \Sigma \cup \{\perp,\Delta\}$ pointwise:

$$M \setminus Z = \{\sigma \setminus Z \mid \sigma \in M\} \cup \{\perp \mid \perp \in M\} \cup \{\Delta \mid \Delta \in M\}.$$

For state transformers $\mathcal{M}_1,\mathcal{M}_2 : \Sigma \rightarrow \mathcal{P}(\Sigma \cup \{\perp,\Delta\})$ we write

$$\mathcal{M}_1 = \mathcal{M}_2 \ \underline{mod}\ Z$$

if $\mathcal{M}_1(\sigma)\setminus Z = \mathcal{M}_2(\sigma)\setminus Z$ holds for every state $\sigma \in \Sigma$.

Theorem 5.3 There is no admissible transformation $T:L(\|) \longrightarrow L(\| ,?)$ such that for every program $S \in L(\|)$

$$\mathcal{M}_{imp}[\![S]\!] = \mathcal{M}[\![T(S)]\!] \ \underline{\text{mod}}\ Z$$

holds where Z is the set of auxiliary variables used in T(S).

The theorem states that it is more difficult to find transformations T realizing fairness (here impartiality) for parallel programs than for nondeterministic ones. The reason is that transformations $T:L(\|) \longrightarrow L(\| ,?)$ would have to terminate the presently executed component S_i of a program $S \in L(\|)$ in order to force a shift of control to another component S_j. But after terminating S_i there is no possibility of resuming S_i later on. To achieve this effect we necessarily need an additional language construct in T: the await-statement.

Third attempt

First we extend Definition 5.2 of admissibility to transformations $T:L(\|) \longrightarrow L(\| ,\text{await},?)$ by allowing in T(S) also

(3) new await-statements <u>await</u> c <u>then</u> S_1 <u>end</u> where S_1 is a sequence of assignments of the form (1) of Definition 5.2.

To conduct a finer analysis, we introduce further concepts:

Definition 5.4 A transformation $T:L(\|) \longrightarrow L(\| ,\underline{\text{await}},?)$ is sequential (in every component) if it is admissible, i.e. if it is of the form

$$T(\ S_0; (S_1 \| \ldots \| S_n)\ ) = T_o^n(S_0); (\ T_1^n(S_1) \| \ldots \| T_n^n(S_n)\ )\ ,$$

and if it preserves sequential composition in every component, i.e. if for every $i = 1,\ldots,n$

$$T_i^n(S_1'\ ;\ S_2') = T_i^n(S_1')\ ;\ T_i^n(S_2')$$

holds. A transformation scheme $\mathbb{T}$ is sequential if every instance T of $\mathbb{T}$ is.

Sequentiality yields particularly simple transformations.

Definition 5.5 A transformation $T:L(\|) \longrightarrow L(\| ,\underline{\text{await}},?)$ is faithful if T does not introduce deadlocks, i.e. $\Delta \notin \mathcal{M}[\![\ T(S)\ ]\!](\sigma)$ holds for every $S \in L(\|)$ and $\sigma \in \Sigma$. A transformation scheme $\mathbb{T}$ is faithful if every instance T of $\mathbb{T}$ is. Otherwise T and $\mathbb{T}$ are called deadlocking.

Transformations implementing schedulers should be faithful as schedulers should never run into any deadlocked configuration. The notion of a faithful transformation was first introduced for nondeterministic do-od-programs in /AO/ where it meant absence of guard-failures. Unfortunately, we cannot find a simple sequential transformation which is faithful:

Theorem 5.6 There is no faithful, sequential transformation $T: L(\|) \longrightarrow L(\|, \underline{await}, ?)$ such that for every program $S \in L(\|)$

$$\mathcal{M}_{imp}[\![S]\!] = \mathcal{M}[\![T(S)]\!] \underline{mod}\ Z$$

holds where Z is the set of auxiliary variables in T(S).

Faithful, but non-sequential transformations will be presented in Sec. 6.

A Solution

However, we can find a deadlocking transformation (scheme)

$$T_{imp+\Delta} : L(\|) \longrightarrow \mathcal{P}(L(\|, \underline{await}, ?)) \setminus \{\emptyset\}$$

which is sequential and realizes impartiality. Certainly, deadlocking transformations T are not suitable as implementations of fair schedulers, but - as first observed in /APS/ - may lead to simplified correctness proofs of transformed programs T(S). This is why we are also interested in deadlocking transformations.

For a given program $S = S_0; (S_1 \| \dots \| S_n)$ in $L(\|)$ let $T_{imp+\Delta}$ (S) be the set of all programs resulting from S by

(1) prefixing S with an initialisation part

$$INIT = z_1 := ?; \; \dots \; ; z_n := ?$$

(2) replacing in every loop <u>while</u> b <u>do</u> S' <u>od</u> of a component S_i <u>some</u> atomic statement A in S' by

$$\begin{aligned} TEST_i(A) = \; & \underline{await}\ \bar{z} \geqslant 1\ \underline{then} \\ & z_i := ?;\ \underline{for}\ j \neq i\ \underline{do}\ z_j := z_j - 1\ \underline{od}; \\ & A \\ & \underline{end} \end{aligned}$$

(for i = 1,...,n).

Here we use new variables $z_1, \dots, z_n$ not already present in S and the following abbreviations:

$$\bar{z} \geqslant 1 \; = \; z_1 \geqslant 1 \wedge \dots \wedge z_n \geqslant 1$$

$$\underline{for}\ j \neq i\ \underline{do}\ z_j := z_j - 1\ \underline{od} \; =$$

$$z_1 := z_1 - 1; \dots ; z_{i-1} := z_{i-1} - 1; z_{i+1} := z_{i+1} - 1; \dots ; z_n := z_n - 1$$

To see its impact, we apply $T_{imp+\Delta}$ to the program

$$S^* = \underline{while}\ b\ \underline{do}\ x := x+1\ \underline{od} \ \|\ b := false$$

of Sec. 4. Here there is exactly one program $T \in T_{imp+\Delta}$ (S), viz.

```
T = z1:=?; z2:=?;
    ( while b do await z1,z2 ≥ 1 then
                      z1:=?; z2:=z2-1;
                      x:=x+1
                  end
      od
    || b:=false )
```

T uses variables z_1,z_2 for scheduling purposes. The variable z_2 counts how many times we may enter the while-loop of the first component of T without switching control to the second component. (The variable z_1 is introduced for analogous purposes but not relevant for this particular program T without a while-loop in its second component.) Initially z_2 is set to an arbitrary non-negative integer. Each time the while-loop is entered z_2 is decremented by 1. This ensures that this loop cannot be executed arbitrarily long without falsifying $z_1,z_2 \geqslant 1$. Note that as soon as the Boolean expression $z_1,z_2 \geqslant 1$ of the await-statement is false, it remains so even after executing the second component b:=false. Hence T can deadlock from states σ with $\sigma(b)$ = true.

Thus $T_{imp+\Delta}$ is a deadlocking transformation which transforms all diverging non-impartial computations of S into deadlocking computations of T. Indeed $T_{imp+\Delta}$ realizes the assumption of impartiality in the sense of:

Theorem 5.7 For every L(‖)-program S and $T \in T_{imp+\Delta}$ (S) the equation

$$\mathcal{M}_{imp}[\![S]\!] = \mathcal{M}_{-\Delta}[\![T]\!] \text{ mod } Z$$

holds where Z is the set of auxiliary variables in T.

6. Liveness

Consider the L(‖)-program

$$S^{**} = \text{while } b \text{ do } x:=x+1 \text{ od } \| \text{ skip } .$$

Intuitively, S^{**} should diverge for states σ with $\sigma(b)$ = true - independently whether the interleaving or a concurrent, i.e. "fair" semantics is chosen. However, with our definition of impartiality S^{**} always terminates: $\perp \notin \mathcal{M}_{imp}[\![S^{**}]\!](\sigma)$ for every state σ.

Thus impartility is not adequate to capture the idea of fairness even for L(‖). Therefore we introduce the refined concept of liveness which distinguishes between terminated and running components of parallel programs.

Definition 6.1 A computation $\xi : \langle S,\sigma\rangle = \langle T_1,\sigma_1\rangle \rightarrow \ldots \rightarrow \langle T_j,\sigma_j\rangle \rightarrow \ldots$ of a program $S = S_0;(S_1 \| \ldots \| S_n)$ in $L(\|,\underline{await})$ is live if ξ is finite or the following holds for every $i \in \{1,\ldots,n\}$: either component S_i has terminated in some $\langle T_j,\sigma_j\rangle$ or there are infinitely many j such that component S_i is active in step $\langle T_j,\sigma_j\rangle \rightarrow \langle T_{j+1},\sigma_{j+1}\rangle$.

Thus in a live computation every non-terminated component will eventually be active and make progress. Analogously to $\mathcal{M}_{imp}$ we define a semantics $\mathcal{M}_{live}$ which captures this assumption of liveness:

$$\begin{aligned}\mathcal{M}_{live}[\![S]\!](\sigma) = \; & \{\tau \mid \langle S,\sigma\rangle \rightarrow^* \langle E\| \ldots \| E,\tau\rangle\} \\ & \cup \{\bot \mid \exists \text{ infinite } \underline{\text{live}} \text{ computation of S starting in } \sigma\} \\ & \cup \{\Delta \mid \text{S can deadlock from } \sigma\}\end{aligned}$$

Let us first establish an interesting relation between $\mathcal{M}_{imp}$ and $\mathcal{M}_{live}$.

Definition 6.2 A program S in $L(\|)$ is called strong if whenever $\langle S,\sigma\rangle \rightarrow^* \langle T_1\| \ldots \| T_n,\tau\rangle$ with $T_i = E$ holds for some $i \in \{1,\ldots,n\}$ then $T_1 \| \ldots \| T_n$ cannot diverge from τ.

Informally, S cannot diverge with one component terminated. This property is not decidable but it is often easy to check whether a given program is strong. E.g. program S^* of Sec. 4 is strong.

Proposition 6.3 For strong programs S in $L(\|)$ the equation $\mathcal{M}_{live}[\![S]\!] = \mathcal{M}_{imp}[\![S]\!]$ holds.

As done for impartiality we are looking for structure preserving transformations which realize the assumption of liveness. Clearly, for strong $L(\|)$-programs we can use $T_{imp+\Delta}$ due to Proposition 6.3. But in general things are more complicated:

Theorem 6.4 There is no sequential transformation $T: L(\|) \rightarrow L(\|,\underline{await},?)$ such that for every $S \in L(\|)$

$$\mathcal{M}_{live}[\![S]\!] = \mathcal{M}_{-\Delta}[\![T(S)]\!] \;\underline{\text{mod}}\; Z$$

holds where Z is the set of auxiliary variables in T(S).

The result is based on the fact that sequential transformations T cannot distinguish whether a certain substatement is the final statement in a component of a parallel program or whether it is followed by some other statement. To accomplish this distinction we use in our transformations further auxiliary variables end_i which record termination of the component programs.

We present a faithful (but non-sequential) transformation scheme

$$T_{live}: L(\|) \longrightarrow \mathcal{P}(L(\|,\underline{await},?)) \setminus \{\emptyset\}.$$

For a given program $S = S_0;(S_1 \parallel \ldots \parallel S_n)$ in $L(\parallel)$ let $T_{live}(S)$ be the set of all programs resulting from S by

(1) prefixing S with an initialisation part

$$INIT = z_1:=?;\ \ldots;z_n:=?;\ end_1:=false;\ \ldots\ ;end:=false$$

(2) replacing in every loop <u>while</u> b <u>do</u> S' <u>od</u> of a component S_i <u>some</u> atomic statement A in S' by

```
TEST_i(A) = await turn = i ∨ z̄ ≥ 1 then
                z_i:=?; for j ≠ i do
                           if ¬end_j then z_j:=z_j-1 fi
                        od;
                A
            end
```

(for i = 1,...,n).

(3) suffixing every component S_i by

$$END_i = end_i:=true$$

(for i = 1,...,n).

Again the z_i's and end_i's are new variables not already present in S. As additional abbreviation we use

$$turn = \min\{\, j \mid z_j = \min\{z_k \mid end_k = false\}\}\ .$$

Due to (3) all components of transformed programs $T \in T_{live}(S)$ have terminated when all variables end_i are true. Thus the expression turn is properly defined whenever a test $TEST_i(A)$ is executed in T.

<u>Theorem 6.5</u> For every program $S \in L(\parallel)$ and $T \in T_{live}(S)$ the equation

$$\mathcal{M}_{live}[\![S]\!] = \mathcal{M}[\![T]\!]\ \underline{mod}\ Z$$

holds where Z is the set of auxiliary variables z_i and end_i in T.

The proof of Theorem 6.5 shows that the transformation scheme T_{live} not only models the input-output behaviour of S but in fact provides a one-one correspondence between live computations of S and arbitrary computations of $T \in T_{live}(S)$. Therefore we can view T_{live} as an <u>abstract specification</u> of schedulers which guarantee liveness for parallel programs S. By Theorem 6.5 every deterministic scheduler can be <u>implemented</u> by replacing the random assignments z:=? in $T \in T_{live}(S)$ by deterministic assignments and by refining the Boolean conjuncts "$\bar{z} \geq 1$" in await-statements $TEST_i(A)$. (See /Pa/ for the notion of implementation in the context of specifications with unbounded nondeterminism.) Moreover Theorem 6.5 guarantees that all these implemented schedulers are <u>deadlock-free</u> and therefore never require any rescuing or backtracking from deadlocked configurations /Ho/.

7. Weak Fairness

In this section we extend our programming language to L(‖ ,<u>await</u>). Though liveness is an adequate formalization of the concept of concurrency for the language L(‖), it is not sufficient for L(‖ ,<u>await</u>). Consider the program

$$S^{***} = \underline{\text{while}}\ b\ \underline{\text{do}}\ x:=x+1\ \underline{\text{od}}\ \|\ \underline{\text{await}}\ \neg b\ \underline{\text{then}}\ \text{skip}\ \underline{\text{end}}\ .$$

We expect computations of S^{***} starting in a state σ with $\sigma(b)$ = true to diverge - independently whether the interleaving or a concurrent semantics is chosen. But with the simple defintion of liveness S^{***} always terminates: $\perp \notin \mathcal{M}_{live}[\![S^{***}]\!](\sigma)$ for every state σ.

In the presence of await's we have to refine the idea of liveness by replacing the notion of termination by the notion of enabledness of components (cf. Sec.3). This leads to the following concept of <u>weak fairness</u> /AO,FP/ (called <u>justice</u> in /LPS/).

<u>Definition 7.1</u> A computation $\xi : \langle S,\sigma\rangle = \langle T_1,\sigma_1\rangle \rightarrow \ldots \rightarrow \langle T_j,\sigma_j\rangle \rightarrow \ldots$ of an L(‖ ,<u>await</u>)-program $S = S_0;(S_1 \| \ldots \| S_n)$ is <u>weakly fair</u> if ξ is finite or the following holds for every $i \in \{1,\ldots,n\}$: if for all but finitely many j the component S_i is enabled in $\langle T_j,\sigma_j\rangle$, then there are infinitely many j such that component S_i is active in step $\langle T_j,\sigma_j\rangle \rightarrow \langle T_{j+1},\sigma_{j+1}\rangle$.

Thus in a weakly fair computation every component which is from some moment on continuously enabled will eventually make progress. This definition induces a semantics $\mathcal{M}_{wfair}$ analogously to $\mathcal{M}_{live}$.

<u>Remark 7.2</u> $\mathcal{M}_{wfair}[\![S]\!] = \mathcal{M}_{live}[\![S]\!]$ holds for all programs $S \in L(\|)$.

As for impartiality and liveness we wish to develop transformations which realize the assumption of weak fairness. (Note that the previous definitions of ‖ -preserving, admissible, sequential, faithful and deadlocking have straightforward extensions to transformations $T : L(\|,\underline{await}) \rightarrow L(\|,\underline{await},?)$.) These transformations are again more sophisticated than the previous ones because we have to check enabledness of components in front of <u>every</u> atomic statement inside of while-loops.

We refine the transformation scheme T_{live} of Sec.6 to an admissible, faithful scheme T_{wfair}. (Clearly T_{wfair} cannot be sequential by Theorem 6.4 and Remark 7.2.) Given a program $S = S_0;(S_1\| \ldots \| S_n)$ in L(‖ ,<u>await</u>) this scheme T_{wfair} will use sets of new variables, viz. z_i, end_i, pc_i for i = 1,...,n. The z_i's and end_i's are used as in T_{live}. The pc_i's are a restricted form of program counters which indicate when the component S_i is in front of an await-statement and if so in front of which one.

To this end, we assign to every occurrence of an await-statement in S_i a unique number $l \geq 1$ as label. Let L_i denote the set of all these labels for S_i and b_l denote the Boolean expression of the await-statement labelled by l. Further on we introduce for S_i the abbreviation

$$enabled_i \;=\; \neg end_i \wedge \bigwedge_{l \in L_i} (pc_i = l \rightarrow b_l) \; .$$

By the following construction of T_{wfair}, $enabled_i$ will be true iff the component S_i of S is indeed enabled.

The transformation scheme

$$T_{wfair} : L(\parallel, \underline{await}) \longrightarrow \mathcal{P}(L(\parallel, \underline{await}, ?)) \setminus \{\emptyset\}$$

maps a given program $S = S_o; (S_1 \parallel \ldots \parallel S_n)$ in $L(\parallel)$ into the set $T_{wfair}(S)$ of all programs resulting from S by

(1) prefixing S with

INIT = <u>for</u> i = 1,...,n <u>do</u> z_i:=?; end_i:=false; pc_i:=0 <u>od</u>

(2) replacing every substatement <u>await</u> b_l <u>then</u> S' <u>end</u> with $l \in L_i$ in S_i by

pc_i:=l; <u>await</u> b_l <u>then</u> S'; pc_i:=k <u>end</u>

where $k \notin L_i$ holds, e.g. k = 0 (for i = 1,...,n).

(3) transforming in the so prepared program every loop <u>while</u> b <u>do</u> S' <u>od</u> in a component S_i as follows:

(i) replace <u>some</u> atomic statement A in S' by

```
TEST_i(A) = await turn = i ∨ z̄ ≥ 1 then
                z_i:=?; for j ≠ i do
                            if enabled_j then z_j:=z_j-1
                                         else z_j:=?   fi
                        od;
                A
            end
```

(ii) replace every <u>other</u> atomic statement B in S' not affected under (i) by

```
RESET_i(B) = await true then
                 for j ≠ i do if ¬enabled_j then z_j:=? fi od;
                 B
             end
```

<u>Comment</u>: If A or B are already await-statements, we "amalgamate" their Boolean expressions with turn = i $\wedge$ $\bar{z} \geqslant 1$ or true to avoid nested await's. The expression turn is here defined as follows:

$$\text{turn} = \min\left\{ j \mid z_j = \min\left\{ z_k \mid \text{enabled}_k = \text{true} \right\}\right\}.$$

(4) suffixing every component S_i by

$$\text{END}_i \equiv \text{end}_i := \text{true}$$

Inside $\text{RESET}_i(B)$ and $\text{TEST}_i(A)$ each of the variables z_j associated with S_j is reset as soon as S_j gets disabled. Thus z_j is continuously decremented by $z_j := z_j - 1$ inside $\text{TEST}_i(A)$ only if S_j is continuously enabled. This formalizes the idea of weak fairness where only those components which are continuously enabled are guaranteed to progress eventually.

<u>Theorem 7.3</u> For every program $S \in L(\,\|\,,\underline{\text{await}})$ and $T \in T_{wfair}(S)$ the equation

$$\mathcal{M}_{wfair}[\![S]\!] = \mathcal{M}[\![T]\!] \ \underline{\text{mod}}\ Z$$

holds where Z is the set of auxiliary variables z_i, end_i and pc_i in T.

8. Strong Fairness

Weak fairness guarantees progress of those components which are continuously enabled. A more ambitious version of fairness is <u>strong fairness</u> /AO,FP/ (called <u>fairness</u> in /LPS/) where progress is already guaranteed if the component is infinitely often enabled.

<u>Definition 8.1</u> A computation $\xi : \langle S,\sigma\rangle = \langle T_1,\sigma_1\rangle \rightarrow \ldots \rightarrow \langle T_j,\sigma_j\rangle \rightarrow \ldots$ of an $L(\,\|\,,\underline{\text{await}})$-program $S = S_0;(S_1 \| \ldots \| S_n)$ is <u>strongly fair</u> if ξ is finite or the following holds for every $i \in \{1,\ldots,n\}$: if for infinitely many j the component S_i is enabled in $\langle T_j,\sigma_j\rangle$, then there are infinitely many j such that component S_i is active in the step $\langle T_j,\sigma_j\rangle \rightarrow \langle T_{j+1},\sigma_{j+1}\rangle$.

Analogously to $\mathcal{M}_{wfair}$ we define $\mathcal{M}_{sfair}$. We refine the previous transformation scheme T_{wfair} to a scheme

$$T_{sfair} : L(\,\|\,,\underline{\text{await}}) \longrightarrow \mathcal{P}(L(\,\|\,,\underline{\text{await}},?)) \setminus \{\emptyset\}$$

for strong fairness. For a given program $S = S_0;(S_1 \| \ldots \| S_n)$ in $L(\,\|\,,\underline{\text{await}})$ let $T_{sfair}(S)$ result from S by applying the steps (1), (2) and (4) as in T_{wfair} but with the following new step (3):

(3) replace in the so prepared program <u>every</u> atomic statement A occurring in a while-loop of S_i by

$TEST_i(A)$ = $\underline{await}$ turn = i $\vee$ $\bar{z} \geq 1$ $\underline{then}$

z_i:=?; $\underline{for}$ j $\neq$ i $\underline{do}$

$\underline{if}$ $enabled_j$ $\underline{then}$ $z_j := z_j - 1$ $\underline{fi}$

$\underline{od}$;

A

$\underline{end}$

As with T_{wfair} we have to test the enabledness of the components S_j of S in front of every atomic statement. But in contrast to T_{wfair} the transformed programs $T \in T_{sfair}(S)$ do not reset the variables z_j for component S_j when S_j gets disabled. Instead we have to decrement z_j (and be prepared for switching to component S_j) whenever S_j is enabled. This change ensures that those S_j which are infinitely often enabled make eventually progress. These observations are formalized in:

Theorem 8.2 For every program $S \in L(\|,\underline{await})$ and $T \in T_{sfair}(S)$ the equation

$$\mathcal{M}_{sfair}[\![S]\!] = \mathcal{M}[\![T]\!] \ \underline{mod}\ Z$$

holds where Z is the set of auxiliary variables z_i, end_i and pc_i in T.

9. Conclusion

We presented here a series of structure preserving transformations which reduce different notions of a concurrent or fair semantics for parallel programs to a simple interleaving semantics. These transformations can be viewed as abstract specifications of schedulers guaranteeing only fair computations.

But they also provide a basis for syntax-directed correctness proofs for parallel programs under fairness assumptions. We outline this idea with help of a simple example. Consider the $L(\|)$-program

S = $\underline{while}$ x > 0 $\underline{do}$ skip; x:=x-1 $\underline{od}$ $\|$ $\underline{while}$ x > 0 $\underline{do}$ skip $\underline{od}$.

Under the interleaving semantics $\mathcal{M}$ this program can diverge but under the semantics $\mathcal{M}_{live}$ modelling the assumption of liveness S always terminates. We write this fact as

(1) $\models_{live} \{true\}\ S\ \{true\}$

in the sense of total correctness modulo liveness.

First observe that S is a strong $L(\|)$-program. Thus to prove (1) it suffices to apply the transformation scheme $T_{imp+\Delta}$ modelling impartiality and prove for $\underline{some}$ program $T \in T_{imp+\Delta}(S)$

(2) $\models_{-\Delta} \{true\}\ T\ \{true\}$

where $\models_{-\Delta}$ refers to the interleaving semantics $\mathcal{M}_{-\Delta}$ ignoring deadlocks. The equivalence of (1) and (2) follows from Theorem 5.7 and Proposition 6.3.

To prove (2) we will use a simple extension of the proof system /OG/ which ignores deadlocks but deals with termination in the presence of random assignments z:=? , i.e. the extension deals with "total correctness modulo deadlocks". As in /OG/ the extended proof system proceeds in two steps: first it proves correctness of the components of a parallel program T and then it uses a proof rule for parallel composition to prove correctness of the whole program T.

Note that in our particular example S there are two transformed programs $T \in T_{imp+\Delta}(S)$ for which we could prove correctness in the sense of (2) with the extended proof system of /OG/ - one, say T_1, is obtained by applying the expansion $TEST_1(A)$ of $T_{imp+\Delta}(S)$ to the atomic statement A = skip in the first component of S, another one, say T_2, by applying $TEST_1(A)$ to A = x:=x-1. It turns out that for T_2 claim (2) is considerably simpler to prove correct in the extended proof system than for T_1. This observation explains the advantage of having nondeterministic transformation schemes like $T_{imp+\Delta}$ to our disposal: they can be applied flexible according to the needs of particular examples like S.

Finally, we stress the fact that for proving (1) about S we simply need to prove total correctness modulo deadlocks for $T_2 \in T_{imp+\Delta}(S)$ in (2). This connection explains why in correctness proofs deadlocking transformation schemes like $T_{imp+\Delta}$ are often desirable. For describing schedulers we are of course advised to use faithful transformation schemes only.

Acknowledgement. Research on this paper was supported by the German Research Council (DFG) under grant La 426/3-1.

References

/AO/ K.R. Apt, E.-R. Olderog, Proof rules and transformations dealing with fairness, Science of Computer Programming 3 (1983) 65-100; extended abstract appeared in: D. Kozen (Ed.), Proc. Logics of Programs 1981, Lecture Notes in Computer Science 131 (Springer, Berlin, 1982) 1-8.

/AP/ K.R. Apt, G.D. Plotkin, Countable nondeterminism and random assignment, Technical Report, Univ. of Edinburgh (1982); extended abstract appeared in: S. Even, O. Kariv (Eds.), Proc. 8th Coll. Automata, languages and Programming, Lecture Notes in Computer Science 115 (Springer, Berlin, 1981) 479-494.

/APS/ K.R. Apt, A. Pnueli, J. Stavi, Fair termination revisited - with delay, in: Proc. 2nd Conf. on Software Technology and Theoretical Computer Science, Bangalore (1982).

/Br1/ M. Broy, Transformational semantics for concurrent programs, Inform. Proc. Letters 11 (1980) 87-91.

/Br2/ M. Broy, Are fairness assumptions fair? , in: Proc. 2nd Intern. Conf. on Distributed Computing Systems (IEEE, Paris, 1981) 116-125.

/Di/ E.W. Dijkstra, A Discipline of Programming (Prentice Hall, 1976).

/FP/ M.J. Fisher, M.S. Paterson, Storage requirements for fair scheduling, Manuscript, Univ. of Warwick (1982).

/FS1/ L. Flon, N. Suzuki, Nondeterminism and the correctness of parallel programs, in: E.J. Neuhold (Ed.), Formal Description of Programming Concepts I (North Holland, Amsterdam, 1978) 589-608.

/FS2/ L. Flon, N. Suzuki, The total correctness of parallel programs, SIAM J. Comp. 10 (1981) 227-246.

/Fr/ N. Francez, Fairness, Unpublished Manuscript, Technion Univ. (1983).

/HP/ M.C.B. Henessy, G.D. Plotkin, Full abstraction for a simple programming language, in: J. Bečvář (Ed.), Proc. 8th Symp. on Mathematical Foundations of Computer Science 74 (Springer, Berlin, 1979) 108-120.

/Ho/ C.A.R. Hoare, Some properties of predicate transformers, J. ACM 25 (1978) 461-480.

/LPS/ D. Lehmann, A. Pnueli, J. Stavi, Impartiality, justice and fairness: the ethics of concurrent termination, in: S. Even, O. Kariv (Eds.), Proc. 8th Coll. Automata, Languages and Programming, Lecture Notes in Computer Science 115 (Springer, Berlin, 1981) 264-277.

/MP/ Z. Manna, A. Pnueli, Verification of concurrent programs: the temporal framework, in: R.S. Boyer, J.S. Moore (Eds.), The Correctness Problem in Computer Science, International Lecture Series in Computer Science (Academic Press, London, 1981).

/OG/ S. Owicki, D. Gries, An axiomatic proof technique for parallel programs, Acta Informatica 6 (1976) 319-340.

/OL/ S. Owicki, L. Lamport, Proving liveness properties of concurrent programs, ACM TOPLAS 4 (1982) 455-495.

/Pa/ D. Park, On the semantics of fair parallelism, in: D. Bjørner (Ed.), Proc. Abstract Software Specifications, Lecture Notes in Computer Science 86 (Springer, Berlin, 1979) 504-526.

/Pl/ G.D. Plotkin, A structural approach to operational semantics, Technical Report DAIMI-FN 19, Comp. Sci. Dept., Aarhus Univ. (1981).

/Pn/ A. Pnueli, The temporal semantics of concurrent programs, Theoretical Computer Science 13 (1981) 45-60.

COMPUTING THE LARGEST EMPTY RECTANGLE

B. Chazelle[1], R. L. Drysdale III[2], and D. T. Lee[3]
1. Dept. Computer Science, Brown University
2. Dept. Mathematics and Computer Science, Dartmouth College
3. Dept. Electrical Engineering/Computer Science, Northwestern Univeristy

ABSTRACT

We consider the following problem: Given a rectangle containing N points, find the largest area subrectangle with sides parallel to those of the original rectangle which contains none of the given points. If the rectangle is a piece of fabric or sheet metal and the points are flaws, this problem is finding the largest-area rectangular piece which can be salvaged. A previously known result[13] takes $O(N^2)$ worst-case and $O(N\log^2 N)$ expected time. This paper presents an $O(N \log^3 N)$ time, $O(N \log N)$ space algorithm to solve this problem. It uses a divide-and-conquer approach similar to the ones used by Strong and Bentley[1] and introduces a new notion of Voronoi diagram along with a method for efficient computation of certain functions over paths of a tree.

Introduction

We consider the following problem: Given a rectangle containing n points, find the largest area subrectangle with sides parallel to those of the original rectangle which contains none of the given points. The special case in which a largest empty square is desired has been solved in $\Theta(n \log n)$ time using Voronoi diagrams in L_1-(L_∞-) metric[7,12], which is just a variation of the largest empty circle problem studied by Shamos[14,15]. In [13] an $O(n^2)$ worst-case and $O(n\log^2 n)$ expected-time algorithm is presented for the largest empty rectangle problem. Other related problem can be found in [3,5].

Note that the largest area rectangle with sides parallel to the bounding rectangle has each edge supported by either an edge of the bounding rectangle or by at least one of the given points. Any rectangle is uniquely determined by its four supports (points or edges of the bounding rectangle).

Let $p_1, p_2, \ldots, p_n$ be the n points sorted by x-coordinate and x_{min}, x_{max}, y_{min}, and y_{max} be the boundaries of the bounding rectangle. Let the coordinates of point p_i be (x_i, y_i). Our algorithm splits the points into two halves by x-coordinate and

*Supported in part by the National Science Foundation under Grants MCS 83-42862, and ECS 81-21741.
#A full version of this paper can be found in [4].

recursively solves the problem for the sets $\{p_1, \ldots, p_{\lfloor n/2\rfloor}\}$ and $\{p_{\lfloor n/2\rfloor+1}, \ldots, p_n\}$. (The bounding rectangles of these recursive calls must be adjusted. The right boundary for the left call is $x_{\lfloor n/2\rfloor}$ and the left boundary for the right call is $x_{\lfloor n/2\rfloor+1}$.) These calls determine the largest rectangles with all four supporting points or edges in one half or the other. What remains are rectangles with supports in both halves. These rectangles contain either three supports in one half and one support in the other or two supports in each half (see Fig. 1). Our algorithm finds the largest rectangle of each type, and then returns the largest rectangle found with either all four supports in one half, three supports in one half and one in the other, or two on each side as the largest rectangle. Therefore the run time of our algorithm is governed by the time required to find the largest rectangle with three supports in one half and one in the other and the time to find the largest rectangle with two supports in each half. That is, we have

(1) $T(N) \leq 2T(N/2) + C(N) + D(N)$,

where $T(N)$ denotes the run time of the algorithm for the largest empty rectangle problem for N points, $C(N)$ the time for finding the largest empty rectangle with three supports in one half and one support in the other half and $D(N)$ the time for finding the rectangle with two supports in each half.

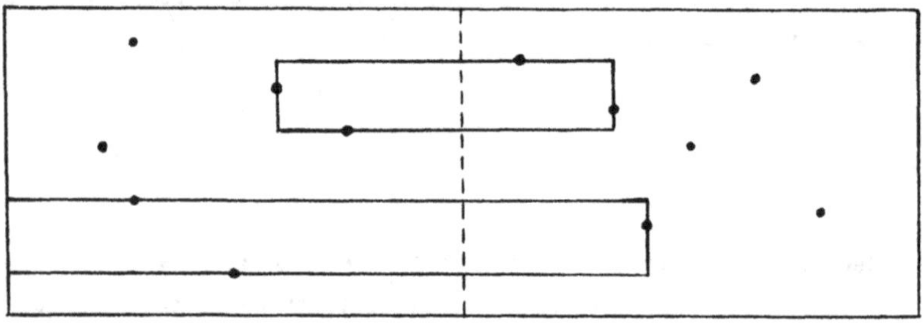

Figure 1. Possible empty rectangles

Three supports in one half, one in the other.

We will look at the case of three supports in the left half and one in the right and present a linear time algorithm for this case. The other case is symmetrical, and is solved the same way.

If the left support is a given point p_j, the rectangle is completely determined. The upper edge is supported by the first point above p_j which also lies to its right. If no such point exists, the rectangle is supported by the top edge of the bounding rectangle. Similarly the bottom edge is supported by the first point below p_j which also lies to its right if such a point exists, and the bottom edge of the bounding rectangle otherwise. Let $upper_i$ and $lower_i$ denote, resp. the upper and lower supports of the rectangle whose left support is p_i. The right support $right_i$

is found by extending the rectangle supported above by $upper_i$ and below by $lower_i$ to the right until it encounters either a point in the right half or the right edge of the bounding rectangle.

We present below a linear time algorithm to find the upper, lower and right supports of each rectangle supported on the left by a point p_i in the left half. Suppose that the points in the left half are sorted from top to bottom as p_1, p_2, ..., p_m. gap_i is defined to be the right support of the rectangle supported above by p_{i-1} and below by p_i, with $p_0 = (x_{max}, y_{max})$ and $p_{m+1} = (x_{min}, y_{min})$, and right(i) initialized to be the point with the leftmost point in the right half with y-coordinate y_i, or to $q_i = (x'_{max}, y_i)$ if no such point exists, where x'_{max} is the right boundary of the bounding rectangle for the right half. The arrays above and below are used to hold the points with running minimum x-coordinates.

1. Initialize the stack with upper support p_0 and $q_0 = (x'_{max}, y_{max})$ so that top is p_0, $x(top) = x_{max}$, $y(top) = y_{max}$, $above(top) = q_0$ and $x(q_0) = x'_{max}$.
2. Scan the points p_1, p_2, ..., p_m from top to bottom. For each point p_j encountered we do the following.
   2.1 If x(gap(j)) < x(right(j)) then above(j) is set to gap(j) and to right(j) otherwise.
   2.2 While x(top) $\leq$ x(j) do;
   if x(above(j)) $\geq$ x(above(top)) then above(j) is set to above(top); pop the stack.
   2.3 upper(j) is set to top.
   2.4 Push p_j onto the stack.
3. Re-initialize the stack with lower support p_{m+1} and $q_{m+1} = (x'_{max}, y_{min})$ so that top is p_{m+1}, $x(top) = x_{min}$, $y(top) = y_{min}$, $below(top) = q_{m+1}$ and $x(q_{m+1}) = x'_{max}$.
4. Scan the points p_1, p_2, ..., p_m from bottom to top. For each point p_j encountered we do the following.
   4.1 If x(gap(j+1)) < x(right(j)) then below(j) is set to gap(j+1) and to right(j) otherwise.
   4.2 While x(top) $\leq$ x(j) do;
   if x(below(j)) $\geq$ x(below(top)) then below(j) is set to below(top); pop the stack.
   4.3 lower(j) is set to top.
   4.4 Push p_j onto the stack.
5. For each point p_j, j = 1, 2, ..., m do;
   if x(above(j)) < x(below(j))
   then right(j) is set to above(j)
   else right(j) is set to below(j).

Lemma 1: The time C(N) for finding the largest empty rectangle for N points with three supports in one half and one support in the other half is O(N).

The proofs of this and following lemmas can be found in [4].

Two supports in each half

Notice that the two supports in the left half must determine either the upper left corner or the lower left corner of the rectangle and the other two supports in the right half determine the lower right corner or the upper right corner of the rectangle respectively. Since these two cases are similar, we consider only the case where the two supports in the left half determine the lower left corner and the two supports in the right half determine the upper right corner of the rectangle, and address ourselves to the problem of finding the so-called largest empty corner rectangle (LECR) determined by a corner point in each half.

Computation of corner points

We observe that two points p_i and p_j determine the lower left corner point of an empty rectangle iff p_j is $lower_i$. Thus, the point LC_i, i= 1, 2, ..., m, determined by p_i and $lower_i$ is a lower left corner point and has as its x- and y-coordinates equal to x_i and $y(lower_i)$ respectively. In addition to these lower left corner points we include the points $L_i = (x_{min}, y_i)$, i=1,2,...,m, i.e., the points on the left boundary, and the original set of points to form the set CL = $\{LC_1, LC_2, \ldots, LC_s\}$ where $s \leq 3*m$. All the possible upper right corner points in the right half can be computed in an analogous manner. We now have two sets of corner points CL $=\{LC_1, LC_2, \ldots, LC_s\}$ and CR $=\{RC_1, RC_2, \ldots, RC_t\}$ and want to find the largest empty (corner) rectangle whose lower left corner and upper right corner are from CL and CR respectively. Fig. 2 shows the corner points in each half, with • and x representing given and newly created points, respectively. Notice that not every point in CL can be paired with a point in CR. The empty rectangle that we seek must be a rectangle with exactly two supports in each half. For example, in Figure 2 the point P in CL can only be paired with point Q in CR (but not Q'). Specifically, the following pairing condition must be satisfied: the corner point LC_i with left support p_ℓ and bottom support p_b can only be paired with a point RC_j whose corresponding top support is higher than p_ℓ and right support higher than p_b. Secondly, since original points are included in CL and CR, we should not use any of these points as corner points of the corner rectangle. However, as we will see in the following two lemmas, these problems will not arise as far as the computation of the LECR is concerned. Inclusion of the given points in CL and CR is to ensure that the corner rectangle thus determined contains no given points in its interior.

Lemma 2: The largest empty corner rectangle cannot use any of the given points as corner points. Furthermore, its corner points satisfy the pairing condition.

Lemma 3: If the corner rectangle thus obtained does not contain any given point in its interior, then it must also not contain any newly created corner points.

they can be trimmed is that they cannot form the LECR with a point in CL_2. Similar remarks can be made about CL_2, and we can trim this set in a similar way. We can also apply this clean-up to CL_1 and CR_2. Note that this final clean-up removes from CL_1 the points that have the same y-coordinate except the rightmost one and removes from CR_2 the points that have the same y-coordinate except the leftmost one. This clean-up procedure can be accomplished in O(N) time. In what follows we assume that these sets have been trimmed.

The next step is to determine, for each point in CL_2, the set of points in CR_1 with which the point can be paired. This set is clearly a contiguous subsequence of the points $M_1, M_2, \ldots, M_u$ of CR_1 given in ascending x-order. We will therefore precompute the functions $\ell(P)$, and $r(P)$ such that the set $\{M_{\ell(P)}, M_{\ell(P)+1}, \ldots, M_{r(P)}\}$ contains exactly the points of CR_1 which can be paired with P to form an empty corner rectangle (Fig. 4). It is easy to precompute the function ℓ (and by the same token, r) in linear time. Once the set $\{M_{\ell(P)}, M_{\ell(P)+1}, \ldots, M_{r(P)}\}$ associated with P is computed, in order to facilitate searching of a point M_i in the set with which to pair P to form the LECR we make use of the notion of so called LL-diagram, which is similar to the notion of Voronoi diagram (See, e.g. [10,11,15]).

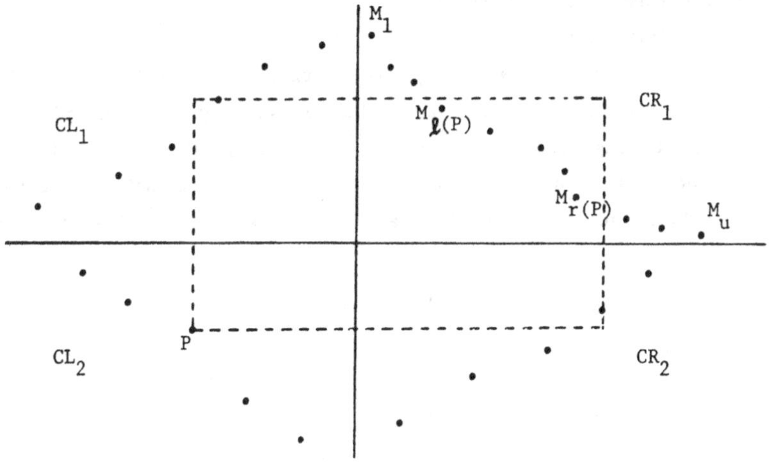

Figure 4. Points in CR_1 that can be paired with P in CL_2

Computing the LL-diagram

The LL-diagram of a set $S = \{M_1, M_2, \ldots, M_N\}$, denoted LL(S), is defined as follows: LL(S) is a set of regions $\{V(M_1), V(M_2), \ldots, V(M_N)\}$, where

$$V(M_i) = \{ M \in NE^* \mid d(M,M_i) \geq d(M,M_j) \text{ for all } j = 1,2,\ldots,N\}$$

and d(A,B) measures the area of the corner rectangle between A and B if B dominates

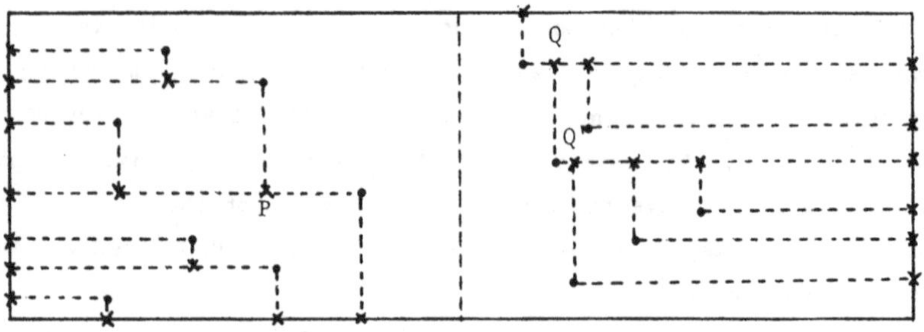

Figure 2. Newly created corner points

Computing the largest empty corner rectangle

Divide the sets CL and CR each into two subsets CL_1, CL_2 and CR_1, CR_2, respectively, with CL_1 above CL_2 and CR_1 above CR_2, using a horizontal line such that $CL_1 \cup CR_1$ is approximately of the same size as $CL_2 \cup CR_2$ (Fig. 3). Assume recursively that we have computed the LECR in $CL_1 \cup CR_1$ and in $CL_2 \cup CR_2$. So we may concentrate on the case where the lower left corner is in CL_2 and upper right corner is in CR_1. If E(N) denotes the time complexity of the latter problem and D(N) denotes that of the former problem, we have

(2) $D(N) \leq 2D(N/2) + E(N)$

We may discard all the points of CR_1 that "dominate" any other, and for points with the same y-coordinate we further trim them by keeping only the rightmost one that does not dominate any other point in CR_1. Similarly, for points with the same x-coordinate we keep only the topmost point that does not dominate any other point in CR_1. See Fig. 3, in which points eliminated are marked as ×. The reason why

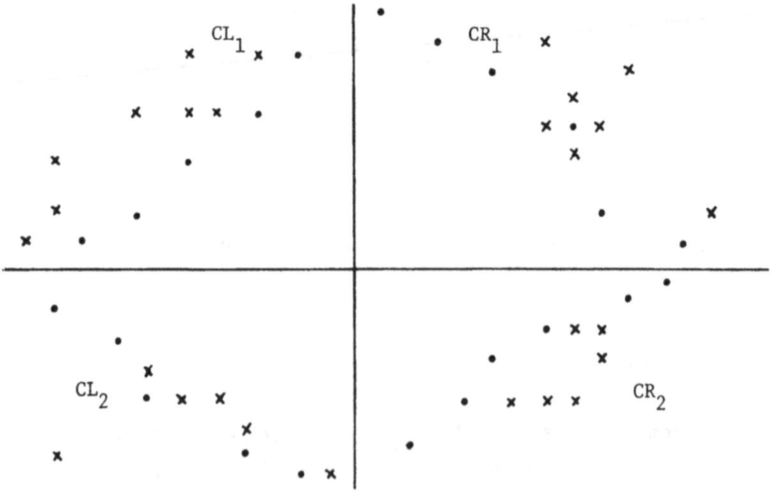

Figure 3. Subdivision of points and trimming operation

A and is zero otherwise; NE^* denotes the region $(-\infty, x_{max}] \times (-\infty, y_{max}]$ excluding the smallest enclosing rectangle of S, where x_{max} and y_{max} are maximum x-and y-coordinates of S respectively, and is the crossed-line area shown in Fig 5. Note that if a point M of S is dominated by another, its associated region V(M) is empty. The LL-diagram of S has the following properties (Lemmas 4, 5 and 6).

Lemma 4: Let S be a set of N maxima, M_1, M_2, ..., M_N. Then LL(S) consists of a set of possibly unbounded polygons which partitions NE^*. All the polygons (except one) are convex, and LL(S) involves only O(N) edges.

Lemma 5: Let M_1, M_2, ..., M_N occur in this order with ascending x-coordinate and let L be any line parallel to the x-axis. It is impossible to find two points A and B on L in NE^* with increasing coordinates such that A and B lie in $V(M_i)$ and $V(M_j)$, respectively, with $i > j$.

Lemma 6: The LL-diagram of a set of N points can be computed in O(N log N) time using divide-and-conquer technique.(See [10,11,15] for a general approach.)

Consider the complete binary tree T that has M_1, M_2,..., M_u of CR_1 for leaves, from left to right. Letting SL be the set of sequences of leaves of each subtree of T, we can use the segment-tree technique[2] to decompose any contiguous subsequences of M_1, M_2, ..., M_u into a concatenation of O(log u) sequences in SL. We also use a technique similar to the one used in Gowda, et. al.[6] to precompute the LL-diagrams associated with each sequence of points in SL and attach to each of internal nodes so that searches for the "farthest" neighbor of P in each of the sequences can be performed.(Fig.6) Searching for the farthest neighbor is, in this case, equivalent to determining in which region of the LL-diagram P lies. This can be accomplished in logarithmic time, using only linear space with Kirkpatrick's planar point location algorithm[8].

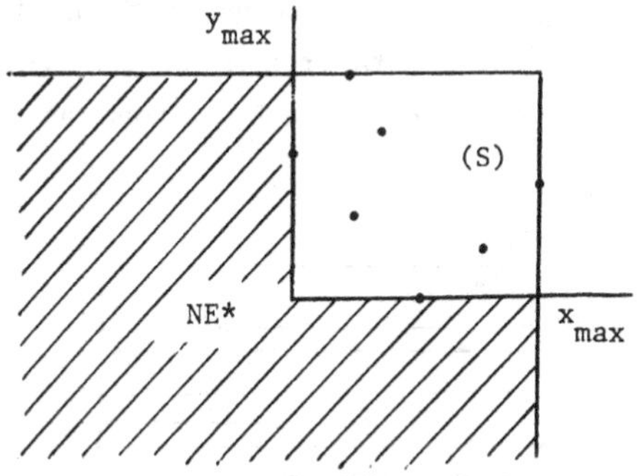

Figure 5. Domain of definition of LL-diagram

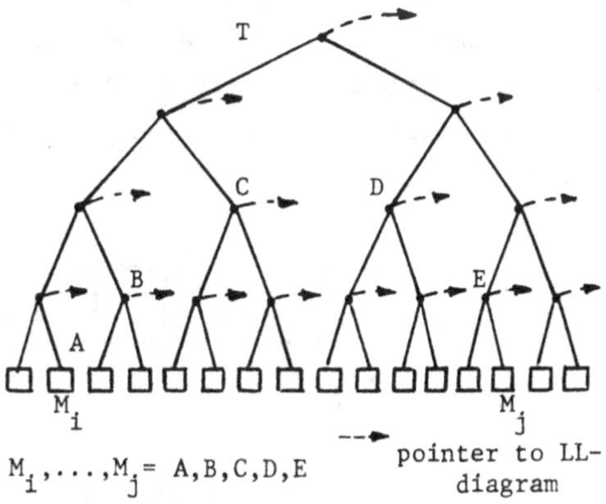

Figure 6. Decomposition of interval (M_i, M_j)

To summarize, the preprocessing of the recursive step consists of:

1. Trimming CL_1, CL_2, CR_1 and CR_2 in O(N) time and space.
2. Precomputing the functions ℓ, and r in O(N) time and space.
3. Setting up the tree T for CR_1, and computing the LL-diagram of each sequence of points in SL in O(N log N) time and space. (See Lemma 6 and [6])
4. Setting up the preprocessing required by Kirkpatrick's planar point location algorithm for each LL-diagram computed, which requires O(k) time and space for a set of k points.

The computation of the farthest neighbor in $\{M_{\ell(P)}, \ldots, M_{r(P)}\}$ of each point P in CL_2 is done by performing O(log u) planar point searches, each requiring O(log u) time. We conclude that it is possible to find the LECR with corners in CR_1 and CL_2 in time $E(N) = O(N \log^2 N)$ and space O(N log N). From the relations (1) and (2) we therefore have the following.

Lemma 7: The largest empty corner rectangle with corner points in CL and CR can be computed in $D(N) = O(N \log^3 N)$ time and O(N log N) space.

Theorem 1: The largest empty rectangle problem for N points in the plane can be solved in $T(N) = O(N \log^4 N)$ time and O(N log N) space.

An improved algorithm for computing LECR

The previous result can still be improved using a less redundant representation. Let $M_1, \ldots, M_u$ be the points of CR. We will arrange the points to be the nodes of a rooted tree T_{CR} that is constructed as follows. The root is an imaginary point situated entirely above and to the left of CR. First of all, the points with the same y-coordinates are connected to form chains, ordered in y-coordinate. Then for each chain we connect the leftmost point to the point in a higher chain that is directly above it. (Fig.7) We note that if P is an arbitrary point in CL and M_i is the lowest (rightmost) point of CR higher than P, the path from M_i to the root of the tree contains the only points which can be paired with P to form an LECR (Fig.7).

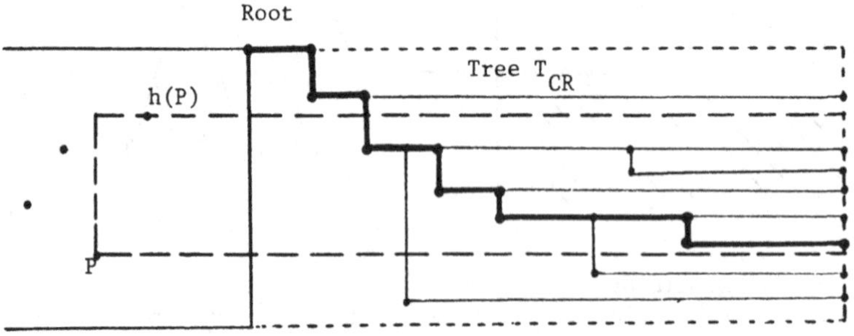

Figure 7. Construction of the tree T_{CR}

By analogy with the previous paragraph, we will precompute for each point in CL the functions ℓ and r, which will now point to nodes in T_{CR}. Notice that $M_{r(P)}$ is simply the lowest (rightmost) point of CR higher than P, and can be computed in linear time for each P in CL. Similarly, we can compute the "vertical" obstacle h(P) = upper(P), in CL for each point P in linear time. The function ℓ is computed in O(N log N) time by scanning the points from top to bottom; maintaining a path for points in T_{CR} and performing binary searches for points P in CL to find the highest point below h(P) in the path.

Computing path functions in a free tree

Let T be a free tree with N vertices, each of degree at most 3. We consider functions of the form F(v,w), defined for any pair of vertices v, w of T. These functions are assumed to have the following property: there exists an associative operator OP computable in O(1) time, such that for any vertex z on the path from v to w, we have

$$F(v,w) = F(w,v) = OP(F(v,z), F(z,w)).$$

Suppose now that in order to compute F(v,w) we can use a data structure L(v,w), which requires O(P) space and can be computed in O(P log P) time, where P is the number of nodes on the path between v and w, so that F(v,w) can then be evaluated in O(f(P)) time. Instead of precomputing all possible structures L(v,w) for all pairs of nodes v, w, we compute only a subset of them $R=L(v_i,w_i)$, which takes only O(N log N) space, and has the property that the path between any pair of nodes in T is the concatenation of disjoint paths between O(log N) pairs (v_i,w_i). The availability of R clearly allows us to evaluate F(v,w) in O(f(N)log N) time, assuming that we can express the path (v,w) as a sequence in R in O(log N) time.

The structure R is constructed recursively as follows. We represent T, as a rooted ternary tree G: let C, the centroid[9] of T be the root of G. We assume without loss of generality that we have exactly 3 subtrees, T_1, T_2, T_3, rooted at C. We then proceed to compute their centroids, C_1, C_2, C_3, which we insert in G as the sons of the root C. We iterate on this process for each subtree, labeling the nodes in the following manner. Assume that T_i has exactly N_i vertices ($N_1 + N_2 + N_3 = N - 1$). The root C is labeled N and the general rule is that T_1 will be labeled recursively with the integers $\{1,\dots,N_1\}$, T_2 with $\{N_1+1,\dots,N_1+N_2\}$, and T_3 with $\{N_1+N_2+1,\dots,N-1\}$ and the root of each subtree is labeled with the highest label available.

Our next task is to augment G with new edges, called <u>extra-edges</u>. For each vertex v of G we, in turn, apply the following procedure to all the vertices which are adjacent to v in T and are labeled lower than v in G. Let w be such a vertex. Since it clearly must lie in the subtree of G rooted at v, we link to v every node including w on the path in G from v to w, thus adding the so-called extra-edges (Fig. 8).

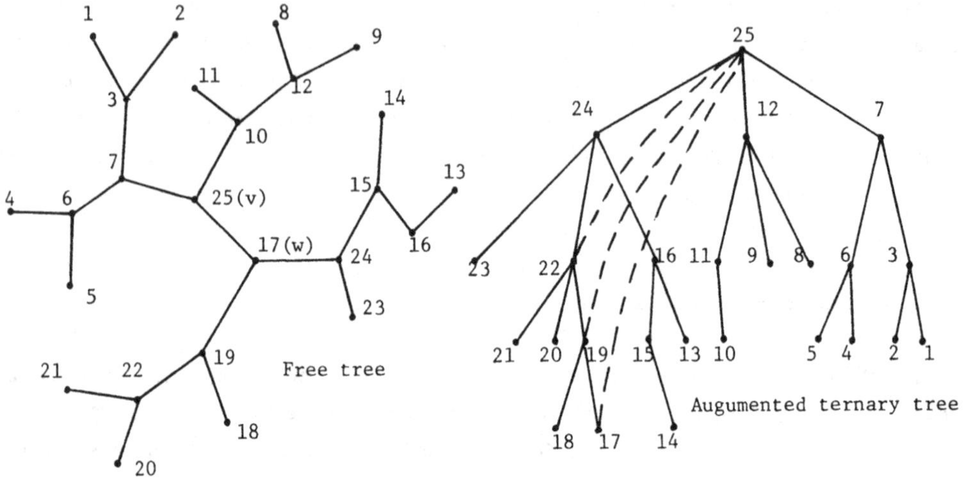

Since we can compute centroids in linear time[9] and G clearly has height O(log N), it is easy to construct the tree in time O(N log N). The final addition to G is to set pointers from each edge (u,v) of G to the structure L(u,v). The overall time and space complexities can be shown to be $T(N) = O(N \log^2 N)$ and $S(N) = O(N \log N)$ respectively. We state without proof that F(u,v) can be computed in O(f(N)log N) time for any pair (u,v) of nodes in T.

Lemma 8: With O(N log N)-space, $O(N \log^2 N)$-time preprocessing, it is possible to evaluate F(u,v) in O(f(N)log N) time for any pair of vertices u,v in T.

Computing the LECR efficiently

A simple application of the previous paragraph provides an improved algorithm for computing the LECR of the set S = CL U CR. Clearly T is our tree T_{CR}, the structure L(u,v) is the LL-diagram of the points of CR on the path between u and v, preprocessed so as to allow for Kirkpatrick's planar point location algorithm, the function F(u,v) simply returns the regions in L(u,v) where a given point P of CL lies; its complexity is therefore f(N) = O(log N). Note that the only discrepancy comes from the fact that T_{CR} is not necessarily a tree with degree ≤ 3. There is an easy fix, however. We simply introduce dummy vertices to reduce any excessive degree to 3. This adds only O(N) vertices and thus does not affect the complexity of the our algorithm. We are now in a position to compute the LECR in S. To do so, compute $F(M_{\ell(P)},M_{r(P)})$ for all P in CL, and return the point which gives the largest area along with its upper right neighbor. Thus, with Lemma 8 and the above discussion we have the following.

Lemma 9: It is possible to compute the LECR in $D(N) = O(N \log^2 N)$ time and in $O(N \log N)$ space.

Using relation (1) we can state our main result:

Theorem 2: The largest empty rectangle problem for a set of N points can be computed in $O(N \log^3 N)$ time and $O(N \log N)$ space.

Conclusion

We have presented an $O(N \log^3 N)$-time and $O(N \log N)$ space algorithm for computing the largest area rectangle which contains none of the N points in its interior. A simpler version of the algorithm with running time $O(N \log^4 N)$ and space $O(N \log N)$ has also been given. The algorithms are primarily based on the divide-and-conquer strategy. We have addressed only the problem of locating a rectangle whose sides are parallel to those of the bounding rectangle of the given set of points. If the rectangle sought is arbitrarily oriented, the problem seems a lot more difficult. Naturally one may ask for an arbitrary polygon instead of a rectangle within a bounded region. For instance, find a largest empty triangle within a rectangle. If the sides of the triangle have been predetermined, then the largest empty triangle can be found in $O(n \log n)$ time and $O(n)$ space using divide-and-conquer technique. As for general polygons no efficient algorithms are known.

References

1. Bentley, J. L., "Divide-and-conquer algorithms for closest point problems in multidimensional space," Ph. D. thesis, Dept. Comput. Sci., Univ. of North Carolina, Chapel Hill, NC., 1976.

2. Bentley J. L. and D. Wood, "An optimal worst case algorithm for reporting intersections of rectangles," IEEE Trans. Comput., (July 1980), 571-577.

3. Boyce, J. E., D. P. Dobkin, R. L. Drysdale III, and L. J. Guibas, "Finding extremal polygons," Proc. ACM Symp. Theory of Comput., (May 1982), 282-289.

4. Chazelle, B. M., R. L. Drysdale III, and D. T. Lee, "Computing the largest empty rectangle," Dept. Comput. Sci. Brown Univ. Tech. Rep. CS 83-20, Sept. 1983.

5. Dobkin, D. P., R. L. Drysdale III, and L. J. Guibas, "Finding smallest polygons," in Advances of Computing Research, Vol. 1, (F. P. Preparata, ed.), JAI Press Inc. (1983), 181-224.

6. Gowda, I. G., D. G. Kirkpatrick, D. T. Lee and A. Naamad, "Dynamic Voronoi diagrams," IEEE Trans. Information Theory., IT-29,5 (Sept. 1983), 724-731.

7. Hwang, F. K., "An O(n log n) algorithm for rectilinear minimal spanning trees," J. ACM, 26,2 (April 1979), 177-182.

8. Kirkpatrick, D. G., "Optimal search in planar subdivisions," SIAM J. Comput., 12 (1983), 28-35.

9. Knuth, D. E., The Art of Computer Programming, Vol. I: Fundamental Algorithms, Addison-Wesley, Reading, Mass., 1968.

10. Lee, D. T., "Two dimensional Voronoi diagrams in the L_p-metric," J. ACM, 27,4 (Oct. 1980), 604-618.

11. Lee, D. T. and R. L. Drysdale III, "Generalization of Voronoi diagrams in the plane," SIAM J. Comput. 10,1 (Feb. 1981), 73-87.

12. Lee, D. T. and C. K. Wong, "Voronoi diagrams in L_1-(L_∞-)metrics with 2-dimensional storage applications," SIAM J. Comput. 9 (1980), 200-211.

13. Naamad, A., W. L. Hsu, and D. T. Lee, "On maximum empty rectangle problem," Disc. Applied Math., to appear.

14. Shamos, M. I., "Computational geometry," Ph. D. dissertation, Dept. Computer Sci., Yale Univ., 1978.

15. Shamos, M. I. and D. Hoey, "Closest-point problem," Proc. 16th IEEE Symp. on Foundations of Computer Science, (Oct. 1975), 151-162.

APPROXIMATION SCHEMES FOR COVERING AND PACKING PROBLEMS IN ROBOTICS AND VLSI

Extended Abstract

Dorit S. Hochbaum and Wolfgang Maass
350 Barrows Hall Department of Computer Science
University of California, Berkeley
Berkeley, California 94720

1. Introduction

Polynomial approximation schemes for strongly NP-complete problems have rarely been reported in the literature. We describe in this paper a powerful technique and illustrate its use in deriving polynomial approximation schemes for a variety of strongly NP-complete geometric problems. The problems that we consider are defined in a Euclidean space given a specific geometric object. The input is a set of points distributed in some region in the space and the problem is to find the minimum number of objects needed to cover all points. Another type of problem is the packing (with no overlap) of maximum number of objects in a region of space specified by an input of points.

Such problems often occur in practical applications. We illustrate the technique for several applications that were discussed in the literature. For none of these problems has there been an approximation algorithm with guaranteed worst case bound previously reported (with the exception of the scheduling problem in [1] for which 100% error bound is guaranteed).

One of the problems is the square packing problem. This problem comes up in the attempt to increase yield in VLSI chip manufacture. For example, 64K RAM chips, some of which may be defective, are available on a rectilinear grid placed on a silicon wafer. 2x2 arrays of such nondefective chips could be wired together to produce 256K RAM chips. In order to maximize yield, we want to pack a maximal number of such 2x2 arrays into the array of working chips on a wafer. (See Berman, Leighton and Snyder's result [2] reviewed by Johnson [7] and NP-completeness result due to Fowler, Paterson and Tanimoto [3].)

Another problem is covering with disks. Given points in the plane, the problem is to identify a minimally sized set of disks (of prescribed radius), covering all points. One of the applications of the problem is in the area of locating emergency facilities such that all potential customers will be within a reasonably small radius away from the facility. (The complexity results for this problem are reviewed in [7].)

(*)This research was supported in part by the National Science Foundation under grant ECS-8204695.

(**)Address after Fall 1984: Department of Mathematics, Statistics and Computer Science, University of Illinois at Chicago, Chicago, Illinois 60680.

A third problem considered is covering with squares (or rectangles). This problem has an important application to image processing discussed in Tanimoto and Fowler [9]. Frequently most of the areas of images do not include any interesting information (these are the "background" pixels). The problem is then to cover all nontrivial information in minimum number of square "patches" (the position and size of which are constrained by a specified grid) which are then stored in a database.

The problem of covering with rings (referred to as the ring cover problem in this paper) is a generic example of covering with nonconvex objects. The covering objects are the regions bounded between two concentric spheres which we call rings. This problem has an interesting application in the area of planning motion and positions of robots. Many robot constructions are such that any object that is placed between the minimum and maximum range of the robot arm can be reached by the robot. The problem is to identify a minimum number of robot positions such that all points (objects to be handled) are accessible. When the minimum range of the robot arm is zero, the reachability region forms a disk (or a ball), in which case the problem falls in the previously discussed category of covering with disks or balls.

Nonconvex covering problems also arise in the context of scheduling theory. Realistic models take into account resources that are only intermittently available. This may be due to, say, lunch breaks for workers or preventive maintenance for machines (see Bartholdi [1]).

We shall call an algorithm a δ-approximation, $\delta > 0$, for a certain problem if the error of the value of the solution delivered by the algorithm divided by the value of the optimal solution does not exceed δ. Obviously, we would like to identify a δ-approximation algorithm such that δ is as small as possible. In some cases one can specify a family of algorithms such that for each $\varepsilon > 0$ there is an ε-approximation algorithm in the family that solves a given problem instance within relative error ε. Such a family is called an approximation scheme. The running time of an ε-approximation algorithm will be monotonically increasing with $\frac{1}{\varepsilon}$. If the functional dependence of the running time on the size of the input and $\frac{1}{\varepsilon}$ is polynomial, then the scheme is said to be fully polynomial; if, on the other hand, it is polynomial only in the input size, the scheme is called polynomial.

All the problems described and consequently their extensions are NP-complete in the strong sense (the reader is referred to Garey and Johnson's [4] comprehensive review of this concept). As such, there are no fully polynomial approximation schemes for these problems, unless NP=P ([4]). This negative result does not exclude, however, the existence of a polynomial approximation scheme for these problems, i.e., a family of algorithms such that for any specified relative error $\varepsilon > 0$, there is an ε-approximation algorithm in the scheme that is polynomial. Though such schemes are conceptually feasible, their existence has been rarely reported.

Our main results are the construction of polynomial approximation schemes for the above problems which, given the negative result above, are the best possible results of this type. We present a unified methodology that is helpful for numerous geometric covering and packing problems, and could potentially be applicable to problems beyond this context. We call this fundamental technique the "shifting strategy" and outline the necessary conditions for its applicability.

Throughout the paper the following notation will be used. Z^A denotes the value of the solution delivered by algorithm A. An optimal solution set is denoted by OPT and its size by $|OPT|$. We define a d-dimensional ring to be the volume enclosed between two concentric d-dimensional spheres and we say that such a ring is of size $\langle r,w \rangle$ if the difference between the outer and inner radius of the ring is w and the inner radius is equal to r. The diameter of such ring is denoted by D, where $D = 2r + 2w$.

In this paper we omitted many of the details and proofs. For a complete description and extensions see [5], [6] and [8].

2. The "Shifting Strategy"

We illustrate the use of the shifting strategy via the problem of covering with disks. The shifting strategy allows us to bound the error of the simple divide-and-conquer approach by repetitive applications of it, followed by the selection of the single most favorable resulting solution.

Let the set N of the n given points in the plane be enclosed in an area I. The goal is to cover these points with a minimal number of disks of diameter D. Let the shifting parameter be ℓ. In the first phase the area I is subdivided into vertical strips of width D. Each such strip will be considered left closed and right open. These strips are then considered in groups of ℓ consecutive strips resulting in strips of width $\ell \cdot D$ each. For any fixed subdivision of I into strips of width D, there are ℓ different ways of partitioning I into strips of width $\ell \cdot D$. These partitions can be ordered such that each can be derived from the previous one by shifting it to the right over distance D. Repeating the shift ℓ times we end up with the same partition we started from. We denote such ℓ distinguished shift partitions by $S_1, S_2, \ldots, S_\ell$.

Let A be any algorithm that delivers a solution in any strip of width $\ell \cdot D$ (or less). For a given partition S_i, let $A(S_i)$ be the algorithm that applies algorithm A to each strip in the partition S_i, and outputs the union of all disks used. Such set of disks is clearly a feasible solution to the global problem defined on I. This process of finding a global solution is repeated for each partition $S_i, i=1,2,\ldots,\ell$. The shift algorithm S_A, defined for a given local algorithm A, delivers the set of disks of minimum cardinality among the ℓ sets delivered by $A(S_1), \ldots, A(S_\ell)$.

Let the performance ratio of an algorithm B be denoted by r_B, i.e., r_B is defined as the supremum of $Z^B/|OPT|$ over all problem instances.

Lemma 2.1 (the shifting lemma)

Let A be a local algorithm and ℓ be the shifting parameter then

$$r_{S_A} \leq r_A\left(1 + \frac{1}{\ell}\right) . \tag{2.1}$$

Proof: We produce an upper bound on the sum of errors caused by all algorithms $A(S_i)$.

By the definition of r_A we have

$$Z^{A(S_i)} \leq r_A \cdot \sum_{J \text{ in } S_i} |OPT_J|, \qquad (2.2)$$

where J runs over all strips in partition S_i and $|OPT_J|$ is the number of disks in an optimal cover of the points in strip J.

Let OPT be the set of rings in an optimal solution and $OPT^{(1)},\ldots,OPT^{(\ell)}$ the set of disks, in OPT, covering points in two adjacent $\ell \cdot D$ strips in the $1,2,\ldots,\ell$ shifts, respectively. It can easily be seen that

$$\sum_{J \text{ in } S_i} |OPT_J| \leq |OPT| + |OPT^{(i)}|. \qquad (2.3)$$

There can be no disk in the set OPT that covers points in two adjacent strips in more than one shift partition. Therefore, the sets $OPT^{(1)},\ldots,OPT^{(\ell)}$ are disjoint. It follows that

$$\sum_{i=1}^{\ell} (|OPT| + |OPT^{(i)}|) \leq (\ell+1) \cdot |OPT|. \qquad (2.4)$$

(2.3) and (2.4) imply

$$\min_{i=1,\ldots,\ell} \sum_{J \text{ in } S_i} |OPT_J| \leq \frac{1}{\ell} \sum_{i=1}^{\ell} \Big(\sum_{J \text{ in } S_i} |OPT_J| \Big) \leq \left(1 + \frac{1}{\ell}\right) |OPT|. \qquad (2.5)$$

Joining the inequality (2.5) with (2.2) we derive that

$$Z^{S_A} = \min_{i=1,\ldots,\ell} Z^{A(S_i)} \leq r_A \cdot \left(1 + \frac{1}{\ell}\right) \cdot |OPT|, \qquad (2.6)$$

which establishes (2.1).

Q.E.D.

The local algorithm A may itself be derived from an application of the shifting strategy in lower dimensional space. Repetitive applications of this type yield an approximation scheme as described in the following section.

3. Polynomial Approximation Schemes for Covering Problems in Arbitrary Dimensions

We first illustrate in Theorem 3.1 the method of repetitive applications of the shifting for the problem of covering with balls in a d-dimensional space. The remainder of this section consists of a generalization of this concept for other objects.

Theorem 3.1 Let $d \geq 1$ be some finite dimension, then there is a polynomial time approximation scheme H^d s.t. for every given natural number $\ell \geq 1$, the algorithm H^d_ℓ delivers a cover of n given points in a d-dimensional Euclidean space by d-dimensional balls of given diameter D in $O((\ell \cdot \sqrt{d})^d \cdot (2n)^{d\lceil \ell\sqrt{d}\rceil^d+1})$ steps with performance ratio $\leq (1 + \frac{1}{\ell})^d$.

Proof: The considered problem is NP-complete only for $d > 1$. For $d = 1$ one can actually compute an optimal solution in linear time with the following algorithm: we always place the next interval (= 1-dimensional ball) with its left end at the leftmost point that is not yet covered.

For $d = 2$ and fixed $\ell > 1$ we use two nested applications of the shifting strategy from section 2. We first cut the plane into vertical strips of width $\ell \cdot D$. Then in order to cover the points in such a strip we apply again the shifting strategy to the other dimension. Thus, we cut the considered strip into squares of side length $\ell \cdot D$. We then find optimal coverings of points in such a square by exhaustive search. With $\lceil \ell \cdot \sqrt{2} \rceil^2$ disks of diameter D we can cover an $\ell \cdot D \times \ell \cdot D$ square completely, thus we never need to consider more disks for one square. Further, we can assume that any disk that covers at least two of the given points has two of these points on its border. (For disks that cover only one point the following estimate holds trivially.) Since there are only two ways to draw a circle of given diameter through two given points, we only have to consider $2 \cdot \binom{\tilde{n}}{2}$ possible disk positions--where $\tilde{n}$ is the number of given points in the considered square. Thus we have to check at most $O(\tilde{n}^{2\lceil \ell \cdot \sqrt{2} \rceil^2})$ arrangements of disks.

The two nested applications of the shifting stragegy add another factor ℓ^2 to our global time bound.

For $d > 2$ one proceeds analogously with d nested applications of the shifting strategy.

Q.E.D.

We have considered in Theorem 3.1 the problem of covering given points with a minimal number of balls of given size. The method of Theorem 3.1 can easily be generalized to yield approximation schemes for problems where one covers with other objects than balls. For a fixed type of object (of arbitrary fixed shape) we define D as the maximum diameter of such an object. In a manner similar to Theorem 3.1 we cut the considered d-dimensional space in a number of different ways ("shifting") into d-dimensional cubes with sides of length $\ell \cdot D$. One can always find a local algorithm that proceeds by enumeration in the same way as the one for balls in Theorem 3.1. But now the number of objects of the considered type that are needed to cover a d-dimensional cube with sides of length $\ell \cdot D$ will depend on the ratio between D and the maximal $\tilde{D}$ s.t. a d-dimensional cube with sides of length $\tilde{D}$ is contained in a covering object of the considered type. The running time of the resulting approximation algorithm H_ℓ^d will depend exponentially on this ratio $D/\tilde{D}$. We will show in Theorem 5.3 that at least in one important case one can eliminate the ratio $D/\tilde{D}$ from the exponent of the running time by replacing the local enumeration algorithm by another approximation scheme.

In certain applications the covering problem is defined in terms of objects with fixed orientation. This is the case, for instance, with the covering with squares problem in the context of image processing [9]. This additional constraint simplifies the problem in that the following trick often suffices to eliminate $D/\tilde{D}$ from the exponent of the running time. An example is the following corollary.

Corollary 3.2

Consider the problem of covering n given points in d-space with a minimal number of rectilinear blocks (the sides of which have given lengths $D_1,\ldots,D_d$) oriented with sides parallel to the axes. There is a polynomial time approximation scheme H^d such that for every given integer $\ell > 1$, the algorithm H^d_ℓ delivers a cover in $O(\ell^d \cdot n^{2\ell^d+1})$ steps with performance ratio $\leq (1+\frac{1}{\ell})^d$.

This corollary is proved in the same way as Theorem 3.1, except that the cuts orthogonal to the ith axis are introduced at a distance $\ell \cdot D_i$ from each other.

4. Application of the Technique to Packing Problems

In a packing problem one wants to place without overlap a maximal number of objects of given shape within a given area. Since the error analysis of the shifting strategy remains true for such problems, we can use similar algorithms as in section 3. We consider as an example the problem of packing with squares discussed in the introduction. The squares in this case have to be placed such that their sides coincide with lines of an overlaying rectilinear grid. The following theorem can also be generalized to packing problems without such a restriction.

Theorem 4.1 There is a polynomial time approximation scheme for the problem of packing a maximal number of $k \times k$ squares (for a natural number k) into an area that is given by n squares of unit size on a rectilinear grid. The approximation algorithm with parameter ℓ has an error ratio $\leq (1+\frac{1}{\ell})^2$ and runs in time $O(k^2 \cdot \ell^2 \cdot n^{\ell^2})$.

The idea of the proof is to reduce the problem via two nested applications of the shifting strategy to a local packing problem in an $\ell{\cdot}k \times \ell{\cdot}k$ square.

Remark: We also get polynomial approximation schemes for many packing problems in higher dimensions, with arbitrary orientations and with objects other than squares.

5. Covering with Nonconvex Objects in One Dimension: The Ring Cover Problem

In one dimension a ring of size $\langle r,w\rangle$ is simply a pair of closed intervals of length w with distance $2r$ in between. Unlike most other geometric location problems, the ring cover problem does not become easy in one dimension (in one dimension one has to cover n given points on a line by a minimal number of pairs of intervals as above).

Theorem 5.1 (Maass [8]) The ring cover problem in one dimension is strongly NP-complete.

On the other hand, we have noted in the proof of Theorem 3.1 that one can solve (optimally) this problem for $\frac{r}{w} = 0$ in linear time. A natural question is then, how does the running time of an optimal algorithm depend on the "nonconvexity measure" $\frac{r}{w}$ for the covering rings of size $\langle r,w\rangle$.

Theorem 5.2 (Maass [8]) The ring cover problem in one dimension for n given points and rings of size <r,w> can be solved optimally in time $O(\lceil \frac{r}{w} \rceil^2 \cdot \log n \cdot n^{16 \cdot \lceil \frac{r}{w} \rceil + 18})$. In particular for every fixed bound on $\frac{r}{w}$ the problem is in P.

Concerning approximation algorithms two issues arise. The large degree of the polynomial time bound in Theorem 5.2 leads to the question, whether at least for common values of the parameters one can find reasonably fast approximation algorithms. We consider this topic in section 6. Second, from a more theoretical point of view one would like to know whether for unbounded values of $\frac{r}{w}$ (i.e., the strongly NP-complete problem of Theorem 5.1) a polynomial time approximation scheme exists. We give a positive answer in Theorem 5.3. According to the general discussion in section 3 the parameter $D/\tilde{D}$ --which is equal to $2\frac{r}{w} + 2$ in the present situation--appears in the exponent of the time bound for the approximation algorithms of section 3. Thus, the methods of section 3 do not suffice.

The following result relies on a more subtle method where one employs a nested application of the shifting strategy even in the considered one-dimensional case (see [5] for details).

Theorem 5.3 There is a polynomial time approximation scheme C s.t. for every given natural number $\ell > 1$ the algorithm C_ℓ computes for any given <r,w> and any given n points on a line in time $O(\ell^4 (4n)^{\ell^2})$ an approximate solution to the one-dimensional ring cover problem with performance ratio $\leq (1 + \frac{1}{\ell})^2$.

6. Fast Approximation Algorithms

The time bounds of many approximation algorithms in this paper can be improved considerably by using more efficient algorithms for the computation of optimal solutions in combination with the shifting strategy. We mention in this section two examples in the case of the one-dimensional ring cover problem: a nearly quadratic time algorithm with at most 50% error and, further, for rings with $\frac{r}{w} \leq \frac{1}{2}$ (this appears to be the more typical case in robotics) for every $\varepsilon > 0$ an approximation algorithm that is linear in n. Both results require a more detailed analysis of the mathematical structure of optimal local coverings (see [4]). On the basis of such insight one can drastically shorten the exhaustive search for an optimal local solution: we show that it is enough to try out only a few representative types of local solutions.

Theorem 6.1 There is an algorithm that computes a $\frac{1}{2}$-approximate solution of the one-dimensional ring cover problem in $O(\lceil \frac{r}{w} \rceil \cdot n^2 \cdot \log n)$ steps.

Theorem 6.2 For rings of size <r,w> with $\frac{r}{w} \leq \frac{1}{2}$ there is a polynomial time approximation scheme for the one-dimensional ring cover problem that covers n given points on the line for any $\varepsilon > 0$ in $O(\lceil \frac{1}{\varepsilon} \rceil \cdot 2^{2\lceil \frac{1}{\varepsilon} \rceil} \cdot n \cdot \log n)$ steps with ratio $\leq 1 + \varepsilon$.

7. Summary

The approach described in this paper, the shifting strategy, has proved useful in a large variety of contexts. Via the use of this approach we were able to derive algorithms that are the best possible in the sense that the exponential dependence on $\frac{1}{\varepsilon}$ cannot be removed unless NP=P. We also note that all other polynomial approximation schemes that we are familiar with rely on dynamic programming. The technique we introduced is an alternative to dynamic programming for the construction of polynomial approximation schemes for strongly NP-complete problems.

References

[1] John J. Bartholdi III, "A Guaranteed-Accuracy Round-Off Algorithm for Cyclic Scheduling and Set Covering," Operations Research, Vol. 29, No. 3 (1981).

[2] F. D. Berman, F. T. Leighton and L. Snyder, "Optimal Tile Salvage," unpublished manuscript (1982).

[3] R. J. Fowler, M. S. Paterson, and S. L. Tanimoto, "Optimal Packing and Covering in the Plane Are NP-Complete," Inform. Process. Lett., 12 (1981), 133-137.

[4] M. R. Gary and D. S. Johnson, Computers and Intractability: A Guide to the Theory of NP-Completeness, W. H. Freeman (1978).

[5] D. S. Hochbaum and W. Maass, "Fast Approximation Algorithms for the Robot Placement Problem," manuscript, U.C. Berkeley (1983), submitted.

[6] D. S. Hochbaum and W. Maass, "Approximation Algorithms for Covering and Packing Problems in Image Processing and VLSI," manuscript, U.C. Berkeley (May 1983), submitted.

[7] D. S. Johnson, "The NP-Completeness Column: An Ongoing Guide," Journal of Algorithms, 3, 182-195 (1982).

[8] W. Maass, "On the Complexity of Computing Optimal Positions for Industrial Robots," U.C. Berkeley, manuscript, submitted.

[9] S. L. Tanimoto and R. J. Fowler, "Covering Image Subsets with Patches," Proc. 5th Inter. Conf. on Pattern Recognition, (1980) 835-839.

COVERING POLYGONS WITH MINIMUM NUMBER OF RECTANGLES

Christos Levcopoulos

Andrzej Lingas

The Department of Computer and Information Science
Linköping University

581 83 Linköping, Sweden

Abstract: In the fabrication of masks for integrated circuits, it is desirable to replace the polygons comprising the layout of a circuit with as small as possible number of rectangles. Let Q be the set of all simple polygons with interior angles $\geq$ 90 degrees. Given a polygon $P \in Q$, let $\theta(P)$ be the minimum number of (possibly overlapping) rectangles lying within P necessary to cover P, and let $r(P)$ be the ratio between the length of the longest edge of P and the length of the shortest edge of P. For every natural $n \geq 5$, and k, a uniform polygon $P_{n,k}$ with n corners is constructed such that $r(P_{n,k}) \geq k$ and $\theta(P_n) \geq \Omega(n loglog(r(P_{n,k})))$. On the other hand, by modifying a known heuristic it is shown that for all convex polygons P in Q with n vertices $\theta(P) \leq O(n log(r(P)))$.

Introduction

To produce a photolithographic mask of an integrated circuit, a layer of the circuit is printed on a photographic plate. First, the polygonal area of the layer is decomposed into rectangles. Then, the rectangles are flashed onto the plate. To minimize the cost of the mask production, the number of rectangles should be as small as possible.

Acute angles can only approximately be covered by rectangles. Here, we consider only polygons with interior angles $\geq$90 degrees whose class is denoted by Q. Rectilinear polygons form a subclass of Q. Chaiken *et. al* [1] proved a weakened conjecture of Chvatal that if the polygon P is a set of squares with integer coordinates, convex in the horizontal and vertical direction then $\theta(P)$ is equal to the maximum number of squares in P, no two of which are in a common rectangle lying within P. Their method of proof can be used to obtain a polynomial time algorithm achieving $\theta(P)$. Hegedus [2] developed two algorithms for covering polygons with rectangles. One of this algorithms is for polygons from Q, the other for rectilinear polygons. The general idea of the former, so called GENCOV algorithm, is as follows:

(1) On each edge of P place the rectangle whose width is the length of the side, and whose height is the maximum height such that the rectangle lies within P.

(2) If the rectangles set on the edges do not cover P totally then cover the remaining,

polygonal holes by the same method, with the exception that not the boundaries of holes but the perimeter of P is still the limit of the maximum height of covering rectangles.

Hegedus has not presented any analysis of GENCOV algorithm in [2]. We observe that if three consecutive edges of P form an acute funnel then the number of iterations of GENCOV algorithm is $\Omega(log(a/b))$ where a is the length of the arms of the funnel and b is the length of the basis of the funnel. Hence, we can easily construct the polygons $P'_{n,k}$, with n vertices and $r(P'_{n,k}) \geq k$, that are covered with $\Omega(nlog(r(P'_{n,k})))$ rectangles by GENCOV algorithm. For analogously constructed polygons $P_{n,k}$ with n vertices and $r(P) \geq k$, we are able to prove $\theta(P_{n,k}) \geq \Omega(nloglog(r(P_{n,k})))$ '. Thus, the number of rectangles necessary to cover a polygon in Q with n vertices may be arbitrarily large.

To obtain an upper bound on $\theta(P)$ in terms of $r(P)$ and n, we modify GENCOV algorithm. At the beginning of a consecutive iteration, maximal sets of aligned hole edges, in the one-to-one correspondence with edges of P, are sought. Then, on each shortest segment totally covering such a maximal set of hole edges, a single maximal rectangle is placed instead of separate maximal rectangles placed on consecutive aligned hole edges. When the polygon $P \in Q$ is convex, the modified algorithm produces $O(nlog(r(P)))$ rectangles '.

The $\Omega(nloglog(r(P)))$ lower bound

An acute angle cannot be covered with a finite number of rectangles. We may approximate the angle with funnels of smaller and smaller basis. Clearly, the funnels can be covered with a finite number of rectangles. The necessary number of rectangles to cover such a funnel increases when the size of the funnel basis decreases. In the proof of the following theorem, we construct figures composed of several uniform funnels and estimate the asymptotic growth of the cardinality of rectangular covering of the figures when the funnel basis relatively decreases.

Theorem 1. For all integers $n \geq 5$, k, there exists a polygon $P_{n,k} \in Q$ with n vertices such that $r(P) \geq k$ and $\theta(P) \geq \Omega(nloglog(r(P))$.

Proof. Consider the polygon $P_{n,k} \in Q$ in the form of a circle with $\lfloor n/4 \rfloor$ copies of a funnel, and $n \bmod 4$ additional vertices on its perimeter, shown in Fig. 1 . Any rectangle within $P_{n,k}$ can overlap with at most two of the funnel copies. Therefore, it is sufficient to show that $\Omega(loglog(r(P_{n,k})))$ rectangles are necessary to cover the funnel. Note that $r(P_{n,k})$ is equal to the ratio between the basis and the side edge of the funnel. We assume $r(P_{n,k}) \geq k$.

' In his dissertation, Christos Levcopoulos has recently improved the $\Omega(nloglog(r(P_{n,k})))$ bound to $\Omega(nlog(r(P_{n,k}))$, and generalized the algorithm to include any polygons in Q [3].

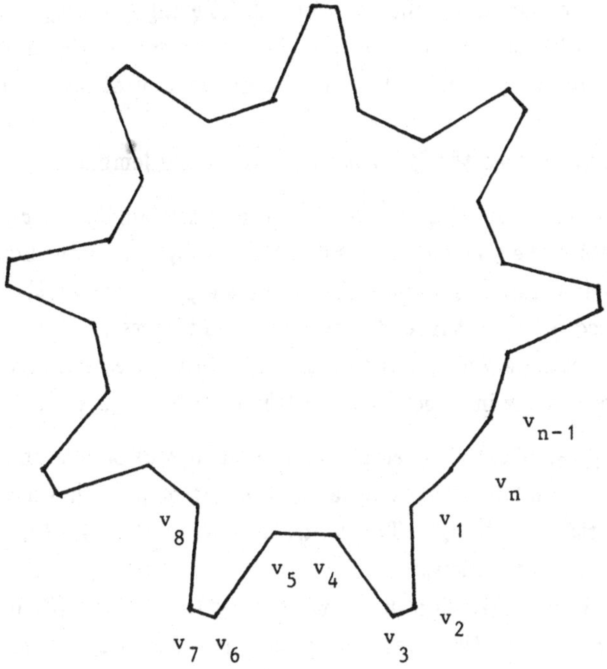

Fig. 1. The polygon $P_{n,k}$

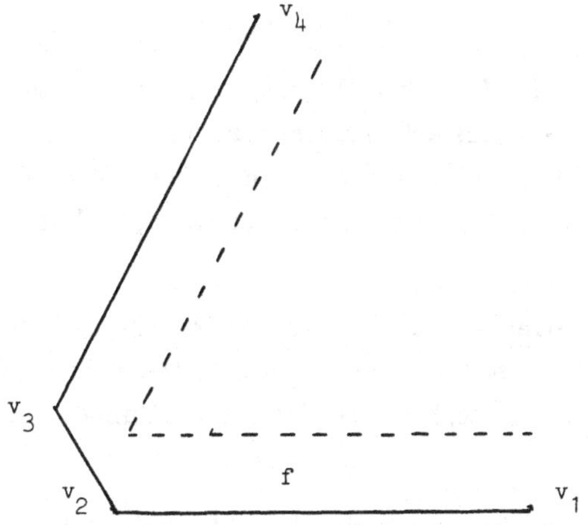

Fig. 2. The funnel and the interior triangle T (marked with broken lines).

Consider a single copy of the funnel shown in Fig. 2. The angles (v_1, v_2, v_3) and (v_2, v_3, v_4) are of 120 degrees. Inside the funnel, the triangle T is drawn in Fig. 2. The edges of T are parallel to edges of the funnel, and are in the distance of at least f from the funnel perimeter.
To prove the theorem, we need the following definitions and lemmas.

Definition 1. Given a rectangle r, a real number d, and a triangle (a, b, c), the rectangle r is said to d-overlap with the triangle (a, b, c) if the following conditions hold (see Fig. 3):
(1) the rectangle r lies within the angle whose arms are parallel to (a, b) and (a, c) respectively, and are located in the distance of d over (a, b) and below (a, c), respectively;
(2) there exists no rectangle which satisfies (1) and whose intersection with the triangle (a, b, c) properly contains the intersection of r with the triangle (a, b, c).

Definition 2. Let (v_1, v_2, v_3, v_4) be a rectangle, and let (a, b, c) be a triangle where $[v_1, v_2]$ crosses $[a, b]$ and $[a, c]$, and the vertex a lies to the left of $[v_1, v_2]$, whereas the vertices v_3, v_4, b, c lie to the right of $[v_1, v_2]$. The *contraction* of the triangle (a, b, c) with respect to the rectangle is defined as follows:
remove the belt between the straight-lines induced by (v_1, v_4) and (v_2, v_3). If two pieces of the triangle has remained, stick them along the line induced by $[v_1, v_4]$ by moving the bottom piece along the line induced by (b, c). The contraction is the greatest equilateral triangle with sides parallel to these of the triangle (a, b, c), lying within the remained, stuck pieces, see Fig. 4.

Lemma 1. Let the triangle (a, b, c) be an equilateral triangle of height $x \times d$ where x, d are real numbers and $x \geq 16$. Let r be a rectangle d-overlapping with the triangle (a, b, c). Either (1) or (2) hold:

(1) there exists a contraction of the triangle (a, b, c) with respect to r of height $\geq x \times d - c \times \sqrt{x} \times d$, where $c \geq 7$ is a constant uniform in x and d,
(2) there exists an equilateral triangle (a, b', c') such that $b' \in (a, b]$, $c' \in (a, c]$, the height of (a, b', c') is $\Omega(\sqrt{x} \times d)$, and the inside of the triangle (a, b', c') is disjoint from the inside of r.

Proof. Let us draw the straight-line K parallel to (c, b) in the distance of $\sqrt{x} \times d$ from a (see Fig. 5). If the intersection $r \cap (a, b, c)$ lies to the right of K, then the condition (2) in Lemma 1 holds. Otherwise, the condition (1) in Lemma 1 holds, since r is of width $< 3\sqrt{x} \times d$. ∎

Lemma 2. Let (v_1, v_2, v_3, v_4) be a rectangle where $|(v_1, v_2)| \leq 3 \times d \times y$, where $y \geq 1$, and let (a, b, c) be an equilateral triangle such that the contraction of (a, b, c) with respect to (v_1, v_2, v_3, v_4) exists (see Def. 2). The minimum number of rectangles d-overlapping with the triangle (a, b, c) necessary to cover it is greater at least by one than the minimum number of rectangles $7d \times y$-overlapping with the contraction, necessary to cover the contraction.
Proof. Consider any rectangle r d-overlapping with the triangle (a, b, c). Remove the belt

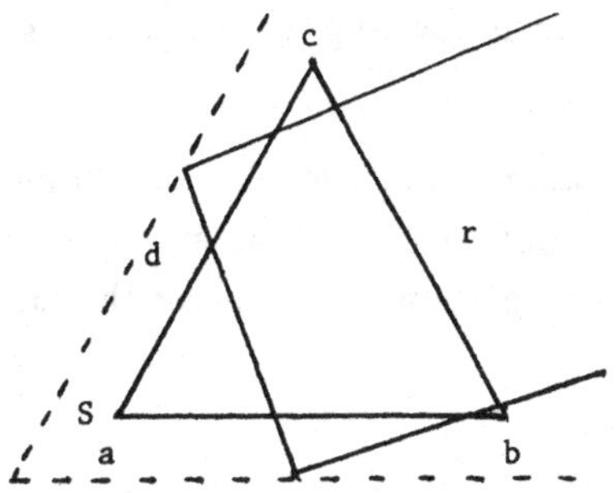

Fig. 3. An example of the rectangle r d-overlapping with the triangle (a,b,c).

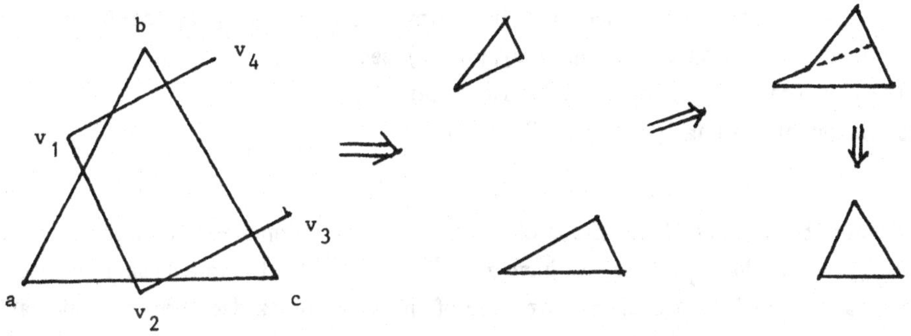

Fig. 4. The process of contraction of the triangle (a,b,c) with respect to the rectangle (v_1, v_2, v_3, v_4).

between the lines induced by $[v_1, v_4]$ and $[v_2, v_3]$. We may assume w.l.o.g. that two pieces of the rectangle remain. They are shifted by at most $3 \times d \times y$. Therefore, there exists a rectangle $7d \times y$-overlapping with the contraction, totally covering the two pieces (see Fig. 6). ∎

To prove the theorem it is sufficient to show that the minimum number of rectangles f-overlapping with the internal triangle $T = (w_1, w_2, w_3)$ (see Fig. 2) necessary to cover T is $\Omega(loglog(h/f))$ where h is the height of T. For this purpose, we consider the following procedure:

$(a, b, c) \leftarrow (w_1, w_2, w_3)$;
$d \leftarrow f$;
$x \leftarrow$ the height of the triangle (a, b, c) divided by d;
<u>*while*</u> $x \geq 16$<u>*do*</u>
  guess a rectangle r d-overlapping with the triangle (a, b, c);
  $t \leftarrow$ the first triangle satisfying the condition (1) or (2) in Lemma 1 with respect to (a, b, c), r, x and d;
  $d \leftarrow$ <u>*if*</u> t is a contraction of (a, b, c) <u>*then*</u> $2 \times c \times d \times \sqrt{x}$ <u>*else*</u>
  $d +$ ***maximum***{ ***distance***$((a, b), (v_3, v_4))$, ***distance***$((a, c), (v_1, v_2))$ };
  <u>*comment*</u> c is the constant specified in (1) in Lemma 1, and v_1, v_2, v_3, v_4 are the vertices of the funnel surrounding the triangle (w_1, w_2, w_3), see Fig. 2;
  $(a, b, c) \leftarrow t$, where a stands for the leftmost vertex of t;
  $x \leftarrow$ the height of the triangle (a, b, c) divided by d
<u>*end*</u>

Let us estimate the number of iterations of the while block independently of the guesses of the rectangle r. At the beginning, we have $x \geq 2^{2^{\lfloor loglog(h/f) \rfloor}}$. By Lemma 1, there exists a positive constant c', such that each performance of the while block decreases x to at least $\sqrt{x}/c'$. Straightforward calculations show that the number of iterations is $\Omega(loglog(h/f))$. Let (a_i, b_i, c_i) stand for the triangle (a, b, c) resulting from the $i-th$ iteration of the while block. Next, let t_i be the minimum number of rectangles d-overlapping with (a_i, b_i, c_i) and covering (a_i, b_i, c_i). Next, let t_0 be analogously defined for the original triangle (w_1, w_2, w_3). By the definition of the triangle $(a_{i+1}, b_{i+1}, c_{i+1})$, the new d and Lemma 1, 2, we have $t_i \geq 1 + t_{i+1}$. Hence, $\theta(P_{n,k}) \geq \Omega(nloglogr(P_{n,k}))$ by a straightforward inductive argument. ∎

By slightly modifying the polygons $P_{n,k}$, we also obtain the following theorem.

Theorem 2. For all integers $n \geq 5$, k, there exists a polygon $P'_{n,k} \in Q$ with n vertices such that $r(P'_{n,k}) \geq k$ and GENCOV algorithm produces $\Omega(nlog(r(P'_{n,k}))$ rectangles to cover $P'_{n,k}$.

Proof. Consider the funnel that is half of the funnel from Theorem 1, shown in Fig. 7. Now, the angle (v_1, v_2, v_3) is of 90 degrees, and the angle (v_2, v_3, v_4) is of 120 degrees. To

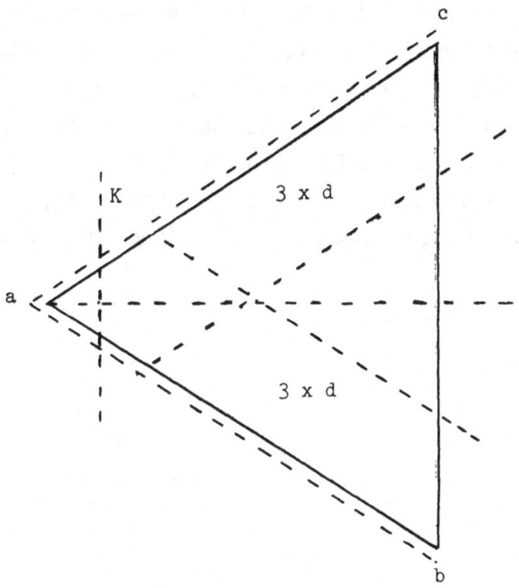

Fig. 5. The triangle (a,b,c) and the line K.

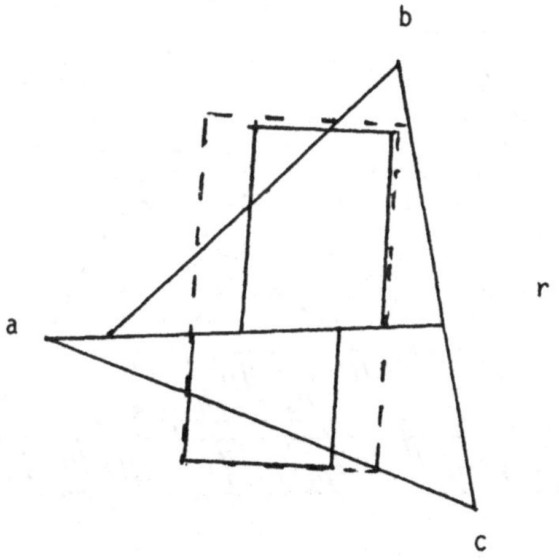

Fig. 6. Covering the two remaining pieces of the rectangle r.

construct $P'_{n,k}$, we replace all the copies of the funnel from Theorem 1, occurring in $P_{n,k}$, by copies of the new funnel. It is sufficient to show that GENCOV algorithm produces $\Omega(log(r(P'_{n,k}))$ rectangles to cover the new funnel. Let r_i, $i = 1, 2, ..., m$, be the rectangles alternately placed by GENCOV algorithm parallelly to (v_1, v_2) or (v_3, v_4) such that for $i < j$ the rectangle r_i is placed before the rectangle r_j. The height of the rectangles r_1 and r_2 is less than $2f$. For $i = 3, 4, ..., m$, the height of the rectangle r_i is not greater than the triple height of the rectangle r_{i-2}. Hence, $m \geq \Omega(log(r(P'_{n,k})))$. ∎

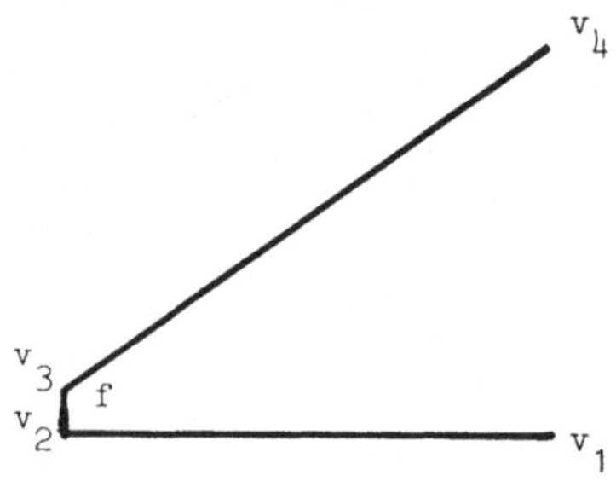

Fig. 7. The new funnel.

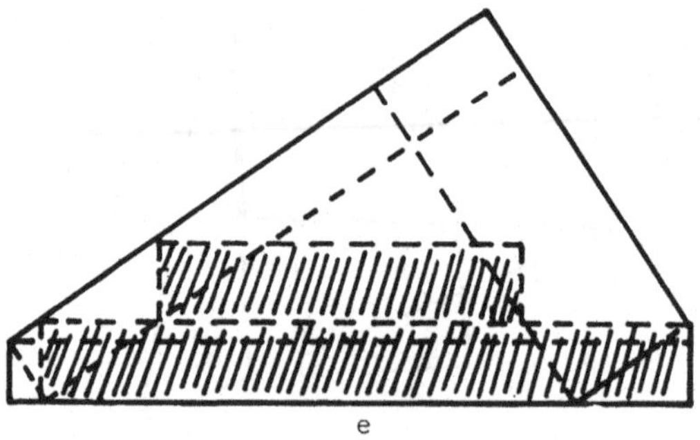

Fig. 8. The shadowed rectangles are associated with the edge e.

The $O(nlog(r(P)))$ upper bound for convex polygons

Each rectangle placed by GENCOV algorithm applied to a convex polygon P in Q can be uniquely associated with a parallel edge of P (see Fig. 8). To derive the upper bound on $\theta(P)$, we consider the following modification of GENCOV algorithm (applied only to convex polygons in Q) :

If e is en edge of P, r is the rectangle associated to e, placed in the $i-th$ iteration, and $HE(e,i)$ is the union of all hole edges that occur on the distant edge of r parallel to e, then only a single maximal rectangle, whose edge is the shortest segment including $HE(e,i)$, is placed instead of separated maximal rectangles placed on distinct components of $HE(e,i)$ and other edges of r.

Lemma 3. After i iterations of the modified GENCOV algorithm applied to a convex polygon P in Q with the shortest edge of length s, all of the points within P that lie within the distance of $2^{i-1} \times s$ from the perimeter of P are covered.

Proof. It is sufficient to prove that the distance of each hole edge from the perimeter of P is at least $2^{i-1}s$ after the $i-th$ iteration. Obviously, after the first iteration, the hole edges are in the distance of at least s from the perimeter of P. Consider any rectangle r placed during the $i+1$ iteration. By the inductive assumption, the height of r is at least $2^{i-1}s$. We may assume w.l.o.g. that some pieces of the more distant edge of r parallel to the associated edge of P are hole edges after the $i+1$ iteration. Hence, these edge pieces are in the distance of at least $2 \times 2^{i-1} = 2^{(i+1)-1}$ from the associated edge of P. By transitivity, any hole edge is in the distance of at least $2^{(i+1)-1}$ from any other edge of P. ∎

By Lemma 3, and a simple geometric argument, we obtain the following theorem :

Theorem 3. The modified GENCOV algorithm applied to a convex polygon P in Q with n vertices produces $O(nlog(r(P)))$ rectangles.

Proof. Let l, s be the the length of longest and the shortest edge of P respectively. It follows from Lemma 3 that after $\lceil log(l/s) \rceil$ iterations, all of the points within P that lie within the distance of l from the perimeter of P are covered by rectangles.

Now, assume that there exist a point p within P which is not covered after $\lceil log(l/s) \rceil$ iterations. Thus, the distance of p from the perimeter of P is greater than l. Since P is convex, there exists at least one edge $e = (a,b)$ of P, such that a line perpendicular to e and crossing e contains p. Since p is uncovered, the maximal rectangle $r = (a,b,c,d)$ in P does not cover p (see Fig. 9). Since r is maximal, either d or c lie on the perimeter of P. Assume that c lies on the perimeter of P, see Fig. 9. That means, that if we follow the perimeter of P from c clockwise between the lines induced by a,d, and b,c, then, by convexity of P, we reach some perimeter point within the distance of l from p. We have

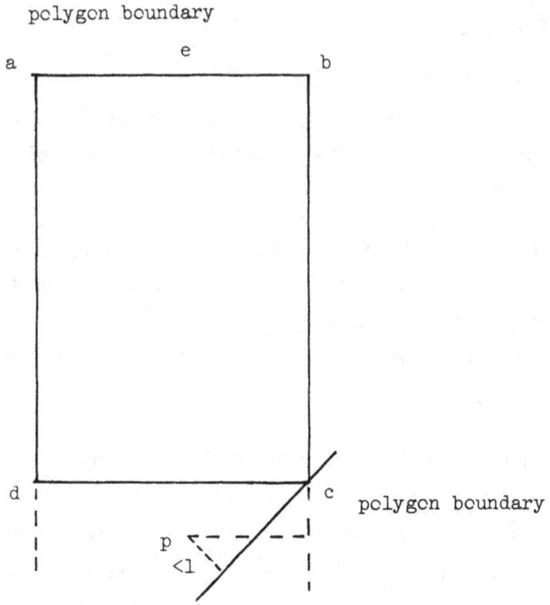

Fig. 9. The rectangle r=(a,b,c,d) and the point p.

got a contradiction. ∎

Corollary 1. For any convex polygon P in Q, $\theta(P) \leq O(n\log(r(P)))$.

Acknowledgments

We are greatly indebted to Piotr Siemienski for telling us about the problem of covering polygons with rectangles, discussions and encouragement.

References

[1] Chaiken, S., D.J. Kleitman, M. Saks and J. Shearer, *Covering regions by rectangles*, SIAM J. Alg. Disc. Meth., vol. 2, no. 4, 1981.
[2] Hegedus, A., *Algorithms for covering polygons by rectangles*, Computer Aided Design, vol. 14, no. 5, 1982.
[3] Levcopoulos, C.,*On Covering Regions with Minimum Number of Rectangles* ,dissertation in preparation, 1984.

ON EXPRESSIVE INTERPRETATIONS OF A HOARE-LOGIC FOR CLARKE'S LANGUAGE L_4

Bernhard Josko
Lehrstuhl für Informatik II, RWTH Aachen
Büchel 29 - 31, D-5100 Aachen, West-Germany

Introduction

In his 1979 paper [Cl] Clarke proved, that there exists no sound and relatively complete Hoare-logic for a programming language which simultaneously uses the features: (1) procedures are allowed in parameter positions (without self-application), (2) recursion, (3) static scope, (4) global variables in procedure bodies, (5) nested procedure declarations. In the same paper he claimed, that the languages L_i obtained by disallowing feature (i) do have a relatively complete Hoare-logic. While for $i \neq 4$ these claims were either proved in [Cl] or established subsequently by Olderog [Ol1], the claim regarding the language L_4 turned out to be "a challenge to develop new tools and methods in the field of Hoare-like systems" [LO]. This arises from the fact, that the execution tree of a program of L_4 does not need to be regular while the construction of prooftrees by present-day Hoare-like systems depends essentially on regularity of execution trees [Ol2]. Meanwhile several papers [BKM], [DJ], [GCH], [La2], [Ol3] have appeared which investigate the existence of Hoare-style proof-systems for (sublanguages of) L_4. Our investigations in this paper are based on the Hoare-logic developed in [DJ]. The crucial idea to obtain a complete proof-system was to prove the correctness of a call $P(\bar{x}:q_1,\ldots,q_n)$ by *seperately* proving a partial correctness assertion for P and its actual procedure parameters $q_1,\ldots,q_n$. This seperation increases the complexity of correctness formulae, proving P now means proving a partial correctness assertion no longer of a program transforming *states into states* but rather *state-transformations into state-transformations*. Hence in order to allow the proof to proceed inductively on applications, all concepts for Hoare-style proof-systems have to be lifted to higher levels: the assertion language, partial correctness assertions, the notion of strongest postcondition etc. As the notion of expressive interpretations depends on the assertion language, extending all the concepts mentioned above raises the question for which interpretations the assertion language is expressive. It will turn out that there is no difference to the usual notion of expressive interpretations. By a theorem of Lipton [Li] we know that (with respect to the usual notion) the expressive interpretations are essentially the arithmetic ones and finite ones. Hence we consider these interpretations and prove in this paper that they are expressive in our extended notion.

In the case that I is a finite interpretation, the proof is straightforward and it is omitted here. In the case that I is an arithmetic interpretation we proceed as follows. We use the fact that all semantic cpo's $Pred^{\tau}$ are effectively (relative to some oracle O_I given by the interpretation of the function and relation symbols) given domains. We show that every computable element of such a domain can be described by a formula of the assertion language. As the input-output relation of a statement S is some computable element and the strongest postcondition of $\bar{x}=\bar{z}$ and S is essentially this input-output relation, we obtain a formula for the strongest postcondition of $\bar{x}=\bar{z}$ and S , from which a formula describing the strongest postcondition of an arbitrary formula f and S can easily be derived. The fact that I is arithmetic will essentially be used to obtain formulae defining r.e. sets.

<u>The programming language</u>

First we will give the syntax of Clarke's language L_4 in a denested version, but with complex procedure terms in parameter positions. (For a (schematological) denesting of procedure declarations cf. [La1], [DF], [TMH].) Furthermore we consider here only programs without sharing of variables. (A treatment of sharing is given e.g. in [Jo2]). As no self-application is allowed every procedure has a finite mode in the sense of ALGOL 68 [Wi]. Hence we will give the syntax in a typed version. The sets *Type* of *types* and *Ptype* of *procedure types* are given by

- $\underline{n} \in Ptype$ for every $n \in \mathbb{N}$
  ($\hat{=}$ <u>proc</u>(<u>ref</u> <u>int</u>,...,<u>ref</u> <u>int</u>)<u>void</u> in ALGOL 68)
  (<u>ref</u> <u>int</u> repeated n times)
- if $\tau_0,\ldots,\tau_n \in Ptype$, $n \geq 1$, then $(\tau_1\ldots\tau_n \to \tau_0) \in Ptype$
  ($\hat{=}$ <u>proc</u>$(\tau_1,\ldots,\tau_n)\tau_0$ in ALGOL 68)
- $Type := Ptype \cup \{\underline{c}\}$ ($\underline{c}$ $\hat{=}$ <u>void</u> in ALGOL 68)

We start from the disjoint, infinite sets $(x,z\in)$ *Var* of *variables*, $(P,P_{\tau}\in)$ $Pvar^{\tau}$, $\tau\in Ptype$, of *procedure identifiers of type* τ and $(y,y_{\tau}\in)$ Par^{τ}, $\tau\in Ptype$, of *(formal procedure) parameters of type* τ. The sets (e∈) *Expr* of *expressions* and (b∈) *BExpr* of *boolean expressions* are defined in the usual way. We assume that there is a special 0-ary symbol "ω" (denoting the initial value of a new variable) and a binary relation symbol "=". We use the $\bar{\ }$-operator to denote some non-empty list. In connection with set-theoretic operations $\bar{a} = (a_1,\dots,a_n)$ is identified with $\{a_1,\dots,a_n\}$. α is used to denote some non-empty word $\tau_1\dots\tau_n$ over *Ptype* and y_α stands for a list $(y_{\tau_1},\dots,y_{\tau_n})$.

The sets $(S^\tau\in)$ $Stat^\tau$ of *statements of type* τ, (D∈) *Decl* of *declarations* and of *units* (U) are then defined by

$$S^{\underline{c}} ::= \underline{skip} \mid x := e \mid S_1^{\underline{c}};S_2^{\underline{c}} \mid \underline{if}\ b\ \underline{then}\ S_1^{\underline{c}}\ \underline{else}\ S_2^{\underline{c}}\ \underline{fi} \mid$$

$$\underline{while}\ b\ \underline{do}\ S^{\underline{c}}\ \underline{od} \mid \underline{begin}\ \underline{new}\ x;\ S^{\underline{c}}\ \underline{end} \mid S^{\underline{n}}(x_1,\dots,x_n),$$

where $x_1,\dots,x_n$ are distinct variables

$$S^\tau ::= P_\tau \mid y_\tau \mid S^{(\tau_1\dots\tau_n\rightarrow\tau)}(S_1^{\tau_1},\dots,S_n^{\tau_n})$$

$$D ::= \varepsilon \mid \underline{proc}\ P(y_{\alpha_1})\dots(y_{\alpha_m})(x_1,\dots,x_n) \Leftarrow S^{\underline{c}}\ \underline{corp};\ D$$

$$\mid \underline{proc}\ P(y_{\alpha_1})\dots(y_{\alpha_m}) \Leftarrow S^{\tau_o}\ \underline{corp};\ D$$

where

$P \in Pvar^\tau$, $\tau = (\alpha_1 \rightarrow \dots \rightarrow (\alpha_m \rightarrow \tau_o)\dots)$ (in the first case $\tau_o = \underline{n}$), $\alpha_j = \tau_1^j\dots\tau_{i_j}^j$, $y_{\alpha_j} = (y_{\tau_1^j},\dots,y_{\tau_{i_j}^j})$ $1 \le j \le m$, $y_{\tau_1^1},\dots,y_{\tau_{i_m}^m}$ are distinct procedure parameters and all parameters occurring in $S^{\underline{c}}$ resp. S^{τ_o} are contained in these parameters (i.e. procedures are closed terms); $x_1,\dots,x_n$ are distinct variables and all free variables of $S^{\underline{c}}$ are contained in $\{x_1,\dots,x_n\}$ (i.e. no global variables).

$U ::= \langle D,S\rangle$, where $D \equiv \underline{proc}\ P_1\dots\Leftarrow S_1\ \underline{corp};\dots;\ \underline{proc}\ P_k\dots\Leftarrow S_k\ \underline{corp}$; such that all procedure identifiers occurring in D and S are contained in $\{P_1,\dots,P_k\}$ and $P_1,\dots,P_k$ are distinct procedure identifiers.

A program is some unit $\langle D,S^{\underline{c}}\rangle$, where $S^{\underline{c}}$ contains no formal procedure parameters.

To define the semantics we assume that some *interpretation* $I = \langle I,\varphi\rangle$ is given, where I is some domain and φ a mapping which interprets the function and relation symbols. The semantics of a statement of type $\underline{c}$

will be some relation between states (Σ will denote the set of *states* $\sigma: Var \to I$), the semantics of a statement $S^{\underline{n}}$ is determined by some relation $R \subseteq I^n \times I^n$ as $S^{\underline{n}}$ contains no global variables. (If we allow sharing, the semantics of $S^{\underline{n}}$ is not determined by one relation, but by several relations, one for every sharing class.) The meaning of higher-type statements are functionals. Accordingly the semantic domains $Cont^{\tau}$, *continuations of type* τ, are given by the following cpo's:

$$Cont^{\underline{c}} := \langle P(\Sigma \times \Sigma), \subseteq \rangle$$

$$Cont^{\underline{n}} := \langle \{\theta_R \mid R \subseteq I^n \times I^n\}, \subseteq \rangle, \text{ where } \theta_R \subseteq \theta_{R'} \text{ iff } R \subseteq R' \text{ and}$$

$$\theta_R : Var^n \to P(\Sigma \times \Sigma) : \bar{x} \longmapsto \{(\sigma,\sigma') \mid \sigma =_{\bar{x}} \sigma' \text{ and } (\sigma(\bar{x}),\sigma'(\bar{x})) \in R\}$$ [1]

$$Cont^{(\tau_1 \ldots \tau_n \to \tau_o)} := [Cont^{\tau_1} \times \ldots \times Cont^{\tau_n} \to Cont^{\tau_o}]$$

As the semantics of a statement $S^{\underline{c}}$ in an environment depends only on its free variables, only those relations $\theta \subseteq \Sigma \times \Sigma$ are of interest which *operate on* a finite subset X of Var, i.e. which satisfy:

(1) $(\sigma,\sigma') \in \theta \leadsto \sigma =_X \sigma'$

(2) $(\sigma,\sigma') \in \theta,\ \tilde{\sigma}_{|X} = \sigma_{|X}, \tilde{\sigma}'_{|X} = \sigma'_{|X},\ \tilde{\sigma} =_X \tilde{\sigma}' \leadsto (\tilde{\sigma},\tilde{\sigma}') \in \theta.$

Let $Cont^X$ be the set of all continuations $\theta \subseteq \Sigma \times \Sigma$ which operates on X, then $\bigcup_{X \subseteq Var} Cont^X$ is the relevant part of $Cont^{\underline{c}}$. Assuming that Var is wellordered we can define an isomorphism between $Cont^X$ and $Cont^{\underline{n}}$.

Env denotes the set of *environments*, $\rho : Par \to Cont$, which assigns to every parameter y_τ some continuation of type τ. Then the meaning of a unit $\langle D,S \rangle$ in an environment ρ is denoted by $C[\![D,S]\!]\rho$. For more details of the language and its semantics we refer to [DJ] or [Jo2], the reader may assume some standard denotational or approximating semantics here.

The assertion language

The assertion language reflects the main features of the programming language. While in the programming language declarations allow to

---

[1] $\sigma =_{\bar{x}} \sigma'$ denotes that $\sigma(z) = \sigma'(z)$ for all $z \in Var \setminus \bar{x}$

avoid explicit abstractions, this feature is needed in the assertion language. The assertion language is a typed λ-calculus with predicate variables of higher types (which stand for some postconditions of procedure parameters with respect to some canonical preconditions). Let *Predvar* := {post-y | y ∈ *Par*} be the set of *predicate variables* and *Aux* be a countable set of *auxiliary variables* with typical element $\tilde{x}$. Syntactically auxiliary variables are used in the same manner as variables, but their values are given not by states but by environments. This allows to fix some value in a higher type formula. The set of auxiliary variables in an expression e is denoted by *aux*(e). The set ($f^\tau \in$) $Form^\tau$, $\tau \in Type$, of *formulae of type* τ are defined as follows:

$$f^{\underline{c}} ::= \underline{\text{true}} \mid \underline{\text{false}} \mid e_1 = e_2 \mid R(e_1,\ldots,e_n) \mid f_1^{\underline{c}} \vee f_2^{\underline{c}} \mid f_1^{\underline{c}} \wedge f_2^{\underline{c}} \mid \forall x.f^{\underline{c}} \mid \exists x.f^{\underline{c}} \mid$$
$$\forall\tilde{x}.f^{\underline{c}} \mid \exists\tilde{x}.f^{\underline{c}} \mid \neg f^{\underline{c}}\ ,\ \text{where } frpred(f^{\underline{c}}) = \emptyset \mid f^{\underline{n}}(e_1,\ldots,e_{2n})$$

$$f^\tau ::= \text{post-}y_\tau \mid \underline{\text{abs}}\ x_1,\ldots,x_{2n}.f^{\underline{c}}\ \underline{\text{sba}}\ ,\ \text{where } \tau = \underline{n} \text{ and } free(f^{\underline{c}}) \subseteq$$
$$\{x_1,\ldots,x_{2n}\} \mid \underline{\text{abs}}\ \text{post-}y_\alpha.f^{\tau_o}\ \underline{\text{sba}}\ ,\ \text{where } \tau = (\alpha \to \tau_o) \mid$$
$$f^{(\tau_1\ldots\tau_n \to \tau)}(f_1^{\tau_1},\ldots,f_n^{\tau_n})$$

frpred(f) is the set of free predicate variables in a formula f which is defined as in the classical setting of λ-calculus. We use *free*(f) and *fraux*(f) to denote the set of free variables, resp. auxiliary variables, of f .

Note that we allow negation only for closed formulae, since we want the semantics of a formula to be continuous in its free predicate variables. Formulae of type $\underline{n}$ denote some sets ($\underline{\text{abs}}\ \bar{x}.f^{\underline{c}}\ \underline{\text{sba}}$ will be interpreted as $\{\bar{x}\}f^{\underline{c}}$ in simple type theory [Ta]), whereas formulae of higher types, $(\alpha \to \tau)$, denote some continuous predicate transformers. The cpo's $Pred^\tau$, $\tau \in Type$, are given by

$$Pred^{\underline{c}} := \langle P(\Sigma), \subseteq \rangle \qquad Pred^{\underline{n}} := \langle P(I^{2n}), \subseteq \rangle$$

$$Pred^{\tau_1\ldots\tau_n} := Pred^{\tau_1} \times \ldots \times Pred^{\tau_n} \qquad Pred^{(\alpha \to \tau_o)} := [Pred^\alpha \to Pred^{\tau_o}]$$

We will give only the non-obvious clauses in the definition of the semantics of formulae. Clearly, formulae will have to be evaluated in an environment ρ, which binds predicate variables to higher type predicate transformations while associating domain-values to auxiliary variables. The set of such environments is called *Predenv*. The semantics of formulae $F : Form \to Predenv \to Pred$ is then given by

$$F[\![f^{\underline{n}}(e_1,\ldots,e_{2n})]\!]\rho := \{\sigma \mid (E[\![e_1]\!]\rho\sigma,\ldots,E[\![e_{2n}]\!]\rho\sigma) \in F[\![f^{\underline{n}}]\!]\rho\}$$

$F[\![\text{post-}y_\tau]\!]\rho := \rho(\text{post-}y_\tau)$

$F[\![\underline{\text{abs}}\ x_1,\ldots,x_{2n}.f^{\underline{c}}\ \underline{\text{sba}}]\!]\rho := \{(\sigma(x_1),\ldots,\sigma(x_{2n}))\mid\sigma\in F[\![f^{\underline{c}}]\!]\rho\}$

$F[\![f(f_1,\ldots,f_n)]\!]\rho := F[\![f]\!]\rho(F[\![f_1]\!]\rho,\ldots,F[\![f_n]\!]\rho)$

$F[\![\underline{\text{abs}}\ \text{post-}y_\alpha.f\ \underline{\text{sba}}]\!]\rho := (\pi_\alpha \mapsto F[\![f]\!]\rho[\text{post-}y_\alpha/\pi_\alpha])$

Note that the semantics of a formula of type τ is a predicate of type τ. The relation $R\sim\theta_R$ defines natural isomorphisms between $Cont^\tau$ and $Pred^\tau$, $\tau\in Ptype$, which are denoted by $relpred^\tau$ and their inverses by $predrel^\tau$. Using the isomorphism between $Cont^X$ and $Cont^{\underline{n}}$ we obtain an isomorphism between $Cont^X$ and $Pred^{\underline{n}}$, too. The isomorphisms $relpred^\tau$ allow to associate to every predicate environment $\rho\in Predenv$ a continuation environment $predrel(\rho)$, which is given by $predrel(\rho)(y_\tau) := predrel^\tau(\rho(\text{post-}y_\tau))$.

The *strongest postcondition* of a formula $f^{\underline{c}}$ and a unit $<D,S^{\underline{c}}>$ is defined by

$$sp(f,<D,S>)\rho := \{\sigma\mid\exists\sigma'\in F[\![f]\!]\rho\ \text{ with }\ (\sigma',\sigma)\in C[\![D,S]\!]predrel(\rho)\}$$

The assertion language *Form* is *expressive* for an interpretation I iff for every formula $f^{\underline{c}}$ and every unit $<D,S^{\underline{c}}>$ there is a formula f' such that $F_I[\![f']\!] = sp(f,<D,S>)$.

<u>Lemma 1</u>

(i) Let f' be a formula which expresses the strongest postcondition of $\bar{x}=\bar{z}$ and $<D,S^{\underline{c}}>$, where $\bar{x}$ are the free variables of $S^{\underline{c}}$. Then $sp(f,<D,S>) = F_I[\![\exists\bar{w}.(f'[\bar{z}/\bar{w}]\wedge f[\bar{x}/\bar{w}])]\!]$

(ii) $relpred^{\bar{x}}(C[\![D,S]\!]predrel(\rho)) = \{\sigma(\overline{zx})\mid\sigma\in sp(\bar{x}=\bar{z},<D,S>)\rho\}$

For a proof see [Jo3] resp. [DJ], [Jo2]. □

<u>Interpretations</u>

As mentioned above there are two classes of interpretations which are of interest, the arithmetical ones and finite ones. In this chapter we will use the terminology of [CGH], where an extension of Lipton's result has been proved.

Let FOL_Ω be the set of *first order formulae* built up from the variable set *Var* and the signature Ω, and $F_I : FOL_\Omega\to\Sigma$ its standard semantic function.

I is *(weakly) arithmetic*, if we can find first-order formulae Nat($\bar{x}$), Eq($\bar{x},\bar{y}$), Zero($\bar{x}$), Succ($\bar{x},\bar{y}$), Add($\bar{x},\bar{y},\bar{z}$), Mult($\bar{x},\bar{y},\bar{z}$) (with respectively k, 2k, k, 2k, 3k, 3k free variables for some k), such that Eq defines an equivalence relation on I^k and, if $eq := \{(\bar{a},\bar{b})\mid F[\![Eq(\bar{x},\bar{y})]\!]\sigma[\bar{x}/\bar{a}][\bar{y}/\bar{b}] =$

true} and if $[\bar{a}]_{eq} := \{\bar{b} \in I^k \mid (\bar{a},\bar{b}) \in eq\}$, there is a bijection $\Psi : \{[\bar{a}]_{eq} \mid F[\![\mathrm{Nat}(\bar{x})]\!]\sigma[\bar{x}/\bar{a}] = \mathrm{true}\} \to \mathbb{N}$ such that

(i) $F[\![\mathrm{Nat}(\bar{x}) \wedge \mathrm{Zero}(\bar{x})]\!]\sigma = \mathrm{true}$ iff $\Psi([\sigma(\bar{x})]_{eq}) = 0$

(ii) $F[\![\mathrm{Nat}(\bar{x}) \wedge \mathrm{Nat}(\bar{y}) \wedge \mathrm{Succ}(\bar{x},\bar{y})]\!]\sigma = \mathrm{true}$ iff $\Psi([\sigma(x)]_{eq}) + 1 = \Psi([\sigma(\bar{y})]_{eq})$

(iii) $F[\![\mathrm{Nat}(\bar{x}) \wedge \mathrm{Nat}(\bar{y}) \wedge \mathrm{Nat}(\bar{z}) \wedge \mathrm{Add}(\bar{x},\bar{y},\bar{z})]\!]\sigma = \mathrm{true}$ iff $\Psi([\sigma(\bar{x})]_{eq}) + \Psi([\sigma(\bar{y})]_{eq}) = \Psi([\sigma(\bar{z})]_{eq})$

(iv) $F[\![\mathrm{Nat}(\bar{x}) \wedge \mathrm{Nat}(\bar{y}) \wedge \mathrm{Nat}(\bar{z}) \wedge \mathrm{Mult}(\bar{x},\bar{y},\bar{z})]\!]\sigma = \mathrm{true}$ iff $\Psi([\sigma(\bar{x})]_{eq}) * \Psi([\sigma(\bar{y})]_{eq}) = \Psi([\sigma(\bar{z})]_{eq})$

Given an arithmetic interpretation I we denote by k_I some integer k given by the definition above.
If FOL_{PA} is the set of first order formulae of Peano Arithmetic, I_{PA} the standard interpretation of Peano Arithmetic and I an arithmetic Ω-interpretation, then for every formula $f(x_1,\dots,x_n) \in FOL_{PA}$ with n free variables there is a corresponding formula $\tilde{f}(\bar{x}_1,\dots,\bar{x}_n) \in FOL_\Omega$ with $n \cdot k_I$ free variables such that $F_I[\![\mathrm{Nat}(\bar{x}_1) \wedge \dots \wedge \mathrm{Nat}(\bar{x}_n) \wedge \tilde{f}(\bar{x}_1,\dots,\bar{x}_n)]\!]\sigma = \mathrm{true}$ iff $F_{I_{PA}}[\![f(x_1,\dots,x_n)]\!]\sigma[(x_1,\dots,x_n)/(\Psi([\sigma(\bar{x}_1)]_{eq}),\dots,\Psi([\sigma(\bar{x}_n)]_{eq}))] = \mathrm{true}$.
Using this fact and the fact that all r.e. sets are arithmetical, we can conclude that every r.e. set is expressible in FOL_Ω w.r.t. an arithmetic interpretation. We use $F_z(x)$ as a denotation for a formula of FOL_{PA} which expresses the r.e. set W_z. The *Herbrand universe* H_Ω of Ω is the set of all variable-free terms over Ω. An interpretation I is *Herbrand definable* (or *finitely generated*) iff for all a∈I there is a term $t \in H_\Omega$ whose semantics is a . In such an interpretation every element can be effectively described and all elements can be encoded into the natural numbers, which allows to give a notion of computability. Now assume that I is a Herbrand definable interpretation and let *code* : $H_\Omega \to \mathbb{N}$ be some effective encoding of Herbrand terms such that the set of codenumbers $code(H_\Omega)$ is deciable. As I is Herbrand definable this encoding of Herbrand terms yields an encoding of all elements a∈I. We denote by $Enc \subseteq \mathbb{N} \times I$ the predicate, which is true for a pair (n,a) iff n is the codenumber of a Herbrand term equal to a . Using the encoding of elements a∈I we can define computability of functions and predicates over I . As the functions and predicates given by the signature Ω are considered as basic functions and predicates computability means here computability relative to these basic operations. The encoding of a function $h : I^n \dashrightarrow I$ is given by $cdgraph(h) := \{< m_1,\dots,m_{n+1} > \mid$

$\exists a_1,\ldots,a_{n+1} \in I : (m_i,a_i) \in Enc,\ 1 \leq i \leq n+1$, and $h(a_1,\ldots,a_n) = a_{n+1}\}$[2]; similarly we define *cdgraph*(M) for a relation $M \subseteq I^n$. The oracle O_I is then given by combining all code-graphs of the functions and relations given by the signature Ω. A function $h : I^n \dashrightarrow I$ (resp. a predicate $M \subseteq I^n$) is *computable* iff *cdgraph*(h) is r.e. in O_I.
An enumeration of the sets $M \subseteq \mathbb{N}$ which are r.e. in O_I is given by (cf. [Ro] §9.2,9.3):

$$W_z^{O_I} := \{m \mid \exists l,i,j : \langle m,l,i,j \rangle \in W_{\rho(z)} \text{ and } fs(i) \subseteq O_I \text{ and } fs(j) \subseteq \mathbb{N} \setminus O_I\}$$ [3]

Considering Peano Arithmetic, all computable sets are definable by a first order formula. To obtain an analogous result for arithmetic interpretations we have to require that the predicate *Enc* is definable. We call an arithmetic interpretation I *code-definable* iff there is a formula $ENC(\bar{x},y)$ of k_I+1 free variables such that $F[\![Nat(\bar{x}) \wedge ENC(\bar{x},y)]\!]\sigma$ = true iff $(\Psi([\sigma(\bar{x})]_{eq}),\ \sigma(y)) \in Enc$.
During the rest of the paper we will call a Herbrand-definable, arithmetic and code-definable interptretation briefly an arithmetical one. Now assume that I is such an interpretation, then for every function and relation symbol $g \in \Omega$ we can define a formula which describes *cdgraph*(φ(g)). Hence there is a formula $F_{O_I}(\bar{x})$ of k_I free variables which describes the oracle O_I. From this we can easily construct formulae $F_z^{O_I}(\bar{x})$, $z \in \mathbb{N}$, defining the sets $W_z^{O_I}$.

Main results

In this section we will prove that the assertion language is expressive for arithmetical interpretations. To define some formula which expresses the strongest postcondition of a given formula f and a unit $\langle D,S \rangle$ we will precede as follows. First we investigate the semantic cpo's $Pred^\tau$ and prove that for every procedure type τ, $Pred^\tau$ is an O_I-effectively given domain. Then we define formulae $E^\tau(\bar{x})$ which describe the finite elements of $Pred^\tau$. Using these formulae we can construct for every computable function $h : Pred^{\tau_1} \times \ldots \times Pred^{\tau_n} \to Pred^{\tau_0}$ a formula F_h which describes this function. As the semantics of a unit can be considered as such a computable function (using the isomorphisms between $Cont^\tau$ and $Pred^\tau$), we obtain a formula describing the strongest postcondition of $\bar{x} = \bar{z}$ and $\langle D,S \rangle$, and from this formula we can easily derive a formula defining the strongest postcondition on an arbitrary

[2] $\langle -,\ldots,- \rangle$ is the standard encoding of n-tuples of natural numbers into the natural numbers.

[3] *fs* denotes the standard enumeration of finit subsets of $\mathbb{N}$

formula f and $< D,S >$.

First we recall some definitions concerning effectively given domains. For more details the reader is refered to [Ka], [CE].

For an ω-algebraic bounded complete cpo $D = < D,\sqsubseteq >$, we denote the set of all finite elements by Fin_D. A mapping $\varepsilon : \mathbb{N} \to Fin_D$ is an enumeration of Fin_D iff ε is onto and $\varepsilon(0) = \bot$. $< D,\varepsilon >$ is then called an *indexed domain*. For an indexed domain $< D,\varepsilon >$ the predicates $bd(i)$ and $lub(i,k)$ are defined by

$$bd(i) = \text{true} \quad \text{iff} \quad \{\varepsilon(j) \mid j \in fs(i)\} \quad \text{is bounded}$$
$$lub(i,k) = \text{true} \quad \text{iff} \quad \varepsilon(k) = \bigsqcup\{\varepsilon(j) \mid j \in fs(i)\}$$

Given an indexed domain $< D,\varepsilon >$ and some oracle $\mathcal{O} \subseteq \mathbb{N}$, we say that $< D,\varepsilon >$ is an *$\mathcal{O}$-effectively given domain* iff the predicates bd and lub are decidable in $\mathcal{O}$. An element of an $\mathcal{O}$-effectively given domain is *computable w.r.t.* ε iff $\{i \mid \varepsilon(i) \sqsubseteq d\}$ is r.e. in $\mathcal{O}$ and a continuous function $f : D_1 \to D_2$, where $< D_1,\varepsilon_1 >$ and $< D_2,\varepsilon_2 >$ are $\mathcal{O}$-effectively given domains, is *computable w.r.t.* $(\varepsilon_1,\varepsilon_2)$ iff $graph(f) := \{< n,m > \mid \varepsilon_2(m) \sqsubseteq f(\varepsilon_1(n))\}$ is r.e. in $\mathcal{O}$. Given indexed domains $< D_1,\varepsilon_1 >$ and $< D_2,\varepsilon_2 >$ the canonical enumerations $\varepsilon_1 \times \varepsilon_2$ and $\varepsilon_1 \to \varepsilon_2$ of the finite elements of $D_1 \times D_2$ and $[D_1 \to D_2]$ are given by

$$\varepsilon_1 \times \varepsilon_2(i) := (\varepsilon_1(i_1),\varepsilon_2(i_2)) \qquad \text{where } i = < i_1,i_2 >$$

$$\varepsilon_1 \to \varepsilon_2(i) := \begin{cases} \bigsqcup M & \text{if } M := \{[\varepsilon_1(i_1),\varepsilon_2(i_2)] \mid < i_1,i_2 > \in fs(i)\} \text{ is bounded} \\ \bot & \text{otherwise} \end{cases}$$

where $[a,b] : D_1 \to D_2$ is a *stepfunction* which yields for an argument $d \in D_1$ b if $a \sqsubseteq d$ and $\bot$ if $a \not\sqsubseteq d$.

If $< D_1,\varepsilon_1 >$ and $< D_2,\varepsilon_2 >$ are $\mathcal{O}$-effectively given domains, then $< D_1 \times D_2, \varepsilon_1 \times \varepsilon_2 >$ and $<[D_1 \to D_2],\varepsilon_1 \to \varepsilon_2 >$ are $\mathcal{O}$-effectively given domains too.

Evidently, $Pred^\tau$ is a bounded complete cpo, moreover it is a complete lattice and it is algebraic ($Pred^{\underline{n}}$ is the power set of I^{2n}, and the class of algebraic bounded complete cpo's is closed under cartesian product and function space). A canonical enumeration ε^τ of the finite elements of $Pred^\tau$, such that $< Pred^\tau,\varepsilon^\tau >$ is an $\mathcal{O}_I$-effectively given domain, is given in the case that τ is $\underline{n}$ by a standard numbering of the finite subsets of I^{2n} and in the case that τ is a composed type $(\tau_1 \ldots \tau_n \to \tau_0)$ by the canonical enumeration obtained from the enumerations of its components. Let us make this more precise. The standard numbering of finite subsets of I^n is given by

$$fs_{I,n}(i) := \{(a_1,\ldots,a_n) \mid \exists\, m_1,\ldots,m_n \in \mathbb{N} \text{ s.t. } (m_j,a_j) \in Enc\ 1 \leq j \leq n, \text{ and } < m_1,\ldots,m_n > \in fs(i)\}$$

Then the enumerations $\varepsilon^\tau : \mathbb{N} \to Fin_{Pred^\tau}$, $\tau \in Ptype$ are defined as follows:

$\tau = \underline{n} : \varepsilon^\tau := fs_{I,2n}$; $\tau = (\tau_1 \ldots \tau_n \to \tau_o) : \varepsilon^\tau := \varepsilon^{\tau_1} \times \ldots \times \varepsilon^{\tau_n} \to \varepsilon^{\tau_o}$

It can be proved that for all $\tau \in Ptype$, $< Pred^\tau, \varepsilon^\tau >$ is an O_I-effectively given domain.

Next we turn to definability of the finite elements. We define formulae $E^\tau(\tilde{x})$[4] which describe the enumerations ε^τ. Simultaneously we define for every formula f of type τ a formula $\text{LESS}^\tau(\tilde{x},f)$ which expresses that a finite element $\varepsilon^\tau(i)$ is less than the semantics of f .

$\tau = \underline{n}$:

(i) $E^\tau(\tilde{x}) :\equiv \underline{\text{abs}}\ \overline{zx}.\ \exists \bar{u}_o,\ldots,\bar{u}_{2n}.\ \text{Nat}(\bar{u}_o) \wedge \ldots \wedge \text{Nat}(\bar{u}_{2n}) \wedge$
$\widetilde{\text{PAIR}}_{2n}(\bar{u}_o,\bar{u}_1,\ldots,\bar{u}_{2n}) \wedge \text{ENC}(\bar{u}_1,x_1) \wedge \ldots \wedge \text{ENC}(\bar{u}_n,x_n) \wedge$
$\text{ENC}(\bar{u}_{n+1},z_1) \wedge \ldots \wedge \text{ENC}(\bar{u}_{2n},z_n) \wedge \widetilde{\text{FS}}(\tilde{x},\bar{u}_o)\ \underline{\text{sba}}$ [5]

(ii) $\text{LESS}^\tau(\tilde{x},f) :\equiv \forall \overline{zx}.\ E^\tau(\tilde{x})(\overline{zx}) \to f(\overline{zx})$

$\tau = (\tau_1 \ldots \tau_k \to \tau_o)$: let $\tau_o = (\alpha_m \to \ldots \to (\alpha_1 \to \underline{n})\ldots)$

(i) $E^\tau(\tilde{x}) :\equiv \underline{\text{abs}}\ \text{post-y}_{\tau_1},\ldots,\text{post-y}_{\tau_k}.\underline{\text{abs}}\ \text{post-y}_{\alpha_m}.\ \ldots\ \underline{\text{abs}}\ \text{post-y}_{\alpha_1}.$
$\underline{\text{abs}}\ \overline{zx}.\ \exists \tilde{z},\tilde{z}',\tilde{z}''.\text{Nat}(\tilde{z}) \wedge \text{Nat}(\tilde{z}') \wedge \text{Nat}(\tilde{z}'') \wedge \widetilde{\text{PAIR}}_2(\tilde{z},\tilde{z}',\tilde{z}'') \wedge$
$\widetilde{\text{FS}}(\tilde{x},\tilde{z}) \wedge \exists \tilde{z}_1,\ldots,\tilde{z}_k\ .\ \text{Nat}(\tilde{z}_1) \wedge \ldots \wedge \text{Nat}(\tilde{z}_k) \wedge \widetilde{\text{PAIR}}_k(\tilde{z}',\tilde{z}_1,\ldots,\tilde{z}_k) \wedge$
$\text{LESS}^{\tau_1}(\tilde{z}_1,\text{post-y}_{\tau_1}) \wedge \ldots \wedge \text{LESS}^{\tau_k}(\tilde{z}_k,\text{post-y}_{\tau_k}) \wedge$
$E^{\tau_o}(\tilde{z}'')(\text{post-y}_{\alpha_m})\ldots(\text{post-y}_{\alpha_1})(\overline{zx})\ \underline{\text{sba}}\ \underline{\text{sba}}\ \ldots\ \underline{\text{sba}}\ \underline{\text{sba}}$

(ii) $\text{LESS}^\tau(\tilde{x},f) :\equiv \forall \tilde{z},\tilde{z}',\tilde{z}''.(\text{Nat}(\tilde{z}) \wedge \text{Nat}(\tilde{z}') \wedge \text{Nat}(\tilde{z}'') \wedge$
$\widetilde{\text{PAIR}}_2(\tilde{z},\tilde{z}',\tilde{z}'') \wedge \widetilde{\text{FS}}(\tilde{x},\tilde{z})) \to (\exists \tilde{z}_1,\ldots,\tilde{z}_k.\text{Nat}(\tilde{z}_1) \wedge \ldots \wedge \text{Nat}(\tilde{z}_k) \wedge$
$\widetilde{\text{PAIR}}_k(\tilde{z}',\tilde{z}_1,\ldots,\tilde{z}_k) \wedge \text{LESS}^{\tau_o}(\tilde{z}'',f(E^{\tau_1}(\tilde{z}_1),\ldots,E^{\tau_k}(\tilde{z}_k))))$

These formulae result from the definition of the enumerations ε^τ and from the observations that (1) $\sigma \in \varepsilon^{(\tau_1\ldots\tau_k\to\tau_o)}(i)(\pi_{\tau_1},\ldots,\pi_{\tau_k})(\pi_{\alpha_m})\ldots(\pi_{\alpha_1})(\bar{x})$ iff $\sigma \in \varepsilon^{\tau_o}(j)(\pi_{\alpha_m})\ldots(\pi_{\alpha_1})(\bar{x})$ and $(\varepsilon^{\tau_1}(i_1),\ldots,\varepsilon^{\tau_k}(i_k)) \subseteq (\pi_{\tau_1},\ldots,\pi_{\tau_k})$ for some $<<i_1,\ldots,i_k>,j> \in fs(i)$ and (2) $\bigsqcup\{[(\varepsilon^{\tau_1}(i_1),\ldots,\varepsilon^{\tau_k}(i_k)),\varepsilon^{\tau_o}(j)]$ $|<<i_1,\ldots,i_k>,j> \in fs(i)\} \subseteq \pi$ iff $\varepsilon^{\tau_o}(j) \subseteq \pi(\varepsilon^{\tau_1}(i_1),\ldots,\varepsilon^{\tau_k}(i_k))$ for all $<<i_1,\ldots,i_k>,j> \in fs(i)$. Hence we can prove the following theorem.

Theorem 1

(1) For all ρ with $F[\![\text{Nat}(\tilde{x})]\!]\rho\sigma = \text{true}$ it holds: $F[\![E^\tau(\tilde{x})]\!]\rho = \varepsilon^\tau(\Psi([\rho(\tilde{x})]_{eq}))$

---

[4] Here and in the following $\tilde{x}$ stands not for a single auxiliary variable but for a tuple of k_I distinct auxiliary variables

[5] $\text{PAIR}_n(x,x_1,\ldots,x_n)$ denotes a formula of FOL_{PA} defining $m=<m_1,\ldots,m_n>$ and $\text{FS}(x_1,x_2)$ denotes a formula defining $m_2 \in fs(m_1)$

(2) For all formulae $f \in Form^{\tau}$ it holds:

$$F[\![Nat(\tilde{x}) \wedge LESS^{\tau}(\tilde{x},f)]\!]\rho\sigma = true \quad iff \quad \varepsilon^{\tau}(\Psi([\rho(\tilde{x})]_{eq})) \subseteq F[\![f]\!]\rho$$

□

Next we use these formulae $E^{\tau}(\tilde{x})$ and $LESS^{\tau}(\tilde{x},f)$ to find formulae defining the computable functions. Assume that h is some computable function, $h: Pred^{\tau_1} \times \ldots \times Pred^{\tau_n} \to Pred^{\tau_o}$, then its graph $\{<<i_1,\ldots,i_n>,i_0> \mid \varepsilon^{\tau_o}(i_0) \subseteq h(\varepsilon^{\tau_1}(i_1),\ldots,\varepsilon^{\tau_n}(i_n))\}$ is r.e. in O_I, i.e. $graph(h) = W_z^{O_I}$ for some z. Let τ_o be $(\alpha_m \to \ldots \to (\alpha_1 \to \underline{k})\ldots)$, we define :

$$\begin{aligned} F_h :\equiv\; & \underline{abs}\ post\text{-}y_{\tau_1},\ldots,post\text{-}y_{\tau_n} .\ \underline{abs}\ post\text{-}y_{\alpha_m} .\ \ldots\ \underline{abs}\ post\text{-}y_{\alpha_1} .\ \underline{abs}\ \overline{zx}. \\ & \exists\, \tilde{x}_1,\ldots,\tilde{x}_{n+3}.\ Nat(\tilde{x}_1) \wedge \ldots \wedge Nat(\tilde{x}_{n+3}) \wedge \widetilde{PAIR}_n(\tilde{x}_{n+1},\tilde{x}_1,\ldots,\tilde{x}_n) \wedge \\ & \widetilde{PAIR}_2(\tilde{x}_{n+3},\tilde{x}_{n+1},\tilde{x}_{n+2}) \wedge F_z^{O_I}(\tilde{x}_{n+3}) \wedge LESS^{\tau_1}(\tilde{x}_1,post\text{-}y_{\tau_1}) \wedge \ldots \wedge \\ & LESS^{\tau_n}(\tilde{x}_n,post\text{-}y_{\tau_n}) \wedge E^{\tau_o}(\tilde{x}_{n+2})(post\text{-}y_{\alpha_m})\ldots(post\text{-}y_{\alpha_1})(\overline{zx})\ \underline{sba}\ \underline{sba} \\ & \ldots\ \underline{sba}\ \underline{sba} \end{aligned}$$

Observing that $h(\pi_1,\ldots,\pi_n) = \bigsqcup\{\varepsilon^{\tau_o}(i_0) \mid \varepsilon^{\tau_j}(i_j) \subseteq \pi_j \quad 1 \leq j \leq n$ and $<<i_1,\ldots,i_n>,i_0> \in graph(h)\}$, it is obvious that $F[\![F_h]\!]\rho = h$. Hence we have proved the following theorem.

<u>Theorem 2</u>

For every computable function $h: Pred^{\tau_1} \times \ldots \times Pred^{\tau_n} \to Pred^{\tau_o}$ there is a formula F_h s.t. $F[\![F_h]\!]\rho = h$.

□

Now we turn to the programming language. Assume that D is a declaration and S a statement of type $\underline{c}$ with free parameters $y_{\tau_1},\ldots,y_{\tau_m}$ and free variables $x_1,\ldots,x_n$. If an environment ρ assigns to these parameters computable elements, then $C[\![D,S]\!]\rho$ is a computable element too. (i.e. the semantics of S abstracted to its free variables is a computable element of $Cont^{\underline{n}}$.) This can easily be seen by the fact that the program constructors, as composition, conditional, while-loop, abstraction, application and fixpoint-operator, are effective operators, and the functions and predicates occurring on the right hand sides of assignments and in tests of conditionals are contained in the oracle O_I. As a function is computable iff it maps computable elements to computable elements, the function

$$\Phi_{<D,S>} : Pred^{\tau_1} \times \ldots \times Pred^{\tau_m} \to Pred^{\underline{n}} \qquad \text{defined by}$$

$$\Phi_{<D,S>}(\pi_1,\ldots,\pi_m) := relpred^{\underline{n}}(C[\![D,S]\!]\rho[y_{\tau_1},\ldots,y_{\tau_m}/predrel(\pi_1,\ldots,\pi_m)])$$

is a computable function. Hence by theorem 2 there is a formula $F_{<D,S>}$

which defines this function. Then by Lemma 1(ii) the formula $F_{<D,S>}(\text{post-}y_{\tau_1},\ldots,\text{post-}y_{\tau_m})(\overline{zx})$ defines the strongest postcondition of $\overline{x}=\overline{z}$ and <D,S>. The strongest postcondition of an arbitrary formula $f^{\underline{c}}$ and <D,S> is then given by

$$F_{sp(f,<D,S>)} :\equiv \exists\,\overline{v}\,.\,F_{<D,S>}(\text{post-}y_{\tau_1},\ldots,\text{post-}y_{\tau_m})(\overline{vx}) \wedge f^{\underline{c}}[\overline{x}/\overline{v}]$$

where $\overline{v} \cap (\overline{xz} \cup \mathit{free}(f)) = \emptyset$.

Theorem 3

The assertion language *Form* is expressive for arithmetic interpretations. □

Moreover we can prove that *Form* is expressive for finite interpretations. The proof is straightforward (see [Jo2] or [Jo1]) and is omitted here.

References

[BKM] de Bakker, J.W./Klop, J.W./Meyer, J.-J.Ch.: *Correctness of programs with function procedures.* Report IW 17o/81, Mathematisch Centrum, Amsterdam (1981)

[Cl] Clarke, E.M.: *Programming language constructs for which it is impossible to obtain good Hoare-like axioms.* JACM 26, 129-147 (1979)

[CGH] Clarke, E.M./German, S.M./Halpern, J.Y.: *On effective axiomatizations of Hoare-logics.* 9th Annual ACM Symp. on Principles of Programming Languages, 3o9-321 (1982)

[CE] Constable, R./Egli, H.: *Computability concepts for programming language semantics.* TCS 2, 133-145 (1976)

[DJ] Damm, W./Josko, B.: *A sound and relatively* complete Hoare logic for a language with higher type procedures.* Acta Informatica 2o, 59-1o1 (1983)

[GCH] German, S.M./Clarke, E.M./Halpern, J.Y.: *A stronger axiom system for reasoning about procedures as parameters.* Workshop on Logics of Programs, Pittsburgh (1983)

[Ho] Hoare, C.A.R.: *An axiomatic basis for computer programming.* CACM 12, 576-583 (1969

[Jo1] Josko, B.: *On expressive interpretations of a Hoare-logic for a language with higher type procedures.* Schriften z. Inf. u. Angewandt. Math. Nr.88, Aachen (1983

[Jo2] Josko, B.: *A Hoare-calculus for ALGOL-like programs with finite mode procedures without global variables.* (in preparation)

[Jo3] Josko, B.: *A note on expressivity definitions in Hoare-logics.* Schriften z. Inf. u. Angewandt. Math. Nr.8o, TH Aachen (1982)

[Ka] Kanda, A.: *Effective solutions of recursive domain equations.* Warwick (1979)

[La1] Langmaack, H.: *On procedures as open subroutines I, II.* Acta Informatica 2, 311-333 (1973) and 3, 227-241 (1974)

[La2] Langmaack, H.: *Aspects of programs with finite modes.* Proc. of the Int. Conf. on Foundations of Computation Theory (1983)

[LO] Langmaack, H./Olderog, E.-R.: *Present-day Hoare-like systems for programming languages with procedures: power limits and most likely extensions.* Proc. 7th Coll. Automata, Languages and Programming, LNCS 85, 363-373 (198o)

[Li] Lipton, R.J.: *A necessary and sufficient condition for the existence of Hoare-logics.* 18th IEEE Symp. on Foundations of Computer Science, 1-6 (1977)

[Ol1] Olderog, E.-R.: *Sound and complete Hoare-like calculi based on copy rules.* Acta Informatica 16, 161-197 (1981)

[Ol2] Olderog, E.-R.: *Hoare-style proof and formal computations.* 11.GI-Jahrestagung, IFB 5o, 65-71 (1981)

[Ol3] Olderog, E.-R.: *Correctness of programs with PASCAL-like procedures without global variables.* (to appear in TCS)

[Ro] Rogers, H.: *Theory of recursive functions and effective computability.* McGraw-Hill

[TMH] Trakhtenbrot, B.A./Meyer, A.E./Halpern, J.Y.: *From denotational to operational and axiomatic semantics for ALGOL-like languages.* Workshop on Logics of Programs, Pittsburgh (1983)

[Ta] Takeuti, G.: *Proof theory.* North-Holland (1975)

TOWARDS EXECUTABLE SPECIFICATIONS USING CONDITIONAL AXIOMS +)

K. Drosten
TU Braunschweig, Institut fuer Informatik
Postfach 3329, D-3300 Braunschweig

ABSTRACT

Executing algebraic specifications is done by considering the equations as directed rules from left to right in order to compute normal forms. To improve the expressiveness of algebraic specifications, we not only admit pure equations but conditional ones having the form of positive Horn clauses. Based on a hierarchical approach where conditions have to be evaluated by means of axioms at lower levels, syntactical criteria are provided which guarantee the Church-Rosser property and, therefore, the well-definedness of the operational semantics. Besides, these criteria turn out to be sufficient for the termination of the full substitution strategy as well. Automatic computation of normal forms is possible if each proper subspecification has the finite termination property additionally.

1. INTRODUCTION

Ever since initiated by Guttag and Liskov & Zilles [Gu 75, LZ 74], algebraic specifications have met a lot of research activities. Today, they are considered to be a promising tool in software system development. A precise mathematical semantics as investigated in ADJ 78, Wa 77 and WB 82 makes correctness proofs possible. Besides, the concepts of implementation and parametrization [ADJ 79, Eh 79, EKMP 80, EKTWW 81, SW 82] support a structured software design by providing methods for stepwise refinement and modularization resp.. More practical works led to the definition of specification languages as CLEAR [BG 81] and OBJ [GT 79]. Implementations of these languages treat specifications as term rewriting systems and reduce terms to normal forms. The theoretical foundations on term rewriting systems concerning confluence, finite termination and termination of reduction strategies trace back to KB 70, Ro 73, Hu 77 and O'D 77, but all these papers are limited to pure equations. Work on conditional ones has not come up before in recent years [PEE 81, BK 82, DGEL 82, Re 82, Dr 83].

+) An extended version can be found in Dr 83 where detailed proofs are included.

2. MOTIVATION

The operational semantics of algebraic specifications bases on considering the symmetric equations as rewrite rules from left to right. By this way, it's often possible to reduce terms to a distinguished form, the so-called normal form. A simple example for illustration is the abstract data type nat (natural numbers).

Example 2.1

SORTS:		bool, nat
OPNS:		true, false: $\rightarrow$ bool
		0: $\rightarrow$ nat
		succ: nat $\rightarrow$ nat
		add, mult: $\text{nat}^2 \rightarrow$ nat
		eq: $\text{nat}^2 \rightarrow$ bool
VARS:		n, m: nat
AXMS:	(n1)	add(0,n) = n
	(n2)	add(succ(m),n) = succ(add(m,n))
	(n3)	mult(0,n) = 0
	(n4)	mult(succ(m),n) = add(mult(m,n),n)
	(n5)	eq(0,0) = true
	(n6)	eq(succ(n),0) = false
	(n7)	eq(0,succ(n)) = false
	(n8)	eq(succ(m),succ(n)) = eq(m,n)

The axioms (n1)-(n8) describe all possible reduction steps in nat: For a term t, a subterm of t matching a lefthand side of an axiom can be replaced by the righthand side. t then reduces to a normal form if there is a finite sequence of reduction steps starting with t and ending in a term where no further axiom can be applied to.

***

The operational semantics of a specification is given by the normal form algebra which is obtained as follows: For each sort s, there is a set NF_s containing all normal forms of sort s. For each operation symbol $\sigma: s_1 x \ldots x s_k \rightarrow s$ $(k \in N_0)$ there is a corresponding function $\sigma_{NF}: NF_{s_1} x \ldots x NF_{s_k} \rightarrow NF_s$ which, when applied to normal forms $n_1, \ldots, n_k$, returns the normal form of $\sigma(n_1, \ldots, n_k)$.
It's obvious that the normal form algebra induced by nat is isomorphic to the intended natural numbers.

Example 2.2
nat gets on with pure equations but it's useful to have conditional ones as well in many cases. Therefore, consider the data type bounded-stack. Informally spoken, the data of bounded-stack are stacks of natural numbers that don't have more than four

entries. The manipulation on stacks is done by the usual operations push, pop and top. An application of these operations introduces an error situation in case it shall be tried to push an element on a 'full' stack, to pop an element from the empty stack or to read the top entry of the empty stack.
The specification of bounded-stack is given in two steps. The first part, called b-stack1, builds up unbounded stacks (new, insert) and takes the number of entries as a measure for the size of a stack. bounded-stack is completed by the second part, called b-stack2, which specifies the operations push, pop and top.
Take care that, in the following, b-stack2 contains all sorts, operation symbols and variables of b-stack1 and that they are dropped for convenience only.

b-stack1

SORTS:		bool, nat, stack	
OPNS:		true, false: → bool	
		0: → nat	
		succ: nat → nat	
		_≤_: nat^2 → bool	
		new: → stack	
		insert: stack x nat → stack	(hidden)
		size: stack → nat	(hidden)
		in-b-stack1: nat → bool	(hidden)
VARS:		s: stack	
		m, n: nat	
AXMS:	(b1)	0 ≤ 0 = true	
	(b2)	succ(n) ≤ 0 = false	
	(b3)	0 ≤ succ(n) = true	
	(b4)	succ(m) ≤ succ(n) = n ≤ m	
	(b5)	size(new) = 0	
	(b6)	size(insert(s,n)) = succ(size(s))	
	(b7)	in-b-stack1(n) = true	

b-stack2

SORTS:			
OPNS:		push: stack x nat → stack	(unsafe)
		pop: stack → stack	(unsafe)
		top: stack → nat	(unsafe)
VARS:			
AXMS:	(B1)	size(s) ≤ $succ^3(0)$ = true ∧ in-b-stack1(n) = true ==> push(s,n) = insert(s,n)	
	(B2)	size(insert(s,n)) ≤ $succ^4(0)$ = true ==> pop(insert(s,n)) = s	
	(B3)	size(insert(s,n)) ≤ $succ^4(0)$ = true ==> top(insert(s,n)) = n	

A conditional axiom (B1)-(B3) only applies to a term t of bounded-stack if both the lefthand side matches a subterm of t and the actual condition holds. A condition is satisfied if for each '='-symbol occurring in the condition the lefthand side and the righthand side have a common reduct w.r.t. b-stack1. For example, we have

$$
\begin{array}{lll}
 & \text{pop(push(new,0))} & \\
\xrightarrow{(B1)} & \text{pop(insert(new,0))} & \\
 & [\text{for:} & \text{size(new)} \leqslant \text{succ}^3(0) \\
 & \xrightarrow{(b5)} & 0 \leqslant \text{succ}^3(0) \\
 & \xrightarrow{(b3)} & \text{true} \\
 & \text{and} & \text{in-b-stack1(0)} \\
 & \xrightarrow{(b7)} & \text{true} \quad] \\
\xrightarrow{(B3)} & \text{new} & \\
 & [\text{for:} & \text{size(insert(new,0))} \leqslant \text{succ}^4(0) \\
 & \xrightarrow{(b6)} & \text{succ(size(new))} \leqslant \text{succ}^4(0) \\
 & \xrightarrow{(b5)} & \text{succ}(0) \leqslant \text{succ}^4(0) \\
 & \xrightarrow{(b4)} & 0 \leqslant \text{succ}^3(0) \\
 & \xrightarrow{(b3)} & \text{true} \quad]
\end{array}
$$

Pay attention to the different signatures (i.e. declarations of sorts and operations) for b-stack1 and b-stack2. In order to apply an axiom A the variables occurring in A may only be substituted by constant terms built over the signature which belongs to A. Consequently, the variables in the axioms (b1)-(b7) mustn't be actualized by constant terms containing push, pop and top resp.. For instance, (b7) can't be applied to in-b-stack1(top(new)) so that push(new,top(new)) is in normal form.
As in OBJ, the hidden operations are internal to bounded-stack and mustn't be used from outside for data access. That is why we only take those normal forms for data representation which are a reduct of at least one term where no hidden operation symbol occurs in. bounded-stack then specifies the intended data type in the sense that ok-values are represented by those normal forms that don't contain any unsafe operation symbol whereas the other normal forms describe error situations.

***

Based on a precise notion of 'hierarchical conditional specifications', the following chapters investigate

- the well-definedness of the operational semantics
- automatic computation of normal forms

These results are most crucial for an interpreter which for any given term computes its normal form according to a given specification. Executing a specification this way, the interpreter would make possible

- to test whether terms reduce to normal forms as intended
- to evaluate operations when applied to argument values

and by this way realizes a prototype of the specified data type.

3. PRELIMINARIES

A signature is a pair $<S,\Sigma>$ where S is a set of sorts and $\Sigma = <\Sigma_{w,s}>_{w\in S^*, s\in S}$ is an S^*xS-indexed family of disjoint sets of operation symbols.
Let a signature $<S,\Sigma>$ and a set of formal variables $V=<V_s>_{s\in S}$ be given such that Σ and V have no elements in common. $T_{\Sigma\&V} = <T_{\Sigma\&V,s}>_{s\in S}$ denotes the set of Σ-terms with variables in V, $T_\Sigma = <T_{\Sigma,s}>_{s\in S}$ is the set of constant Σ-terms.
An assignment (of the variables V to T_Σ) is an S-indexed mapping $h:V\to T_\Sigma = <h_s:V_s\to T_{\Sigma,s}>_{s\in S}$. The homomorphic extension of h to $T_{\Sigma\&V}$ is denoted by $h^*:T_{\Sigma\&V}\to T_\Sigma = <h^*_s:T_{\Sigma\&V,s}\to T_{\Sigma,s}>_{s\in S}$. $\tilde{A}$ is an occurrence of a Σ&V-term A iff there is an assignment $h:V\to T_\Sigma$ such that $\tilde{A}=h^*A$.
Σ&V-terms can be regarded as labelled trees. In the following the nodes of a tree are addressed by strings over the natural numbers, by the way that () denotes the root and, for $x\in N^*$, $i\in N$, $x\cdot(i)$ is the address of the i-th son of x. For a Σ&V-term A, the set of node addresses of the tree representing A (tree(A) for short) is referred to as the address domain of A (denoted by domA). domA seperates into $dom_\Sigma A$ and $dom_V A$ containing all node addresses marked by operation symbols and variables resp. The function $A:domA \to \Sigma\cup V$ which maps each node $x\in domA$ to the operation symbol or variable x is labelled by, is called tree representation function of A. $A^{-1}:V\to \mathcal{P}(N^*)$ maps each variable X to the set of node addresses of tree(A) which are labelled by X.
To compare node addresses or to claim special properties of a set of node addresses, the following notations are used

anc is the ancestor relation on N^*: x anc y iff $\exists w\in N^*: x\cdot w=y$

anc≠ is the proper ancestor relation on N^*: x anc≠ y iff x anc y and $x\neq y$

$\perp$ is the independence relation on N^*: $x\perp y$ iff $\neg$(x anc y) and $\neg$(y anc x)

$\perp S$ iff $S\subseteq N^*$ and $\forall x,y\in S: (x\perp y) \vee (x=y)$ ("S is an independent set")

$\mathcal{P}^\perp(N^*) = \{S \mid S\subseteq N^* \wedge \perp S \wedge S \text{ is finite}\}$

For a Σ&V-term A and $x\in domA$, the subterm A/x of A at position x is represented by $A/x: D\to\Sigma\cup V$ where $D=\{y\in N^* \mid x\cdot y\in domA\}$ and $(A/x)y = A(x\cdot y)$ for all $y\in D$
Let A,B be Σ&V-terms and $x\in domA$ such that A/x and B are of the same sort. The Σ&V-term $A(x\leftarrow B)$ resulting from the substitution of the subterm A/x by B is represented by $A(x\leftarrow B): D\to\Sigma\cup V$ where $D=\{x\cdot y \mid y\in domB\}\cup\{y\in domA \mid \neg(x \text{ anc } y)\}$

$$\text{and} \quad A(x\leftarrow B)y = \begin{cases} Bz & ,\text{if } y=x\cdot z \\ Ay & ,\text{otherwise} \end{cases} \quad \text{for all } y\in D$$

Term replacement can be done simultaneously if independent subterms are indicated:
$A(x\leftarrow B_x \mid x\in M) := A(x_1\leftarrow B_{x_1})\ldots(x_n\leftarrow B_{x_n})$ where $M=\{x_1,\ldots,x_n\}\subseteq domA$ is an independent set.

A *term rewriting system* is a triple $T=\langle S,\Sigma,R\rangle$ where $\langle S,\Sigma\rangle$ is a signature and $R = \langle R_s\rangle_{s\in S} \subseteq \langle T_{\Sigma,s}\times T_{\Sigma,s}\rangle_{s\in S}$ is a set family of rules. $rhs_T(A) := \{A' \mid \langle A\to A'\rangle \in R\}$ is the set of all valid rewritings for A within T.

The *reduction relation* $\xrightarrow{T}$ is an S-indexed family of relations on T_Σ:

$$A \xrightarrow{T}_s B \;:\Longleftrightarrow\; A,B\in T_{\Sigma,s} \text{ and } \exists \langle C\to D\rangle \in R,\ x\in \underline{dom}A:\ A/x=C \wedge B=A(x\leftarrow D)$$

$\xrightarrow{T}{}^* = \langle \xrightarrow{T}{}^*_s\rangle_{s\in S}$ is the reflexive and transitive closure of $\xrightarrow{T}$.

$\overset{T}{\downarrow} = \langle \overset{T}{\downarrow}_s\rangle_{s\in S}$ is a relation family on T_Σ:

$$A \overset{T}{\downarrow}_s B \;:\Longleftrightarrow\; A,B\in T_{\Sigma,s} \text{ and } \exists C\in T_{\Sigma,s}:\ A \xrightarrow{T}{}^*_s C \;\wedge\; B \xrightarrow{T}{}^*_s C$$

$\xrightarrow{T}$ is called *noetherian* iff there isn't an infinite chain $A_0 \xrightarrow{T} A_1 \xrightarrow{T} A_2 \ldots$

Sometimes we write $A \xrightarrow[x]{T} B$ in place of $A \xrightarrow{T} B$ to indicate that A is reduced at position x. The set of *redexes* in A is then given by $red_T(A) := \{x \mid \exists B:\ A \xrightarrow[x]{T} B\}$ and we say x to be an *innermost* (*outermost*) *redex* in A iff $x\in red_T(A)$ and $\neg\exists y\in red_T(A):\ x\ \underline{anc}{\neq}\ y\ \ (y\ \underline{anc}{\neq}\ x)$

T has the *Church-Rosser property* (or *Confluence property*) iff for all $A,B,C\in T_\Sigma$ such that $A \xrightarrow{T}{}^* B$ and $A \xrightarrow{T}{}^* C$ there is a $D\in T_\Sigma$ such that $B \xrightarrow{T}{}^* D$ and $C \xrightarrow{T}{}^* D$.

If a TRS has the Church-Rosser property, then the normal form of any given term if it exists is unique. This gives reason for the interest in confluent TRSs because the uniqueness of normal forms is necessary the well-definedness of the normal form algebra (see 2.).

A confluent TRS guarantees that any two reduction sequences starting with a term A and ending in a normal form end in the same normal form, but it doesn't make sure that all reduction sequences really end. Thus, A may have a normal form and also an infinite sequence of reductions. This is the reason why reduction strategies don't find existing normal forms in general (if they do they are called *terminating*).

A well-known reduction strategy is the *strategy of full substitution*:

while normal form not found
  do reduce the given term at all redexes from innermost to outermost

4. HIERARCHICAL CONDITIONAL SPECIFICATIONS AND THEIR OPERATIONAL SEMANTICS

From an operational point of view, algebraic specifications are treated as term rewriting systems. The operational semantics construction is then given by the diagram below.

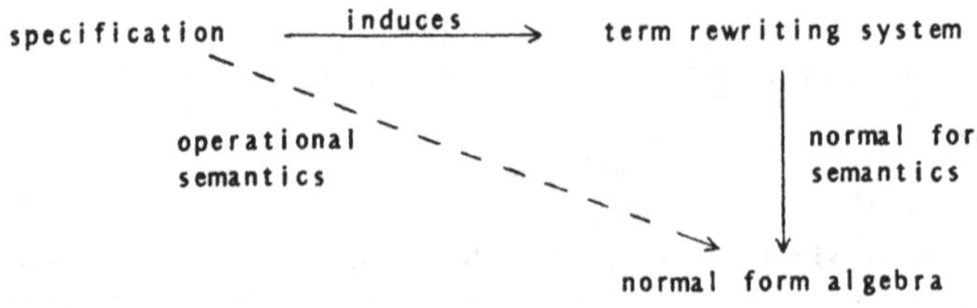

For unconditional specifications one obtains a TRS by simply regarding all occurrences of the equations as rewrite rules. bounded-stack, however, motivates that it is often useful not to take all occurrences of an equation as rules but a subset of them. This leads to the definition of conditional axioms. The conditions admitted are conjunctions of equations so that the axioms have the form of positive Horn clauses.

Definition 4.1

A Σ&V-axiom of sort s is of the form $\alpha_1=\beta_1 \wedge .. \wedge \alpha_n=\beta_n \Rightarrow A=B$ ($n \in N_0$) where $A,B \in T_{\Sigma\&V,s}$ and, for i=1,..,n , $\alpha_i,\beta_i \in T_{\Sigma\&V,s_i}$ ($s_i \in S$).

$\alpha_1=\beta_1 \wedge .. \wedge \alpha_n=\beta_n$ is called condition, A lefthand side and B righthand side.
In case of n=0 we speak of an unconditional Σ&V-equation (and often simply write A=B) otherwise of a conditional Σ&V-equation.

Definition 4.2

A hierarchical conditional specification (HCS for short) is a finite sequence of quadruples $D=(\langle S_1,\Sigma_1,V_1,E_1\rangle,...,\langle S_n,\Sigma_n,V_n,E_n\rangle)$,$n \in N$, where for i=1,...,n

(1) $\langle S_i,\Sigma_i\rangle$ is a signature such that $\langle S_1,\Sigma_1\rangle \subseteq ... \subseteq \langle S_n,\Sigma_n\rangle$

(2) $V_i=\langle V_{i,s}\rangle_{s \in S_i}$ is a set family of variables with $(V_i \cap \Sigma_i)=\emptyset$ such that $V_1 \subseteq ... \subseteq V_n$
Assume for convenience $\forall i \in \{1,..,n\}: X \in V_{i,s} \Rightarrow T_{\Sigma_i,s} \neq \emptyset$

(3) $E_i=\langle E_{i,s}\rangle_{s \in S_i}$ is a set family of Σ_i&V_i-axioms where E_1 only contains unconditional equations.

- For n=1, we have the special case of an unconditional specification.
- For i=1,..,n: D|i $:=(\langle S_1,\Sigma_1,V_1,E_1\rangle,...,\langle S_i,\Sigma_i,V_i,E_i\rangle)$ is a HCS as well.
- Let E_u denote the smallest set of Σ_n&V_n-axioms such that $(\alpha_1=\beta_1 \wedge .. \wedge \alpha_l=\beta_l \Rightarrow A=B) \in \bigcup_{i=1}^{n} E_i$ implies $(A=B) \in E_u$ ($l \in N_0$). Then, $D_u := \langle S_n,\Sigma_n,V_n,E_u\rangle$ is an unconditional specification.
- The number H(D) of hierarchy levels of D is given by n.- Furthermore, we agree upon that $S(D):=S_n$, $\Sigma(D):=\Sigma_n$, $V(D):=V_n$ and $E(D):=E_n$.

The main step from a HCS to a TRS is the rule generating process. For unconditional specifications one only has to actualize the variables by constant terms and consider all occurrences of the equations as directed rules from left to right. Conditional axioms restrict the set of generated rules to those occurrences for which the actual condition holds: a condition is satisfied iff, for each '='-symbol occurring in the condition the lefthand side term and the righthand side one have a common reduct w.r.t. the underlying system. Evaluating conditions at lower levels avoids circularity problems which usually arise in a non-hierarchical approach (see BK 82) by applying axioms to themselves for conditional evaluation.

Definition 4.3

The TRS induced by a HCS $D=(\langle S_1,\Sigma_1,V_1,E_1\rangle,\ldots,\langle S_n,\Sigma_n,V_n,E_n\rangle)$ is given by $T(D)=\langle S_n,\Sigma_n,R(D):=\langle\bigcup_{i=1}^{n}R^i(D)_s\rangle_{s\in S_n}\rangle$ where, for $i\in\{1,\ldots,n\}$ and $s\in S_n$, $R^i(D)_s$ denotes the set of rules of sort s generated by the axioms at hierarchy level i of D:

$$R^n(D)_s = \bigcup_{(\alpha_1=\beta_1\wedge..\wedge\alpha_l=\beta_l \Rightarrow A=B)\in E_{n,s}\ (l\in N_0)} \{\langle\tilde{A}\to\tilde{B}\rangle \mid \exists(h:V_n\to T_{\Sigma_n}):\ \tilde{A}=h^*A \wedge \tilde{B}=h^*B \wedge (\forall j\in\{1,..,l\}:\ h^*\alpha_j \xrightarrow[\downarrow]{T(D|n-1)} h^*\beta_j)\}$$

$$R^j(D)_s = \begin{cases} R^j(D|n-1)_s & ,\text{if } s\in S_{n-1} \\ \emptyset & ,\text{otherwise} \end{cases} \qquad \text{for } 1\leqslant j\leqslant n-1$$

- Notice that the recursion ends for we don't need an underlying TRS in order to define $R^1(D|1)$: according to def. 4.2, E_1 only contains unconditional equations so that, for $s\in S_1$, $R^1(D|1)_s$ simplifies to

$$R^1(D|1)_s = \bigcup_{(A=B)\in E_{1,s}} \{\langle\tilde{A}\to\tilde{B}\rangle \mid \exists(h:V_1\to T_{\Sigma_1}):\ \tilde{A}=h^*A \wedge \tilde{B}=h^*B\}$$

5. CHURCH-ROSSER AND TERMINATION RESULTS

Recall that the Church-Rosser property assures the well-definedness of the operational semantics. It is well-known, there isn't a decision procedure which checks the property of confluence for arbitrary (already unconditional) specifications. Therefore, this chapter provides syntactical criteria which are sufficient for the Church-Rosser property. Moreover, they turn out to guarantee the termination of the full substitution strategy as well.

Definition 5.1

A Σ&V-axiom $\alpha_1=\beta_1\wedge..\wedge\alpha_l=\beta_l \Rightarrow A=B$ $(l\in N_0)$ is called a rule scheme iff:

(1) $A() \notin V$

(2) $\forall y\in \underline{dom_V}B\ \exists x\in\underline{dom_V}A:\ Ax=By$

(3) $\forall y\in\underline{dom_V}\alpha_i\ \exists x\in\underline{dom_V}A:\ \alpha_i y=Ax\quad (i=1,..,l)$

$\forall y\in\underline{dom_V}\beta_i\ \exists x\in\underline{dom_V}A:\ \beta_i y=Ax\quad (i=1,..,l)$

(4) $\forall x,y\in\underline{dom_V}A:\ (Ax=Ay \Rightarrow x=y)$

- Informally, clause (1) says that the lefthand side doesn't consist of a single variable, (2) and (3) say that each variable occurring in the righthand side or in the condition also occurs in the lefthand side, (4) says that each variable occurs at most once in the lefthand side.

Definition 5.2

A set E of Σ&V-rule schemes is called consistent iff, for all pairs $\alpha_1=\beta_1\wedge..\wedge\alpha_l=\beta_l \Rightarrow A=B$ and $\gamma_1=\psi_1\wedge..\wedge\gamma_m=\psi_m \Rightarrow C=D$ $(n,m\in N_0)$ in E, the following holds: If $g^*A=h^*C$ for any two assignments $g,h:V\to T_\Sigma$, then

(1) $\underline{dom_\Sigma}A = \underline{dom_\Sigma}C$ and $\underline{dom_\Sigma}B = \underline{dom_\Sigma}D$

(2) $\forall x\in\underline{dom_\Sigma}A$: $Ax=Cx$ and $\forall x\in\underline{dom_\Sigma}B$: $Bx=Dx$

(3) $\forall x\in\underline{dom_V}A$: $B^{-1}(Ax) = D^{-1}(Cx)$

- The clauses (1)-(3) express that A and C as well as B and D are identical up to renaming of variables.

Definition 5.3

A set E of Σ&V-rule schemes is called nonoverlapping iff, for all pairs of (not necessarily different) schemes $\alpha_1=\beta_1\wedge..\wedge\alpha_l=\beta_l \Rightarrow A=B$ and $\gamma_1=\psi_1\wedge..\wedge\gamma_m=\psi_m \Rightarrow C=D$ $(l,m\in N_0)$ in E, the following holds: Let $g,h:V\to T_\Sigma$ be any two assignments and let $X_1,...,X_k$ $(k\in N_0)$ denote the variables occurring in A. Then, for any $x\in(\underline{dom}(g^*A)-\{()\})$, $(g^*A)/x=h^*C$ implies that there are $y\in N^+$, $z\in N^*$ and $i\in\{1,...,k\}$ such that $Ay=X_i$ and $x=y\cdot z$.

- Assume that, for each variable, there is at least one constant term for substitution. Then a set E of Σ&V-axioms is nonoverlapping iff for all pairs A and C of (not necessarily different) lefthand sides, there isn't an $x\in N^+$ for which
  (1) $(\underline{dom_\Sigma}C \cap \underline{dom_\Sigma}(A/x)) \neq \emptyset$ and
  (2) $\forall y\in(\underline{dom_\Sigma}C \cap \underline{dom_\Sigma}(A/x))$: $Cy = (A/x)y$

  Hence, a finite set of Σ&V-axioms can be tested for nonoverlapping (as well as for consistency) by means of a tree pattern matching algorithm.

Definition 5.4

A HCS $D=(\langle S_1,\Sigma_1,V_1,E_1\rangle,...,\langle S_n,\Sigma_n,V_n,E_n\rangle)$ is called homogeneous iff, for all pairs $j\in\{2,3,...,n\}$ and $(\alpha_1=\beta_1\wedge..\wedge\alpha_l=\beta_l \Rightarrow A=B)\in E_j$:

$\forall i\in\{1,2,...,j-1\}$: $(\exists y\in\underline{dom_{\Sigma_j}}B$: $By\in(\Sigma_j-\Sigma_i) \Longrightarrow \exists x\in\underline{dom_{\Sigma_j}}A$: $Ax\in(\Sigma_j-\Sigma_i))$

- Informally the homogeneousness says that at each hierarchy level, the righthand side of an axiom may only introduce a 'new' operation symbol if the lefthand side does ('new' means new w.r.t. the signature of any underlying level).

  It's an easy work to give an algorithm which tests an arbitrary finite HCS for homogeneousness. Besides, there are some forms of homogeneousness that can be checked very efficiently. For instance, $D=(\langle S_1,\Sigma_1,V_1,E_1\rangle,...,\langle S_n,\Sigma_n,V_n,E_n\rangle)$ is homogeneous if it has one of the following properties:

  - $\langle S_1,\Sigma_1\rangle=...=\langle S_n,\Sigma_n\rangle$

- $\forall j\in\{2,\ldots,n\}$: $(\alpha_1=\beta_1\wedge..\wedge\alpha_l=\beta_l \Rightarrow A=B) \in E_j \implies \exists x\in \underline{dom_\Sigma}A$: $Ax \in (\Sigma_j-\Sigma_{j-1})$

  Due to PEE 81, we call this property lefthand side extensiveness. Informally, a HCS is lefthand side extensive iff each axiom has a lefthand side which contains at least one operation symbol that isn't declared at any lower level.

Theorem 5.5

Let $D=(\langle S_1,\Sigma_1,V_1,E_1\rangle,\ldots,\langle S_n,\Sigma_n,V_n,E_n\rangle)$ be a HCS which is lefthand side extensive and where $\bigcup_{i=1}^{n} E_i$ is a consistent and nonoverlapping set of Σ_n&V_n-rule schemes. Then,

1. T(D) has the Church-Rosser property
2. the full substitution strategy is terminating for T(D)

Theorem 5.6

Let $D=(\langle S_1,\Sigma_1,V_1,E_1\rangle,\ldots,\langle S_n,\Sigma_n,V_n,E_n\rangle)$ be a homogeneous HCS where $E=\bigcup_{i=1}^{n} E_i$ is a consistent and nonoverlapping set of Σ_n&V_n-rule schemes. Assume for each $(\alpha_1=\beta_1\wedge..\wedge\alpha_l=\beta_l \Rightarrow A=B) \in E$ that $\beta_j\in NF_{T(D_u)}$ $(j=1,..,l)$. Then,

1. T(D) has the Church-Rosser property
2. the full substitution strategy is terminating for T(D)

- Theorem 5.5 and 5.6 indicate a trade-off: the more general property of homogeneousness must be 'paid' for by restrictions to the conditions or, the other way round, arbitrary forms of conditions must be 'bought' by restrictions to the lefthand sides.

6. AUTOMATIC COMPUTATION OF NORMAL FORMS

Reducing terms automatically by an interpreter requires an algorithm to decide the set of redexes for any given term. For unconditional (finite) specifications, there is no problem since the redexes can be obtained by a tree pattern matching algorithm. If conditional equations occur, one has to evaluate the conditions additionally. That is why the set of redexes is undecidable in general (for a proof see BK 82). It is decidable, however, for those HCSs which satisfy the preconditions of Theorem 5.5 or 5.6 resp. and where each proper sub-HCS induces a TRS having a normal form for each valid term.

Theorem 6.1

Let $D=(\langle S_1,\Sigma_1,V_1,E_1\rangle,\ldots,\langle S_n,\Sigma_n,V_n,E_n\rangle)$ be a finite HCS satisfying the preconditions of Theorem 5.5 or 5.6 resp. Assume for $i=1,..,n-1$, $\forall A\in T_{\Sigma_i}\ \exists B\in NF_{T(D|i)}$: $A \xrightarrow{T(D|i)}{}^{*} B$

Then, $rhs_{T(D)}: T_{\Sigma_n} \rightarrow \mathcal{P}(T_{\Sigma_n})$ is computable.

A procedure which computes $rhs_{T(D)}$ can be obtained from Dr 83 (we can't give it here owing to space limitations). Because of $x \in red_{T(D)}(A) \Longleftrightarrow rhs_{T(D)}(A/x) \neq \emptyset$, the procedure makes redexes decidable for specifications which satisfy the preconditions of Theorem 6.1.

As already mentioned, the preconditions in Theorem 5.5 or 5.6 resp. can be checked syntactically . The following lemma gives a clūe how to derive syntactical criteria for the remaining preconditions in Theorem 6.1.

Lemma 6.2

Let a HCS $D=(\langle S_1,\Sigma_1,V_1,E_1\rangle,\ldots,\langle S_n,\Sigma_n,V_n,E_n\rangle)$ be given.

$\xrightarrow{T(D_u)}$ is noetherian $\Longrightarrow$ $\forall A \in T_{\Sigma_i}\ \exists B \in NF_{T(D|i)}: A \xrightarrow{T(D|i)}{}^{*} B \quad (i=1,\ldots,n)$

Lemma 6.2 justifies to adopt criteria developped by Dershowitz, Plaisted and others.

Concluding Remark

As an application of the above results, bounded-stack (see 2.) can be executed by an interpreter for early protyping. Further examples for executable HCSs (library system, error recovery stack) can be found in Dr 83.

REFERENCES

ADJ 78 Goguen,J.A./ Thatcher,J.W./ Wagner,E.G.:
An Initial Algebra Approach to the Specification, Correctness and Implementation of Abstract Data Types. Current Trends in Programming Methodology, Vol.IV (R.T.Yeh ed.), Prentice Hall, Englewood Cliffs, 1978

ADJ 79 Thatcher,J.W./ Wagner,E.G./ Wright,J.B.:
Data Type Specification: Parameterization and the Power of Specification Techniques. ACM Transactions on Programming Languages and Systems, Vol.4, 1982
also: IBM Research Report RC 7757, 1979

BG 81 Burstall,R.M./ Goguen, J.A.:
An Informal Introduction to Specifications Using CLEAR. The Correctness Problem in Computer Science (R.Boyer/J.Moore eds.), Academic Press, New York, 1981

BK 82 Bergstra,J.A./ Klop,J.W.:
Conditional Rewrite Rules: Confluency and Termination. Report No. IW 198/82, Dept. of Computer Science, Mathematisch Centrum Amsterdam, 1982

DGEL 82 Drosten,K./ Gogolla,M./ Ehrich,H.-D./ Lipeck,U.:
A Hierarchical Approach to an Operational Semantics for Conditional Algebraic Specifications. Forschungsbericht Nr. 144/82, Abt. Informatik, Univ. Dortmund, 1982

Dr 83 Drosten,K.:
Towards Executable Specifications Using Conditional Axioms. Bericht Nr. 83-01, Institut fuer Informatik, TU Braunschweig, 1983

Eh 79 Ehrich,H.-D.:
On the Theory of Specification, Implementation and Parameterization of Abstract Data Types. Journal ACM, Vol.29, 1982
also: Bericht Nr. 82/79, Abt. Informatik, Univ. Dortmund, 1979

EKMP 80 Ehrig,H./ Kreowski,H.-J./ Mahr,B./ Padawitz,P.:
Algebraic Implementation of Abstract Data Types. Theoretical Computer Science, Vol.20, 1982
also: Bericht Nr. 80-32, Fachbereich 20, TU Berlin, 1980

EKTWW 81 Ehrig,H./ Kreowski,H.-J./ Thatcher,J.W./ Wagner,E.G./ Wright,J.B.:
Parameter Passing in Algebraic Specification Languages. Proc. Workshop on Program Specification 1981 (J.Staunstrup ed.), LNCS 134, Springer-Verlag, Berlin, 1982

GT 79 Goguen,J.A./ Tardo,J.J.:
An Introduction to OBJ: a Language for Writing and Testing Formal Algebraic Program Specifications. Specification of Reliable Software, IEEE, Cambridge (Mass.), 1979

Gu 75 Guttag,J.V.:
The Specification and Application to Programming of Abstract Data Types. Technical Report CSRG-59, Univ. of Toronto, 1975

Hu 77 Huet,G.:
Confluent Reductions: Abstract Properties and Applications to Term Rewriting Systems, Journal ACM, Vol.27, 1980
also: Proc. 18th IEEE Symposium on Foundations of Computer Science, 1977

KB 70 Knuth,D.E./ Bendix,P.:
Simple Word Problems in Universal Algebras. Computational Problems in Abstract Algebra (J.Leech ed.), Pergamon Press, 1970

LZ 74 Liskov,B./ Zilles,S.:
Programming with Abstract Data Types. SIGPLAN Notices, Vol.9, 1974

O'D 77 O'Donnell,M.:
Computing in Systems Described by Equations. LNCS 58, Springer-Verlag, Berlin, 1977

PEE 81 Pletat,U./ Engels,G./ Ehrich,H.-D.:
Operational Semantics of Algebraic Specifications with Conditional Equations. 7th CAAP, Lille, 1982
also: Forschungsbericht Nr. 118/81, Abt. Informatik, Univ. Dortmund, 1981

Re 82 Remy,J.L.:
Proving Conditional Identities by Equational Case Reasoning, Rewriting and Normalization. Technical Report, C.R.I.N., Nancy, 1982

Ro 73 Rosen,B.K.:
Tree Manipulating Systems and Church-Rosser Theorems. Journal ACM, Vol.20, 1973

SW 82 Sannella,D./ Wirsing,M.:
Implementation of Parameterized Specifications. Proc. 9th ICALP (M.Nielsen-E.M.Schmidt eds.), LNCS 140, Springer-Verlag, Berlin, 1982

Wa 77 Wand,M.:
Algebraic Theories and Tree Rewriting Systems. Technical Report No.66, Indiana University, Bloomington, 1977

WB 82 Wirsing,M./ Broy,M.:
An Analysis of Semantics Models for Algebraic Specifications. Theoretical Foundations of Program Methodology (M.Broy/G.Schmidt eds.), Reidel Publ. Co., Dordrecht, 1982

PROPRIETES CHURCH-ROSSER DE SYSTEMES DE REECRITURE EQUATIONNELS AYANT LA PROPRIETE DE TERMINAISON FAIBLE

H. Perdrix
Université de Paris-Sud
Laboratoire de Recherche en Informatique
Bât. 490 - 91405 ORSAY CEDEX - FRANCE
ERA 452 du CNRS

Introduction:

Les systèmes de réécriture ont de nombreuses applications en intelligence artificielle : démonstration automatique, preuve, synthèse de programmes, ... Nous nous intéressons ici au problème du mot: étant donné une théorie axiomatique A, on cherche à décider si deux termes sont égaux modulo A. Pour cela, classiquement, on oriente les axiomes de A et on tente de construire à l'aide de l'algorithme de Knuth et Bendix un système de réécriture possédant les propriétés de confluence et de terminaison. Une implémentation de cet algorithme est décrite dans (LES,83). Toutefois, on ne peut traiter de cette façon des axiomes tels que la commutativité car on perd alors la propriété de terminaison. Les systèmes de réécriture équationnels (en abrégé SRE) obtenus en divisant les axiomes en un ensemble de règles R et un ensemble d'equations E, permettent de lever cette restriction. J.P. Jouannaud (JOU,83b) en a unifié et généralisé les différentes approches et l'algorithme de Knuth et Bendix a été étendu à ces théories (KIR,83). Dans cette approche, la terminaison des règles modulo E est exigée. Padawitz (PAD,82), puis Jouannaud-Kirchner-Remy (JKR,83) se sont intéressés aux SRE où seule la terminaison de l'ensemble des règles était vérifiée. Dans ce cas, les SRE doivent vérifier les deux propriétés de confluence et de cohérence locale en un coup modulo E. Ces propriétés se testent sur des ensembles de paires critiques qui dépendent de l'égalité modulo E choisie. Trois types d'égalité en un coup sont examinés : l'égalité classique |-|, l'égalité parallèle |=| et enfin l'égalité récursive |=r=|. Dans les trois cas, R doit être linéaire gauche. L'égalité |=| conduit à exiger la confluence en 0 coup de paires critiques parallèles de E dans R. L'égalité récursive autorise la confluence en un coup de ces paires critiques mais entraine des restrictions importantes :

1) Les superpositions des règles dans les équations sont interdites sauf en tête.
2) Les superpositions des équations dans les règles doivent être des filtres qui instancient les règles sans instancier les équations.
Nous présentons ici une généralisation des résultats de JKR, basée sur l'introduction de paires critiques récursives, ce qui permet de lever les restrictions 1 et 2. Dans la partie qui suit, nous donnons un certain nombre de définitions et de notations et rappelons les résultats axiomatiques dont nous avons besoin. Dans la seconde partie, nous introduisons le concept de paires critiques récursives et le lemme correspondant qui permet l'obtention de nouveaux résultats. Enfin nous donnons des exemples montrant l'intérêt de la méthode.

I - Préliminaires:

Les notations et les définitions utilisées sont concordantes avec celles de (JKR,83) et (H & O,80). Un terme t est considéré comme étant un arbre étiqueté. O(t) désigne l'ensemble des occurrences des symboles de fonctions de t, y compris les occurrences de constantes et V(t) l'ensemble des variables de t. Un terme est dit linéaire si chacune de ses variables a une seule occurrence. On note t/u le sous terme de t à l'occurrence u et t [u←t1] le terme obtenu en remplaçant t/u par t1 dans t. x, y, z désignent généralement des variables f, g, h des symboles de fonctions d'arité non nulle, a, b, c des constantes, s1, ..., sn des substitutions. Un système de réécriture R est un ensemble de règles g->d. Un terme t se réduit en t' noté t->t' avec la règle g->d s'il existe un filtre s de g vers t/u tel que t' = t [u←s(d)], les variables de g->d ont été éventuellement renommées afin que V(g)∩V(t) = ∅.
-+-> désigne la fermeture transitive de la relation de réécriture ->.
-*-> désigne la fermeture transitive, réflexive de ->. Un système de réécriture est linéaire gauche si tous les membres gauches de ses règles sont linéaires. On appelle forme normale de t, noté t!, tout terme irréductible issu de t pour la relation de réécriture considérée. Un système de réécriture est à terminaison finie si aucun terme n'admet de suite infinie de réduction. Soit A un ensemble d'axiomes, |-|A (en abrégé |-|) désigne une relation symétrique dont la fermeture transitive, réflexive est l'égalité modulo A (= A), |-n-|A (ou |-n-|) la composition de n étapes de |-|A, |-0,1-|A (ou |-0,1-|) la fermeture réflexive de |-|A.
Définition 1: Soit A un ensemble d'axiomes, on le sépare en un ensemble de règles R et un ensemble d'équations E (A = R∪E).

. Un couple de terme (p,q) est confluent en un coup |-|E ssi il existe (p',q') tel que p -*->p' |-0,1-|E q'<-*-q.
. R est uniformément Church Rosser modulo E ssi pour tout t1,t2 tel que t1 = A t2, il existe t1!,t2! forme normale de t1,t2 tel que t1! = E t2!
. R est localement confluent en un coup modulo E ssi pour tout t,t1,t2 tel que t1←t->t2, (t1,t2) est confluent en un coup |-|E.
. R est localement cohérent en un coup modulo E ssi pour tout t,t1,t2 tel que t1←t|-|t2, (t1,t2) est confluent en un coup |-|E.
Shéma:

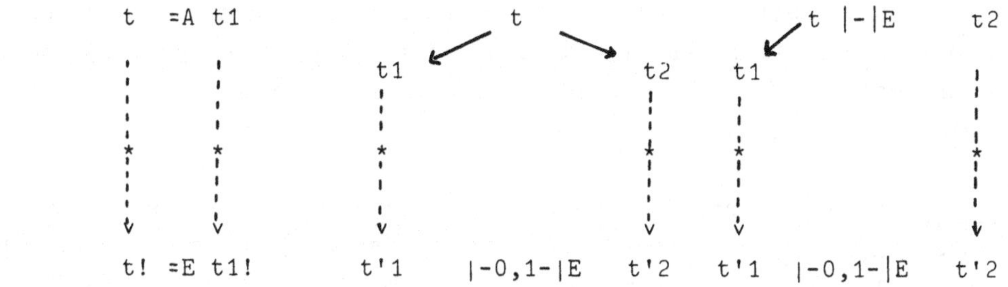

R est uniformément Church Rosser modulo E

R est localement confluent en un coup modulo E

R est localement cohérent en un coup modulo E

Les traits pleins représentent des hypothèses quantifiées universellement et les traits pointillés des conclusions quantifiées existentiellement.

<u>Proposition 1</u>:(JKR,83) : soit R à terminaison finie. Si R est localement confluent en un coup modulo E et R est localement cohérent en un coup modulo E alors R est uniformément Church-Rosser modulo E.
Nous allons utiliser comme égalité modulo E, l'égalité récursive notée |=r=|E ou |=r=|.

<u>Définition 2</u>: égalité récursive.
t |=r=| t' ssi t=t' ou bien il existe des occurrences disjointes v1, ..., vn de t, des substitutions s, s', des équations gi = di telles que t/vi = s(gi), t' = t[(vi←s'(di))i=1,n] et pour tout x de (∪ V(gi))i, s(x) |=r=| s'(x). Les variables des équations des gi = di ont été renommées de telle sorte que V(t) ∩ V(gi) = ∅ et V(gi) ∩ V(gj) = ∅ pour tout i,j distincts.

<u>Exemple 1</u>: E = (x + y = y + x, x.y = y.x), x.y + z.t |=r=| t.z + y.x

II - Paires critiques récursives:

Définition 3: Profondeur de la récursivité de t |=r=| t' : P(t |=r=| t'). soit t,t' tels que t |=r=| t', si t = t' alors P(t |=r=| t') = 0 sinon on a avec les notations de la définition 2, t/vi = s(gi) t' = t[(vi←s'(di))i] et P(t |=r=| t') = 1 + P(t[(vi←s(di))i] |=r=| t'). Dans l'exemple 1, la profondeur de la récursivité est 2. Afin de définir les paires critiques récursives simplement nous allons introduire l'égalité récursive basée sur un terme t notée (t)|=r=|. Intuitivement t1 (t)|=r=| t2 si on a t1 = s(t), t1 |=r=| t2 et si les premières occurrences vi de superposition des gi = di sont dans O(t), à l'étape suivante, elles sont dans O(s" (x)), s" étant l'unificateur principal des paires (t/vi,gi) et ainsi de suite.

Définition 4: t1 (t)|=r=| t2 ssi t1 = t2 = s(t) ou bien t1 = s(t), t1/vi = s(gi), t2 = t1[(vi←s'(di))i] et s(x) (s"(x))|=r=| s'(x) pour tout x de (∪ V(gi))i. Les vi sont des occurrences disjointes de O(t), s, s' des substitutions et s" l'unificateur principal des paires (t/vi, gi).

Définition 5: (t1, t2) est un couple canonique basé sur t ssi t1 ≠ t2, t1 (t)|=r=| t2 et il n'existe pas de termes t'1, t'2, ni de substitution non triviale s tels que t1 = s(t'1), t2 = s(t'2), t'1 (t)|=r=| t'2 et les équations et leurs occurrences d'applications intervenant dans t1 |=r=| t2 sont identiques à celles intervenant dans t'1 |=r=| t'2.

Exemple 2: E = {(x*y)*z = x*(y*z), x+0 = 0+x}
t0 = (x*y)*(z+t), t2 = x*(y*(z+t)), t = (x*y)*(z+t)
t1 = (x*y)*(z+0), t3 = x*(y*(0+z)
(t0,t2) et (t1,t3) sont des couples canoniques basés sur t.
t' = ((x*1)*0)*(z+0), t'3 = (x*1)*(0*(0+z)) on a t' (t)|=r=| t'3.

Lemme 1: Soient t,t1,t2 tels que t1 (t)|=r=| t2 avec t1 ≠ t2 alors il existe un couple canonique basé sur t et une substitution s tel que t1 = s(t'1), t2 = s(t'2).

Preuve: Récurrence sur la profondeur n de la récursivité de t1 |=r=| t2.
n = 1 : évident
n > 1 : par définition de (t)|=r=| on a t1/vi = s(gi), t2 = t1[(vi←s'(di))i] et s(x) (s"(x))|=r=| s'(x). Par hypothèse de récurrence il existe un couple canonique (s1(x), s1'(x)) tel que s(x) = s2.s1(x) et s'(x) = s2.s'1(x). On a t1 = s2.s1(t),

t2 = s2.(s1(t)[(vi←s'1(di))i]) et (s1(t),s1(t)[(vi←s'1(di))i]) est un couple canonique.
Rappelons brièvement la définition des paires critiques de R.

<u>Définition 6</u>: (p,q) est une paire critique de R ssi il existe deux règles l→r et g→d telles que p = s(d), q = s(g[u←r]) avec u ∈ O(g) et s unificateur principal de g/u et de l.

<u>Définition 7</u>: Ensemble des paires critiques récursives de E dans R : EPCRec(E,R). (p,q) ∈ EPCRec(E,R) ssi il existe une règle g→d et une substitution s telles que p = s(d) et (s(g),q) soit un couple canonique basé sur g.

<u>Exemple 3</u>: E = {(x*y)*z = x*(y*z), x+0 = 0+x}
R = {x*(y+z) → x*y + x*z}
Une première unification entre la première équation et la règle donne le terme t = (x*y)*(z+t) qui se réécrit en t1 = (x*y)*z + (x*y)*t et qui est égal en un coup à t2 = x*(y*(z+t)).(t1,t2) est une paire critique récursive dont la profondeur de récursivité est de 1. Mais on peut continuer à superposer des équations dans le sous terme z+t de t2 d'où la nouvelle paire critique (t'1,t'2) avec t'1 = (x*y)*z + (x*y)*0, t'2 = x*(y*(0+z)).

<u>Définition 8</u>: Ensemble des paires critiques récursives de R dans E : EPCRec(R,E).
(p,q) ∈ EPCRec(R,E) ssi il existe une règle g→d et une équation g1 = d1 telles que p = s'(d1), q = s(g1[u←d]), u ∈ O(g1)et (s(g1),p) soit un couple canonique basé sur s"(g1), s" étant l'unificateur principal de (g1/u,g).

<u>Exemple 4</u>: Construction de paires critiques récursives de R dans E.
gi = di sont des équations, g→d une règle.

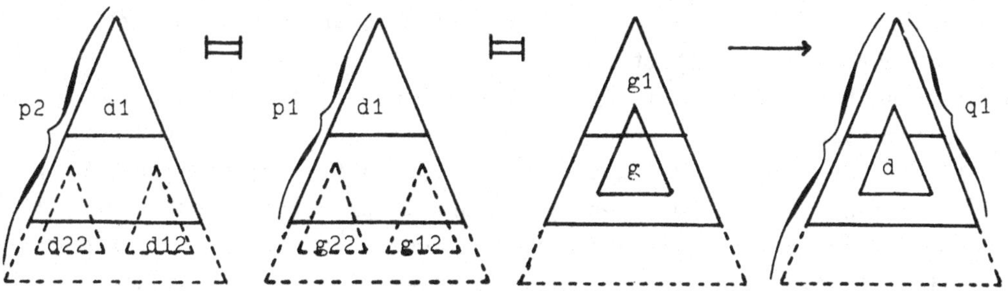

$p1 = s(d1)$, $q1 = s(g1[u \leftarrow d])$, $(p1,q1)$ est une paire critique récursive, s est l'unificateur principal de $g1/u$ et de g. $p2 = s'1(d1) = s1(p1[(u2i \leftarrow d2i)i]))$, $q2 = s1(q1)$, $u2i \notin O(d1)$, s1 est l'unificateur principal de $s(p1/u2i, g2i)$, $(p2,q2)$ est une paire critique récursive (de profondeur 2). On dit que $(p2,q2)$ est issue de $(p1,q1)$.

Lemme 2:

a) Lemme des paires critiques récursives de E dans R. Soient $g \rightarrow d$ une règle et t, t1,t2 tels que: $t = s(g) \rightarrow t1 = s(d)$, $t\ (g) |{=}r{=}|\ t2$ alors il existe une substitution s1 et une paire critique (p,q) de EPCRec(E,R) tel que $t1 = s1(p)$ et $t2 = s1(q)$.

b) Lemme des paires critiques récursives de R dans E. Soient $g1 = d1$ une équation, $l \rightarrow r$ une règle et t,t1,t2 tels que $t = s(g1)\ |{=}r{=}|\ t1 = s'(d1)$ $t \rightarrow t2$ à l'occurrence u de O(g1) avec la règle $l \rightarrow r$ et $t\ (s''(g1))|{=}r{=}|\ t1$, s" étant l'unificateur principal de t/u et de l. Alors il existe une substitution s1 et une paire critique (p,q) de EPCRec(R,E) tel que $t1 = s1(p)$ et $t2 = s1(q)$.

Preuve: Application immédiate du lemme 1.

Proposition 2 (JKR,83): R est localement confluent en un coup $|{=}r{=}|$ modulo E ssi toutes les paires critiques de R sont confluentes en un coup $|{=}r{=}|E$.

Proposition 3: On suppose que R est linéaire à gauche et que les paires critiques récursives de E dans R et de R dans E sont confluentes en un coup $|{=}r{=}|$. Alors pour tous termes t1,t2,t tels que $t = s(g) \rightarrow t1 = s(d)$ et $t\ |{=}r{=}|\ t2$, $g \rightarrow d$ étant une règle, (t1,t2) est confluent en un coup $|{=}r{=}|$.

Preuve:

1er cas : les occurrences de superpositions des équations lors de $t\ |{=}r{=}|\ t2$ se font en dehors de O(g). Puisque g est linéaire on a $t1 = s(d)$ et $t2 = s'(g)$ avec $s(x)\ |{=}r{=}|\ s'(x)$ pour tout x de $V(g) \cup V(d)$ d'où la confluence de (t1,t2).

2e cas : soit (vi)i l'ensemble non vide des occurrences de superpositions d'équations $gi = di$ appartenant à O(g) et s" l'unificateur principal des (g/vi,gi). On décompose $t\ |{=}r{=}|\ t2$ en $t\ |{=}r{=}|\ t'2\ |{=}r{=}|\ t2$; t'2 est obtenu à partir de t en appliquant le plus grand nombre d'équations intervenant lors de $t\ |{=}r{=}|\ t2$ aux mêmes occurrences de sorte que l'on ait $t\ (s''(g))|{=}r{=}|\ t'2$. D'après le lemme 2 appliqué à (t1,t'2), $t1 = s1(p)$ et $t'2 = s1(q)$, $(p,q) \in$ EPCRec(E,R). De par la construction de t'2, l'égalité t'2 |=r=| t2 ne s'effectue pas à des occurrences de O(q) et comme g est linéaire on a t2 = s'1(q) avec pour x de V(q), s1(x) |=r=| s'1(x). Par hypothèse (p,q) conflue en un coup |=r=| et on conclut en appliquant le lemme de composition. Cette preuve se visualise sur le shéma suivant.

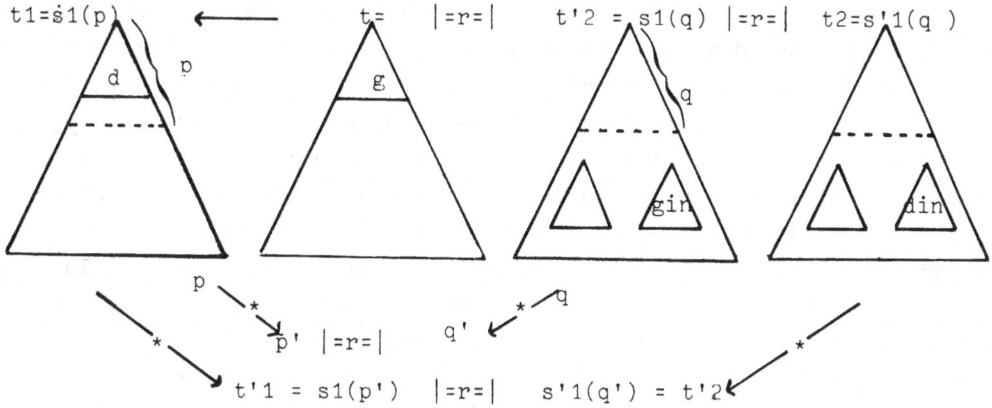

Proposition 4: Si toutes les paires critiques récursives de R dans E sont confluentes en un coup |=r=| **alors** pour tout t,t1,t2, g1 = d1 tels que t = s(g1)→ t2 à une occurrence de O(g1) et t |=r=| t1 = s'(d1) alors (t1,t2) est confluente en un coup |=r=|.

Preuve: On décompose comme précédemment t |=r=| t1 en t |=r=| t'1 |=r=| t1 avec t (s(g1))|=r=| t'1, on a alors t1 = s1(p), t'1 = s'1(p), t2 = s'1(q) avec (p,q) ∈ EPCRec(R,E) et s1(x) |=r=| s'1(x) pour x ∈ V(p) et on conclut comme précédemment.

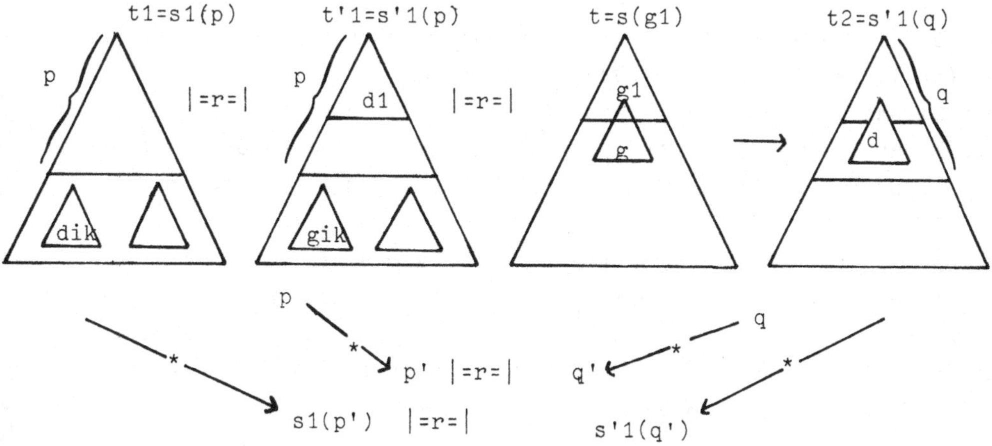

Proposition 5: On suppose que R est linéaire gauche et que toutes les paires récursives de E dans R et de R dans E sont confluentes en un coup |=r=|. Alors R est localement cohérent en un coup |=r=| modulo E.

Preuve: Soient t,t1,t2 tels que t→t2, t |=r=| t1. Soient v1,...,vn les plus petites occurrences disjointes de superpositions d'équations gi=di lors de l'égalité récursive t |=r=| t1 (ie les occurrences de superpositions à la profondeur 1 de récursivité) et u celle de la règle g→d. On définit une relation d'induction d par : si aucun des vi n'est préfixe de u, ou si l'un des vi est préfixe de u, u = vi.u' avec u' ∈ O(gi) alors d(u, t |=r=| t1)=0. Sinon u se met sous la forme u = vi.w.u" avec gi/w = x ∈ V(gi) et on pose d(u,t |=r=| t1) = 1+d(u",si(x) |=r=| s'i(x)) avec si(x) = t/vi.w, s'i(x) = t1/vi.w.
Premier cas: d(u,t |=r=| t1) = 0. Alors si u est disjoint des vi, la confluence en un coup de (t1,t2) est évidente sinon celle-ci s'obtient en appliquant la proposition 1 ou 2 puis la compatibilité.
Deuxième cas: d(u,t |=r=| t1) = n, n ≠0. On a d(u, t |=r=| t1) = 1 + d(u", si(x) |=r=| s'i(x)), on a si(x) → t'2 à l'aide de la règle g → d, t'2 = t2/vi.w (on reprend les notations de la définition de d) et par hypothèse de récurrence (t'2, s'(x)) est confluente en un coup |=r=|. Le lemme de compatibilité permet alors de déduire que (t1,t2) est confluente en un coup |=r=|.
Il découle des propositions 1,2,5 le théorème suivant :

Théorème : Soit E un ensemble d'équations et R un ensemble de règles linéaires gauche à terminaison finie. Si les paires critiques de R et les paires critiques récursives de E dans R sont confluentes en un coup |=r=| alors R est uniformément Church Rosser modulo E.
On remarque que les paires critiques récursives peuvent être en nombre infini. Par exemple si on prend R = {x*0 → 0}, E = {x*x → x}. On a l'ensemble infini de paires critiques suivant {(0,(x*0)*(x*0)), (0,((x*0)*(x*0))*((x*0)*(x*0))), ...}
Nous allons donner un critère de finitude de l'ensemble des paires critiques récursives et un critère permettant de se restreindre à un nombre fini de paires critiques quand celles-ci sont en nombre infini.

Proposition 6: Finitude des ensembles de paires critiques. Soit R un système de réécriture linéaire gauche et E un ensemble d'équations dont aucune n'est de la forme t(x) = x (où x ∈ V(t)). Alors l'ensemble des paires critiques récursives de E dans R et de R dans E est de cardinal fini.

Définition 9: Profondeur d'un terme t: p(t). Si t = x alors p(t) = 0 sinon t = f(t1,...,tn) et p(t) = 1 + sup(p(ti))i = 1,n

Lemme 3: Soient (ti)i = 1,n des termes linéaires tels que v(ti) ∩ v(tj) = ∅ pour i ≠ j, alors l'unifié des (ti)i est, s'il existe, linéaire et p(t) = sup{p(ti)}i.

Preuve de la proposition 6: Elle consiste a vérifier en utilisant le lemme précédent que lors de la construction des paires critiques récursives, au fur et à mesure que l'on augmente la profondeur de la récursivité, la profondeur des termes où l'on peut superposer des équations diminue strictement.

Lorsqu'on a des équations de la forme t(x) = x, on peut se ramener à ne tester que les paires critiques obtenues en considérant toutes les équations sauf les membres droits des équations t(x) = x. Le nombre de paires critiques ainsi obtenu est fini si R est linéaire gauche.

Proposition 7: On suppose R linéaire gauche, soit P1 l'ensemble des paires critiques récursives obtenues en interdisant les superpositions de membres droits des équations de la forme ti(x) = x. Si, à partir de chacunes des paires critiques récursives de P1, pour chaque occurrence u où l'on peut superposer le membre droit de ti(x) = x pour obtenir une nouvelle paire critique, tous les symboles de fonction préfixes de u ou d'une occurrence de non variable d'un membre gauche de règle vérifient : f(y1,...,yi-1,t(yi),yi+1,...,yn) -*-> t(f(y1,...,yn)) alors la confluence de l'ensemble infini des paires critiques récursives est équivalente à la confluence de l'ensemble des paires de P1.

Preuve: Elle s'appuie sur la remarque suivante : soit t1 un terme, t = x une équation, u une occurrence dans t1 tel que les symboles de fonction de t1 qui sont préfixes de u, vérifient l'hypothèse ci-dessus. Alors, t1 |-| t1[u <-- t(t1/u)] et t1[u <-- t(t1/u)] -*-> t(t1) |-| t1, ce qui se visualise sur le schéma suivant :

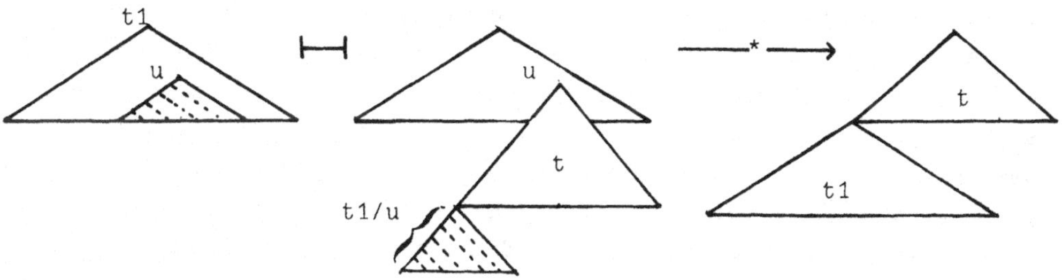

Ceci permet de traiter avec succès l'idempotence associée à des règles de distributivité.

Exemples :

R = {x* (y+z) --> x*y + x*z, (x+y) * z --> x*z + y*z}

E = {x+y = y+x , (x+y) + z = x + (y+z),

(x+y) + (z+t) = (x+z) + (y+t) , (x*y) = (y*x)

(x*y) * z = x * (y*z)}

La troisième équation semble à priori redondante mais elle est indispensable pour assurer la confluence de la paire critique de R en un coup.

2) R = {x* (y+z) --> x*y + x*z, (x+y) * z --> x*z + y*z}

E = {x+y = y+x , (x+y) + z = x + (y+z), x+x=x ,

(x+y) + (z+t) = (x+z) + (y+t) , (x*y) = (y*x)

(x*y) * z = x * (y*z)}

3) Spécification des entiers

E = {x+y=y+x , (x+y)+z=x+(y+z) , x + OPP(x)=0 , x+0=0}

R = {x*(y+z)-->x*y + x*z , x*OPP(y)-->OPP(x*y),

x*0-->0, x*1-->x}

Remarques: On remarque sur ces exemples que la confluence des paires critiques a lieu à l'aide des équations intervenant dans leur formation. Cela suggère que l'égalité récursive est "trop forte". On peut remplacer l'égalité |=r=|E par l'égalité (∪|=r=|Ei)i où E = (∪ Ei)i, et tous les résultats précédents restent valables pour cette nouvelle égalité. (Il suffit de remplacer dans les propositions |=r=|E par (∪ |=r=|Ei)i=1,n), ce qui permet de limiter le nombre de paires critiques à tester et fournit une méthode incrémentale puisqu'on peut, si besoin, fusionner les ensembles d'équations Ei.

Conclusion:

Il s'avère que l'égalité récursive définie dans (JKR,83) est bien adaptée pour traiter un certain nombre de théories équationnelles ayant seulement la propriété de terminaison faible. Le concept de paires critiques récursives permet de généraliser les résultats de (JKR,83). La principale restriction tient à la linéarité gauche des règles. Pour s'en affranchir, il semble nécessaire de changer de relation de réécriture.
Les conditions que l'on a cherchées à tester ici ne sont que des conditions suffisantes pour avoir la propriété Church-Rosser. Il serait intéressant de connaître soit des conditions nécessaires et suffisantes soit d'autres conditions suffisantes plus faibles et plus variées.

Remerciements:

Je remercie toute l'équipe EURECA du CRIN et plus particulièrement J.P. Jouannaud pour ses nombreux conseils ainsi que J.L. Remy. Je remercie Madame G. Sabater qui a assuré avec beaucoup de gentillesse et de patience la frappe de cet article.

Bibliographie:

[DER,82] Dershowitz N. : "Computing with term rewriting systems". soumis à publication.

[H&O,80] Huet G. Oppen D.C.: "Equations and rewrite rules: a survey". In Formal Languages: Perspectives and Open Problems". Book R. Editor, Academic Press (1980).

[JOU,83a] Jouannaud J.P.: "Confluent and Coherent sets of reductions with equations. Application to proofs in data types". Proc. 8th Colloquium on Trees in Algebra and Programming (1983).

[JOU,83b] Jouannaud J.P.: "Church-Rosser computations in equational term rewriting systems". Soumis à publication.

[JKR,83] Jouannaud J.P., Kirchner h., Remy J.L.: "Church-Rosser properties of weakly terminating term rewriting systems". 10th IJCAI (1983).

[KIR,83] Kirchner H.:"A general completion algorithm for equationnal term rewriting systems and its proof of correctness". Rapport interne CRIN.

[LES,83] Lescanne P.: "Computer experiments with the REVE term rewriting system generator". Proc. 10th POPL conference (1983).

[PAD,82] Padawitz P.: "Equational data type specification and recursive program scheme". In "Formal Description of Programming Concepts 2". Ed. Bjorner D. (1982).

[PER,83] Perdrix H.: "Propriété Church-Rosser de systèmes de réécriture équationnels ayant la propriété de terminaison faible". Rapport interne CRIN.

Résumé:

L'algorithme de Knuth et Bendix permet de calculer un système de réécriture convergent à partir d'un ensemble d'axiomes. Cet algorithme a été étendu aux systèmes de réécriture équationnels (SRE en agrégé) obtenus en séparant les axiomes en un ensemble de règles et un ensemble d'équations (JOUA,83a et b), (KIR,83). Nous décrivons ici une généralisation des résultats de Jouannaud, Kirchner, Rémy (JKR,83) concernant les SRE où seule la terminaison de l'ensemble des règles est supposée vérifiée et non pas la terminaison modulo les équations. Nous introduisons le concept de paires critiques récursives, cela permet de traiter des ensembles d'axiomes comprenant la commutativité, l'associativité, l'idempotence.

Mots clés:

Système de réécriture, Théorie équationnelle, Unification, Paire critique, Confluence, Cohérence, Terminaison uniforme, Forme normale, Church-Rosser, Preuve automatique.

Remerciements:

Je remercie toute l'équipe EURECA du CRIN et plus particulièrement J.P. Jouannaud pour ses nombreux conseils ainsi que J.L. Remy. Je remercie également Madame G. Sabater qui a assuré avec beaucoup de gentillesse et de patience la frappe de cet article.

ON A GENERAL WEIGHT OF TREES

R. Kemp
Johann Wolfgang Goethe-Universität
Fachbereich Informatik (20)
D-6000 Frankfurt a. M.

Abstract. We define a general weight of the nodes of a given tree T; it depends on the structure of the subtrees of a node, on the number of interior and exterior nodes of these subtrees and on three weight functions defined on the degrees of the nodes appearing in T. Choosing particular weight functions, the weight of the root of the tree is equal to its internal path length, to its external path length, to its internal degree path length, to its external degree path length, to its number of nodes of some degree r, etc.
For a simply generated family of rooted planar trees $\mathcal{F}$ (e.g. all trees defined by restrictions on the set of allowed node degrees), we shall derive a general approach to the computation of the average weight of a tree $T \in \mathcal{F}$ with n nodes and m leaves for arbitrary weight functions, on the assumption that all these trees are equally likely. This general result implies exact and asymptotic formulas for the average weight of a tree $T \in \mathcal{F}$ with n nodes for arbitrary weight functions satisfying particular conditions. Furthermore, this approach enables us to derive explicit and asymptotic expressions for the different types of average path lengths of a tree $T \in \mathcal{F}$ with n nodes and of all ordered trees with n nodes and m leaves.

I. Introduction

Let T=(N,L,r) be an unlabelled rooted planar tree with the set of nodes N, the set of leaves L and the root $r \in N$. Throughout this paper we shall constantly use the convention that the one node tree has no interior nodes and exactly one leaf. The *weight* $\xi_{f,g,h}(x)$ of a node $x \in N$ is recursively defined by

$$\xi_{f,g,h}(x) := \text{IF } x \in L \text{ THEN } 0 \text{ ELSE } \sum_{1 \leq i \leq d} \xi_{f,g,h}(x_i) + \{g(d)+h(d)\} \sum_{1 \leq i \leq d} |L_i| + g(d) \sum_{1 \leq i \leq d} |N_i \setminus L_i| + f(d); ,$$

where $x \in N$ has the d subtrees $T_i=(N_i,L_i,x_i)$, $1 \leq i \leq d$, and $f,g,h: \mathbb{N} \to \mathbb{R}$ are given mappings, the so-called *weight functions*. A tree T has weight w if $\xi_{f,g,h}(r)=w$.
For example, consider the tree T=(N,L,r) drawn in Figure 1. We obtain

the following weights of the nodes for given weight functions f,g and h:

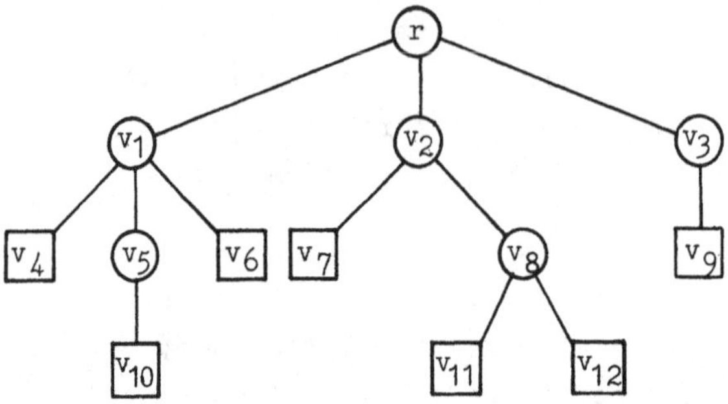

<u>Figure 1.</u> An unlabelled rooted planar tree T. (Here, ○ denotes an internal node and □ denotes a leaf.)

$\xi_{f,g,h}(v) = 0$ for $v \in \{v_4, v_6, v_7, v_9, v_{10}, v_{11}, v_{12}\}$,

$\xi_{f,g,h}(v_5) = \xi_{f,g,h}(v_3) = f(1)+g(1)+h(1)$,

$\xi_{f,g,h}(v_8) = f(2)+2g(2)+2h(2)$,

$\xi_{f,g,h}(v_1) = f(1)+f(3)+g(1)+4g(3)+h(1)+3h(3)$,

$\xi_{f,g,h}(v_2) = 2f(2)+6g(2)+5h(2)$

$\xi_{f,g,h}(r) = 2f(1)+2f(2)+2f(3)+2g(1)+6g(2)+16g(3)+2h(1)+5h(2)+10h(3)$.

Choosing particular weight functions f,g and h, the weight w of a tree corresponds to important parameters which are directly related to the analysis of algorithms. Here are some typical examples:

- Let $f(\lambda)=0$ and $g(\lambda)=-h(\lambda)=1$ for $\lambda \in \mathbb{N}$.
  Obviously, the weight of a tree T=(N,L,r) is equal to the *internal path length* of T which is defined to be the sum - taken over all interior nodes $N \setminus L$ - of the lengths of the paths from the root to each node. This quantity is related to the execution time of particular algorithms, e.g. binary search in an ordered table ([7;p.410]), binary tree searching ([7;p.427]) or digital searching ([7;p.495]).
- Let $f(\lambda)=g(\lambda)=0$ and $h(\lambda)=1$ for $\lambda \in \mathbb{N}$.
  In this case, the weight of a tree T=(N,L,r) is equal to the *external path length* of T which is defined to be the sum - taken over all leaves L - of the lengths of the paths from the root to each node. This parameter plays a part in problems dealing with optimum patterns for merging on a tape ([7;p.306]) or with the number of comparisons and the time required by particular sorting methods ([7;pp.194,367,410, 427,495]).
- Let $f(\lambda)=g(\lambda)=0$ and $h(\lambda)=\lambda$ for $\lambda \in \mathbb{N}$.
  Evidently, the weight of a tree T=(N,L,r) is equal to the *external degree path length* of T which is defined by the sum - taken over all

leaves - of the degrees of the nodes on the paths from the root to the leaves. This quantity is related to the time required to do a P-way merge on characters ([7;p.367]).

- Let $f(\lambda)=0$ and $g(\lambda)=-h(\lambda)=\lambda$ for $\lambda \in \mathbb{N}$.
  The weight of a tree $T=(N,L,r)$ is equal to the *internal degree path length* of T which is defined by the sum - taken over all interior nodes $x \in N \setminus L$ - of the degrees of the nodes on the paths from the root to the nodes x, excluding x.
- Let $f(\lambda)=1$ and $g(\lambda)=h(\lambda)=0$ for $\lambda \in \mathbb{N}$.
  In this case, the weight of a tree $T=(N,L,r)$ is equal to the *number of the interior nodes* of T.
- Let $f(\lambda)=\delta_{\lambda s}$, $s \in \mathbb{N}$, and $g(\lambda)=h(\lambda)=0$ for $\lambda \in \mathbb{N}$.
  The weight of a tree $T=(N,L,r)$ is equal to the *number of all nodes of degree s* appearing in T.

Following [8], a family $\mathcal{F}$ of rooted planar trees is said to be *simply generated* if the generating function

$$T(z) = \sum_{n \geq 1} \tau(n) z^n \tag{1}$$

of the numbers $\tau(n)$ of all trees $T \in \mathcal{F}$ with n nodes satisfies a functional equation of the form

$$T(z) = z\,\Theta(T(z)) , \tag{2}$$

where $\Theta(y) = 1 + \sum_{\lambda \geq 1} c_\lambda y^\lambda$ is a regular function of y when $|y|<R<\infty$. If Θ is a polynomial, then the family $\mathcal{F}$ is said to be *bounded*. This definition obviously includes all families of unlabelled rooted planar trees defined by restriction on the set of allowed node degrees that is, c_λ is zero or one. In this paper, we shall restrict our attention to these *families of simply generated unlabelled rooted planar trees (FSGURPT $\mathcal{F}(\Theta)$)*. As examples, we mention:

- the FSGURPT $\mathcal{F}(\Theta)$ consisting of all *q-ary trees* for which $\Theta(y)=1+y^q$ (if q=2, $\mathcal{F}(\Theta)$ is the set of all *extended binary trees* ([6;p.399]);
- the FSGURPT $\mathcal{F}(\Theta)$ consisting of all *s,s+1-trees* for which $\Theta(y)=1+y^s+$ $+y^{s+1}$ (if s=1, $\mathcal{F}(\Theta)$ is the set of all *unary-binary trees*; if s=2, $\mathcal{F}(\Theta)$ is the set of all *unbalanced 2,3-trees)*;
- the FSGURPT $\mathcal{F}(\Theta)$ consisting of all *planar trees (ordered trees)* for which $\Theta(y)=(1-y)^{-1}$.

If $\mathcal{F}(\Theta)$ is a FSGURPT, then the numbers $\tau(n)$ and the enumerator $T(z)$ satisfy the following conditions which can be easily proved by an application of the implicit function theorem and the Darboux-Polya theorem (see [3],[8]):

(C1) $T(z)$ is a regular function for $|z|<\rho$, where $\rho=\tau/\Theta(\tau)$ and τ is the smallest positive root of the equation $\tau\Theta'(\tau) - \Theta(\tau)=0$;

(C2) $T(z)$ has algebraic singularities at the points $\tau_j=\omega^j\tau, 0 \leq j<d$, where

$d=GCD\{\lambda \in \mathbb{N} \mid \langle y^\lambda;\Theta(y)\rangle \neq 0\}$, ω is a primitive d-th root of unity and τ is defined by the equation given in (C1); (the abbreviation $\langle z^n;f(z)\rangle$ denotes the coefficient of z^n in the expansion of $f(z)$);

(C3) Let $\rho_j=\omega^j\rho$, $0\leq j<d$, where ρ,ω and d have the same meaning as in (C1) and (C2). If $|z|=\rho$ but $z \neq \rho_j$, $0\leq j<d$, then $|T(z)|<\tau$; furthermore, $T(\rho_j)=\tau_j$ for $0\leq j<d$.

(C4) $T(z)$ has an expansion in the neighbourhood of $z=\rho_j$, $j\in [0:d[$, of the form

$$T(z) = \sum_{n\geq 0} a_n^{(j)}(\rho_j-z)^{n/2},$$

where $a_0^{(j)}=\tau_j$ and $a_1^{(j)}=-\omega^j \rho_j^{-1/2}\{2\Theta(\tau)/\Theta''(\tau)\}^{1/2}$;

(C5) The numbers $\tau(n)=\langle z^n;T(z)\rangle$ have an asymptotic representation of the form

$$\tau(n) \sim d\,[\Theta(\tau)/\{2\pi\Theta''(\tau)\}]^{1/2}\rho^{-n}\,n^{-3/2}$$

for $n\equiv 1 \pmod d$. If $n\not\equiv 1 \pmod d$, then $\tau(n)=0$.

If we are interested in the number $\tau(n,m)$ of all trees in a given FSGURPT $\mathcal{F}(\Theta)$ with n nodes and m leaves, then we have to consider the generating function

$$L(z,u) = \sum_{n\geq 1}\sum_{m\geq 1} \tau(n,m)\, z^n u^m . \tag{3}$$

It is not hard to see that this function is defined by the functional equation

$$L(z,u) = z(u-1) + z\Theta(L(z,u)), \tag{4}$$

where Θ is the same power series as in (2). Note that $L(z,1)=T(z)$.

II. A General Approach to the Computation of the Average Weight

This section is devoted to the derivation of some basic results. First, we will prove the following

Theorem 1.

Let $\mathcal{F}(\Theta)$ be a FSGURPT and $t_{\xi_{f,g,h}}(n,m,w)$ be the number of all trees $T\in \mathcal{F}(\Theta)$ with n nodes, m leaves and weight w. The generating function

$$P_{\xi_{f,g,h}}(z,u,t) = \sum_{n\geq 1}\sum_{m\geq 1}\sum_{w\geq 0} t_{\xi_{f,g,h}}(n,m,w)\, z^n u^m t^w$$

satisfies the functional equation

$$P_{\xi_{f,g,h}}(z,u,t) = zu + z\sum_{\lambda\geq 1} t^{f(\lambda)}\, P^{\lambda}_{\xi_{f,g,h}}(zt^{g(\lambda)},ut^{h(\lambda)},t)\,\langle y^\lambda;\Theta(y)\rangle.$$

Proof. We obtain all trees $T\in \mathcal{F}(\Theta)$ with n nodes, m leaves and weight w by taking a root node and attaching zero (n=m=1) or $\lambda\in\{s \mid \langle y^s;\Theta(y)\rangle\neq 0\}$ subtrees $T_i\in \mathcal{F}(\Theta)$ with n_i nodes, m_i leaves and weights w_i, $1\leq i\leq\lambda$, where $\sum_{1\leq i\leq\lambda} n_i=n-1$, $\sum_{1\leq i\leq\lambda} m_i=m$ and $\sum_{1\leq i\leq\lambda}[w_i+\{g(\lambda)+h(\lambda)\}m_i+g(\lambda)(n_i-m_i)+f(\lambda)]=w$

that is $\sum_{1\leq i<\lambda} w_i + (n-1)g(\lambda) + mh(\lambda) + f(\lambda) = w$.
Hence

$$P_{\xi_{f,g,h}}(z,u,t) = z\left[u + \sum_{\lambda\geq 1} t^{f(\lambda)} P^{\lambda}_{\xi_{f,g,h}}(zt^{g(\lambda)}, ut^{h(\lambda)}, t) \langle y^{\lambda};\Theta(y)\rangle\right]. \square$$

Assuming that all trees $T\in\mathcal{F}(\Theta)$ with n nodes and m leaves are equally likely, the quotient $q_{\xi_{f,g,h}}(n,m,w)=t_{\xi_{f,g,h}}(n,m,w)/\tau(n,m)$ is the probability that such a tree has a weight w. The s-th moment about the origin $\mu_{\xi_{f,g,h}}(s,n,m)$ of the random variable X taking on the value w with probability $q_{\xi_{f,g,h}}(n,m,w)$ is given by

$$\mu_{\xi_{f,g,h}}(s,n,m) = \sum_{w\geq 0} w^s q_{\xi_{f,g,h}}(n,m,w) = \tau^{-1}(n,m) \sum_{w\geq 0} w^s t_{\xi_{f,g,h}}(n,m,w) .$$

Introducing the function

$$G^{[s]}_{\xi_{f,g,h}}(z,u,t) = \sum_{n\geq 1}\sum_{m\geq 1}\sum_{w\geq 0} w^s t_{\xi_{f,g,h}}(n,m,w) z^n u^m t^w ,$$

we find immediately

$$\mu_{\xi_{f,g,h}}(s,n,m) = \tau^{-1}(n,m) \langle z^n u^m; G^{[s]}_{\xi_{f,g,h}}(z,u,1)\rangle , \tag{5}$$

where

$$G^{[0]}_{\xi_{f,g,h}}(z,u,t) = P_{\xi_{f,g,h}}(z,u,t) \quad\text{and}\quad G^{[s+1]}_{\xi_{f,g,h}}(z,u,t) = t\frac{\partial}{\partial t} G^{[s]}_{\xi_{f,g,h}}(z,u,t),\ s\geq 0.$$

<u>Theorem 2.</u>

Let $\mathcal{F}(\Theta)$ be a FSGURPT and let $\tau(n,m)$ be the number of all trees $T\in\mathcal{F}(\Theta)$ with n nodes and m leaves. Assuming that all these $\tau(n,m)$ trees are equally likely, the average weight $\mu_{\xi_{f,g,h}}(1,n,m)$ is given by

$$\mu_{\xi_{f,g,h}}(1,n,m) = \tau^{-1}(n,m) \langle z^n u^m; G^{[1]}_{\xi_{f,g,h}}(z,u,1)\rangle,$$

where

$$G^{[1]}_{\xi_{f,g,h}}(z,u,1) = z^2 L_z L^{-2}\left[L\tilde{f}(L) + zLL_z\tilde{g}'(L) + z^2uL_z\tilde{h}'(L)\right] .$$

Here, L and L_z denote the functions L(z,u) and $L_z(z,u)$ and $\tilde{\eta}$ denotes the power series $\tilde{\eta}(v) = \sum_{\lambda\geq 1} \eta(\lambda) \langle y^{\lambda};\Theta(y)\rangle v^{\lambda}$, $\eta\in\{f,g,h\}$. L(z,u) is the enumerator of $\mathcal{F}(\Theta)$ given by (3).

Proof. Consider the functional equation presented in Theorem 1. Taking the partial derivative with respect to t, we obtain

$$\begin{aligned} G^{[1]}_{\xi_{f,g,h}}(z,u,t) &= t\frac{\partial}{\partial t} P_{\xi_{f,g,h}}(z,u,t) \\ &= z\sum_{\lambda\geq 1} f(\lambda)t^{f(\lambda)} P^{\lambda}_{\xi_{f,g,h}}(zt^{g(\lambda)}, ut^{h(\lambda)}, t) \langle y^{\lambda};\Theta(y)\rangle \; + \\ &\quad + z\sum_{\lambda\geq 1} \lambda t^{f(\lambda)+1} P^{\lambda-1}_{\xi_{f,g,h}}(zt^{g(\lambda)}, ut^{h(\lambda)}, t)\, F(\lambda) \langle y^{\lambda};\Theta(y)\rangle, \end{aligned}$$

where

$$F(\lambda) = zg(\lambda)t^{g(\lambda)}\frac{\partial}{\partial z} P_{\xi_{f,g,h}}(zt^{g(\lambda)}, ut^{h(\lambda)}, t) + t\frac{\partial}{\partial t} P_{\xi_{f,g,h}}(zt^{g(\lambda)}, ut^{h(\lambda)}, t) +$$

$$+uh(\lambda)t^{h(\lambda)}\frac{\partial}{\partial u}P_{\xi_{f,g,h}}(zt^{g(\lambda)},ut^{h(\lambda)},t).$$

Since $P_{\xi_{f,g,h}}(z,u,1)=L(z,u)$, $\frac{\partial}{\partial z}P_{\xi_{f,g,h}}(z,u,1)=L_z(z,u)$, $\frac{\partial}{\partial u}P_{\xi_{f,g,h}}(z,u,1)=L_u(z,u)$ and $\frac{\partial}{\partial t}P_{\xi_{f,g,h}}(z,u,1)=G^{[1]}_{\xi_{f,g,h}}(z,u,1)$, we obtain further

$$G^{[1]}_{\xi_{f,g,h}}(z,u,1) = z\left[1-z\sum_{\lambda\geq 1}\lambda L^{\lambda-1}(z,u)\ \langle y^\lambda;\Theta(y)\rangle\right]^{-1}\times$$
$$\sum_{\lambda\geq 1}L^{\lambda-1}(z,u)\left[f(\lambda)L(z,u)+\lambda g(\lambda)zL_z(z,u)+\lambda h(\lambda)uL_u(z,u)\right]\langle y^\lambda;\Theta(y)\rangle$$

On the other hand, the functional equation (4) implies

$$L_u(z,u) = z^2\,L_z(z,u)L^{-1}(z,u) \tag{6}$$

and

$$\sum_{\lambda\geq 1}\lambda L^{\lambda-1}(z,u)\langle y^\lambda;\Theta(y)\rangle = z^{-2}\left[zL_z(z,u)-L(z,u)\right]L_z^{-1}(z,u) \tag{7}$$

Using these relations and the definition of the functions $\tilde{f}$, $\tilde{g}$ and $\tilde{h}$, the above formula for $G^{[1]}_{\xi_{f,g,h}}(z,u,1)$ can easily be transformed into the expression given in our proposition. □

III. On the Average Weight of A Tree With N Nodes

In this section we shall derive asymptotic expressions for particular average weights of a tree $T\in\mathcal{F}(\Theta)$ with n nodes, where $\mathcal{F}(\Theta)$ is a FSGURPT. First we shall prove a rather general result.

Theorem 3.

Let $\tilde{\eta}(v)$, $\eta\in\{f,g,h\}$, be the functions defined in Theorem 2, $T(z)$ be the enumerator of the number of all trees with n nodes in the FSGURPT $\mathcal{F}(\Theta)$, $d=GCD\{\lambda\in\mathbb{N}\,|\,\langle y^\lambda;\Theta(y)\rangle\neq 0\}$ and suppose that the series $\tilde{f}(T(z))$, $\tilde{g}'(T(z))$ and $\tilde{h}'(T(z))$ converge when $|z|<\rho+\varepsilon$ for some $\varepsilon>0$, where $\rho=\tau/\Theta(\tau)$ and τ is the smallest positive root of the equation $\Theta(\tau)-\tau\Theta'(\tau)=0$. Assuming that all trees $T\in\mathcal{F}(\Theta)$ with n nodes are equally likely, the average weight $\mu_{\xi_{f,g,h}}(1,n)$ is asymptotically given for $n\equiv 1 (mod\ d)$ by

$$\mu_{\xi_{f,g,h}}(1,n) \sim \rho\tau^{-1}\tilde{f}(\tau)n + \tau^{-1}b\left[\tau\tilde{g}'(\tau)+\rho\tilde{h}'(\tau)\right]n^{3/2},$$

where $b=(\rho\pi/\{2\tau\Theta''(\tau)\})^{1/2}$.

Proof. Since $T(z)=L(z,1)$, an inspection of Theorem 2 shows that

$$\mu_{\xi_{f,g,h}}(1,n) = B_1(n)+B_2(n)+B_3(n),$$

where

$$B_1(n) = \tau^{-1}(n)\ \langle z^n;z^2T'(z)T^{-1}(z)\ \tilde{f}(T(z))\rangle, \tag{8}$$
$$B_2(n) = \tau^{-1}(n)\ \langle z^n;z^3\{T'(z)\}^2T^{-1}(z)\ \tilde{g}'(T(z))\rangle, \tag{9}$$
$$B_3(n) = \tau^{-1}(n)\ \langle z^n;z^4\{T'(z)\}^2T^{-2}(z)\ \tilde{h}'(T(z))\rangle. \tag{10}$$

Since $\tilde{f}(T(z))$, $\tilde{g}'(T(z))$ and $\tilde{h}'(T(z))$ converge when $|z|<\rho+\varepsilon$ for some $\varepsilon>0$, we obtain by condition (C4) the following expansions around $z=\rho_j$, $j\in[0:d]$

$$z^2T'(z)T^{-1}(z)\tilde{f}(T(z)) = (\rho_j-z)^{-1/2}\sum_{\lambda\geq 1}\frac{1}{2}\bar{a}_1^{(j)}\rho_j^2\tau_j^{\lambda-1}f(\lambda)\langle y^\lambda;\Theta(y)\rangle + x_1^{(j)} + x_2^{(j)}(\rho_j-z)^{1/2} + \ldots ,$$

$$z^3\{T'(z)\}^2T^{-1}(z)\tilde{g}'(T(z)) = (\rho_j-z)^{-1}\sum_{\lambda\geq 1}\frac{1}{4}\{\bar{a}_1^{(j)}\}^2\rho_j^2\tau_j^{\lambda-2}\lambda g(\lambda)\langle y^\lambda;\Theta(y)\rangle + y_1^{(j)}(\rho_j-z)^{-1/2} + y_2^{(j)} + \ldots ,$$

$$z^4\{T'(z)\}^2T^{-2}(z)\tilde{h}'(T(z)) = (\rho_j-z)^{-1}\sum_{\lambda\geq 1}\frac{1}{4}\{\bar{a}_1^{(j)}\}^2\rho_j^4\tau_j^{\lambda-3}\lambda h(\lambda)\langle y^\lambda;\Theta(y)\rangle + z_1^{(j)}(\rho_j-z)^{-1/2} + z_2^{(j)} + \ldots ,$$

where $\bar{a}_1^{(j)}=\omega^j\rho_j^{-1/2}\{2\Theta(\tau)/\Theta''(\tau)\}^{1/2}$. Hence by a result of Darboux ([2]) and by definition of ρ_j and τ_j given in the conditions (C2) and (C3):

$$\langle z^n;z^2T'(z)T^{-1}(z)\tilde{f}(T(z))\rangle =$$
$$= \sum_{\lambda\geq 1}f(\lambda)\langle y^\lambda;\Theta(y)\rangle\left[\frac{1}{n}\sum_{0\leq j<d}\frac{1}{2}\bar{a}_1^{(j)}\rho_j^{3/2}\tau_j^{\lambda-1}n^{1/2}\Gamma^{-1}(\tfrac{1}{2})\rho_j^{-n}\right]+o(\rho^{-n}n^{-1/2})$$
$$\sim \sum_{\lambda\geq 1}f(\lambda)\langle y^\lambda;\Theta(y)\rangle\left[\{\Theta(\tau)/(2\pi\Theta''(\tau))\}^{1/2}\tau^{\lambda-1}n^{-1/2}\rho^{-n+1}\sum_{0\leq j<d}\omega^{j\lambda-j(n-1)}\right]$$

$$\langle z^n;z^3\{T'(z)\}^2T^{-1}(z)\tilde{g}'(T(z))\rangle =$$
$$= \sum_{\lambda\geq 1}\lambda g(\lambda)\langle y^\lambda;\Theta(y)\rangle\left[\frac{1}{n}\sum_{0\leq j<d}\frac{1}{4}\{\bar{a}_1^{(j)}\}^2\rho_j^2\tau_j^{\lambda-2}n\Gamma^{-1}(1)\rho_j^{-n}\right] +o(\rho^{-n})$$
$$\sim \sum_{\lambda\geq 1}\lambda g(\lambda)\langle y^\lambda;\Theta(y)\rangle\left[\frac{1}{2}\Theta(\tau)\tau^{\lambda-2}\rho^{-n+1}/\Theta''(\tau)\sum_{0\leq j<d}\omega^{j\lambda-j(n-1)}\right] ,$$

$$\langle z^n;z^4\{T'(z)\}^2T^{-2}(z)\tilde{h}'(T(z))\rangle =$$
$$= \sum_{\lambda\geq 1}\lambda h(\lambda)\langle y^\lambda;\Theta(y)\rangle\left[\frac{1}{n}\sum_{0\leq j<d}\frac{1}{4}\{\bar{a}_1^{(j)}\}^2\rho_j^3\tau_j^{\lambda-3}n\Gamma^{-1}(1)\rho_j^{-n}\right] +o(\rho^{-n})$$
$$\sim \sum_{\lambda\geq 1}\lambda h(\lambda)\langle y^\lambda;\Theta(y)\rangle\left[\frac{1}{2}\Theta(\tau)\tau^{\lambda-3}\rho^{-n+2}/\Theta''(\tau)\sum_{0\leq j<d}\omega^{j\lambda-j(n-1)}\right].$$

Since $d=GCD\{\lambda\in\mathbb{N}\,|\,\langle y^\lambda;\Theta(y)\rangle\neq 0\}$, we have

$$\langle y^\lambda;\Theta(y)\rangle\sum_{0\leq j<d}\omega^{j\lambda-j(n-1)} = \begin{cases} d & \text{if } \lambda\equiv 0 \pmod d \wedge n\equiv 1 \pmod d\\ 0 & \text{otherwise}\end{cases}$$

and therefore

$$B_1(n) \sim n\rho\sum_{\lambda\geq 1}f(\lambda)\ \langle y^\lambda;\Theta(y)\rangle\tau^{\lambda-1} = \rho\tau^{-1}\tilde{f}(\tau)n ,$$

$$B_2(n) \sim \{\pi\Theta(\tau)/(2\Theta''(\tau))\}^{1/2}\rho n^{3/2}\sum_{\lambda\geq 1}\lambda g(\lambda)\langle y^\lambda;\Theta(y)\rangle\tau^{\lambda-2} = b\tilde{g}'(\tau)n^{3/2} ,$$

$$B_3(n) \sim \{\pi\Theta(\tau)/(2\Theta''(\tau))\}^{1/2}\rho^2n^{3/2}\sum_{\lambda\geq 1}\lambda h(\lambda)\langle y^\lambda;\Theta(y)\rangle\tau^{\lambda-3} =b\rho\tau^{-1}\tilde{h}'(\tau)n^{3/2},$$

where $b=\{\rho\pi/(2\tau\Theta''(\tau))\}^{1/2}$. This implies the desired result. □

Note that the assumption about $\tilde{f}(T(z))$, $\tilde{g}'(T(z))$ and $\tilde{h}'(T(z))$ is clearly satisfied if the sums $\tilde{f}(\tau)$, $\tilde{g}'(\tau)$ and $\tilde{h}'(\tau)$ are absolutely convergent; this fact is implied by the principle of the maximum because $T(z)$ fulfils the conditions (C1), (C2) and (C3). Let us discuss a simple example! Consider the FSGURPT $\mathcal{F}(\Theta)$ consisting of all rooted planar trees with even degrees of the nodes (i.e. $\Theta(y)=(1-y^2)^{-1}$) and choose the weight functions $f(\lambda)=\lambda^{-1}$, $g(\lambda)=\lambda!^{-1}$, $h(\lambda)=\sin(\lambda)$ for $\lambda\geq 1$. The first few values of the average weight are $\mu_{\xi_{f,g,h}}(1,1)=0$, $\mu_{\xi_{f,g,h}}(1,3)=3/2+2\sin(2)$, $\mu_{\xi_{f,g,h}}(1,5)=101/66 + 10\sin(2)/3 + 4\sin(4)/3$, $\mu_{\xi_{f,g,h}}(1,7)=6301/1440 + 31\sin(2)/6 + 7\sin(4)/3 + \sin(6)/2$. We have $\Theta'(y)=2y(1-y^2)^{-2}$ and $\Theta''(y)=2(1+3y^2)/(1-y^2)^{-3}$. Thus $\tau=\sqrt{3}/3$, $\rho=2\sqrt{3}/9$ and $b=\sqrt{2\pi}/9$. Since the sums $\tilde{f}(\tau)$, $\tilde{g}'(\tau)$ and $\tilde{h}'(\tau)$ are absolutely convergent, we can apply Theorem 3 and obtain for $n\equiv 1 \pmod 2$:

$$\begin{aligned}\mu_{\xi_{f,g,h}}(1,n) &\sim \frac{2}{3}\, n \sum_{\lambda\geq 1}(2\lambda)^{-1}\tau^{2\lambda} + \\ &\quad + \frac{1}{9}(6\pi)^{1/2}\left[\frac{1}{3}\sqrt{3}\sum_{\lambda\geq 1}\frac{2\lambda}{(2\lambda)!}\tau^{2\lambda-1} + \frac{2}{9}\sqrt{3}\sum_{\lambda\geq 1} 2\lambda\sin(2\lambda)\tau^{2\lambda-1}\right]n^{3/2} \\ &= \frac{1}{3}\, n \ln(\tfrac{3}{2}) + \frac{1}{27}(6\pi)^{1/2}\left[\sqrt{3}\sinh(\tfrac{\sqrt{3}}{3}) + 24\sin(2)/(5-3\cos(2))^2\right]n^{3/2} \\ &= 0.135\ n + 0.259\ n^{3/2}.\end{aligned}$$

It is not hard to see that the result of Theorem 3 describes the asymptotic behaviour of the average weight $\mu_{\xi_{f,g,h}}(1,n)$ for arbitrary weight functions f,g and h if $\{\lambda \mid \langle y^\lambda;\Theta(y)\rangle \neq 0\}$ is finite, in other words, if the FSGURPT is bounded. Furthermore, Theorem 3 may also be applied in the case of non-bounded FSGURPT's $\mathcal{F}(\Theta)$ if the weight functions f,g and h are polynomials in λ, because in this case $0<\tau<1$. Therefore, using the particular weight functions f, g and h given in section I, we obtain the following

Corollary 1.

Let $\mathcal{F}(\Theta)$ be a FSGURPT, τ be the smallest positive root of the equation $\Theta(\tau)-\tau\Theta'(\tau)=0$, $d=GCD\{\lambda\in\mathbb{N} \mid \langle y^\lambda;\Theta(y)\rangle\neq 0\}$, $C=\{\pi/2\}^{1/2}\{\Theta''(\tau)\}^{-1/2}\{\Theta(\tau)\}^{-3/2}$ and assume that all trees $T\in\mathcal{F}(\Theta)$ with n nodes are equally likely.

(a) The average internal path length $p_{in}(n)$ of a tree $T\in\mathcal{F}(\Theta)$ with n nodes is given for $n\equiv 1 \pmod d$ by

$$p_{in}(n) \sim C\ \Theta'(\tau)\ \{\Theta(\tau) - 1\}\ n^{3/2}.$$

(b) The average external path length $p_{ex}(n)$ of a tree $T\in\mathcal{F}(\Theta)$ with n nodes is given for $n\equiv 1 \pmod d$ by

$$p_{ex}(n) \sim C\ \Theta'(\tau)\ n^{3/2}.$$

(c) The average internal degree path length $p_{ind}(n)$ of a tree $T\in\mathcal{F}(\Theta)$ with n nodes is given for $n\equiv 1 \pmod d$ by

$$p_{ind}(n) \sim C\ \{\Theta'(\tau) + \tau\Theta''(\tau)\}\ \{\Theta(\tau) - 1\}\ n^{3/2}.$$

(d) The average external degree path length $p_{exd}(n)$ of a tree $T\in\mathcal{F}(\Theta)$ with n nodes is given for $n\equiv 1 \pmod d$ by

$$p_{exd}(n) \sim C\ \{\Theta'(\tau) + \tau\Theta''(\tau)\}\ n^{3/2}.$$

(e) The average number $I(n)$ of interior nodes in a tree $T\in\mathcal{F}(\Theta)$ with n nodes is given for $n\equiv 1 \pmod d$ by

$$I(n) \sim \{\Theta(\tau)\}^{-1}\{\Theta(\tau) - 1\}\ n.$$

(d) The average number $N_r(n)$ of nodes of degree $r\in\mathbb{N}_0$ in a tree $T\in\mathcal{F}(\Theta)$ with n nodes is given for $n\equiv 1 \pmod d$ by

$$N_r(n) \sim \{\Theta(\tau)\}^{-1}\ \tau^r\ \langle y^r;\Theta(y)\rangle\ n.$$

f(λ)	g(λ)	h(λ)	q-ary trees (q≥2) $\Theta(y)=1+y^q$; $\tau=(q-1)^{-1/q}$; d=q; n≡1(mod q)	extended binary trees $\Theta(y)=1+y^2$; τ=1 ; d=2; n≡1(mod 2)	s,s+1-trees $\Theta(y)=1+y^s+y^{s+1}$; $\tau=\tau_0$; d=1; $n\in\mathbb{N}$	unary-binary trees $\Theta(y)=1+y+y^2$; τ=1 ; d=1; $n\in\mathbb{N}$	2,3-trees $\Theta(y)=1+y^2+y^3$; $\tau=\tau_1$; d=1; $n\in\mathbb{N}$	rooted planar trees $\Theta(y)=\frac{1}{1-y}$; τ=1/2 ; d=1; $n\in\mathbb{N}$	meaning
0	1	-1	$Aq^{-1}\ n^{3/2}$	$\frac{1}{2}\sqrt{\frac{\pi}{2}}\ n^{3/2}$	$B\tau^{3s/2}(\tau+1)\ \times$ $\times\{s+\tau(s+1)\}\ \times$ $\times\ n^{3/2}$	$\sqrt{\frac{\pi}{3}}\ n^{3/2}$	$\approx .4275\ n^{3/2}$	$\frac{1}{4}\sqrt{\pi}\ n^{3/2}$	average int. path length
0	0	1	$Aq^{-1}(q-1)\ \times$ $\times\ n^{3/2}$	$\frac{1}{2}\sqrt{\frac{\pi}{2}}\ n^{3/2}$	$B\tau^{s/2}\ \times$ $\times\{s+\tau(s+1)\}\ \times$ $\times\ n^{3/2}$	$\frac{1}{2}\sqrt{\frac{\pi}{3}}\ n^{3/2}$	$\approx .5970\ n^{3/2}$	$\frac{1}{4}\sqrt{\pi}\ n^{3/2}$	average ext. path length
0	λ	-λ	$A\ n^{3/2}$	$\sqrt{\frac{\pi}{2}}\ n^{3/2}$	$B\tau^{3s/2}(\tau+1)\ \times$ $\times\{s^2+\tau(s+1)^2\}\times$ $\times\ n^{3/2}$	$\frac{5}{3}\sqrt{\frac{\pi}{3}}\ n^{3/2}$	$\approx 1.0672\ n^{3/2}$	$\frac{3}{4}\sqrt{\pi}\ n^{3/2}$	average int. degree path l.
0	0	λ	$A(q-1)\ n^{3/2}$	$\sqrt{\frac{\pi}{2}}\ n^{3/2}$	$B\tau^{s/2}\ \times$ $\times\{s^2+\tau(s+1)^2\}\times$ $\times\ n^{3/2}$	$\frac{5}{6}\sqrt{\frac{\pi}{3}}\ n^{3/2}$	$\approx 1.4905\ n^{3/2}$	$\frac{3}{4}\sqrt{\pi}\ n^{3/2}$	average ext. degree path l.
1	0	0	n/q	n/2	$\frac{\tau^s(\tau+1)}{1+\tau^s+\tau^{s+1}}\ n$	2n/3	$\approx .4172\ n$	n/2	average number of int. nodes
$<y^r;$ $\Theta(y)>$	0	0	n/q if r=q; $\frac{q-1}{q}n$ if r=0	n/2 if r=0; n/2 if r=2	$\frac{\tau^r}{1+\tau^s+\tau^{s+1}}\ n$ if $r\in\{0,s,s+1\}$	n/3 if $r\in\{0,1,2\}$	$\approx .5827\ \times$ $\times\ (.6573)^r\ n$ if $r\in\{0,2,3\}$	$n/2^{r+1}$	average number of nod. of deg. r

Table 1. The asymptotic behaviour of particular average weights of some important FSGURPT's. ($A=\{\pi/(2q-2)\}^{1/2}$; τ_0 is the smallest positive root of $(s-1)\tau^s+s\tau^{s+1}-1=0$; $B=\{s-1+\tau(s+1)\}^{-1/2}\{\pi/(2s)\}^{1/2}\ \times$ $\times\{1+\tau^s+\tau^{s+1}\}^{-3/2}$; $\tau_1=\{53/216+(13/216)^{1/2}\}^{1/3}+\{53/216-(13/216)^{1/2}\}^{1/3}-1/6$)

Note that the asymptotic expression for the total path length $p_{in}(n) + p_{ex}(n)$ is implicitly derived in [8]. The asymptotic behaviour of $\mu_{\xi_{f,g,h}}(1,n)$ for some important weight functions and FSGURPT's is displayed in Table 1. In order to obtain explicit formulae for the average weights appearing in Table 1 for a particular FSGURPT, we can use the following Corollary 2 with u=1; it is a simple specialization of Theorem 2 to linear weight functions f,g and h.

Corollary 2.

Let $\mathcal{F}(\Theta)$ be a FSGURPT and let $\tau(n,m)$ be the number of all trees $T\in\mathcal{F}(\Theta)$ with n nodes and m leaves. If the weight functions are defined by $\eta(\lambda)=\eta_0+\lambda\eta_1$, $\eta\in\{f,g,h\}$, then the average weight $\mu_{\xi_{f,g,h}}(1,n,m)$ is given by $\mu_{\xi_{f,g,h}}(1,n,m)=\tau^{-1}(n,m)<z^n u^m; G^{[1]}_{\xi_{f,g,h}}(z,u,1)>$, where

$$G^{[1]}_{\xi_{f,g,h}}(z,u,1) = \{zL_z-L\}\{f_1L^2+(g_0+g_1)zLL_z+(h_0+h_1)uz^2L_z\}L^{-2} + \{zLL_{zz}+2LL_z-2zL_z^2\}\{g_1L+h_1uz\}L^{-1}L_z^{-1} + f_0z\{L-uz\}L^{-1}L_z.$$

Here, L, L_z, L_{zz} denote the functions $L(z,u)$, $L_z(z,u)$ and $L_{zz}(z,u)$, respectively. □

IV. On the Average Path Lengths of a Rooted Planar Tree with N Nodes and M Leaves

This section is devoted to the computation of explicit and asymptotic expressions for the different types of average path lengths of a tree $T\in\mathcal{F}(\Theta)$ with n nodes and m leaves, where $\mathcal{F}(\Theta)$ is the FSGURPT consisting of all rooted planar trees. We shall describe the behaviour of these path lengths by the parameters n, m and the quotient $\sigma=m/n\in]0,1[$, σ fixed. Unfortunately, very little is known about obtaining asymptotics from multivariate generating functions (e.g. [1]); therefore, we cannot prove a general result like that given in Theorem 3. Nevertheless, we can prove the following

Theorem 4.

Let $\mathcal{F}(\Theta)$ be the FSGURPT consisting of all rooted planar trees. We have for $n\geq 2$ and $m\geq 1$:

(a) The average internal path length of a tree $T\in\mathcal{F}(\Theta)$ with n nodes and m leaves is given by

$$p_{in}(n,m) = \frac{1}{2}n\left[\binom{2n-2}{2m}-\binom{n-1}{m}^2\right]\Big/\left[\binom{n}{m}\binom{n-2}{m-1}\right].$$

(b) The average external path length of a tree $T\in\mathcal{F}(\Theta)$ with n nodes and m leaves is given by

$$p_{ex}(n,m) = \frac{1}{2}n\binom{2n-2}{2m-1}\Big/\left[\binom{n}{m}\binom{n-2}{m-1}\right].$$

(c) The average internal degree path length of a tree $T\in\mathcal{F}(\Theta)$ with n nodes and m leaves is given by

$$p_{ind}(n,m) = \frac{1}{2}\, n\left[\frac{2n+2m-1}{2m}\binom{2n-2}{2m-1} - \frac{n+3m}{n-m}\binom{n-1}{m}^2\right]\Big/\left[\binom{n}{m}\binom{n-2}{m-1}\right].$$

(d) The average external degree path length of a tree $T \in \mathcal{F}(\Theta)$ with n nodes and m leaves is given by

$$p_{exd}(n,m) = \frac{1}{2}\, n\left[\frac{n+m-1}{n-m}\binom{2n-2}{2m-1} - 2\binom{n-1}{m-1}^2\right]\Big/\left[\binom{n}{m}\binom{n-2}{m-1}\right].$$

Proof. We shall show part (a); the other parts can be proved in a similar way. Since $L(z,u)=z(u-1)+z\{1-L(z,u)\}^{-1}$, Lagrange-Bürman's formula yields (see also [4],[5])

$$<z^n;L^s(z,u)> = \frac{s}{n} <y^{n-s};\{u-1+(1-y)^{-1}\}^n> = \frac{s}{n} <y^{n-s};\{u+y(1-y)^{-1}\}^n> =$$
$$= \frac{s}{n}\sum_{\lambda\geq 0}\binom{n}{\lambda}\binom{n-s-1}{n-s-\lambda} u^{n-\lambda}.$$

Hence

$$<z^n u^m;L^s(z,u)> = \frac{s}{n}\binom{n}{m}\binom{n-s-1}{m-s} \qquad (11)$$

and

$$\tau(n,m) = <z^n u^m;L(z,u)> = \frac{1}{n}\binom{n}{m}\binom{n-2}{m-1}, \quad 1\leq m<n.$$

Choosing $f_0=f_1=g_1=h_1=0$, $g_0=-h_0=1$, Corollary 2 implies

$$p_{in}(n,m) = \tau^{-1}(n,m)<z^n u^m;zL_z(z,u)\{L(z,u)-uz\}\{zL_z(z,u)-L(z,u)\}L^{-2}(z,u)>.$$

Using the above functional equation for $L(z,u)$ and (11), we obtain further

$$<z^n u^m;zL_z(z,u)\{L(z,u)-uz\}\{zL_z(z,u)-L(z,u)\}L^{-2}(z,u)> =$$
$$= <z^n u^m;z^3L_z(z,u)\{1-L(z,u)\}^{-3}\{1-z/(1-L(z,u))^2\}^{-1}> =$$
$$= <z^n u^m;\sum_{\lambda\geq 0} z^{\lambda+3}\{1-L(z,u)\}^{-(2\lambda+3)}L_z(z,u)> =$$
$$= <z^n u^m;\sum_{\lambda\geq 0}\sum_{i\geq 0}\binom{2\lambda+2+i}{i} z^{\lambda+3}(i+1)^{-1}\frac{\partial}{\partial z}L^{i+1}(z,u)> =$$
$$= \sum_{\lambda\geq 0}\sum_{i\geq 0}\binom{2\lambda+2+i}{i}(i+1)^{-1}<z^{n-\lambda-3}u^m;\frac{\partial}{\partial z}L^{i+1}(z,u)> =$$
$$= \sum_{\lambda\geq 0}\sum_{i\geq 0}\binom{2\lambda+2+i}{i}(i+1)^{-1}(n-\lambda-2)<z^{n-\lambda-2}u^m;L^{i+1}(z,u)> =$$
$$= \binom{2n-m-3}{m-1} + \sum_{0\leq\lambda\leq n-m-3}\sum_{i\geq 0}\binom{2\lambda+2+i}{i}\binom{n-\lambda-2}{m}\binom{n-\lambda-i-4}{m-i-1}$$
$$= \sum_{0\leq\lambda\leq n-m-2}\binom{n-\lambda-2}{m}\binom{n+\lambda-1}{m-1}.$$

Here, we have used the general identity $\sum_{0\leq k\leq r}\binom{r-k}{m}\binom{s+k}{n} = \binom{r+s+1}{m+n+1}$ for $n,m,s\in\mathbb{N}_0$ with $n\geq s$ ([6;p.58]).

Thus, $p_{in}(n,m)=\tau^{-1}(n,m)\,\Omega(n,m)$, where $\Omega(n,m)=\sum_{0\leq\lambda\leq n-m-2}\binom{n-\lambda-2}{m}\binom{n+\lambda-1}{m-1}$.

Now, we have to derive an explicit expression for the sum $\Omega(n,m)$. This can be done as follows: Expanding the second binomial coefficient appearing in the terms of $\Omega(n,m)$, we find $\Omega(n,m)=\Omega_1(n,m)-\Omega_2(n,m)$, where

$$\Omega_1(n,m) = \sum_{0\leq\lambda\leq n-m-2}\binom{n-\lambda-2}{m}\binom{n+\lambda}{m}, \quad \Omega_2(n,m) = \sum_{0\leq\lambda\leq n-m-2}\binom{n-\lambda-2}{m}\binom{n+\lambda-1}{m}.$$

Let us first consider the sum $\Omega_1(n,m)$. We get by the above general identity:

$$\binom{2n-1}{2m+1} = \sum_{0\le\lambda\le 2n-m-2} \binom{2n-m-2-\lambda}{m}\binom{m+\lambda}{m}$$
$$= \sum_{0\le\lambda\le n-m-2} \binom{2n-m-2-\lambda}{m}\binom{m+\lambda}{m} + \sum_{n-m-1\le\lambda\le 2n-m-2} \binom{2n-m-2-\lambda}{m}\binom{m+\lambda}{m}$$
$$= \Omega_1(n,m) + \sum_{-1\le\lambda\le n-2} \binom{n-\lambda-2}{m}\binom{n+\lambda}{m} = 2\Omega_1(n,m) + \binom{n-1}{m}^2 .$$

Using the same procedure for $\Omega_2(n,m)$ and combining our results, we get part (a) of our theorem.□

We obtain immediately by the preceding theorem and Stirling's formula the following

Corollary 3

Let $\mathcal{F}(\Theta)$ be the FSGURPT consisting of all rooted planar trees. We have for fixed $\sigma=m/n$, $0<\sigma<1$:

(a) $p_{in}(n,m) = \frac{1}{2}(1-\sigma)\{\pi(\sigma^{-1}-1)\}^{1/2}n^{3/2} + O(n)$

(b) $p_{ex}(n,m) = \frac{1}{2}\{\pi\sigma(1-\sigma)\}^{1/2}n^{3/2} + O(n^{1/2})$

(c) $p_{ind}(n,m) = \frac{1}{2}(1+\sigma)\{\pi(\sigma^{-1}-1)\}^{1/2}n^{3/2} + O(n)$

(d) $p_{exd}(n,m) = \frac{1}{2}(1+\sigma)\{\pi\sigma/(1-\sigma)\}^{1/2}n^{3/2} + O(n)$.□

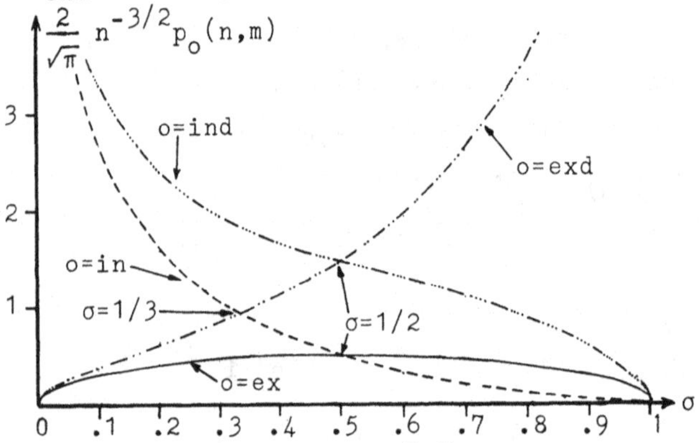

Figure 2. The average path lengths of a rooted planar tree as a function of the proportion σ of the number of leaves m to the whole number of nodes n.

References

[1] Bender,E.A.: Central and Local Limit Theorems Applied to Asymptotic Enumeration, *J. Comb. Theory (Ser.B)* 15, 95-111 (1973)

[2] Bender,E.A.: Asymptotic Methods in Enumeration, *SIAM Rev.* 16(4), 485-515 (1974)

[3] Flajolet,Ph., Odlyzko,A.: The Average Height of Binary Trees and Other Simple Trees, *JCSS* 25(2), 171-213 (1982)

[4] Kemp,R.: On the Average Oscillation of a Stack, *Combinatorica* 2(2), 157-176 (1982)

[5] Kemp,R.: The Average Height of Planted Plane Trees with M Leaves, *J. Comb. Theory (Ser.B)* 34(2), 191-208 (1983)

[6] Knuth,D.E.: The Art of Computer Programming, vol.1, 2nd ed., Addison Wesley, Reading, Mass. 1973

[7] Knuth,D.E.: The Art of Computer Programming. vol.3, Addison Wesley, Reading, Mass. 1973

[8] Meir,A., Moon,J.W.: On the Altitude of Nodes in Random Trees, *Can. Math.* 30, 997-1015 (1978)

FROM EXPANDERS TO BETTER SUPERCONCENTRATORS WITHOUT CASCADING

ELI SHAMIR

Institut of Mathematics and Computer Science
Hebrew University, Jerusalem.

Abstract

Superconcentration is a strong property of interconnection diagraphs. We characterize its negation by existence of two disjoint and seperated sets which shrink under the forward and backward neighbor relation, respectively. This enables a better, non-cascaded design of superconcentrators, explicit ones with edge density ≤ 118, random ones with edge density ≤ 13.

Introduction

Consider a digraph $G = (V, E)$ where $V = I + N + O$, + denotes a disjoint set union. Vertices in I are inputs, vertices in O are outputs, G is a *superconcentrator* (abbreviated SC), if for every source - sink pair (A, B) - $A \subseteq I$, $B \subseteq O$, $|A| = |B| = k$, there exist k - vertex - disjoint paths from A to B.

The search for economic, linear SCs with K.m edges (where $|I| = |O| = m$) attracted considerable attention. The standard design is based on a cascade of shrinking pieces H_i, where each piece is a bipartite graph with nice concentration properties. An explicit construction of such pieces is given in [2,4] resulting is a SC of about 270 edges.

Using the existence of these H_i and the latest result had about $36m$ edges for a non-explicit SC.

Our key observation is that cascading is superfluous. By a deeper analysis of the SC property, we arrive at much better direct designs, random and explicit.

In section 1, we use Menger's Theorem to prove Theorem 1.1, characterizing the path property " G is non SC " by a direct neighbor propery, the existence of two disjoint and seperated sets T_I and T_O which shrink under forward and backward neighbor relation, respectively. Thus universal non - shrinking (on expansion) up to half the size of G implies superconcentration.

In section 2 we piece together explicit expander graphs in a double trapezoid design to get superconcentrators of edge density ≤ 118. In section 3 we force expansion on every vertex by an equi - probable neighbors choice and get full spaces of random superconcentrators of edge density ≤ 13.

1. A Characterization of Superconcentrators

Consider an interconnection digraph of the form

(1.1) $G = (V, E)\ ,\ V = I + N + O\ ,\ E \subseteq (I + N) \times (N + O)$

We are interested in vertex - disjoint paths from inputs (of I) to outputs (of O). In particular G is a *superconcentrator* if

(1.2) for each $A \subseteq I\ ,\ B \subseteq O\ ,\ |A| = |B| = k$ *there exists* k disjoint path from A to B

For a set $T \subseteq V$, we take the forward and backward neighbors

(1.3)
$$\Gamma(T) = \{y \in N \mid (x,y) \in E \text{ and } x \in T\}$$
$$\Gamma^*(T) = \{x \in N \mid (x,y) \in E \text{ and } y \in T\}$$

Note that we restrict neighbors to N, and disregard "express" edges $(x,y) \in I \times O$.

THEOREM 1.1 : Assume a graph G of the form (1.1) is not a superconcentrator, then there exist sets A, B, A', B', F satisfying the relations.

(1.4) $A \subseteq I\ ,\ B \subseteq O\ ,\ A' + B' + F \subseteq N\ ,\ |F| < |A| = |B| = k$

(1.5) $\Gamma(A + A') \subseteq F + A'\ ,\ \Gamma^*(B + B') \subseteq F + B\ ,\ E(A', B') = \phi$

These disjoinness and size relations state that F , $A + A'$, $B + B'$ are disjoint; T_I and T_O are shrinked by Γ and Γ^* respectively. Conversely, these

relations imply that F is a cut in N, disallowing k disjoint paths from A to B through N.

Proof : This is a simple consequence of Menger's Theorem. One can find a triplet (A, B, F) such that the source - sink pair (A, B) violates (1.1) and a set F, $|F| < k$, seperating A from B. For the triplet with minimal k and minimal $F \cap (A + B)'$ there are no "express" edges from A to B and actually $F \subseteq N$, since by (1.1) a vertex $x \in A \cap F$ (say) seperates itself only and can be dropped together with a $b \in B$ from the triplet. Now let

(1.6) $\quad A' = \{x \in N - F \mid \textit{there is a path in } G - F \textit{ from } A \textit{ to } x\}$

then clearly $\Gamma(A + A') \subseteq A' + F$. Similarly, $y \in B'$ if there is a path from y to $b \in B$. Then $\Gamma^*(B + B') \subseteq B' + F$. Finally an edge from $A + A'$ to $B + B'$ or a common vertex, will establish a path from A to B avoiding F which is impossible.

Two observations are useful in the sequel. First,

(1.7) $\quad \mathit{Min}\ \{|A'|, |B'|\} \le \frac{|N| - |F|}{2} \le \frac{|N|}{2}$.

Secondly, we may assume all self - loops (x, x), $x \in N$ are edges. By (1.5), this will not increase $\Gamma(A + A')$ or $\Gamma^*(B + B')$.

2. An Explicit Superconcentrator with 205m Directed Edges but only 118m edges.

A bipartite digraph $H = (C, D, E)$ where $E \subseteq C \times D$ is α - concentrating if

(2.1) $\quad$ for *all* $A \subseteq C\ [|A| \le \alpha |C|$ *implies* $|\Gamma(A)| \ge |A|]$

This condition is more interesting if $|D| < |C|$. Consider now the double trapezoid design G depicted in Figure 1a, where $V = I + O + N$. The set of edges E_C consists of the edges of the bipartite digraph $H_1(N + I, N, E_1)$

edges E_G consists of the edges of the bipartite digraph $H_1(N + I , N , E_1)$ plus the edges of $H_2(N + O , N , E_2)$ *in reverse*, plus "identity edges" from number i in I to number i in O.

LEMMA 2.1 : If each trapezoid is $\frac{1}{2}$ - concentrating then G is a superconcentrator. [see also proof of Th. 2.2].

PROOF : Assume (1.2) is violated by (A , B). Due to the identity edges, we may assume $k = |A| \le \frac{m}{2}$ (where $m = |I|$). We take the smaller shrinking set provided by Theorem 1.1. We may assume it is $A + A' \subseteq I + N$ and

(2.2) $\quad |A + A'| \le \frac{n+m}{2} \; , \; \Gamma_N(A + A') < |A + A'|$

(we observed that Γ_N accounts also for all self - loops (x , x) , $x \in N$). But even the edges of the first trapezoid H_1, which is $\frac{1}{2}$ - concentrating, already contradict (2.2).

In [2], an explicit expander $D(N , N , E)$ is constructed. This is a bipartite digraph with 1 edges (including $j \longrightarrow j$) coming out of each $v \in N$ and

$$\text{for all } X \subseteq N \; , \; |\Gamma(X)| \ge |X| \cdot (1 + d_0 \frac{|N - X|}{|N|})$$

where $d_0 > \frac{2}{15}$. Further, a $\frac{1}{2}$ - concentrator

(2.3) $\quad H(I + N , N , E_H)$, with $|N| = 15|I|$

is obtained as follows: Take the edges of the above expander from N to N. Also, the range N is divided into 15 parts equal to $|I|$, and I is connected to each part in a 1 – 1 fashion. This H has $(7 \times 15 + 15 \times 1)m = 120m$ edges.

Now the double trapezoid based on (2.3) will have at most $(2 \times 105 + 1)m = 211m$ edges. We gained $(15 + 15)m$ by not counting the edges $j \longrightarrow j$ of D which became self - loops in the double trapezoid G. We can gain six more, and many more if we count undirected edges.

THEOREM 2.2 : The double trapezoid design (Figure 1a) provides explicit superconcentrators of edge - density ≤ 205. *If the trapezoids* H_1 , H_2 *are isomorphic, the undirected edge - density is* ≤ 118.

PROOF : From (1.1) it follows that (2.2) can be improved and

$$(2.4) \qquad \alpha = \frac{|A + A'|}{n + m} \leq [A' + (N - |F|)/2]/(n + m)$$

For $|A| \leq \frac{m}{2}$ and $|F| = |A| - 1$, the maximal ratio α is obtained for $|A'| = \frac{m}{2}$ where it value is $\frac{n}{2} - \frac{m}{4}$ (plus 1 if both m and $n - \frac{m}{2} + 1$ are even, but anyway this 1 is negligable). The ratio will be $\leq \frac{14}{29}$ if $n = 14.5m$.

Now if we take 14.5 instead of 15 in (2.3), the trapezoid H (with the I part still having out - degree 15 into N but expansion ratio 14.5)will be β - concentrating with $\beta > \frac{14}{29}$. Then the double trapezoid must be a superconcentrator with edge density ≤ 205. (we gained $6 \times \frac{1}{2} \times 2$ edges).

If H_1 is isomorphic to H_2 then for $u, v \in N$

$$(u , v) \in H_1 \Longrightarrow (u , v) \in H_2 \Longrightarrow (v , u) \in G$$

So the total number of edges is $[14.5 \times 6 + 15 + 15 + 1]m = 118$.

3. Superconcentrators of $13m$ = (*random* 8 + 5)m edges

Here we replace the explicit expander $N \Longrightarrow N$ by a random one. Each vertex of N chooses in an equiprobable manner d neighbors in N. We leave the edges $I \Longrightarrow N$, $N \Longrightarrow O$ as before : N is devided into equal pieces of size $m = |I|$, each piece is connected to I, and O, in a $1 - 1$ fashion. This gives an optimal $\frac{n}{m}$ - expansion. We also leave the $I \Longrightarrow O$ identity edges $i \longrightarrow i$. This hybrid design, depicted in Figure 1b, defines a probability space of random digraphs with parameters (n , m , d), each G has $n \cdot d$ random directed edges.

THEOREM 3.1 : For $n = 2m$, $d = 4$

(3.1) $\quad Prob\ \{G \text{ is not a } SC\} = o(1)\ ,\ m \Rightarrow \infty$

The edge density is 13 = (*random* 8 + 2 + 2 + 1).

PROOF : Assume G is not a SC. There is a pair violating (1.2). We use Theorem 1.1. Since $I \Rightarrow N$ is a 2 - expander, it is clear that

(3.2) $\quad A' + F \subset N\ ,\ \Gamma(A') \subset A' + F\ ,\ t = |A'| \geq |F|$

Similarly for B (with Γ^*). We may assume A' is the smaller one and due to the identity edges $I \Rightarrow O$, $|A| \leq \frac{m}{2}$ and

(3.3) $\quad S = |A' + F| \leq \frac{n}{2} + \frac{m}{4} = \frac{5}{8}n$

The expactation of a configuration in N satisfying (3.2) , (3.3), with parameters s , t, is

(3.4) $\quad \binom{s}{t}\cdot\binom{n}{s}\cdot\left(\frac{s}{n}\right)^{td}\left(\frac{n-t}{n}\right)^{(n-s)d}$

Set

(3.5) $\quad s = \sigma n\ ,\ t = \alpha s = \alpha\sigma n\ ,\ \alpha \geq \frac{1}{2}$

For small s , t the expression (3.4) is $O[n - (\alpha d - 1)s]$. Since $d = 4$, the expectation tends to O even after summing over all possible (small) values of s , t.

In general, we factor out from (3.4)

$$\binom{n}{s}\sigma^{s}(1-\sigma)^{n-s} \text{ and } \binom{s}{t}\sigma^{t}(1-\sigma)^{s-t}\ ,$$

which clearly tend to O. We are left with

(3.6) $\quad \sigma^{\sigma(d\alpha - \alpha - 1)n}\cdot(1-\alpha\sigma)^{(1-\sigma)dn}\cdot\left(\frac{1}{1-\sigma}\right)^{(1-\alpha\sigma)n}$

It suffices to check (3.6) for $\alpha = \frac{1}{2}$ and $\sigma_{max} = \frac{5}{8}$. In $\log_2$ - scale we have

$$n[\frac{1}{2}\sigma \log \sigma + 4(1-\sigma)\log(1-\frac{\sigma}{2}) - (1-\frac{\sigma}{2})\log(1-\sigma)]$$

For $\sigma_{max} = (.625)$ we get

$$n[-(.212) - (.810) + (.962)] = [-.06]n$$

This concludes the proof. Actually we can take d slightly below 4.

REMARK 3.1 : If one tests all small sets X, $|X| \le L$ for non - shrinking and all $O(n^k)$ tests succeed, then

$$Prob\ (G \text{ is non } SC) = O(n^{-L})$$

Thus one can cheaply increase one's confidence in a chasen graph to any desired level.

4. Concluding Remarks

Once a digraph is established to be a superconcentrator, the actual constructor of k disjoint paths from A to B is done by a standard maxflow algorithm.

Our results show that the edge - density threshold for random graph to be SC is very near the threshold for connecting and perfect matching (cf. [5]). Using the design 1b, but giving each edge independently the probability p to occur, we get a random graph space of $G_{n,p}$ type. Using Theorem 1.1 we get that for $p > \log n / n$, the threshold for connectivity, superconcentration also holds almost surely. This is related to our results about factors in [6], but is actually simpler. Analogous results for flows in planar lattices are proved in [3].

Acknowledgements :

Even simple arguments take time and discussions. Together with Eli Upfal we analysed the non - cascaded random design in Figure 1b on the basis of a moderate expansion result. The shrinking condition was found later, with a complicatedproof. Nogah Alon suggested and Nathan Linial insisted that Menger's Theorem will give a simpler argument and a better condition, and contributed to the final form of Theorem 1.1.

REFERENCES

[1] L.A. Bassalygo, Asymptotically optimal swiching circuits. *Problems of Information Transmission* (1981), 206-211. [in Russian].

[2] O. Gabber and Z Galil, Explicit construction of linear size superconcentrators. *Proc. of IEEE 20th FOCS Conference* 1971, 364-370.

[3] G.R. Grimmett and H. Kesten, First - passage perculation, network flows and electrical resistances 1982 (to appear).

[4] G. A. Margulis, Explicit construction of concentrators. Problems of Information Transmissiom 9 (1973), 71-80 [in Rusian, English translation plenum 1975]

[5] E. Shamir and E. Upfal, 1 - factor in random graphs based on vertex choice. *Discrete Math. 41* (1982), 281-286.

[6] E. Shamir and E. Upfal, On factors in random graphs. *Israel J. of Math. 39* (1981), 296-301.

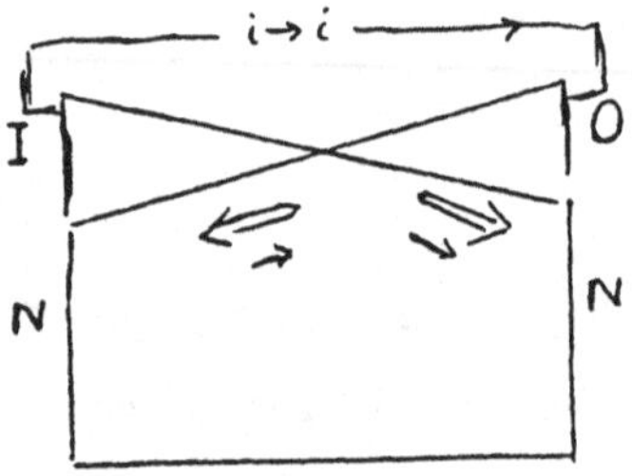

Figure 1a

The double trapezoid

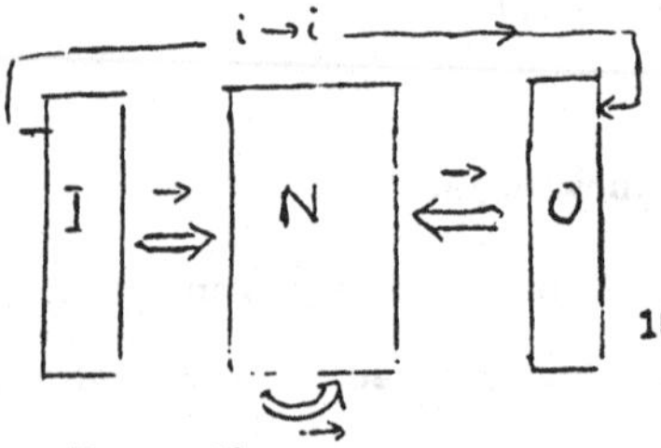

10

Figure 1b

a random design

Edges introduction follow double arrow, edge direction in the digraph follow single arrow.

LOCALLY SYNCHRONOUS COMPLEXITY

IN THE LIGHT OF THE TRANS-BOX METHOD

(Extended Abstract)

Edward G. Belaga
C.N.R.S.
Université Louis Pasteur
67084 Strasbourg Cédex, France

> When pouring balm from one flask into another, the oil easily passes, but the perfume evaporates.
> Midrash-Rabbah, Canticles 1.3.

1. Introduction.

This text is a brief survey of our paper [10] which will appear elsewere. Its aim is a presentation of the new theory of straight-line algorithms, or circuits, namely : the transparent-box (trans-box, or TB-) method [3-10]. To this end we begin by formalizing the notion of a circuit over an arbitrary operator domain and its functional representation. Then we proceed to three (nontraditional) operation modes of a circuit and introduce, on the base of these modes, a new technique of "lower-bounds-to-circuits-complexity" proving.

And we finish with a description of the general notion of an operation mode which we have arrived at in our search for an adequate, insightful, and creative framework for investigation of circuits and the circuits complexity. In particular, in this framework can be naturally unified and become of indistinguishable difference so called structured and (instead of vs, as in [12]) general circuits models.

2. Circuit.

A circuit can be defined over an arbitrary operator base $\{K, \Omega\}$, with K being a set and Ω an operator domain over K (see e.g. [13]). Syntactically, a circuit is a linear list of operators from Ω which can use repeatedly as arguments foregoing items of the list together with a finite number of fixed input symbols : this definition includes both Boolean [19] and arithmetical [1], as well as mixed Boolean-arithmetical (as in ALGOL), continuous (as in A. Kolmogorov's solution of Hilbert's XIII-th problem [17]), and other circuits.

As a model of computation, circuits were introduced by Shannon [20] for Boolean computations and by the author [1, 2] for arithmetical ones. In spite of their simplicity, circuits and the corresponding (combinational, or circuits) complexity measure play an outstanding rôle in modern complexity investigations of both sequential [11, 19] and parallel [15, 16] computations.

3. Shannon representation.

Semantically, a circuit turns out to be a much more complicated and powerful instrument than it is traditionally anticipated. Usually, nobody suspects here a trap, and all the more, - a trapdoor to a hoard. As people say [16 ; p. 79], if a circuit $\mathfrak{A}$ has m inputs and n outputs, then $\mathfrak{A}$ computes a function

$$(3.1) \quad f : K^m \to K^n$$

"in an obvious way". We have precised (see any of the papers [3-6]) this naïve definition and have called the function (3.1) the Shannon (S-)representation of a circuit :

$$(3.2) \quad f = \underline{\mathrm{rep}}(\mathfrak{A}, S) = S(\mathfrak{A}) .$$

Such thoroughness is obligatory : a circuit has other functional representations as well (§§ 6, 7, 10).

Let $\mathfrak{U}(K, \Omega)$ be a set of all circuits over $\{K, \Omega\}$, and $\mathfrak{F}(K)$ be a set of all functions f (3.1) over K . Then S-representation is a mapping (3.2) :

$$(3.3) \quad S : \mathfrak{U}(K, \Omega) \to \mathfrak{F}(K) .$$

4. Circuits complexity.

Let $\mathfrak{A}$ be a circuit over $\{K, \Omega\}$ and f its S-representation (3.1-2). Then the size of $\mathfrak{A}$,

$$s = \mathrm{size}(\mathfrak{A}) ,$$

i.e. the length of the corresponding list of operators, can be naturally regarded as the cost of the realization of f by $\mathfrak{A}$.

Let now $\mathfrak{F}_1$ be a subset of $\mathfrak{F}(K)$ and $\mathfrak{U}_1$ be a subset of $\mathfrak{U}(K, \Omega)$ (see § 3); examples : sets of linear [7] , bilinear [8] , monotone (both Boolean and arithmetical) [19, 21] functions and circuits, sets of synchronous and locally-synchronous (both Boolean [5] and arithmetical [6]) circuits. And let us suppose that (3.3)

$$(4.1) \quad \mathfrak{F}_1 \subseteq S(\mathfrak{U}_1) .$$

Then for any $f \in \mathfrak{F}_1$ can be defined its circuits complexity with respect to $\mathfrak{U}_1$:

$$(4.2) \quad c(f, \mathfrak{U}_1) = \min\{\text{size}(\mathfrak{A}) | \mathfrak{A} \in \mathfrak{U}_1 \ \& \ f = S(\mathfrak{A})\} .$$

This very natural measure of complexity is closely related to computational time for sequential computations and, when the total number of processors is uniformly bounded, for parallel computations as well (if we assume that the computation of an operator from Ω takes a unit of time).

We shall write simply $c(f)$, or $c(f ; K, \Omega)$, instead of (4.1), if the set $\mathfrak{U}_1 = \mathfrak{U}(K, \Omega)$ includes all circuits over $\{K, \Omega\}$.

Sometimes, it is necessary to deal with a restriction of a function f over K^m to a subset K_1^m, $K_1 \subset K$ (and $f(K_1^m) \subset K_1^n \subset K^n$), and/or a restriction of realizations of f over $\{K, \Omega\}$ to a base $\{K_1, \Omega_1\}$, $K_1 \subset K$, $\Omega_1 \subset \Omega$ (i. e. use $\mathfrak{U}(K_1, \Omega_1)$ instead of the bigger set $\mathfrak{U}(K, \Omega)$). Then one has to distinguish between different mesures $c(f ; K, \Omega)$ and $c(f ; K_1, \Omega_1)$, and we have obviously :

$$(4.3) \quad c(f ; K, \Omega) \le c(f ; K_1, \Omega_1) .$$

5. <u>The problem.</u>

<u>Let</u> f <u>and</u> $\mathfrak{U}_1(K, \Omega)$ <u>be given ; find</u> $c(f, \mathfrak{U}_1)$. Indeed, this problem comprises two different and central for all complexity theory problems, the first one of "pure" constructive nature (find a circuit $\mathfrak{A} \in \mathfrak{U}_1$ realizing f), and the second a "pure" theoretical one (prove that $\mathfrak{A}$ gives the minimum in (4.2)).

Explicitely, they were for the first time stated, in just this form, and completely solved in [1, 2] in a concrete case ; namely, for complex polynomials of one variable, $f \in \mathbb{C}[x] = \mathfrak{F}_1$ and for circuits with preprocessing,

$$\begin{cases} \mathfrak{A} \in \mathfrak{U}(\mathbb{C}, \Omega), \ \Omega = \{\Omega_1, \Omega_2\} , \\ \Omega_1 = \{\alpha+, \alpha-, \alpha., \alpha: ; \alpha \in \mathbb{C}\} , \quad \Omega_2 = \{+, -, ., :\} . \end{cases}$$

These results remain a dream for almost all other interesting functions. Namely, the constructive problem (which is really more important, taking in consideration direct applications) was successfully solved for such functions as number and matrix multiplications (NM and MM), discrete Fourier transform (DFT), etc.(see the surveys [11, 21]). But the second problem, even in its modest form, -

PROBLEM 5.1. Find an effective lower bound to $c(f, \mathfrak{U}_1)$.

- remained until recently surprisingly stubborn. However, without a solution of this problem, one never can be sure that any constructed algorithm is optimal.

This "samewhat embarassing state of affairs in computational complexity" [12 ; p. 48] is now substantially improved : using the TB-method, we have already arrived [7] at a general nontrivial lower bound to linear circuits complexity of a linear function over an arbitrary field $\mathbb{K}$. The proof of the corresponding lower bound to DFT-complexity is in preparation [9], as well as lower bounds to bilinear circuits complexity of bilinear functions [8], including the MM-case. One of our goals here is to describe a general "lower-bounds-to-circuits-complexity" proving scheme. And as the first step in this direction, we formulate [6] :

6. Multipurpose-Thesis.

A circuit $\mathfrak{A}$ can be used for computational purposes according to different modes of operation, and the Shannon mode (§ 3) is only one of them.

Let μ be such a mode of operation (see § 10 for a general definition, § 7 for examples, and our papers [3-6, 10] for detailed exposition). Then, according to μ, $\mathfrak{A}$ computes a function

(6.1) $g = \underline{\text{rep}}(\mathfrak{A}, \mu) : K^p \to K^q$,

where p and q depend on $\mathfrak{A}$ and μ. Using notations of § 3, we have :

(6.2) $\mu : \mathfrak{U}(K, \Omega) \to \mathfrak{F}(K)$.

The consclusive power of the TB-method is based, in particular, on the possibility to compare one functional representation of $\mathfrak{A}$ to others.

7. Injection, Ejection, and Mincing modes.

Let $\mathfrak{A}$ be a circuit over a base $\{K, \Omega\}$ with m inputs, n outputs, size s, and depth d :

(7.1) $$\mathfrak{A} = \mathfrak{A}(m, n, s, d) = \mathfrak{A}(m, n, s, d ; K, \Omega) .$$

Then (see our papers [3-6]) $\mathfrak{A}$ computes according to the Injection mode the function

(7.2) $$G = \underline{\mathrm{rep}}(\mathfrak{A} ; I) : K^{m(d+1)} \to K^{s} ,$$

according to the Ejection mode, - the function

(7.3) $$H = \underline{\mathrm{rep}}(\mathfrak{A} ; E) : K^{s} \to K^{n(d+1)} ,$$

and according to the Mincing mode, - the function

(7.4) $$F = \underline{\mathrm{rep}}(\mathfrak{A} ; M) : K^{m(d+1)} \to K^{n(d+1)} ,$$

so that the following diagram is commutative :

(7.5) $$\begin{array}{ccc} K^{m(d+1)} & \xrightarrow{\quad F \quad} & K^{n(d+1)} \\ & {\scriptstyle G} \searrow \quad \nearrow {\scriptstyle H} & \\ & K^{s} & \end{array}$$

8. Lower bound to a circuit size.

For some sets K and operator domains Ω, an image of a mapping

$$g : K^{p} \to K^{q} ,$$

produced as a superposition of operators from Ω, can be naturally supplied with a structure of a "manifold", so it can be defined a finite "dimension" of $\mathrm{Image}(g) \subseteq K^{q}$. Those are, e.g., the cases

(8.1) $$K = \mathbb{B},\ GF(p^{r}),\ \mathbb{Q},\ \mathbb{R},\ \mathbb{C} .$$

Then, according to the diagram (7.5), one has for a function F (7.4) :

(8.2) $$\dim(\mathrm{Image}(F)) \le \mathrm{size}(\mathfrak{A}) .$$

This fundamental inequality represents, in our opinion, the most far going generalization of the dimension idea for the "lower-bounds-to-complexity" proving, which was firstly hinted at by T. Motzkin [18] and established by the author [1, 2].

Here are some applications of (8.2).

If $K = \mathbb{R}$ is a real field and Ω is its natural arithmetical domain, then a function F has (almost everywhere) a Jacobian $\mathcal{J}(F)$, and according to (8.2),

(8.3) $\quad \operatorname{rank}(\mathcal{J}(F)) \le s = \operatorname{size}(\mathfrak{A})$.

Another interesting aspect of the inequality (8.2) : if $K' \subset K$ is an extension of a field K' by another field K, then dim(Image(F)) depends on a choice of the basic field. This fact demonstrates the very important sensibility of our method to change of a base $\{K, \Omega\}$ (cf. the inequality (4.3)).

9. Mincing complexity.

On conditions of §§4, 8, we can define the mincing complexity of a function f with respect to $\mathfrak{U}_1(K, \Omega)$:

(9.1) $\quad m(f, \mathfrak{U}_1) = \min\{\dim(\mathrm{Image}(F)) \mid f = S(\mathfrak{A}) \;\&\; F = M(\mathfrak{A}) \;\&\; \mathfrak{A} \in \mathfrak{U}_1\}$.

Now, according to (8.2), we have

(9.2) $\quad m(f, \mathfrak{U}_1) \le c(f, \mathfrak{U}_1)$,

so any lower bound to m(f) is at the same time a lower bound to c(f) :

PROBLEM 9.1. Find an effective lower bound to $m(f, \mathfrak{U}_1)$.

The definition (9.1) seems rather complicated, if compared with (4.2), but the object of matter is much more simpler : it is a function F instead of an algorithm (circuit) $\mathfrak{A}$.

And the function F is much more tractable because it is connected with the function f of (9.1) by a number of simple functional equations [5, 6].

10. The general notion of an operation mode.

"Any machine worth the name will want to communicate with its environment by means of suitable input and output facilities" [14 ; p. 1].

Returning to the subject of circuits after more then twenty years, the author ventures to contend that the seminal ideas of his papers [1, 2] were oversimplified and, subsequently, overused : along with the dimension method [11, 21], it was introduced there an algorithmical procedure of reorganizing a circuit which can be regarded as the first example of an operation mode. But the perfume evaporated ...

A general (but still effective, if compared to Definition 10.1 below), definition of an operation mode [4] includes three separate and essential but not completely reciprocally independent parts :

(1) a description of an input domain together with a mode (procedure) of input ;
(2) a description of an output domain together with a mode of output ;
(3) a description of a mode of processing.

Four previously introduced operation modes (§§ 3, 7, [3-6]) are covered by this general definition. (Some applications to VLSI-complexity of these and other special modes will appear elsewere.)

Speaking modern slang, μ-representation is a recursive functor from the category of circuits into the category of functions (see for details [10]).

Here is a "right" general definition :

DEFINITION 10.1. Let $\mathfrak{U}_1(K, \Omega)$ and $\mathfrak{I}_1(K, \Omega)$ be defined as in § 4, and let (4.1) be true. Then an operation mode μ^* is a recursive mapping

(10.1) $\mu^* : \mathfrak{U}_1 \to \mathfrak{U}_1$

and the μ-representation is such a mapping

(10.2) $\mu : \mathfrak{U}_1 \to \mathfrak{I}_1$

that the following diagram is commutative (see (3.3)) :

(10.3)
$$\begin{array}{ccc} \mathfrak{U}_1 & \xrightarrow{\ \mu\ } & \mathfrak{I}_1 \\ & {\scriptstyle \mu^*}\searrow \quad \nearrow{\scriptstyle S} & \\ & \mathfrak{U}_1 & \end{array}$$

Therefore, for any $\mathfrak{A} \in \mathfrak{U}_1$ we have :

$g = \underline{rep}(\mathfrak{A}, \mu) = \underline{rep}(\mu^*(\mathfrak{A}), S)$.

Obviously, for practical reasons such a general recursivness of the definition must be restricted ; see for details [4, 10] .

11. Locally synchronous complexity.

As an application of our general proving scheme (§§ 4, 10), let us discuss here at some length the locally synchronous (LS-)case (see for details [5, 6]).

DEFINITION 11.1. A circuit $\mathfrak{A}$ is called locally synchronous (LC-circuit) if for any pair (a, b) of an input a and output b all paths from a to b have the same length $\ell(a, b)$ (which can be different for different pairs). Then $\mathfrak{U}^{\ell s}$ is the subset of all LS-circuits, and (4.2)

(11.1) $\ell sc(f) = c(f, \mathfrak{U}^{\ell s})$.

DEFINITION 11.2 [5]. LS-circuit is called synchronous (S-circuit) if $\ell(a, b) =$ const.(i.e. if all paths from inputs to outputs have the same length). Then $\mathfrak{U}^s$ is the subset of all S-circuits, and (4.2)

(11.2) $sc(f) = c(f, \mathfrak{U}^s)$.

The following inequalities are trivial corollaries of the definitions (4.2) (11.1), (11.2) and the inclusions $\mathfrak{U}^s \subsetneq \mathfrak{U}^{\ell s} \subsetneq \mathfrak{U}$:

$$c(f) \le \ell sc(f) \le sc(f) .$$

THEOREM 11.3 [5, 6]. If $K = \mathbb{B}, \mathbb{Q}, \mathbb{R}$, or $\mathbb{C}$ (with natural operator domains Ω) then there exists a function

$$g^0 : K^m \to K^m \quad , \quad m \ge 6 ,$$

so that

(11.3) $c(g^0) \le \ell sc(g^0) \le 20m < \frac{m-1}{2} \log_2 m \le sc(g^0)$.

The following function is a well known touchstone for various complexity techniques :

$$(11.4)\quad \begin{cases} g^* : K^{2m} \to K^m \\ g_1^* = x_1 \cdot y_1 + x_2 \cdot y_2 + \ldots + x_m \cdot y_m \\ g_2^* = x_m \cdot y_1 + x_1 \cdot y_2 + \ldots + x_{m-1} \cdot y_m \\ \ldots \\ g_m^* = x_2 \cdot y_1 + x_3 \cdot y_2 + \ldots + x_1 \cdot y_m \end{cases}$$

where the signs $\{+\,,\ .\}$ of operations stand for :

(1) arithmetical case : as usually ;
(2) Boolean case : OR and AND respectively .

The definition (11.4) can be also expressed in words : g^* is the product of a circulant $C(x_1, x_2, \ldots, x_m)$ and a vector $y \in K^m$.

THEOREM 11.4 [5, 6]. $m\log_2 m + m/2 \le \ell sc(g^*)$.

Compare this result with the well known conjecture :

$$m\log_2 m \le c(g^*) .$$

The notion of a locally synchronous (LS-) circuit is of independent interest : it is based on the least restrictive condition (among recently existing) on a circuit.

Another application of the TB-method (namely : a nonlinear lower bound to linear complexity of almost all linear functions over $K = \mathbb{R}$ or $\mathbb{C}$) can be found in [7] .

12. <u>Concluding remarks.</u>

12.1. In our opinion, introduction of the notion of an operation mode represents a new step in our understanding of how a circuit works and dramatically improves our methods of complexity investigations for both sequential and parallel computations.

12.2. Moreover, the same approach can be applied to some other models of computation, both sequential and parallel, excluding may be various sorts of Turing machines. We hope to return to this theme in due course.

12.3. Our general lower bounds proving scheme (§§ 7-9) instigates some questions about the algebraic meaning of "lower-bounds-to-complexity" problem and some implications of the related solutions [1, 2, 7-9] for algebra, algebraic geometry and number theory. We intend to elucidate some of these questions elsewhere.

Acknowlegements.

My interest in the themes of this paper dates back to my friendly discussions with my teachers and colleagues, Professors V. I. Arnold, A. N. Kolmogorov, Yu. P. Ofman and A. G. Vitushkin, in Moscow, during the late Fifties.

I am deeply grateful to my French colleagues for the assistance and hospitality, and especially to Professors C. Choffrut, P. Cohendet, J. Françon, J.-C. Lafon, M. Mignotte, M. Nivat.

I appreciate the patience [5-8] and excellent printing of Madame Sylvie Braun.

This paper is among the first ones which I hope to bring to the attention of my colleagues after about five years of silence. To leave the Soviet Union in ones forties is a terrible test. To live there until ones forties is a far worse test. I am now able to continue my research only because I have here, as I have had there my L-rd and my friends.

References.

1. E. Belaga. - Some problems involved in the calculation of polynomials (Russian), Dokl. Akad. Nauk SSSR, vol. 123 (1958) 775-777.

2. E. Belaga. - Evaluation of polynomials of one variable with preliminary processing of the coefficients, Problems of Cybernetics, vol. 5 (1964) 1-13.

3. E. Belaga. - An introduction to the trans-box method, Report, Université Louis Pasteur, Strasbourg, France, January 1983.

4. E. Belaga. - The trans-box method fundamentals, Parts 1-3, Université Louis Pasteur, Strasbourg, France, January 1983.

5. E. Belaga. - Through the mincing machine with a layer cake, Part 1, Report, Université Louis Pasteur, Strasbourg, France, Avril 1983.

6. E. Belaga. - Through the mincing machine with a layer cake, Part 2, Report, Université Louis Pasteur, Strasbourg, France, October 1983.

7. E. Belaga. - Through the mincing machine with a layer cake, Part 3 : Linear functions and algorithms, To appear.

8. E. Belaga. - Through the mincing machine with a layer cake, Part 4 : Bilinear functions and algorithms, To appear.

9. E. Belaga. - Rank resistibility, In preparation.

10. E. Belaga. - A new look at a straight-line algorithm, To appear.

11. A. Borodin and I. Munro. - The Computational Complexity of Algebraic and Numerical Problems, American Elsevier, New York, 1975.

12. A. Borodin. - Structured vs general models in computational complexity, Monographie n°30 de l'Enseignement Mathématique, (1982) 47-65.

13. P. Cohn. - Universal Algebra, Harper & Row, New York, Evanston & London, and John Weatherhill, Inc. Tokyo, 1965.

14. J. Conway. - Regular Algebra and Finite Machines, London, 1971.

15. S. Cook. - Towards a complexity theory of synchronous parallel computation, Monographie n°30 de l'Enseignement Mathématique, Université de Genève (1982), 75-100.

16. S. Cook. - The classification of problems which have fast parallel algorithms, Lecture Notes in Computer Science 158, Springer-Verlag, Berlin, etc. (1983) 78-93.

17. G. Lorentz. - Approximation of Functions, New York, etc. 1966.

18. T. Motzkin. - Evaluation of polynomials and evaluation of rational functions, Bull. Amer. Math. Soc., vol. 61 : 2 (1955), p. 163.

19. J. Savage. - The complexity of computing, New York, 1965.

20. C. Shannon. - A symbolic analysis of relay and switching circuits, Trans. AIEE, vol. 57 (1938) 713-723.

21. A. Slisenko. - Complexity problems in computation theory, Russian Math. Surveys, vol. 36, n°6 (1981) 23-125.

A NEW DEFINITION OF MORPHISM ON PETRI NETS
(Extended Abstract)

Glynn Winskel
University of Cambridge
Computer Laboratory
Corn Exchange Street
Cambridge CB2 3QG

Introduction

Petri nets are a fundamental model of concurrent processes and have a wide range of applications (see [Br], [Pe]). In this paper we address the problem of how to structure nets, define constructions on them and understand the behaviour of a compound process, represented as a net, from the behaviour of its components. The constructions follow from a new definition of morphism on Petri nets--it is not the same as Petri's original. The morphisms respect the "token game"--the dynamic behaviour of nets--unlike Petri's. The category of nets with the new morphisms has a product which is closely related to various parallel compositions which have been defined on labelled Petri nets for synchronising processes (see e.g. the compositions on nets defined in [LSC] and section 3). It has a coproduct which is a generalised form of the "sum" operation as used for example in [M]. There are pleasing relations with other categories too.

One can use Petri nets to give semantics to programming languages. But, what is the semantics of nets? In themselves nets are complicated objects whose behaviour is rather intricate. When, for instance, do Petri nets have the same behaviour? Attempting to answer these questions leads naturally to occurrence nets first introduced in [NWP1,2]. Occurrence nets form a subcategory which bears a pleasant relation to the larger category of nets; the inclusion functor has a right adjoint which is an operation taking a net to its unfolding to a net of condition and event occurrences. (This construction was introduced in [NWP1,2, W] but without this abstract characterisation.) It is argued that the meaning, or semantics, of a net is its occurrence net unfolding so that two nets are regarded as having essentially the same behaviour if they have isomorphic unfoldings. In a similar way there is an adjunction between the category of occurrence nets and the category of (prime) event structures. Thus allied with the work of [W1,2] there are functors which serve as a bridge between Petri net models and the interleaving models used in e.g. [M] and [HBR].

These successes give force to the new definition of morphism on nets. They counter a criticism frequently levelled at Petri nets, that their mathematics is unwieldy.

Unfortunately for lack of space all proofs have been omitted. They will be included in a report of the Computer Laboratory, University of Cambridge.

1. Petri nets

Petri nets model processes in terms of how the occurrences of events incur changes in local states, called conditions. This is expressed by a causal dependency (or flow) relation between sets of events and conditions, and it is this structure which determines the dynamic behaviour of nets once the causal dependency relation is given a natural interpretation.

1.1 Definition. A Petri net is a 3-tuple (B,E,F) where
B is a non-null set of conditions
E is a set of events, and
$F \subseteq (B \times E) \cup (E \times B)$ is the causal dependency relation which satisfies the restriction $\{b \in B \mid bFe\}$ is non-null for all events $e \in E$.

Nets are often drawn as graphs in which events are represented as boxes and conditions as circles with directed arcs between them to represent the flow relation. Here is an example.

1.2 Example.

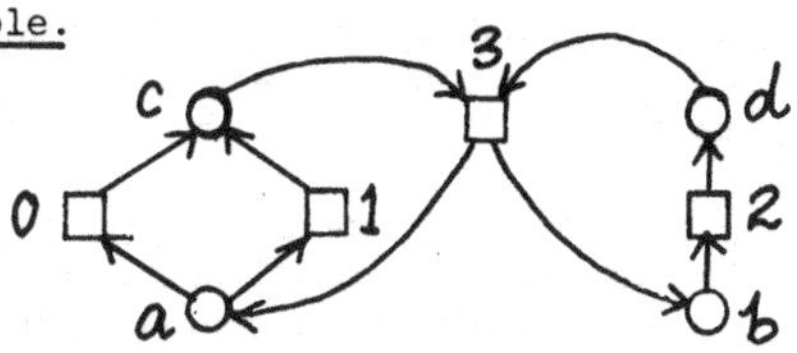

1.3 Notation. Let N = (B,E,F) be a net. Let $A \subseteq B \cup E$.
Define $^{\bullet}A = \{y \in B \cup E \mid \exists a \in A.\ yFa\}$ and
$A^{\bullet} = \{y \in B \cup E \mid \exists a \in A.\ aFy\}$.
When A is a singleton $\{a\}$ we abbreviate $\{a\}^{\bullet}$ to $a^{\bullet}$ and $^{\bullet}\{a\}$ to $^{\bullet}a$. When e is an event we call $^{\bullet}e$ its set of preconditions and $e^{\bullet}$ its postconditions.

The dynamic behaviour of nets is based on these principles which specify how the occurrence of events affect the holding of conditions--a condition is said to hold when it is true. They express the intended meaning of the causal dependency relation.

(i) An occurrence of an event e ends the holding of its preconditions $^{\bullet}e$ and begins the holding of its postconditions $e^{\bullet}$.

(ii) (a) The holding of a condition b, when it ends, ends because of the occurrence of a unique event in $b^{\bullet}$.
(b) The holding of a condition b, when it begins, begins because of the occurrence of a unique event in $^{\bullet}b$.

Of course we need a way to specify what conditions hold. We introduce an idea of global state which just specifies what subset of conditions hold.

1.4 Definition. A marking of a net is a non-null subset of conditions.

The marking of a net changes over time according to rules, commonly called "the token game" because a marking is often specified by laying tokens on those conditions in the marking; as events occur tokens are picked-up and put-down in accord with the principles above. From the principles it follows, only informally, of course, that an event can occur only once all its preconditions hold and none of its postconditions which are not preconditions hold. Then the event is said to have concession. Nets allow more than one event to occur together but there are situations where the occurrence of one event excludes the occurrence of another and vice versa - a phenomenon called conflict. Consider two events which both have concession but which have a precondition in common. From the principle (ii)(a) it follows that only one of them can occur; otherwise they would both end the holding of the condition b. They are in forwards conflict. Now consider two events which both have concession but which have a postcondition in common. By (ii)(b) only one of them can occur. They are in backwards conflict. We formally define the token game which specifies how the marking changes as events occur.

1.5 Definition. (The token game) Let N = (B,E,F) be a Petri net. Let M be a marking. Say an event $e \in E$ has concession at M iff $^{\bullet}e \subseteq M$ & $(e^{\bullet} \setminus {}^{\bullet}e) \cap M = \emptyset$.
Let e,e' be events with concession at M. Say e and e' are in forwards conflict at M iff $e \neq e'$ & $^{\bullet}e \cap {}^{\bullet}e' \neq \emptyset$.
Say they are in backwards conflict at M iff $e \neq e'$ & $e^{\bullet} \cap e'^{\bullet} \neq \emptyset$.
Let M and M' be markings. Let A be a finite subset of E. Define $M \xrightarrow{A} M'$ iff

(i) $\forall e \in A.$e has concession at M and
(ii) $\forall e,e' \in A.$e,e' are not in conflict, and
(iii) $M' = (M \setminus {}^{\bullet}A) \cup A^{\bullet}$.

In this situation the events A are said to occur concurrently.

A marking M' is said to be reachable from a marking M iff $M = M_0 \xrightarrow{A_0} M_1 \xrightarrow{A_1} \cdots \xrightarrow{A_{n-1}} M_n = M'$ for subsets of events $A_0, A_1, \ldots, A_{n-1}$ and markings $M_0, M_1, \ldots M_n$.

Remark. There are other versions of the token game in which more than one token is allowed on a condition; conditions are allowed a certain multiplicity so that they can model, for example, the availability of a number of resources. We shall not allow more than one token on a condition, partly for simplicity and partly because it is intended that more complicated nets should ultimately be abbreviations for the simpler nets we consider (see e.g. [GR]). The nets we consider are almost, but not quite, those nets called condition-event systems in [Br].

1.6 Example. Consider the net of example 1.2. Initially the net is marked {a,b}. The events 0, 1 are in both forwards and backwards conflict so either 0 or 1, but not both can occur. Certainly the event 2 can occur. It is not in conflict with either 0 or 1 so 2 can occur concurrently with 0 or 1, but not both. For example, taking M' = {c,d} and A = {0,2} we have $M \xrightarrow{A} M'$. Of course from the marking M' the event 3 can occur giving rise to the marking M again, and we can start all over again, perhaps letting event 1 occur this time.

Generally a process is modelled by a Petri net with an initial marking from which it reaches other markings as events occur.

1.7 Definition. A Petri net with initial marking is a structure (B,E,F,M) where (B,E,F) is a Petri net and M is a marking called the initial marking. Markings reachable from the initial markings are called reachable markings. An event e is said to be in contact at a marking M' if $^\bullet e \subseteq M' \,\&\, (e^\bullet \setminus {}^\bullet e) \cap M' \neq \emptyset$.

A net with initial marking is contact-free iff there is not contact at any reachable marking.

The event e in the net 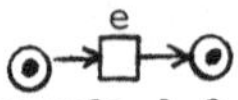 is in contact and the net  is not contact-free. The net of example 1.2 with initial marking {a,b} is contact-free however.

Contact-free nets have the pleasant property that an event can occur at a reachable marking iff its preconditions are included in the marking. If one accepts the earlier principles, the behaviour of nets with contact is weird; it seems an event is prevented from occurring by the knowledge of what would happen in the future if it did--see the above examples. For this reason it is difficult to understand their behaviour. Later when we come to associate an occurrence net unfolding with the behaviour of a net--thus giving nets a formal semantics in terms of more basic nets--we shall be able to do this only for nets which are contact-free. One view of nets with contact is that they are improper descriptions. As has been remarked, there are other token games in which conditions can have multiple holdings. For such nets the above principles are invalid. The understanding of such nets is less settled; for example the question of how to unfold such a net to an occurrence net (as in §5) is unsettled, though a start has been made in [GR].

2. The new definition of morphism on nets

Our definition of morphism on nets involves binary relations, sometimes specialised to being partial or total functions. Here are the elementary notations, properties and operations on relations we shall use:

2.1 Notation. A relation from a set X to a set Y is a subset $R \subseteq X \times Y$. When $(x,y) \in R$ we write xRy. A relation R has an opposite or (converse) relation, R^{op}, given by $R^{op} = \{(y,x) \mid xRy\}$. Clearly $xRy \Leftrightarrow yR^{op}x$.

When the relation R satisfies the property $\forall y,y' \in Y\ \forall x \in X.xRy \ \&\ xRy' \Rightarrow y = y'$ the relation R is said to be a partial function. A partial function R is said to be total when it satisfies the additional property $\forall x \in X \exists y \in Y.xRy$.

The composition of relations is defined as follows: Let R be a relation from a set X to a set Y and S a relation from the set Y to a set Z. The composition of R with S is the relation $S \circ R$ from X to Z given by $S \circ R = \{(x,z) \in X \times Z \mid \exists y \in Y.xRy \ \& \ ySz\}$. Note the order of the composition which follows that generally used for functions. We shall frequently miss-out the composition symbol $\circ$ and write $S \circ R$ as just SR.

When a relation R is a partial function, and we are thinking of it as taking an argument x and giving a value R(x), it is useful to have a symbol to invoke when the value R(x) does not exist. We use * to represent undefined and so write $R(x) = * \Leftrightarrow \nexists y.xRy$ when R is a partial function from X to Y.

If R is a relation from X to Y and $A \subseteq X$ we define the image of A under R to be the set RA given by $RA = \{y \in Y \mid \exists x \in A.xRy\}$. Note the clash with abbreviated relation composition; any ambiguities can be resolved from the context.

A morphism from a net $N_0 = (B_0, E_0, F_0, M_0)$ to a net $N_1 = (B_1, E_1, F_1, M_1)$ specifies how the dynamic behaviour of N_0 induces the dynamic behaviour of N_1. It consists of two parts.

One is a partial function $\eta \subseteq E_0 \times E_1$ on events where $e_0 \,\eta\, e_1$ means the occurrence of e_0 implies the simultaneous occurence of e_1. Think of the event e_1 as being a component of the event e_0. We assume an event e_1 only occurs in N_1 if some e_0 occurs in N_0 with $e_0 \eta e_1$.

The other part of the morphism is a relation $\beta \subseteq B_0 \times B_1$ between conditions. A relation $b_0 \,\beta\, b_1$ means the holding of b_0 implies the coincident holding of b_1 i.e. when b_0 begins or ends holding then so does b_1 --they have the same extent. We assume a condition b_1 holds in N_1 only if there is a unique condition b_0 which holds in N_0 with $b_0 \,\beta\, b_1$.

This understanding implies several properties of a morphism $(\eta, \beta): N_0 \rightarrow N_1$ which we take as our formal definition below. Firstly every condition which holds initially in N_1 should be the image under β of a unique condition which holds initially in N_0 property (i). Secondly if $b_0 \,\beta\, b_1$ the occurrence of an event beginning the holding of b_0 should imply the simultaneous occurrence of an event beginning the holding of b_1, and similarly the occurrence of an event ending b_0 should imply the simultaneous occurrence of an event ending b_1, property (ii). Thirdly if $e_0 \,\eta\, e_1$ the occurrence of e_0 should imply the conditions $^{\bullet}e_1$ end holding and the conditions $e_1^{\bullet}$ begin holding which gives property (iii).

2.2 Definition. Let $N_i = (B_i, E_i, F_i, M_i)$ be nets for i=0,1. Define a morphism of nets from N_0 to N_1 to be a pair of relations (η, β) with $\eta \subseteq E_0 \times E_1$, a partial function, and $\beta \subseteq B_0 \times B_1$ such that:

(i) $M_1 = \beta M_0$ and $\forall b_1 \in M_1 \exists! b_0 \in M_0.\ b_0 \beta b_1$,

(ii) If $b_0 \beta b_1$ then $\eta \cap ({}^{\bullet}b_0 \times {}^{\bullet}b_1)$ is a total function ${}^{\bullet}b_0 \rightarrow {}^{\bullet}b_1$
and $\eta \cap (b_0^{\bullet} \times b_1^{\bullet})$ is a total function $b_0^{\bullet} \rightarrow b_1^{\bullet}$,

(iii) If $e_0 \eta e_1$ then $\beta^{op} \cap ({}^{\bullet}e_1 \times {}^{\bullet}e_0)$ is a total function ${}^{\bullet}e_1 \rightarrow {}^{\bullet}e_0$
and $\beta^{op} \cap (e_1^{\bullet} \times e_0^{\bullet})$ is a total function $e_1^{\bullet} \rightarrow e_0^{\bullet}$.

If further η is total we say the morphism (η, β) is synchronous. When η and β are total functions we say the morphism (η, β) is a folding. When η and β are the inclusion relations $\eta: E_0 \subseteq E_1$ and $\beta: B_0 \subseteq B_1$ we say N_0 is a subnet of N_1.

Subnets provide the simplest example of morphisms on nets. They have a simple characterisation and arise naturally by restricting a net to a subset of events.

2.3 Proposition. Let $N_0 = (B_0, E_0, F_0, M_0)$ and $N_1 = (B_1, E_1, F_1, M_1)$ be nets. Then N_0 is a subnet of N_1 iff $B_0 \subseteq B_1, E_0 \subseteq E_1, M_0 = M_1$ and $\forall e_0 \in E_0 \forall b \in B_1 . e_0 F_1 b \Leftrightarrow e_0 F_0 b$,
& $\forall e_0 \in E_0 \forall b \in B_1\ b F_1 e_0 \Leftrightarrow b F_0 e_0$.

2.4 Proposition. Let N = (B,E,F,M) be a net. Let $E' \subseteq E$. Define the restriction of N to E', written $N \upharpoonright E'$, to be (B,E',F',M) where $F' = F \cap ((B \times E') \cup (E' \times B))$. The restriction $N \upharpoonright E'$ is a subnet of N.

Of course morphisms can be more complicated as the following examples show.

2.5 Examples of morphisms:

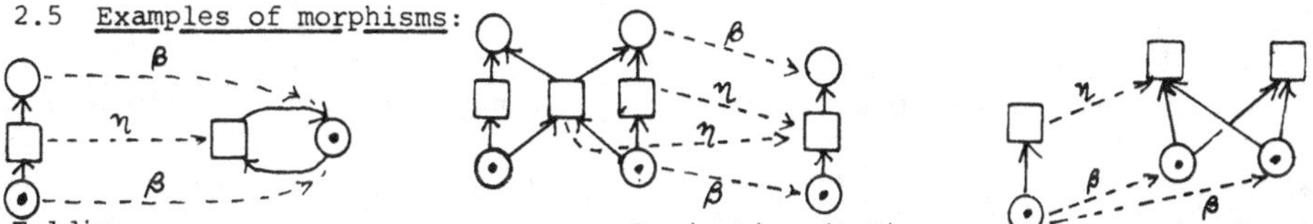

Folding Projection (3.3) Injection (3.9)

When $(\eta, \beta): N_0 \rightarrow N_1$ is a morphism β preserves the pre and postconditions of a set of events. Far more, when N_1 is contact-free the morphism respects the dynamic behaviour of nets; a play of the token game in N_0 induces a play of the token game in N_1. This further justifies our definition of morphism.

2.6 Lemma. Let $(\eta,\beta):N_0 \to N_1$ be a morphism between nets N_0 and N_1. Let A be a subset of the events N_0. Then $\beta({}^{\bullet}A) = {}^{\bullet}(\eta A)$ and $\beta(A^{\bullet}) = (\eta A)^{\bullet}$.

2.7 Theorem. Let $N = (B_i, E_i, F_i, M_i)$ be nets for $i = 0,1$. Let N_1 be contact-free. Let $(\eta,\beta): N_0 \to N_1$ be a morphism of nets. Let C be a reachable marking of N_0 and suppose $C \xrightarrow{A} C'$ in N_0. Then βC is a reachable marking of N_1 and $\beta C \xrightarrow{\eta A} \beta C'$ in N_1. Further, for all reachable markings C of N_0, $\forall b_1 \in \beta C \exists! b_0 \in C. b_0 \beta b_1$.

From now on we shall insist all nets are contact-free. Contact-free nets with morphisms of nets form a category.

2.8 Definition. Define Net to be the category of contact-free nets with morphisms as above and composition given by $(\eta_0,\beta_0) \circ (\eta_1,\beta_1) = (\eta_0 \circ \eta_1, \beta_0 \circ \beta_1)$. Define Net_{syn} to be the subcategory with synchronous morphisms on nets.

3. Categorical constructions

The categorical constructions in Net and Net_{syn} which we introduce will depend on the properties of two more basic categories. One is well-known; it is the category of sets with partial functions. It corresponds to that part of morphisms on nets which act between sets of events. The other is the category of marked sets and corresponds to that part of morphisms on nets which act between sets of conditions while respecting the initial marking.

3.1 Lemma. Let Set_* be the category of sets and partial functions given in definition 2.1. Set_* has products and coproducts of the following form where E_0 and E_1 are sets:

Their product, to within isomorphism, is $E_0 \times_* E_1$ with projections π_0, π_1 where

$$E_0 \times_* E_1 = \{(e_0,*) \mid e_0 \in E_0\} \cup \{(*,e_1) \mid e_1 \in E_1\} \cup \{(e_0,e_1) \mid e_0 \in E_0 \,\&\, e_1 \in E_1\},$$

and $\pi_0(x,y) = x$, $\pi_1(x,y) = y$.

Their coproduct, to within isomorphism, is $E_0 + E_1 =_{def} \{0\} \times E_0 \cup \{1\} \times E_1$ with injections $in_0(e_0) = (0,e_0)$ and $in_1(e_1) = (1,e_1)$ for $e_0 \in E_0$ and $e_1 \in E_1$.

3.2 Lemma. Define a marked set to be a pair of sets (B,M) where $M \subseteq B$. Define a morphism of marked sets from (B_0,M_0) to (B_1,M_1) to be a relation $R \subseteq B_0 \times B_1$ such that $RM_0 = M_1$ and

$$\forall b_0, b'_0 \in M_0 \forall b_1 \in M_1. b_0 R b_1 \;\&\; b'_0 R b_1 \Rightarrow b_0 = b'_0.$$

Define composition to be the usual composition of relations given in 2.1. Then marked sets with the morphisms above form a category with identity morphisms the identity relations. It has products and coproducts of the following form, where (B_0,M_0) and (B_1,M_1) are marked sets:

Their product, to within isomorphism, is $(B_0 + B_1, M_0 + M_1)$ with projections the relations ρ_0 and ρ_1 given by $(b,0)\rho_0 b$ for $b \in B_0$ and $(b,1)\rho_1 b$ for $b \in B_1$.

Their coproduct, to within isomorphism, is (B,M) with injections ι_0 and ι_1 where

$$B = \{(b_0,*) \mid b_0 \in B_0 \setminus M_0\} \cup \{(*,b_1) \mid b_1 \in B_1 \setminus M_1\} \cup \{(b_0,b_1) \mid b_0 \in B_0 \;\&\; b_1 \in B_1\},$$

$$M = M_0 \times M_1,$$

$$b_0 \iota_0 b \Leftrightarrow \exists b_1 \in B_1 \cup \{*\}.\ b = (b_0, b_1),$$

$$b_1 \iota_1 b \Leftrightarrow \exists b_0 \in B_0 \cup \{*\}.\ b = (b_0, b_1).$$

We shall use the above facts and notation in defining the constructions as nets.

3.3 Definition. (The products of nets) Let $N_0 = (B_0, E_0, F_0, M_0)$ and $N_1 = (B_1, E_1, F_1, M_1)$ be contact free nets. Let $\pi_0 : E_0 \times_* E_1 \to E_0$ and $\pi_1 : E_0 \times_* E_1 \to E_1$ be the projections from the product of sets in Set_* given in 3.1. Let $\rho_0: (B_0 + B_1, M_0 + M_1) \to (B_0, M_0)$ and $\rho_1: (B_0 + B_1, M_0 + M_1) \to (B_1, M_1)$ be the projections from the product of marked sets given in 3.2.

Define the product of the nets, $N_0 \times N_1$, to be the net (B,E,F,M) where $B = B_0 + B_1$, $M = M_0 + M_1$, $E = E_0 \times_* E_1$ and

$$eFb \Leftrightarrow (\exists e_0 \in E, b_0 \in B_0 .\ e\pi_0 e_0 \ \&\ b\rho_0 b_0 \ \&\ e_0 F_0 b_0) \text{ or } (\exists e_1 \in E, b_1 \in B_1 .\ e\pi_1 e_1 \ \&\ b\rho_1 b_1 \ \&\ e_1 F_1 b_1),$$

$$bFe \Leftrightarrow (\exists e_0 \in E, b_0 \in B_0 .\ e\pi_0 e_0 \ \&\ b\rho_0 b_0 \ \&\ b_0 F_0 e_0) \text{ or } (\exists e_1 \in E, b_1 \in B_1 .\ e\pi_1 e_1 \ \&\ b\rho_1 b_1 \ \&\ b_1 F_1 e_1).$$

Define projection morphisms of nets: $\Pi_0 = (\pi_0, \rho_0) : N_0 \times N_1 \to N_0$

$\Pi_1 = (\pi_1, \rho_1) : N_0 \times N_1 \to N_1$.

The product construction can be summarised in a simple picture. Disjoint copies of the two nets N_0 and N_1 are juxtaposed and extra events of synchronisation of the form (e_0, e_1) are adjoined, for e_0 an event of N_0 and e_1 an event of N_1; an extra event (e_0, e_1) has as preconditions those of its components ${}^\bullet e_0 \cup {}^\bullet e_1$ and similarly postconditions $e_0^\bullet \cup e_1^\bullet$.

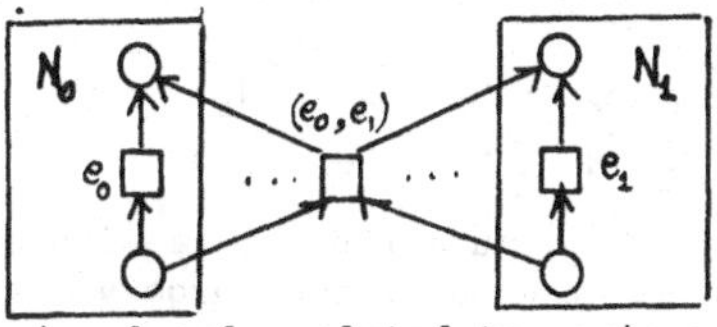

The product on nets is closely related to various forms of parallel composition which have been defined on nets to model synchronised communication--see [LSC]. Imagine that the events of nets are labelled in order to specify how they can or cannot synchronise with events in the environment--the synchronisation algebras of [W1,W2] are a way of formalising this idea. Then the parallel composition of two labelled nets will be modelled as a restriction of the product of those synchronised events--of the from (e_0, e_1)--and those unsynchronised events--of the form $(e_0, *)$ and $(*, e_1)$--allowed by the discipline of synchronisation.

3.4 Theorem. The above construction $N_0 \times N_1$, Π_0, Π_1 is a product in Net, the category of nets.

Of course the token game tells us how we can view a net as giving rise to a transition system in which the arrows between states are associated with sets of events imagined to occur concurrently. Let us see how the product construction looks from this point of view.

3.5 Theorem. Let $N_0 \times N_1$, $\Pi_0 = (\pi_0, \rho_0)$ and $\Pi_1 = (\pi_1, \rho_1)$ be a product of nets. Then M is a reachable marking of $N_0 \times N_1$ and $M \xrightarrow{A} M'$ iff

$\rho_0 M$ is a reachable marking of N_0 and $\rho_0 M \xrightarrow{\pi_0 A} \rho_0 M'$ and
$\forall e, e' \in A\ \forall e_0 \in E_0 .\ e\pi_0 e_0 \ \&\ e'\pi_0 e_0 \Rightarrow e = e'$ and

$\rho_1 M$ is a reachable marking of N_1 and $\rho_1 M \xrightarrow{\pi_1 A} \rho_1 M'$ and
$\forall e, e' \in A\ \forall e_1 \in E_1 .\ e\pi_1 e_1 \ \&\ e'\pi_1 e_1 \Rightarrow e = e'$.

A similar story can be told for Net_{syn}.

3.6 Definition. (Synchronous product) Let $N_0 = (B_0, E_0, F_0, M_0)$ and $N_1 = (B_1, E_1, F_1, M_1)$ be contact-free nets. Define their synchronous product $N_0 \otimes N_1$ to be the restriction $N_0 \times N_1 \lceil (E_0 \times E_1)$ with synchronous projections $\Pi_0' = (\pi_0', \rho_0)$ and $\Pi_1' = (\pi_1', \rho_1)$ where $\pi_0'(e_0, e_1) = e_0$ and $\pi_1'(e_0, e_1) = e_1$.

3.7 Theorem. The above construction $N_0 \otimes N_1$, Π_0', Π_1' is a product of Net_{syn}, the category of nets with synchronous morphisms.

3.8 Example. One can repeat a ticking clock as the simple net $\Omega =$ . Given an arbitrary contact-free net N it is a simple matter to serialise, or interleave, its event occurrences; just synchronise them one at a time with the ticks of the clock. This amounts tc forming the synchronous product $N \otimes \Omega$ of N with Ω.

Now we give the form of coproducts in Net and Net_{syn}.

3.9 Definition. (The coproduct of nets)

Let $N_0 = (B_0, E_0, F_0, M_0)$ and $N_1 = (B_1, E_1, F_1, M_1)$ be contact-free nets.

Let $in_0 : E_0 \to E_0 + E_1$ and $in_1 : E_1 \to E_0 + E_1$ be the injections into the coproduct of sets in $\underset{\sim}{Set}_*$ given in 3.2. Let $\iota_0 : (B_0, M_0) \to (B,M)$ and $\iota_1 : (B_1, M_1) \to (B,M)$ be the injections into the coproduct of marked sets given in 3.3.

Define the coproduct of the nets, $N_0 + N_1$, to be the net (B,E,F,M) where

(B,M) is the coproduct of marked sets

$$E = E_0 + E_1,$$

$$eFb \Leftrightarrow (\exists e_0 \in E_0, b_0 \in B_0 . e_0 \, in_0 \, e \ \& \ b_0 \, \iota_0 \, b \ \& \ e_0 F_0 b_0)$$
$$\text{or } (\exists e_1 \in E_1, b_1 \in B_1 . e_1 \, in_1 \, e \ \& \ b_1 \, \iota_1 \, b \ \& \ e_1 F_1 b_1),$$
$$bFe \Leftrightarrow (\exists e_0 \in E_0, b_0 \in B_0 . e_0 \, in_0 \, e_0 \ \& \ b_0 \, \iota_0 \, b \ \& \ b_0 F_0 e_0)$$
$$\text{or } (\exists e_1 \in E_1, b_1 \in B_1 . e_1 \, in_1 \, e \ \& \ b_1 \, \iota_1 \, b \ \& \ b_1 F_1 e_1).$$

Define injection morphisms of nets:

$$I_0 = (in_0, \iota_0) : N_0 \to N_0 + N_1$$
$$I_1 = (in_1, \iota_1) : N_1 \to N_0 + N_1 .$$

The coproduct construction can be summarised in a simple picture. The two nets N_0 and N_1 are laid side by side and then a little surgery is performed on their initial markings. For each pair of conditions b_0 in the initial marking of N_0 and b_1 in the initial marking of N_1 a new condition (b_0, b_1) is created and made to have the same pre and post events as b_0 and b_1 together--think of it as exclusive or of b_0 and b_1. The conditions in the original initial markings are removed and replaced by a new initial marking consisting of these newly created conditions. Here is the picture:

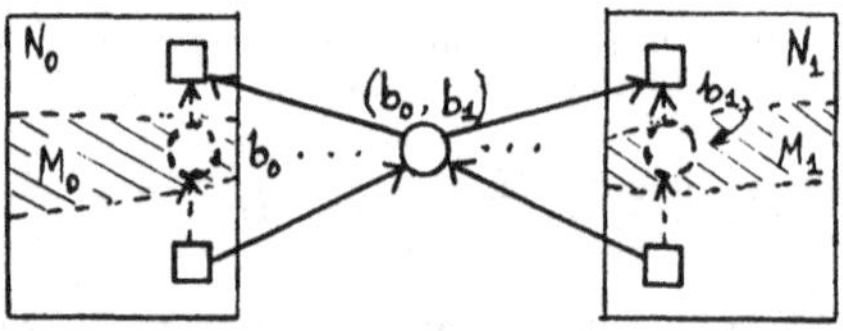

3.10 Theorem. The above construction $N_0 + N_1$, I_0, I_1 is a coproduct in the categories $\underset{\sim}{Net}$ and $\underset{\sim}{Net}_{syn}$.

Again the construction translates over to a natural construction on transition systems.

3.11 Theorem. Let $N_0 + N_1$, $I_0 = (in_0, \iota_0)$ and $I_1 = (in_1, \iota_1)$ be the coproduct of nets. Then M is a reachable marking of $N_0 + N_1$ and $M \to M'$ iff

$$\exists M_0, A_0, M_0' . \ M_0 \xrightarrow{A_0} M_0' \ \& \ A = in_0 A_0 \ \& \ M = \iota_0 M_0 \ \& \ M' = \iota_0 M_0' \quad \text{or}$$
$$\exists M_1, A_1, M_1' . \ M_1 \xrightarrow{A_1} M_1' \ \& \ A = in_1 A_1 \ \& \ M = \iota_1 M_1 \ \& \ M' = \iota_1 M_1' .$$

4. The semantics of Petri nets

Here we show how an occurrence net, in which conditions and events stand for occurrences, can be associated with a contact-free net. The occurrence net we associate with a contact-free net will be built up essentially by unfolding the net to its occurrences. This unfolding is a canonical representative of the behaviour of the original net. Occurrence nets and the operation of unfolding a net to an occurrence net were first introduced in [NPW1,2 and W] and the reader should look there for more motivation. (Note causal nets were rechristened "occurrence nets" in [Br]--such nets are not as general as the ones here.)

In general because of the presence of backwards conflict that part of a net causing an event or condition need not be unique. We wish events and conditions of an occurrence net to correspond to occurrences (as in the case for Petri's causal nets). From this point of view backwards conflict is undesirable as it allows a holding of a condition to occur in more than one way, so we impose (i). Following this view we ban loops in the F^+ relation and ensure any occurrence depends on only a finite number of event occurrences —axiom (iii) — and insist no event is in conflict with itself —axiom (iv). For occurrence nets there is an especially simple definition of a concurrency relation and conflict relation which was previously only defined with respect to a marking. We take the initial marking to consist of those conditions such that $^{\cdot}b = \emptyset$.

4.1 Definition. An occurrence net is a net (B,E,F,M) for which the following restrictions are satisfied:

(i) $\forall b \in B. |{}^{\cdot}b| \leq 1$,

(ii) $b \in M \Leftrightarrow {}^{\cdot}b = \emptyset$,

(iii) F^+ is irreflexive and $\forall e \in E.\ \{e' \in E | e' F^* e\}$ is finite.

(iv) # is irreflexive where $e \#_1 e' \underset{def}{\Leftrightarrow} e \in E \ \& \ e' \in E \ \& \ {}^{\bullet}e \cap {}^{\bullet}e' \neq \emptyset$ and

$$x \# x' \underset{def}{\Leftrightarrow} \exists e,e' \in E. e \#_1 e' \ \& \ e F^* x \ \& \ e' F^* x'.$$

Suppose N = (B,E,F,M) is an occurrence net. We call the relation $\#_1$ defined above the immediate conflict relation and # the conflict relation. We define the concurrency relation, co, between pairs $x,y \in B \cup E$ by:

$$x \text{ co } y \underset{def}{\Leftrightarrow} \neg(x F^+ y \text{ or } y F^+ x \text{ or } x \# y).$$

4.2 Proposition. Let N = (B,E,F,M) be an occurrence net. Then N is contact-free and every event has concession at some reachable marking and every condition holds at some reachable marking.

Let e,e' be two events of N. Let b,b' be two conditions of N.

The relations $\#_1 \subseteq E^2$ and $\# \subseteq (B \cup E)^2$ are binary, symmetric, irreflexive relations. The relation of immediate conflict $e \#_1 e'$ holds iff there is a reachable marking of N at which the events e and e' are in conflict.

The relation co is a binary, symmetric, reflexive relation between conditions and events of N. We have b co b' iff there is a reachable marking of N at which b and b' both hold. We have e co e' iff there is a reachable marking at which e and e' can occur concurrently.

4.3 Definition. Write Occ for the category of occurrence nets with net morphisms.

We can define the unfolding contact-free net inductively to obtain an occurrence net satisfying the following theorem.

4.4 Theorem. Let N = (B,E,F,M) be a contact-free net. There is a unique occurrence net $\mathcal{N} = (\mathcal{B},\mathcal{E},\mathcal{F},\mathcal{M})$ and folding $f = (\eta,\beta)$ which satisfy:

$\mathcal{B} = \{(\emptyset,b) | b \in M\} \cup \{(\{e'\},b) | e' \in \mathcal{E} \ \& \ b \in B \ \& \ \eta(e') F b\}$,

$\mathcal{E} = \{(S,e) | S \subseteq \mathcal{B} \ \& \ e \in E \ \& \ \beta S = {}^{\bullet}e \ \& \ \forall b',b'' \in S.\ b' \text{ co } b''\}$,

$x \mathcal{F} y \Leftrightarrow \exists w,z.\ y = (w,z) \ \& \ x \in z$,

$\mathcal{M} = \{(\emptyset,b) | b \in M\}$

and $e' \eta e \Leftrightarrow \exists S \subseteq \mathcal{B}.\ e' = (S,e)$,

$b' \beta b \Leftrightarrow (b \in M \ \& \ b' = (\emptyset,b)) \text{ or } \exists e' \in \mathcal{E}.\ b' = (\{e'\}),b)$.

4.5 Definition. Write $\mathcal{U}$N for the occurrence net defined above. Call it the unfolding of N.

4.6 Example. The unfolding of the net of example 1.2 with initial marking {a,b} looks like this:

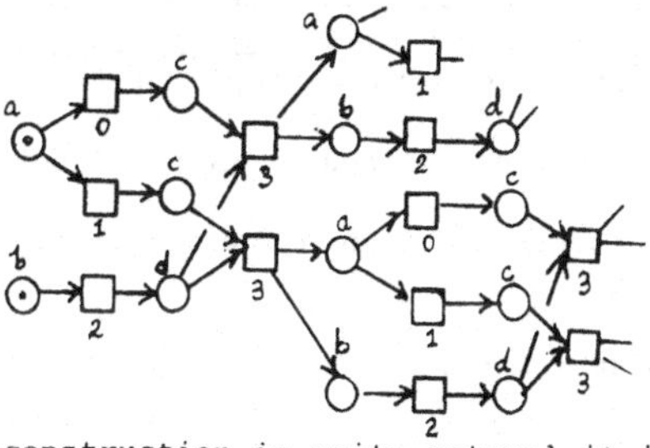

Although the unfolding construction is quite natural it is, by itself, quite unwieldy. Imagine proving for example that unfolding preserves products. Fortunately the unfolding construction has an abstract characterisation which implies such facts immediately. Unfolding is cofree. It is a right adjoint to the inclusion functor

Occ → Net, and right adjoints preserve limits and in particular products (see [Mac]). The unfolding of an occurrence net is naturally isomorphic to the original net which makes this adjunction a coreflection.

4.7 Theorem. Let N be a contact-free Petri net. Then the occurrence net unfolding $\mathcal{U}N$ and folding f are cofree over N i.e. for any morphism $g : N_1 \to N$ with N_1 an occurrence net there is a unique morphism $h : N_1 \to \mathcal{U}N$ such that $f \circ h = g$. In fact Occ is a coreflective subcategory of Net.

Thus, from the coreflection we know the product of two occurrence nets N_0, N_1 in Occ is $N_0 \times_{Occ} N_1 \cong \mathcal{U}N \times_{Occ} \mathcal{U}N \cong \mathcal{U}(N_0 \times_{Net} N_1)$, the unfolding of their product in Net. Although we cannot make the full case here, the coreflection relates parallel compositions using contact-free nets to parallel compositions using occurrence nets and vice versa. The idea is to label events by elements of a synchronisation algebra, specifying how events synchronise, and to obtain parallel compositions by restricting events of the product in accord with the algebra--see [W1,2]. The coproduct of occurrence nets in Occ is their coproduct in Net--this follows from the coreflection. Coproducts are not always preserved by $\mathcal{U}$ however (right adjoints only preserve limits not necessarily colimits). Still they are preserved on a full subcategory of Net with objects those nets whose initial markings consist solely of conditions with no pre-events.

5. A coreflection between nets and event structures

We show there is a coreflection between the category of occurrence nets and a category of event structures. The functors provide a translation between the Petri net model of computation and that based on event structures. The work [W1,2] provides another coreflection which bridges the gap between event structures and synchronisation trees, at the basis of the interleaving models of CCS and CSP (see e.g. [M] and [HBR]). Coreflections compose so relating Petri nets to other established work in concurrency.

The event structures are of the simple form introduced in [NPW1,2]. They are essentially occurrence nets with the conditions stripped away to leave the causal dependency and conflict relations. (They are called prime event structures in [W1].)

5.1 Definition. A (prime) event structure is a triple $(E, \leq, \#)$ consisting of

(i) E a set of events,

(ii) $\leq$ the causal dependency relation, a partial order on E and

(iii) # the conflict relation a binary symmetric relation on E

which satisfy $e \# e' \leq e'' \Rightarrow e \# e''$ and $\{e' \in E \mid e' \leq e\}$ is finite.

Event structures carry a natural idea of configuration (or state), the left-closed, conflict-free subsets of events. Intuitively a configuration is a set of events that occur in some history of a process; it should only be possible for an event to occur once the events on which it causally depends have occurred and it should be impossible for two events in conflict to occur in the same history.

5.2 Definition. Let $(E, \leq, \#)$ be an event structure. Let $x \subseteq E$. Say x is left-closed iff $\forall e, e' \in E. e \leq e' \in x \Rightarrow e \in x$. Say x is conflict-free iff $\forall e, e' \in x. \neg(e \# e')$. Write $\mathcal{L}(E, \leq, \#)$ for the set of left-closed conflict-free subsets.

Clearly an occurrence net determines an event structure.

5.3 Definition. Le $N = (B,E,F,M)$ be an occurrence net. Define $\mathcal{E}(N) = (E, F^* \restriction E, \# \restriction E)$ where # is defined in 4.1.

Event structures possess a definition of morphism which is respected by $\mathcal{E}$ making $\mathcal{E}$ into a functor.

5.4 Definition. Define $\mathbb{P}$, the category of event structures, to have prime event structures as objects and morphisms $\theta : (E_0, \leq_0, \#_0) \to (E_1, \leq_1, \#_1)$ those partial functions $\theta : E_0 \to_* E_1$ which satisfy

$$\forall x \in \mathcal{L}(E_0).\ (\theta x \in \mathcal{L}(E_1)\ \&\ (\forall e,e' \in x.\ \theta(e) = \theta(e) \neq * \Rightarrow e = e'))$$

The identity morphisms are the identity functions and composition is the usual composition of partial functions.

5.5 <u>Theorem.</u> Let $N_i = (B_i, E_i, F_i, M_i)$ be occurrence nets for $i = 0,1$. Let $f = (\eta, \beta) : N_0 \to N_1$ be a morphism of nets. Then $\mathcal{E}f = \eta : \mathcal{E}N_0 \to \mathcal{E}N_1$ is a morphism of event structures, making $\mathcal{E}$ a functor $\underline{\underline{Occ}} \to \underline{\underline{P}}$.

Conversely an event structure can be identified with a canonical occurrence net. The basic idea is to produce an occurrence net with as many conditions as are consistent with the causal dependency and conflict relations of the event structure. But we do not want more than one condition with the same beginning and ending events --we want an occurrence net which is "condition-extensional" in the terms of [Br]. Thus we can identify the conditions with pairs of the form (e,A) where e is an event and A is a subset of events causally dependant on e and with every distinct pair of events in A in conflict. But not quite, we also want initial conditions $(\emptyset, A)$ with no beginning events (see [NPW], though note a small but important change; we introduce the isolated condition $(\emptyset,\emptyset)$.)

5.6 <u>Definition</u>. Let $(E, \leqslant, \#)$ be an event structure. Define $\mathcal{N}(E,\leqslant,\#)$ to be (B,E,F,M) where

$$M = \{(\emptyset, A) \mid A \subseteq E\ \&\ \forall a,a' \in A.\ a(\# \cup 1)a'\},$$
$$B = M \cup \{(e,A) \mid e \in E\ \&\ A \subseteq E\ \&\ (\forall a \in A.\ e < a)\ \&\ \forall a,a' \in A.\ a(\# \cup 1)a'\},$$
$$F = \{((c,A),e) \mid (c,A) \in B\ \&\ e \in A\} \cup \{(e,(e,A)) \mid (e,A) \in B\}.$$

As promised there is a coreflection between event structures and occurrence nets; the construction $\mathcal{N}$ provides the free occurrence net over an event structure.

5.7 <u>Theorem.</u> Let E be an event structure. Then $\mathcal{N}E$ is an occurrence net. Moreover, $\mathcal{E}\mathcal{N}E = E$. In fact $\mathcal{N}E$, $1_E : E \to \mathcal{E}\mathcal{N}E$ is free over E with respect to $\mathcal{E}$ i.e. for any morphism $g : E \to \mathcal{E}N$ in $\underline{\underline{P}}$ with N an occurrence net there is a unique morphism $h : \mathcal{N}E \to N$ in $\underline{\underline{Occ}}$ such that $\mathcal{E}h = \mathcal{E}h \circ 1_E = g$.

5.8 <u>Example.</u> Left adjoints preserve colimits, and so coproducts. Thus by 5.7 we can deduce $\mathcal{N}(E_0 + E_1) \cong \mathcal{N}E_0 + \mathcal{N}E_1$ so $E_0 + E_1 = \mathcal{E}\mathcal{N}(E_0 + E_1) \cong \mathcal{E}(\mathcal{N}E_0 + \mathcal{N}E_1)$, which expresses the coproduct of event structures in terms of the coproduct of nets. Right adjoints preserve limits, and so products. By 5.7 and 4.7 we deduce : $E_0 \times_P E_1 = \mathcal{E}\mathcal{N}E_0 \times_P \mathcal{E}\mathcal{N}E_1 \cong \mathcal{E}(\mathcal{N}E_0 \times_{Occ} \mathcal{N}E_1) \cong \mathcal{E}\mathcal{U}(\mathcal{N}E_0 \times_{Net} \mathcal{N}E_1)$ which expresses the product of event structures in terms of the product of nets.

In fact whole denotational semantics for a wide range of languages ($Proc_L$ of [W1,2]) can be translated back and forth between different models using these techniques. The demonstration of this and the use of "net-embeddings" to define nets recursively must await the complete version of this paper.

<u>Acknowledgements</u> Thanks to Mogens Nielsen and Gordon Plotkin for helpful discussions. Thanks to Alison Emery for the typing which had to be carried out in a hurry. This work was partially supported by the Computer Science Department, Carnegie-Mellon University.

References

[Br] Brauer, W. (editor), Net theory and its applications, Lecture notes in Comp. Sc. No. 84, Springer-Verlag (1979).

[GR] Goltz, U. and Reisig, W., Processes of Place/Transition Nets. Icalp 83.

[HBR] Hoare, C.A.R., Brookes, S.D., and Roscoe, A.W., A Theory of Communicating Processes. Technical Report PRG-16, Programming Research Group, Oxford University (1981).

[LSC] Lauer, P.E., Shields, M.W. and Cotronis, J.Y., Formal behaviour specification of concurrent systems without globality assumptions. Springer-Verlag Lecture notes in Comp. Sc. vol. 107 (1981).

[Mac] Maclane, S., Categories for the Working Mathematician. Graduate Texts in Mathematics, Springer-Verlag (1972).

[M] Milner, R., A Calculus of Communicating Systems. Springer-Verlag Lecture Notes in Comp. Sc. vol. 92 (1980).

[NPW1] Nielsen, M., Plotkin, G., Winskel, G., Petri nets, Event structures and Domains. Proc. Conf. on Semantics of Concurrent Computation, Evian, Springer-Verlag Lecture Notes in Comp. Sc. 70 (1979).

[NPW2] Nielsen, M., Plotkin, G., Winskel, G., Petri nets, Event structures and Domains, part 1. Theoretical Computer Science, vol. 13 (1981) pp. 85-108.

[Pe] Peterson, J.L., Petri Net Theory and the Modelling of Systems. Prentice-Hall (1981).

[W] Winskel, G., Events in Computation. Ph.D. thesis, University of Edinburgh (1980).

[W1] Winskel, G., Event structure semantics of CCS and related languages, Springer-Verlag Lecture Notes in Comp. Sc. 140 (1982). Also as a full version in Report of the Computer Sc. Dept., University of Aarhus, Denmark (1982).

[W2] Winskel, G., Synchronisation trees. ICALP '83, Springer-Verlag Lecture Notes in Comp. Sc. and fully in Technical Report, Comp. Sc. Dept., Carnegie-Mellon University (1983).

BLOCAGE ET VIVACITÉ
DANS LES RÉSEAUX A PILE-FILE.

A. FINKEL

L.R.I. & L.I.T.P.
Université de Paris Sud
Centre d'Orsay - Bât. 490
91405 - ORSAY Cedex - FRANCE.

ABSTRACT. :

We show that under certain structural conditions in a finite biparti valued graph the absence of local deadlock is equivalent to the possibility for the system to have an infinite behaviour.

RESUME. :

Nous montrons que sous certaines conditions structurelles dans un graphe fini biparti valué, on a l'équivalence entre l'absence de blocage local et la possibilité pour le système d'avoir un comportement infini.

I. - INTRODUCTION. :

Le but de ce papier est d'étudier comment, dans un système parallèle, un blocage local peut devenir un blocage global.
Nous avons choisi les réseaux à Pile-File pour modéliser un système parallèle. Les réseaux à Pile-File sont une extension naturelle des réseaux à File [12][7], eux mêmes généralisant les réseaux de Pétri [3][15] qui sont le principal modèle du parallélisme utilisé actuellement. Rappelons qu'un réseau de Pétri est un graphe fini biparti, valué par des nombres entiers, sur lequel on spécifie une règle de franchissements d'une partie des sommets appellés transitions. Les réseaux à File [7] sont des réseaux de Pétri dans lesquels on a remplacé les nombres valuant les arcs par des mots sur un alphabet fini des messages. Les places se comportent alors comme des files modélisant ainsi le fonctionnement FIFO (First In, First Out). Les réseaux à Pile-File sont tout naturellement des réseaux à File dans lesquels ... il y a aussi des piles modélisant le fonctionnement LIFO (Last In, First Out).

Le modèle des réseaux à Pile-File a clairement la puissance des machines de Turing puisque les réseaux à File l'ont déjà [6]. Ainsi il s'agit de définir de "bonnes" sous-classes de réseaux à Pile-File. Nous avons choisi les réseaux à Pile-File Libres ayant une structure Equilibrée-Alimentée.

Un réseau à Pile-File est Libre quand chaque ensemble de mots valuant les sorties de chaque pile (respectivement de chaque file) forme un code à délai de déchiffrement fini [2] . Celui-ci assure que le déchiffrage de la pile et de la file se fait "presque" de manière unique. En effet, si on déclenche une transition qui ne décode pas le mot présent dans la pile p ou dans la file f de manière à assurer l'unicité on sait qu'au bout d'au plus d_p ou d_f franchissements la pile (la file) sera bloquée pour toujours c'est-à-dire toutes les transitions de $\Gamma(p)$ ($\Gamma(f)$) ne seront plus jamais franchissables.

La structure Equilibrée-Alimentée exige que chaque pile, chaque file soit Equilibrée ou Alimentée : une file est Equilibrée lorsqu'elle a autant d'entrées que de sorties et que l'ensemble des mots valuant les entrées est exactement celui valuant les sorties. On sait [8] que les graphes marqués [5] , qui sont une sous-classe importante des réseaux de Pétri, pour laquelle on dispose de beaucoup de résultats [4] [11] , sont "inclus" dans les réseaux à File Equilibrée. Dans [8] nous y avons généralisé la condition nécessaire et suffisante de vivacité connue pour les graphes marqués. Cela suffirait à motiver l'étude des réseaux à Pile-File Equilibrée si ceux ci n'intervenaient pas aussi dans le problème de la sérialisation [9] .

La définition des piles, files Alimentées est duale de celle des piles, files Equilibrées : une pile, file est Alimentée quand chacun des mots valuant ses entrées contient au moins une occurrence de chaque mot valuant ses sorties. De façon intuitive, le déclenchement d'une transition en entrée d'une pile, file Alimentée la remplit suffisamment pour éviter certains blocages dus à des famines.

Notre modèle bien défini, nous cherchons à disposer de critères structuraux (graphiques) assurant l'équivalence entre un blocage local et un blocage global du réseau. L'intérêt de critères structuraux est que la construction d'un arbre de couverture [10] , quand elle est possible, est un procédure non primitive récursive [18] donc très coûteuse. Une foule de résultats "du genre" que nous établirons existent déjà pour les machines à états [11] , les réseaux de Pétri à choix libre [4] [13] , les graphes marqués [5] . Les nôtres sont originaux car les réseaux à Pile-File Libre à structure Equilibrée-Alimentée ne sont inclus dans aucune des classes précédemment citées. Nous définissons quatre applications qui "propagent" un blocage local et à partir de ces applications nous introduisons une relation d'équivalence donc une partition sur l'ensemble des transitions. Nous montrons alors que cette relation d'équivalence structurelle est incluse dans la relation d'équivalence "dynamique" suivante notée P ; P(X, Y) : X est bloqué $\Longleftrightarrow$ Y est bloqué. Nous obtenons donc un critère structurel (graphique) assurant l'équivalence, au niveau du comportement entre deux parties du réseau.

II. - RAPPELS ET DEFINITIONS. :

II. 1. Rappels :

A^* est le monoïde libre sur l'alphabet A. A^ω est l'ensemble des mots infinis sur A et on pose $A^\infty = A^* \cup A^\omega$. Pour $x \in A^\infty$ on note $|x|$ la longueur de x . On notera

$A^{\leqslant k}$ l'ensemble des mots de longueur au plus égale à k. $X \subseteq A^*$ est un code si tout mot de X^* admet une unique factorisation en mots de X, c'est-à-dire si X^* est un monoïde libre. Un code X est à délai de déchiffrement fini (ddf) égal à d si $\forall x_1, x_2 \in X \ \forall u \in A^* \ \forall x \in X^d \ \forall u' \in X^* \quad x_1 u = x_2 x u' \Rightarrow x_1 = x_2$.
Autrement dit une "mauvaise" factorisation est dévoilée au plus tard après le d-ième mot de X.

<u>Exemples</u> : A et $X \subseteq A^*$ préfixe sont deux codes à ddf égal à 0 . $X = \{ab, a\}$ est un code à ddf égal à 1 car il faut lire la lettre après "a" pour savoir comment factoriser : ab mais aab . $X = \{b, ba, aa\}$ n'est pas un code à ddf car pour tout $n \geqslant 1$ on a : $ba(aa)^n = b(aa)^n a$. Ici le délai est infini. Enfin $X = \{a, ab, b\}$ n'est pas un code car $a.b = ab$.
Soit $x \in A^*$, $x = x_1 x_2 \ldots x_k$, $x_i \in A$ on note $\tilde{x}$ le mot miroir de x : $\tilde{x} = x_k x_{k-1} \ldots x_1$.

II. 2. <u>Définition d'un réseau à Pile-File</u> :

Définition : Un réseau à Pile-File est un cinquplet $N = (P \cup F, T, A, V, M_0)$ où

- $P = \{p_1, \ldots, p_r\}$ est un ensemble fini de piles ;
- $F = \{f_1, \ldots, f_p\}$ est un ensemble fini de files ;
- $T = \{t_1, \ldots, t_n\}$ est un ensemble fini de transitions, avec P, F, T deux à deux disjoints ;
- A est un alphabet fini ;
- V est une application de $[(P \cup F) \times T] \cup T \times (P \cup F)$ dans A^* ;
- $M_0 : F \to A^*$ est le marquage initial.

Nous adoptons et adaptons les traditions en usage dans les réseaux de Pétri en représentant un réseau à Pile-File par un graphe fini biparti et valué. Les sommets seront soit des piles soit des files soit des transitions. Un rond représentera une pile ou une file et une barre représentera une transition. Si $V(x, y) = \lambda$ il n'y aura pas d'arc de x vers y . Si $V(x, y) = a \in A^+$ il y aura un arc, étiqueté par a, de x vers y . On notera PB (respectivement FB) l'ensemble des piles bornées (respectivement l'ensemble des files bornées).

Par la suite nous aurons besoin des notations suivantes :

<u>Notations</u> : Pour tout $x \in P \cup F \cup T$ on pose

$\Gamma(x) = \{y \in P \cup F \cup T \ / \ V(x, y) \neq \lambda\}$

$\Gamma^-(x) = \{y \in P \cup F \cup T \ / \ V(y, x) \neq \lambda\}$

On appellera entrées de x les éléments de $\Gamma^-(x)$ et sorties de x les éléments de $\Gamma(x)$

<u>Exemple 1.</u> : Soit N_1 le réseau à Pile-File ci-dessous :

Figure 1. :

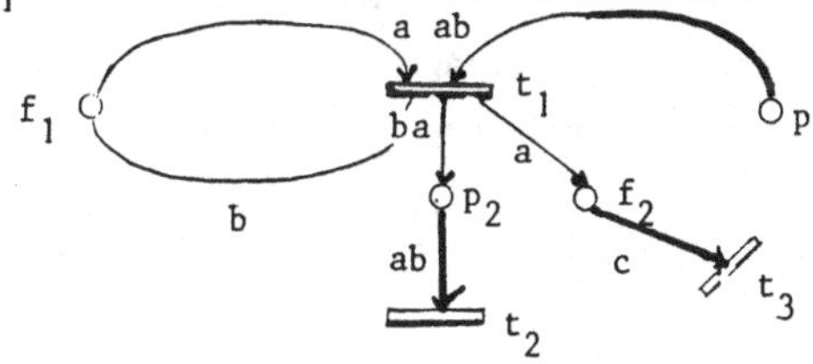

$M_0 = (aab, \lambda, ababa, \lambda)$
f_1, f_2, p_3, p_4

On a $P = \{p_1, p_2\}$, $F = \{f_1, f_2\}$, $T = \{t_1, t_2, t_3\}$, $A = \{a, b, c\}$ et par exemple $V(t_1, p_2) = ba$ ... etc.

II. 3. Fonctionnement d'un réseau à Pile-File.

L'état global d'un réseau à Pile-File est donné par les mots dans chaque pile et dans chaque file du réseau. Par le franchissement d'une transition t, les mots qui sont dans les piles et files entrées ou sorties de t peuvent être modifiés. La règle de fonctionnement des réseaux à Pile-File leur donne une dynamique, en précisant à quelles conditions une transition est franchissable et de quelle manière le frnchissement de celle-ci modifie l'état du réseau.

Un marquage est une application $M : P \cup F \to A^*$, aussi représentée par un vecteur $M \in (A^*)^{r+p}$ avec $r + p = \mathrm{card}(P \cup F)$. $M(x)$ est le mot dans x pour le marquage M. $M_0 = (M_0(f_1), \ldots, M_0(f_p), M_0(p_1), \ldots, M_0(p_r))$.

Définition : Une transition t est franchissable pour un marquage M ssi pour toute pile $p \in P$ $V(p, t)$ est facteur gauche de $\tilde{M}(p)$ et pour toute file $f \in F$, $V(f, t)$ est facteur gauche de $M(f)$.

Dans le cas où t est franchissable pour M, on notera $M(t >$. On définit maintenant le franchissement d'une transition de façon à modéliser le fonctionnement LIFO et FIFO. Plus formellement on a :

Définition : Le franchissement de t à partir de M donne un nouveau marquage M' ; $M(t > M'$ ssi

$$\forall p \in P \quad M'(p) = d(\tilde{V}(p, t), M(p)) . V(t, p)$$

$$\forall f \in F \quad M'(f) = g(V(f, t), M(f)) . V(t, f)$$

où $d(x, yx) = y$ et $g(x, xy) = y$.

Reprenons avec l'exemple 1 le fonctionnement du réseau. A partir de $M_0 = (aab, \lambda, ababa, \lambda)$ je ne peux plus faire que t_1 et j'ai $M_0(t_1 > M_1$ avec $M_1 = (abb, a, aba, ba)$. Puis je franchis t_1 ou t_2. Soit $M_1(t_2 > M_2$ avec $M_2 = (abb, a, ab, \lambda)$ etc. La relation de franchissement est étendue de façon naturelle aux séquences de franchissements ; ainsi on a $M_0 (t_1 t_2 > M_2$.

Définition : Une séquence s de T^* est franchissable pour un marquage M et donne un marquage M' ssi : - $s = \lambda \Rightarrow M' = M$;

- $s = s't$ avec $s' \in T^*$, $t \in T$ alors $\exists M''$ tel que $M(s' > M''$ et $M''(t > M'$.

On dira qu'un marquage M' est accessible à partir de M ssi il existe $s \in T^*$ $M(s > M'$. On notera $[M > = \{M' / \exists s ; M(s > M'\}$ l'ensemble des marquages accessibles à partir de M. L'ensemble des marquages accessibles ("the reachability set") d'un réseau N est $[M_0 >$. On notera $Acc(N) = [M_0 >$.

Enfin on aura besoin de deux langages associés à un réseau à Pile-File N.

$L(N) = \{s \in T^{*} \ / \ M_0(s >\}$

$L^{\omega}(N) = \{u \in T^{\omega} \ / \ \forall\, n \in N^{+} \ M_0(u[n]>\}$ où $u[n]$ est le facteur gauche de u, de longueur égale à n.

II. 4. Evolutions d'un réseau à Pile-File. :

On définit les notions de réseau borné, vivant, équitable et sans blocage de façon similaire à [3].

Définition : Une pile p ou une file f d'un réseau N est bornée si $\exists\, k \in \mathbb{N}$ tel que $\forall\, M \in Acc(N)$ on a $|M(p)|$ ou $|M(f)| \leqslant k$. Un réseau est borné si chaque pile et chaque file du réseau est bornée.

Il est clair que : N borné $\Longleftrightarrow$ Acc(N) fini.

Définition : Une transition t d'un réseau N est vivante si $\forall\, M \in Acc(N)$ $\exists\, M' \in [M >$ tel que $M'(t >$. N est vivant si $\forall\, t \in T$ t est vivante.

Un réseau N est sans blocage si $\forall\, x \in L(N)$ $\exists\, t \in T$; $x\,t \in L(N)$ ou encore $\forall\, M \in Acc(N)$ $\exists\, t \in T$ $M(t >$.

Un réseau N est équitable si N est sans blocage et $\forall\, u \in L^{\omega}(N)$ $\forall\, t \in T$ $|u|_t = \omega$.

On utilisera la Proposition [6] : N équitable $\Rightarrow$ N vivant $\Rightarrow$ N sans blocage.

III. - RESEAUX A PILE-FILE LIBRE. :

III. 1. Définitions :

On définit les réseaux à Pile-File Libre à structure Equilibrée-Alimentée. Puis on construit une relation d'équivalence, associée à quatre applications de propagation des blocages, sur le graphe fini biparti valué.

Notations : $\forall\, i = 1, \ldots, r$ $\quad P_i^{-} = \{V(t, p_i) \ / \ t \in T\}$

$\quad P_i = \{V(p_i, t) \ / \ t \in T\}$

$\forall\, j = 1, \ldots, p$ $\quad F_j^{-} = \{V(t, f_j) \ / \ t \in T\}$

$\quad F_j = \{V(f_j, t) \ / \ t \in T\}$

Définition : Un réseau à Pile-File est Libre ssi :

1) $\forall\, i = 1, \ldots, r$ $\quad P_i$ est un code à ddf égal à d_{p_i}

2) $\forall\, j = 1, \ldots, p$ $\quad F_j$ est un code à ddf égal à d_{f_j}.

Remarque 1. : L'intérêt des réseaux à Pile-File Libre réside dans le fait suivant : soit $x_1 \ldots x_k \in \tilde{P}_i^{k}$ (ou bien F_j^{k}) un mot dans une pile p_i (ou une file f_j) ; si on franchit une transition qui enlève un mot différent de $x_m \ldots x_n$ $\quad 1 \leqslant m \leqslant n \leqslant k$ alors au bout d'un temps fini au plus égal à d_{p_i} (ou d_{f_j}) la pile p_i (ou la file f_j) est bloquée c'est-à-dire que toutes les transitions de $\Gamma(p_i)$ (ou de $\Gamma(f_j)$) sont mortes à partir de M_{p_i} (M_{f_j}) avec $M(x_1\, x_2 \ldots x_{k-d_{p_i}} > M_{p_i}$ (ou bien

$M(x_{k-d_{f_j}} \dots x_k > M_{f_j})$.

Ainsi le "décodage" d'un mot dans une pile p_i (ou dans une file f_j) se fait de manière unique ou s'arrête au bout d'un temps fini égal au délai de déchiffrage du code P_i (ou du code F_j).

Dans toute la suite on étudiera des réseaux à Pile-File Libre dans lesquels les piles et les files sont soit équilibrées soit alimentées.

<u>Définition</u> : Un réseau à Pile-File Libre possède une structure Equilibrée-Alimentée quand :

1) - $\forall\, i = 1, \dots, r$ on a $P_i^- = P_i$ (équilibrée) <u>ou</u> (alimentée) $P_i^- \subseteq (\tilde{P}_i)^*$ et $\forall\, x \in P_i^-$ $\forall\, y \in P_i$ $|x|_y \geq 1$;

2) - $\forall\, j = 1, \dots, p$ on a $F_j^- = F_j$ (équilibrée) <u>ou</u> (alimentée) $F_j^- \subseteq F_j^*$ et $\forall\, x \in F_i^-$ $\forall\, y \in F_i$ $|x|_y \geq 1$

3) - $\forall\, i = 1, \dots, r$ $\forall\, j = 1, \dots, p$ $M_0(p_i) \in (\check{P}_i)^*$ et $M_0(f_j) \in F_j^*$.

<u>Notations</u> : On posera $P = P_1 \cup P_2$ avec $P_1 = \{p_1, \dots, p_s\}$ et $P_2 = \{p_{s+1}, \dots, p_r\}$ et $F = F_1 \cup F_2$ avec $F_1 = \{f_1, \dots, f_q\}$ et $F_2 = \{f_{q+1}, \dots, f_p\}$ avec la légende suivante : 1 : équilibrée 2 : alimentée

Intuitivement une pile ou une file équilibrée est une généralisation [10] d'une place d'un graphe marqué, c'est-à-dire que le déclenchement d'une transition t en sortie de p (ou de f) est conditionné par le déclenchement d'une transition t', en entrée de p (ou f), associée à t de la manière suivante :

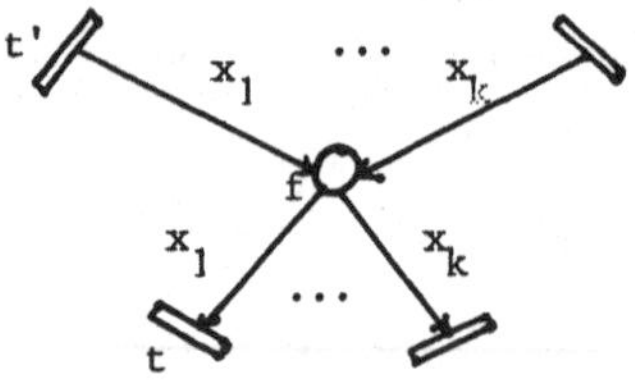

<u>Figure 2</u>

On appellera <u>chemin apparié</u> tout chemin de la forme :

$$t \xrightarrow{x_1} \circ \xrightarrow{x_1} t' \xrightarrow{x_2} \circ \xrightarrow{x_2} t'' \xrightarrow{x_4} \circ \xrightarrow{x_4} t''' \dots$$

Une pile p ou une file f alimentée possède la propriété suivante : si on déclenche une transition t' en entrée de p ou de f alors on a remplit la pile p ou la file f "suffisamment" pour éviter certains blocages sur toutes les transitions t en sortie de p ou de f .

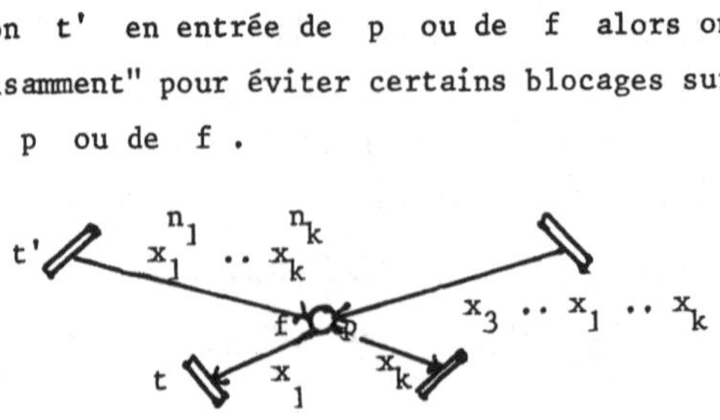

<u>Figure 3</u>

La dernière condition est posée afin d'être sûr qu'à tout moment le mot dans une pile p_i (dans une file f_j) appartient à $(\tilde{P}_i)^*$ respectivement à F_j^*.

<u>Définitions</u> : Pour tout $i = 1,\dots,7$ on définit une suite d'applications $(g_i^k)_{k \geq 1}$ de la manière suivante :

$$g_i = g_i^1 : \begin{array}{l} T \to 2^T \\ t \mapsto g_i(t) \end{array} \quad \text{et} \quad \forall\, k \geq 1 \quad \text{on pose} \quad g_i^{k+1}(t) = g_i(g_i^k(t)) \cup g_i^k(t)$$

1) $g_1(t) = \Gamma(\Gamma^-(t) \cap (F_2 \cup P_2\, B))$ est l'application qui associe à une transition t la <u>chaîne alternée</u> suivante :

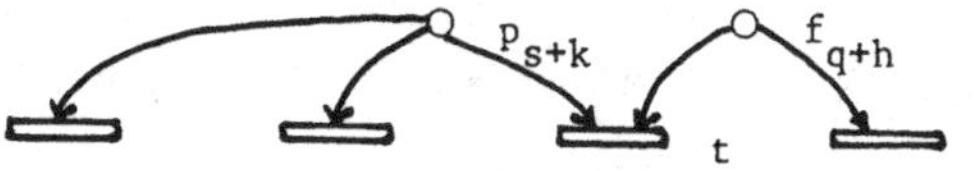

p_{s+k} est bornée.

2) $g_2(t) = \Gamma_e(\Gamma(t) \cap (F_1 \cup P_1))$; g_2 associe à une transition t l'ensemble des transitions qui sont sur un <u>chemin apparié</u> de longueur 1

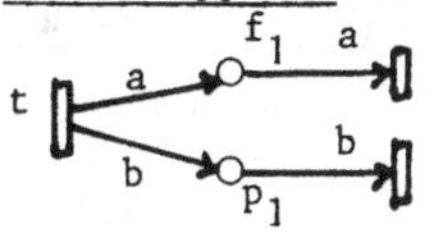

3) $g_3(t) = \Gamma_e^-(\Gamma^-(t) \cap (F_1 \cup P_1))$ est l'application duale de g_2

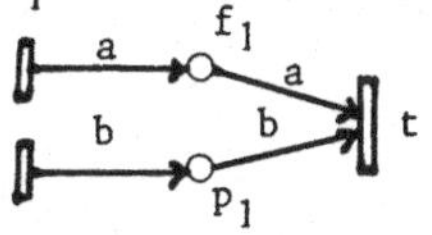

4) $g_4(t) = \Gamma_e(\Gamma(t) \cap (F_1\, B \cup P_1\, B))$ est la restriction de l'application g_2 aux piles et files bornées.

5) $g_5(t) = \Gamma_e^-(\Gamma^-(t) \cap (F_1\, B \cup P_1\, B))$ est la restriction de l'application g_3 aux piles et files bornées.

6) $g_6(t) = \Gamma^-(\Gamma^-(t) \cap (F_2\, B \cup P_2\, B))$

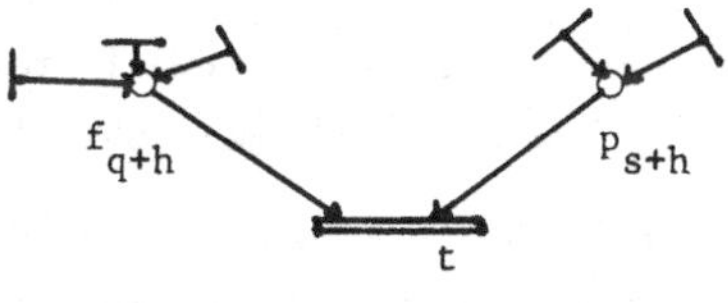

f_{q+h} et p_{s+h} sont bornées.

7) $g_7(t) = \Gamma(\Gamma(t) \cap (F_2\, B \cup P_2\, B))$ est l'application duale de g_6 (au lieu de remonter les transitions en amont de t, on les "descend").

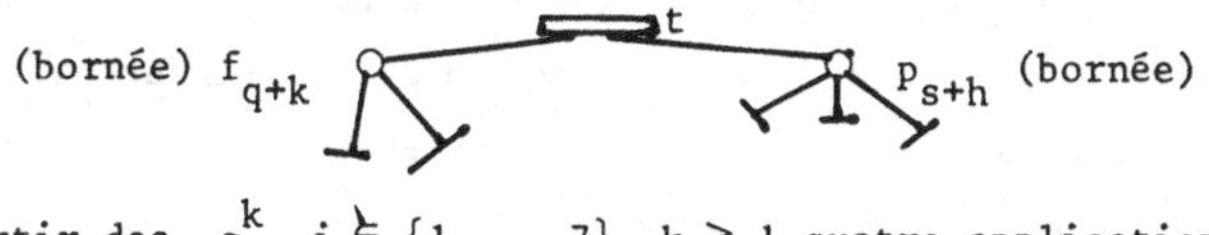

On définit à partir des g_i^k, $i \in \{1,\dots,7\}$, $k \geq 1$ quatre applications h_i de propagation qui auront la bonne propriété suivante : deux transitions t et t' ayant même image par h_i pour $i \in \{1,\dots,4\}$ seront vivantes toutes les deux ou mortes toutes les deux.

DDéfinitions : $h_1(t) = g_1^n(t)$ est la chaîne alternée associée à t .
$h_2(t) = g_2^n(t) \cap g_3^n(t)$ est l'ensemble des circuits appariés contenant t.
$h_3(t) = g_4^n(t) \cup g_5^n(t)$ est l'ensemble des chemins appariés contenant t où les piles et les files du chemin sont bornées.
$h_4(t) = g_6^n(t) \cap g_7^n(t)$ est l'ensemble des circuits alimentés, où les piles et les files sont bornées, passant par t.

Lemme 1. : $\begin{cases} \text{Pour tout } k \geqslant 1 \text{ on a } h_i^k(t) \subseteq h_i^{k+1}(t) . \\ \text{Pour tout } k \geqslant n \text{ on a } h_i^k(t) = h_i^n(t) . \\ \text{Si } h_i^k(t) = h_i^{k+1}(t) \text{ alors } h_i^k(t) = h_i^{k+p}(t) \quad \forall p \geqslant 1 . \end{cases}$

Preuve : Découle immédiatement des définitions. ■

Pour chaque entier $k \geqslant 1$ on définit une relation d'équivalence, notée $\sim_k$, de la manière suivante : $\forall t , t' \in T \quad t \sim_k t' \overset{def}{\iff} \exists\, m \in (h_1, h_2, h_3, h_4)^{\leqslant k}$ tel que $m(t) = m(t')$ et, de façon naturelle, on pose pour $X, Y \subseteq T$

$$X \sim_k Y \overset{def}{\iff} \forall t \in X \quad \forall t' \in Y \quad t \sim_k t'$$

Remarque 2. : Il est clair que pour tout entier $k \geqslant 1$, $\sim_k$ est une relation d'équi valence dans 2^T ; de plus on a $\sim_k \subseteq \sim_{k+1}$.

Remarque 3. : En posant $\sim = \bigcup_{k=1}^{\infty} \sim_k$ on a $\sim = \bigcup_{k=1}^{4n^2} \sim_k$. En effet les applications h_i pour $i = 1, 2, 3, 4$ sont croissantes et "majorées" par le nombre n de transitions.

Définition : On pose $\bar{T} = T / \sim$ et pour tout $X, Y \subseteq T$
$P(X, Y)$: $(\forall M \in (A^*)^{r+p})(\forall t \in X)(\forall t' \in Y)$($t$ franchissable seulement un nombre fini de fois à partir de $M \iff t'$ franchissable seulement un nombre fini de fois à partir de M).

Remarque 4 : Cette relation P est "plus faible" que la relation Q définie par :
$Q(X, Y)$: (X vivant $\iff$ Y vivant) ; on a $P \Rightarrow Q$ mais pas l'inverse.

Remarque 5 : Il est clair que $\forall X, Y, Z \subseteq T$.On a $P(X, X)$, $P(X, Y) \Rightarrow P(Y, X)$, P(X
$P(X, Y)$ et $P(Y, Z) \Rightarrow P(X, Z)$. Autrement dit P est une relation d'équivalence.

Notre but : Tout notre travail, maintenant, est de montrer que la relation d'équivalence $\sim$, qui est structurelle dans le sens qu'elle ne dépend que du graphe biparti valué, est incluse dans la relation d'équivalence P , qui au contraire n'est pas structurelle mais dynamique puisqu'elle relie deux ensembles de transitions qui ont le même comportement vis à vis de la vivacité.

III. 2. Le résultat principal. :

Enonçons le théorème que nous voulons montrer :

Théorème. : Soit N un réseau à Pile-File Libre où les piles et les files sont soit équilibrées soit alimentées. Si card $\bar{T} = 1$ alors N sans blocage $\iff$ N vivant $\iff$ N équitable.

Preuve : Pour démontrer le théorème nous aurons besoin des deux lemmes suivants :

Lemme 2. : $\forall$ i = 1, ..., 4 $\forall X \subseteq T$ $P(X, h_i(X))$.

Lemme 3. : $\forall X, Y \subseteq T$ $X \sim Y \Rightarrow P(X, Y)$.

Il suffira alors de remarquer que card($\bar{T}$) = 1 équivaut à $\forall t \in T$ $\{t\} \sim T$. En utilisant le Lemme 3 on aura pour tout $t \in T$, $P(t, T)$. Ayant déjà vu que N équitable $\Rightarrow$ N vivant $\Rightarrow$ N sans blocage, il nous suffit de montrer que N sans blocage $\Rightarrow$ N équitable ou encore N non équitable $\Rightarrow$ N a un blocage.

Soit donc N non équitable : $\exists u \in L^{\omega}(N)$ $\exists t \in T$ $|u|_t < \omega$ donc il existe un mot fini x tel que u = xv avec $|v|_t = 0$. Autrement dit il existe une transition t qui n'est pas déclenchée à partir de x. Alors le non-déclenchement de t et le fait que $\{t\} \sim T$ impliquent qu'au bout d'un temps fini on ne peut plus déclencher aucune transition de T, c'est-à-dire qu'on est arrivé à un blocage. ■

Exemple 2. :

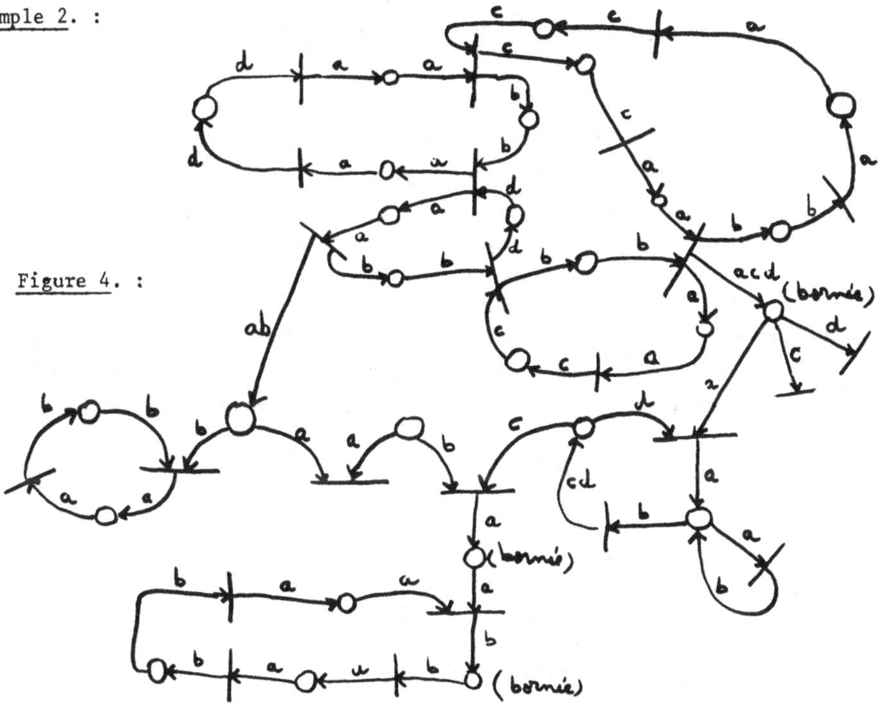

Figure 4. :

Toutes les transitions du réseau sont équivalentes pour la relation $\sim$, d'où l'absence de blocage est équivalent à la vivacité du réseau.

Preuve du lemme 2. : Remarquons qu'on a $\forall$ i = 1, ..., 4 $\forall X \subseteq T$

$$h_i(X) = h_i(\bigcup_{t \in X} \{t\}) = \bigcup_{t \in X} h_i(t)$$

Il nous suffit alors de montrer que $\forall$ i = 1, ..., 4 $\forall t \in T$ $P(t, h_i(t))$; autrement dit $(\forall M)(\forall t \in T)(\forall t' \in h_i(t))$ (t franchissable seulement un nombre fini de fois à partir de M $\Longleftrightarrow$ t' franchissable seulement un nombre fini de fois à partir de M).

1er cas. : $i = 1$ $h_1 = g_1^n$

il s'agit de montrer que $\forall k \geq 1$ $P(t, g_1^k(t))$.

Nous traitons le cas : $k = 1$

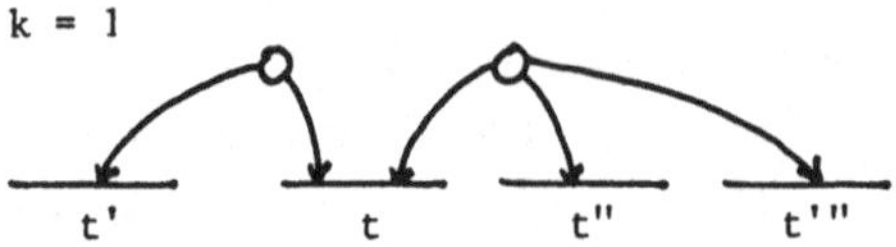

chaîne alternée

figure 5

$g_1^1(t) = g_1(t) = \{t, t', t'', t'''\}$.

Si t n'est franchissable qu'un nombre fini de fois à partir d'un marquage M alors il arrive un moment M à partir duquel t n'est jamais franchissable. En utilisant la remarque 1 on voit que toutes les transitions de $g_1(t)$ sont infranchissables au bout d'un mot fini de longueur au plus égale à

$$\begin{bmatrix} \mathrm{Sup}(d_f, d_p) \\ f \in \Gamma^-(t) \\ p \in \Gamma^-(t) \text{ et bornée} \end{bmatrix} \times \begin{bmatrix} \mathrm{Sup}(|x| \ ; \ x \in P_p \cup F_f) \\ p \in \Gamma^-(t) \text{ bornée} \\ f \in \Gamma^-(t) \end{bmatrix}$$

Toutes les transitions de $g_1(t)$ jouant le même rôle on voit que ce qu'on dit de t reste vrai pour tout $t' \in g_1(t)$; d'où $P(t, g_1^1(t))$.

Il est alors clair que $P(t, g_1^k(t))$ est vrai pour tout $k \geq 2$ donc $P(t, g_1^n(t)) = P(t, h_1(t))$ est vrai, ce qui termine le premier cas.

2éme cas. : $i = 2$ $h_2(t) = g_2^n(t) \cap g_3^n(t)$

Il s'agit de montrer que $P(t, h_2(t))$ est vrai ; autrement dit que toutes les transitions situées sur un circuit apparié contenant t sont infranchissables au bout d'un temps fini si c'est déjà le cas pour t et que si un $t' \in h_2(t)$ est morte alors t aussi.

figure 6. :

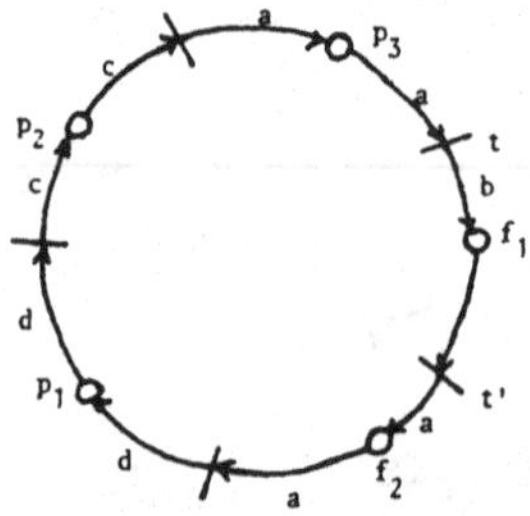

Soit t jamais franchissable à partir de M alors les "b" n'arriveront plus dans f_1. Comme ceux-ci ne viennent que par le déclenchement de t, que $\Gamma(f_1)$ est un code à délai de déchiffrement fini et que f_1 est équilibrée, t' est aussi infranchissable au tout d'un temps (c'est-à-dire un mot) fini x tel que :

$$|x| \leq |M(f_1)| + (d_{f_1}) \times (\mathrm{Sup}\ \{|y| \ ; \ y \in F_1\}) .$$

En continuant ce raisonnement un nombre fini de fois on "bloque" toutes les transitions $t' \in h_2(t)$. Réciproquement il est clair que si une transition t' de $h_2(t)$

est infranchissable à partir de M elle va bloquer au bout d'un temps fini la tran sition t - on a donc $P(t, h_2(t))$ vrai.

3éme cas. : $i = 3 \quad h_3(t) = g_4^n(t) \cup g_5^n(t)$

4éme cas. : $i = 4 \quad h_4(t) = g_6^n(t) \cap g_7^n(t)$.

Les preuves des troisième et quatrième cas ne présentent pas de difficulté particu lière. Ce qui termine la preuve du lemme 2. ■

Donnons la preuve du preuve du Lemme 3.

Rappellons qu'on veut montrer que $\forall X, Y \subseteq T \quad X \sim Y \Rightarrow P(X, Y)$. On raisonne par récurrence sur le "degré"de l'équivalence.

- $X \sim_1 Y \Longleftrightarrow \exists i = 1, \ldots, 4 \quad h_i(X) = h_i(Y)$

Or le lemme 2 nous assure que $P(X, h_i(X))$ et $P(Y, h_i(Y))$ sont vrais donc on a $P(X, Y)$ vrai.

- Supposons que $X \sim_k Y \Rightarrow P(X, Y)$

Soit donc $X \sim_{k+1} Y \Longleftrightarrow \exists i = 1, \ldots, 4 \quad h_i(X) \sim_k h_i(Y)$. Avec hypothèse de récurrence on a : $\exists i = 1, \ldots, 4 \quad P(h_i(X), h_i(Y))$. En utilisant le Lemme 2 on a

$$\left.\begin{array}{l} P(X, h_i(X)) \\ P(Y, h_i(Y)) \\ P(h_i(X), h_i(Y)) \end{array}\right\} \Rightarrow P(X, Y)$$

Le théorème est enfin démontré. ■

Enonçons trois cas particuliers du théorème précédent :

Corollaire 1. : Soit N un réseau à Pile-File Libre borné et connexe tel que $F_1 \cup P_1 = \emptyset$ alors N sans blocage $\Longleftrightarrow$ N vivant $\Longleftrightarrow$ N équitable.

Preuve : Les hypothèses "borné, connexe et $F_1 \cup P_1 = \emptyset$" impliquent que $\mathrm{card}(\bar{T}) = 1$; on applique alors le théorème principal. ■

Corollaire 2. : Soit N un réseau à Pile-File Libre fortement connexe tel que $\forall t \in T, \Gamma^-(t)$ est borné et tel que $F_1 \cup P_1 = \emptyset$ alors

N sans blocage $\Longleftrightarrow$ N vivant $\Longleftrightarrow$ N équitable.

Corollaire 3. : Soit N un réseau à Pile-File Libre tel que les files, piles équilibrées et les piles alimentées soient bornées, tel que les files alimentées soient monogènes alors $\mathrm{card}(\bar{T}) = 1$ implique que l'absence de blocage, la vivacité et l'équité sont équivalents et décidables.

Preuve : Les files alimentées étant monogènes [6] et les autres piles et files étant bornées on peut construire un arbre de couverture qui permet de décider l'absence de blocage donc la vivacité et l'équité en utilisant le théorème principal. ■

IV. - CONCLUSION. :

Nous avons montré que dans les réseaux à Pile-File Libre, il était possible de réduire le nombre de transitions à observer car certaines étaient équivalentes vis à vis de la vivacité. Nous avons ainsi construit une relation d'équivalence structurelle et donc une partition de l'ensemble des transitions du réseau. Nous pensons qu'il est possible de raffiner notre théorème principal en observant les piles et files qui relient un élément de la partition à un autre.

V. - REMERCIEMENTS. :

C'est à Gérard ROUCAIROL que je dois l'intuition qu'il existait des circuits propageant la mortalité d'une transition dans les réseaux à File équilibrée. Par la suite j'ai généralisé cette idée aux réseaux à Pile-File Libre (équilibré et alimenté).

VI. - BIBLIOGRAPHIE. :

[1] C. BERGE. - "Graphes et hypergraphes" - Dunod, Paris 1970.

[2] J. BERSTEL, D. PERRIN, M.P. SCHUTZENBERGER. - "Théorie des codes" - rapport LITP n° 82-33.

[3] G.W. BRAMS. - "Réseaux de Pétri : théorie et pratique" (tome 1) - Masson, Paris (1982).

[4] F. COMMONER. - "Deadlocks in Petri nets" CA-7206-2311, Applied Data Research, Wakefield, Mess, June 1972.

[5] F. COMMONER, A. HOLT, S. EVEN, A. PNUELI. - "Marked directed graphs" - JCSS octobre 1971.

[6] A. FINKEL. - "Deux classes de réseaux à file : les réseaux monogènes et les réseaux préfixes" - Thèse de 3° cycle - Paris VII (octobre 1982) - rapport LITP n° 83-3.

[7] A. FINKEL, G. MEMMI. - "FIFO Nets : a new model of computation" - Proc. of the 6th. G.I. Conf. on Theor. Comp. Sc. - Dortmund, L.N.C.S. 150 Springer Verlag (janvier 1983).

[8] A. FINKEL, G. ROUCAIROL. - "La vivacité d'un réseau à file équilibrée" anusc (manuscript).

[9] M.P. FLE, G. ROUCAIROL. - "On serializability of iterated transactions" ACM SIGACT-SIGOPS Symposium on Principles of Distributed Computing, Ottawa, Canada (1982).

[10] R.M. KARP, R.E. MILLER. - "Parallel program schemata" JCSS 3(4) (1969).

[11] Y.E. LIEN. - "A note on transition systems" K. Inf. Sciences 1976 vol 10 n° 4.

[12] R. MARTIN, G. MEMMI. - "Spécification et validation de systèmes temps réel à l'aide de réseaux de Petri à files". - Revue Technique THOMSON-CSF, vol. 13, n° 3, pp. 635-653 (september 1981).

[13] G MEMMI. - "Fuites et semi-flots dans les réseaux de Pétri" - Thèse de Docteur Ingénieur - Paris VI (1978).

[14] G. MEMMI. - "Méthode d'analyse des réseaux de Pétri, réseaux à files et applications aux systèmes temps réel". - Thèse d'Etat - Paris VI (1983).

[15] J. PETERSON. - "Petri net theory and the modelling of systems" - Prentice Hall INC, Englewood Cliffs, N.J. 07632 (1981).

[16] G. ROUCAIROL. - "Mots de synchronisation" - RAIRO, Inf. vol. 12, n° 4 (1978).

[17] A. SACHE. - "La Théorie des graphes" - PUF n° 1554 (1975).

[18] R. VALK, G. VIDAL-NAQUET. - "Petri nets and regular languages" - JCSS vol. 23 n° 3, (décembre 1981).

Denotational Semantics of Concurrent Programs with Shared Memory

Manfred Broy

Universität Passau
Fakultät für Informatik
Postfach 2540
D-8390 Passau

Abstract

For a simple classical procedural programming language for writing concurrent programs with protected access to shared memory a denotational semantics is given. It is, in particular, based on techniques developed for giving semantic models for languages for describing tightly coupled communicating systems based on the rendezvous concept like CSP and CCS and others for describing loosely coupled systems based on implicit buffering using notations as found in applicative multiprogramming such as nondeterministic stream processing and data flow networks.
13 Dec 83

1. Introduction

Historically concurrent programs where first studied in the form of concurrent systems of processes working on some form of shared memory. For synchronizing access to this shared memory (and more generally also to other resources) a number of synchronization primitives have been introduced such as test-and-set and later semaphors (cf. [Dijkstra 68]). Gradually more and more general protection mechanisms have been suggested such as conditional critical regions (cf. [Hoare 71]) and monitors (cf. [Hoare 74]).

Recently more abstract views of concurrent systems have been developed where communication is taken as being more fundamental than synchronization. Examples are languages for writing tightly coupled systems like CCS (Calculus of Communicating Systems, [Milner 80]) and CSP (Communicating Sequential Processes, [Hoare 78]), and loosely coupled systems like those described by nondeterministic stream-processing functions ([Broy 82]). Following these lines attempts for giving a denotational semantics for concurrent systems focused on those more abstract languages.

Now, where we are at a situation where we begin to have formal (denotational) semantic models for those languages (cf. [Hoare et al. 81], [Broy 83]) it seems not uninteresting to go back to the historical roots of those languages for describing concurrent computations trying out how the developed techniques for semantic specification apply to concepts of synchronized access to shared memory. So in the following for a simple procedural language for writing concurrent systems of processes with protected access to shared memory a denotational semantics is given. It is not based on the concepts of powerdomains and shows in particular an alternative to resumptions as advocated in [Plotkin 76].

2. The Syntax of the Language

We consider a very simple but classical language (cf. [Hoare 71]) for representing concurrent processes. It allows to write a concurrent program that is composed of a finite number of sequential processes running in parallel and having access to shared programming variables within conditional critical regions indicated by **await**-statements.

The syntax of this language is given in BNF:

<statement> ::= **nop** |
abort |
<id> := <exp> |
if <exp> **then** <statement> **else** <statement> **fi** |
while <exp> **do** <statement> **od** |
<statement>; <statement>

<sequential process> ::= <statement> |
await <exp> **then** <statement> **endwait** |
if <exp> **then** <sequential process>
else <sequential process> **fi** |
while <exp> **do** <sequential process> **od** |
<sequential process>; <sequential process>

<parallel process> ::= <sequential process> |
<parallel process> || <parallel process>

<program> ::= ⟦ <parallel process> ⟧

As additional context conditions we require that in a program and in the composition of parallel process all access to shared memory is **orderly protected.** A parallel process

p1 || p2

is called orderly protected if both p1 and p2 are orderly protected (sequential processes are trivially assumed to be orderly protected) and whenever there occurs an assignment to a program variable x in p1 (or in p2 resp.) and x is used also in p2 (or in p1 resp.), then x only occurs exclusively within **await**-statements both in p1 and p2.

3. Semantics

Generally procedural programs, i.e. programs using assignments are semantically represented by state-to-state mappings. For a process working in parallel to other processes this does not suffice, however, since a process may be interrupted, delayed or it may interrupt other processes by virtue of **await**-statements, and in this case some intermediate states become important. This indicates that the meaning of a parallel composition of a set of processes depends on the sequence of intermediate states a process produces.

3.1. Explanation of the Semantic Representation

For motivating our particular semantic representation intuitively we consider a computation of a process for the moment as a finite or infinite sequence of assignments, **nop**-statements, **await**-statement and (only possibly as last action) **abort**. So a computation of a process P can be seen as a sequence

S_1; **await** C_2 **then** K_2 **endwait**; S_2; **await** C_3 **then** K_3 **endwait**; S_3; ...

where the C_i are simple boolean expressions and the S_i and K_i are (sequences of assignment-)statements. For the moment it is sufficient to look at this simplified situation where we ignore the fact that the actual selection of the sequence is done dynamically with help of our control structures such as the conditional or the **while**-loop.

Intuitively the process P executes such a sequence by obtaining an initial state σ_1, and then applying the statement S_1 to σ_1 leading to the result state τ_1. However τ_1 is **not** necessarily the input state for

await C_2 **then** K_2 **endwait**...

It may be the input state for some other process running in parallel. Only after a number (including zero) of state transformations performed by other processes running in parallel the process P may be allowed to continue with a possibly transformed input state σ_2. (The fact that the values of the local variables of P in σ_1 coincide with the local variables in σ_2 is just a theorem in our language.) So τ_1 is considered as part of the output and σ_2 is considered as part of the input of our process P. Now either C_2 is true on σ_2 and our process performs K_2 and S_2 and produces a state τ_2 and is interrupted again. Or C_2 is false on σ_2; then the process P rejects to continue and is interrupted immediately. This is indicated in our semantics by producing the special symbol R.

So a process can be seen as a mapping from a sequence σ_i of input states to a sequence τ_i of either output states or R. This is expressed by the following scheme:

stream of input states				stream of output states
σ_1	$\rightarrow$	S_1;	$\rightarrow$	τ_1
σ_2	$\rightarrow$	**await** C_2 **then** K_2 **endwait**; S_2;	$\rightarrow$	τ_2
σ_3	$\rightarrow$	**await** C_3 **then** K_3 **endwait**; S_3;	$\rightarrow$	τ_3
σ_4	$\rightarrow$	**await** C_4 **then** K_4 **endwait**; S_4;	$\rightarrow$	τ_4
σ_5	$\rightarrow$	**await** C_5 **then** K_5 **endwait**; S_5;	$\rightarrow$	τ_5
.		.		.
.		.		.
.		.		.

According to this explanation we choose the semantic representation of a process. It can be seen as a mapping of the sequence $\langle \sigma_1 \sigma_2 \ldots \rangle$ of input states to a sequence $\langle \tau_1 \; \tau_2 \; \ldots \rangle$ of output states, R (for rejection) or $\perp$ (for nonterminating statements). In the case one output state τ_i is $\perp$, then of course for the input states σ_j with j>i there cannot exist a defined output state τ_j. This can be best modelled by streams.

3.2. Streams

For giving a semantics to agents we introduce the notion of streams. Basically a stream is defined by a sequence of atoms. So let ATOM be some given set of atomic values (including the natural numbers and the truth values for instance). By $\text{ATOM}^{\perp}$ the classical flat domain over ATOM is denoted, i.e. the partially ordered set with just $\perp$ as the least element and all other elements incomparable. By ATOM^* we denote the finite sequences of elements from ATOM, by ATOM^{∞} the infinite sequences. Then the set of streams is defined by

$$\text{STREAM(ATOM)} =: (\text{ATOM}^* \times \{\perp\}) \cup \text{ATOM}^* \cup \text{ATOM}^{\infty}$$

This definition represents the union of all finite partial streams with all finite total and all infinite (and total) streams, if we use the ordering $\sqsubseteq$ for streams s1, s2, defined by

$$s1 \sqsubseteq s2 \iff s1 = s2 \text{ or } s1 = s3 \circ \langle \perp \rangle \text{ and } s3 \text{ is prefix of } s2$$

By <a> the one-element sequence is denoted consisting just of the atom a from ATOM. The symbol "$\circ$" is used to denote the usual concatenation of sequences to sequences. By "&" we denote the operator adding an atomic element as first element to a stream, i.e.

$$a \,\&\, s = \langle a \rangle \circ s, \text{ for } a \in \text{ATOM}, \quad \perp \&\, s = \langle \perp \rangle$$

is assumed. Note, that "&" is leftstrict. By ε the empty stream is denoted. For streams we use the following two functions:

$$\text{first: STREAM(ATOM)} \rightarrow \text{ATOM}^{\perp}, \qquad \text{rest: STREAM(ATOM)} \rightarrow \text{STREAM(ATOM)}$$

which are defined by

$$\text{first}(\varepsilon) = \text{first}(\langle \perp \rangle) = \perp, \qquad \text{first}(\langle a \rangle \,\&\, s) = a,$$
$$\text{rest}(\varepsilon) = \text{rest}(\langle \perp \rangle) = \langle \perp \rangle, \qquad \text{rest}(\langle a \rangle \,\&\, s) = s.$$

With these definitions we immediately may prove:

<u>Lemma:</u>
STREAM(ATOM) forms an algebraic domain; the functions first, ".&.", and rest are monotonic and continuous.

As pointed out in [Broy 82] streams are a very basic notion in concurrent communicating systems. As it is demonstrated in the following this even holds for systems of processes communicating via shared memory.

3.3. Formal Semantics

In our formal semantics states are simple total mappings between identifiers and data. The set of states is turned into a flat domain by adding $\perp$. A statement is a continuous state-to-state mapping. According to what has been said in the previous section a sequential process is a mapping from streams of input-states into either streams of output states or the symbol R for rejection.

We use the particular semantic domains (where DATA is assumed to be an arbitrary set of basic data objects):

STATE = {<id> → DATA} (total functions)

STATEMENT = [STATE$^\perp$ → STATE$^\perp$] (monotonic and continuous functions)

SEQUENTIAL-PROCESS = [STREAM(STATE) → STREAM(STATE ∪ {R})]

PARALLEL-PROCESS = P(SEQUENTIAL-PROCESS)

PROGRAM = {STATE$^\perp$ → P(STATE$^\perp$)}

Here P(SEQUENTIAL-PROCESS) denotes the powerset over SEQUENTIAL-PROCESS, i.e. the set of all sets with elements from SEQUENTIAL-PROCESS, and P(STATE$^\perp$) denotes the powerset over STATE$^\perp$. According to our syntax a sequential process is a deterministic function on streams of states. A parallel process is nondeterministic and therefore represented semantically by a set of such functions. Note that for very particular reasons that are explained below we do not represent parallel processes by functions mapping streams of states into sets of streams of states and R.

We use the following semantic functions.

V: <exp> → STATE$^\perp$ → DATA$^\perp$

S: <statement> → STATEMENT

F: <sequential process> → SEQUENTIAL-PROCESS

Q: <parallel process> → PARALLEL-PROCESS

R: <program> → PROGRAM

The semantic function V is assumed to be given. It can be defined by standard techniques of denotational semantics.

3.4. Semantics of Statements

The meaning of statements can also simply be described by standard techniques of denotational semantics. As usual for a state σ by $\sigma[d/x]$ we denote the state that is obtained by updating the state s, i.e. the state that is identical to σ apart for the argument x for which it yields d. However, if σ or d are $\perp$ the $\sigma[d/x]$ is assumed to be $\perp$, too.

$S[\![\textbf{nop}]\!](\sigma) = \sigma$

$S[\![\textbf{abort}]\!](\sigma) = \bot$

$S[\![x := E]\!](\sigma) = \sigma[V[\![E]\!](\sigma)/x]$

$S[\![\textbf{if } E \textbf{ then } S1 \textbf{ else } S2 \textbf{ fi}]\!] = IF(V[\![E]\!], S[\![S1]\!], S[\![S2]\!])$

where

$$IF(c,f1,f2)(\sigma) = \begin{cases} f1(\sigma) & \text{if } c(\sigma) = \text{true} \\ f2(\sigma) & \text{if } c(\sigma) = \text{false} \\ \bot & \text{otherwise} \end{cases}$$

$S[\![S1;S2]\!](\sigma) = S[\![S2]\!](S[\![S1]\!](\sigma))$

$S[\![\textbf{while } E \textbf{ do } S1 \textbf{ od}]\!] = \textbf{fix } \lambda f : IF(V[\![E]\!], \lambda\sigma: f(S[\![S1]\!](\sigma)), \lambda\sigma: \sigma)$

Here as usual **fix** denotes the operator that selects the least fixed point of the (monotonic) function to which it is applied.

3.5. Semantics of Sequential Processes

Since all our statements are deterministic (there is no local nondeterminism in our language) a sequential process is a deterministic object. According to our chosen semantic representation a sequential processes is a mapping from the stream of input states to the stream of output states. The first input state is used to produce the first output state that is reached before entering the first **await**-statement. The second input state then is used to either produce R (in case of rejection) and trying the next input state for this **await**-statement or for producing the next output state that is reached before entering the next **await**-statement.

$F[\![S1]\!](s) = S[\![S1]\!](first(s))\ \&\ \varepsilon$ if S1 is a statement

$F[\![\textbf{if } E \textbf{ then } P1 \textbf{ else } P2 \textbf{ fi}]\!] = IFP(V[\![E]\!], F[\![P1]\!], F[\![P2]\!])$

where

$$IFP(c,f1,f2)(s) = \begin{cases} f1(s) & \text{if } c(first(s)) = \text{true} \\ f2(s) & \text{if } c(first(s)) = \text{false} \\ \langle\bot\rangle & \text{otherwise} \end{cases}$$

$F[\![P1;P2]\!](s) = CONC(F[\![P1]\!](s), F[\![P2]\!](DROP(t, F[\![P1]\!](s))))$

where DROP and CONC are the least fixed points of

$CONC(\sigma\ \&\ \varepsilon, s) = s,$
$CONC(\sigma1\ \&\ \sigma2\ \&\ s1, s2) = \sigma1\ \&\ CONC(\sigma2\ \&\ s1, s2),$

$DROP(\sigma\ \&\ \varepsilon, s) = \sigma\ \&\ rest(s),$
$DROP(\sigma1\ \&\ \sigma2\ \&\ s1, s2) = DROP(\sigma2\ \&\ s1, rest(s2)),$

Here the function CONC simply denotes the left-strict concatenation of streams and the function DROP deletes all the input states that are needed for the first process p1 and yields the remaining stream of states that are given as inputs to p2. So in a sequential composition P1;P2 the sequence of input states is given to the first process P1 until P1 has properly terminated and the remaining sequence is given to P2. The result sequence of P1;P2 simply consists of the concatenation of the result sequence of P1 with the result sequence of P2. If P1 does not terminate properly then DROP(F[P1](s), s) is $\langle \bot \rangle$.

The **while**-loop can be explained in a straightforward way:

$$F[\textbf{while}\ E\ \textbf{do}\ P1\ \textbf{od}] = \\ \textbf{fix}\ \lambda f.\ IFP(V[E],\ \lambda s.\ CONC(F[P1](s),\ f(DROP(F[P1](s),\ s))),\ \lambda s.\ first(s)\ \&\ \varepsilon)$$

Again **fix** selects the least fixed point of the function.

$$F[\textbf{await}\ E\ \textbf{then}\ S1\ \textbf{endwait}](t) = \\ first(s)\ \&\ AWAIT(\lambda z.\ V[E](first(z)),\ S[S1])(rest(s))$$

where AWAIT is defined as the least fixed point of

$$AWAIT(c,g)(t) = \begin{cases} R\ \&\ AWAIT(c,g)(rest(t)) & \text{if } c(t) = false \\ g(first(t))\ \&\ \varepsilon & \text{if } c(t) = true \\ \langle \bot \rangle & \text{otherwise} \end{cases}$$

Note that the least fixed points all are trivially well-defined due to the fact that STREAM(STATE) is a domain.

Note, moreover, that according to our standard representation of processes the first output (more precisely the first element of the stream of output states) represents the state that is reached by the process **before** it enters the first critical section. In the case of an await statement this is trivially the first input state.

3.6. Semantics of Parallel Processes

The parallel composition of two processes leads to a nondeterministic process in general: the "scheduler" is free to choose some interleaving. Basically the idea of specifying the meaning of a parallel composition is as follows. We are free to choose any pair of instantiations (deterministic stream-processing functions) for the two processes that are composed. Now the stream of input states has to be split into two streams (expressed by the function FORK below) such that each of the instantiations of the two processes obtains a substream of the input stream according to the choice of the scheduler (expressed by d). The resulting two output streams are merged again according to the scheduler d. However, a scheduler d is only working correct (expressed by FEASIBLE below) if a state in the input stream is rejected only of both processes are ready to do so, i.e. it is sent to both processes iff both processes are ready to reject this state.

For a sequential process S we simply have

$$Q[S] = \{F[S]\}$$

The parallel composition of processes is defined by:

$$Q[R1\ ||\ R2] = \\ \{f \in SEQUENTIALPROCESS:\ \exists\ g1 \in Q[R1],\ g2 \in Q[R2]:\ \forall s \in STREAM(STATE):\ \exists d \in \{0,1,2\}^{\infty}: \\ FEASIBLE(g1(FORK(s,d,1)),\ g2(FORK(s,d,2)),d) \sqsubseteq true \\ \wedge\ f(s) = MERGE(g1(FORK(s,d,1)),\ g2(FORK(s,\bar{d},2)),d)\}$$

where FORK is the least fixed point of

$$\mathrm{FORK}(s, i \,\&\, d, i) = \mathrm{FORK}(s, 0 \,\&\, d, i) = \mathrm{first}(s) \,\&\, \mathrm{FORK}(\mathrm{rest}(s), d, i)$$
$$i \neq j \wedge i \neq 0 \Rightarrow \mathrm{FORK}(s, i \,\&\, d, j) = \mathrm{FORK}(\mathrm{rest}(s), d, j)$$

and MERGE and FEASIBLE are the least fixed points of

$$\mathrm{MERGE}(R \,\&\, r1, R \,\&\, r2, 0 \,\&\, d) = R \,\&\, \mathrm{MERGE}(r1, r2, d)$$
$$(r2 = \varepsilon \vee \sigma \in \mathrm{STATE}) \Rightarrow \mathrm{MERGE}(\sigma \,\&\, r1, r2, 1 \,\&\, d) = \sigma \,\&\, \mathrm{MERGE}(r1, r2, d)$$
$$(r1 = \varepsilon \vee \sigma \in \mathrm{STATE}) \Rightarrow \mathrm{MERGE}(r1, \sigma \,\&\, r2, 2 \,\&\, d) = \sigma \,\&\, \mathrm{MERGE}(r1, r2, d)$$
$$\mathrm{MERGE}(\varepsilon, \varepsilon, d) = \varepsilon$$

$$\mathrm{FEASIBLE}(R \,\&\, r1, R \,\&\, r2, 0 \,\&\, d) = \mathrm{FEASIBLE}(r1, r2, d)$$
$$(r2 = \varepsilon \vee \sigma \in \mathrm{STATE}) \Rightarrow \mathrm{FEASIBLE}(\sigma \,\&\, r1, r2, 1 \,\&\, d) = \mathrm{FEASIBLE}(r1, r2, d)$$
$$(r1 = \varepsilon \vee \sigma \in \mathrm{STATE}) \Rightarrow \mathrm{FEASIBLE}(r1, \sigma \,\&\, r2, 2 \,\&\, d) = \mathrm{FEASIBLE}(r1, r2, d)$$
$$\mathrm{FEASIBLE}(\varepsilon, \varepsilon, d) = \mathrm{true}$$

$$\sigma \in \mathrm{STATE} \Rightarrow \mathrm{FEASIBLE}(\sigma \,\&\, r1, r2, 0 \,\&\, d) = \mathrm{FEASIBLE}(r1, \sigma \,\&\, r2, 0 \,\&\, d) = \mathrm{false},$$
$$\sigma \in \mathrm{STATE} \cup \{R\} \Rightarrow$$
$$\mathrm{FEASIBLE}(\varepsilon, \sigma \,\&\, r2, 1 \,\&\, d) = \mathrm{FEASIBLE}(\sigma \,\&\, r1, \varepsilon, 2 \,\&\, d) = \mathrm{false}.$$

This definition simply defines that a state σ can only be rejected by the process p1 || p2 if both p1 and p2 are going to reject σ, otherwise it has to be accepted. A scheduling d is only accepted as proper scheduling (i.e. as FEASIBLE) if a state is given to both processes iff both are ready to reject it and none of them has terminated yet.

Note, that the definition of parallel composition fulfils a number of monotonicity and continuity properties as dealt with in [Broy 83]. For instance, all our language constructs are monotonic and continuous in the classical ordering on power-domains such as Egli-Milner (cf. [Plotkin 76],). However, we need not make use of these properties since parallel processes cannot be recursively defined in our language. If we would have also recursive definitions of parallel processes such as

proc p =: S1 || <u>if</u> B <u>then</u> p <u>else</u> S2 <u>fi</u>

then we would need powerdomains and more sophisticated fixed point theory (cf. [Broy 82]) as used for CSP in [Broy 83]. If we were only interested in fair schedulers, then the predicate FEASIBLE just has to be chosen more sophisticated.

3.7. Semantics of the Parallel Compound

If we use a system of parallel processes for forming a parallel compound, i.e. a closed system of parallel processes, then of course the sequence of produced output states has to be taken as input states, too, apart from the initial input state. So the system starts with the initial state as first element of the computation and produces some output state that is taken as second input state and so on. As soon as one of these input states is rejected the system has produced a deadlock. If the system terminates (i.e. produces a finite sequence of states) then the last state is the result state of the program. This particular way of considering parallel computations can be nicely expressed by a fixed point equation for streams.

$$R[\![P]\!](\sigma) = \{LAST(\mathbf{fix}\ \lambda s: f(\sigma \& CLEAN(s))): f \in Q[P]\}$$

where LAST and CLEAN are the least fixed points of the equations.

$$CLEAN(\varepsilon) = \varepsilon,$$
$$CLEAN(R \& t) = \langle \bot \rangle,$$
$$CLEAN(\sigma \& s) = \sigma \& CLEAN(s),$$

$$LAST(\sigma \& \varepsilon) = \sigma,$$
$$LAST(\sigma 1 \& \sigma 2 \& s) = LAST(\sigma 2 \& s),$$

Note, that in the above formula the stream s of intermediate states (at interrupt points) that an instantiation f of system produces is the least fixed point of the equation (where σ is the initial state)

$$t = f(\sigma \& CLEAN(t))$$

If this stream is finite and total, than its last state is the defined endstate of the system; otherwise the system does not terminate in a defined state (this is represented by $\bot$). If one is interested in nonterminating systems of processes working on shared memory then the (infinite) stream s could also be taken for representing the meaning of the system.

Here deadlock and nontermination is both represented by $\bot$. It is technically not complicated to change our definitions slightly to represent deadlock by an error element different from $\bot$ if wanted.

The very particular representation of parallel processes by sets of stream-processing functions follows [Broy 82] where such a semantic representation has been used for resolving the so-called merge anomaly (cf. [Keller 78]). Every instantiation of a system of parallel processes is represented by one particular stream-processing function. The instantiation of such a system within a parallel compound, i.e. without any other processes in parallel, can be modelled by the least defined stream of states that is a fixed point of this function. If the produced stream has a defined last element (i.e. it is finite with a last element distinct from bottom) this is the final state of the system, otherwise the final state is not defined.

4. Concluding Remarks

The meaning of the simple language for parallel processing with shared memory has been given formally combining techniques of denotational semantics developed for languages like CSP and CCS (cf. [Broy 83]) as well as those used for nondeterministic stream processing functions (cf. [Broy 82]). This explains some of the problems people had to find appropriate denotational models for concurrent systems with shared memories: the difficulties of tightly coupled systems (with the problems of hand-shaking communication and respectively the capabilities of rejection in particular) as well as those of loosely coupled systems (i.e. nondeterministic system of stream-processing functions with the problem of the merge anomaly) occur side by side. As demonstrated in the previous section they can be solved just by applying techniques developed for those more abstract languages (cf. [Broy 82, 83]).

Note, however, that due to the fact that we did not have recursion nor iteration over the parallel systems (i.e. there was just iteration within a sequential, deterministic process), we could avoid completely using power domain concepts.

In [Plotkin 76] another semantics for parallel processes has been suggested based on resumptions. Resumptions are closely related to sets of stream-processing functions (cf. [Broy 82]). However, they lead into severe technical problems concerning powerdomains and continuity (cf. [Broy 83]).

We close with a short attempt to assess out semantics. There are several criteria about the quality of a semantic model:

(a) The semantic equivalence should be a congruence. This is certainly true for our definition.

(b) The semantic model should be "sufficiently" abstract. Ideally it should be fully abstract. Our semantic model surely is reasonably abstract. But is it sufficiently or even fully abstract?

Full abstractness is a relative notion. Something can only be fully abstract w.r.t. some notion of observability. If we assume, that the meaning of a parallel compound is just the function mapping states into sets of states including $\perp$ for nontermination (which is surely a clear and abstract notion of observablity), then we can ask now the question of full abstractness more precisely: A semantic model of our language is fully abstract, if program constructs are mapped onto distinct semantic representations iff there are program contexts in the form of parallel compounds for them in which they lead to distinct results. Our representation of expressions and statements surely is fully abstract. So there remains the question whether sequential or parallel processes are represented fully abstract in our model.

The answer is definitely "No". Always nonterminating programs as those producing infinite streams of output for infinite streams of input are always mapped to $\perp$ in the context of parallel compounds. However, if we change our notion of observability for also studying nonterminating processes, than our notion of observability changes and also the notion of full abstractness. Then a new notion of observability has to be fixed to assess full abstractness.

Acknowledgement

This work has been carried out during the preparation of a seminar on the semantics of concurrency held at the Escuela Tecnica Sperior de Ingenieros de Telecomunicacion at the University of Madrid in the July 1983. The pleasant atmosphere at the seminar and the stimulating discussions with the participants and my co-lecturer Carlos Delgado-Kloos have definitly influenced this work.

References

[Broy 82]
M. Broy: Fixed Point Theory for Communication and Concurrency. In: D. Bjørner (ed): IFIP TC2 Working Conference on Formal Description of Programming Concepts II, Garmisch, June 1982, North Holland 1983, 125-147

[Broy 83]
M. Broy: Semantics of Communicating Processes. Information and Control (to appear)

[Dijkstra 68]
E.W. Dijkstra: Co-Operating Sequential Processes. In: F. Genuys (ed.): Programming Languages. Academic Press, 1968, 43 - 112

[Hoare 71]
C.A.R. Hoare: Towards a Theory of Parallel Programming. In: C.A.R. Hoare, R.H. Perrot (eds.): Operating Systems Techniques, Academic Press, New York 1972, 61 - 71

[Hoare 74]
C.A.R. Hoare: Monitors: An Operating Systems Structuring Concept. Comm. ACM **17**: 10, October 1974, 549-557

[Hoare 78]
C.A.R. Hoare: Communicating Sequential Processes. Comm. ACM 21:8, August 1978, 666-677

[Hoare et al. 81]
C.A.R. Hoare, S.D. Brookes, A.W. Roscoe: A Theory of Communicating Sequential Processes. Oxford University Computing Laboratory, Programming Research Group, Technical Monograph PRG-21, Oxford 1981

[Keller 78]
R.M. Keller: Denotational Models for Parallel Programs with Indeterminate Operators. In: E.J. Neuhold (ed.): Formal Description of Programming Concepts. Amsterdam: North-Holland 1978, 337-366

[Milner 80]
R. Milner: A Calculus of Communicating Systems. Lecture Notes in Computer Science **92**, Berlin-Heidelberg-New York: Springer 1980

[Plotkin 76]
G. Plotkin: A Powerdomain Construction. SIAM J. Computing 5, 1976, 452-486

HIGHER ORDER DATA STRUCTURES

- Cartesian Closure Versus λ-Calculus -

Axel Poigné

Informatik II
Universität Dortmund
Postfach 50 05 00
D-4600 Dortmund 50, F.R.G.

ABSTRACT We discuss connections of typed λ-calculus and cartesian closure and prove equivalence of the theories 'up to abstraction'. This is a working out of ideas of Scott and Lambeck but in an abstract data type environment. The results serve as a basis for the discussion of higher order specifications. We demonstrate that higher order equations based on λ-calculus are more appropiate if the equivalence of λ-calculus and cartesian closure is to be preserved. We construct higher order theories for higher order specifications. For higher order models we discuss existence of initial models and completeness of higher order theories.

0.INTRODUCTION

Abstract data types as originally introduced by Guttag and Zilles by now are widely accepted for software development. There are several papers on the theoretical foundations of abstract data types (f.e. /1/) and on modularization techniques (f.e. /7/,/8/,/13/). Being based on universal algebra abstract data type theory up to now essentially is a first order approach (except for the Munich school /4/). An appropiate handling of functions, especially those of higher types, is not - at least not in a natural way - in the scope of abstract data type theory. But a specification technique which includes the handling of functions seems to be useful in denotational semantics /9/, and in general as a more flexible method of specification.

It is not too surprising that in computer science first investigations on higher order structures are to be found in the field of semantics of programming languages because denotational semantics cannot be imagined not to use functions of higher order. First approaches to higher order data types are Milner's investigations on type polymorphism /17/ and the language ML as outcome /10/. Functional programming languages /2/ may be taken as another root, their definition being based on higher order operators. But being mainly interested in the programming language aspect, little attention has been paid to specification techniques. It seems that the combination of data type specification and higher order operations is at first explicitly expressed in the work of Parsaye-Ghomi /19/, while implicitly being considered for instance in the work of Mosses /18/. Another reference is /6/ where Dybjer expresses a similar view (the reader is refered to his PhD-thesis where a lot of the connections to be found in the literature are worked out).

ur interest in the subject stems from a project on compiler generation where we have sed an intermediate language based on cartesian closure to express semantics. It soon ecame apparent that modularization techniques for denotational semantics are needed to ake compiler generation comfortable and efficient. At that time only abstract data type heory has provided such techniques, but for denotational semantics abstract data types eemed too unhandy. Hence in /20/ we have made some suggestions how to combine abstract ata type theory with higher order structures. The ideas were based on the work of Scott 23/ and Lambeck /11/. Somewhat later we learned of the thesis of Parsaye-Ghomi /19/. his paper may be understood as a reaction to and extension of his work.

ue to lack of space we are only able to give the core of the definitions and construc-ions and only a few short examples. Full proofs are given in /20/ and /21/. We must ssume that the reader is familiar with the standard approach to abstract data type heory. For category theory we refer to /14/,/15/ but we hope that the 'algebraic' pecification of cartesian closed categories at least gives a good imagination of this tructure.

. CARTESIAN CLOSURE VERSUS λ-CALCULUS

e introduce cartesian closed categories by a two-level specification technique. To put t roughly a two-level specification is of the form

```
SPEC = first:  Spec
         var:  A_o,A_1,...:s_o,  B_o,B_1,...;s_1, ...
      second:  Spec'
```

here Spec is a specification in the standard sense, and $s_o, s_1 \ldots$ are sorts of Spec. ne declaration of sorts and operators of the 'specification scheme' Spec' may contain ec-terms with variables $A_o, A_1, \ldots, B_o, B_1, \ldots$. Given a Spec-algebra A the specifica-ion Spec'(A) is obtained by substituting all Spec-variables by elements of A, and by en evaluating all Spec-terms occuring in Spec' in A. Similarly, we use axiom schemes. is is a way to handle polymorphism of operators.

r categories we replace the keywords 'first' by the more suggestive 'dom' and 'second' 'functs'. Then a cartesian closed category is specified by

```
CART =   dom:    sorts:  dom
                   ops:  1: → dom                        "terminal object"
                         _×_: dom dom → dom              "products"
                         _→_: dom dom → dom              "function space"
         var:  A,B,C,D : dom

       functs:    sorts:    (A,B)
                    ops:    1_A:  →  (A,A)                   "unit"
                            _∘_: (A,B)(B,C)  →  (A,C)         "composition"
```

$0_A: \ \to (A,1)$ "tupling"

$<\_,\_> : (A,B)(A,C) \to (A,B\times C)$

$p_{A,B}: \ \to (A\times B,A)$ "projections"

$q_{A,B}: \ \to (A\times B,B)$

$\Lambda\_ : (C\times A,B) \to (C,A\to B)$ "abstraction"

$ev_{A,B}: \ \to ((A\to B)\times A,B)$ "evaluation"

var: $f:(A,B),\ g:(B,C),\ h:(C,D),\ t:(A,1), f_o:(A,B), f_1:(A,C), k:(A,B\times C), r:(C\times A,B)$
$s:(C,A\to B)$

axioms: "category" "products"

$$f\circ(g\circ h) = (f\circ g)\circ h \qquad 0_A = t$$

$$1_A\circ f = f \qquad <f_o,f_1>\circ p_{B,C} = f_o$$

$$f\circ 1_B = f \qquad <f_o,f_1>\circ q_{B,C} = f_1$$

$$<k\circ p_{B,C}, k\circ q_{B,C}> = k$$

"function space"

$$<p_{C,A}\circ \Lambda r,\ q_{C,A}>\circ ev_{A,B} = r$$

$$\Lambda(<p_{C,A}\circ s, q_{C,A}>\circ ev_{A,B}) = s$$

An algebra C with regard to this specification is a small cartesian closed category: We have an algebra of objects with operations 'terminal object','products' and 'function spaces', carriers $C(d,d')$ are sets of morphisms from d to d', d,d' objects, composition, units etc. are given by the interpretation of the 'functs'-operators. Observe that the Λ-operator corresponds to the curry-operator in denotational semantics, and the derived operator $<p_{C,A}\circ \_, q_{C,A}>\circ ev_{A,B}$ to the uncurry-operator.

As pointed out by Lambeck and Scott /11/,/23/.there exists a close connection between cartesian closed categories and typed λ-calculus. In fact cartesian closure is like the theory of combinators /3/ a variable-free approach towards a theory of functions. The type structure of our λ-calculus is more elaborated because of the addition of products. We shall again use a two level specification technique. On the first level we introduce the type structure, on the second the calculus is introduced. We shall index the λ-operators by type expressions, and use the same conventions as for two-level specifications.

XTENDED TYPED -CALCULUS

et Dom be a homogeneous specification with sort dom such that

$$\underline{\Lambda Dom} \;=\; \text{sorts: } \underline{dom}$$
$$\text{ops: } 1: \to \underline{dom}$$
$$\_\times\_,\ \_\to\_: \underline{dom}\ \underline{dom} \to \underline{dom}$$

s a subspecification. Dom is called the specification of *domains* or *types*. Type-orted sets of λ-terms are defined by induction using an operator scheme indexed by Dom-terms with type variables A,B,... . Replacing variables by elements of a given Dom-algebra D and evaluating Dom-terms in D then yields concrete operators and axioms.

et $V_A := \{x_o{:}A,\ x_1{:}A, \ldots\}$ be a set of A-variables. Then λ-terms are defined by

(i) $V_A \subseteq \Lambda_A$

(ii) $M \in \Lambda_{A\to B},\ N \in \Lambda_A \quad \Rightarrow \quad (MN) \in \Lambda_B$

$x \in V_A,\ M \in \Lambda_B \quad \Rightarrow \quad (\lambda x.M) \in \Lambda_{A\to B}$

(iii) $\emptyset \in \Lambda_1 \ ,\ p_{A,B} \in \Lambda_{A\times B \to A} \ ,\ q_{A,B} \in \Lambda_{A\times B\to B}$

$M \in \Lambda_A \ ,\ N \in \Lambda_B \quad \Rightarrow \quad \langle M,N\rangle \in \Lambda_{A\times B}$.

ree and bound variables are defined as usual. We use FV(M) to denote the set of vari-bles occuring free in M. Substitution is denoted by M(x/N). As in /3/ we assume that ubstitution does not influence the binding structure, i.e. we consider terms modulo -conversion. The set of closed terms of type A is denoted by Λ^o_A.

he λ-terms are to satisfy the following axiom scheme

(β) $(\lambda x.M)N = M(x/N)$

(π) $p_{A,B}\langle M,N\rangle = M \qquad q_{A,B}\langle M,N\rangle = N$

(η) $M \in \Lambda_1 \quad \Rightarrow \quad M = \emptyset$

$\lambda x.(Mx) = M \quad \text{if} \quad x \notin FV(M)$

$\langle p_{A,B}M,\ q_{A,B}M\rangle = M$

lus congruence axioms. Given a Dom-algebra D the resulting calculus is denoted by Λ(D).

ample: Untyped = ΛDom + ops: U: → dom
axioms: U → U = U

Given an Untyped-algbra D untyped λ-calculus can be interpreted in Λ(D) by $I(\lambda x.M) = \lambda x{:}U.M$, $I(x) = x{:}U$, $I(MN) = I(M)I(N)$. Self-application is possible as $(\lambda x{:}U.M)(\lambda x{:}U.M)$ is well defined.

In order to prove the equivalence of the theories we need translations of CART-terms to λ-terms and vice versa. The translation follows the lines of /23/. Let $T_{\Sigma CART}(D)$ denote the set of CART-terms with respect to a domain algebra D, and $\Lambda(D)$ be the corresponding set of λ-terms. We then define the

TRANSLATION OF CARTESIAN CLOSED CATEGORIES TO λ-CALCULUS

$\# f \# = f:A \to B$ if f is a variable of sort (A,B)

$\# 1_A \# = \lambda x:A.x$

$\# p_{A,B} \# = p_{A,B}$ $\# q_{A,B} \# = q_{A,B}$ $\# 0_A \# = \lambda x:A.\emptyset$

$\# ev_{A,B} \# = \lambda x:(A \to B) \times A.(p_{A\to B,A}x)(q_{A \to B,A}x)$

$\# T \circ T' \# = \lambda x:A.\# T \#(\# T' \# x)$ if $T:(A,B)$

$\# <T,T'> \# = \lambda x:A. <\# T \# x, \# T' \# x>$ if $T:(A,B)$

$\# \Lambda T \# = \lambda x:A.\lambda y:B.(\# T \# <x,y>)$ if $T:(A \times B, C)$

(for convenience we use 'x' instead of 'x:A' for variables if the typing is obvious).

TRANSLATION OF λ-TERMS TO CARTESIAN CLOSED CATEGORIES

Any λ-term M of type B is interpreted by a morphism (= constant CART-term)

$$|M|: \prod_{x:A \in FV(M)} A \to B$$

with a suitably chosen product. To shorten notation we shall use $\underline{M}$ for $\prod_{x:A \in FV(M)} A$.
We use diagramatic definitions.

$|x:A| = 1_A$ $|\emptyset| = 1_1$

$|p_{A,B}| = 'p_{A,B}'$ $|q_{A,B}| = 'q_{A,B}'$ with

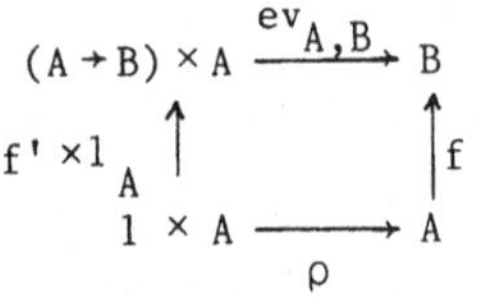

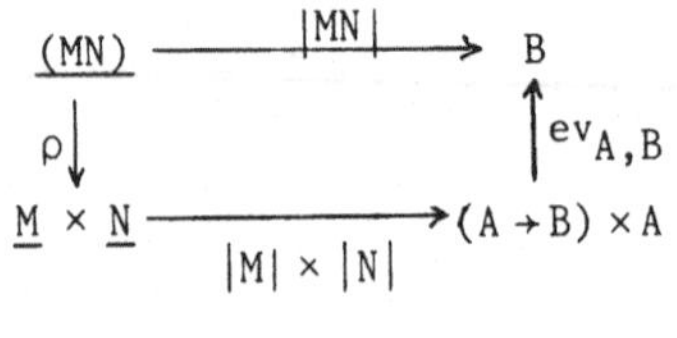

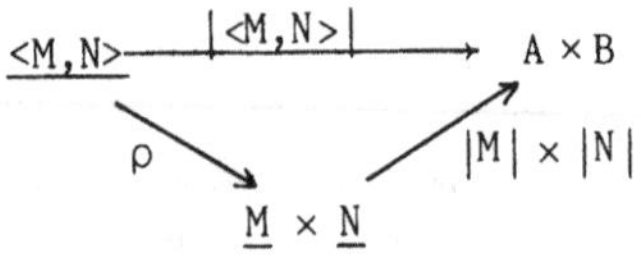

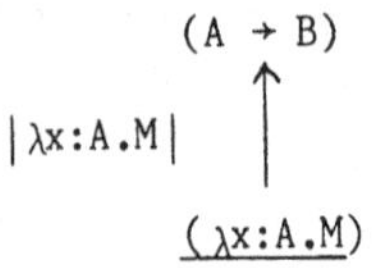

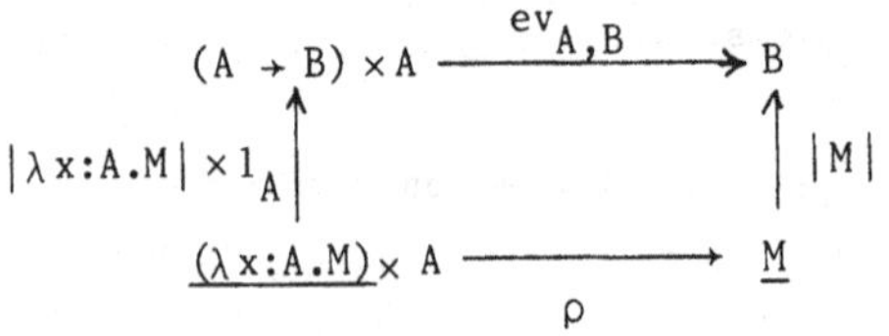

where the 'substitution mapping ρ are defined using tupling and projections (in the obvious way).

Remark : Another very elegant interpretation of λ-calculus, based on the variable concept of de Brujn /3/, is given by Curien in /5/. There the projection maps are explicitly computed from the index of the variables.

ith this translations we are able to state the

1.1 *Theorem* : The theories $\Lambda(D)$ and CART(D) are *equivalent up to abstraction* for every domain algebra D, i.e.

(i) $\Lambda(D) \vdash \#|M|\# = \lambda x{:}A_o \times \ldots \times A_{n-1}.M(x_o/(p_0 x),\ldots,x_{n-1}/(p_{n-1}x))$
with $FV(M) = \{x_o{:}A_o,\ldots,x_{n-1}{:}A_{n-1}\}$ and p_i
being the projection to the i-th component

(ii) $CART(D) \vdash |\#T\#| = \bar{T}$

(iii) $\Lambda(D) \vdash M = N \iff CART(D) \vdash \rho_M \circ |M| = \rho_N \circ |N|$

(iv) $CART(D) \vdash T = T' \iff \Lambda(D) \vdash \#T\# = \#T'\#$

where $\rho_M{:}<M,N> \to M$, $\rho_n{:}<M,N> \to N$ are the canonical projections, and where
$\bar{T}: \prod_{f:(A,B)\,\varepsilon\,FV(T)} (A\to B) \to (C\to D)$ if T is a term of sort (C,D) with

$\bar{f} = 1_{A\to B}$ if $f{:}(A,B)$

and $\overline{\gamma(T_o,\ldots,T_{m-1})} = \rho \circ (\bar{T}_o \ldots \bar{T}_{m-1}) \circ \bar{\gamma}$

where $\bar{\gamma}{:}(A_0\to B_o)\times\ldots\times(A_{m-1}\to B_{m-1}) \to (A\to B)$ is the the CART-morphism which corresponds to the CART-operator $\gamma{:}(A_o,B_o)\ldots(A_{m-1},B_{m-1}) \to (A,B)$, for example

$$\begin{array}{ccc} (A\to C)\times A & \xrightarrow{\;ev_{A,C}\;} & C \\ {\scriptstyle \_\bar{\circ}\_\times 1_A}\uparrow & & \uparrow{\scriptstyle ev_{B,C}} \\ (A\to B)\times(B\to C)\times A \simeq (B\to C)\times(A\to B)\times A & \xrightarrow[\;1_{(A\to B)}\times ev_{A,B}\;]{} & (B\to C)\times B \end{array}$$

emark: The transition from γ to $\bar{\gamma}$ is well known in the category of sets where for instance composition is a mapping and hence a morphism of the category. This works for all cartesian closed categories.

he theorem is not fully satisfactory as it shows a certain asymmetry being inconsitent with our intuition (which is the intuition expressed by Scott /23/). A closer ook immediately shows the problems: Given two λ-terms which are identical except for he free variables, the terms are identified by the above interpretation (for example $x{:}A| = 1_A = |y{:}A|$ and thus $\#\,|x{:}A|\,\# = \lambda x{:}A.x$!). This contradicts the use of free ariables in λ-calculus, free variables being handled as being bound. On the other way ound category theory distinguishes between 'functions' and 'function names', i.e. lements of a function space, while λ-calculus does not - at a first look. Implicitly he distinction holds as well in λ-calculus: A λ-term is a function in its free varibles, while a function name is obtained by abstraction. To cut it short a stronger quivalence result is to be exspected if both the concepts of 'functions' and 'funcion names' are preserved by the translations. This is demonstrated in /21/ but we ave to extend λ-calculus by 'function types'.

2. HIGHER ORDER SPECIFICATIONS AND HIGHER ORDER THEORIES

Our concept of higher order specifications follows that of /19/. Our specification mechanism allows polymorphic operators (in fact the above specifications of categories are polymorphic higher order specifications in some sense). Extending the approach of Parsaye-Ghomi we shall allow domain generation and domain equations in higher order specifications. We shall discuss the implications of equations with regard to the equivalence of the theories of cartesian closed categories and extended typed λ-calculus.

2.1 *Definition*: A *higher order specification* consists of a *domain specification* Dom s.t. that ΛDom is a subspecification, a set $H\Sigma$ of *higher order operators* of the form

$$\sigma : t_0 t_1 \ldots t_{n-1} \to t$$

with t_i, t being Dom-terms and a set HE of equations of the form $M = N$ where M,N are $\Lambda(H\Sigma)$-terms, i.e. λ-terms where the term construction is enriched by the rule

$$\sigma: t_0 t_1 \ldots t_{n-1} \to t \in \Lambda_{t_0 \times \ldots \times t_{n-1} \to t} \quad .$$

Examples: We suggest the following specification schemes (for convenience in domain specifications only the data added to ΛDom is to be specified)

(i) Fix = functs: ops: $Y: (B \to B) \to B$
var: $f:(B \to B)$
axioms: $Y(f) = f(Y(f))$

defines a fixpoint operator.

(ii) Sums = doms: ops: $\_+\_$: dom dom → dom
var: A,B,C:dom
functs: ops: $u_{A,B}: A \to A + B$
$v_{A,B}: B \to A + B$
case _ , _ esac: $(A \to C)(B \to C) \to (A + B \to C)$
var: $M:(A \to C)$, $N:(B \to C)$, $L:A$, $L':B$, $P:(A + B \to C)$

axioms: case M,N esac $(u_{A,B}L) = ML$
case M,N esac $(v_{A,B}L') = NL'$
case $\lambda x{:}A.P(u_{A,B}x)$, $\lambda y{:}B.P(v_{A,B}y)$ esac $= P$
if $x,y \notin FV(P)$

adds coproducts (disjoint sums).

(iii) Lists = Sums +
var: A:dom
sorts: ops: list(A): → dom
axioms: $list(A) = 1 + list(A) \times A$

Trees = Sums +
var: A:dom
sorts: ops: tree(A): → dom
axioms: $tree(A) = A + tree(A) \times tree(A) \times A$

The definitions are polymorphic and, due to the use of variables for domains (which we do not discuss formally here), recursive. The standard operations are a consequence of the 'sum' and 'product' structure. For instance

$$\text{case } v_{A,1},\ \lambda x{:}list(A)\times A.u_{A,1}(q_{list(A)\ ,A}\ y) \text{ esac}: list(A) \to A + 1$$

yields the head of the list and an 'error' if the list is empty.

We now consider cartesian closed categories resp. λ-calculus over a higher order specification.

CARTESIAN CLOSED CATEGORIES OVER HIGHER ORDER SPECIFICATIONS

Let HSpec = (Dom, HΣ, HE) be a higher order specification. Then

CART(HSpec) = CART + doms: Dom
var: A,B:dom
functs: ops: $\sigma_A: (A,t_o)\ldots(A,t_{n-1}) \to (A,t)$
var: $f:(A,B),\ g_i:(B,t_i)$
axioms: $f\circ\sigma_B(g_o,\ldots,g_{n-1}) = \sigma_A(f\circ g_o,\ldots,f\circ g_{n-1})$
$\rho_M \circ |M| = \rho_N \circ |N|$

for $\sigma: t_o\ldots t_{n-1} \to t \in H\Sigma$, $M = N \in HE$.

EXTENDED λ-CALCULUS OVER HIGHER ORDER SPECIFICATIONS

We add the axioms HE to the λ-calculus Λ(HΣ). The resulting calculus is denoted by Λ(HSpec).

Not too surprisingly we state

2.2 *Theorem*: Given a higher order specification HSpec the theories CART(HSpec) and Λ(HSpec) (resp. CART(HSpec)(D) and Λ(HSpec)(D) with a fixed domain algebra D) are equivalent up to abstraction.

Remark: The choice to use λ-terms in higher order equations is essential. Otherwise 2.2 would not hold. This can be demonstrated by the following example. Let stop: → A be a higher order operator and stop ∘ f = stop be an equation of CART-terms. To ensure

$\Lambda(H\Sigma) + \{\#stop \circ f\# = \#stop\#\} \vdash M = N$

$\Rightarrow \quad CART(H\Sigma) + \{stop \circ f = stop\} \vdash \rho_M\circ|M| = \rho_N\circ|N|$

we need commutativity of the diagram

$$\begin{array}{ccc} (A\to B)\times 1 & \longrightarrow & 1 \\ {\scriptstyle 1_{(A\to B)}\times stop}\downarrow & & \downarrow{\scriptstyle stop} \\ (A\to B)\times A & \underset{ev_{A,B}}{\longrightarrow} & B \end{array}$$

which does not hold in general.

Theorem 2.2 has several corollaries which are of interest for abstract data type theory. Let HSpec be a higher order specification. Then the category CART(HSpec) consists of all CART(HSpec)-algebras or all small cartesian closed categories with additional properties induced by the higher order specification, and of functors preserving cartesian closure and the HSpec-structure (CART(HSpec)-homomorphisms). If we fix the domain algebra D let CART(HSpec)(D) denote the subcategory of CART(HSpec) such that D is the set of objects and that functors are the identity on objects.

2.3 *Proposition*: Let HSpec be a higher order specification and D be a domain algebra w.r.t. HSpec. Then a CART(HSpec)(D)-algebra $\underline{C}$ can be defined by

$$\underline{C}(d,d') := \{ [M] \mid M \in \Lambda^{o}_{d \to d'} \text{ w.r.t. } \Lambda(\text{HSpec}) \}$$

$$\gamma([M_o],\ldots,[M_{n-1}]) := [\# \gamma(X_o,\ldots,X_{n-1}) \# (X_o/M_o,\ldots,X_{n-1}/M_{n-1})]$$

with $[M]$ being the congruence class of M in Λ(HSpec) and $\gamma\colon (d_o,d'_o)\ldots(d_{n-1},d'_{n-1}) \to (d,d')$ being a CART(HSpec)-operator and X_i variables of sort (d_i,d'_i). Then

(i) $\underline{C}$ is an initial object in CART(HSpec)(D).

(ii) If $D = T_{\text{Dom}}$ is the initial domain algebra w.r.t. HSpec = (Dom,HΣ,HE) then $\underline{C}$ is an initial object in CART(HSpec).

We will call $\underline{C}$ the *higher order theory* generated by HSpec (and D).

Now let HSIG be the category of *concrete higher order signatures* which can be specified by a two-level specification as follows

```
HSIG =  doms: ops: 1: → dom
                  _ × _: dom dom → dom
                  _ → _: dom dom → dom
              var:  A,B:dom
        functs: sorts:  (A,B)
```

A HSIG-algebra consists of a domain algebra D and a D×D-sorted set. The inclusion HSIG ⊆ CART induces a forgetful functor V: CART → HSIG.

2.4 *Proposition*: V: CART → HSIG has a left adjoint, a free CART-algebra being defined by the higher order theory generated by the HSIG-algebra (D,HΣ).

The last result states that free cartesian closed categories over a higher order signature exist . This extends the result stated in /19/ as type generators are allowed. In contrast to our proceeding Parsaye-Ghomi /19/ constructs a free cartesian closed category over a given signature category, and then factorizes by the least cartesian closed congruence containing the relation generated by the higher order equations. Concrete higher order theories then are introduced via an extended λ-calculus (in the same way we did) and it is stated that higher order theories are isomorphic to concrete

higher order theories. The development depends on the statement that the construction of free cartesian closed categories over categories preserve products and exponentiation, what may be doubted.
Dybjer gives in his thesis /6/ a construction of initial CART(HSpec)-algebras by pure algebraic arguments (which in our context are immediate because of the two-level specification) and points out the connection to λ-calculus.

To conclude the section we remark that restriction of the whole development to products yield the standard results of categorical algebra /12/ except that we use theories in product form. Especially higher order signatures cut down to ordinary specifications. The proofs then are to be slightly modified as we cannot use higher types for translations (compare /20/).

3. REMARKS ON HIGHER ORDER ALGEBRAS

It is at hand that the notion of a higher order theory deserves the notion of *higher order algebras* as counterpart. Higher order algebras are discussed in the thesis of Parsaye-Ghomi /19/, but we shall choose a slightly different approach. Even if our approach is equivalent to Parsaye-Ghomi's (what we cannot demonstrate because of lack of space) some of our results contradict his statements.

3.1 *Definition*: (i) An object A in a category C is called a *generator* if for all morphisms $f,g: B \to C$ such that $f \neq g$ there exists an 'element' $x: A \to B$ such that $x \circ f \neq x \circ g$. A cartesian closed category is called *concrete* if 1 is a generator.
(ii) Let C be a higher order theory. A concrete cartesian closed category D together with a functor $F: C \to D$ which preserves cartesian closure is called a *higher order algebra*. Given two higher order algebras $F: C \to D$, $F': C \to D'$ a *homomorphism between higher order algebras* is a functor $H: D \to D'$ such that $F \circ H = F'$. This defines a category C-Alg of C-*algebras*.

Remark: An equivalent 'functorial' definition is to state that an C-algebra is a functor $F: C \to$ Set which preserves finite products and for which the canonical embedding $\Phi_{A,B}: F(A \to B) \to (F(A) \to F(B))$ is a monomorphism. Such a functor may be called *weakly cartesian closed*. (For functorial definitions compare /12/)

Now Parsaye-Ghomi states that the 'hom-category' C(1,_) defined by

objects C(1,A) for A being an object of C

morphisms $C(1,f): C(1,A) \to C(1,B)$, $a \mapsto a \circ f$ with $f: A \to B \in C$

with the canonical functor is an initial C-algebra.

3.2 *Remark*: C(1,_) is an initial C-algebra iff C is concrete.

The problem is that C(1,_) not necessarily is cartesian closed (for cartesian closure we need that $f = g: A \to B \in C$ implies $C(1,f) = C(1,g)$).

Clearly, not every cartesian closed category is concrete.

Example: Consider the specification

$$\underline{\underline{\text{Simple}}} = \text{functs: sorts: } s$$
$$\text{ops: } a: \to s$$
$$f,g: s \to s$$
$$\text{axioms: } f(a) = g(a) = a$$

Then in the initial CART(Simple)-algebra $f \neq g$ (as morphisms) but $\underline{C}(1,f) = \underline{C}(1,g)$.

3.2 only tells us that the hom-category $\underline{C}(1,\_)$ is an initial $\underline{C}$-model only if $\underline{C}$ is concrete. So one may wonder if there exists a $\underline{C}$-model which is initial. The problem is not as simple as we originally believed, and we have not the space to give the full development. But we will give a few propositions which are all based on Lambecks idea of adding indeterminates to a cartesian closed category /11/.

3.3 *Proposition*: Let $\underline{C}$ be a cartesian closed category such that for all objects A either A is weakly initial or 0_A: A → 1 is epi. Such a category is called *sensible* (A is weakly initial if a morphism f: A → B is the unique such morphism).
Then $\underline{C}$ has an initial model iff $\underline{C}$ is concrete.

Remark: A category is sensible if any object has an element.

Corollary: The CART(Simple)-theory does not have an initial object.

The problem is that in a category an equation $0_A \circ a = 0_A \circ b$ may hold even if $a \neq b$.

Example: Consider the specification $\underline{\underline{\text{Strange}}}$ = functs: sorts: A,B

$$\text{ops: } f,g: A \to B$$
$$\text{axioms: } 0_A \circ 'f' = 0_A \circ 'g'$$

In the initial CART(Strange)-category $\underline{C}$ we have that $f \neq g$ but in any $\underline{C}$-model $f = g$ (either f and g are identified or there exists an $a: 1 \to A$). Hence any $\underline{C}$-model is as well a $\underline{C}'$-model where $\underline{C}'$ is the higher model theory w.r.t.

$$\underline{\underline{\text{Sound}}} = \text{functs: sorts: } A,B$$
$$\text{ops: } f,g: A \to B$$
$$\text{axioms: } f = g$$

We conclude that there exists an initial $\underline{C}$-model. Moreover - again in contrast to /19/ - the higher order theory is not complete as f and g are identified in any $\underline{C}$-model.

3.4 *Proposition*: Sensible theories are complete.

We do not know if the converse holds, but

3.5 *Proposition*: Complete theories which have an initial object are sensible.

It may be asked if the notion of a $\underline{C}$-model is sensible.

Acknowledgements: I like to thank Harald Ganzinger for helpful comments.

REFERENCES

/1/ ADJ-group: An Initial Algebra Approach to the Specification, Correctness and Implementation of Abstract Data Types, IBM Res. Rep. RC-6487, 1976

/2/ Backus,J.: Can Programming be Liberated from the von Neumann Style?, CACM 21,1978

/3/ Barendregt,H.: The Lambda Calculus, North Holland 1981

/4/ Bauer,F.L. & al (the CIP Language Group): Report on a Wide Spectrum Language for Program Specification and Development, Rep. TUM - I8104, TU München 1981

/5/ Curien,P.L.: Combinateur Catégoriques, Algorithmes Séquentiels et Programmation Applicative, Thèse d'Etat, Université Paris VII, 1983

/6/ Dybjer,P.: Category-Theoretic Logics and Algebras of Programs, PhD, Göteborg 1983

/7 Ehrig,H./Kreowski,H.-J./Thatcher,J./Wagner,E.G./Wright,J.B.: Parameterized Data Types in Algebraic Specification Languages, ICALP'80, LNCS 85, 1980

/8/ Ganzinger,H.: Parameterized specifications: Parameter Passing and Implementation, Rep. TUM I8110, TU München 1981, To appear in TOPLAS

/9/ Gordon,M.J.C.: The Denotational Description of Programming Languages, Springer 1979

/10/ Hupbach,U.L.: Abstract Implementation of Abstract Data Types, MFCS'80, LNCS 88,1980

/11/ Lambeck,J.: From λ-Calculus to Cartesian Closed Categories, In: To H.B. Curry: Essays on Combinatory Logic, Lambda Calculus and Formalism, Seldin,J.P. & Hindley,J.R. eds., Academic Press 1980

/12/ Lawvere,F.W.: Functorial Semantics of Algebraic Theories, Proc. of the National Academy of Sciences 1963

/13/ Lipeck,U.: Ein algebraischer Kalkül für einen strukturierten Entwurf von Datenabstraktionen, PhD-thesis, Dortmund 1982

/14/ MacLane,S,: Kategorien, Springer 1972

/15/ Manes,E.G.: Algebraic Theories, Springer 1974

/16/ Martin-Löf,P.: Constructive Mathematics and Computer Programming, 6th Int. Congress for Logic,Methodology and Philosophy of Sciences, Hannover 1979

/17/ Milner,R.: A Theory of Type Polymorphism in Programming, JCSS 17, 1979

/18/ Mosses,P.: Abstract Semantic Algebras!, In: Proc. IFIP TC-2 Working Conf. on Formal Description of Programming Concepts II, Garmisch-Partenkirchen 1982

/19/ Parsaye-Ghomi,K.: Higher Order Abstract Data Types, PhD-thesis, UCLA 1981

/20/ Poigné,A.: On Semantic Algebras, Techn. Rep. 156, Abt. Informatik, Univ. Dortmund 1983

/21/ Poigné,A.: Higher Order Data Structures - Cartesian Closure Versus λ-Calculus -, Rep. 166, Abt. Informatik, Univ. Dortmund 1983 (Extended version of this paper)

/22/ Poigné,A./Voss,J.: Programs over Abstract Data Types - On the Implentation of Abstract Data Types, Techn. Rep. Abt. Informatik, Univ. Dortmund 1983

/23/ Scott,D.S.: Relating Theories of the λ-Calculus, In: compare /11/

COMPUTABILITY IN HIGHER TYPES AND THE UNIVERSAL DOMAIN $P\omega$.

G. Longo and S. Martini
Dipartimento di Informatica
Università di Pisa, Corso Italia 40, I-56100 Pisa

Introduction and summary. When dealing with denotational semantics of programming languages, the natural question one may ask is whether the interpretation of a program is an effective object (function) in the given semantical domain. An answer to this question first requires a sound notion of computability in abstract structures, for computability of number theoretic functions may not suffice, i.e. not any program may be interpreted just as a (partial) recursive function. As a matter of fact, mathematical domains for the semantics of type-free and typed languages need to be much richer than ω (the natural numberes): ω, say, does not yield a model for type-free λ-calculus (see LM [1984] for a discussion) and, by definition, the semantics of typed languages, such as typed λ-calculus, whose programs may act also an programs, immediately invòlve function spaces at any finite higher type. As a further motivation, just notice that Computer Science often deals with different and various sorts of data, besides ω.

In the early 50's, Myhill and Shepherdson, MS [1955], gave an elegant characterization of type two functionals, the recursive operators, by a simple notion of application over $P\omega$. Shortly later, papers by Gödel, Kleene and Kreisel (Göd [1958], Kle [1959], Kre [1959], for example) introduced higher type recursion theory, i.e. recursion on the type structure generated by ω. Gödel and Kreisel work was also motivated by consistency results for intuitionistic arithmetic and constructive mathematics.

Some 10-15 years ago, Scott's work an posets (lattices, in particular) provided the category theoretic framework for computability in abstract structures, by a suitable topological notion of approximation. Later on, Ershov (Er [1972,1976] and a lot more in Algebra and Logic

Research partially supported by Min.P.I. (fondi 60%).

and ZML) and Hyland (Hy [1979]) studied the effective type structures over ω of partial and total objects (respectively) as subcategories of topological or limit categories, relating by this higher type recursion theory to computability in abstract structures.

Scott's domains, Scott [1981], and Ershov's complete f_0-spaces are readely seen to be equivalent (see GL [1982] for a discussion and LM [1983] for recent recursion theoretic applications). Similarly to Hyland's approach, an element (function) of a domain is computable when it is the limit of a countable sequence with an r.e. set of indices. In particular the ideal of compact elements below (see later) must be indexed by an r.e. set.

For increasing types, though, the intuition of the "ideal below", say, gets more and more vague. The purpose of this paper is to take back to Myhill-Shepherdson $\langle P\omega,\cdot\rangle$ as much as possible of the abstract (higher types) approach.

More precisely, for $A,B \subseteq P\omega$, set $A \to B = \{d\in P\omega / \forall a\in A\ da\in B\}$. We first show that any effectively given domain can be embedded into $P\omega$ by a continuous and computable retraction (notation: $X \lhd_c A_X$, for some $A_X \subseteq P\omega$, which is also an effectively given domain). Then, if $X \lhd_c A_X$ and $Y \lhd_c A_Y$, one has

(1) $\qquad \mathrm{Cont}(X,Y) \lhd_c A_X \to A_Y$ and $X \times Y \lhd_c A_X \underset{\omega}{\times} A_Y$

(for some simple product in $P\omega$). Also $A_X \to A_Y$ and $A_X \underset{\omega}{\times} A_Y$ are effectively given domains.

Thus an (effective) functional in a given type, over an arbitrary domain, is represented by the application "." and an (r.e.) set in the corresponding type as a subset of $P\omega$.

In particular, let $P \subseteq P\omega$ be the single valued sets, i.e. P is isomorphic to the effectively given domain of the partial functions on ω. Then, for $P^{(1)} = P$, $P^{(n+1)} = P^{(n)} \to P^{(n)}$ extend the classical recursive operators at higher types (this is done for any finite type $\sigma \in T$).

By (1), Ershov's model of the Kleene-Kreisel countable functionals can be effectively embedded, by some G_σ's, into the type structure $\{P^\sigma\}_{\sigma\in T}$ in $P\omega$. Thus the recursive functionals correspond to the r.e. sets in the due types, e.g. f has type $\sigma \to \tau$ iff $G_{\sigma\to\tau}(f)$ is an r.e. set in $P^\sigma \to P^\tau$.

§.1. Domains and $P\omega$

For the notion of domain we refer to Scott [1981]. Shortly, in a poset $(X,\leq)$, set $\check{x} = \{y \in X / x \leq y\}$; then a domain is an algebraic c.p.o. $(X,X_0,\leq)$, where $X_0 = \{x \in X/\check{x}$ is open in Scott topology$\}$, the set of compact elements, and X_0 has bounded joins. That is, if $x_0,y_0 \in X_0$ are compatible (i.e. $\exists z \in X\ x_0,y_0 \leq z$; notation: $x_0 \uparrow y_0$) then $x_0 \sqcup y_0$ exists and is in X_0. An effectively given domain $(X,X_0,\nu,\leq)$ is a countably based domain such that, for the given numbering $\nu : \omega \longrightarrow X_0$, $\nu(n) \uparrow \nu(m)$ is decidable in n,m and $\nu(n) = \nu(p) \sqcup \nu(q)$ is decidable in n,p,q. An element x of an effectively given domain $(X,X_0,\nu,\leq)$ is computable if $\{n/\nu(n) \leq x\}$ is r.e. (notation: $x \in X_c$). As a matter of fact Scott [1981] introduces domains as the completion over filtres of neighbourhoods systems. The equivalence with the above definition can be readily seen (cf. GL [1982])

Of course, for a given canonical numbering $e : \omega \to P\omega_0$ of the finite sets, $(P\omega,P\omega_0,e,\subseteq)$ is an effectively given domain.

The category of (effectively given) domains is cartesian closed with continuous functions (w.r. t. Scott topology) as morphisms (notation: Cont(X,Y) are the continuous functions from X to Y). Thus the notions of compact and computable elements are inherited at higher types. In particular $\mathrm{Cont}(X,Y)_c$ are the continuous and computable maps from X to Y.

Notation (i) $<,> : \omega^2 \leftrightarrow \omega$ is a bijective pairing and $\{e_n\}_{n\in\omega} = P\omega_0$, the finite subsets of ω.

(ii) Given domains $(X,X_0,\leq)$ and $(Y,Y_0,\leq)$ set step $xy = \lambda z \cdot$ (if $x \leq z$ then y else $\bot$); step xy is continuous if $x \in X_0$. As well known, the elements of $\mathrm{Cont}(X,Y)_0$ are exactly the finite sups of compatible step functions over X_0,Y_0. If (X,X_0,ν) and (Y,Y_0,μ) are effectively given, then for $g_n \in \mathrm{Cont}(X,Y)_0$ one has $g_n = \bigsqcup_{<i,j>\in e_{k(n)}}$ step $\nu(i)\mu(j) = \bigsqcup_{e_{k(n)}}$ step $\nu(i)\mu(j)$ where $k : \omega \to \omega$ is a recursive function such that $e_{k(n)} = e_n$ if for every $J \subseteq e_n$, $J = \{<i_1,j_1>,\dots,<i_p,j_p>\}$, one has step $\nu(i_1)\mu(j_1)\uparrow\dots\uparrow$ step $\nu(i_p)\nu(j_p)$ and $e_{k(n)} = \emptyset$ otherwise.

1.1 Lemma. Let ν and μ be the given numbering of X_0 and Y_0 (respect.), then $f \in \mathrm{Cont}(X,Y)_c$ iff $f \in \mathrm{Cont}(X,Y)$ and $\mu(j) \leq f(\nu(i))$ is semidecidable in i,j.

Proof. Let $\{g_n\}_{n\in\omega} = \mathrm{Cont}(X,Y)_0$, then $g_n = \bigsqcup_{e_{k(n)}}$ step $\nu(i)\mu(j) \leq f$ iff $\forall <i,j> \in e_{k(n)}\ \mu(j) \leq f(\nu(i))$. The result easily follows. ∎

Any domain $(X,X_0,\leq)$ induces a structure on its subsets by the induced Scott topology. That is:

1.2 <u>Remark</u>. Let $(X,X_0,\leq)$ be a domain and $Y \subseteq X$. Define $Y_0 = \{y \in Y/\check{y} \subseteq Y$ is open in the induced topology). Then $(Y,Y_0,\leq)$ is a domain iff

1) Y is a (sub-) c.p.o.

2) Y_0 has bounded joins (w.r.t.Y)

3) $\forall y,y' \in Y(y \nleq y' \Rightarrow \exists y_0 \in Y_0\ y_0 \leq y$ and $y_0 \nleq y')$.

1.3 <u>Lemma</u>. Let $(X,X_0,\leq)$ be a domain. Then any closed subset of X, with the induced structure, is a domain.

<u>Proof</u>. Let Y be a closed subset of X. Then $y \in Y$ <u>and</u> $y' \leq y \Rightarrow y' \in Y$ and $x \notin Y \Rightarrow \exists x_0 \in X_0\ x_0 \notin Y$ <u>and</u> $x_0 \leq x$, since $\bar{Y}$ is open and $\{x_0/x_0 \in X_0\}$ is a basis for the topology on X. Thus 1,2,3 in 1.2 easily follow.

Of course, if $Y \subseteq X$ is closed, $Y_0 = X_0 \cap Y$.

1.4 <u>Definition</u>. Let $(X,X_0,\nu,\leq)$ be an effectively given domain. $Y \subseteq X$ is <u>effective</u> if $\nu(n) \in Y$ is decidable in n.

Clearly, any closed effective subset Y of an effectively given domain X is also an effectively given (sub-)domain. Moreover $Y_c = Y \cap X_c$.

Recall now that, for sets X and Y, a <u>retraction</u> (f,g) is a pair $g : X \to Y$ and $f : Y \to X$ such that $f \circ g = id_X$ (notation: $X < Y$, via (g,f)). In case X and Y are effectively given domains and $X \lhd Y$ via some continuous and computable functions f and g, we write $X \lhd_c Y$. We show next that any effectively given domain is a continuous and computable retraction of an effectively given subdomain of $P\omega$ (see also remark 1.6).

1.5 <u>Theorem</u>. Let $(X,X_0,\nu,\leq)$ be an effectively domain. Then there exists $A_X \subseteq P\omega$ closed an effective such that $X \lhd_c A_X$.

<u>Proof</u>. For sake of simplicity, write x_n for $\nu(n)$ in X_0. By assumption, X is a countably based T_0-space. Thus we can use the embedding $G : X \to P\omega$ given in Scott [1976], i.e. $G(x) = \{n/x_n \leq x\}$. Define then $A_X = \{a \in P\omega/\exists x \in X\ a \subseteq G(x)\}$ and $F : A_X \to X$ by $F(a) = \sqcup\{x_n/n \in a\}$.

<u>Claim 1</u>. F is well defined and $F \circ G = id_X$. Just notice that $\forall a \in A_X\ \exists x \in X\ \forall n \in a\ x_n \leq x$ and then $F(a) = \sqcup\{x_n/n \in a\}$ exists in X. $F(G(x)) = x$ is immediate.

<u>Claim 2</u>. A_X is closed.

A_X is clearly downward closed. Take now an arbitrary directed set $\{e_i\}_{i\in I}$ in A_X. We only need to show that $\bigcup_I e_i \in A_X$. Notice that $F(e_i) = \sqcup\{x_n/n \in e_i\} \in X_0$ and that $\forall i,j \in I$ $F(e_i) \sqcup F(e_j) = F(e_i \cup e_j)$ Thus $x = \sqcup\{F(e_i)/i \in I\} \in X$ exists and $\bigcup_I e_i \subseteq G(x) \in A_X$. This proves claim 2.

<u>Claim 3</u>. A_X is effective.

In fact $e_n \in A_X \Leftrightarrow \exists z\ \forall p \in e_n\ x_p \leq z$, which is decidable.

By the claims and 1.3, A_X is an effectively given domain.

<u>Claim 4</u>. $G \in \mathrm{Cont}(X,A_X)_c$ and $F \in \mathrm{Cont}(A_X,X)_c$, i.e. G and F are continuous and computable.

The proof of the continuity is a simple exercise.

Let now $\{e^A_n\}_{n\in\omega}$ be a numbering of $(A_X)_0 = P\omega_0 \cap A_X$. Then $e^A_n \subseteq G(x_m)$ is clearly decidable in n,m and lemma 1.1 applies. Similarly for F. ▪

1.6 <u>Remark</u>. (i) Let X, A_X, G and F be as in 1.5 (and its proof). Clearly $G \circ F \geq id_{A_X}$. Does $G \circ F$ give a retract $a_X \in P\omega$ (a closure, actually) such that $A_X = \mathrm{range}\ a_X$ (see Scott [1976])? This is not true in general, since the range of any $a_X \in P\omega$ is a lattice, whereas X is a lattice iff A_X is a lattice iff $A_X = P\omega$. Moreover it is easy to give a domain X such that the corresponding A_X does not admit any $\bar{F} \in \mathrm{Cont}(P\omega,X)$ extending $F \in \mathrm{Cont}(A_X,X)$. (Recall that continuous lattices are exactly the injective spaces (see Scott [1972])).

Therefore, one may define, using 2.1 below,
$a_X = \mathrm{Graph}(G \circ F) = \{\langle n,m\rangle/m \in G \circ F(e_n)\} \in P\omega_c$ (the r.e. sets) iff X is a lattice.

(ii) Then main aim of this paper is to interpret within $P\omega$ the higher types objects over abstract structures, i.e. to interpret in $P\omega$ the space of morphisms (the "arrow" objects) of some interesting categories. Taking domains which are lattices, by (i), we could use he full strenght of the theory of retracts in §.4 of Scott [1976], with the corresponding notion of "$\to$" in $P\omega$. We prefer to deal with the more general cases for two reasons. First, in Plo [1978] general sound motivations are given for the computational and semantic interest of posets which are not lattices (see also Scott [1981]). The domain P, say, of partial functions from ω to ω is not a lattice; the interest of this space is obvious and our main applications will deal with it. Second, by the interpretation of "$\to$" in $P\omega$ used below our wotk directly relates to classical recursion theory.

(iii) Another possibility would be to consider Plotkin's universal domain $T\omega$, which is not a lattice. Then any (effectively given) domain would be (isomorphic to) a retract of $T\omega$, namely the range of an element a_X of $T\omega$, representing, via "$\cdot$" in $T\omega$, the continuous (and computable) function which corresponds to $G \circ F$ above. a_X would also be a closure (and a computable element of $T\omega$, i.e. a pair of disjoint r.e. sets), see Plo [1977; theor. 11,20,21]. Plotkin gives a theory of retracts corresponding to Scott's work for $P\omega$. We would miss though the natural extension to higher types of Myhill- Shepherdson recursive operators, which motivated Lo [1982b;§.2] and this paper, as well as the simple notion of "application" they are based on (see below). As a matter of fact, what is gained by dealing with a c.p.o. instead of a lattice is lost in simplicity and transparency, since the notion of application over $T\omega$ is not so immediate (see BL [1980,1981] for some work on $T\omega$ as a model of type-free λ-calculus and as a tool for type two recursion theory).

§.2. Type structures in $P\omega$

Let $a,b \in P\omega$. Define

$$a \cdot b = \{m / \exists e_n \subseteq b \ \langle n,m\rangle \in a\}.$$

Given $A,B \subseteq P\omega$, set now

$$A \to B = \{d \in P\omega / \forall a \in A \ da \in B\}.$$

As for products, for $a,b \in P\omega$, define

$$[a,b] = \{\langle 1,n\rangle / n \in a\} \cup \{\langle 2,n\rangle / n \in b\}.$$

Set then

$$A \underset{\omega}{\times} B = \{[a,b] / a \in A \ \text{and} \ b \in B\}.$$

For $e_1 = \{0\}$ and $e_2 = \{1\}$, $\underset{\omega}{\times}$ in $P\omega$ has projections $\lambda y \cdot y\{0\}$ and $\lambda y \cdot y\{1\}$.

2.1 Remark. (i) For $a \in P\omega$ and $f \in \mathrm{Cont}(P\omega,P\omega)$ set $\mathrm{Funct}(a) = \lambda x . ax \in \mathrm{Cont}(P\omega,P\omega)$ and $\mathrm{Graph}(f) = \{\langle n,m\rangle / m \in f(e_n)\}$. Then $\mathrm{Cont}(P\omega,P\omega) \lhd P\omega$, via (Graph, Funct). Both Funct and Graph are continuous. Moreover, given "$\cdot$", Graph is the unique continuous function such that $\mathrm{Graph}(f) \cdot a = f(a)$. In other words the interpretation of λ-abstraction is unique in $P\omega$ (in Lo [1982a] this is shown in a general setting).

(ii) Graph and Funct are also computable, in the due types. Let $\mathrm{Cont}(P\omega,P\omega)_0 = \{g_n\}_{n\in\omega}$. Then $g_n = \bigsqcup_{e_{k(n)}} \mathrm{step}\, e_i e_j \le \mathrm{Funct}(e_p) =$

$= \bigcup_{<r,s> \in e_p} \text{step}\, e_r\{s\}$ is decidable in n,p. Moreover $e_p \subseteq \text{Graph}(g_n) = \{<m,q>/q \in (\bigcup_{e_{k(n)}} \text{step}\, e_i e_j)(e_m)\}$ is also decidable in p and n. Thus lemma 1.1 applies.

2.2 Lemma. Let A,B closed (and effective) subsets of $P\omega$. Then $A \to B$, $A \underset{\omega}{\times} B$ and $A \cap B$ are closed (and effective).

Proof. Let $d' \subseteq d \in A \to B$. Then $\forall a \in A$ $d'a \subseteq da \in B$ and, by the assumption, $A \to B$ is downward closed.

Let $d \notin A \to B$. Then for some $a \in A$, $da \notin B$. By the assumption, $\exists e_n \subseteq da$ $\check{e}_n \subseteq \bar{B}$. Set then

$$e_q = \{<p,m>/m \in e_n \text{ and } p = \min i\, [e_i \subseteq a \text{ and } <i,m> \in d]\}.$$

Clearly $e_n = e_q a \subseteq da$ and $d \in \check{e}_q \subseteq A \to B$. Thus $A \to B$ is closed.

Finally $e_p \in A \to B$ iff $\forall J \subseteq e_p$ $(\bigcup_{<r,s>\in J} e_r \in A \quad \bigcup_{<r,s>\in J} \{s\} \in B)$ (This is trivial in view of $e_p a = \bigcup_{e_n \subseteq a} \{m/<n,m> \in e_p\}$). This proves that, if A and B are effective, then also $A \to B$ is effective.

The result is immediate for $A \underset{\omega}{\times} B$ and $A \cap B$. ∎

2.3 Definition. A collection T of generalized type symbols is the least set containing the set AT of atomic types $\phi,\psi\ldots$ and such that, if $\sigma,\tau \in T$, then $\sigma\to\tau$, $\sigma \times \tau \in T$.

The extended type symbols are the least set T_E such that $T \subseteq T_E$ and if $\sigma,\tau \in T_E$ then $\sigma \cap \tau \in T_E$.

2.4 Remark. The set T_E is just a little bigger than the set of extended type symbols in BCD [1981] (except for type ω). We introduced $\sigma \times \tau$ just for uniformity with respect to the category of domain, which is cartesian closed. Nearly all the results below dealing with $\underset{\omega}{\times}$, though, are trivial and carry little information. This is not so for $\sigma \cap \tau$. However our structure with "$\to$" in $P\omega$ is not a category for quite trivial reasons: there are too many morphisms for each function (in the sense of the category of sets), see §.3. This is the price we pay for having a classical and natural "." and $\cap$, also.

2.5 Definition. Let $V : AT \to PP\omega$ and set $V^\phi = V(\phi)$. Extend then V to $V : T_E \to PP\omega$ by $V^{\sigma\to\tau} = V^\sigma \to V^\tau$, $V^{\sigma\times\tau} = V^\sigma \underset{\omega}{\times} V^\tau$ and $V^{\sigma\cap\tau} = V^\sigma \cap V^\tau$.

By induction, lemma 2.2 immediately gives the following theorem:

2.6 Theorem. Let $V^\phi \subseteq P\omega$ be closed (and effective) for all $\phi \in AT$. Then $\forall\sigma \in T_E$ V^σ is closed (and effective).

The following facts give some structural information on $\{V^\sigma\}_{\sigma\in T_E}$ as a type structure in $P\omega$.

2.7 Lemma.

1) $\forall\phi \in AT\ \emptyset \in V^{\phi} \Rightarrow \forall\sigma \in T_E\ \emptyset \in V^{\sigma}$

2) $\forall\phi \in AT\ \omega \notin V^{\phi} \Rightarrow \forall\sigma \in T_E\ \omega \notin V^{\sigma}$

Proof. Notice that $\forall a \in P\omega\ \emptyset a = \emptyset$ and $\omega a = \omega$ ∎

Of course, for a closed set $V, V = P\omega$ iff $\omega \in V$.

2.8 Proposition. Let $V^{\phi} \neq P\omega$ be closed for all $\phi \in AT$. Then one has, for all $\sigma,\tau,\rho,\nu \in T_E$:

(i) $V^{\sigma\to\tau} \subseteq V^{\rho\to\nu} \Leftrightarrow V^{\rho} \subseteq V^{\sigma}$ and $V^{\tau} \subseteq V^{\nu}$.

(ii) $V^{\sigma\times\tau} \subseteq V^{\rho\times\nu} \Leftrightarrow V^{\sigma} \subseteq V^{\rho}$ and $V^{\tau} \subseteq V^{\nu}$.

Proof. (i) $\Leftarrow$ Easy.

$\Rightarrow$ We first show $V^{\tau} \subseteq V^{\nu}$. Otherwise, let $a \in V^{\tau}\setminus V^{\nu}$. Then Graph $(\lambda x\, .\, a) \in V^{\sigma} \to V^{\tau}$ and Graph $(\lambda x\, .\, a) \notin V^{\rho\to\nu}$, impossible. As for $V^{\rho} \subseteq V^{\sigma}$, assume that $b \in V^{\rho} \setminus V^{\sigma}$. Since V^{ρ} and V^{σ} are closed, for some $e_n \in V^{\rho}\setminus V^{\sigma}$, $b \in \check{e}_n \subseteq V^{\nu}$. Take now $e_m \notin V^{\nu}$ (e_m exists by 2.6) and $f = \text{step}\ e_n e_m$. Then $f \in \text{Cont}(P\omega,P\omega)$ and $\text{Graph}(f) \in V^{\sigma} \to V^{\tau}$, while $\text{Graph}(f) \notin V^{\rho} \to V^{\nu}$.

(ii) Obvious ∎

Thus $\to$ (and $\underset{\omega}{\times}$) are injective type constructors, except for $\lambda x\, .\, (x \to P\omega)$. (Note that "$\to$" is controvariant in the first argument). Moreover, if $\forall\phi \in AT\ \omega \notin V^{\phi}$, then $\bigcup_{\sigma\in T_E} V^{\sigma} \neq P\omega$.

Recall now that any closed (and effective) subset of $P\omega$ is an (effectively given) domain.

2.9 Lemma. Let $A \subseteq P\omega$ and $f \in \text{Cont}(A,P\omega)$. Define $\text{Ext}(f) \in \text{Cont}(P\omega,P\omega)$ by $\text{Ext}(f)(b) = \bigcup_{e_n \subseteq b} \cap \{f(a)/e_n \subseteq a \in A\}$. Then, if A is closed (and effective),

$$\text{Ext} \in \text{Cont}(\text{Cont}(A,P\omega),\ \text{Cont}(P\omega,P\omega))_{(c)}.$$

Proof. Ext(f) is a continuous extensions of f. Notice that $\text{Ext}(f)(b) = \cup \{f(e_n)/e_n \subseteq b$ and $e_n \in A\}$, for A is a downward closed and f is monotone. Then the continuity of Ext follows by an easy computation. Assume now that A is also effective: let $\{e^A_n\}_{n\in\omega}$ be a numbering of $A_o = P\omega_o \cap A$; $\{g_n\}_{n\in\omega} = \text{Cont}(A,P\omega)_o$ and $\{h_n\}_{n\in\omega} = \text{Cont}(P\omega,P\omega)_o$. Recall now that $g_n = \bigsqcup_{e_{k(n)}} \text{step}\ e^A_i e^A_j$, where k is the "compatibility function" with respect to A. Define then a (total) computable fucntion t such that if $e_{k(n)} = \emptyset$, $t(n) = k(n)$; and, if $e_{k(n)} \neq \emptyset$, $e_{t(n)}$ is obtained by substituting for every $\langle i,j\rangle \in e_{k(n)}$ the pair $\langle r,s\rangle$ with $e^A_i = e_r$ and $e^A_j = e_s$ (remember that $e^A_i = e_i$ if $e_i \in A$, or $e^A_i = \emptyset$). Therefore $g_n = g_{t(n)}$, $\text{Ext}(g_n) = \text{Ext}(g_{t(n)}) = h_{t(n)}$ and, hence, $h_m \le h_{t(n)}$ is decidable.

Thus lemma 1.1 applies and Ext is computable. ∎

2.10 Lemma. Let $A,B \subseteq P\omega$ be closed (and effective). Then

$$\mathrm{Cont}(A,B) \lhd_{(c)} A \to B$$

Proof. Let Graph and Funct as in 2.1. Set $\overline{\mathrm{Graph}} = \mathrm{Graph} \circ \mathrm{Ext}$. Then $(\overline{\mathrm{Graph}}, \mathrm{Funct})$ is the required continuous (and computable) embedding, by 2.1 and 2.9. ∎

Our main result (2.12 below) uses a generalized version of Myhill-Shepherdson theorem GMS). This is stated in Er [1976]; a proof may be found in GL [1982]. GMS theorem relates effective operators over numbered sets to continuous and computable functions in the category of domains. Recall that F from $\{c_n\}_{n\in\omega}$ to $\{d_n\}_{n\in\omega}$ is an effective operator iff, for some recursive function f, $F(c_n) = d_{f(n)}$. It is easy to give some "natural" (gödel-) numbering to the computable part X_c of an effectively given domain (see the principal computable enumeration in Er [1976] or GL [1982] or CDL [1983], where GMS is discussed in domains with a suitable notion of application). Of course, in the interesting cases this (gödel-) numbering is not one one.

2.11 Theorem. (GMS) Let $(X,X_0,\nu,\leq)$ and $(Y,Y_0,\mu,\leq)$ be effectively given domains. Let $X_c = \{c_n\}_{n\in\omega}$ and $Y_c = \{d_n\}_{n\in\omega}$ as above and let f map X to Y. Then f is (induces) an effective operator from X_c to Y_c iff $f \in \mathrm{Cont}(X,Y)_c$.

Consider now the category of domains and assume that for any $\phi \in AT$, $(X^\phi,X_0^\phi,\leq)$ is a domain. Set then, for $\sigma,\tau \in T$, $X^{\sigma\to\tau}=\mathrm{Cont}(X^\sigma,X^\tau)$ and $X^{\sigma\times\tau} = X^\sigma \times X^\tau$, as usual.

2.12 Theorem. Let $(X^\phi,X_0^\phi,\nu,\leq)$ be an effectively given domain, for all $\phi \in AT$. Assume that, for all $\phi \in AT$, $A^\phi \subseteq P\omega$ is closed, effective and satisfies $X^\phi \lhd_c A^\phi$. Then

$$\forall\sigma \in T\ X^\sigma \lhd_c A^\sigma.$$

(As for the definition of A^σ, see 2.5)

Proof. (By induction). Let $X^\sigma \lhd_c A^\sigma$, via (G_σ,F_σ), and $X^\tau \lhd_c A^\tau$, via (G_τ,F_τ). We first prove

(1) $\quad X^{\sigma\to\tau} = \mathrm{Cont}(X^\sigma,X^\tau) \lhd_c A^\sigma \to A^\tau = A^{\sigma\to\tau}$

Define $\mathrm{Gra}_{\sigma\to\tau}$ from $X^{\sigma\to\tau}$ to $\mathrm{Cont}(A^\sigma,A^\tau)$ and $\mathrm{Fun}_{\sigma\to\tau}$ from $\mathrm{Cont}(A^\sigma,A^\tau)$ to $X^{\sigma\to\tau}$ by

$$\mathrm{Gra}_{\sigma\to\tau} = \lambda x.\ G_\tau \circ x \circ F_\sigma$$
$$\mathrm{Fun}_{\sigma\to\tau} = \lambda x.\ F_\tau \circ x \circ G_\sigma$$

(The following diagram visualizes the definition

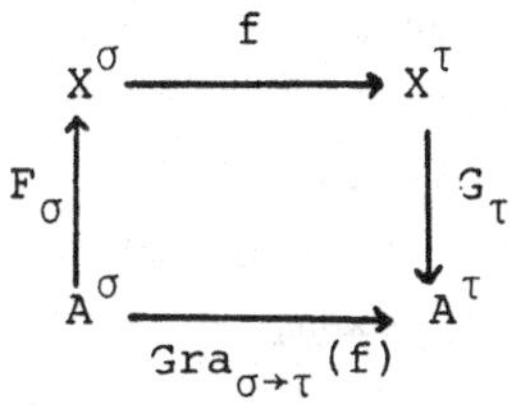

Similarly for $Fun_{\sigma\to\tau}$).

In the category of effectively given domains the composition operator "o" is continuous and computable, (see Scott [1981]). Let $X_c^{\sigma\to\tau} = \{c_n\}_{n\in\omega}$ and $Cont(A^\sigma,A^\tau)_c = \{d_n\}_{n\in\omega}$. By assumption G_τ and F_σ are continuous and computable. Then, by GMS theorem for "o", for some recursive function f

$$Gra_{\sigma\to\tau}(c_n) = G_\tau \circ c_n \circ F_\sigma = d_{f(n)}$$

(of course, f depends uniformely effectively on (the indices for) G_τ and F_σ). By GMS again, $Gra_{\sigma\to\tau} \in Cont(X^{\sigma\to\tau}, Cont(A^\sigma,A^\tau))_c$. Similarly for $Fun_{\sigma\to\tau}$.

Set now $G_{\sigma\to\tau} = \overline{Graph} \circ Gra_{\sigma\to\tau}$, where $\overline{Graph} = Graph \circ Ext$, and

$$F_{\sigma\to\tau} = Fun_{\sigma\to\tau} \circ Funct.$$

For $f \in Cont(P\omega,P\omega)$ such that range $(f \restriction A^\sigma) \subseteq A^\tau$, set

(*) $$Fun_{\sigma\to\tau}(f) = Fun_{\sigma\to\tau}(f \restriction A^\sigma).$$

Compute then, for $f \in X^{\sigma\to\tau}$,

$$\begin{aligned} F_{\sigma\to\tau} \circ G_{\sigma\to\tau}(f) &= Fun_{\sigma\to\tau} \circ Funct \circ \overline{Graph} \bullet Gra_{\sigma\to\tau}(f) \\ &= Fun_{\sigma\to\tau} \circ Gra_{\sigma\to\tau}(f), \text{ by 2.1 (i) and (*)} \\ &= F_\tau \circ G_\tau \circ f \circ F_\sigma \circ G_\sigma \\ &= f. \end{aligned}$$

$G_{\sigma\to\tau}$ and $F_{\sigma\to\tau}$ are clearly continuous and computable.

As for

(2) $$X^{\sigma\times\tau} = X^\sigma \times X^\tau \triangleleft_c A^\sigma \underset{\omega}{\times} A^\tau = A^{\sigma\times\tau},$$

recall first that, in $P\omega$, $[a,b]\{0\} = a$ and $[a,b]\{1\} = b$, for $e_1 = \{0\}$ and $e_2 = \{1\}$. Set then

$$G_{\sigma\times\tau}(x,y) = [G_\sigma(x), G_\tau(y)]$$

and

$$F_{\sigma\times\tau} = \lambda y.F_\sigma(y\{0\}) \times F_\tau(y\{1\}).$$

Thus $G_{\sigma\times\tau}$ is continuous and computable, since so are the projections in the category of domains and $[\cdot,\cdot]$ in $P\omega$. Similarly for $F_{\sigma\times\tau}$. Finally compute

$$\begin{aligned} F_{\sigma\times\tau} \circ G_{\sigma\times\tau}(x,y) &= F_\sigma(G_\sigma(x)) \times F_\tau(G_\tau(y)) \\ &= (x,y). \end{aligned}$$

■

In view of theorem 1.5, any effectively given domain is (canonically) a computable retraction of some closed and effective subset of

$P\omega$. In the sequel, though, we will also use another natural embedding.

Note now that computable maps, such as G_σ and F_σ, take computable objects to computable objects. Then, by theorem 2.12, one may understand computable functionals in an anstract structure simply by r.e. sets and "$\cdot$" over $P\omega$. For example, in the notation of 2.12, let $f \in Cont(X^\sigma, X^\tau)_c$. By the definition, this means that the "ideal below" f has an r.e. set of indices. The ideal below, though, as a set of finite sups of step functions (and their indices), is not an immediate notion to hanbled. By theorem 2.12, f is characterized by $G_{\sigma\to\tau}(f) \in A^\sigma \to A^\tau \cap RE$, i.e. by an r.e. set which takes, by "$\cdot$", A^σ into A^τ.

Concluding Remark.

The work done so far may be applied to the number theoretic hierarchy of functionals. In particular we relate a type structure in $P\omega$ to the continuous and computable functionals, in any finite type, over the flat cpo $\omega^\perp$ of the integer, with the Scott topology. Ershov, see Er [1976] for an account and references, characterized by this the Kleene-Kreisel countable (continuous) functionals (Kle [1959], Kre [1959] and the Hereditarely Effective Operations (HEO; Tro [1973]).

Let $\omega^\perp$ be as above and embed ω with the discrete topology. Then $E = Cont(\omega, \omega^\perp)$ are the partial functions from ω to ω. E is an effectively given domain and is isomorphic to

$$P = \{\{\langle n,m\rangle / m = f(n)\} / f \in E\} \subseteq P\omega$$

Let T be a collection of generalized type symbols, as in 2.3, with only one atomic type, (1), say. Set then, for $\sigma, \tau \in T$, $E^{(1)} = E$, $E^{\sigma\to\tau} = Cont(E^\sigma, E^\tau)$, $E^{\sigma\times\tau} = E^\sigma \times E^\tau$; and $P^{(1)} = P$, $P^{\sigma\to\tau} = P^\sigma \to P^\tau$, $P^{\sigma\times\tau} = P^\sigma \underset{\omega}{\times} P^\tau$.

Theorem. $\forall\sigma \in T\ E^\sigma \triangleleft_c P^\sigma$, via (G_σ, F_σ)

Proof. In view of the isomorphism between $E^{(1)}$ and $P^{(1)}$, via $(G_{(1)}, F_{(1)})$ say, the result follows from theorem 2.12. ∎

As pointed out after 2.12, one then has, for each $\sigma \in T$, $f \in E^\sigma_c$ iff $G_\sigma(f) \in P^\sigma_c$, where by 2.2 P^σ_c is well defined and $P^\sigma_c = P^\sigma \cap RE$.

References

BL [1980] Barendregt,H., Longo,G., Equality of lambda-terms in the model $T\omega$, in: To H.B. Curry: Essays on Combinatory Logic Lambda Calculus and Formalism, Hindley and Seldin (Eds), Academic Press, New York, 303-337.

BL [1981] Barendregt,H., Longo,G., Recursion theoretic operators and morphisms of numbered sets, Fundamenta Mathematicae, CXIX (1982), to appear.

CDL [1983] Coppo,M., Dezani-Ciancaglini,M., Longo,G., Applicative Information Systems, Conference on Trees in Algebra and Programming Ausiello, Protasi (eds), Springer-Verlag LNCS 159 (revised: Info. Contr., to appear).

Er [1972] Ershov,Yu.L., Computable Functionals of finite types, Algebra and Logic vol. 11 n. 4.

Er [1976] Ershov,Yu.L., Model C of partial continuous functionals, in: Logic Colloquium 76, Gandy, Hyland (Eds), North-Holland, 1977.

GL [1982] Giannini,P., Longo,G., Effectively given domains and lambda-calculus semantics, Nota Scientifica, D.I. Università di Pisa.

Gö [1958] Gödel,K., Uber eine bicher noch nicht benützte Erweiterung des finiten Standpunktes, Dialettica vol. 12 (1958), 280-287.

Hyl [1979] Hyland,M., Filter Spaces and Continuous functionals, Annals Math Logic, 16 (1979) 101-143.

KP [1979] Kanda,A., Park,D., When are two effectively given domains identical?, Proc. 4th GI Conf in T.C.S., Aachen, LNCS 67, Springer-Verlag.

Kle [1959] Kleene,S., Countable Functionals, in: Constructivity in Mathematics, Heyting (Ed), North-Holland.

Kre [1959] Kreisel,G., Interpretation of analysis by means of constructive functionals of finite types, in Constructivity in Mathematics, Heyting (Ed), North-Holland.

Lo [1982a] Longo,G., Set-theoretical models of lambda-calculus: theories, expansions, isomorphisms, Annals Pure Applied Logic (formely: Ann. Math. Logic) 24, 153-188.

Lo [1982b] Longo,G., Hereditary Partial Effective Functionals in any finite type, Preliminary note, Forshungsinstitut f. Math. ETH Zřich.

LM [1983] Longo,G., Moggi,E., The Hereditary Partial Effective Functionals and Recursion Theory in higher types, J. Symb. Logic (to appear).

LM [1984] Longo,G., Moggi,E., Gödel-numberings, principal morphisms, combinatory algebras, Nota Sci. 9-83-21. Dip. Informatica, Pisa.

MS [1955] Myhill,J., Shepherdson,C., Effective operations on partial recursive functions, Zeit. Math. Logik, 1, 310-317.

Nor [1980] Normann,D., Recursion on the Countable Functionals LNM 811 Springer-Verlag, Berlin.

Pl [1978] Plotkin,G., $T\omega$ as a universal domain, J. Comp. and Syst. Sciences vol. 17, 2(1978), 209-236.

Ro [1967] Rogers,H., Theory of Recursive Functions and Effective Computability, Mc Graw-Hill, New York.

Scott [1972] Scott,D., Continuous lattices, in Toposes, Algebraic Geometry and Logic (Law v ere ed), Springer-Verlag LNM 274, 97-136.

Scott [1976] Scott,D., Data types as lattices, SIAM J. Comp. 5,3,522-587.

Scott [1981] Scott;D., Lectures on a Mathematical Theory of Computation. Oxford University Computing Laboratory, Technical Monogragh PRG-19.

Smyth [1977] Smyth,M., Effectively given domains, Theor. Comp. Science 5 (1977) 257-274.

Smyth [1979] Smyth,M., Computability in Categories, Theory of Computation Report, University of Warwick.

Tro [1973] Troelstra,A., Metamathematical Investigation of Intuitionistic Arithmetic and Analysis, LNM 344 Springer-Verlag, Berlin.

ON THE STRUCTURE OF POLYNOMIAL TIME DEGREES.

Klaus Ambos-Spies
Lehrstuhl für Informatik II
Universität Dortmund
D-4600 Dortmund 50
W.Germany.

ABSTRACT. The main results of this paper are the following. 1) For both the polynomial time many-one and the polynomial time Turing degrees of recursive sets, every countable distributive lattice can be embedded in any interval of degrees. Furthermore, certain restraints - like preservation of the least or greatest element - can be imposed on the embeddings. 2) The upper semi-lattice of polynomial time many-one degrees is distributive, whereas that of the polynomial time Turing degrees is nondistributive. This gives the first (elementary) difference between the algebraic structures of p-many-one and p-Turing degrees, respectively.

INTRODUCTION.

Cook [6] and Karp [7] introduced two notions of polynomial time bounded reducibilities, namely polynomial time Turing (p-T) and many-one (p-m) reducibilities, respectively. These notions proved to be of great value for investigations into the nature of NP-sets as well as sets of other complexity classes. Ladner [8] was the first to study the polynomial time (p-) degrees induced by these reducibility notions. He showed that, for both notions, the p-degrees of recursive sets form an upper semilattice (u.s.l) but not a lattice, that the p-degrees are dense, that every nonzero p-degree splits, i.e. is the join of two lesser ones, and that minimal pairs of p-degrees exist, i.e. pairs of incomparable degrees $\underset{\sim}{a}$ and $\underset{\sim}{b}$ such that $\underset{\sim}{a} \cap \underset{\sim}{b} = \underset{\sim}{0}$, $\underset{\sim}{0}$ the degree of P-sets. A second step towards a characterization of the structure of p-degrees was done by Landweber, Lipton and Robertson [10] and Chew and Machtey [5]. They introduced a refinement of Ladner's diagonalization technique, which allowed to simplify and extend some of the results in [8]. E.g. they showed that every nonzero p-degree bounds a minimal pair.

Here we continue the investigations into the structure of the polynomial degrees. The purpose of this paper is twofold.

We first state quite general results on sublattices of the p-degrees: Every countable distributive lattice can be embedded in any interval of polynomial degrees. Furthermore, the embeddings can be chosen to preserve the greatest or least element. Our embedding results unify and extend most of the previously obtained results on the polynomial degrees. E.g. we obtain the density, splitting and minimal pair theorems of [8,10,5] by considering embeddings of the 2-atom Boolean lattice.

The second aim of this paper is to distinguish the degree structures for p-many-one reducibility and p-Turing reducibility, respectively. Though it is wellknown that these reducibility notions differ on the recursive sets ([9]), so far no algebraic property had been found which distinguishes the degree structures of the respective reducibility notions on the recursive non-polynomial sets (due to a minor pathology of the p-m-reducibility the structure of p-m-degrees differs from that of the p-T-degrees on P). In fact, the way results on the p-degrees are usually proved might suggest that the upper semi-lattices of the p-m and p-T degrees of recursive but non-polynomial sets are isomorphic. Namely the typical arguments that the p-degrees (with respect to some reducibility notion) have a certain property usually show that the reductions which are required to hold in fact hold for (the strong) p-m-reducibility while the reductions which are required to fail in fact fail for (the weak) p-T-reducibility. So one obtains the result simultaneously for many-one and Turing reducibility (as well as for any intermediate reducibility). As we will show here, however, this argument is misleading. The structures of p-m and p-T degrees are not isomorphic: The u.s.l. of polynomial time many-one degrees is distributive, that of polynomial time Turing degrees is not. So in fact the elementary theories of the partial orderings of p-many-one respective p-Turing degrees are not elementarily equivalent.

We will state our results only for p-m and p-T reducibilities, which we consider to be the most important polynomial time reducibilities. Similar results can be obtained, however, for the intermediate p-reducibilities. Moreover the results transfer to various other complexity classes in place of P.

§0. PRELIMINARIES.

The set of nonnegative integers is denoted by $\mathbb{N}$. Lower case letters i,j,k,l, m,n,s stand for elements of $\mathbb{N}$. $\Sigma = \{0,1\}$. x,y,z denote strings over Σ, i.e. elements of Σ^*; capital letters A, B, C, ... stand for *recursive* subsets of Σ^*. $|x|$ is the length of x. We identify a set and its characteristic function, i.e. $x \in A$ iff $A(x) = 1$ and $x \notin A$ iff $A(x) = 0$. $\bar{A}$ is the complement of A, $A \upharpoonright n = \{x : x \in A \text{ and } |x| < n\}$ is the restriction of A to arguments of length less than n. We let $xA = \{xy : y \in A\}$. For $n \in \mathbb{N}$, $\underline{n} = 1^n0$ and $A^{(n)} = \{x : \underline{n}x \in A\}$. The p-effective disjoint union $A \oplus B$ of A and B is defined by $A \oplus B = 0A \cup 1B$.

P (NP) is the class of subsets of Σ^* which can be recognized in polynomial time by a (non)deterministic Turing machine. $\{f_n : n \in \mathbb{N}\}$ and $\{M_n(X) : n \in \mathbb{N}\}$ are standard enumerations of the p-time computable functions from Σ^* to Σ^* and of the polynomially bounded deterministic oracle machine acceptors (with oracle X), respectively. We write $M_n(X)(x) = 1$ (0) iff $M_n(X)$ accepts (refutes) x. A is polynomial time many-one (p-m) reducible to B, $A \leq_m^P B$, if $A(x) = B(f_n(x))$ for some n and all x. A is polynomial time Turing (p-T) reducible to B, $A \leq_T^P B$, if $A = M_n(B)$ for some n. We write $A \equiv_{m(T)}^P B$ if $A \leq_{m(T)}^P B$ and $B \leq_{m(T)}^P A$. The p-m (p-T) degree of A, $deg_m^P A$ $(deg_T^P A)$, is the equivalence class of A w.r.t. $\equiv_m^P$ $(\equiv_T^P)$. P-degrees (w.r.t. both reducibility notions) are denoted by $\underset{\sim}{a}, \underset{\sim}{b}, \underset{\sim}{c}, \ldots$. $\underset{\sim}{R}_m$ and $\underset{\sim}{NP}_m$ ($\underset{\sim}{R}_T$ and $\underset{\sim}{NP}_T$) denote the set of p-m (p-T) degrees of recursive sets and NP-sets, respectively. The partial orderings of the p-degrees induced by $\leq_m^P$ and $\leq_T^P$, respectively, are both denoted by $\leq$ In the context of p-m-reducibility we systematically ignore the sets $\emptyset$ and Σ^*; so the class P consists of a single p-m(T)-degree, which is denoted by $\underset{\sim}{0}$. If we drop the subscripts m and T then we do so to indicate that the given statement holds for both reducibility notions likewise. Note that, for any sets A and B, $deg^P A \cup deg^P B = deg^P A \oplus B$. So $\langle \underset{\sim}{R}, \leq \rangle$ $(\langle \underset{\sim}{NP}, \leq \rangle)$ is an upper semi-lattice with least element $\underset{\sim}{0}$. For $\underset{\sim}{a}, \underset{\sim}{b}$ such that $\underset{\sim}{a} < \underset{\sim}{b}$, $[a,b]$ denotes the interval $\{\underset{\sim}{c} : \underset{\sim}{a} \leq \underset{\sim}{c} \leq \underset{\sim}{b}\}$; $\underset{\sim}{a} \mid \underset{\sim}{b}$ abbreviates that $\underset{\sim}{a}$ and $\underset{\sim}{b}$ are incomparable.

A class C of recursive sets is called recursively presentable (or uniformly recursive) if, for some recursive set A, $C = \{A^{(n)} : n \in \mathbb{N}\}$. A class $\underset{\sim}{C}$ of recursive p-degrees is recursively presentable if, for some recursively presentable class C, $\underset{\sim}{C} = \{deg^P C : C \in C\}$. Note that any finite nonempty class of degrees is recursively presentable and that every recursively presentable class of p-degrees is bounded in $\langle \underset{\sim}{R}, \leq \rangle$.

Finally we need some notions from lattice theory. A partial ordering $L = \langle L, \leq \rangle$ is a lattice if, for all $a,b \in L$, the supremum $a \cup b$ and the infimum $a \cap b$ (both w.r.t. $\leq$) exist. If only the former holds then L is called an upper semi-lattice (u.s.l.). A lattice L is distributive if $\forall\, a,b,c \in L$ $((a \cup b) \cap (a \cup c) = a \cup (b \cap c))$. The least (greatest) element of a partial ordering $\langle L, \leq \rangle$ (if it exists) is denoted by 0_L (1_L) or simply by 0 (1).

For the following definitions let $L_1 = \langle L_1, \leq \rangle$ and $L_2 = \langle L_2, \leq \rangle$ be partial orderings. If L_1 is a lattice and L_2 a u.s.l. then a one-to-one map $f : L_1 \to L_2$ is a (lattice) embedding of L_1 in L_2 if

$\forall\, a,b \in L_1$ ($f(a \cup b) = f(a) \cup f(b)$, $f(a) \cap f(b)$ exists and $f(a \cap b) = f(a) \cap f(b)$).

We say f preserves 0 (1), i.e. the least (greatest) element, if $f(0_{L_1}) = 0_{L_2}$ $(f(1_{L_1}) = 1_{L_2})$ or 0_{L_1} (1_{L_1}) does not exist. We write $L_1 \overset{}{\underset{f}{===>>}} L_2$ ($L_1 \overset{0}{\underset{f}{===>>}} L_2$, $L_1 \overset{1}{\underset{f}{===>>}} L_2$) if f embeds L_1 in L_2 (preserving 0,1), and $L_1 ===>> L_2$ ($L_1 \overset{0}{===>>} L_2$,

$L_1 \overset{1}{===>>} L_2$) if such an embedding f exists. A one-to-one map $f : L_1 \to L_2$ is an order embedding of L_1 in L_2, $L_1 \underset{f}{===>} L_2$ for short, if

$$\forall\, a,b \in L_1 \;(\, a \le b \quad \to \quad f(a) \le f(b)\,).$$

If such an f exists then we say that L_1 is order embeddable in L_2 and write $L_1 ===> L_2$. Note that any lattice embedding is an order embedding but not vice versa.

§1. SUBLATTICES OF THE POLYNOMIAL TIME DEGREES.

In this section we state embedding theorems for the p-degrees which unify and extend most of the previous work on the structure of the p-degrees. Proofs for the theorems of this section will appear in [1]. The proofs exploit the diagonalization techniques of [5] and [10].

1.1. Theorem. Let $\underset{\sim}{a},\underset{\sim}{b} \in \underset{\sim}{R}$ be given such that $\underset{\sim}{a} < \underset{\sim}{b}$ and let L be any countable distributive lattice. Then

(i) $L \overset{1}{===>>} [\underset{\sim}{a},\underset{\sim}{b}]$ and

(ii) $L \overset{0}{===>>} [\underset{\sim}{a},\underset{\sim}{b}]$.

Moreover, if $\underset{\sim}{a},\underset{\sim}{b} \in \underset{\sim}{NP}$ then

(i') $L \overset{1}{===>>} [\underset{\sim}{a},\underset{\sim}{b}] \cap \underset{\sim}{NP}$ and

(ii') $L \overset{0}{===>>} [\underset{\sim}{a},\underset{\sim}{b}] \cap \underset{\sim}{NP}$.

To illustrate the theorem we consider some special cases. If we let L be a 3-element total ordering then the theorem yields Ladner's density theorem for the p-degrees [8, Corollary 2.3] and the fact that, under the assumption $P \ne NP$, there are p-T-incomplete NP-sets in $NP-P$ [8,Corollary 1.1]. If we let L be a 2-atom Boolean algebra then (i) gives Ladner's result that any nonzero p-degree splits over any lesser one, i.e.

$$\forall\, \underset{\sim}{a},\underset{\sim}{b} \in \underset{\sim}{R}\;(\,\underset{\sim}{a} < \underset{\sim}{b} \quad \to \exists\, \underset{\sim}{c}_0 > \underset{\sim}{a}\; \exists\, \underset{\sim}{c}_1 > \underset{\sim}{a}\;(\,\underset{\sim}{c}_0 \mid \underset{\sim}{c}_1 \text{ and } \underset{\sim}{b} = \underset{\sim}{c}_0 \cup \underset{\sim}{c}_1\,))$$

[8,Corollary 2.2], while (ii) gives the following generalized minimal pair theorem [10, Theorem 17]

$$\forall\, \underset{\sim}{a},\underset{\sim}{b} \in \underset{\sim}{R}\;(\,\underset{\sim}{a} < \underset{\sim}{b} \quad \to \exists\, \underset{\sim}{c}_0 < \underset{\sim}{b}\; \exists\, \underset{\sim}{c}_1 < \underset{\sim}{b}\;(\,\underset{\sim}{c}_0 \mid \underset{\sim}{c}_1 \text{ and } \underset{\sim}{a} = \underset{\sim}{c}_0 \cap \underset{\sim}{c}_1\,)).$$

In particular, for $\underset{\sim}{a} = \underset{\sim}{0}$, (ii) shows that any nonzero p-degree bounds a minimal pair ([10, Theorem 14],[5, Theorem 3]). If L is taken to be a Boolean algebra with infinitely many atoms (e.g. the set of finite and co-finite subsets of $\mathbb{N}$) then the theorem shows that any interval of p-degrees contains infinitely many mutually incomparable p-degrees (Schmidt [11, Corollary 15]). While the last result can also be obtained by iterated applications of Ladner's splitting theorem above, we can obtain stronger new results on suborderings of the p-degrees: Any interval of p-degrees contains all countable partial orderings as suborderings.

1.2. Corollary. Let $\underset{\sim}{a},\underset{\sim}{b} \in \underset{\sim}{R}(\underset{\sim}{NP})$ be given such that $\underset{\sim}{a} < \underset{\sim}{b}$ and let L be any countable partial ordering. Then

$$L \Longrightarrow [\underset{\sim}{a},\underset{\sim}{b}] \ (\cap \ \underset{\sim}{NP}).$$

Proof. By Theorem 1.1, since any countable partial ordering can be order embedded in some countable distributive lattice.

Theorem 1.1 and Corollary 1.2 imply that if $P \neq NP$ then any countable distributive lattice (partial ordering) can be embedded in the p-degrees of NP-sets. Similarly, if NP-completeness for p-m and p-T reducibilities do not coincide then any such lattice (partial ordering) can be embedded in the p-m degrees of p-T-complete NP sets. More generally, we get the following result on the p-m degrees contained in a p-T-degree.

1.3. Corollary. Let $\underset{\sim}{a}$ be any p-T degree and let $\underset{\sim}{A}$ be the set of p-m-degrees contained in $\underset{\sim}{a}$. Then either $\underset{\sim}{A}$ consists of a single p-m-degree or any countable distributive lattice (countable partial ordering) can be lattice (order) embedded in $\underset{\sim}{A}$.

Proof. W.l.o.g. assume that $|\underset{\sim}{A}| \geq 2$, say $\underset{\sim}{b},\underset{\sim}{c} \in \underset{\sim}{A}$ and $\underset{\sim}{b} \nleq \underset{\sim}{c}$. Then $\underset{\sim}{c} < \underset{\sim}{b} \cup \underset{\sim}{c}$ and $[\underset{\sim}{c},\underset{\sim}{b} \cup \underset{\sim}{c}] \subseteq \underset{\sim}{A}$. So the claim follows from Theorem 1.1 (Corollary 1.2).

We conclude this section with the discussion of possible extensions of Theorem 1.1.

As we have shown, the embeddings of distributive lattices in intervals of p-degrees can be chosen so that they preserve the least *or* greatest element. So it is natural to ask if, for lattices with at least two elements, we can always obtain embeddings which preserve both the least *and* the greatest elements. In [2] we answer this question negatively for p-m-degrees: There is a nonzero p-m-degree $\underset{\sim}{a}$ which is not the supremum of a minimal pair. So the 2-atom Boolean algebra cannot be embedded in the interval $[\underset{\sim}{0},\underset{\sim}{a}]$ by a map which preserves least and greatest elements.

By Theorem 1.1 the structure of any interval of p-degrees is extremely rich. This suggest the question whether the embeddings of Theorem 1.1 can be chosen in such a way that they avoid the lower or upper cones of given intermediate degrees. We show that this is possible for any recursively presentable (so in particular for any finite) collection of intermediate degrees.

1.4. Theorem. Let $\underset{\sim}{a},\underset{\sim}{b} \in \underset{\sim}{R}(\underset{\sim}{NP})$ be given such that $\underset{\sim}{a} < \underset{\sim}{b}$, let $L = \langle L,\leq \rangle$ be a countable distributive lattice and let $\underset{\sim}{C}$ be a recursively presentable class of p-degrees such that

(1.1) $\forall \underset{\sim}{c} \in \underset{\sim}{C} \; (\underset{\sim}{b} \nleq \underset{\sim}{c} \text{ and } \underset{\sim}{c} \nleq \underset{\sim}{a})$.

Then there exist embeddings f_o and f_1 such that, for $i = 0,1$,

$L \overset{i}{\underset{f_i}{\Longrightarrow}} [\underset{\sim}{a},\underset{\sim}{b}] \; (\cap \underset{\sim}{NP})$ and $\forall x \in L-\{0_L, 1_L\} \; \forall \underset{\sim}{c} \in \underset{\sim}{C} \; (f_i(x) \mid \underset{\sim}{c})$.

By using Theorem 1.4 in place of Theorem 1.1, we obtain similar extensions of Corollaries 1.2 and 1.3. The following special case of Theorem 1.4, where L is taken to be a 3-element linear ordering, gives an extension of the main theorem of Balcazar and Diaz [3].

1.5. Corollary. Let $\underset{\sim}{a},\underset{\sim}{b} \in \underset{\sim}{R}\,(\underset{\sim}{NP})$ be given such that $\underset{\sim}{a} < \underset{\sim}{b}$ and let $\underset{\sim}{C}$ be any recursively presentable class of p-degrees satisfying (1.1). Then there is a p-degree $\underset{\sim}{d}$ $(\in \underset{\sim}{NP})$ such that $\underset{\sim}{a} < \underset{\sim}{d} < \underset{\sim}{b}$ and $\forall \underset{\sim}{c} \in \underset{\sim}{C} \; (\underset{\sim}{c} \mid \underset{\sim}{d})$.

The results of this section hold not only for p-m and p-T-reducibilities but also for any of the intermediate reducibilities introduced in [9] (see [1]).

§2. DISTRIBUTIVITY OF THE POLYNOMIAL TIME MANY-ONE DEGREES.

Like all previously obtained results on p-degrees, the embedding results of §1 hold for p-Turing and p-many-one degrees likewise. In this and the following section we give a first example of an algebraic property which holds for the p-degrees of one of the notions but fails for the other one. This property is distributivity. In this section we show that the p-m degrees are distributive and in section 3 that the p-Turing degrees fail to be distributive. These results indicate that the structure of p-m degrees is much more well behaved than that of p-T degrees.

Since the p-degrees do not form a lattice, we first have to give an adequate definition of distributivity for upper semi-lattices.

2.1. Definition. An upper semi-lattice $L = \langle L, \leq \rangle$ is *distributive* if, for all $a,b,c \in L$,

(2.1) $a \leq b \cup c \rightarrow \exists d \leq b \; \exists e \leq c \; (a = d \cup e)$.

It is known from lattice theory that this definition is compatible with the standard definition of distributivity for lattices:

2.2. Proposition. Let L be any distributive u.s.l. Then any sublattice of L is distributive (as a lattice).

Proof. Since any nondistributive lattice contains a copy of one of the two non-distributive 5-element lattices M_5 or N_5 as a sublattice (cf. Birkhoff [4, Theorems I.12 and II.13]), it suffices to show that neither M_5 nor N_5 can be embedded

M_5: 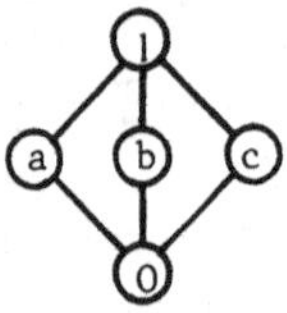

N_5: 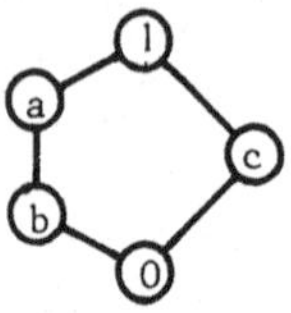

in L. But this is immediate, since, for the above given labelings of M_5 and N_5, condition (2.1) fails.

2.3. Theorem. The u.s.l. $\langle \mathbf{R}_m, \leq \rangle$ of the p-m-degrees of recursive sets is distributive.

Proof. Fix $\mathbf{a},\mathbf{b},\mathbf{c} \in \mathbf{R}_m$ such that $\mathbf{a} \leq \mathbf{b} \cup \mathbf{c}$. We will show that there are degrees $\mathbf{d},\mathbf{e} \in \mathbf{R}_m$ such that $\mathbf{d} \leq \mathbf{b}$, $\mathbf{e} \leq \mathbf{c}$ and $\mathbf{a} = \mathbf{d} \cup \mathbf{e}$. Choose recursive sets $A \in \mathbf{a}$, $B \in \mathbf{b}$ and $C \in \mathbf{c}$. Then $A \leq^P_m B \oplus C$, say via f. Now let $F = \{x : f(x) \in 0\Sigma^*\}$, and set $D = A \cap F$, $E = A \cap \bar{F}$, $\mathbf{d} = \deg^P_m D$ and $\mathbf{e} = \deg^P_m E$. Obviously, $F \in P$. Hence $A \equiv^P_m D \oplus E$, i.e. $\mathbf{a} = \mathbf{d} \cup \mathbf{e}$. Moreover, $D \leq^P_m B \oplus \emptyset$ via f and $E \leq^P_m \emptyset \oplus C$ via f, whence $\mathbf{d} \leq \mathbf{b}$ and $\mathbf{e} \leq \mathbf{c}$.

From Theorems 1.1 and 2.3 we obtain a complete characterization of the sublattices of the u.s.l. of polynomial time many-one degrees.

2.4. Corollary. Let L be any lattice and let $\mathbf{a}$ and $\mathbf{b}$ be any p-m degrees of recursive sets such that $\mathbf{a} < \mathbf{b}$. Then the following are equivalent:

(a) L is countable and distributive

(b) $L \Longrightarrow\!\!> \mathbf{R}_m$

(c) $L \overset{0}{\Longrightarrow\!\!>} \mathbf{R}_m$

(d) $L \overset{0}{\Longrightarrow\!\!>} [\mathbf{a},\mathbf{b}]$

(e) $L \overset{1}{\Longrightarrow\!\!>} [\mathbf{a},\mathbf{b}]$.

Distributivity implies strong restrictions on the possible algebraic properties of a structure. Various properties of lattices which in general are independent coincide -or are at least related- for distributive lattices. In the following we give an example.

Two incomparable elements a,b of a semi-lattice $L = \langle L, \leq \rangle$ are called *strongly incomparable* if $\forall c \in L\ ([\, a \leq b \cup c \rightarrow a \leq c\,]\ \&\ [\, b \leq a \cup c \rightarrow b \leq c\,])$. Intuitively speaking, if A,B are sets whose polynomial degrees are strongly incomparable then the knowledge of B is of no help for giving a fast (relativized) algorithm for computing A and vice versa. One migth expect that sets whose degrees form a minimal pair have this property, since - again intuitively speaking - such sets are hard to compute for completely different reasons. The following shows that this is so for p-m-degrees.

<u>2.5. Proposition.</u> Let $L = \langle L, \le \rangle$ be a distributive u.s.l. and a,b a minimal pair of L. Then a and b are strongly incomparable.

<u>Proof.</u> Obviously, $a \mid b$. So fix c such that $a \le b \cup c$ (the case $b \le a \cup c$ is symmetric). We have to show $a \le c$. Since $a \le b \cup c$, by (2.1), there are elements d and e of L such that $d \le b$, $e \le c$ and $a = d \cup e$. So in particular $d \le a$ and $d \le b$. Since a and b form a minimal pair, it follows $d = 0$, whence $a = d \cup e = e \le c$.

For nondistributive u.s.ls. the proposition in general fails. For example in the lattice M_5 given above the elements a and b form a minimal pair but are not strongly incomparable since $a \le b \cup c$ but $a \not\le c$.

Theorem 2.3 and Proposition 2.5 applied to Theorem 1.1 (or the minimal pair theorem [10, Theorem 14]) yield the following result.

<u>2.6. Corollary.</u> For any nonzero recursive p-m degree $\underset{\sim}{a}$ there is a strongly incomparable pair of p-m degrees below $\underset{\sim}{a}$. In particular, if $P \ne NP$ then there are NP-sets whose p-m degrees are strongly incomparable.

§3. NONDISTRIBUTIVITY OF THE POLYNOMIAL TIME TURING DEGREES.

We now show that in contrast to the p-m degrees the p-T degrees do not form a distributive upper semi-lattice.

<u>3.1. Theorem.</u> The u.s.l. $\langle \underset{\sim}{R}_T, \le \rangle$ of polynomial time Turing degrees of recursive sets is not distributive.

<u>Proof.</u> It suffices to show that there are recursive sets A, B and C such that

(3.1) $A \le^P_T B \oplus C$ and

(3.2) $\forall D,E\ (A \equiv^P_T D \oplus E \rightarrow D \not\le^P_T B \text{ or } E \not\le^P_T C)$.

Then, for $\underset{\sim}{a} = \deg^P_T A$, $\underset{\sim}{b} = \deg^P_T B$ and $\underset{\sim}{c} = \deg^P_T C$, $\underset{\sim}{a} \le \underset{\sim}{b} \cup \underset{\sim}{c}$ but, for any $\underset{\sim}{d} \le \underset{\sim}{b}$ and $\underset{\sim}{e} \le \underset{\sim}{c}$, $\underset{\sim}{a} \ne \underset{\sim}{d} \cup \underset{\sim}{e}$. So (2.1) fails for the p-T degrees $\underset{\sim}{a}, \underset{\sim}{b}, \underset{\sim}{c}$.

In the following we construct sets A, B, C with the desired properties by a diagonalization argument. Condition (3.1) will be satisfied by ensuring

(3.3) $\forall x \in \Sigma^* \ (\ x \in A \ \text{ iff } \ x \in B \ \text{ or } \ x \in C\ ).$

Moreover, for every $i,j,k,l,m \in \mathbb{N}$, we will meet the requirement

$$R_{<i,j,k,l,m>} \ : \ A \neq M_k(A_i \oplus A_j) \ \text{ or } \ A_i \neq M_l(B) \ \text{ or } \ A_j \neq M_m(C),$$

where A_n denotes the set $\{x : M_n(A) \text{ accepts } x\}$ $(n \in \mathbb{N})$ and $<\ldots>$ is a recursive bijection from $\mathbb{N}^5$ onto $\mathbb{N}$. As one can easily see, this implies (3.2).

The sets A,B,C are effectively constructed in stages s, $s \in \mathbb{N}$. At stage s we ensure that requirement R_s is met. In the course of the construction we define a strictly increasing *length* function l, where l(s) is defined at stage s, such that for the parts A^s, B^s, C^s of A, B, C, respectively, enumerated by the end of stage s,

(3.4) $A^s = A \upharpoonright l(s) \ \ \& \ \ B^s = B \upharpoonright l(s) \ \ \& \ \ C^s = C \upharpoonright l(s).$

So, by effectiveness of the construction, the constructed sets are recursive. Given A^s, we let A_i^s denote the set $\{x : M_i(A^s)(x) = 1\}$ and we set $A^{-1} = B^{-1} = C^{-1} = \emptyset$ and $l(-1) = 0$. Finally, let $\{p_n : n \in \mathbb{N}\}$ be a sequence of polynomials such that, for any oracle X, the running time of $M_n(X)$ is bounded by p_n. W.l.o.g. we assume that $p_n(m) > m$ for all $n,m \in \mathbb{N}$. Note that in a computation $M_n(X)(x)$ only strings of length less than $p_n(|x|)$ are used in oracle queries. So $M_n(X)(x) = M_n(Y)(x)$ for any set Y such that $X \upharpoonright p_n(|x|) = Y \upharpoonright p_n(|x|)$.

We are now ready to describe the construction.

<u>Stage s</u>, say $s = <i,j,k,l,m>$. Let $x = 0^{l(s-1)}$ and set $u = p_k(l(s-1))$, $v = \max\{p_i(u),p_j(u)\}$ and $w = \max\{p_l(u),p_m(u)\}$.

Then $l(s) = \max\{v,w\}$. For the definition of A^s, B^s and C^s distinguish the following cases.

<u>Case 1</u>: $A^{s-1}(x) \neq M_k(A_i^{s-1} \oplus A_j^{s-1})(x)$ or $A_i^{s-1} \upharpoonright u \neq M_l(B^{s-1}) \upharpoonright u$ or $A_j^{s-1} \upharpoonright u \neq M_m(C^{s-1}) \upharpoonright u$. Then let $A^s = A^{s-1}$, $B^s = B^{s-1}$ and $C^s = C^{s-1}$.

<u>Case 2</u>: Otherwise. Then let $A^s = A^{s-1} \cup \{x\}$ and distinguish the following subcases.

<u>Case 2.1</u>: $A_i^s \upharpoonright u \neq A_i^{s-1} \upharpoonright u$. Then let $B^s = B^{s-1}$ and $C^s = C^{s-1} \cup \{x\}$

<u>Case 2.2</u>: Otherwise. Then let $B^s = B^{s-1} \cup \{x\}$ and $C^s = C^{s-1}$.

This completes the construction.

We now show that the constructed sets have the desired properties. Obviously the construction is effective and, by a straightforward induction on s, the function l is strictly increasing and satisfies (3.4) and $A^s - A^{s-1} = (B^s - B^{s-1}) \cup (C^s - C^{s-1})$. It follows that the constructed sets are recursive and that condition (3.3) is satisfied. It remains to show that requirement R_s is met for each $s \in \mathbb{N}$.

So fix $s = \langle i,j,k,l,m \rangle$, let $x = 0^{l(s-1)}$ and define u,v,w as in the description of stage s above. Note that $l(s-1) < u < v,w \leq l(s)$ and that, by (3.4), $x \notin A^{s-1} \cup B^{s-1} \cup C^{s-1}$.

Now first assume that Case 1 holds. Then no string enters A, B and C at stage s, whence by (3.4) and $w \leq l(s)$, $A^{s-1} \restriction w = A \restriction w$, $B^{s-1} \restriction w = B \restriction w$ and $C^{s-1} \restriction w = C \restriction w$. By definition of w, this implies that one of the equalities stated in Case 1 is preserved, i.e. $A(x) \neq M_k(A_i \oplus A_j)(x)$ or $A_i \restriction u \neq M_l(B) \restriction u$ or $A_j \restriction u \neq M_m(C) \restriction u$. So R_s is met in this case.

Now assume that Case 2 holds. Then

(3.5) $A^{s-1}(x) = M_k(A_i^{s-1} \oplus A_j^{s-1})(x) = 0$,

(3.6) $A_i^{s-1} \restriction u = M_l(B^{s-1}) \restriction u$ and

(3.7) $A_j^{s-1} \restriction u = M_m(C^{s-1}) \restriction u$.

Moreover, by construction,

(3.8) $A(x) = A^s(x) = 1$

and, by (3.4),

(3.9) $A_i \restriction u = A_i^s \restriction u$ & $A_j \restriction u = A_j^s \restriction u$ & $B \restriction w = B^s \restriction w$ & $C \restriction w = C^s \restriction w$.

So, if $A_i^s \restriction u = A_i^{s-1} \restriction u$ and $A_j^s \restriction u = A_j^{s-1} \restriction u$, then, by (3.5) and (3.9), $M_k(A_i \oplus A_j)(x) = 0$ and thus, by (3.8), $A \neq M_k(A_i \oplus A_j)$ and R_s is met. So w.l.o.g. we may assume that $A_i^s \restriction u \neq A_i^{s-1} \restriction u$ or $A_j^s \restriction u \neq A_j^{s-1} \restriction u$. Now, if the former holds, then Case 2.1 applies to stage s, whence $B^{s-1} = B^s$. It follows, by (3.6) and (3.9), that

$$A_i \restriction u = A_i^s \restriction u \neq A_i^{s-1} \restriction u = M_l(B^{s-1}) \restriction u = M_l(B^s) \restriction u = M_l(B) \restriction u$$

and thus that R_s is met. Otherwise, Case 2.2 applies and thus $C^{s-1} = C^s$. So it follows , by a similar argument using (3.7) and (3.9), that $A_j \neq M_m(C)$.

So in any case requirement R_s is met. This completes the proof.

3.2. Corollary. The upper semi-lattices $\underset{\sim}{R}_m$ and $\underset{\sim}{R}_T$ of polynomial time many-one and Turing degrees, respectively, are not isomorphic.

Proof. By Theorems 2.3 and 3.1.

Since the fact that a partial ordering is a distributive upper semi-lattice can be expressed by a first order formula in the language of partial orderings, we have indeed shown the following stronger result.

3.3. Corollary. The first order theories of the partial orderings of recursive p-m and p-T degrees, respectively, are not elementarily equivalent.

By a straightforward modification, the sets A, B, C in the proof of Theorem 3.1 can be constructed to be computable in exponential time ($DTIME(2^n)$). So the structures of p-m and p-T degrees differ already on the class of exponential time computable sets. We do not know, however, whether -under the assumption $P \neq NP$- the structure $\underset{\sim}{NP}_T$ of p-T degrees of NP-sets is nondistributive.

Finally, the proof of Theorem 3.1 actually shows that any p-reducibility between $\leq^P_{2-tt}$ (see [9]) and $\leq^P_T$ is nondistributive. On the other hand a straightforward variant of the proof for Theorem 2.3 shows that $\leq^P_{1-tt}$ is distributive. So, roughly speaking, reducibilities which allow only one query are distributive, the others not.

REFERENCES.

1. K.Ambos-Spies, Sublattices of the polynomial time degrees, in preparation.
2. K.Ambos-Spies, Splittings of recursive sets and their polynomial degrees, preprint.
3. J.L.Balcazar and J.Diaz, A note on a theorem by Ladner, Inform. Proc. Letters 15 (1982) 84-86.
4. G.Birkhoff, Lattice Theory, Amer. Math. Soc. Colloquium Publications, vol.25, Third Edition, Providence, 1973.
5. P.Chew and M.Machtey, A note on structure and looking back applied to relative complexity of computable functions, JCSS 22 (1981) 53-59.
6. S.A.Cook, The complexity of theorem proving procedures, Proc. Third Annual ACM Symp. on Theory of Comp., 1971, 151-158.
7. R.M.Karp, Reducibility among combinatorial problems, In: R.E.Miller and J.W.Thatcher, Eds., Complexity of computer computations, Plenum, New York, 1972, 85-103.
8. R.E.Ladner, On the structure of polynomial time reducibility, JACM 22 (1975) 155-171.
9. R.E.Ladner, N.A.Lynch and A.L.Selman, A comparision of polynomial time reducibilities, TCS 1 (1976) 103-123.
10. L.H.Landweber, R.J.Lipton and E.L.Robertson, On the structure of sets in NP and other complexity classes, TCS 15 (1981) 181-200.
11. D.Schmidt, On the complexity of one complexity class in another, In: E.Börger G.Hasenjäger and D.Rödding, Eds., Logic and Machines: Decision problems and complexity, SLNCS (to appear in 1984).

OPTIMAL LAYOUTS OF THE TREE OF MESHES WITH VERTICES ON THE PERIMETER OF THE BOUNDING CONVEX REGION

O. Sýkora and I. Vrťo
Institute of Technical Cybernetics
Slovak Academy of Sciences
Dúbravská cesta 9, Bratislava 842 37
Czechoslovakia

Abstract

The lower bound for the minimal bisection width of the tree of meshes with respect to all vertices (w.r.t. all leaves) is determined in both cases. On the basis of these results the lower bounds of layout area with all vertices (leaves) on the perimeter of the bounding convex region, which coincide with upper bounds, are stated.

1. Introduction

One of the most important problems of VLSI-circuits layouts is the minimization of the layout area. The total area of VLSI-circuit is composed of some functional elements (processors, memories, I/0-nodes), wires connecting them and empty space, whereby already in relatively simple circuits the wires usually occupy much more area than functional elements.

The total area of the circuit is typically expressed as the area of the smallest bounding convex region. Abstracting from the VLSI-circuit to a graph (by substitution of vertices (edges) for functional elements (wires) respectively), and basing on the practical constraints, there arises the problem how to lay out a given graph into the square mesh so that it occupies the smallest area. Then the total area of the circuit layout is typically the area of the smallest bounding rectangle. The main results of the graph layouts are in the papers [1], [2], [3], [4]. Much attention has been paid to planar graphs. From papers [2] and [3] it follows that every planar graph of N vertices can be embedded into $O(N \log^2 N)$ - area rectangle. On the other hand Leighton constructed a graph, the so-called tree of meshes, which requires so far the greatest area $\Theta(N \log N)$ among planar graphs. Some vertices of the graph represent I/0-nodes of the VLSI-circuit. According to the actual state of technology they are placed on the margin of the chip. There arises the question how to embed a graph into the square mesh using the minimal area and placing a subset of vertices of the graph on the perimeter of the bounding convex region.

In [1] Brent and Kung analysed the layout of the complete binary tree with all leaves lying on the perimeter. They showed that such a layout requires $\Theta(N \log N)$ area. From [2] follows that even if all leaves would lie on the perimeter, the layout need not more than $\Theta(N \log N)$ area. Of interest is the fact that if we drop the requirement of the special placing of vertices, the complete binary tree can be embedded into $\Theta(N)$ area [1] .

In this paper, we show that the N-vertices tree of meshes, whose all vertices (leaves) are on the perimeter of the bounding convex region requires $\Theta(N^{3/2}/\log^{1/2} N)$ $(\Theta((N/\log N)^{3/2}))$ area respectively. These results are heavily based upon the finding of minimal bisection width of the graph for both cases.

In the second section of the paper, the basic concepts and results are introduced. In the third and fourth sections the minimal bisection widths of the tree of meshes with respect to all its vertices and with respect to all its leaves respectively, are stated. In the fifth section we use these results to derive the optimal layouts.

2. Basic concepts and results

In this section, we define all concepts that are used in the next sections and introduce two theorems serving the derivation of main results. One of the most important concepts is the so-called layout of a graph and its area. (Hereinafter a graph G is given by the set V of vertices and by the set E of edges.)

2.1. Definition: A layout (or embedding) of the graph G into the square mesh (with edges of unit length) is an injective mapping of the set V into the set of unit squares of the sqaure mesh and an injective mapping of the set E into the set of paths in the square mesh such that it holds:

a/ end-vertices of the image of edge (u,v) lie on the perimeters of images of vertices u and v,

b/ no edge of mesh belongs to two different images of edges of G and no image of an edge passes through the image of the vertex which is not incident upon the edge.

2.2. Remark: From the definition follows that the degree of the vertices of G is not greater than 8 and the images of two different edges can intersect.

2.3. Definition: The layout area A of the given graph G is the area of the minimal (with respect to the area) bounding rectangle with the sides parallel to the mesh edges.

In the lower bound estimation of the layout area of a graph the next important concept is used: the concept of bisection and its width.

2.4. Definition: Let $V_0 \subset V$. Then the bisection R of the graph G with respect to the set V_0 is the set of edges $R \subset E$ such that by removing its elements from the graph G one obtains two mutually disjoint subgraphs $G_1 = (V_1, E_1)$, $G_2 = (V_2, E_2)$ such that $|V_0 \cap V_1| \leq |V_0 \cap V_2| \leq |V_0 \cap V_1| + 1$. The bisection width of the graph G with respect to the set V_0 is the number of elements of the set R and it is indicated as $|R(G,V_0)|$. The minimal bisection width is the number $w(G,V_0) = \min_R \{|R(G,V_0)|\}$.

The importance of the minimal bisection width is evident from the results of Thompson [5] and Leiserson [2]. Thompson showed that there exists the following relation between layout area and minimal bisection width:
$A \geq \frac{w^2(G,V_0)}{4}$, which confirms the practical experience from VLSI-circuits creation. Leiserson's result is expressed in the following theorem.

2.5. Theorem: Let the images of the vertices from the set V_0 lie on the perimeter of the convex region that is bounding a layout of a graph G. Then it holds $A = \Omega(|V_0| \cdot w(G,V_0))$.

The finding of the minimal bisection is the NP-complete problem [6] but fortunately for the majority of problems it is enough to know that there exists a set of edges which is the minimal bisection. Another concept important for determining the upper bound layout area is the concept of separator, which we define in the following definition and introduce its application in the theorem 2.7 from [2].

2.6. Definition: Let $|V| = N$. A graph G has f(x)-separator if by removing at most f(N) edges, G can be partitioned into disjoint subgraphs $G_1 = (V_1, E_1)$ and $G_2 = (V_2, E_2)$ such that $|V_1| = \left\lceil \frac{N}{2} \right\rceil$, $V_2 = \left\lfloor \frac{N}{2} \right\rfloor$ and both subgraphs G_1 and G_2 have f(x)- separator.

2.7. Theorem: Let a graph G have the f(x) - separator. If $f(N) = \Omega(N^q)$ for some $q > 0$ and there exists a constant c, where $0 < c < 1$, such that for sufficiently great N it holds $f(\frac{N}{2}) \leq c\, f(N)$, then the layout of the graph G with all vertices on the perimeter of the bounding convex region requests the area $A = O(N f(N))$.

In the following definition we define an important graph the so-called tree of meshes.

2.8. Definition: Let $n = 2^k$. The tree of meshes can be obtained from the complete binary tree with n^2 leaves so that the root of the tree is replaced by the square mesh of the type n x n, the successors of the root are replaced by the rectangle meshes of the type n/2 x n, their successors are replaced by the square meshes of the type n/2 x n/2, etc., finally the leaves of the tree are replaced by the meshes of the type 1 x 1 . The edges of the binary tree are replaced by the sets of edges according to Fig. 1., where the tree of meshes having the root-mesh of the type n x n = 4 x 4 and having $N = 2n^2 \log n + n^2 = 80$ vertices, is depicted.

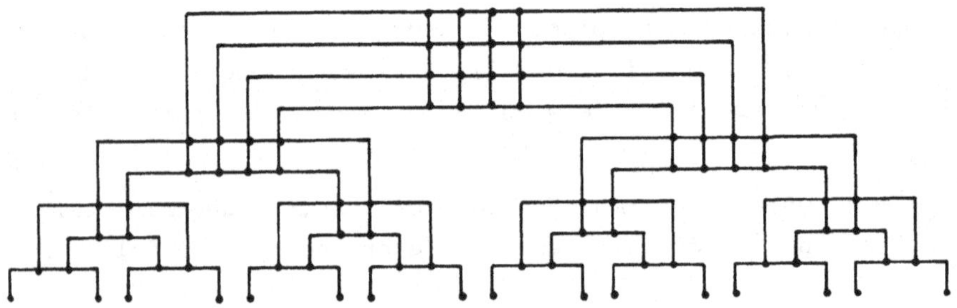

Fig. 1 .

Similarly a tree of meshes with the rectangle root-mesh of the type n/2 x n can be defined. The tree of meshes with the root-mesh of the type n x n (n/2 x n) will be indicated by $T_{n,n}$ ($T_{\frac{n}{2},n}$) . It is evident, that the number of vertices of the tree of meshes $T_{\frac{n}{2},n}$ is $n^2 \log n$.

The tree of meshes is important on the following grounds:

a/ Owing to the fact that the layout area of the tree of meshes is $A = \Theta(N \log N)$, there is a contradiction to the hypothesis of Leiserson and Valiant about the linear layout area of the planar graphs. Till now no planar graph is known of a greater layout area than the layout area of the tree of meshes.

b/ Leighton [4] has shown that any N-vertex planar graph can be embedded in an $O(N \log N)$ - vertex tree of meshes, whereby no method is known of how to embed an N-vertex planar graph into the less than $O(N \log^2 N)$ - vertex square mesh.

c/ According to Leighton's hypothesis [4] any graph that has $f(x) = O(\sqrt{x})$ - separator can be embedded in an $O(N \log N)$ - vertex tree of meshes.

3. Minimal bisection width of the tree of meshes

In this section we determine a lower bound for the minimal bisection width of the tree of meshes with respect to all vertices of the tree of meshes (thereby $V_0 = V$). The following lemma states the evident fact, therefore it is introduced without a proof.

3.1. Lemma: Let the graph G' be a factor of the graph G. Then $w(G', V_0) \leq w(G, V_0)$.

3.2. Theorem: $w(T_{n,n}, V) > n/4$.

Proof: Without loss of generality, let us assume that $n = 2^{2k}$, $n > 4$. Then the tree of meshes has $4k + 1$ levels. If l is odd, then on the l-th level there are the square meshes of the type $\frac{n}{2^{(l-1)/2}} \times \frac{n}{2^{(l-1)/2}}$.

If l is even, then on the l-th level there are the rectangle meshes of the type $\frac{n}{2^{l/2}} \times \frac{n}{2^{l/2-1}}$. Notice that on the $\log n+1$ -th level there are the square meshes of the type $\sqrt{n} \times \sqrt{n}$.

By removing the edges from the tree of meshes according to Fig. 2 ($n = 16$) we get the factor graph of $T_{n,n}$ that will be indicated by $T'_{n,n}$.

We will prove that $w(T'_{n,n}, V) > n/4$, from what, on the basis of the previous lemma, follows the assertion of the theorem. By removing the root mesh from the graph $T'_{n,n}$ one gets the set of $2n$ trees: $U = \{U_1, U_2, \ldots, U_{2n}\}$. We will show that each of them has at most $\frac{3}{2} n \log n$ vertices.

Let us choose an arbitrary tree U_i. We will calculate how many vertices are on the levels:

a/ from the $\log n+2$ -th till the $2 \log n+1$ -th

b/ from the 2-nd till the $\log n+1$ -th.

a/ It is evident from Fig. 2 that the tree U_i contains on these levels the factor graph of the graph $T_{\frac{\sqrt{n}}{2}, \sqrt{n}}$ and therefore it has on these levels $\frac{n}{2} \log n$ vertices.

b/ One can prove that the tree U_i has at most $n-2^{l-2}$ vertices on the l-th level.

Fig. 2.

Therefore it has from the 2-nd level till the log n+1 -th level less than n log n vertices.
Hence the tree U_i has at most $\frac{3}{2}$ n log n vertices.
Let the graph $T'_{n,n}$ have the minimal bisection that bisects it in two subgraphs T_1 and T_2. Minimal bisection induces decomposition of the set U into three mutually distinct subsets: A,B,C.
$A = \{U_i : U_i$ is subgraph of $T_1\}$
$B = \{U_i : U_i$ is subgraph of $T_2\}$
$C = U - A \cup B$.
According to the cardinality of the set C we will consider two cases.
a/ Let $|C| > \frac{n}{4}$. Then it is evident that $w(T'_{n,n}, V) > \frac{n}{4}$.
b/ Let $|C| \leq \frac{n}{4}$. Let $|A| \leq \frac{n}{4}$. Then $|A| + |C| \leq \frac{n}{2}$ and therefore the number of the vertices of the graph T_1 is at most: $(|A| + |C|) \cdot \frac{3}{2}$ n log $n + n^2 \leq \frac{3}{4} n^2 \log n + n^2 < n^2 \log n + \frac{n^2}{2}$ what is the contradiction with the definition of bisection.
Hence $|A| > \frac{n}{4}$.
Analogically one can show that $|B| > \frac{n}{4}$.
Let is indicate the vertices from the top level of the trees of the set U as the root-vertices. In the following part of the proof we will show that one can construct $\frac{n}{4} + 1$ edge-distinct paths between the root-vertices from the set A and the root-vertices from the set B. Hence $w > \frac{n}{4}$, because in the opposite case one can find a path that has no edge in bisection and therefore there exists an edge with endpoints from T_1 and T_2 what is a contradiction.
Let us consider a subgraph of the graph $T_{n,n}$ induced by the set of the vertices from the root-mesh of $T_{n,n}$ and by the root-vertices of the trees from the sets A and B. Let us assume that there exist exactly m paths between the root vertices from A and B of the length n + 1 and such that their one endvertex is from the left root-vertices and the second one is from the right root-vertices (with respect to the root-mesh of $T_{n,n}$). Let us indicate other root-vertices from the set A from the left to the right $a_1, a_2, \ldots, a_{n/4-1-m}, \ldots$ Analogically let us indicate other root-vertices from the set B: $b_1, b_2, \ldots, b_{n/4-1-m}, \ldots$
Let us construct paths between the root-vertices from A and root-vertices from B as follows:
Let us indicate the columns of the root-mesh from the left to the right by the indices: 1, 2, ..., n.
Connect the root-vertex a_i to the i-th column by the shortest path (it is exactly determined), that ends in a vertex d_i. Analogically create the shortest path between the root-vertex b_i and the i-th column, that ends in a vertex e_i . Finally connect the vertices d_i and e_i by the shortest path. In this way there are $\frac{n}{4} + 1$ edge-distinct paths between

the root-vertices of the sets A and B.

3.3. Remark: The proof of the theorem 3.2. can be easily reformulated to prove that $w(T_{n,n}, V) > \frac{n}{3+\varepsilon}$, where $\varepsilon > 0$ and $n > n_0(\varepsilon)$. The authors conjecture that it holds $w(T_{n,n}, V) = n$.

4. Minimal bisection width with respect to the leaves of the tree of meshes

Let V_0 be the set of all vertices of the graph $T_{n,n}$ with the degree 1 and let us call all its elements leaves (evidently $|V_0| = n^2$).

4.1. Theorem: $w(T_{n,n}, V_0) = n$.

Proof: We will show that $w(T'_{n,n}, V_0) = n$.

Let R be minimal bisection of the graph $T'_{n,n}$ with respect to the set of leaves. Let R_1 be the subset of R containing only the edges from the trees U_i, i=1, 2, ..., 2n. Let $R_2 = R - R_1$. Let us consider again the decomposition of the set U in the sets A,B,C induced by minimal bisection R as it is in the proof of the theorem 3.2. Then it holds $|R_1| \geq |C|$, $|R_2| \geq \min(|A|, |B|)$. Further it holds $|A| \leq n$, $|B| \leq n$, because if $|A| > n$ ($|B| > n$), then in T_1 (T_2) there are more than $\frac{n^2}{2}$ leaves.

Now we will estimate the number of the elements of the set R:

$$|R| = |R_1| + |R_2| \geq |C| + \min(|A|, |B|) = 2n - |A| - |B| + \min(|A|,|B|) = 2n - \max(|A|, |B|) \geq n.$$

Bisection of the width equal to n can be obtained for example by removing all edges between two neighbou[r] columns of the root-mesh.

4.2. Remark: If V_0 is the set of all vertices from p arbitrary levels of the tree of meshes (therefore $|V_0| = p.n^2$), then by the methods used in the section 3 one can show that $w(T_{n,n}, V_0) \geq cn$, where c is a suitable constant.

5. The optimal layouts

In this section we use the results of the theorems 2.5., 3.2. and 4.1. to prove the lower bounds for the layout areas with the vertices on the perimeter of the bounding convex region and to construct optimal upper bounds.

a/ Let $V_0 = V$. Then on the basis of the theorems 2.5. and 3.2. it holds: $A = \Omega(|V| \,.\, w(T_{n,n}, V)) = \Omega(N \,.\, n) = \Omega(N^{3/2} / \log^{1/2} N)$.
From [4] follows, that the separator of the graph $T_{n,n}$ is $f(x) = O(x^{1/2} / \log^{1/2} x)$. On the basis of theorem 2.7. there exists

a construction of the layout of the graph $T_{n,n}$ with all vertices on the perimeter of the bounding convex region that requests the area $A = O(N \,.\, f(N)) = O(N^{3/2} / \log^{1/2} N)$, therefore this layout is optimal.

b/ Let V_0 be the set of the vertices of degree 1 of the graph $T_{n,n}$. Then on the basis of theorems 2.5. and 4.1. it holds
$A = \Omega\ (|V_0| \,.\, w(T_{n,n}, V_0)) = \Omega\ (n^3) = \Omega\ ((N/\log N)^{3/2})$.
The layout of the graph $T_{n,n}$ constructed in the way evident from Fig. 1. requires the area $A = O(n^3) = O((N/\log n)^{3/2})$. Hence this layout is optimal too.

5. . Remark: From remark 4.2., in the case that V_0 is the set of all vertices from p arbitrary levels of $T_{n,n}$, follows:

$$A = \Omega\ (p \,.\, (\frac{N}{\log N})^{3/2})\ .$$

References

[1] Brent, R.P., Kung, H.T.: On the area of binary tree layouts. Information Processing Letters, 11, 1980, pp. 44-46.

[2] Leiserson, C.E.: Area - efficient graph layouts (for VLSI). Proc. of the 21-st Annual IEEE Symp. on Found. of CS, Oct. 1980, pp. 270-281.

[3] Valiant, L.G.: Universality considerations in VLSI circuits. IEEE Transactions on Computers, Vol. C-30, No. 2, Feb. 1981, pp. 135-140.

[4] Leighton, F.T.: New lower bound techniques for VLSI. Proc. of the 22-nd Annual IEEE Symp. on Found. of CS, 1981, pp. 1-12.

[5] Thompson, C.D.: A complexity theory for VLSI. CMU-CS-80-140, Carnegie - Mellon University, 1980.

[6] Garey, M.R., Johnson, D.S., Stockmeyer, L.: Some simplified polynomial complete problems. SIGACT, 1974, pp. 47-63.

Efficient Simulations among Several Models of Parallel Computers (Extended Abstract)

Friedhelm Meyer auf der Heide
Fachbereich Informatik
Johann Wolfgang Goethe-Universität
6000 Frankfurt am Main
Fed. Rep. of Germany

Abstract: We consider parallel computers (PC's) with fixed communication network and deal with the question, how fast can we simulate PC's with n processors whose communication network has unbounded degree (unfair PC's) by PC's where this degree is bounded (fair PC's). An important class of unfair PC's is thatone of PC's with predictable communication (pred.com.). In such a PC each processor can compute in O(t) steps the sequence of processors it wants to communicate with during the next t steps. A famous example of such PC's are cubes initialized with ascend-and descend programs as introduced by Preparata and Vuillemin in [5]. They could simulate such unfair PC's with pred.com. with constant time loss using only as many processors as the cube has. We generalize this result by presenting a fair PC which can simulate each unfair PC with pred.com., n processors, and O(log(n)) storage locations per processor with constant time loss using $O(n^{1+\varepsilon})$ processors for an arbitrary $\varepsilon>0$.

I. Introduction

In this paper we deal with the following question:
How efficiently can one parallel computer (PC) with fixed communication network with bounded degree simulate all members of a certain class of PC's?

By a PC we mean a finite set of n processors which have usual sequential capabilities. They are partially joint by wires. The graph defined by the processors and the wires is its communication network. In one step each processor is allowed to read an information from a (relative to the communication network) neighboring processor. We allow that several processors read from the same processors at the same time. We assume the PC is syncronized.

Technological restrictions demand the degree of a PC, i.e. the degree of its communication network to be bounded by a small constant.

We shall call such PC's fair. Those with large degree we call unfair. Later we shall always assume that their degree is n-1, i.e. that their communication network is the complete graph. We furthermore assume that each processor only has $0(\log(n))$ storage locations, each for one integer.

An important class of unfair PC's are those with predictable communication (unfair PC's with pred.com.).

Such a PC has the additional property that for each integer t, each processor can compute for itself the sequence of addresses of processors it wants to read from during the next t steps in $0(t)$ steps.

Famous examples of unfair PC's with pred.com. are the ascend-and descend- programs for cubes defined by Preparata and Vuillemin in [5].

This unfair PC has $N=2^k$ processors, and its communication network is a k-dimensional cube. The prediction of the communication is very easy for each processor: neighbour in direction of the first dimension, neighbour in the direction of the second dimension, and so on.

Preparata and Vuillemin could simulate this special, very regular PC with pred.com. by a fair PC which N processors- the Cube-Connected Cycles- and constant time loss.

In this paper we shall present a fair PC which can simulate each unfair PC with pred.com. with n processors, a so-called n-simulator. This n-simulator can for an arbitrary $\varepsilon>0$ be constructed such that it has $0(n^{1+\varepsilon})$ processors and only a constant time loss. (For a more detailed construction see [10].)

In [10] the above method of simulating and ideas from [4] are combined for constructing a so-called n-universal PC. Such a fair PC can simulate each fair PC with n processors and fixed degree. In [3] an n-universal PC with $0(n)$ processors and time loss $0(\log(n))$ is constructed. In [4] an n-universal PC with $0(n^{1+\varepsilon})$ processors for some arbitrary $\varepsilon>0$ is constructed which has only a time loss $0(\log\log(n))$.

The n-universal PC constructed in [10] has the same number of processors as above but a constant time loss only. This result even holds if we remove the restriction of the storage capacity of the processors.

In [10], it is also shown that we cannot hope for fast simulations if we want to build a general n-simulator. Such a fair PC is able to simulate each unfair PC, also those whose communication is not predictable. A lower bound of $\Omega(\log(n))$ is proved for the time loss of a general n-simulator, independent on the number of its processors. This result holds when assuming some reasonable properties of the design of simulations as they are already defined in [4] for proving a time-processor trade-off for n-universal PC's. By results from [1], [6], [7] or [8] one can prove that this lower bound is tight.

II. The Construction of an n-Simulator.

In this chapter we shall construct an n-simulator. The construction of the n-simulator proceeds in three steps. First we describe for each integer t a fair PC T_t^* which can simulate t steps of each unfair PC with pred.com. in $O(t)$ steps. Afterwards we define what we mean by weak n-simulators. Based on such fair PC's we construct our n-simulators. Finally we quote from [10] some ways of constructing weak n-simulators which completes our construction.

First we describe a fair PC T_t^* for some fixed integer t. T_t^* can simulate t steps of each unfair PC with pred.com. in $O(t)$ steps if it is initialized in an appropriate way. T_t^* consists of n exemplaries $T_t^1,\ldots,T_t^n$ of a fair PC T_t which we will define now.

Its communication network is a tree whose vertices are replaced by cycles. The cycle corresponding to its root is called the root cycle, each processor on it is a root processor and one of them is the main root.

T_t is inductively defined as follows:

T_0 consists of one processor, it is its main root and forms its root cycle.

For t>0, T_t consists of exemplaries of $T_0,\ldots,T_{t-1}$ and t new processors $P_0,\ldots,P_{t-1}$. These processors form the root cycle of T_t by wires between P_p and $P_{(p+1)\bmod(t)}$ for $p \in \{0,\ldots,t-1\}$.

P_0 is the main root. Furthermore, for each $p \in \{0,\ldots,t-1\}$, P_p is joint to the main root of T_p.

An example of this fair PC is shown in figure 1.

The following lemma can easily be proved by evaluating the obvious recursion for the number of processors of T_t and by the above definition.

<u>Lemma 1:</u> For $t \geq 1$, T_t has $3\cdot 2^{t-1}-1$ processors and degree 3.

Now let H be an unfair PC with pred.com. and n processors $R_1,\ldots,R_n$. A configuration $K=(K_1,\ldots,K_n)$ of H consists of configurations K_i for each processor R_i of H, $i \in \{1,\ldots,n\}$. Recall that each processor only has $O(\log(n))$ storage areas. Thus each K_i can be represented by a coding of its program and a list of the contents of its storage locations. This representation is a string of integers of length

$O(\log(n))$. In the sequel we shall identify this string with the configuration.

Now suppose that H started with K executes p steps for some integer p. The resulting configuration $\bar{K}=(\bar{K}_1,\ldots,\bar{K}_n)$ then is called the p'th successor configuration of K and for $i \in \{1,\ldots,n\}$, $\bar{K}_i$ is the p'th successor configuration of K for R_i.

For an integer p and $i \in \{1,\ldots,n\}$, $Com(K,R_i,p)$ denotes the string of addresses of processors R_i reads from during p steps of H started with K. For $q \in \{1,\ldots,p\}$, $Com(K,R_i,p)_q$ denotes the q'th element of $Com(K,R_i,p)$. If for some such q, H doesn't read from another processor in the q'th step started with K, we assume that $Com(K,R_i,p)=i$.

Let $i \in \{1,\ldots,n\}$. We say T_t is prepared for K and R_i for t steps, if the following holds:

If t=0 the T_t contains K_i.

Let t>0. Then each root processor contains K_i, and for each $p \in \{0,\ldots,t-1\}$ the exemplary T_p joint to the p'th root processor is prepared for K and R_j for p steps, if $j=Com(K,R_i,t)_{p+1}$ and $j \neq i$. If j=i, T_p may be arbitrary.

T_t^* is prepared for K if for each $i \in \{1,\ldots,n\} T_t^i$ is prepared for K and R_i for t steps.

The processor of H being attached by the above preparation to some processor P of T_t^* is said to be represented by P relative to K.

We say T_t^* simulates t steps of H started with K, if T_t^* executes a computation which finishes with the t'th successor configuration of K for R_i in each root processor of T_t^*, $i \in \{1,\ldots,n\}$.

<u>Lemma 2:</u> If T_t^* is prepared for K, it can simulate t steps of H started with K in O(t) steps.

<u>Proof:</u> Let $i \in \{1,\ldots,n\}$ be fixed, $P_0,\ldots,P_{n-1}$ be the root processors of T_t^i. Suppose that T_t^* is prepared for K.

For $p \in \{1,\ldots,t\}$ we say that the root cycle of T_t^i is p-prepared if P_{p-1} and $P_{p \bmod (t)}$ contain the p'th successor configuration of K for R_i and for each $q \in \{1,\ldots,p-1\}$, $P_{(p+q) \bmod (t)}$ contains the (p-q)'th successor configuration of K for R_i.

We now want to find an algorithm which transfers a p-prepared root cycle to a (p+1)-prepared one. For this purpose we first assume that for each $q \in \{0,\ldots,t-1\}$ the main root Q of the exemplary of T_q joint to P_q contains the q'th successor configuration of K for the processor R_j being represented by Q. Thus Q contains the message R_i

wants to read from R_j in the (q+1)'th step of H started with K.

Now if the root cycle is p-prepared for $p \in \{0,\ldots,t-2\}$, it becomes (p+1)-prepared by the following algorithm.

Part 1: For each $q \in \{1,\ldots,p\}$, $P_{(p+q) \bmod (t)}$ simulates the (p-q+1)'th step of R_i with the help of $P_{(p+q-1) \bmod (t)}$.

Remark 1: As $P_{(p+q-1) \bmod (t)}$ has already executed this step by definition of "p-prepared", Part 1 can be done in constant time.

Part 2: P_p simulates the (p+1)'th step of R_i.

Remark 2: This can be done in constant time because we have assumed that the message R_i perhaps wants to read from another processor is stored in the main root of the T_p joint to P_p.

Part 3: For each $q \in \{1,\ldots,p+1\}$, $P_{(p+q) \bmod (t)}$ simulates the (p-q+2)'th step of R_i with the help of $P_{(p+q-1) \bmod (t)}$.

Remark 3: This works in constant time, because in step 1 resp. step 2, $P_{(p+q-1) \bmod (t)}$ just has simulated this step.

Thus T_t^* is (p+1)-prepared in a constant number s' of steps. Now we may inductively assume that after s' • p steps, the root cycle of the exemplary of T_p joint to P_p is p-prepared. But this means that its main root contains the message R_i needs to execute its (p+1)'th step after s' • p steps.

By our algorithm this message is needed after s'• p+(time for step 1) many steps that means it is available when it is required by P_p. Thus P_0 contains the t'th successor-configuration of K for R_i after s' • t steps. Clearly in further s" • t steps each root processor can have stored this configuration.

Executing this algorithm in parallel for each $i \in \{1,\ldots,n\}$ we have simulated t steps of M started with K in (s'+s")•t steps.

Figure 2 shows the states of the p-prepared root cycle of T_8^i for some $i \in \{1,\ldots,n\}$ and each $p \in \{1,\ldots,8\}$. A number ℓ in the q'th column and p'th row, $q \in \{0,\ldots,7\}$, $p \in \{1,\ldots,8\}$ means:
If T_8 is p-prepared, P_q contains the ℓ'th successor configuration of K for R_i.

In order to obtain a fast simulation of arbitrarily many steps of H we have to prepare T_t^* before each phase of t steps for the appropriate configuration of H. In order to obtain an n-simulator of at most polynomial size we have to choose $t=O(\log(n))$ because of lemma 1. But then we have to prepare T_t^* before each phase of t steps in $O(\log(n))$ time in order to obtain a constant time loss. Unfortunately such algorithms would need at least $\Omega(\log(n)^2)$ steps. Therefore we will execute an initialization each time before d such phases of t steps, where d is chosen suitably. It turns out that this initialization for d preparations can be done in parallel and doesn't neede much more time than one preparation.

This initialization effects that afterwards d preparations can become executed, each in $O(\log(n))$ steps. This trick will guarantee the constant time loss. Let in the sequel $\varepsilon>0$ be fixed and $t:=\lfloor \varepsilon\log(n)\rfloor$. Then by lemma 1, T_t^* has at most $3n^{1+\varepsilon}$ processors

Now we shall first define a type of fair PC's, so-called weak n-simulators, which will be used for constructing n-simulators. Explicit constructions of weak n-simulators can be found in [10].

A weak n-simulator M is a fair PC with the following properties:

- M contains an exemplary of T_t^*.
- If $K=(K_1,\ldots,K_n)$ is some configuration of H and for each $i \in \{1,\ldots,n\}$, each root processor of T_t^i contains $Com(K,R_i,t)$, then M can initialize itself such that afterwards the following holds: If for each $i \in \{1,\ldots,n\}$, each root processor of T_t^i contains K_i, then M can prepare T_t^* for K in $O(\log(n))$ steps.

The above initialization we call the initialization of M for K and the time it needs the initialization time of M.

We now shall construct n-simulators.

Let M be some weak n-simulator with initialization time d. Then the fair PC M* consists of $r:=\lceil d/_t\rceil$ exemplaries of M called $M^0,\ldots,M^{r-1}$. For each $\ell \in \{0,\ldots,r-1\}$, $i \in \{1,\ldots,n\}$, each root processor of T_t^i in M^ℓ is joint to the corresponding processor in $M^{(\ell+1)\bmod(r)}$.

<u>Theorem 1:</u> Let M be a weak n-simulator with initialization time d. Then M* is an n-simulator which can simulate ℓ steps pf some arbitrary unfair PC with pred.com. and n processors in $O(d+\ell)$ steps. If M has m processors, M* has $\lceil d/t\rceil \cdot m$ processors.

<u>Proof:</u> The computation of the number of processors of M* is clear. We will construct an algorithm which simulates $d':=t\cdot r$ steps of H started with $K^0=(K_1^0,\ldots,K_n^0)$. For $j \in \{1,\ldots,r\}$ let $K^j=(K_1^j,\ldots,K_n^j)$ be the $(t\cdot j)$'th successor-configuration of K^0.

Assume that for each $i \in \{1,\dots,n\}$, $q \in \{0,\dots,r-1\}$, K_i^0 is stored in each root processor of T_t^i in M^q.

Now d' steps of H started with K^0 can be simulated as follows.

Part 1: For each $q \in \{0,\dots,r-1\}$, $i \in \{1,\dots,n\}$, each root processor of T_t^i in M^q computes $Com(K^q, R_i, t)$.

Remark 1: This can be done in $O(r \cdot t) = O(d')$ steps because of the definition of predictable communication.

Part 2: For each $q \in \{0,\dots,r-1\}$, M^q initializes itself for K^q.

Remark 2: This can (after having executed Part 1) be done in d steps as d is the initialization time of the M^q's.

Part 3: For $q=0,\dots,r-1$ do (sequentially)

Begin

a) M^q prepares the exemplary T' of T_t^* in M^q for K^q.

b) T' simulates t steps of H started with K^q.

Comment: Now for each $i \in \{1,\dots,n\}$ each root processor of T_t^i in T' contains $K_i^{(q+1)}$.

c) For each $i \in \{1,\dots,n\}$, each root processor of T_t^i in T' transports $K_i^{(q+1)}$ to the corresponding processor in $M^{(q+1)\bmod(r)}$.

End

Remark 3: Now for each $i \in \{1,\dots,n\}$, each root processor of T_t^i in M^0 has stored K_i^r, the d'-th successor-configuration of K^0 for R_i.

Remark 4: Each pass of the loop of part 3 needs $O(t)=O(\log(n))$ steps: $O(\log(n))$ for a) because of the definition of a weak n- simulator, $O(t)$ for b) because of lemma 2, $O(\log(n))$ for c) because we have assumed that each configuration of a processor is represented by an integer string of length $O(\log(n))$. Thus part 3 needs $O(r \cdot t) = O(d')$ steps.

Part 4: For each $q \in \{0,\dots,r-1\}$, $i \in \{1,\dots,n\}$, K_i^r is transported to each root processor of T_t^i in M^q.

Remark 5: This can be done in $O(r \cdot \log(n)) = O(d')$ steps because of the above bound for the lengthes of the representations of configurations.

Now we have achieved all preconditions for starting this algorithm again with $K^0 \leftarrow K^r$. Remark 1,2,4 and 5 guarantee that we have only needed $O(d')$ steps for simulating d' steps of H. Repeating this algorithm we obtain that we need $O(\ell)$ steps for simulating ℓ steps of H, if $\ell = \Omega(d)$. If ℓ is smaller, we still have to execute Part 1 and 2 once. Thus we need $O(d)$ steps also in this case. Therefore in general we need $O(d+\ell)$ steps for simulating ℓ steps of H.

Now the problem of constructing n-simulators is reduced to constructing weak n-simulators.

For this construction we define so-called (a,b)-distributors $D_{a,b}$ for integers a,b, $a \leq b$.
Such a fair PC has a+b distinguished processors, a input processors $A_1,\ldots,A_a$ and b output processors $B_1,\ldots,B_b$, and has the following property:

If each B_i, $i \in \{1,\ldots,b\}$, has stored an integer $c_i \in \{1,\ldots,a+1\}$, then $D_{a,b}$ can initialize itself such that afterwards the following holds:
If each A_j, $j \in \{1,\ldots,a\}$, contains an integer string x_j of length $O(\log(n))$, then $D_{a,b}$ can distribute $(x_1,\ldots,x_a)$ according to $(c_1,\ldots,c_b)$, i.e. can transport each x_j, $j \in \{1,\ldots,a\}$, to each B_i with $c_i = j$, $i \in \{1,\ldots,a\}$, in $O(\log(b) + \log(n))$ steps.
The above initialization is called the initialization of $D_{a,b}$ for $(c_1,\ldots,c_b)$, and the time it needs is the initialization time of $D_{a,b}$.
Now we shall construct weak n-simulators with the help of (a,b)-distributors.
Let for $j \in \{0,\ldots,t-1\}$ L_j be the following subset of the set of processors of T_t^*.
L_0 is the set of root processors of $T_t^1,\ldots,T_t^n$.
For $j > 0$, L_j is the set of all processors which belong to cycles which are joint to processors of L_{j-1} and which do not belong to L_{j-2} or L_{j-1}.

Informally, L_j consists of those processors which belong to a cycle in depth j of some T_t^i in T_t^*. Let $\#L_j =: m_j$, $j \in \{0,\ldots,t-1\}$.
Let for $j \in \{0,\ldots,t-1\}$ D_j be a (n,m_j) distributor with initialization time d_j.

Then the fair PC M based on $D_0,\dots,D_{t-1}$ is defined as follows:

M consists of T_t^* and $D_1,\dots,D_{t-1}$ where for $j \in \{0,\dots,t-1\}$ L_j is the set of output processors of D_j and the j'th root processors of $T_t^1,\dots,T_t^n$ are its input processors.

<u>Lemma 3:</u> M is a weak n-simulator with initialization time $0(\log(n)^2 + \sum_{j=0}^{t-1} d_j)$.

<u>Proof:</u> Let $K=(K_1,\dots,K_n)$ be a configuration of H, and suppose that for each $i \in \{1,\dots,n\}$, each root processor of T_t^i has stored $\text{Com}(K,R_i,t)$.

Let for each processor P of T_t^* $\ell(P)$ be the address of the processor of H being represented by P relative to K. Clearly, for each $i \in \{1,\dots,n\}$, $\ell(P)=i$ for each root processor P of T_t^i.

The following algorithm initializes M for K.

For $j=0,\dots,t-1$ do (sequentially)

Begin

a) D_j initializes itself for $(\ell(P),\ P \in L_j)$.

b) D_j distributes $(\text{Com}(K,R_i,t),\ i \in \{1,\dots,n\})$ according to $(\ell(P),\ P \in L_j)$.

c) For each $P \in L_j$; if for $q \in \{1,\dots,t-1\}$, $p \in \{0,\dots,q-1\}$, P is the p'th root processor of an exemplary of T_q in T_t^*, then P sends $z:=\text{Com}(K,R_{\ell(P)},t)_{p+1}$ to its neighbour Q in L_{j+1} and $\ell(Q):=z$.

<u>Comment:</u> Now for each cycle whose processors belong to L_j, one of its processors Q knows $\ell(Q)$.

d) For each $Q \in L_{j+1}$, which knows $\ell(Q)$: Q transports $\ell(Q)$ to each processors Q' of the cycle it belongs to, and $\ell(Q'):=\ell(Q)$.

<u>End</u>

Obviously this algorithm attaches the correct address $\ell(P)$ to each processor P of T_t^*. Because of the initializations of $D_0,\dots,D_{t-1}$ in step a) of the passes of the loop, finally M is initialized for K.

For $j \in \{0,\dots,t-1\}$, the j'th pass of the loop needs $d_j+0(\log(n))+0(t)=0(d_j+\log(n))$ steps. Thus the initialization time of M is $0(\log(n)^2 + \sum_{j=0}^{t-1} d_j)$. Now a preparation of T_t^* in M can be

executed in $0(\max_j \{\log(d_j) + \log(n)\}) = 0(\log(n))$ steps
Using ideas from [4] one can construct an (a,b)-distributor with $0(b \log(b))$ processors ans initialization time $0(\log(b)^4)$ with the help of Waksman permutation networks [9]. (See [10]).

Applying lemma 3 and theorem 1 we obtain:

Theorem 2: M_1^* is an n-simulator with $0(n^{1+\varepsilon})\log(n)^5)$processors. M_1^* can simulate ℓ steps of some arbitrary unfair PC with pred.com. and n processors in $0(\log(n)^5 + \ell)$ steps.

Finally we note two possible improvements of this theorem. We can construct (a,b)-distributors with initialization time $0(\log(b))$ if we are able to sort b numbers in $0(\log(b))$ steps. Ajtai, Komlos and Szemeredi [1] have done so with the help of a fair PC with $0(b\log(b))$ processors. This fair PC can also sort packets of length s according to some keys in $0(\log(b)+s)$ steps. With this result we can construct an (a,b)-distributor with $0(b\log(b))$ processors and initialization time $0(\log(b))$. Call the associated weak n-simulator M_2.

A similar result can be achieved when using the sorting algorithm from [6] due to Reif and Valiant. They have sorted b numbers on Cube-Connected Cycles using $0(\log(b))$ steps with overwhelming probability. In order to sort packets of length $0(\log(n))$ we here need $0(\log(n))$ such fair PC's in order to do so in $0(\log(b)+\log(n))$ steps. Thus we obtain an (a,b)-distributor with $0(b\log(n))$ processors and initiatisation time $0(\log(b)^2)$ which allows distributions using $0(\log(b)+\log(n))$ steps with overwhelming probability.

The associated weak n-simulator let be called M_3. M_2 and M_3 both have $0(n^{1+\varepsilon}\log(n))$ processors.

Applying M_2 and M_3 to theorem 1 we obtain:

Theorem 3: M_2^* (M_3^*) is an n-simulator with $0(n^{1+\varepsilon}\cdot\log(n)^2)$ processors. M_2^* (M_3^*) can simulate ℓ steps of some arbitrary unfair PC with pred.com. and n processors in $0(\log(n)^2+\ell)$ steps (with overwhelming probability).

References:

[1] M.Ajtai, J.Komlos, E.Szemeredi:
An O(nlog(n)) Sorting Network, Proc. of the 15'th Annual ACM Symposium on Theory of Computing (1983), Boston, USA, 1-9.

[2] K.Batcher:
Sorting Networks and their Applications, AFIPS Spring Joint Comp. Conf. 32 (1968), 307-314.

[3] Z.Galil, W.J.Paul:
A General Purpose Parallel Computer, Journal of the ACM 30(2) (1983), 360-387.

[4] F.Meyer auf der Heide:
Efficiency of Universal Parallel Computers, Acta Informatica 19 (1983) 269-296.

[5] F.P.Preparata, J.Vuillemin:
The Cube-Connected Cycles: A Versatile Network for Parallel Computation, Communications of the ACM 24 (1981), 300-310.

[6] J.H.Reif, L.G.Valiant:
A Logarithmic Time Sort for Linear Size Networks, 15'th Annual ACM Symposium on Theory of Computing (1983), Boston, USA,10-16.

[7] E.Upfal:
Efficient Schemes for Parallel Communication, Proc. of the ACM Symposium on Principles of Distributed Computing (1982), Ottawa, Canada.

[8] L.G.Valiant, G.J.Brebner:
Universal Schemes for Parallel Communication, Proc. of the 13'th Annual ACM Symposium on Theory of Computing (1981), Milwaukee, USA, 263-267.

[9] A.Waksman:
A Permutation Network, Journal of the ACM, 15(1) (1968), 159-163.

[10]F.Meyer auf der Heide:
Efficient Simulations among Several Models of Parallel Computers, Interner Bericht des Fachbereichs Informatik der J.W.Goethe-Universität, Frankfurt, 2/83, to appear in SIAM J.on Comp.

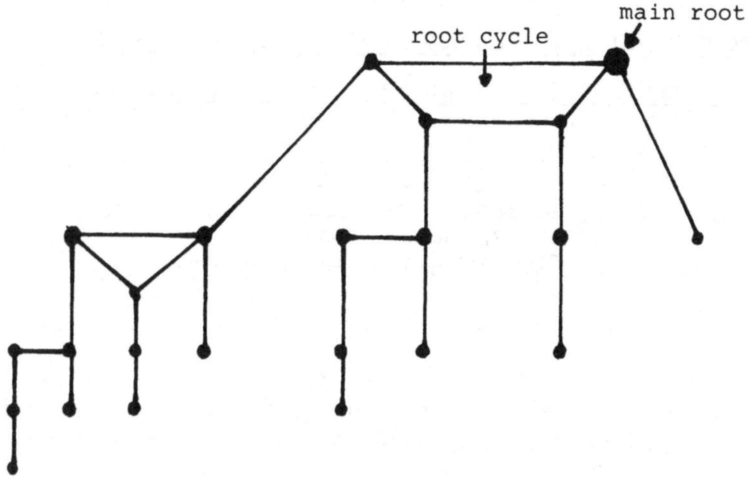

Figure 1: The fair PC T_4.

	p_0	p_1	p_2	p_3	p_4	p_5	p_6	p_7
1	1	1	0	0	0	0	0	0
2	0	$\underline{2}$	2	1	0	0	0	0
3	0	0	$\underline{3}$	3	2	1	0	0
4	0	0	0	$\underline{4}$	4	3	2	1
5	2	1	0	0	$\underline{5}$	5	4	3
6	4	3	2	1	0	$\underline{6}$	6	5
7	6	5	4	3	2	1	$\underline{7}$	7
8	8	7	6	5	4	3	2	$\underline{8}$

Figure 2: The design of a p-prepared root cycle.

BORNES INFERIEURES SUR LA COMPLEXITE DES FACTEURS DES MOTS INFINIS ENGENDRES PAR MORPHISMES ITERES

Jean-Jacques Pansiot
Centre de Calcul de l'Esplanade
7, rue René Descartes
67084 Strasbourg Cédex, France

Résumé. Ehrenfeucht, Lee et Rozenberg ont montré que la complexité des facteurs des DOL langages (et donc des mots infinis engendrés par morphismes itérés) était majorée par cn^2 (resp. cnlogn, cn) suivant que le morphisme est quelconque, croissant ou uniforme. Nous introduisons une classe intermédiaire dont la complexité est majorée par cnloglog n. De plus nous montrons que tout mot infini engendré par morphisme a une complexité en $O(n^2)$, $O(n \log n)$, $O(n \log \log n)$, $O(n)$ ou $O(1)$ suivant la nature du morphisme.

1. Introduction et préliminaires.

La complexité des facteurs d'un mot infini $\mathcal{S}$ (resp. d'un langage L) est la fonction f(n) égale au nombre de facteurs distincts de longueur n de $\mathcal{S}$ (resp. des mots de L). Un DOL système (cf [RS]) est la donnée d'un triplet $\langle X, g, \alpha \rangle$, où X est un alphabet fini, g un morphisme de X^*, et l'axiome α un mot de X^*. Le DOL langage engendré par un tel système est $L = \{g^i(\alpha), i \geq 0\}$. Ehrenfeucht, Lee et Rozenberg [ELR] ont étudié la complexité des facteurs des DOL langages en fonction des propriétés de g (voir aussi [ER 81a], [ER 81b], [ER 82], [ER 83a], [ER 83b], [R]). Un morphisme g est croissant (resp. uniforme de module $m \geq 2$) si $|g(x)| \geq 2$ pour tout x (resp. $|g(x)| = m$). Il est montré dans [ELR] que la complexité des facteurs d'un DOL langage est majorée par $c\,n^2$ (resp. $c\,n \log n$, $c\,n$) suivant que le morphisme à itérer est quelconque, croissant ou uniforme. De plus il existe des langages atteignant ces bornes.

Dans ce travail nous donnons des bornes inférieures pour la complexité des facteurs. Nous nous plaçons dans le cadre des mots infinis engendrés par itération de morphisme, qui permet des preuves plus simples que pour les DOL langages.

Soit g un morphisme prolongeable en x_0, c'est-à-dire tel que $g(x_0) = x_0u$. Alors $g^{i+1}(x_0)$ commence par $g^i(x_0)$, $i \geq 0$ et la suite $g^i(x_0)$, $i \geq 0$, converge vers un mot unique, en général infini que l'on note $g^{\omega}(x_0)$.

Résultat. Soit $\mathcal{S} = g^{\omega}(x_0)$ un mot infini. Alors il existe des constantes c_1 et c_2, $0 < c_1 \leq c_2$ telles que la complexité des facteurs $f(n)$ de $\mathcal{S}$ vérifie

$$c_1\ c(n) \leq f(n) \leq c_2\ c(n)$$

où $c(n)$ est l'une des fonctions 1, n, nloglogn, nlogn, ou n^2.

En particulier la complexité de $\mathcal{S}$ ne peut pas croître comme $n^{3/2}$, $n(\log n)^2$ ou $n\log^3 n$.

Le comportement asymptotique de la complexité dépend essentiellement d'un critère : la vitesse relative de croissance des images itérées des lettres. On sait (cf [SS] chap. III. 7), que $|g^n(x)|$ est soit bornée, soit croissante comme $n^{a_x} b_x^{\,n}$ appelé ordre de x pour un entier $a_x \geq 0$, et un nombre $b_x \geq 1$. Nous allons voir que la complexité croît comme n (resp. nloglogn, nlogn, n^2) seulement si tous les a_x et tous les b_x sont égaux (resp. les b_x sont égaux et les a_x différents, les b_x sont différents et plus grands que 1, certains b_x sont égaux à 1 et a_x plus grands que zéro).

Dans le paragraphe 2 nous donnons un lemme général permettant d'établir des bornes inférieures sur la complexité. Au paragraphe 3 nous traitons des morphismes croissants, et au paragraphe 4 des morphismes non croissants.

2. Résultat général sur les bornes inférieures pour la complexité.

Soit $\mathcal{S}$ un mot infini et $f(n)$ sa complexité. Appelons biprolongeable un facteur u de $\mathcal{S}$ tel qu'il existe des lettres x et y, $x \neq y$ avec ux et uy facteurs de $\mathcal{S}$. Soit $b(n)$ le nombre de facteurs biprolongeables de $\mathcal{S}$ de longueur

n. En tenant compte du fait que tout facteur se prolonge d'au moins une façon, on obtient

$$f(n+1) \geq f(n) + b(n) \quad \text{et} \quad f(n) \geq \sum_{i=0}^{n-1} b(n)$$

Il suffit donc de minorer $b(n)$ pour minorer la complexité.

<u>Lemme 2.1</u>. Soit $\mathcal{S} = \alpha_0 x\beta_0 = \alpha_1 x\beta_1 = \ldots = \alpha_i x\beta_i \ldots$ une suite infinie de factorisations de $\mathcal{S}$ et des fonctions $p(n)$, $s(n)$, telles que

(i) le plus grand préfixe commun p_i de β_i et β_{i+1} vérifie p_i ne contient pas de x, $|p_i| < |p_{i+1}|$ et $|p_i| \leq p(i)$;

(ii) le plus grand suffixe commun s_i de α_i et α_{i+1} vérifie $|s_i| \geq s(i)$;

Alors $b(n)$ est minoré par le nombre d'entiers i vérifiant

(1) $1 + p(i) \leq n \leq 1 + p(i) + s(i)$.

<u>Preuve</u>. Soit α un suffixe de s_i. Alors $\alpha\, x\, p_i$ est biprolongeable puisque $s_i\, x\, p_i$ se prolonge différemment dans $\alpha_i\, x\beta_i$ et dans $\alpha_{i+1}\, x\beta_{i+1}$ (sinon p_i ne serait pas maximal).

Pour chaque n et chaque i vérifiant $|x\, p_i| \leq n \leq |s_i\, x\, p_i|$ on a donc un mot prolongeable de longueur n. De plus pour n fixé et i variable, tous ces mots sont distincts, puisque la dernière occurrence de x apparaît à distance $|p_i|$ de la fin du mot et $i \neq i'$ entraîne $|p_i| \neq |p_{i'}|$ d'après i). Pour n fixé le nombre de mots est donc bien minoré par le nombre de i vérifiant (1) ■

Pour différents choix de $p(n)$ et $s(n)$ on obtient les minorations suivantes :

Corollaire 2.2. Il existe des constantes c et d telles que

a) Si $p(n) = k_1 n$ et $s(n) = k_2 n$, $k_1 > 0$, $k_2 > 0$ alors

$b(n) \geq c\, n$, $f(n) \geq d\, n^2$.

b) Si $p(n) = b_1^n$ et $s(n) = b_2^n$, $1 < b_1 < b_2$ alors

$b(n) \geq c \log n$, $f(n) \geq d\, n \log n$

c) Si $p(n) = n^{a_1} b^n$ et $s(n) = n^{a_2} b^n$, $a_1 < a_2$ alors

$b(n) \geq c \log \log n$, $f(n) \geq d\, n \log \log n$.

Nous allons maintenant appliquer ce résultat aux différents types de morphismes.

3. Morphismes croissants.

Pour obtenir des bornes inférieures non triviales, on remarque que tout mot infini $\mathcal{S}$ a une complexité $f(n) \leq n$ si et seulement si $\mathcal{S}$ est ultimement périodique. Dans ce cas il existe des constantes c_1 et c_2, $0 < c_1 < c_2$ telles que $c_1 \leq f(n) \leq c_2$, et $\mathcal{S}$ peut être engendré par morphisme uniforme. Tout mot infini $\mathcal{S} = g^{\omega}(x_0)$ non ultimement périodique avec g uniforme vérifie donc

$$c_1\, n \leq f(n) \leq c_2 n\,, \quad 1 \leq c_1 \leq c_2\,,$$

d'après les résultats de [ELR].

Néanmoins il existe des mots $\mathcal{S} = g^{\omega}(x_0)$ où g n'est pas uniforme, mais où la complexité est linéaire, comme par exemple le mot de Fibonacci engendré par $\varphi : a \to a\,b$, $b \to a$.

Nous allons caractériser la classe des morphismes engendrant des mots de complexité linéaire.

Définition. Un morphisme g est quasi-uniforme si toutes les lettres ont le même ordre de croissance, de la forme b^n. Il est polynomialement divergent si toute lettre x a un ordre de la forme $n^{a_x} b^n$, avec certains a_x non nuls. Finalement il est <u>exponentiellement divergent</u> si il existe des lettres x et y d'ordre $n^{a_x} b_x^n$ et $n^{a_y} b_y^n$ avec $1 < b_x < b_y$.

Remarques.

1. Nous utiliserons une définition des morphismes croissants un peu plus large que celle de [ELR] : un morphisme est croissant si pour toute lettre x $|g^n(x)|$ est non borné, ou de façon équivalente l'ordre de x est non constant. Ceci entraîne que g^i est croissant au sens de [ELR] pour i assez grand.
2. Tout morphisme croissant est soit quasi-uniforme, soit polynomialement divergent soit exponentiellement divergent.
3. Un morphisme uniforme de module b est quasi-uniforme avec des lettres d'ordre b^n.
4. Si pour tout couple (x, y) il existe i tel que $g^i(x)$ contienne y, alors g est quasi-uniforme (l'inverse n'est pas toujours vrai).

Exemple. Le morphisme de Fibonacci est quasi-uniforme car $\varphi(a)$ contient b et $\varphi(b)$ contient a.

Lemme 3.1. Tout mot infini non ultimement périodique $\mathcal{S} = g^{\omega}(x_0)$ où g est quasi-uniforme a une complexité f(n) vérifiant

$$c_1\, n \le f(n) \le c_2\, n\ ,\quad 1 \le c_1 \le c_2\ .$$

La borne inférieure est déjà établie. Pour la borne supérieure, $f(n) \le c_2 n$, on peut adapter la preuve donnée dans [ELR] pour le cas uniforme.

Nous allons voir que pour un morphisme croissant non quasi-uniforme la complexité des facteurs croît au moins comme n log log n. Pour un morphisme croissant, la complexité est donc linéaire si et seulement si le morphisme est quasi-uniforme mais non périodique.

Lemme 3.2. Pour tout mot infini $\mathcal{S} = g^{\omega}(x_0)$ où g est polynomialement divergent il existe des constantes c_1 et c_2 telles que la complexité $f(n)$ vérifie

$$c_1 \, n \log \log n \leq f(n) \leq c_2 \, n \log \log n \, .$$

Exemple. Soit g_1 le morphisme défini par $g_1(x) = xyxy$ et $g_1(y) = yy$. On a $|g_1^n(y)| = 2^n$ et $|g_1^n(x)| = (n+1)2^n$, g_1 est donc polynomialement divergent, et la complexité de $g_1^{\omega}(x)$ est en nloglogn.

Preuve du lemme 3.2. Montrons tout d'abord la borne supérieure. Soit g un morphisme polynomialement divergent, et b^n, $n\, b^n$, ..., $n^a b^n$ l'ordre de croissance de ses lettres, $a \geq 1$ (voir [SS, chap. III.7]). En particulier il existe des constantes c'_1 et c'_2 telles que pour tout u, $c'_1 b^n |u| \leq |g^n(u)| \leq c'_2 n^a b^n |u|$. Soit u_0 un mot de longueur n facteur de $\mathcal{S} = g^{\omega}(x_0)$. Soit u_1 le plus court facteur de $\mathcal{S}$ couvrant u_0 , c'est-à-dire tel que u_0 soit facteur de $g(u_1)$ (voir [ELR]). Si $|u_0| \geq 4$ alors $|u_1| < |u_0|$. On peut ainsi construire une suite $u_0, u_1, \ldots u_k$ telle que $|u_k| \leq 3$ et $|u_{k-1}| \geq 4$.

Il y a un nombre fini de possibilités pour u_k . Il suffit donc de majorer le nombre de u_0 provenant d'un $u = u_k$ fixé. On a $g(u) = x_1 \, v \, x_2$ et $g^{k-1}(v)$ est un facteur de u_0, lui-même facteur de $g^{k-1}(x_1 \, v \, x_2)$. Pour k fixé, il y a au plus $n - |g^{k-1}(v)| + 1$ possibilités, soit au plus n . Pour u et n fixés comptons maintenant le nombre de valeurs possibles pour k . On a $|g^{k-1}(v)| < n < |g^{k-1}(x_1 v x_2|$, soit $|v| \, c'_1 b^{k-1} \leq n \leq |x_1 \, v \, x_2| c'_2 (k-1)^a b^{k-1}$. Le nombre de k vérifiant cette inégalité est majoré par $c''_2 \log \log n$. Pour chaque k il y a au plus n valeurs de u_0 possible. On a donc bien $f(n) \leq c_2 \, n \log \log n$.

Pour la borne inférieure, on considère une lettre x d'ordre de croissance maximum $n^a b^n$. Pour i assez grand, $g^i(x)$ contient au moins deux lettres d'ordre $n^a b^n$, donc $\mathcal{S}$ contient une infinité de telles lettres. Il existe alors un facteur $x_1 \, u_1 \, x'_1$, où x_1 et x'_1 sont d'ordre $n^a b^n$, et les lettres de u_1 sont d'ordre au plus $n^{a-1}b^n$. Soient $g(x_i) = v_{i+1}x_{i+1}u_{i+1}$, $g(x'_i) = u'_{i+1}\ x'_{i+1}\ v'_{i+1}$, où x_{i+1} et x'_{i+1} sont d'ordre $n^a b^n$, et les lettres de u_{i+1} et u'_{i+1} sont d'ordre inférieur. En considérant la suite $x_1\, u_1\, x'_1$, $x_2\, u_2\, g(u_1)\, u'_2 x'_2, \ldots, x_i\, u_i\, g(u_{i-1}) \ldots g^{i-2}(u_2) g^{i-1}(u_1) g^{i-2}(u'_2) \ldots u'_i x'_i$, on observe que les suites x_i, $i \geq 0$ et $x'_i, i \geq 0$ sont ultimement périodiques. En prenant une puissance appropriée de g, on peut donc supposer qu'il existe un facteur $x\, u_0 x'$ de $\mathcal{S}$ avec $g(x) = v\, x\, u$, $g(x') = u'\, x'\, v'$ où x et x' sont d'ordre $n^a b^n$, et u, u_0, u' sont d'ordre inférieur.

Considérons maintenant la suite de factorisations de $\mathcal{S} = \alpha_1\, x\, \beta_1 = \alpha_2\, x\, \beta_2 = \ldots = \alpha_i\, x\, \beta_i = \ldots$, où β_1 commence par $u_0 x'$ et où $\alpha_i = g(\alpha_{i-1})v$, $\beta_i = u\, g(\beta_{i-1})$. Soit p_i le plus long préfixe commun à β_i et β_{i+1}. Si u est non vide il croît strictement. Si u est vide, il faut remplacer g par une de ses puissances telle que le plus grand préfixe commun à $g^i(u_0)$ et $g^{i+1}(u_0)$ soit strictement croissant. Il est clair que p_i qui ne contient que des lettres d'ordre inférieur à $n^a b^n$ ne peut contenir x. Finalement on a

$$\begin{aligned} |p_i| &\leq |u\, g(u) \ldots g^{i-1}(u)\, g^i(u_0)\, g^{i-1}(u') \ldots g(u')u'| \\ &\leq c'_2 |u\, u'| \sum_{j=0}^{i-1} j^{a-1}\, b^j + c'_2\, |u_0|\, i^{a-1}\, b^i \\ &\leq c\, i^{a-1}\, b^i . \end{aligned}$$

D'autre part le plus long suffixe commun s_i à α_i et α_{i+1} croît au moins comme $c'\, i^a\, b^i$, d'où le lemme d'après le corollaire 2.2 ∎

<u>Lemme 3.3</u>. Pour tout mot infini $\mathcal{S} = g^{\omega}(x_0)$ où g est croissant exponentiellement divergent, il existe des constantes c_1 et c_2 telles que la complexité $f(n)$ de $\mathcal{S}$ vérifie

$$c_1\, n \log n \leq f(n) \leq c_2\, n \log n .$$

<u>Preuve</u>. La borne supérieure est donnée dans [ELR]. Pour la borne inférieure on applique le même raisonnement que pour le cas polynomialement divergent :

On considère un facteur $x_1\ u_1\ x'_1$ tel que x_1 et x'_1 sont d'ordre maximal $(n^{a_1}\ b^n$ et $n^{a_2}\ b^n)$ et les lettres de u_1 sont d'ordre au plus $n^a\ b'^n, b' < b$. On obtient cette fois les relations $|p_i| \leq c'_1\ n^a b'^n \leq c''_1 b''^n$ $b' < b'' < b$ et $|s_i| \geq c'_2\ b^n$, d'où le lemme par le corollaire 2.2 ■

Les trois lemmes précédents peuvent se résumer dans le théorème qui suit :

Théorème 3.4. Soit $\mathcal{S} = g^{\omega}(x_0)$ un mot infini non ultimement périodique où g est croissant. Alors il existe des constantes c_1 et c_2 telles que la complexité $f(n)$ de $\mathcal{S}$ vérifie $c_1 n \leq f(n) \leq c_2 n$ (resp. $c_1 n \log\log n \leq f(n) \leq c_2\ n \log\log n$, $c_1 n \log n \leq f(n) \leq c_2\ n \log n$) si et seulement si g est quasi-uniforme (resp. polynomialement divergent, exponentiellement divergent).

4. Morphismes non croissants.

Soit g un morphisme non croissant. Il existe donc une lettre x telle que $|g^n(x)|$ soit bornée. Soit B l'ensemble des lettres bornées et C l'ensemble des lettres croissantes.

Théorème 4.1. Soit $\mathcal{S} = g^{\omega}(x_0)$ un mot infini non ultimement périodique où g est non croissant. Alors l'une (et une seule) des deux propriétés suivantes est vraie :

i) $\mathcal{S}$ contient des facteurs arbitrairement longs dans B^*, et sa complexité $f(n)$ vérifie $c_1 n^2 \leq f(n) \leq c_2 n^2$, $c_1 > 0$.

ii) Les facteurs de $\mathcal{S}$ dans B^* sont de longueur bornée, il existe un alphabet Y, un morphisme croissant $g' : Y^* \to Y^*$, $y_0 \in Y$ et un morphisme ε-free $h : Y^* \to X^*$ tels que $\mathcal{S} = h(\mathcal{S}')$ où

$$\mathcal{S}' = g'^{\omega}(y_0).$$

Dans le second cas, la complexité de $\mathcal{S}$ croît asymptotiquement comme celle de $\mathcal{S}'$, c'est-à-dire en $0(n \log n)$, $0(n \log \log n)$, $0(n)$ suivant g'.

Pour prouver ce théorème nous allons utiliser le lemme suivant

Lemme 4.2. Soient $\mathcal{S}$ et $\mathcal{S}'$ deux mots infinis et h un morphisme ϵ-free tel que $h(\mathcal{S}') = \mathcal{S}$. Alors il existe des constantes c et k telles que les complexités $f(n)$ et $f'(n)$ de $\mathcal{S}$ et $\mathcal{S}'$ vérifient

$$f(n) \leq c\, f'(n+k).$$

Preuve. Soit $f''(n)$ le nombre de facteurs de $\mathcal{S}$ de la forme $h(u)$ et de longueur n. Alors $f''(n) \leq f'(n)$. Soit $m = \max|h(x)|$, et u un facteur de longueur n de $\mathcal{S}$. Alors u est un facteur d'un mot de la forme $h(v)$ où $n \leq |h(v)| \leq n+2m-2$. On a donc

$$f(n) \leq f''(n) + 2\, f''(n+1) + \ldots + m\, f''(n+m) + \ldots + m\, f''(n+2m-2).$$

Comme $f''(n) \leq f'\, n)$, et $f'(n) \leq f'(n+1)$, on a $f(n) \leq c\, f'(n+k)$ ■

Esquisse de preuve du théorème 4.1. Soit $x \in B$. Il existe donc i et j tels que $g^i(x) = g^j(x)$. Quitte à remplacer g par une de ses puissances, on peut supposer que $g^i(x) = g(x)$, $x \in B$, $i \geq 1$.

Premier cas : $\mathcal{S}$ contient des facteurs arbitrairement longs dans B^*. Il existe alors un facteur $x\, u_0\, x'$ de $\mathcal{S}$ avec $g(x) = v\, x\, u$, $g(x') = u'\, x'\, v'$ où $u_0, u' \in B^*$, $u \in B^+$, $x, x' \in C$. On applique le corollaire 2.2 à la suite de factorisations $\mathcal{S} = \alpha_0\, x\, \beta_0 = \alpha_1\, x\, \beta_1 = \ldots = \alpha_i\, x\, \beta_i = \ldots$, où β_0 commence par $u_0 x'$, et où $\alpha_{i+1} = g(\alpha_i)v$, $\beta_{i+1} = u\, g(\beta_i)$. Le plus long préfixe commun p_i à β_i et β_{i+1} vérifie $|p_i| \leq k_1 i$, et le plus long suffixe commun s_i à α_i et α_{i+1} vérifie $|s_i| \geq k_2\, i$ d'où le résultat.

Deuxième cas : Les facteurs de $\mathcal{S}$ dans B^* sont bornés. Soit $Y = \{[\alpha x \beta],$ $\alpha x \beta$ facteur de $\mathcal{S}$, $\alpha, \beta \in B^*$, $x \in C\}$. L'alphabet Y est fini par hypothèse. On effectue une compression d'alphabet suivant Y (cf [P]) c'est-à-dire qu'on définit un morphisme $g' : Y^* \to Y^*$ par $g'([\alpha x \beta]) = [\alpha_1 x_1][\alpha_2 x_2] \ldots [\alpha_k x_k \alpha_{k+1}]$ où $g(\alpha x \beta) = \alpha_1 x_1 \alpha_2 x_2 \ldots \alpha_k x_k \alpha_{k+1}$, $x_i \in C$, $\alpha_i \in B^*$. Soit $y_0 = [x_0]$ et $h : Y^* \to X^*$ défini par $h([\alpha x \beta]) = \alpha x \beta$. Alors le morphisme g' est croissant et on a $g^i(x_0) = h(g'^i(y_0))$. En posant $\mathcal{S} = g'^{\omega}(y_0)$, on a bien $\mathcal{S} = h(\mathcal{S}')$, avec g' croissant et h ε-free. Soient $f(n)$ et $f'(n)$ les complexités de $\mathcal{S}$ et $\mathcal{S}'$. D'après le lemme 4.2, $f(n) \leq c\, f'(n+2k-2)$ où $k = \max |h(y)|$, ce qui donne bien les majorations du théorème. Pour les minorations on peut reprendre les démonstrations des lemmes 3.2 et 3.3 ■

Remarque. Nous avons vu que si la complexité d'un mot infini $\mathcal{S} = g^{\omega}(x_0)$ est en $O(n^2)$, alors il existe un facteur u non vide tel que u^i soit facteur de $\mathcal{S}$, $i \geq 1$. Il en découle immédiatement que si $\mathcal{S} = g^{\omega}(x_0)$ est sans carré, et plus généralement sans $k^{\text{ième}}$ puissance, $k \geq 2$, alors la complexité de $\mathcal{S}$ est au plus en $O(n \log n)$ et au moins en $O(n)$. Ceci est à rapprocher des résultats sur les DOL langages sans carré (cf [ER 81a]).

REFERENCES

[ELR] A. EHRENFEUCHT, K. P. LEE, G. ROZENBERG, Subword complexities of various classes of deterministic developmental languages without interaction, Theoretical Computer Science 1 (1975) 59-75.

[ER 81a] A. EHRENFEUCHT, G. ROZENBERG, On the subword complexity of square-free DOL-languages, Theoretical Computer Science 16 (1981) 25-32.

[ER 81b] A. EHRENFEUCHT, G. ROZENBERG, On the subword complexity of DOL languages with a constant distribution, Information Processing Letters 13 (1981) 108-113.

[ER 82] A. EHRENFEUCHT, G. ROZENBERG, On subword complexities of homomorphic images of languages, R.A.I.R.O. Informatique Théorique 16 (1982) 303-316.

[ER 83a] A. EHRENFEUCHT, G. ROZENBERG, On the subword complexity of locally catenative DOL languages, Information Processing Letters 16 (1983) 7-9.

[ER 83b] A. EHRENFEUCHT, G. ROZENBERG, On the subword complexity of m-free DOL languages, Information Processing Letters 17 (1983) 121-124.

[P] J.-J. PANSIOT, Hiérarchie et fermeture de certaines classes de tag-systèmes, Acta Informatica 20 (1983) 179-196.

[R] G. ROZENBERG, On subwords of formal languages, Lecture Notes in Computer Science 117, (Springer, Berlin 1981) 328-333.

[RS] G. ROZENBERG, A. SALOMAA, The mathematical theory of L systems, Academic Press, New York 1980.

[SS] A. SALOMAA, M. SOITTOLA, Automata theoretic aspects of formal power series, Springer-Verlag New York 1978.

Adherence Equivalence Is Decidable for DOL Languages

Tom Head
Department of Mathematical Sciences

University of Alaska
Fairbanks, Alaska 99701
U.S.A.

Abstract

A procedure is given for deciding whether or not the languages generated by an arbitrary pair of DOL systems have the same adherence.

From arbitrary DOL systems simpler systems are constructed which have the same adherences as the original systems. Representations of the sequences in the adherences of these simpler systems are constructed. Such sequences either have the form uv^{ω} for finite strings u and v or they have a form widely discussed by A.Salomaa: $wsh(s)h^2(s)\ldots h^n(s)\ldots$ where h is an endomorphism of A^* and $h(w)=ws$. The problem of deciding equality of two sequences of the latter type was recently solved by K.Culik II and T.Harju and their algorithm is a major tool used here.

Correspondence with Karel Culik II during the early stages of the present work was helpful and encouraging.

This research was supported in part by Grants MCS-8003348 and MCS-8303922 of the National Science Foundation of the United States of America.

1. Background and introduction.

Let A be an alphabet, i.e. a finite non-empty set. Let A^* be the set of all finite strings of symbols in A including the empty string, 1. Let A^{ω} be the set of infinite sequences, also called ω-words, $a_1a_2\ldots a_i\ldots$ with each a_i in A, $i\geq 1$. By a <u>prefix</u> of either a string in A^* or a sequence in A^{ω} we mean a finite initial segment of the string or the sequence. A prefix of a string is <u>proper</u> if it does not coincide with the string. Thus the empty string is a proper prefix of every non-empty string. Let L be a language over A, i.e. let $L \subseteq A^*$. The adherence of L, Adh L, is the subset of A^ω for which: a sequence is in Adh L precisely if each of its prefixes is a prefix of some string in L. Adherences of context-free languages have been studied by L.Boasson and M.Nivat in [2] and in [1,Part II] Nivat has used the adherence concept in studying the sychronization of concurrent processes.

Adherences of DOL languages were discussed by K.Culik II and A.Salomaa in [4]. However, their main concern was with limit languages in the following sense: The limit of a language L, Lim L, over an alphabet A consists of those sequences in A^ω for which for any positive integer k, the sequence possesses a prefix longer than k that lies in L. Apparently Lim L $\subseteq$ Adh L for all languages. In [4,Sec.3] the relationship between the adherence of a DOL language and the limit of the DOL language was discussed and an equivalent of the following fact, which is fundamental for our work here, was stated without proof [4,Thm.3]: If a DOL language L fails to be a prefix code then Adh L = Lim L. Recall that a subset C of $A^*\setminus\{1\}$ is a prefix code if whenever strings u and uv lie in C it follows that v=1. We devote the next paragraph to a brief review of limits of DOL languages.

If a language is a prefix code then it follows from the definition of the limit of a language that Lim L is empty. Let G=(A,h,w) be a DOL system for which L=L(G) is infinite but fails to be a prefix code. Let $w_i=h^i(w)$ for $i \geq 0$. Then there is a least non-negative integer I for which w_I is a proper prefix of another string in L. Let P be the least positive integer for which w_I is a proper prefix of w_{I+P}. It follows easily that, for each positive integer n, w_{I+n} is a proper prefix of w_{I+n+P}. In particular for each J, $I \leq J \leq I+P-1$, $\{w_{J+kP}:k \geq 0\}$ is an infinite prefix chain, i.e. w_{J+kP} is a proper prefix of $w_{J+(k+1)P}$ for all $k \geq 0$. The initial portion, $\{w_i:0 \leq i \leq I+P-1\}$, of the sequence generated by G is a prefix code. It follows that L is the union of precisely I+P maximal prefix chains. The first I of these chains are singletons and the last P of these chains are the P infinite prefix chains noted above. Further, since the first I+P strings generated by G constitute a prefix code, it follows that these maximal prefix chains are pairwise disjoint and that there are no other maximal prefix chains in L. Apparently Lim L consists of exactly P sequences. We review the method of representing such sequences: Let $u=w_J$ for any J satisfying $I \leq J \leq I+P-1$. Then u is a proper prefix of $h^P(u)$ and $h^P(u)=us$ for a string s which is non-mortal, i.e. $h^i(s)\neq 1$ for all $i\geq 0$. Let $u_i=h^i(u)$ for $i\geq 0$. It follows that the strings in the prefix chain $\{w_{J+kP}:k\geq 0\}$ have the form: u, us_0, us_0s_1, ... , $us_0s_1...s_n$, ... The associated element of Lim L is the infinite sequence $us_0s_1...s_n...$. Thus Lim L consists of exactly P such sequences, one for each J, $I\leq J\leq I+P-1$.

For a DOL language L, the relationship between Adh L and Lim L is as follows: If L is finite then Lim L = Adh L since both are empty. Assume that L is infinite. If L is a prefix code then Lim L $\neq$ Adh L since Lim L is empty but Adh L is not [2]. Finally, let G=(A,h,w) be a DOL system for which L=L(G) is not a prefix code and let I, J, and w_J have the meaning given them in the previous paragraph. Let s be any sequence in Adh L. Since C = $\{w_J:0\leq J\leq I+P-1\}$ is a prefix code there is a unique u in C that is a prefix of s. It follows that u lies in $\{w_J:I\leq J\leq I+P-1\}$ and that s coincides with the unique sequence in Lim L that has u as a prefix. Thus in this case Lim L = Adh L as asserted in [4,Thm.3].

The problem of deciding whether or not two DOL languages have the same limit was raised and discussed in [4]. This limit equivalence problem reduces to the problem of deciding whether for DOL systems F=(A,f,u) and G=(A,g,v) for which f(u)=ux, g(v)=vy, and x,y are non-mortal, we have $ux_0x_1...x_i... = vy_0y_1...y_i...$ where $x_i=f^i(x)$ and $y_i=g^i(y)$ for $i\geq 0$. This latter problem has now been solved by K.Culik II and T.Harju in [3]. From the perspective of the present article, [4] and [3] constitute the solution of the adherence equivalence problem for the class consisting of those DOL languages that are not prefix codes.

Our first objective is to give algorithms for constructing satisfactory representations of each of the sequences belonging to the adherence of an arbitrary DOL language. This is done in Sec.3 through the use of auxiliary DOL systems constructed from the original system. Our second objective is to complete the solution of the adherence equivalence problem for DOL languages by employing the solution of the limit equivalence problem given in [3] to auxiliary systems constructed in Sec.3. The resulting algorithm for deciding adherence equivalence of DOL languages is then given in Sec.4 with one procedure being separated out as Sec.5. In Sec.2 we present a device used in Sec.3 for showing that the adherences of the auxiliary systems coincide with the adherences of the systems from which they are constructed.

A longer version of the present article that includes complete proofs will appear shortly [5].

2. Adherences and a prefix relation between DOL systems.

Let G=(A,h,u) be a DOL system. A DOL system P=(A,k,v) is <u>a prefix of the system</u> G if there is an $m \geq 0$ for which, for all $i \geq 0$, the i-th term of the sequence generated by P is a prefix of the i-th term of the sequence generated by $H=(A,h,h^m(u))$.

The proof of the following Proposition, which uses Thm.11.3 of [6,p.218], is omitted.

Proposition 1. If the DOL system P is a prefix of the DOL system G and L(P) is infinite then Adh P = Adh G.#

3. Representations for each sequence in the adherence of a DOL language.

Let G=(A,h,w) be a DOL system. A symbol a in A is <u>finite</u> or <u>infinite</u> according as (A,h,a) generates a finite or an infinite language. For each string s in A^* define the string s^T as follows: If no infinite symbol occurs in s then $s^T=s$, otherwise s^T is the prefix of s which consists of all occurrences of symbols in s up to and including the first occurrence of an infinite symbol in s. Call s^T <u>the truncation of</u> s. Associate with G the second DOL system $TG=(A,h^T,w^T)$ where h^T is defined by setting $h^T(a)=[h(a)]^T$ for each a in A. Notice that $L(TG) = \{s^T: s \text{ in } L(G)\}$.

Let s be a finite string in A^*. We say that s is <u>primitive</u> if $s=t^n$ holds for a string t and a positive integer n only if t=s and n=1. For every non-null string s there is a unique primitive string r for which $s=r^n$ for some positive integer n. We call r the <u>primitive root</u> of s. By s^ω we mean the sequence sss... .

Theorem 1. Let G=(A,h,w) be a DOL system for which L(TG) is infinite. Then there are strings $x_1,\ldots,x_n,y_1,\ldots,y_n$ in A^* for which Adh G = Adh TG = $\{x_1y_1^\omega,\ldots,x_ny_n^\omega\}$. For each i, $1 \leq i \leq n$, x_i and y_i may be chosen such that y_i is a primitive string and either $x_i=1$ or the right-most symbol of x_i differs from the right-most symbol of y_i. With these choices made the strings x_i and y_i in each representation $x_iy_i^\omega$ are unique.

Proof. Since TG is a prefix of G we have Adh G = Adh TG by Prop.1. We now lighten the notation $TG=(A,h^T,w^T)$ before computing L(TG): We let $k=h^T$ and we express $w^T=ua$ where only finite symbols occur in u and where a is an infinite symbol relative to TG. We may now write TG=(A,k,ua). We will use skip aheads and speed ups to show that $L(TG) = F \cup x_1y_1^*z_1a_1 \cup \ldots \cup x_ny_n^*z_na_n$ where: F is finite; n is a positive integer; $a_1,\ldots,a_n$ are infinite symbols; $x_1,y_1,z_1,\ldots,x_n,y_n,z_n$ are strings, and $y_1,\ldots,y_n$ are not null. The set F will consist of strings skipped over. The value of n will arise from the net effect of two speed ups.

The sequence of infinite symbols, one from each $k^i(a)$,$i\geq 0$, is eventually periodic. Consequently after an appropriate skip ahead and an appropriate speed up we may assume TG=(A,k,ua) where k(a)=va for a string v of finite symbols. Let $v_i=k^i(v)$ for $i\geq 0$. Each v_i is non-null since otherwise L(TG) would be finite. Since only finite symbols occur in v, the sequence v_i, $i\geq 0$, is eventually periodic, i.e. there is a non-negative integer I and a positive integer P for which $v_{K+P}=v_K$ for all $K\geq I$. Let $u_i=k^i(u)$ for $i\geq 0$. Since only finite symbols occur in u, the sequence u_i, $i\geq 0$, is eventually periodic, i.e. there is a non-negative integer J and a positive integer Q for which $u_{K+Q}=u_K$ for all $K\geq J$. Let $M=\max\{I,J\}$ and $R=\mathrm{l.c.m.}\{P,Q\}$. After skipping ahead by M and speeding up by R we may assume $TG=(A,k^R,u_Mv_{M-1}\cdots v_0a)$. For such a TG, $L(TG) = u_M(v_{M+R-1}\cdots v_M)^*v_{M-1}\cdots v_0a$. This language has the form $x_1y_1^*z_1a_1$ where $x_1=u_M$, $y_1=v_{M+R-1}\cdots v_M$, $z_1 = v_{M-1}\cdots v_0$, and $a_1=a$. The union of several speed ups of this form with the finite set that was skipped over gives an expression for L(TG) of the form claimed above.

Since $\mathrm{Adh}\, x_iy_i^*z_ia_i = x_iy_i^\omega$ for each i, $1\leq i\leq n$, we have Adh G= Adh $TG = \{x_1y_1^\omega, \ldots ,x_ny_n^\omega\}$. If for some i, $1\leq i\leq n$, $x_i = x_i'b$ and $y_i = y_i'b$ for a symbol b then $x_iy_i^\omega = x_i'(by_i')^\omega$. Re-denote x_i' by x_i and by_i' by y_i. After iterating this process as many times as necessary we may assume that for each i, $1\leq i\leq n$, either $x_i=1$ or the right-most symbol in x_i differs from the right-most symbol of y_i. If y_i is not primitive it may be replaced by its primitive root which must have the same right-most symbol as y_i. With these adjustments accomplished each x_i and each y_i is unique by an elementary string theoretic argument.#

Let G=(A,h,w) be a DOL system for which L(TG) is finite. Then there is a bound B such that no string in L(TG) has length greater than B. From Thm. 11.3 of [6, p.218], or see [7, ex.3.17 p.42], it follows that there is a non-negative integer J and a positive integer F for which the strings $h^{J+nF}(w)$ have the same prefix of length B for all $n\geq 0$. Let $NG=(A,h,w_J^T)$ where $w_J=h^J(w)$.

Theorem 2. Let G=(A,h,w) be a DOL system for which L(G) is infinite but L(TG) is finite. Then Adh G = Adh NG = Lim NG.

Proof. Let B,J,F,NG, and w_J be as defined in the paragraph preceeding the statement of this Theorem. Since L(G) is infinite it follows that an infinite symbol occurs in $w_J{}^T$ and therefore that L(NG) is also infinite. Since NG is a prefix of G and L(NG) is infinite we have Adh G = Adh NG by Prop.1. From the definition of B it follows that the left-most occurrence of an infinite symbol in w_J occurs in one of the first B locations in w_J. Consequently $h^F(w_J{}^T)=w_J{}^T x$ for some string x. Thus L(NG) is not a prefix code and Adh NG = Lim NG. #

Representations of the individual sequences in Adh G = Lim NG may now be given as described in the third paragraph of Sec.1.

4. The algorithm for deciding adherence equivalence.

Theorem 3. Let F=(A,f,u) and G=(A,g,v) be DOL systems. Then it is decidable whether or not Adh F = Adh G.

Proof. Decide if L(F) is finite. Decide if L(G) is finite. If both languages are finite then the adherences are equal since they are both empty. If one language is finite and the other is infinite then the adherences are not equal since one is empty and one is not. We continue only if both languages are infinite:

Construct the DOL system TF as specified in Sec.3. Decide whether L(TF) is finite. If L(TF) is finite then construct the DOL system NF as specified in Sec.3.

Construct the DOL system TG. Decide whether L(TG) is finite. If L(TG) is finite then construct the DOL system NG. The algorithm now takes a three way branch:

Case 1. If L(TF) and L(TG) are both infinite: From Thm.1 we have Adh F = Adh TF and Adh G = Adh TG. By means of the procedures in the proof of Thm.1 express Adh TF as a finite collection of sequences of the form xy^ω where y is a primitive string and either x=1 or the right-most symbol in x differs from the right-most symbol in y. Do the same for TG. In view of the uniqueness of the strings x and y in such representations, Adh TF = Adh TG precisely if the notations xy^ω for the sequences in Adh TF and in Adh TG are identical.

Case 2. If L(TF) and L(TG) are both finite: By Thm.2 Adh F = Lim NF and Adh G = Lim NG. Apply the algorithm of K.Culik II and

T.Harju [3] to decide whether Lim NF = Lim NG.

Case 3. The only remaining case is that in which one of L(TF) and L(TG) is finite and the other is infinite. We may assume that TF denotes the system for which L(TF) is finite and consequently that L(TG) is infinite. Express Adh G = Adh TG, via Thm.1, as a finite collection of sequences each of which is of the form uv^{ω}. By Thm.2 Adh F = Lim NF. As reviewed in Sec.1, Lim NF consists of a finite collection of sequences each of which has the form $wsh(s)h^2(s)\ldots h^i(s)\ldots$ where w, s, and h are defined via a DOL system (A,h,w) which is constructed via a skip ahead and a speed up from NF and satisfies h(w)=ws with s not mortal. Thus to complete the decision whether Adh F = Adh G we need only make use of a finite number of applications of an algorithm for deciding whether $uv^{\omega} = wsh(s)h^2(s) \ldots h^i(s)\ldots$ where w, s, and h are defined via a DOL system (A,h,w) satisfying h(w)=ws with s not mortal. Such an algorithm is given in Sec.5 as Theorem 4. #

5. A supporting algorithm.

The following Proposition is a key tool for proving the remaining decidability result, Thm.4. The proof, which uses two elementary string theoretic lemmas and several elementary finite induction arguments, is omitted.

Proposition 2. Let r be a primitive string. Let G=(A,h,y) be a DOL system for which: (1) $y=r^4r^ix$ where $i\geq 0$ and x is a proper prefix of r; and (2) length h(r) $\geq$ length r. Let z be the string defined by r=xz if $x\neq 1$ and z=1 if x=1. Let $y_n=h^n(y)$ for all $n\geq 0$. Then $r^{\omega} = y_0y_1\ldots y_n\ldots$ if and only if $h(r) = zr^kx$ for some $k\geq 0$.#

Theorem 4. Let G=(a,h,w) be a DOL system for which h(w)=ws for a string s. Let $s_n=h^n(s)$, for $n\geq 0$. Let u and v be strings over A. Then it is decidable whether or not

$$uv^{\omega} = ws_0s_1 \ldots s_n \ldots .$$

Proof. We begin by assuming that s is not mortal and that v is not null since otherwise at least one of the two sequences degenerates to a finite string. If u is not a prefix of $ws_0s_1\ldots s_n\ldots$ then the sequences are not equal. Otherwise compute the least non-negative integer k for which u is a prefix of $ws_0\ldots s_k$. If $ws_0\ldots s_k$ is not a prefix of uv^{ω} then the sequences are not equal. Otherwise compute the non-negative integer i and the proper prefix x of the string v for which $ws_0 \ldots s_k = uv^i x$. Compute the string z for which v=xz. Compute the primitive string r and the positive integer j for which $zx=r^j$. Since $uv^\omega = uv^i xz(xz)^\omega = uv^i x(zx)^\omega = uv^i xr^\omega$ and we have matched $uv^i x$ successfully with $ws_0 \ldots s_k$, our decision is now reduced to determining whether or not $r^\omega = s_{k+1}s_{k+2}\ldots s_{k+n}\ldots$.

If r^4 is not a prefix of $s_{k+1}s_{k+2}\ldots s_{k+n}\ldots$ then the sequences are not equal. Otherwise compute the least positive integer p for which r^4 is a prefix of $s_{k+1}\ldots s_{k+p}$. Form the DOL system D=(A,H,y) where $H=h^p$ and $y=s_{k+1}\ldots s_{k+p}$. Let $y_n=H^n(y)$ for $i \geq 0$. Since $y_0 y_1 \ldots y_n \ldots = s_{k+1}s_{k+2}\ldots s_{k+n}\ldots$ our decision is now reduced to determining whether or not $r^\omega = y_0 y_1 \ldots y_n \ldots$.

Compute H(r). If length H(r) < length r then the sequences are distinct by the following contradiction argument: Assume $r^\omega = y_0 y_1 \ldots y_n \ldots$. Then for <u>each</u> non-negative integer n, $y_0 \ldots y_n = r^q t$ for an integer $q \geq 4$ and a proper prefix t of r. Consequently when n is sufficiently large the difference d = length $H(y_0 \ldots y_n)$ - length $y_0 \ldots y_n$ assumes negative values that are arbitrarily large in absolute value. However $H(y_0 \ldots y_n) = y_1 \ldots y_{n+1}$ and consequently d = length y_{n+1} - length y_0 > -length y_0 for all $n \geq 0$. This contradiction establishes the assertion.

We continue under the assumption that length H(r) $\geq$ length r. Prop.2 now indicates the remaining steps of the algorithm: Compute the proper prefix x' of r for which $y=r^4 r^i x'$ for an $i \geq 0$. Compute the suffix z' of r so that r=x'z' if x'≠1 and set z'=1 if x'=1. Test the string H(r) to determine whether or not it has the form $z'r^j x'$ for some $j \geq 0$. By Prop.2 the sequences are equal if and only if H(r) has this form. #

References

[1] J.Beauquier and M.Nivat, Application of formal language theory to problems of security and sychronization, in: R.V.Book, Ed., Formal Language Theory (Academic Press, New York, 1980).

[2] L.Boasson and M.Nivat, Adherences of languages, J. Computer and System Sciences 20(1980)285-309.

[3] K.Culik II and T.Harju, The ω-sequence equivalence problem for DOL systems is decidable, J. Assoc. Computing Machinery, to appear; see also: Proc. 13th ACM Symposium on the Theory of Computing (1981)1-6.

[4] K.Culik II and A.Salomaa, On infinite words obtained by iterating morphisms, Theor. Computer Science 19(1982)29-38.

[5] T.Head, Adherences of DOL Languages, Theor. Computer Science, to appear in 1984.

[6] G.T.Herman and G.Rosenberg, Developmental Systems and Languages (North Holland/American Elsevier, New York, 1975).

[7] G.Rozenberg and A.Salomaa, The Mathematical Theory of L Systems (Academic Press, New York, 1980).

PUSDOWN SPACE COMPLEXITY AND RELATED FULL-A.F.L.s.

J.GABARRO.

Facultat d'Informàtica,Universitat Politècnica de Barcelona,c/.Jordi Girona Salgado,31,Barcelona(34) SPAIN,Tel.:204 82 52(ext. 265).

Abstract We study space contraints in p.d.a's.We call pushdown complexity of a language the space needed by a p.d.a. to accept that language.
We prove that every deterministic language has a linear lower bound in pushdown complexity.
We study sublinear bounds.In particular we construct languages with pusdown complexity strictly in $n^{1/q}$ or log n.
We prove that the family of languages with sublinear complexity is a full-A.F.L. containing one infinite decreasing chain of full-A.F.L's.

Introduction One method to study context-free languages is looking at their behaviour in some type of complexity.The most important case arise when this complexity is an integer valued function.Many complexity measures of this type has been proposed:rational index [2] ,initial index [3] ,height of derivation trees [5] .
Given a measure described by a function we can classify the languages with respect to their asymtotic behaviour under that complexity measure.For a fixed asymtotic behaviour we can consider the family of languages that have this complexity.Taking differents types of asymtotic behaviours we can define the corresponding new families of languages.Given a language and a complexity measure the first step is find behaviour upper and lower bounds,and then if it is possible study the sharpness of these bounds.It is interesting to find languages with a sharp bounds for different asymtotic behaviours because in this way we can prove strict inclussion between different complexity families.
Another way to study languages is in the framework given by Ginsburg and Greibach [6] .The main idea consists on the study of families of languages closed under some fixed set of operations.For example a rational cone is a family of languages closed under rational transduction and a full-A.F.L. is a rational cone closed under union,product and star.
One problem is to relate the complexity and A.F.L. approches.For this we study the behaviour of complexity measures through A.F.L. operations [2,5] .When this behaviour is nice the complexity families are full-A.F.L's.In this paper we take as a complexity measure the space needed by a p.d.a. in its stack.We call that measure the pushdown complexity.Obviously every language has a linear upper bound for this complexity measure.Hence it is interesting to study when this bound is sharp.
The section II is devoted to languages with linear lower bound.We prove that $S_=$, $S_{\neq}$, $S_{\leqslant}$ and $S_{\geqslant}$ have linear lower bounds.Using a lemma of Stearns we conclude that every deterministic language has a strictly linear complexity.
Section III is devoted to sublinear languages.We prove that the so-called Goldstine language [7] has complexity strictly in $n^{1/2}$.Two differents generalisations of this language lead to two infinite chains of languages with complexity $n^{1/q}$,$q \geqslant 2$.Finally we give one example of log n complexity.
Section IV is devoted to the relation between the pushdown complexity

and A.F.L. theory. A theorem relating rational transductions and pushdown complexity is given. We prove that the family of languages of sublinear complexity is a substitution closed full-A.F.L., noted p-Sub. Also the family p-Sub contains one infinite chain of full-A.F.L's of decreasing complexity $n^{1/q}$, $q \geq 2$, and a full-A.F.L. of log n complexity.

II.-Pushdown complexity measure. Linear case.

We shall study the space complexity in the p.d.a.s. and its related context-free languages.

Definition 1. Let L be a context-free language we say that L has pushdown complexity f(n) (noted $p_L(n) = O(f(n))$) if L is recognized by a p.d.a. such that every w in L, $|w| \leq n$ has an accepting computation with pushdown space $O(f(n))$.

It is easy to see that every context-free language L satisfies $p_L(n) \leq n$.
When a language L has $p_L(n) = O(f(n))$ and its recognition requires order f(n) infinitely often we say that L has pushdown complexity strictly f(n). In some sense f(n) is the most accurate bound for L.
Let us recall some notations [11] necessary to study lower bounds in pushdown complexity.
Given p.d.a. $\mathcal{A}$ we note the transitions by $(q,z) \overset{x}{\longmapsto} (q',w)$.
A configuration c is a pair (q,w). A scan δ from $c_1 = (q_1,wz_1)$ to $c_2 = (q_2,wz_2)$ is a computation from c_1 to c_2 such that at every step the pushdown contains at least $|wz_1|$ elements.
As usual we call lenght of a computation the number of steps of this computation. The next lemma is a version of Ogden's lemma, and explains that every long scan has a small iterative pair.

Lemma 1. Let $\mathcal{A}$ be a p.d.a. There exits a integer $N \geq 1$ such that for every scan δ from c_0 to c_1 with $|\delta| \geq N$ can be factorized $\delta = \alpha u \beta v \gamma$ with

- For all $n \geq 0$, $\alpha u^n \beta v^n \gamma$ is a scan from c_0 to c_1.
- $0 < |uv| \leq N$.

We call the tuple (α, u, β, v, γ) an iterative pair of computation δ

The relation between the height of stack and the length of the popping computation without iterative pairs is given by:

Lemma 2. Let δ be one computation from $c_0 = (q,w)$ to $c_1 = (q', \varepsilon)$ without iterative pairs; then

$$|\delta| \geqslant |c_0| \geqslant \frac{1}{N}|\delta| - 1$$

Where N is the number given in lemma 1.

Proof. The δ computation can be depicted as:

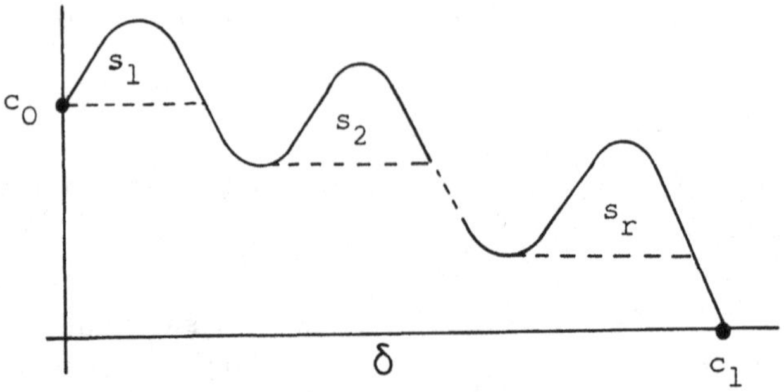

Where the scans s_i are explicited. Then $\delta = s_1 d_1 s_2 d_2 \ldots s_r d_r$. As every scan has no iterative pairs, by Ogden's lemma $|s_i| < N$, then

$$|\delta| \geqslant |c_0| \geqslant \frac{1}{N}|\delta| - 1$$ ■

Roughly speaking this lemma gives us $|c_0| \simeq |\delta|$ when there are no iterative pairs.

We shall deal with languages of strictly linear complexity.

Lemma 3. The languages:

$$S_= = \{ a^n b^p \mid n = p \} \quad , \quad S_{\neq} = \{ a^n b^p \mid n \neq p \}$$

$$S \;\; = \{ a^n b^p \mid n \geqslant p \} \quad , \quad S \;\; = \{ a^n b^p \mid n \leqslant p \}$$

have a pushdown complexity strictly n.

Proof. We shall show it for $S_{\neq}$. The other proofs are very similar.

(a) As every context-free language has linear complexity we have

$$p_{S_{\neq}}(n) = O(n)$$

(b) We shall prove that order n appears infinitely often. Consider the set of words $w_k = a^{2.k!} b^{k!}$, $k > N$, where N is the constant of Ogden's lemma. Any computation for w_k cannot have iterative pairs in the last bloc $b^{k!}$, else the word $a^{2.k!} b^{2.k!}$ could be constructed. By lemma 2 the store has height at least of order $|b^{k!}|$. As $|w_k| = \Theta(k!)$ we obtain the result. ■

Recall a lemma due to Stearns. This lemma relate every deterministic language to one of the last languages by:

Lemma 4. [10]. Let L be a deterministic not regular language. There exits α, u, β, v, γ such that $L \cap \alpha u^* \beta v^* \gamma$ is one of the next four languages:

$$\{ \alpha u^n \beta v^p \gamma \mid n = p \} \quad , \quad \{ \alpha u^n \beta v^p \gamma \mid n \neq p \}$$
$$\{ \alpha u^n \beta v^p \gamma \mid n \geqslant p \} \quad , \quad \{ \alpha u^n \beta v^p \gamma \mid n \leqslant p \}$$

As intersection with regular languages cannot increase pushdown complexity we are lead to:

Theorem 1. Every deterministic not rational language has pushdown complexity strictly linear.

Obviously there are non deterministic languages with a linear pushdown complexity. The language $L = \{ c^p a^m b^n \mid p \geqslant \min(m,n) \}$ gives a regular language for every intersection $L \cap \alpha u^* \beta v^* \gamma$ and its pushdown complexity is strictly linear.

III.-Sublinear pushdown complexity.

We will analyse the sublinear case. We begin with a language given by Goldstine [7] . This language will be called Goldtine's language.

Lemma 5. The language

$$G = \{ a^{i_1} b a^{i_2} b \ldots a^{i_j} \ldots a^{i_k} b \mid k \geqslant 1, \exists\, j, 1 \leqslant j \leqslant k, j \neq i_j \}$$

has pushdown complexity strictly $n^{1/2}$.

Proof. (a) In the first step we will give a upper bound. We will find a p.d.a. accepting in order $n^{1/2}$.

Consider the p.d.a. who tests the existence of a wrong bloc (a bloc $a^{i_j} b$ with $i_j \neq j$). It begins by reading the prefix $a^{i_1} b a^{i_2} b \ldots a^{i_{j-1}} b$ and storing only letters b. In a non deterministic way it chooses a possible wrong bloc $a^{i_j} b$. Then matching letters b with letters a it test $i_j \neq j$. If $i_j \neq j$ reads the end of the word and accepts. The height of computation is in order j. The automaton can test the left-most wrong bloc. In that case the word w can be factorised as

$$w = aba^2ba^3b \ldots a^{j-1}ba^{i_j} \ldots a^{i_k}b$$

We then have $|w| = \Omega(j^2)$. As store height in that case is of order j, and $|w| = \Omega(j^2)$ we conclude that store height is in order $|w|^{1/2}$. The automaton given here accepts in pushdown complexity $n^{1/2}$.

(b) In this second step we will prove that the bound $n^{1/2}$ is optimal. Consider the set of words $w_k = aba^2ba^3b \ldots a^{2.k!}ba^{k!+1}b, k \geqslant N$, where N is the constant of Ogden's lemma. Obviously w_k is in G and

$$|w_k| = \Theta(k!^2)$$

There are no iterative pairs in the computation of the last bloc

$a^{k!+1}b$, else the word $aba^2ba^3b \ldots a^{2.k!}ba^{2.k!+1}b$ could be constructed. In this case the store height is at least in order k!. For every k, the word w_k has pushdown complexity $\Omega(|w_k|^{1/2})$. Then the lower bound $n^{1/2}$ is infinitely often.

■

There are some languages related to Goldstine's language with the same complexity.

Lemma 6. The languages

$$G_< = \left\{ a^{i_1}ba^{i_2}b \ldots a^{i_j}b \ldots a^{i_k}b \mid k > 1, \exists\, 1 \leq j \leq k \text{ with } i_j < j \right\}$$

$$L = \left\{ a^{i_1}ba^{i_2}b \ldots a^{i_j}b \ldots a^{i_k}b \mid k > 1, \exists\, 1 \leq j \leq k \text{ with } i_j \neq k \right\}$$

$$L_< = \left\{ a^{i_1}ba^{i_2}b \ldots a^{i_j}b \ldots a^{i_k}b \mid k > 1, \exists\, 1 \leq j \leq k \text{ with } i_j < k \right\}$$

have pushdown complexity strictly $n^{1/2}$.

We will generalize Goldstine's language. In his way we will obtain a chain of languages with pushdown complexity $n^{1/q}, q \geq 2$.

First method. This method is given by Autebert, Beauquier, Boasson, Latteux in [1] . A minor variation G' of Goldstine language can be founded using the infinite word

$$\underline{\alpha} = 3212112111 \ldots$$

as:

$$G' = 3(21^*)^+ \setminus LF(\underline{\alpha}) =$$
$$= \{ 321^{i_1}21^{i_2} \ldots 21^{i_j} \ldots 21^{i_k} \mid k > 1, \exists j, 1 \leq j \leq k, i_j \neq j \}$$

where $LF(\underline{\alpha})$ is the set of finite left factors of $\underline{\alpha}$.

It is possible to code every bloc 21^x by another word of the same type, for example:

21	is coded by	210
211		210100
2111		2101001000

We obtain the infinite word

$$\underline{\alpha}' = 3210210100210100100 \ldots$$

The word $\underline{\alpha}'$ can be obtained iterating the morphism

$$h_3 = \langle 3 \rightarrow 3210 \; ; \; 2 \rightarrow 210 \; ; \; 1 \rightarrow 10 \; ; \; 0 \rightarrow 0 \rangle$$

We can generalize this method. For every $q \geq 0$ we define $Z_0 = 0^*$, $Z_{q+1} = (q+1)Z_q^*$, $h_q(i) = i(i-1)(i-2) \ldots 10$, we note $h_q^j(q)$ as $w_j^{(q)}$, then [1] $w_i^{(q+1)} = (q+1)w_1^q w_2^q \ldots w_i^q$

Note that $|w_i^q| = \Theta(i^q)$. Using the same techniques as in lemma 5 we can prove.

Theorem 2. The languages, $q \geqslant 2$

$$G_q = \left\{ qu_1u_2 \dots u_j \dots u_k \;\middle|\; k \geqslant 1, u_i \in Z_{q-1}, 1 \leqslant i \leqslant k, \exists\, 1 \leqslant j \leqslant k \text{ such that } u_j \neq w_j^{q-1} \right\}$$

have pushdown complexity $n^{1/q}$.

Using the same technique we can also generalize the languages L and $L_<$ given in lemma 6 [4] .

Second method. The infinite word

$$\underline{\beta} = 1b11b111b111b1111b \dots$$

can be writen

$$\underline{\beta} = 1b\ suc(1)\ b\ suc^2(1)\ b\ suc^3(1)\ b\ suc^4(1)\ b \dots$$

Where $suc(1^x) = 1^{x+1}$. We can obtain other infinite words of the same type. Define a succesor function over the bounded set

$$B_q = q^*(q-1)^* \dots 1^*0^* \setminus \varepsilon \quad , \quad q \geqslant 0$$

as:

. If $w \in B_q$ can be factorized as $w = w_{i+1}ii^x$ with $x \geqslant 0, 0 \leqslant i < q$ and $w_{i+1} \in q^*(q-1)^* \dots (i+1)^*$, then

$$suc_q(w) = w_{i+1}(i+1)0^x$$

. If $w \in B_q$ is $w = q^x, x > 0$ then $suc_q(w) = 0^{x+1}$

Using this succesor function suc_q we define for every $q \geqslant 0$ the infinite word:

$$\underline{\beta}(q) = 0b\ suc_q^1(0)\ b\ suc_q^2(0)\ b \dots$$

We define the second generalisation of Goldstine's language by:

$$G(q) = 0b(B_qb)^* \setminus LF(\underline{\beta}(q)) =$$

$$= \left\{ 0bw_2bw_3b \dots w_{j-1}bw_jb \dots w_kb \;\middle|\; k \geqslant 2, w_i \in B_q, 1 \leqslant i \leqslant k, \exists j, 2 \leqslant j \leqslant k \text{ with } w_j \neq suc_q(w_{j-1}) \right\}$$

We give technical lemma about wrong transitions in the set B_q.

Lemma 7. The language

$$Trans_q = \left\{ w_1bw_2b \;\middle|\; w_1, w_2 \in B_q \text{ and } w_2 \neq suc_q(w_1) \right\}$$

is context-free, one counter, one turn and the word w_1bw_2b can be computed in order $\min \{|w_1|, |w_2|\}$

Proof. $Trans_q$ can be explained as union of the next five languages:

$$L_1 = \left\{ w_{i+1}ii^xbw_1lj^Yb \;\middle|\; l > j, j^Y \neq 0^x \right\}$$

$$L_2 = \left\{ w_{i+1}ii^xbw_1lj^Yb \;\middle|\; l > j, l \neq i+1 \right\}$$

$$L_3 = \left\{ w_{i+1} i i^x b w_1 1 j^y b \mid 1 > j, w_{i+1} \neq w_2 \right\}$$
$$L_4 = \left\{ w_{i+1} i i^x b 1^y b \mid y > 0 \right\}$$
$$L_5 = \left\{ p^x b x b \mid w \neq 0^{x+1} \right\}$$

Using this lemma we come to theorem:

Theorem 3. The language $G(q)$ is context-free, one counter, one turn an has pushdown complexity strictly $n^{1/(q+2)}$, $q \geq 0$.

Proof. (a) Give an upper bound. We shall find j such that $|suc_q^j(0)| = n$.
We have that: $Card \left\{ w \in B_q \mid |w| \leq n \right\} = j$
The generating function of the set $\left\{ w \in B_q \mid |w| \leq n \right\}$ is $\left(\frac{1}{1-z}\right)^{q+2}$. We are lead to:

$$j = [z^n] \left(\frac{1}{1-z}\right)^{q+2} = \binom{q+n+1}{n} = \Theta(n^{q+1})$$

We have then $|suc_q^j(0)| = \Theta(j^{1/(q+1)})$. We study the lenght of the word:

$$m_{q,j} = 0b\ suc_q(0)\ b\ suc_q^2(0)\ b \ldots suc_q^j(0)\ b.$$

We have $|m_{q,j}| = \Theta\left(\int_1^j |suc_q^x(0)|\, dx\right) = \Theta(j^{(q+2)/(q+1)})$

As conclution we obtain $|m_{q,j}| = \Theta(|suc_q^j(0)|^{q+2})$

Considering the last lemma and testing in a word the left-most wrong transition we prove that $G(q)$ is $O(n^{1/(q+2)})$.

(b) To prove that $n^{1/(q+2)}$ is infinitely often needed we consider the following set of words of $G(q)$:

$$w_k = 0\ b\ suc_q(0)\ b\ suc_q^2(0)\ b \ldots b\ q^{2.k!}\ b\ 0^{k!+1}\ b$$

where $k \geq N$, N is the constant of iteration lemma.

■

We have constructed two chains of complexity $n^{1/q}$, the languages G_q and $G(q-2)$. It is an open question wheather for every q, there exits two rational transductions τ_1^q and τ_2^q such that:

$$G(q-2) = \tau_1^q(G_q) \text{ and } G_q = \tau_2^q(G(q-2))$$

In that case the languages G_q and $G(q-2)$ are in some sense the same.

Now weshall give a language with pushdown complexity log n. This language is of the same type of Godstine's language. It is obtained by counting the blocs in binary. It is a modified version of a language given in [8] .

Consider the set $Bin = 1(0+1)^*$ and define the succesor function by $suc_b(w01^x) = w10^x$, $suc(1^x) = 10^x$, then:

Theorem 4. The language

$$G_{Bin} = \left\{ 1bw_2b \ldots w_{j-1}bw_jb \ldots w_kb \mid k \geq 2, w_i \in Bin, 1 \leq i \leq k, \exists 2 \leq j \leq k \text{ with } w_j \neq suc_b(w_{j-1}) \right\}$$

is context-free, one counter, one turn and has pushdown complexity strictly in log n.

The proof is analogous to the previous one. To end this section we define the families of languages with a given complexity.

Definition 2. The family of languages with a sublinear pushdown complexity is

$$p\text{-}\underline{Sub} = \left\{ L \mid p_L(n) = o(n) \right\}$$

. The family of languages with a pushdown complexity bounded by a q-root, $q \geq 2$ is

$$p\text{-}\underline{Root}(q) = \left\{ L \mid p_L(n) = O(n^{1/q}) \right\}$$

. The family of languages with a pushdown complexity bounded by a log is

$$p\text{-}\underline{Log} = \left\{ L \mid p_L(n) = O(\log n) \right\}$$

IV.- Languages operations and full-A.F.L's.

We shall place the families of languages defined by the pushdown complexity in the framework of families of languages defined by Ginsburg and Greibach [6]. We study the behaviour of pushdown complexity through language operation. First we deal with rational operations. The proof of the lemma 8 is straightforward.

Lemma 8. Let L_1, L_2 context-free languages. The following inequalities hold:

- $p_{L_1 \cup L_2}(n) \leq \max \left\{ p_{L_1}(n), p_{L_2}(n) \right\}$
- $p_{L_1 . L_2}(n) \leq \max \left\{ p_{L_1}(n), p_{L_2}(n) \right\} + 1$
- $p_{L_1^*}(n) \leq p_{L_1}(n) + 1$

Recall from Nivat [9] that a rational transduction $\tau : X^* \longrightarrow Y^*$ can be written as $\tau(w) = \psi(\varphi^{-1}(w) \cap R)$, where R is a rational language over finite alphabet Z and φ and ψ are alphabetic morphisms of $Z^* \longrightarrow X^*$ and $Z^* \longrightarrow Y^*$.

We call rational cone or full trio a family closed by rational transduction. A full-A.F.L. [6] is a rational cone closed under rational operations.To deal with morphisms we recall that:

Lemma 9. [4] Let L be a context-free language and φ an alphabetic morphism.Denote $nL = \{ w \in L \mid |w| \leqslant n \}$ .There exists a constant k such that for all n we have $n\,\varphi(L) \subset \varphi(knL)$.

Lemma 10.Let L be a context-free language,R a regular language and an alphabetic morphism.Then:

- There exits a constant k such that $p_{\varphi(L)}(n) \leqslant p_L(kn)$
- $p_{\varphi^{-1}(L)}(n) \leqslant p_L(n) + 1$
- $p_{L \cap R}(n) \leqslant p_L(n)$

Proof.We shall prove the lemma for the direct morphism.Take $w \in n\,\varphi(L)$, by lemma 9 there exists $h \in knL$ such that $\varphi(h) = w$.
Consider an automaton $\mathcal{A}$ with rules $(q,z) \xmapsto{x} (q', \alpha)$ acceptind L with complexity p_L.The word h has complexity at most $p_L(kn)$.Hence the automaton $\varphi(\mathcal{A})$ with rules $(q,z) \xmapsto{\varphi(x)} (q', \alpha)$ accepts $\varphi(L)$,and w has complexity $p_L(kn)$.
Proves for φ^{-1} and $\cap R$ are trivial. ■

This lemma give us the behaviour of pushdown complexity through rational transductions.We state it as follows.

Theorem 5.Let L be a context-free language and τ a rational transduction there exists k such that for all n we have

$$p_{\tau(L)}(n) \leqslant p_L(kn) + 1$$

We shall deal with another language operation.Recall that a syntactical substitution of languages L_1 and L_2 is given by:

$$L_1 \uparrow L_2 = \{ x_1 w_1 x_2 w_2 \dots x_k w_k \quad x_i \text{ are letters}, 1 \leqslant i \leqslant k, \\ x_1 x_2 \dots x_k \in L_1 \text{ and } w_i \in L_2, 1 \leqslant i \leqslant k \}$$

Lemma 10.Let L_1 and L_2 be context-free languages,then

$$p_{L_1 \uparrow L_2}(n) \leqslant p_{L_1}(n) + p_{L_2}(n) + 1$$

Putting together these lemmas we are lead to

Theorem 6.The families p-Sub,p-Root(q),q $\geqslant$ 2,p-Log are substitution closed full-A.F.L's satisfying:

$$\text{p-Log} \subsetneq \dots \text{p-Root}(q+1) \subsetneq \text{p-Root}(q) \subseteq \dots \text{p-Sub}$$

References

[1] Autebert,J;Beauquier,J;Boasson,L;Latteux,M. [1980]"Very small families of algebraic non rational languages" in Formal Language Theory,editor Book,R,Academic Press.

[2] Boasson,L;Courcelle,B;Nivat,M. [1981] ."The rational index a complexity measure for languages".SIAM Journal on Computing 10,2,284-296.

[3] Culik,K;Maurer,H."On the derivation of trees".Internal repport.

[4] Gabarro,J. [1983] ."Funciones de complejidad y su relacion con las familias abstractas de lenguages".Thesis.Universidad Politécnica de Barcelona.Spain.

[5] Gabarro,J. [1983] ."Initial index:a new complexity function for languages".ICALP-83.Lec.not.comp.sci.154,pag 226-236.

[6] Ginsburg,S;Greibach,S. [1969] ."Abstract families of languages" in Abstract families of languages.Mem. of the Amer. Math.Soc.87,1-32.

[7] Goldstine,J. [1972] ."Substitution and bounded languages". J.Comp.Syst.Sci.6,9-29.

[8] Lewis,P;Hartmanis,J;Stearns,R. [1965] ."Memory bounds for the recognition of context-free and context-sensitive languages".IEEE.Conf.Record on Switching Circuit Theory and Logical Dessign,179-202.

[9] Nivat,M. [1968] ."Transductions des langages de Chomsky". Ann.de l'Inst.Fourier 18,339-456.

[10] Stearns,R. [1967] ."A regularity test for pushdown-machines".Inf;and Control 11,323-340.

[11] Valiand,L. [1976] ."A note on the succincstness of description of deterministic languages".Inf.and Control 32, 139-145.

AUTOMATES A PILE SUR DES ALPHABETS INFINIS

Jeanne IDT
Faculté des Sciences Economiques
47 X Centre de tri
38040 GRENOBLE Cédex - FRANCE

RESUME

Soit Σ un alphabet infini dénombrable. Une grammaire $G = <\Sigma,V,P>$ est Σ-algébrique si V est un ensemble fini de non-terminaux et si $P = \{(\alpha \to m) \ / \ \alpha \in V, \ m \in (\Sigma \cup V)^*\}$ est tel que la longueur de m soit bornée. On peut voir que des langages engendrés par de telles grammaires ne peuvent être caractérisés par des automates à pile classiques. C'est pourquoi il a été nécessaire de construire une nouvelle sorte d'automates que j'ai appelé "automates à pile et à tiroirs". La construction et les propriétés de ces automates sont exposés dans cet article.

I - INTRODUCTION

Un langage, d'après la définition de N. CHOMSKY, est un ensemble de mots finis de X^*, où X est un alphabet fini, et les recherches effectuées en théorie classique des langages ont pour but de donner une représentation finie de langages infinis.

Une première manière de définir des langages est d'utiliser un processus fini pouvant les engendrer, appelé grammaire [6].

Une grammaire G est un triplet $G = <X,V,P>$ où V est un alphabet fini non vide, dit alphabet non terminal, où X est un alphabet disjoint de V fini non vide, dit alphabet terminal, et où P est un ensemble fini de règles de la forme $\alpha \to \beta$ où α appartient à $(V \cup X)^* V (V \cup X)^*$ et β à $(V \cup X)^*$.

Parmi les plus étudiées, citons les grammaires algébriques engendrant la famille des langages algébriques, et les grammaires linéaires droites engendrant la famille des langages rationnels. En imposant ainsi des conditions à α et β, il est possible de former différentes familles de langages dont l'ensemble forme la hiérarchie de CHOMSKY.

La seconde manière de définir des langages est d'utiliser un processus fini pouvant les reconnaître, ou automate, [6]. Parmi ces processus classiques de reconnaissance citons :

- les automates finis qui sont des 5-uplets (Q,X,δ,q_o,F) où Q est un ensemble fini, dit ensemble d'états, X l'alphabet fini d'entrée, δ une fonction, dite de transistion, de $Q \times X$ dans Q, $q_o \in Q$ un état initial et $F \subseteq Q$ un ensemble d'états dits terminaux. La famille des langages reconnus par ces automates coïncide avec la famille des langages rationnels.

- les automates à pile qui sont des 7-uplets $(Q,X,\Gamma,\delta,q_o,Z_o,F)$ où Q est un ensemble fini d'états, X l'alphabet d'entrée, Γ un alphabet fini de symboles de pile, q_o un état initial, Z_o un symbole initial de pile, $F \subseteq Q$ un ensemble d'états terminaux et δ une fonction de $Qx(Xx\{\varepsilon\})x\Gamma$ dans l'ensemble des sous ensembles fini de $Qx\Gamma^*$. Ces automates reconnaissent exactement la famille des langages algébriques.

La notion de grammaire s'applique particulièrement bien aux langages de programmation dont la syntaxe est définie en effet par une grammaire, essentiellement algébrique, par exemple dans le cas d'ALGOL. Le problème est de pouvoir dire en un temps fini si un programme donné c'est à dire un mot du langage, est syntaxiquement correct, donc de construire un automate à pile reconnaissant ce langage. Mais pour qu'un tel automate puisse fonctionner rapidement il faut que chacun de ses mouvements soit entièrement déterminé par l'état, la lettre lue et le symbole de sommet de pile. C'est ce qui conduit à la notion d'automate déterministe :

un automate à pile $(Q,X,\Gamma,\delta,q_o,Z_o,F)$ est dit déterministe si δ vérifie :

1) $\forall q \in Q$, $\forall a \in X$, $\forall Z \in \Gamma$, $|\delta(q,a,Z)| \leq 1$
2) si $\delta(q,\varepsilon,Z) \neq \emptyset$ alors $\delta(q,a,Z) = \emptyset$, $\forall a \in X$.

On peut alors définir la famille des langages reconnus par un automate à pile déterministe.

La théorie classique des langages s'est d'abord limitée à l'étude des sous ensembles de X^*, où X est un alphabet fini, puis certaines modifications de ces hypothèses ont été apportées par exemple par Mc.NAUGHTON [7] et M. NIVAT [8] qui ont étudié des mots infinis et enfin par J.M. AUTEBERT, J. BEAUQUIER et L. BOASSON qui ont étudié des langages sur des alphabets infinis [1]. A priori, il apparaît en effet que certains problèmes importants peuvent s'exprimer à l'aide de langages sur des alphabets infinis. C'est le cas, par exemple, des systèmes de sécurité dans lesquels la création de nouveaux objets est autorisée et qui peuvent être considérés comme des langages sur l'alphabet ΣxM où Σ est l'ensemble des sujets et des objets du système et M l'ensemble des modalités d'accès des sujets aux objets [4,5]. Or, parmi ces objets figurent les programmes écrits par les utilisateurs qui sont donc en nombre a priori non borné.

C'est encore le cas, par exemple, des calculs réalisés à l'aide de procédures récursives. L'ensemble des calculs possibles peut être considéré comme un langage. Si les procédures récursives contiennent des variables locales, à chaque appel de la procédure correspond une lettre différente. Il s'agit donc, là encore, d'un langage sur un alphabet non borné.

A posteriori, l'étude des langages sur des alphabets infinis se justifie puisqu'elle a déjà permis de caractériser des cas où la limite d'une suite croissante de langages algébriques était algébrique [3].

Rappelons les principales définitions et propriétés qui ont été données dans l'article [1].

II - RAPPELS

Soit Σ un alphabet infini dénombrable.

<u>Définition 1</u> : Une grammaire $G = <\Sigma,V,P>$ est une p-grammaire si V et P sont infinis dénombrables et si les membres droits des règles de P sont de longueur bornée.

<u>Définition 2</u> : Une p-grammaire $G = <\Sigma,V,P>$ est Σ-algébrique si, de plus V est fini. On dira alors que G est une Σ-grammaire.

<u>Définition 3</u> : Une p-grammaire $G = <\Sigma,V,P>$ est Σ-rationnelle si elle est Σ-algébrique et si, pour toute règle $(v\to m)$ de P, m est dans $\Sigma^*V\cup\{\varepsilon\}$ (autrement dit, si G est linéaire droite).

<u>Définition 4</u> : Un langage L de Σ^* est Σ-algébrique (resp. Σ-rationnel) s'il est engendré par une p-grammaire Σ-algébrique (resp. Σ-rationnelle).

<u>Exemple</u> : L'extension du langage de DYCK à l'alphabet infini dénombrable $\Sigma = \{a_i,\bar{a}_i \ / \ i\in N\}$ est engendré par la Σ-grammaire $G = <\Sigma,V,P>$ où $V = \{S\}$ et $P = \{S\to a_i S\bar{a}_i S \ / \ i\in N\} \cup \{S\to\varepsilon\}$. Il est donc Σ-algébrique.

<u>Définition 5</u> : (Rappel) Soit M un monoïde quelconque. Une partie A de M est un sous ensemble reconnaissable s'il existe un monoïde fini N, un morphisme $\alpha:M\to N$ et un sous ensemble $P\subset N$ tels que $A = \alpha^{-1}(P)$. On note Rec(M) cette famille.

Rappelons maintenant quelques propriétés vérifiées par ces langages.

<u>Proposition 1</u> : L'ensemble des langages reconnaissables de Σ^* est strictement contenu dans l'ensemble des langages Σ-rationnels. $\mathrm{Rec}(\Sigma^*) \subsetneq \Sigma\text{-Rat}$.

<u>Proposition 2</u> : Il existe des langages Σ-algébriques qui ne sont pas engendrables par des Σ-grammaires sous forme normale de GREIBACH (i.e. les règles $(v\to m)$ de P sont telles que m appartient à ΣV^*).

<u>Proposition 3</u> : Tout langage Σ-algébrique peut être engendré par une Σ-grammaire sous forme faible de GREIBACH (i.e. les règles $(v\to m)$ de P sont telles que m appartient à $\Sigma(\Sigma\cup V)^*$).

<u>Proposition 4</u> : La famille des langages Σ-algébriques (resp. Σ-rationnels) est fermée par union, produit, étoile, homomorphisme alphabétique, homomorphisme alphabétique inverse, intersection reconnaissable.

<u>Proposition 5</u> : La famille des langages Σ-algébriques (resp. Σ-rationnels) n'est pas fermée par intersection Σ-rationnelle (resp. par intersection).

<u>Proposition 6</u> : Les langages Σ-algébriques vérifient le lemme d'OGDEN.

<u>Exemple de langage non Σ-algébrique</u> : Soient R_1 et R_2 les deux langages Σ-rationnels suivants :

$R_1 = \{a_{2i}a_{2i+1} \ / \ i\in N\}$ engendré par $P = \{S\to a_{2i}a_{2i+1} S / i\in N\} \cup \{S\to\varepsilon\}$

$R_2 = a_o\{a_{2i+1}a_{2i+2}\ /\ i\in N\}^* \{a_{2i+1}\ /\ i\in N\}$ engendré par

$P = \{S\to a_oT\} \cup \{T\to a_{2i+1}a_{2i+2}T,\ U\to a_{2i+1}\ /\ i\in N\} \cup \{T\to U\}$

Le langage $R_1 \cap R_2 = \{a_oa_1a_2\ldots a_{2i+1}\ /\ i\in N\}$, ne vérifiant pas le lemme d'OGDEN, n'est pas Σ-algébrique.

III - PROBLEME DE LA RECONNAISSANCE DES LANGAGES Σ-ALGEBRIQUES PAR DES AUTOMATES A PILE CLASSIQUES

Soit $L = L_G(S)$ un langage Σ-algébrique engendré par la Σ-grammaire $G = <\Sigma,V,P>$. Il est facile de vérifier qu'il est reconnu par un automate à pile classique, mais avec un alphabet de pile infini, soit $A = (Q,\Sigma,\Gamma,\delta,q_o,S_o,F)$ où $Q = \{q_o,q\}$, où $\Gamma = \Sigma\cup V\cup\{S_o\}$ et où δ vérifie :

1) $\delta(q_o,\varepsilon,S_o) = \{(q,m)\ /\ m\in(\Sigma\cup V)^*$ et $(S\to m)\in P\}$
2) $\forall a\in\Sigma,\ \delta(q,a,a) = (q,\varepsilon)$
3) $\forall T\in V,\ \delta(a,\varepsilon,T) = \{(q,m)\ /\ m\in(\Sigma\ \cup V)^*\ ,\ (T\to m)\in P\}$

Mais réciproquement il existe des automates à pile classiques, dont l'alphabet de pile est infini, et reconnaissant des langages qui ne sont pas Σ-algébriques. Par exemple, l'automate $A = (Q,\Sigma,\Gamma,\delta,q_o,\bar{a}_o,F)$ où $\Sigma = \{a_i\ /\ i\in N\}$, $\Gamma = \{\bar{a}_i\ /\ i\in N\}$, $Q=\{q_o,q\}$ et où δ est donnée par

1) $\delta(q_o,a_o,\bar{a}_o) = (q,\bar{a}_1)$
2) $\forall i\in N^*,\ \delta(q,a_i,\bar{a}_i) = (q,\bar{a}_{i+1})$
3) $\forall i\in N^*,\ \delta(q,\varepsilon,\bar{a}_{2i}) = (q,\varepsilon)$.

Cet automate reconnait $R = \{a_oa_1a_2\ldots a_{2i+1}\ /\ i\in N\}$ qui n'est pas Σ-algébrique.

Les procédés classiques de reconnaissance ne convenant pas, il devenait donc nécessaire d'en définir de nouveaux. C'est pourquoi j'ai construit des automates dits à pile et à tiroirs et caractérisant les langages Σ-algébriques.

IV - EXEMPLE DE FONCTIONNEMENT D'UN AUTOMATE A PILE ET A TIROIRS

Le fonctionnement d'un automate à pile et à tiroirs étant assez complexe, nous allons commencer par étudier un exemple.

Etant donné l'alphabet infini $\Sigma = \{d\} \cup \{a_i,b_i\ /\ i\in N\}$, on considère le langage L engendré par la p-grammaire Σ-algébrique $G = <\Sigma,V,P>$ où $V = \{S\}$ et $P = \{S\to d\} \cup \{S\to a_iSb_i\ /\ i\in N\}$. On utilisera de façon fondamentale les deux nombres :

N = le nombre de variables = $|V|$

p = la longueur maximale des membres droits des règles.

Ici N = 1 et p = 3. On rebaptisera les variables en les notant de 1 (1 pour l'axiome S) à N. Soit x une nouvelle lettre ($x\notin V$). On forme l'ensemble MOT = $\{u\ (\{x\}\cup V)^*,\ |u|\le p\}$. Ici MOT = $\{\varepsilon,x,xx,xxx,xx1,x1,x1x,x11,1,1x,1xx,1x1,11,11x,111\}$ et $|MOT| = 15$. Soit $W = \{1,\ldots,15\}$. Soit l'application m de W dans MOT qui à un nombre i associe le mot de rang i de MOT, écrit dans l'ordre lexicographique, $m:W \to MOT$. Par exemple $m(1) = \varepsilon$, $m(2) = x$, $m(5) = xx1$. Soit z une nouvelle lettre, $z \neq x$ et $z \notin V$. On transforme les mots m(j) en mots de longueur p+1, appelés type (i), en les complétant à droite avec des z. Par exmple type (3) = xxzz, type (4) = xxxz. On appelera <u>tiroir</u> une fonction t qui, au couple (i,j) de VxW tel que $m(j) = x^{n_1} i_1 x^{n_2} i_2 \ldots i_p x^{n_{p+1}}$, fait correspondre une partie de $\{i\} x\ \Sigma^{n_1} i_1\ \Sigma^{n_2} i_2 \ldots i_p\ \Sigma^{n_{p+1}}$. Par exemple, si $V = \{1\}$ et $m(2) = x$, on pourra prendre $t(1,2) = \{(1,d)\}$ ou $t(1,2) = \{(1,a_{2i})/\ i \in N\}$ ou $t(1,2) = \emptyset$ Autre exemple : si $V = \{1,2\}$ et $m(5) = xx1$ on pourra prendre $t(2,5) = \{(2,a_{2i}a_{2i+1}1)\ /\ i \in N\}$. On peut alors définir la fonction <u>début</u>, notée déb, qui à une lettre v de $\Sigma \cup V$ associe l'ensemble des couple (i,j) dont le tiroir t(i,j) contient un membre droit au moins commençant par v. Ainsi supposons les tiroirs définis par :

$t(1,2) = \{(1,d)\}$, $t(1,7) = \{(1,a_i 1 b_i)\ /\ i \in N\}$

T $t(1,j) = \emptyset$ si $j \neq 2$ et $j \neq 7$.

Alors $déb(d) = \{(1,2)\}$, $déb(a_i) = \{(1,7)\}$, $déb(b_i) = \emptyset$

La pile du nouvel automate est constituée de trois parties liées mais distinctes :

- TIR où sera indiqué le nom du tiroir contenant la règle en cours de reconnaissan
- P qui contiendra des mots de longueur p+1 à savoir les mots type(j) dans lesquels les lettres x seront remplacées par les lettres de Σ au fur et à mesure de la lecture du mot à reconnaître,
- C qui est un compteur indiquant à quelle composante du vecteur P on en est arrivé.

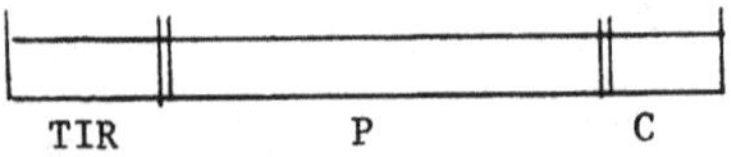

On suppose que les tiroirs sont définis par l'ensemble des relations (T) et l'on cherche à reconnaître le mot $a_1 a_2 d\ b_2 b_1$ de L. Au départ la pile contient le symbole $(\emptyset,\emptyset,\emptyset)$:

1) <u>On lit a_1</u> On cherche parmi les tiroirs t(1,j) s'il en existe possédant des facteurs droits commençant par a_1. On constate, dans les relations (T), que le tiroir t(1,7) appartient à $déb(a_1)$. On empile (1,7) dans TIR, type (7)=x1xz dans P. Puis on remplace $P(1,1) = x$ par $p(1,1) = a_1$. Enfin on met 2 dans C(1) ce qui indique qu'à la prochaine lecture il faudra regarder ce qu'indique la 2ème lettre de P c'est à dire $P(1,C(1)) = P(1,2)$.

1,7	a_1	1	x	z	2

2) <u>$P(1,C(1)) = P(1,2) = 1$</u> (c'est à dire une variable) Puisque l'on trouve une variable, cela signifie que l'on attend l'ouverture d'un nouveau tiroir (i,j) où i est égal à la variable indiquée, ici i = 1. On lit alors dans le mot à reconnaître la lettre suivante c'est à dire a_2. On constate que le tiroir (1,7) appartient à $déb(a_2)$. Alors on augmente C(1) de 1, d'où C(1) = 3, ce qui

signifie que, lorsque cette ligne se trouvera au sommet de pile, il faudra lire la troisième lettre de P, P(1,3). On empile (1,7) dans TIR, type (7)=x1xz dans P, 2 dans C et on remplace P(2,1) = x par P(2,1) = a_2.

2	1,7	a_2	1	x	z	2
1	1,7	a_1	1	x	z	3

3) P(2,C(2)) = P(2,2) = 1 (c'est à dire une variable) Comme en 2), on attend l'ouverture d'un tiroir (1,j). On lit alors dans le mot à reconnaître la lettre d et l'on constate que le tiroir (1,2) appartient à déb(d). On augmente C(2) de 1. On empile (1,2) dans TIR, type (2) = xzzz dans P, 2 dans C et on remplace P(3,1) par d.

3	1,2	d	z	z	z	2
2	1,7	a_2	1	x	z	3
1	1,7	a_1	1	x	z	3

4) P(3,C(3)) = P(3,2) = z On trouve un z, ce qui signifie que l'on doit dépiler la ligne 3 car une règle du tiroir (1,2) vient d'être reconnue entièrement.

2	1,7	a_2	1	x	z	3
1	1,7	a_1	1	x	z	3

5) P(2,C(2)) = P(2,3) = x On lit dans le mot à reconnaître la lettre suivante, soit b_2 et l'on remplace P(2,3) = x par P(2,3) = b_2. On vérifie si le facteur gauche de longueur C(2) = 3, ici $a_2 1 b_2$, du mot écrit dans P, ici $a_2 1 b_2$ z, est un facteur gauche possible d'un facteur droit du tiroir indiqué dans TIR, ici (1,7). D'après les relations (T) on a bien (1,$a_2 1 b_2$) dans t(1,7). On peut alors augmenter C(2) de 1, C(2) = 4.

2	1,7	a_2	1	b_2	z	4
1	1,7	a_1	1	x	z	3

6) P(2,C(2)) = P(2,4) = z Comme en 4), on dépile la ligne 2 puisqu'une règle du tiroir (1,7) vient d'être reconnue entièrement.

7) P(1,C(1)) = P(1,3) = x On procède comme ne 5) et on lit dans le mot à reconnaître la lettre b_1. On constate que $a_1 1 b_1$ est un facteur droit de t(1,7). Donc la ligne 1 devient :

1	1,7	a_1	1	b_1	z	4

8) P(1,C(1)) = P(1,4) = z On dépile. La pile est vide et le mot a été reconnu par pile vide par cet automate à pile et à tiroirs.

V - DEFINITION D'UN AUTOMATE A PILE ET A TIROIRS

Un automate à pile et à tiroirs est donné par :

1) (N,p) un couple d'entiers

Ces 2 entiers déterminent les ensembles :

- $V = \{1,\ldots,N\}$
- $MOT = \{e\} \bigcup_{i=1}^{p} (V \cup \{x\})^i$, où e représente le mot vide et où x est une lettre hors de $V \cup \Sigma$.
- $w = \{1,\ldots,M\}$ où $M = |MOT|$

et les applications :

- m : W →MOT , qui est la numérotation des éléments de MOT par ordre lexicographiqu
- type : $W \rightarrow MOT \, (\bigcup_{q=1}^{p} z^q)$ où z est une lettre hors de $\Sigma \cup V \cup \{x\}$ et où $type(j) = m(j)\, z^{p+1-|m(j)|}$

2) La fonction tiroir t

$$t: V \times N \longrightarrow P(V \times \bigcup_{i=0}^{p} (\Sigma \cup V)^i)$$

$*\ j \neq 1,\ (i,j) \rightsquigarrow t(i,j) \subset \{i\} \times \Sigma^{n_1} i_1\, \Sigma^{n_2} i_2 \ldots \Sigma^{n_{q+1}}$

si $m(j) = x^{n_1} i_1\, x^{n_2} i_2 \ldots i_q\, x^{n_{q+1}}$ (où $i_j \in V$)

$*\ j = 1,\ (i,1) \rightsquigarrow t(i,1) \subset \{(i,e)\}$

On définit de plus la fonction début :

$$déb: \Sigma \cup V \longrightarrow P(V \times W)$$

$$déb(y) = \{(i,j) \ / \ \exists W \in (\Sigma \cup V)^*,\ (i,yw) \in t(i,j)\}$$

La pile de l'automate est formée de mots de longueur 2 +(p+1) +1 :

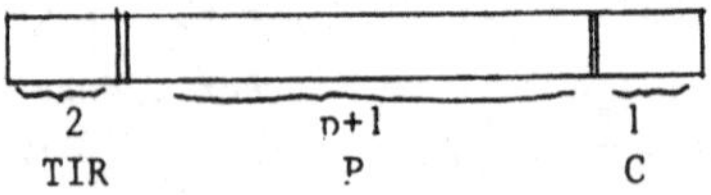

- Dans TIR, seront placés des éléments (i,j) de VxW
- Dans P seront placés d'abord des mots type(j) faisant place petit à petit à des mots de $(\Sigma \cup V)^*$
- Dans C sera placé un pointeur valant de 1 à p+1 indiquant à quelle case de P on en est arrêté dans le remplissage de P.

La fonction de transistion λ indique comment varie l'état de la pile (TIR, P, C) en fonction de la lettre lue.

$$\lambda: \underbrace{\{\emptyset\} \cup V \times W}_{TIR} \times \underbrace{\{\emptyset\} \cup (\{x\} \cup V \cup \{z\} \cup \Sigma)^p z}_{P} \times \underbrace{\{\emptyset\} \cup N}_{C} \times \underbrace{\Sigma \cup \{\varepsilon\}}_{\text{lettre lue}} \longrightarrow$$

$$P((V \times W) \cup x \cup (\{x\} \cup V \cup \{z\} \cup \Sigma)^p z \times N)$$

Au départ la pile convient le symbole de fond de pile $(\emptyset\, \emptyset\, \emptyset)$ et on peut lire une lettre a ou le mot vide.

1 Début

1-a. On lit une lettre a de Σ

$$\lambda(\emptyset\ ,\ \emptyset\ ,\ \emptyset\ ,\ a) = \{((1,j),\ type(j),\ 2) \ / \ (1,j) \in Déb(a)\}$$

$$P(1,1) = a$$

1-b. On lit le mot vide ε

$\lambda(\emptyset, \emptyset, \emptyset, \varepsilon) = \{((1,1), ezz...z, 2) \;/\; t(1,1) \neq \emptyset\}$

1-c. On lit le mot vide ε

$\lambda(\emptyset, \emptyset, \emptyset, \varepsilon) = \{((1,j), type(j), 2) \;/\; (1,j) \in Déb(1)\}$

$P(1,1) = 1$

$1 \in V$

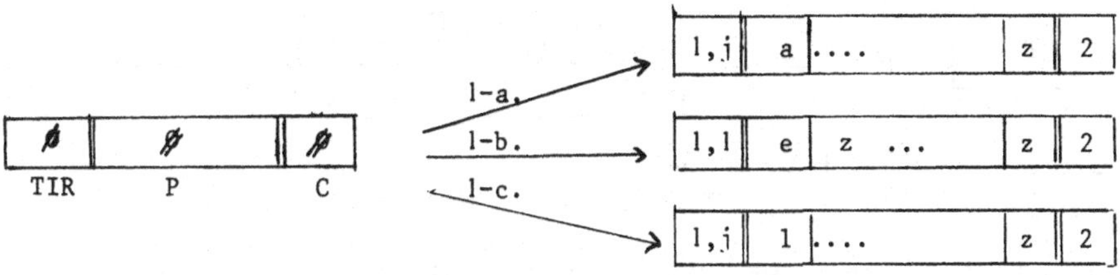

2 On attend la lecture d'une lettre de Σ : $P(k,C(k)) = x$

$\lambda((i,j), u\,x\,vz, |u|+1, a) = ((i,j), uavz, |u|+2)$

Si ua est facteur gauche d'un élément de t(i,j).

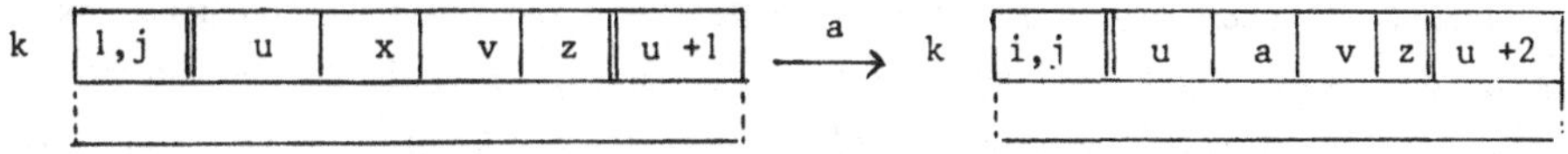

3 On trouve une variable 1 dans P(k,C(k)) et on attend la lecture d'un membre droit de tiroir

3-a. On lit une lettre a de Σ

$\lambda((i,j), ulvz, |u|+1, a) = \{((1,m), type(m), C(k) = C(k)+1) \;/\; (1,m) \in Déb(a)\}$

$P(k+1,1) = a \quad C(k+1) = 2$

3-b. On lit le mot vide ε

$\lambda((i,j), ulvz, |u|+1, \varepsilon) = \{((1,1), ezz..z, C(k) = C(k)+1) \;/\; t(1,1) \neq \emptyset\}$

$C(k+1) = 2$

3-c. On lit le mot vide ε

$\lambda((i,j), ulvz, |u|+1, \varepsilon) = \{((1,j'), type(j'), C(k) = C(k)+1 \;/\; (1,j') \in Déb(1')\}$

$P(k+1,1) = 1' \quad C(k+1) = 1$

Ces règles sont résumées dans le tableau suivant :

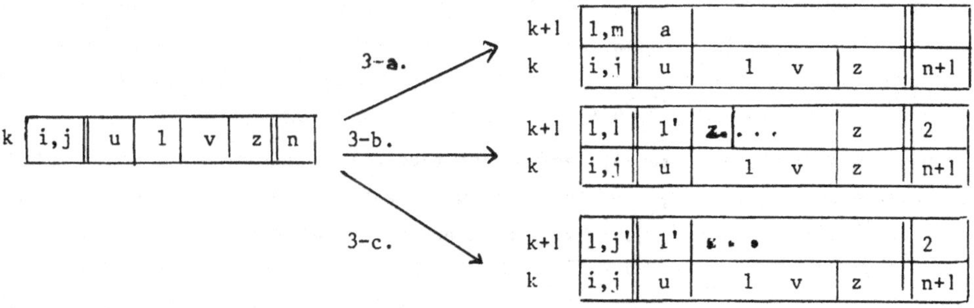

4 On trouve le critère de fin de ligne $P(k,C(k)) = z$

Cela signifie que, au sommet de la pile, dans $P(k)$ est écrit un membre droit (tout entier) du tiroir $t(i,j)$. On dépile alors la ligne k sans rien lire :

$$\lambda((i,j),\ uz\ldots z,\ |u|+1,\ \varepsilon) = (\emptyset,\ \emptyset,\ \emptyset)$$

Remarque sur les ε-move

Les ε-move 1-b. et 3-b donnent la configuration de pile suivante :

i,j	u	1	v	n

$\xrightarrow{\ \varepsilon\ }$

1,j'	e	z	...	z	2
i,j	u	1	v		n+1

$\longrightarrow$

i,j	u	1		n+1

VI - LANGAGES RECONNUS PAR UN AUTOMATE A PILE ET A TIROIRS

Proposition 7 Un langage Σ-algébrique est reconnu par un automate à pile et à tiroirs par pile vide.

Preuve a) Soit L un langage de Σ^* engendré par la Σ-grammaire $G = \langle\Sigma,V,P\rangle$. On peut alors construire l'automate à pile (N,n,t) où $N = |V|$, où n est la longueur maximale des membres droits des règles de P et où la fonction tiroir t est donnée par :

$$t(i,j) = \{(i,u)/i\in V,\ (i\to u)\in P, m(j) = x^{n_1} i_1\, x^{n_2} i_2 \ldots i_q\, x^{n_{q+1}},\ u\in\Sigma^{n_1} i_1\, \Sigma^{n_2} i_2 \ldots i_q \Sigma^{n_{q+1}}$$

soit w un mot de $L = L_G(i)$, où i est dans V. On montre qu'il est reconnu par pile vide par cet automate, par récurrence sur la longueur n des dérivations donnant naissance à w.

- si $n = 1$, soit w est vide et $(i\to\varepsilon)$ est dans P. La pile aura la configuration | i,1 | e | z | ... | z | 1 | puis se videra,

  soit w est différent de ε et $(i\to w)$ est dans P. Après la lecture de w la pile aura la configuration | i,j | w | z | ... | z | \|w\|+1 | puis se videra.
- par hypothèse de récurrence, on suppose que, pour tout i de V, tout mot de L_G (i) de longueur de dérivation inférieure ou égale à n est reconnu par pile vide par l'automate à pile ainsi défini.
- soit w un mot de $L_G(i)$ engendré par les dérivations $i\to u_1\ i_1\ u_2\ i_2\ldots i_q\ u_{q+1}\xrightarrow{n} w$

  Comme dans le cas classique, il existe $v_1,\ldots,v_q$ de Σ^* tels que

  $$i_j \xrightarrow{n_j} v_j,\quad 1\le j\le q,\quad n_j\le n$$

  $$w = u_1\ v_1\ \ldots\ v_q\ u_{q+1}$$

  Par hypothèse de récurrence, les v_j sont reconnus par pile vide par l'automate construit précédemment, pour lequel l'axiome est i_j. La pile aura la configuration | i,j | u_1 | i_1 | u_2 ... | z | \|w\|+1 | puis se videra.

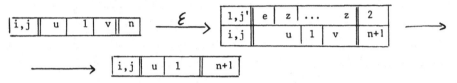

b) Réciproquement ; soit w un mot reconnu par pile vide par l'automate construit ci-dessus, le premier tiroir ouvert étant $t(i,j)$; montrons qu'alors w est dans $L_G(i)$. On fait une récurrence sur le nombre de tiroirs ouverts pour reconnaître le mot (nombre qui représente la hauteur maximale de la pile).

- si $n = 1$, alors (i,w) se trouve dans $t(i,j)$, donc $(i \to w)$ est une règle de P et w est dans $L_G(i)$.
- soit n le nombre de tiroirs ouverts pour reconnaître w et $t(i,j)$ le premier. Supposons que $type(j) = x^{n_1} i_1 \ldots$; alors w s'écrit $w = u_1\ v_1\ u_2\ v_2 \ldots$ avec $(i, u_1\ i_1\ u_2\ i_2 \ldots) \in t(i,j)$, v_k reconnu par pile vide, à partir de l'ouverture du tiroir $t(i_k, j_k)$ donc après l'ouverture de moins de n tiroirs. Par hypothèse de récurrence $v_k \in L_G(i_k)$ et finalement $i \to u_1 i_1 u_2 i_2 \ldots \overset{*}{\to} u_1 v_1 u_2 v_2 \ldots = w$ Donc w est dans $L_G(i)$.

Proposition 8 Un automate à pile et à tiroirs reconnaît par pile vide un langage Σ-algébrique.

Preuve Soient N, p et $t(i,j)$ les caractéristiques de l'automate. On construit la Σ-grammaire $G = \langle \Sigma, V, P \rangle$ de la façon suivante :

$V = \{1, \ldots, N\}$, l'ensemble des variables

$P = \{(i \to m)\ /\ i \in V,\ \exists j \in N,\ (i,m) \in t(i,j)\}$ l'ensemble des règles.

Cette p-grammaire est Σ-algébrique puisque les variables sont en nombre fini et que les membres droits des règles sont de longueur bornée par p. D'après la proposition 7, l'automate reconnaissant les mots engendrés par la grammaire qui vient d'être construite est exactement l'automate initial.

Proposition 9 Un automate à pile et tiroirs reconnaît, par non blocage de la pile, les langages Σ-algébriques.

Preuve Etant donné un automate à pile et à tiroirs, on peut construire une Σ-grammaire $G = \langle \Sigma, V, P \rangle$ comme il a été indiqué dans la proposition 8. Puis on forme une nouvelle grammaire $G' = \langle \Sigma, V', P' \rangle$ où $V' = V \cup \overline{V}$, avec $\overline{V} = \{\overline{i}\ /\ i \in V\}$, et $P' = P \cup \overline{P}$ avec $\overline{P} = \{\overline{i}\ u_1 i_1 \ldots i_p\ u_{p+1}\ /\ i \in V,\ (i \to u_1\ i_1 \ldots u_{p+1}\ i_{p+1} \ldots i_n\ u_{n+1}) \in P$ et $\widehat{u}_{p+1}$ facteur gauche de $u_{p+1}\} \cup$
$\{\overline{i} \to u_1\ i_1 \ldots \overline{i}_p / i \in V,\ (i \to u_1\ i_1 \ldots i_p\ u_{p+1} \ldots\ i_n\ u_{n+1}) \in P\}$

Alors l'automate à pile et à tiroirs reconnaît par non blocage de la pile le langage $L_{G'}$ (T). La démonstration est laissée au lecteur.

Proposition 10 Soit X un alphabet fini. Un langage L de X^* est algébrique si et seulement si il est reconnu par un automate à pile et a tiroirs.
Preuve évident laissée au lecteur.

VII - AUTOMATE A PILE ET A TIROIRS AVEC ETATS

Remarquons que, dans la définition de la fonction de transition des automates à pile et à tiroirs, le choix suivant a été fait : l'action à effectuer en présence d'une variable T dans la pile P dépend de :

- cette variable T
- des tiroirs t(T,j')
- de la lettre lue dans le mot à reconnaître

S,j	u	T	v	z	n+1
TIR		P			C

On peut alors se demander quel résultat on obteindrait en faisant, de plus, dépendre cette action du facteur gauche u qui vient d'être reconnu.

C'est cette nouvelle définition de la fonction de transition qui a permis l'introduction de la notion d'automate à pile, tiroirs et états. Mais ces automates reconnaissant des langages qui ne sont pas forcément Σ-algébriques, il a été nécessaire de poser des conditions supplémentaires pour qu'ils ne reconnaissent que des langages Σ-algébriques.

On dira qu'une <u>boîte</u> est un ensemble de facteurs gauches de la pile P

$$\bar{u} = u_1\, v_1\, u_2\, v_2 \dots u_n \qquad \bar{u}' = u'_1\, v'_1\, u'_2\, v'_2 \dots u'_n \qquad \text{où} \quad \begin{cases} u_i, u'_i, \dots, \in \Sigma^+ \\ v_i, v'_i, \dots, \in V \end{cases}$$

tels que, pour toute lettre lue, a_i ou ε, les piles

i,j	u v u_2 v_2 ...	1	...	c
i',j'	u' v' u'_2 v'_2 ...	1	...	c'

aient le même comportement.

<u>Proposition 11</u> Un automate à pile, tiroirs et états ayant un nombre fini de boîtes reconnaît par pile vide et état quelconque les langages Σ-algébriques.

VIII - AUTOMATES DETERMINISTES

Par analogie avec le cas classique, on définit des automates à pile et à tiroirs avec ou sans état, déterministes et l'on obtient les familles de langages suivantes :

les langages reconnus par des automates à pile et à tiroirs déterministes
- sans état, par pile vide, soit $D\mathcal{L}_1$
- sans états, par non blocage de la pile, soit $D'\mathcal{L}_1$
- avec états et boîtes finies par pile vide, soit, $D\mathcal{L}_2$
- avec états et boîtes finies par non blocage de la pile, soit $D'\mathcal{L}_2$.

Donnons sans démonstration les propriétés vérifiées par ces familles de langages.

<u>Proposition 12</u> Les familles de langages déterministes $D\mathcal{L}_1$, $D'\mathcal{L}_1$, $D\mathcal{L}_2$, $D'\mathcal{L}_2$ vérifient les inclusions suivantes :

$D\mathcal{L}_1 \subset D\mathcal{L}_2 \subset D'\mathcal{L}_2$ et $D'\mathcal{L}_1 \subset D'\mathcal{L}_2$.

Proposition 13 Soit $L \subset X^*$ un langage déterministe au sens de $D'L_2$ (X étant fini) alors L est déterministe au sens classique.

Proposition 14 Soit $L \subset X^*$ (où X est fini) un langage reconnu par un automate à pile classique déterministe, alors il est déterministe au sens de $D'L_2$.

Proposition 15 Soit L_1 un langage reconnu par état final par un automate à pile, tiroirs et états déterministe, c'est à dire un langage de $D'L_2$. Soit L_2 un langage reconnaissable de Σ^*. Alors $L_1 \cap L_2$ est dans $D'L_2$.

Proposition 16 Un langage reconnu par pile vide par un automate à pile et tiroirs avec ou sans état déterministe est préfixe. Autrement dit, les langages de DL_1 et de DL_2 sont préfixes.

Proposition 17 Les langages reconnus par des automates déterministes à boîtes finies ne sont pas fermés par :

- concaténation
- étoile
- union.

Proposition 18 Les langages déterministes ne sont pas fermés par morphisme strictement alphabétique.

Proposition 19 Soit ϕ un morphisme strictement alphabétique de Σ dans Σ'. Soit L' un langage déterministe de Σ'. Alors $\phi^{-1}(L')$ est déterministe.

IX - CONCLUSION

Dans cet article, certains types d'automates à pile classiquement utilisés n'ont pas été abordés. C'est le cas, notamment, des automates quasi-réaltime, realtime et finite turn. Leurs définitions s'étendent sans problème au cas des automates à pile, tiroirs et états. Il reste à étudier si les propriétés vérifiées dans le cas classique le sont toujours pour de telles extensions aux alphabets infinis.

Le problème des langages à compteur est plus complexe. En effet, par analogie avec le cas des automates à pile à un compteur, qui n'ont qu'un symbole de pile, on peut définir des automates à pile et à deux tiroirs (un seul tiroir engendrerait des langages finis sur tout alphabet fini donc peu intéressants). Ils reconnaissent des langages engendrés par des règles de deux types : $S \to v$ et $S \to u_1 \; S \; u_2 \; S \; u_3 \ldots$ Ces langages constituent une famille qu'il est intéressant d'étudier mais qui, cependant rapportée au cas d'un alphabet fini, n'a pas grand chose à voir avec celle des langages à compteur.

On peut par ailleurs se pencher sur les problèmes de décidabilité soulevés dans le cas classique.

Certains sont résolus très facilement. Tout d'abord, étant donnée une p-grammaire -algébrique et un mot $w = x_1 \ldots x_n$ de Σ^*, il existe un algorithme déterminant si w se trouve dans L(G) puisque l'on peut se ramener au cas de l'alphabet fini

$X = \{x_1 ..., x_n\}$ en prenant la trace de la grammaire G sur X.

Ensuite, il est possible de dire si un langage engendré par $G = \langle\Sigma,V,P\rangle$ est vide : en effet, comme on suppose toujours que les règles de la grammaire sont constituées d'ensembles récursivement énumérables, il est possible de former les ensembles :

$W_1 = \{T\in V / \exists\ w\in\Sigma^*,\ (T\to w)\in P\}$

$W_{k+1} = W_k \cup \{T\in V / \exists\alpha\in(\Sigma \cup W_k)^+,\ (T\to\alpha)\in P\}$, (cf. [6]), et le langage est non vide si l'axiome S appartient à W_n (où $n = |V|$).

Enfin, on peut dire si un langage Σ-algébrique est infini ou non. En effet, après avoir réduit la grammaire, deux cas se présentent : ou bien la grammaire est alors réduite à une grammaire sur un alphabet fini et il existe un algorithme décidant si le langage est infini ou non.

ou bien une des règles au moins utilise une infinité de lettres. On est alors certain d'obtenir un langage infini.

Dans ce domaine il reste à étudier la décidabilité de l'égalité de deux langages Σ-algébriques, de leur inclusion.

Maintenant, des problèmes, qui ne sont plus calqués sur ceux de la théorie classique, surgissent. Nous en donnons deux exemples :

- Dans [2], les auteurs ont appelé I-cône la famille des langages de Σ^*fermée par morphismes alphabétiques direct et inverse et par intersection N-rationnelle. Ils ont appelé ombre d'un langage L de la famille des langages images de L dans un morphisme de type fini. Puis ils ont montré que tout cône rationnel fermé par union de langages algébriques est l'ombre d'un I-cône principle admettant comme générateur un langage Σ-algébrique. et ils ont qualifié d'honnête un processus fini de génération de mots dont la Σ-extension vérifie une proposition analogue. On peut alors se demander quelles familles de langages sont engendrées par des processus honnêtes.

- Le deuxième exemple porte sur l'ambiguité. Les notions de grammaires et de langages ambigus s'étendent facilement au cas d'un alphabet infini et la vérification des propriétés classiques ne présente pas de difficultés. Par contre se posent des problèmes d'existence, aux réponses non évidentes ; par exemple :

Conjoncture Il existe un langage Σ-algébrique inhéremment ambigu et non ambigu sur tout partie finie.

BIBLIOGRAPHIE

[1] J.M. AUTEBERT, J. BEAUQUIER, L. BOASSON, "Langages sur des alphabets infinis" Discrete Math.2, 1980, p1-20.

[2] J.M. AUTEBERT, J. BEAUQUIER, L. BOASSON, "Formes de langages et de grammaires", Acta Informatica 7, 1982, p 193-219.

[3] J.M. AUTEBERT, J. BEAUQUIER, L. BOASSON, "Limites de langages algébriques", C.R. Acad. Sc. PARIS, t.29, 1980.

[4] J. BEAUQUIER, "Comptabilité des systèmes de sécurité", In program Transformation B. ROBINET Dunod-1978, p 109-124.

[5] J. BEAUQUIER, M. NIVAT, "Application of formal languages theory to problems of security and synchronization", In Formal language theory, 1980, Academic Press.

[6] M. HARRISON, "Introduction to formal languages theory", Addison Wesley, 1978.

[7] R. McNAUGHTON, "Testing and generating infinite sequences by a finite automaton" Inf. and Control. Vol 9, 1966, p 521-530.

[8] M. NIVAT, "Sur les ensembles de mots infinis engendrés par une grammaire algébrique" RAIRO Info. Théorique, 12, 1978, p 259 270.

LOGIC PROGRAMS AND MANY-VALUED LOGIC

(A fuller version of this paper can be obtained as a report from the address below.)

Alan Mycroft
Institutionen för
Informationsbehandling
Chalmers Tekniska Högskola
S-412 96 Göteborg, Sweden

Abstract: We claim that the well-known equivalence of declarative and procedural interpretations for Horn clauses (predicate logic or Prolog programs) has been unjustifiably used when discussing computation. The reason for this is that the Apt, van Emden and Kowalski theory is based on a 2-valued logic {true, false} whereas computation requires at least a 3-valued logic {true, false, "still computing"}. We introduce such logics and relate the results obtained to the traditional ones. This gives a characterization of under-defined clauses which naturally correspond to looping programs. Moreover, it further supports the view that strong correctness (including termination) should be considered, rather than weak correctness (eg 2-valued logic) together with a separate analysis of termination.

1. Introduction

Logic programming was introduced by Kowalski [6] who observed that a theorem prover for a certain subset of predicate logic could be regarded as an efficient computational mechanism. The word Prolog is somewhat ill-defined, but we will follow the common usag and use it to refer to logic programming with a given evaluation strategy. The logic is that part of predicate logic which can be expressed in definite clause form. A *definite clause* is a statement of the form

$$A \leftarrow B_1 \wedge \ldots \wedge B_n \qquad (n \geq 0)$$

in which $A, B_1 \ldots B_n$ are atomic formulae (atoms for short) given by the grammar

Atom::= Pred(Term*)

Term::= Functor(Term*) | Var

and Pred, Functor and Var are disjoint sets of symbols representing predicates, functor (data constructors) and variables. Such a clause will be interpreted as the (universally quantified) formula $B_1 \wedge \ldots \wedge B_n \supset A$. When $n=0$ this gives an axiom (scheme) and $n>0$ an inference rule. A definite *sentence* P is merely a set of definite clauses interpreted as their conjunction. To forestall misunderstanding we will point out that this is one level of understanding of such clauses. Another is to say that all the clauses are axiom (schemes) and resolution is the (only) inference rule.

Such a sentence, which specifies a logical system, is of little use unless we can use it to determine the truth of a given atom relative to the sentence. Therefore a program is a sentence P followed by an atom A .

There are two ways to determine the truth of A relative to P . Firstly, there is the model-theoretic approach in which we find a model of P (definite sentences always have a model) and test whether (an instance of) A is part of this model. Secondly we try to find a proof-theoretic derivation using the axioms and inference rules of P to reduce A to the empty conjunction which represents truth.

Van Emden and Kowalski [3] observed, upon using a well-determined least model in the above, that the equivalence of these methods is a consequence of Gödel's completeness theorem for predicate calculus, and also that Herbrand (term) models suffice. Moreover, the process of determining a derivation, if one exists, which shows A is satisfiable relative to a definite sentence, is in fact a particularly simple form of resolution-based theorem-proving called SLD-resolution.

Apt and van Emden [1] elucidate these results with many useful lemmas and discuss various notions of A being independent of P (which certainly implies no instance of A being a consequence of P). This is often identified with falsity, but we prefer the word failure. There are at least three such notions including Clark's "finite failure" model [2], the "if-and-only-if" assumption in which clauses are treated as equivalences rather than implications and the "closed world" view in which everything nonprovable is assumed to be false. They extend the above by characterizing these in terms of a greatest model.

Here we will show how a model-theoretic semantics can be built from an arbitrary logic, and as an example with a $\{t,f,\perp\}$-valued logic show how success(t), failure(f) and underdeterminedness ($\perp$, such as would be produced by the definition $p(x) \leftarrow p(x)$) can be exhibited in terms of a single (least) model. This recasts Apt and van Emden's work in a more usual computational form. It turns out that we can also identify underdeterminedness in the model with looping of any uniform proof-seeker. We later find that an ever finer logic can reflect more exactly the details of SLD-tree (proof-tree) searching.

We must emphasise one point- we are not suggesting changing the semantics of predicate logic programs - their internal values will still form part of an "internal" two-valued logic. What we propose is a semantics (or rather a scheme of possible semantics) involving an "external" many-valued logic which contains a $\perp$ element to account for underspecification in the internal view. A similar situation arises when reasoning about programs which calculate boolean values:the logic contains truth and falsity, whilst the program can produce true, false or $\perp$. This is well discussed in the LCF book [4,p12].

Related work includes Lassez and Maher's independent work [7] which gives a 3-valued $\{t,f,\perp\}$ logic interpretation to Horn clauses to characterize an "Optimal fixpoint" of logic programs. However, their transformation τ differs from our corresponding Z_p^3 and the full reasons for this are unclear. Jones and Mycroft [5] give a full denotational semantics to logic programs with the standard depth-first left-right strategy which amongst other things also distinguishes between failure and looping.

This paper is structured in the following manner: Section 2 gives brief definitions o mathematical prerequisites and section 3 introduces resolution, its search space and failure from the literature. Section 4 defines a general logic and shows how to form a model of a given definite sentence with that logic. It also shows how a certain 3-valued logic subsumes and extends Apt and van Emden's least and greatest models. Section 5 stops to consider the question of which particular logic best represents proof searching. The model generated by this logic is then related to the proof-theoretic semantics in section 6. Section 7 discusses further work based on these ideas.

2. Prerequisites

A substitution is a member of $Subst = Var \rightarrow Term$, naturally extended to $Atom \rightarrow Atom$. A Atom or clause is ground if it contains no variables. Textual equality of atoms is indicated by $\equiv$. Given two atoms A,B there may exist a substitution Θ such that $\Theta(A) \equiv \Theta(B)$. Such a Θ is called a unifier of A and B. If A and B have a unifier, then they have a most-general unifier $mgu(A,B)$ which has the property that any unifier Θ can be factored $\Theta = \phi \circ mgu(A,B)$ for some substitution ϕ. Moreover there is an algorithm which finds the most-general unifier of two atoms, or reports that none exists.

A complete partial order or cpo is a pair $(D,\sqsubseteq)$ where D is a set and $\sqsubseteq$ a partial order on D which has a least element $\perp \in D$ and limits of arbitrary ascending chains $(d_i)_{i<\lambda}$. $(D,\sqsubseteq)$ is abbreviated to D where the ordering is clear.
A function $f:D \rightarrow D'$ is monotonic if $x \sqsubseteq y \Rightarrow f(x) \sqsubseteq f(y)$. It is continuous if for an arbitrary ascending chain $(d_i)_{i<\lambda}$ we have that $f(\bigsqcup d_i) = \bigsqcup f(d_i)$.

If $f:D \rightarrow D$ is monotonic then we define the iterates f^n of f for arbitrary ordinals by

$$f^0(x) = \perp$$
$$f^{n+1}(x) = f(f^n(x))$$
$$f^\lambda(x) = \bigsqcup_{n<\lambda} f^n(x) \qquad \text{for a limit ordinal } \lambda.$$

We also define $f{\downarrow}n = f^n(\perp)$ for an arbitrary ordinal n.

For any function $f:D \rightarrow D$, $x \in D$ is a fixpoint of f if $f(x) = x$. If f is monotonic then it has a least fixpoint, $lfp(f) \in D$. This is given by $f{\uparrow}n$ for some ordinal n

Moreover, if f is continuous then we can take $n=\omega$ and $lfp(f) = \bigsqcup_{m<\omega} f\uparrow m$.

Let D be a cpo, and $\bar{D} = (\bar{D}, \sqsupseteq)$ have the partial order opposite to that in D. We will have cause to study cpo's D where $\bar{D}$ is also a cpo (eg complete lattices). Such D have a maximal element $\top$, and we say a function $f:D\to D$ is dual-continuous if f, considered as a map $\bar{D}\to\bar{D}$ is continuous. Dual monontonicity is the the same as monotonicity. Any monotonic function, f, on such a D has a greatest fixpoint $gfp(f)$ given by $f\downarrow n$ for some ordinal n where $f\downarrow n$ is defined (on D) by

$f\downarrow 0 = \top$

$f\downarrow (n+1) = f(f\downarrow n)$

$f\downarrow\lambda = \bigsqcup_{n<\lambda} f\downarrow n$ for a limit ordinal λ.

If f is dual-continuous then $gfp(f) = f\downarrow\omega$.

For future use we will define the symbols $2, \bar{2}, 3$ to stand for the cpo's (later logics)

$2 = (\{t,f\}, f\sqsubseteq t)$

$\bar{2} = (\{t,f\}, t\sqsubseteq f)$

$3 = (\{t,f,\bot\}, (\bot\sqsubseteq t, \bot\sqsubseteq f))$.

3. More on clauses, SLD-resolution

A negative clause is a statement of the form

$\leftarrow A_1 \wedge \ldots \wedge A_n$

and is interpreted as $A_1\wedge\ldots\wedge A_n \supset false$ which denies $A_1\wedge\ldots\wedge A_n$. The case $n=0$ represents contradiction. As earlier P is a definite sentence and A an atom. Rather than attempting to show that (an instance of) A is a logical consequence of P, it is traditional to augment P with the negative clause $\leftarrow A$ obtaining the augmented sentence $P\cup\{\leftarrow A\}$ and showing that this is inconsistent. (The contradiction must arise from $\leftarrow A$ since definite sentences (like P) are always consistent). Accordingly, it is common to talk of refuting the augmented sentence instead of proving A from P. Similarly when A is not provable from P we talk about failure of refutation.

As discussed in the introduction the augmented sentence may be shown to be inconsistent by either showing it has no model, or by showing that it logically implies a sentence containing the empty negative clause $\leftarrow$ which represents falsity or contradiction. The latter idea is the basis of resolution based theorem proving: given a negative clause $N = \leftarrow A_1\wedge\ldots\wedge A_n$ and a sentence P we choose an atom A_k (the selected atom) and a clause $C \leftarrow B_1\wedge\ldots\wedge B_m$ from P (the selected clause). For technical correctness it is necessary to assume that $C\leftarrow B_1\wedge\ldots\wedge B_m$ has had its variables renamed so they do not clash with any in the (finite) clause N. Suppose further that there is $\theta\in Subst$

with $\Theta(A_k) \equiv \Theta(C)$.

Then we can re-write N into

$$\leftarrow \Theta(A_1 \wedge \ldots \wedge A_{k-1} \wedge B_1 \wedge \ldots \wedge B_m \wedge A_{k+1} \wedge \ldots \wedge A_n)$$

This is called the resolvent of N and $C \leftarrow B_1 \wedge \ldots \wedge B_m$ and is logically implied by $P \cup \{N\}$. This technique is more properly called SLD-resolution, being a special case of general resolution based theorem proving [11] which does not concern us here.

Note that resolution with axioms (m=0) serves to reduce the number of atoms in the negative clause. Such a sequence of resolution steps is called an SLD-derivation. An SLD-refutation is an SLD-derivation which ends in a sentence containing the empty clause $\leftarrow$ and this enables us to deduce that the augmented sentence was inconsistent.

3.1 SLD-trees

Apt and van Emden showed that a complete search space for SLD-refutations for the augmented sentence $P \cup \{\leftarrow A\}$ is given by any of the SLD-trees for $P \cup \{\leftarrow A\}$.

An SLD-tree for $P \cup \{\leftarrow A\}$ has root labelled $\leftarrow A$ and for every node ℓ, labelled $\leftarrow A_1 \wedge \ldots \wedge A_n$, we choose an arbitrary integer k $(1 \leq k \leq n)$. The sons of ℓ are defined to be $\leftarrow \Theta(A_1 \wedge \ldots \wedge A_{k-1} \wedge B_1 \wedge \ldots \wedge B_m \wedge A_{k+1} \wedge \ldots \wedge A_n)$ as $C \leftarrow B_1 \wedge \ldots \wedge B_m$ ranges over the clauses in P (again renamed to avoid variable clashes) such that $\Theta = \mathrm{mgu}(A_k, C)$ exists. For each possible choice of k at each node we get a different SLD-tree.

It is apparent that every empty node (node labelled with the empty negative clause $\leftarrow$) in a given SLD-tree and its associated path from the root corresponds to an SLD-refutation above. Not so apparent is the converse [1], that if any SLD-tree contains an empty node then every one does - i.e. every SLD-tree is a complete search space for SLD-refutations.

This is used to justify implementations of logic programming only searching one SLD-tree (k=1 throughout is common). However, see section 3.2 for why this is not strictly valid for finite failure. SLD-trees are usefully thought of as a data structure representing the refutation search space.

As a parenthetical remark, we observe that this result can be seen as a result about a two person game: let player A select an atom and player B then select a clause. Then if B can win by producing an empty node in collaboration with A then he can win regardless of A's strategy.

However, the above result on equivalence of SLD-trees is not without practical problem The SLD-trees for a given sentence can differ dramatically in size - even to the exter of one being infinite and another finite. Note that to guarantee finding a node in an infinite SLD-tree we must search it in a manner that has order-type at most ω i.e. some form of parallel search as in the LOGLISP [12] implementation. The obvious suggestion of selecting an appropriately small SLD-tree (by choice of evaluation strat egy) has received little attention.

We will see one consequence of this size variability in the next section.

3.2 Failure

Besides logical consequence, one other interesting property of an atom relative to a sentence is that of logical independence. Due to definite clauses lacking any notion of denial this is often identified with falsity. There are three views on the 'best' way to interpret falsity with respect to definite clauses. These have been well discussed by Apt and van Emden and we will further clarify understanding of them in section 4.1 when we form a particular model of a sentence. One view is the "closed-world" assumption in which A's independence of P is equated to the fact that $P \cup \{\leftarrow A\}$ cannot be refuted. A second, somewhat weaker formulation (in that it specifies less things to be false) is to treat P as specifying "if-and-only-if" clauses instead of implications and establishing the truth of $\sim A$ in this context (see [1]). Neither of these are effectively computable operations, and a third, still weaker notion is that of "finite failure" [2] in which we treat A as being independent of P if there exists a finite SLD-tree (amongst all SLD-trees) for $P \cup \{\leftarrow A\}$ which does not contain an empty node. Note, however that even this formulation technically requires us to search all SLD-trees (in parallel) for a given sentence, and we return to this later in section 4.2 when we discuss sequentiality. Implementations usually choose the even weaker notion that A is independent of P if that particular implementation's SLD-tree for $P\ \{\leftarrow A\}$ is finite and has no empty node. Lassez and Maher [8] give an interesting discussion of finite failure and relate it to fairness.

4. Model-theoretic semantics

In this section we develop very general concepts of logic, interpretation and model for definite sentences. These will be initially used with a 3-valued logic, but we will exhibit a use for another logic in section 5.

We define a logic $(L,\vee,\wedge,t,f)$, or just L when the context is clear, to be a cpo L, containing two distinguished elements t and f and having continuous binary operations $\wedge$ and $\vee$ which have t and f as respective left-identities. We will use Π and Σ for distributed versions of these operators (ie $\Sigma_{1\leq i\leq n} x_i = x_1 \vee \ldots \vee x_n$) with t or f being used when Π or Σ range over empty sets. For simplicity, rather than technical reasons, we assume that $\wedge$ and $\vee$ are associative and commutative. For a concrete example in the following it may be helpful to take $L=\{f,t\}$ with $f\sqsubseteq t$ which reduces to Apt and van Emden's logic.

Associated with a sentence P there is a standard notion of Herbrand base, U, that is the set of variable-free atoms which can be built from the symbols of P (respecting the arities). As usual, we prescribe that U is non-empty by assuming (if necessary) the existence of a functor of arity 0 and at least one predicate symbol.

We now define an <u>interpretation</u>, I, of P to be any function $U \to L$. Classically an interpretation is a subset of U (those elements which are "true") but this is clearly subsumed if $|L| = 2$. Interpretations are ordered pointwise and the least interpretation is $I_o = \lambda A.\bot$. The set of all interpretations is called Interp. A <u>model</u> M of P is any interpretation which respects P under the given logic. This will be expressed formally as the fact that a model M satisfies an equation $M = Z_P^L(M)$ where Z_P^L is the transformation associated with P and L given by

$$Z_P^L : \text{Interp} \to \text{Interp}$$

$$Z_P^L(I) = \lambda A. \sum_{\substack{(C \leftarrow B_1 \wedge \ldots \wedge B_n) \in P \\ \Theta \in \text{Subst} \\ \Theta(C \leftarrow B_1 \wedge \ldots \wedge B_n) \text{ is ground} \\ \Theta(C) \equiv A}} \left(\prod_{1 \le i \le n} I(\Theta(B_i)) \right)$$

We will omit L and P from Z_P^L if the context is clear.

We can retrieve Apt and van Emden's T_P as Z_P^2 where $2 = \{t,f\}$ which gives

$$T_P(I) = \lambda A. \begin{cases} t & \text{if } \exists (C \leftarrow B_1 \wedge \ldots \wedge B_n) \in P,\ \Theta \in \text{Subst}: \Theta(C) \equiv A \wedge \forall i: I(\Theta(B_i)) = t \\ f & \text{otherwise} \end{cases}$$

However, they define a model to be any pre-fixpoint of T_P - i.e. M is a model if $M \sqsupseteq T_P(M)$, using the ordering $f \sqsubseteq t$ in 2. We choose to adopt the stronger requirement that models are fixpoints in order that the models of Z_P under logics 2 and $\bar{2}$ coincide.

Z_P^L is clearly always monotonic, however it is not necessarily continuous; using logic $\bar{2} = \{t,f\}$ with $t \sqsubseteq f$ to exhibit as a least fixpoint the greatest fixpoint of T_P above and using Apt and van Emden's example

$P(a) \leftarrow P(x) \wedge Q(x)$

$P(s(x)) \leftarrow P(x)$

$Q(b) \leftarrow$

$Q(s(x)) \leftarrow Q(x)$

gives a Z_P with

$$Z_P \uparrow \omega = \lambda A. (\exists i: A = Q(s^i(b)) \vee A = P(s^i(a))) \to t,f$$

$$\text{lfp}(Z_P) = \lambda A. (\exists i: A = Q(s^i(b))) \to t,f$$

with the least fixpoint being obtained after $\omega+\omega$ steps. This corresponds to Apt and van Emden's observation that T_P above is not dual-continuous.
It is interesting to consider where the non-continuity of Z_P comes from, since $\wedge$ and $\vee$ are assumed continuous. The answer is that the Σ in the definition of Z_P can be

infinitary when non-ground clauses occur in P . This causes no mathematical problems (compare the standard use of ∀ and ∃) but deeper investigation of this point could further the understanding of failure. The lack of continuity corresponds to the observation in section 3.2 that two of the methods of treating falsity are not decidable.

4.1 Application : Relating 3-valued logic models to classical results

To show the power of our approach we construct a logic which recreates Apt and van Emden's maximal/minimal fixpoints giving extra insight. Let $L=\{t,f,\bot\}$ with $\bot\sqsubseteq t, \bot\sqsubseteq f$ and $\wedge$ and $\vee$ be defined by the tables

∧	⊥	t	f
⊥	⊥	⊥	f
t	⊥	t	f
f	f	f	f

∨	⊥	t	f
⊥	⊥	t	⊥
t	t	t	t
f	⊥	t	f

(It is not a coincidence that these are the parallel-and and -or functions considered by Plotkin [9] in a computational framework - the model-theoretic semantics of success and finite failure require some form of non-sequential evaluation. See also section 6.2).

This gives us a Z_p for any definite sentence P .
Let $M_1=\mathrm{lfp}(Z_p)$ be the least model of P and $M_0=Z_p\uparrow\omega$ be its computable approximation (not a model in general). Similarly let T_p be Apt and van Emden's functional from the previous section.

Apt and van Emden consider three interpretations of T_p namely $T_p\uparrow\omega=\mathrm{lfp}(T_p)$, $\mathrm{gfp}(T_p)$ and $T_p\downarrow\omega$ (the last is not a model). This can be illustrated in the Venn diagram (fig. 1) below where an interpretation I is associated with the set $\{x:I(x)=t\}$.
They also show that the complements of these areas in the maximal interpretation $\lambda A.t$ can be associated with the three ideas of failure : closed world (cw), if-and-only-if (iff) and finite failure (ff).

Our framework can be illustrated in figure 2 where we partition the set of all (variable-free) atoms into those that are associated with t,f and ⊥ in interpretations M_0 and M_1 :

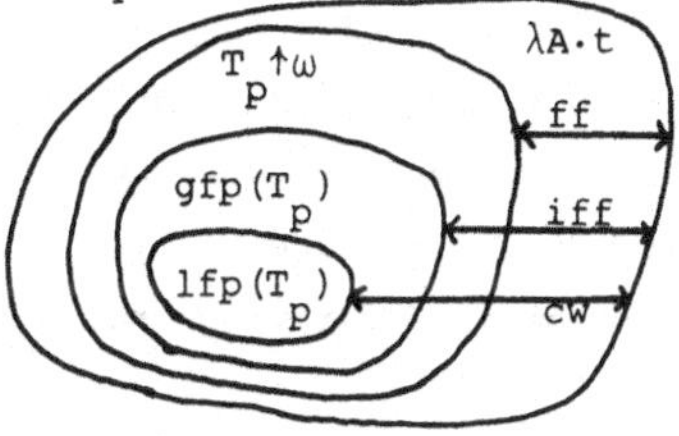

Fig. 1

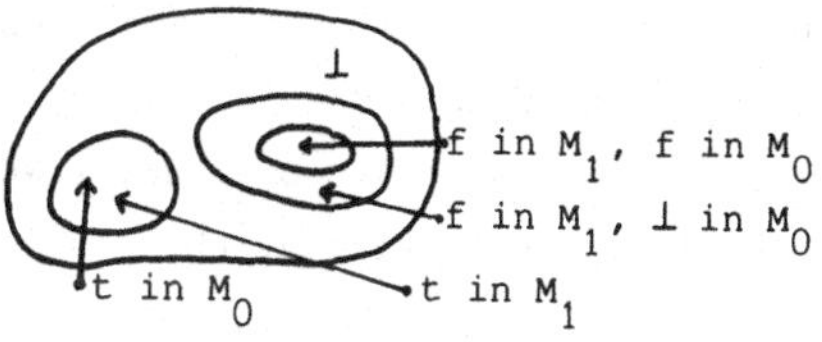

Fig. 2

The failure descriptions can now be written :

$$\text{ff} \longleftrightarrow \text{f in } M_0$$
$$\text{iff} \longleftrightarrow \text{f in } M_1$$
$$\text{cw} \longleftrightarrow \bot \cup (\text{f in } M_1)$$

This can be formally expressed as :

Theorem 4.1

$$lfp(T_p)(A)=t \iff M_0(A)=t \iff M_1(A)=t \qquad \text{(truth)}$$
$$gfp(T_p)(A)=f \iff M_1(A)=f \qquad \text{(iff)}$$
$$(T_p{\downarrow}\omega)(A)=f \iff M_0(A)=f \qquad \text{(finite failure)}$$

Corollary $lfp(T_p)(A)=f \;\&\; gfp(T_p)(A)=t \iff M_1(A)=\bot$

$lfp(T_p)(A)=f \;\&\; (T_p{\downarrow}\omega)(A)=t \iff M_0(A)=\bot$

This corollary duplicates corollaries 5.7 and 7.10 in [1] and is useful because it states that atoms whose values differ in interpretations $lfp(T_p)$ and $(T_p{\downarrow}\omega)$ will in general cause an evaluator to loop[1]. It would seem that use of $\bot$ clarifies this result.

Proof Omitted

The section below (further extended in section 5) provides a method by which we can form a model corresponding to a prescribed SLD-tree search.

4.2 Evaluation order and sequentiality

By allowing $\wedge$ and $\vee$ to be non-commutative (and accordingly defining π and Σ more carefully) we can hope to model particular (e.g. sequential) evaluation strategies for Prolog. These frequently give results different from those given by the least model above. The main reason is associated with sequentiality : our definition of Z_p (following Apt and van Emden's T_p) unavoidably uses the parallel-or and -and functions. However, in practice we only wish to search a single SLD-tree (rather than them all in parallel as required for correct treatment of finite-failure) and to search that given SLD-tree in a depth-first rather than breadth-first (parallel) manner. For example using depth-first left-right evaluation of p(2) in $\{p(2) \leftarrow \quad , \quad p(x) \leftarrow p(x)\}$ gives t , but interchanging the clauses in the sentence would give result $\bot$. The main reason for this behaviour is that depth-first search of an infinite tree does not in general terminate in at most ω steps whereas breadth-first search does. Accordingly fixpoints would have to be replaced with their ω approximations, as is already the case with finite failure.

This whole area needs more study, but a special case of deriving Prolog semantics

1) Of course it is always possible to detect certain looping computations (like $p(x) \leftarrow p(x)$) but this cannot be done uniformly.

which include the concept of looping for depth-first left-right evaluation is given by Jones and Mycroft [5].

In passing, it worth remarking that most of these ideas are parallel to those occurring in the semantics of different evaluation strategies (e.g. innermost left-right) which occur in other programming languages (λ-calculus provides their simplest exposition). Again more research is needed.

5. Natural logic for SLD-tree searching

After seeing that the model theoretic semantics of logic programs can be built on an arbitrary logic, it remains for us to determine the most suitable logic to represent the SLD-tree search. To be true to the spirit of logic programming (most implementations are not) we should attempt to capture properties which might hold in any search of any SLD-tree, and then specialize to a possible prescribed evaluation strategy.

Suppose P is a definite sentence and A an atom. There are five distinguishable forms of behaviour of searches of SLD-trees for $P \cup \{ \leftarrow A\}$:

1. An SLD-tree contains an empty clause (hence all do) :
   - 1a. All SLD-trees finite (guaranteed success)
   - 1b. Some infinite SLD-tree (possible success)
2. No SLD-tree contains an empty clause :
   - 2a. All SLD-trees finite (guaranteed failure)
   - 2b. All SLD-trees infinite (looping)
   - 2c. Some finite, some infinite SLD-trees (possible failure)

Apt and van Emden's finite failure corresponds to behaviours in 2a or 2c.

The set of atoms, A, for a given definite sentence are thus partitioned into five sets independently of which actual SLD-tree is searched in which manner. The non-determinism implicit in the unspecified search strategy means that we can associate these five classes with sets of possible outcomes in the following manner

$$1a \longleftrightarrow \{t\}\ ,\ 1b \longleftrightarrow \{t,\bot\},\ 2a \longleftrightarrow \{f\}\ ,\ 2b \longleftrightarrow \{\bot\}\ ,\ 2c \longleftrightarrow \{f,\bot\}.$$

Unsurprising, perhaps, then is the observation that these elements correspond to five of the seven elements of a certain power domain [10] ordered by the Egli-Milner ordering.

$$P(\{t,f\}_\bot) = P\left(\begin{smallmatrix} t & & f \\ & \bot & \end{smallmatrix}\right) =$$

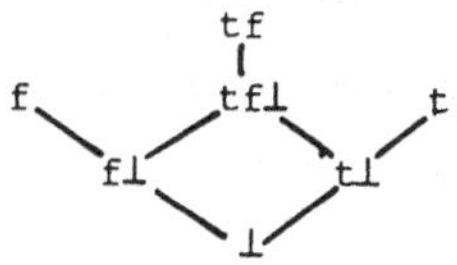

The fact that definite clauses are consistent means that the elements $\{t,f,\bot\}$ and $\{t,f\}$ which represent contradiction (i.e. selection of search strategy can result in either t or f as answer) do not have any analogue in definite clause theory where falsity is a subset of non-truth.

We will pause to comment that selection of a given search strategy serves to remove the non-determinism and distribute the elements corresponding to $\{t,\bot\}$ into $\{t\}$ and $\{\bot\}$ and those corresponding to $\{f,\bot\}$ into $\{f\}$ and $\{\bot\}$. In particular, selection of any breadth-first search (i.e. one with ω steps) moves all elements corresponding to $\{t,\bot\}$ into $\{t\}$. More formally this is seen as an evaluation strategy inducing a continuous map $\psi = (U \longrightarrow P(3)) \longrightarrow (U \longrightarrow 3)$.

We claim that the above 5-valued logic is much more suitable as a model for the proof-theoretic (or procedural) semantics of Prolog, and take this as the definition that the model-theoretic semantics should match. The standard proof-theoretic semantic ideas (success, finite failure etc.), can all be retrieved by considering appropriate images, or equivalently quotients.

6. Relation of model-theoretic and proof-theoretic semantics

Here we present a logic for the model-theoretic semantics which directly models the proof-theoretic semantics given by possible SLD-tree searches as discussed in the previous section. This sharpens Apt and van Emden's results.

Let $3=\{t,f\}_\bot$ be the 3-valued computational logic. We will take as our logic $L=P(3)$ although we will not use elements $\{t,f\}$ or $\{t,f,\bot\}$ as discussed above. We will define $\wedge$ and $\vee$ as below and use t and f for their distinguished left-identities. We define $X \vee Y = \cup\{x \mathring{\vee} y : x \in X, y \in Y\}$ where $\mathring{\vee}: 3 \times 3 \longrightarrow P(3)$ is given by the table

$\mathring{\vee}$	$\bot$	t	f
$\bot$	$\bot$	$t\bot$	$\bot$
t	$t\bot$	t	t
f	$\bot$	t	f

As in the table we will drop the $\{\cdot\}$ brackets where confusion is unlikely and write $t\bot$ for $\{t,\bot\}$.

An equivalent definition is $X \vee Y = \{x \vee_p y, x \vee_s y : x \in X, y \in Y\}$ where $\vee_p$ and $\vee_s$ are the parallel- and strict-or on 3. Similarly $X \wedge Y$ is defined in terms of the parallel- and strict-and by $X \wedge Y = \{x \wedge_p y, x \wedge_s y : x \in X, y \in Y\}$.

For a sentence P this gives an associated transformation $Z_P^{P(3)}$ as in section 4, and the example in the same section shows that it is not continuous.

Let the least model of P in this logic be $M_1 = \mathrm{lfp}(Z_P)$ and its computable approximation $M_0 = Z_P \uparrow \omega$. We would now like to relate M_0 and M_1 to SLD-tree searching. For a given atom A, let $N_0(A)$ give the value of $t, t\bot, f, \bot, f\bot$ according to whether the set of SLD-trees for $P \cup \{\leftarrow A\}$ have property 1a,1b,2a,2b,2c in section 5. The relationship we seek is :

<u>Theorem 6.1</u> $M_0(A) = N_0(A)$ for all variable-free atoms A.

<u>Proof omitted</u>

7. Conclusions and further work

We have exhibited a way to construct models of definite clauses with respect to an arbitrary logic, and shown that a particular 3-valued logic subsumes the work of Apt, van Emden and Kowalski for discussing success and failure. Moreover, we arrive at a model theoretic characterization of non-termination. This subject is particularly important , not only because the theory of logic programming has ignored it , but also because it is very common for programs written without great appreciation of an implementation's evaluation strategy to loop unexpectedly, when the classical models give an answer. The question of termination has previously only been discussed relative to a particular (usually depth-first) evaluation strategy.

It is also pleasant to see how a single semantics can include the notion of termination, rather than having to construct independent termination proofs for Prolog programs.

The previous section provided a model-theoretic semantics which included the notions of guaranteed success or failure. Can a simple characterization of such clauses be found ? Is there a simple characterization of evaluation order in terms of a function ψ used there ? Is there a notion in logic programming corresponding to primitive recursion together with its guaranteed termination properties ?

Acknowledgments

I would like to thank Stuart Anderson, Krzysztof Apt and the referees for their comments on a draft of this paper. I gratefully acknowledge support from the British SERC at Edinburgh and from Chalmers and the Swedish STU.

References

[1] Apt, K.R. and van Emden, M.H.
"Contributions to the theory of logic programming"
JACM, Vol. 29, No. 3, July 1982.

[2] Clark, K.L.
"Negation as failure"
In "Logic and Data Bases", H. Gallaire and J. Minker (eds), 1978.

[3] van Emden, M.H. and Kowalski, R.A.
"The semantics of predicate logic as a programming language",
JACM Vol. 23, No. 3, Oct. 1976.

[4] Gordon, M.J., Milner, R. and Wadsworth, C.P.
"Edinburgh LCF"
Springer-Verlag "Lecture Notes in Computer Science", Vol. 78, 1979.

[5] Jones, N.D. and Mycroft, A.
"Stepwise development of operational and denotational semantics of Prolog"
DIKU report, Copenhagen University 1983, also submitted to "Science of Computer Programming".

[6] Kowalski, R.A.
"Predicate logic as a programming language"
In "Information processing 74", J. Rosenfeld (ed.), 1974.

[7] Lassez, J.L. and Maher, M.J.
"Optimal fixpoints of logic programs"
To appear in TCS, also presented at FST, Bangalore 1983.

[8] Lassez, J.L. and Maher, M.J.
"Closures and fairness in the semantics of predicate logic"
To appear in TCS, also internal report Melbourne University, Australia 1983.

[9] Plotkin, G.D.
"LCF considered as a programming language"
TCS Vol.5, 1976.

[10] Plotkin, G.D.
"A powerdomain construction", SIAM J. Comput., Vol. 5, 1976.

[11] Robinson, J.A.
"A machine-oriented logic based on the resolution principle",
JACM Vol. 12, No. 1, Jan. 1965.

[12] Robinson, J.A. and Sibert, E.E.
"LOGLISP - an alternative to PROLOG"
Technical Report 7-80, School of Comp. and Info. Sci., Syracuse University 1980

ALGEBRE DE MACHINES ET LOGIQUE TEMPORELLE

Max MICHEL

LCR/ENST/LITP-PARIS 7
212 Rue de Tolbiac 75013 PARIS

Résumé: Dans cet article, on étudie la relation qui existe entre la logique temporelle linéaire et la théorie des langages de processus concurrents. Pour ce faire, on propose une correspondance algébrique entre les systèmes de logique temporelle et un certain type de machines séquentielles non déterministes. Cette correspondance est établie par une méthode effective qui compose les machines comme sont composés les opérateurs temporels. On peut ainsi faire de la synthèse de processus à partir de formules de logique temporelle et résoudre des problèmes de logique par les algorithmes d'analyse de machines.

Abstract: This paper shows the relation between linear temporal logic and theory of languages of concurrent processes. To this purpose, we give an algebraic correspondence between temporal logic systems and some non deterministic sequential machines. This correpondence lies on an effective method which composes machines as temporal operators. So we can synthetise processes from temporal logic formulas and solve logic problems by algorithms applied to machines.

Remerciements: L'auteur remercie le Laboratoire de Monsieur G. RUGGIU [LCR Thomson-CSF] où il a effectué l'essentiel de ce travail. Il remercie P. ENJALBERT et K. APT de l'avoir introduit à la logique temporelle et par ailleurs, conseillé. Il remercie également Monique SAKOUN pour la dactylographie de cet article.

Introduction: L'analyse du parallélisme donne lieu actuellement à diverses modélisations: la logique temporelle introduite par Pnueli [PNU1] s'occupe d'exprimer les comportements de programmes parallèles et de faire des preuves; elle est bien adaptée pour exprimer, par exemple, la terminaison, l'équité, l'absence de blocage. Une autre école s'attache à développer la théorie des langages pour exprimer les problèmes de concurrence (Arnold, Nivat [A-N,NIV]): on parle de "langages de processus" et d'autres propriétés sont mises à jour: centralité, normalité.

La méthode exposée ici crée un lien étroit entre ces deux approches en identifiant les opérateurs de la logique temporelle linéaire à des machines séquentielles non déterministes. Une formule de logique temporelle est une composition de formules atomiques et d'opérateurs logiques: ces compositions reviennent à composer des machines. On peut ainsi répondre par l'analyse de machines à des problèmes premiers en logique: décider si un ensemble de formules a un modèle, et même mieux trouver tous les modèles (ce qui permet d'utiliser la logique temporelle pour spécifier des mécanismes de synchronisation [A-N] dans les langages de processus, voire même de synthétiser des programmes parallèles), s'assurer si une formule est satisfaite sur un modèle donné comme, par exemple, une R-structure de Clarke, Emerson, Sistla[CES,CS].

Il existait déjà des procédures de décision basées sur la méthode des tableaux ([BMP,CE,MW,WOL]) qui fournissent des automates comme modèles de formules. L'expression algébrique permet une meilleure modularité, donne des modèles complets et aide à mieux "voir", comme le montre ici l'utilisation de machines pour retrouver des résultats de complexité démontrés auparavant dans [CS].

Le corps de l'article comporte peu de démonstrations qui pourront être trouvées dans [MIC]. Il se compose d'un bref rappel de logique temporelle linéaire, de la définition de nos machines séquentielles non déterministes, qui diffèrent un peu de celles connues, de la façon dont ces machines peuvent "calculer" des formules de logique, de l'exposé des opérations que l'on effectue sur ces machines (produit, composition, complémentation) de l'utilisation de ces opérations pour montrer qu'il suffit de savoir calculer les opérateurs agissant sur des variables muettes pour pouvoir calculer toutes les formules. On finit par l'exemple de calcul de complexité.

I - LOGIQUE TEMPORELLE LINEAIRE PROPOSITIONNELLE

La *logique temporelle linéaire propositionnelle* (cf par exemple, [MP] est une extension de la logique propositionnelle classique où l'on adjoint aux opérateurs habituels (et: $\wedge$, ou: v, non: ~) des opérateurs temporels; les modèles M sur lesquels on raisonne sont des suites infinies de valuation sur des propositions atomiques $\{q_1,\ldots,q_n\}$. (Intuitivement on sait ce qui est vrai ou faux à une date t). Si une formule F est vraie à une date t dans le modèle M, on dit que M valide F à t et on note: $M, t \models F$. Les opérateurs les plus utilisés ont la sémantique suivante :

$M,t \models \Box F$ ssi F est vraie pour tout instant supérieur à t. $\Box$ est l'opérateur "toujours".
$M,t \models \Diamond F$ ssi F est vraie à un instant supérieur à t. <> est l'opérateur "au moins une fois" ("sometime"). Il est dual de $\Box$ ($\Diamond F \leftrightarrow \sim\Box\sim F$).
$M,t \models F_1\, U\, F_2$ ssi F_1 est vraie à partir de t jusqu'à un éventuel instant où F_2 l'est. U est l'opérateur "jusqu'à","Until". Il permet de redéfinir $\Box$.
$M,t \models oF$ ssi F est vraie à t+1: o est l'opérateur "prochaine fois".

Ces opérateurs portent tous sur le futur, on rencontre (moins souvent) des opérateurs qui portent sur le passé :

$M,t \models PF$ ssi F a été vraie à un instant inférieur à t.

Enfin Wolper ([WOL]) a étendu ces opérateurs temporels à des opérateurs "rationnels" définis par une grammaire linéaire à droite (on peut ainsi redéfinir $\Box$, U, o). Ces opérateurs portent sur le futur. Nous définissons ainsi l'opérateur A d'arité 3:

$M,t \models A(F_1, F_2, F_3)$ ssi à partir de t, F_1 et F_2 sont vraies en alternance jusqu'à ce que F_3 soit vraie.

Cet exemple est un peu gratuit mais se prête bien à illustration. L'opérateur dual de A, A': $(A'(F_1, F_2, F_3) \leftrightarrow \sim A(\sim F_1, \sim F_2, \sim F_3))$ dit que F_3 est vraie jusqu'à ce qu'on finisse par observer F_1 vraie et F_2 vraie à des instants dont la différence est paire, ou deux fois F_1 vraie ou deux fois F_2 vraie à des instants dont la différence est impaire.

Si Val_n est l'ensemble des valuations sur des propositions atomiques $\{q_1,\ldots,q_n\}$, un modèle M est un mot infini sur Val_n; et si F est une formule de logique temporelle, elle associe à M le mot infini des "Vrai" ou des "Faux" selon que F est vraie ou fausse à l'instant considéré: elle peut être vue comme une fonction de $(Val_n)^\omega$ dans 2^ω (2 = {Vrai, Faux}): en théorie des langages, les objets susceptibles de calculer ces fonctions sont les machines. Nous allons maintenant les introduire.

II - DEFINITION DES MACHINES SEQUENTIELLES NON DETERMINISTES

Nous appelerons *machine séquentielle non déterministe* sur un alphabet d'entrée Σ et un alphabet de message Γ (en abrégé machine sur Σ, Γ) un objet M constitué de :

1) un ensemble de noeuds N
2) un ensemble d'arcs A: chaque arc a une source: source (a) et un but: but (a) dans N. Il peut y avoir plusieurs arcs entre deux noeuds.
3) une application P de A dans $P(\Sigma)$ (ensemble des parties de l'alphabet d'entrée) qui donne la condition de passage P(a) sur a.

4) une application m de A dans Γ qui donne le message m(a) émis par l'arc a.
5) une partie D de N de noeuds initiaux.
6) un ensemble I de parties de A (chacune définit un sous-graphe partiel de (N,A) dit *graphe instable*).

On notera la machine M = < N, A, P, m, D, I > et on supposera N, A, Σ finis.

Intuitivement une machine effectue un calcul sur un mot infini sur Σ en lisant ce mot et en émettant au fur et à mesure les messages émis par les arcs parcourus.

Plus précisément, pour un mot $s = \sigma_0 \sigma_1 \ldots \sigma_n \ldots$, élément de Σ^ω, on appellera *parcours* p de s sur la machine M une suite infinie d'arcs $a_0 a_1 \ldots a_n \ldots$ telle que:

1) Pour tout entier i: $\sigma_i \in P(a_i)$ (On vérifie la condition de passage).
2) source (a_i) = but (a_{i-1}) pour $i \geq 1$ (On transite par un noeud).
3) source $(a_0) \in D$. (On part d'un noeud initial).
4) Pour tout graphe instable G et tout entier i, si a_i est dans G, il existe j plus grand que i tel que a_j n'est pas dans G (On ne reste pas prisonnier dans un graphe instable).

Le *message émis* par le parcours p sera le mot de Γ^ω, $m(a_0)m(a_1)\ldots m(a_n)\ldots$ noté m(p) ou M(p).

On définit également le *parcours partiel* d'un mot s fini ou infini sur Σ comme une suite d'arcs vérifiant les conditions 1) et 2) et si s est infini 4).

On a choisi de prendre des machines légèrement différente des automates de Büchi ou des systèmes de transition de Nivat: l'utilisation de graphes instables au lieu d'un ensemble de noeuds dans lequel on doit passer infiniment souvent se prête mieux aux opérations algébriques que nous définirons et celle de conditions de passage au lieu d'une simple lettre s'adapte mieux à la logique: en effet si Σ est Val_n, une partie de Σ n'est autre qu'une formule de la logique propositionnelle classique. Cependant on montre que ces machines ont la même puissance de calcul.

M définit une *ω-relation rationnelle* R_M entre mots infinis de Σ et de Γ ainsi:

$R_M(s,g)$ si et seulement si il existe un parcours de s sur M tel que g = M(p).

Le graphe de R_M est une partie de $\Sigma^\omega \times \Gamma^\omega$ (ou $(\Sigma \times \Gamma)^\omega$) et est un langage de mots infinis sur $\Sigma \times \Gamma$, qu'on appelle *langage* accepté par M: L(M). On définit également le *langage de parcours* de M comme le langage rationnel des mots sur Σ qui ont au moins un parcours sur M: on le note $L_p(M)$. Deux machines sont dites *équivalentes* si elles ont le même langage. Nous allons maintenant particulariser certaines de ces machines.

III - MACHINES A FORMULES

On a vu au I comment une formule de logique temporelle pouvait être associée à une fonction rationnelle: on cherche à calculer cette fonction par une machine. Mais calculer toute la fonction est souvent compliqué ou inutile: on va calculer des approximations qui seront des relations rationnelles. Les théorèmes du V permettront à partir d'une approximation de calculer vraiment la fonction, si besoin est. Nous donnons quelques définitions qui ne se limitent pas à la seule logique temporelle.

On se donne un alphabet d'entrée Σ, et on veut exprimer des faits sur Σ^ω. On a alors un ensemble fini $\mathcal{Q} = \{q_1,\ldots,q_n\}$ de formules atomiques et un alphabet OP d'opérateurs: chaque opérateur op a une arité finie ar(op). On appelle formules sur $\mathcal{Q}$,OP l'ensemble FOR des mots définis par induction par :

1) $\mathcal{Q} \subset$ FOR
2) Si $F_1,\ldots,F_n$ sont dans FOR et op est d'arité n $opF_1 \ldots F_n$ est dans FOR.

C'est une sémantique S qui définit la valeur de vérité d'une formule :

Pour chaque formule atomique q_i on a une application $S(q_i)$ de Σ dans 2 (2 est {Faux, Vrai}) et pour chaque opérateur op de OP une application S(op) de $(2^\omega)^{ar(op)}$

dans 2^ω. On définit par induction la valeur de vérité V(F) d'une formule :

V(F) est une application de $\Sigma^\omega \times \omega$ dans 2^ω; si s est un mot de Σ^ω et t un entier, on pourra noter $s,t \models F$ pour V(F)(s)(t) = Vrai et dire que s valide F en t, alors :

1) Si F est la formule atomique q_i: $s,t \models q_i$ ssi $S(q_i)(\sigma_t)$ = Vrai.

2) Si F = op F_1 .. F_n: $V(F)(s)(t) = (S(op)(V(F_1)(s),..,V(F_n)(s)))(t)$

On suppose que l'on dispose dans OP des opérateurs $\wedge,\vee,\sim$ et de leur sémantique traditionnelle. Soit Γ l'ensemble des parties finies de FOR. On appelle *machines à formules* pour Σ, FOR une machine sur Σ,Γ. Une telle machine est donc susceptible d'émettre à la fois plusieurs formules.

Intéressons-nous au cas d'une seule formule F: pour un mot s donné V(F)(s) est un mot de 2^ω, suite de Faux et de Vrai. Si on applique Γ sur 2 en envoyant un ensemble de formules sur Vrai seulement s'il contient F et si M est une machine pour FOR, elle définit une relation R(F) entre Σ^ω et 2^ω: (ici Faux signifie qu'on n'a pas trouvé la formule F, mais cela n'implique pas que l'on ait trouvé $\sim$F): R(F)(s) sera une approximation de V(F)(s). Pour cela on ordonne 2 par Faux < Vrai. On définit alors les classes de machines suivantes:

On suppose données une sémantique S, une machine M = $\langle N,A,P,m,D,I\rangle$ pour Σ,FOR. On dira qu'un parcours p émet F à l'instant t si F appartient à $m(p)_t$. Alors :

1) M sera dite *fidèle* ssi pour tout parcours p d'un mot s, et toute formule F, p émet F à t seulement si s valide F à t. Cela peut aussi se dire par V(F)(s) majore R(F)(s).

Dans la suite les machines seront implicitement fidèles.

2) M *reconnaît* la formule F ssi pour tout mot s et tout entier t où s valide F à t, il existe un parcours p qui émette F à t. Et cela veut dire que V(F)(s) est la borne supérieure de R(F)(s).

Donnons des exemples en logique temporelle: l'alphabet d'entrée Σ sera Val_n ensemble des valuations sur $\mathcal{Q} = \{q_1,..,q_n\}$, on notera $\bar{q}_i$ une lettre, dite conjuguée de q_i et on pourra voir $\bar{q}_i$ comme $\sim q_i$, Val_n sera alors simplement l'ensemble des parties de $\{q_1,..,q_n,\bar{q}_1,..,\bar{q}_n\}$ qui contiennent une et une seule des lettres q_i, $\bar{q}_i$; nous aurons également besoin de $Consis_n$ ensemble des parties qui ne contiennent pas simultanément q_i et $\bar{q}_i$. L'alphabet d'entrée sera Val_n et la sémantique S sera telle que $S(q_i)(\sigma)$ est Vrai ssi $q_i \in \sigma$. Les conditions de passage, partie de Val_n, peuvent se représenter comme des formules classiques sur $\mathcal{Q}$ et $(\wedge,\vee,\sim)$. Toutes les machines de la planche de figures (voir infra) sont fidèles et reconnaissent les formules qu'elles émettent.

On comprend comment on peut émettre sans risque une formule qui porte sur les valeurs futures du mot: par exemple pour la machine M_1, on voit que, un mot qui s'est engagé dans le noeud 2 ne peut manquer de satisfaire $q_1 \mathcal{U} q_2$: on joue sur le non-déterminisme et sur le fait qu'en arrivant sur un noeud, les choix qui se présentent pour en sortir peuvent ne pas recouvrir Val_n. (Les machines ne sont pas "complètes" au sens de la théorie des automates). C'est ce qui nous permet d'avoir des opérateurs avec anticipation et c'est là la différence avec les machines déterministes étudiées par exemple dans Trakhtenbrodt et Barzdin' [T-B].

Nous allons maintenant définir des classes de machines plus performants:

3) M est *réentrante* par rapport à une formule F ssi tout mot s qui valide au moins une fois F a un parcours p sur M qui émet F chaque fois que s la valide: autrement dit R(F)(s) contient V(F)(s) qui en est son plus grand élément. Le mot "réentrant" signifie que la machine est capable de reprendre au début les séquences de vérifications qui correspondent à l'émission d'un F, tout en poursuivant celles déjà en cours.

· Exemple: (cf planche). Les machines M_1 et $M_{\bar{A}}$ ne sont pas réentrantes: une fois qu'un parcours nous a mené au noeud final, on ne peut plus déclencher l'émission pourtant éventuellement valide de la formule. Les autres machines sont réentrantes.

4) M est *précise* par rapport à une formule F ssi tout mot s qui valide au moins une fois F a un parcours sur M et tout parcours p de s émet F chaque fois que s la valide: autrement dit R(F)(s) est réduit à V(F)(s); une machine précise réalise la

FIGURES

Les étiquettes des arcs sont les conditions de passage ou les messages (encadrés).
Un message dans un noeud est émis par tous les arcs qui en sont issus.
Aucune inscription indique un passage libre ou un message vide.
Si seuls certains noeuds d'une machine sont initiaux, ils sont marqués d'un $>$.
Ici, les machines ont au plus un graphe instable représenté en pointillé.

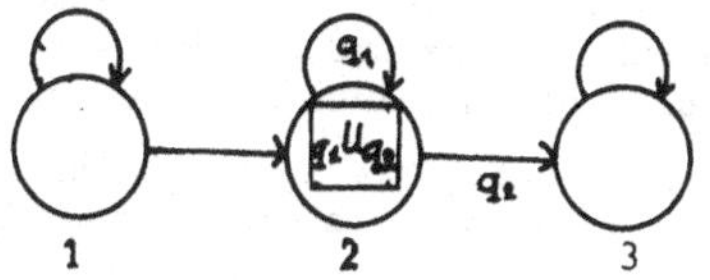

M_1

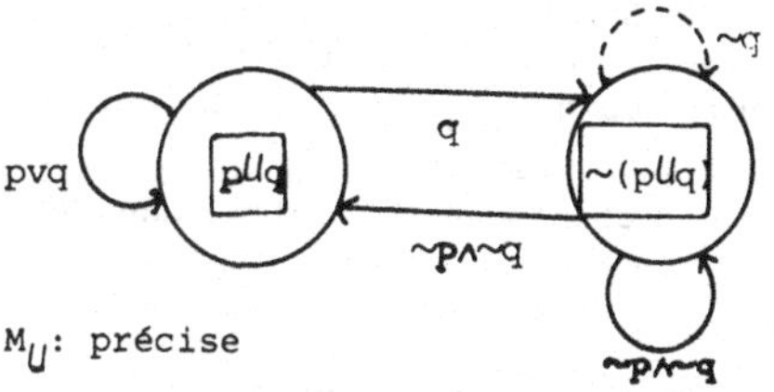

M_U: précise

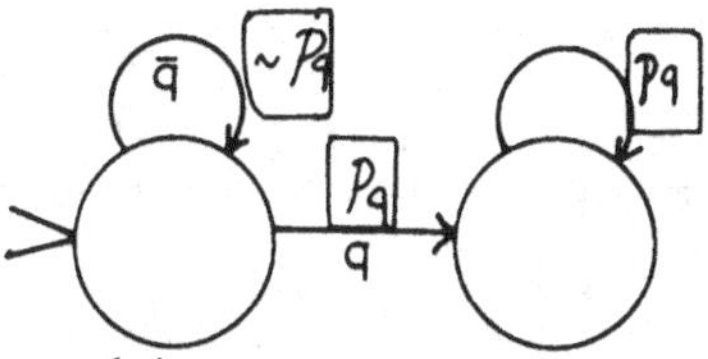

M_P : précise

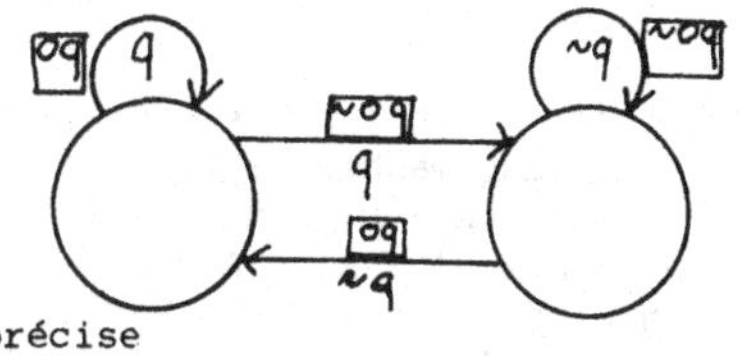

M_O: précise

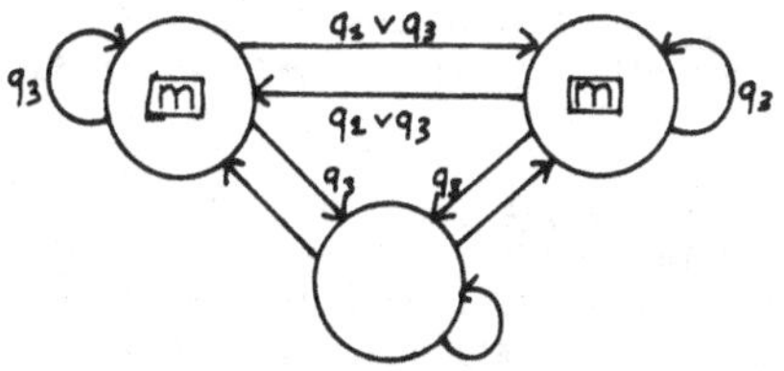

M_A : réentrante, m est $A(q_1,q_2,q_3)$

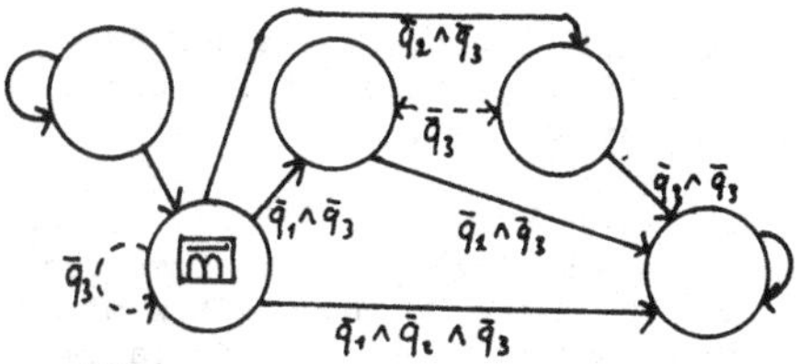

$M_{\bar{A}}$: $\bar{m}$ est $\sim A$ (q_1,q_2,q_3)

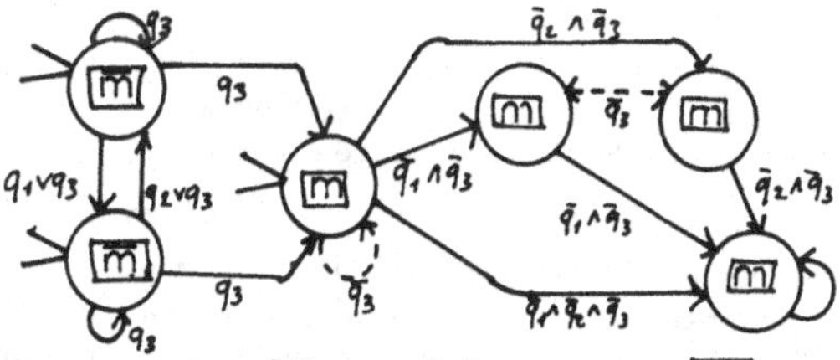

M_ξ : précise m est: $P{\sim}A(q_1,q_2,q_3)$ $\bar{m}$: $\sim m$

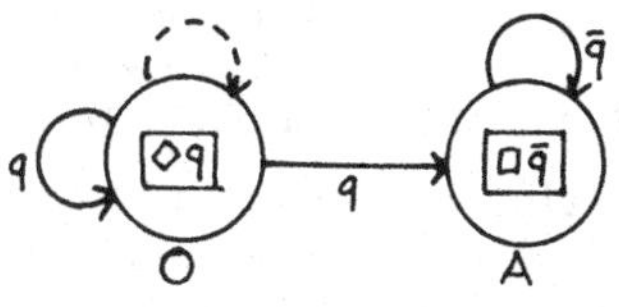

$M_{<>}$: précise

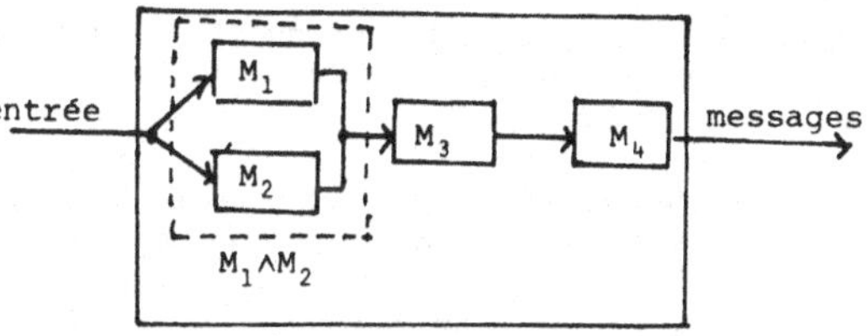

Réseau : $(M_1 \wedge M_2) M_3 M_4$

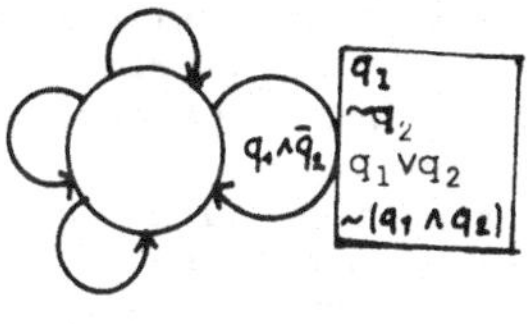

Bool : précise (1 seul arc en détail)

fonction définie par F.

Exemple: Les machines $M_{\mathcal{U}}$, M_o, $M_{<>}$, M_P, M_f sont précises. $M_{\mathcal{A}}$ qui est réentrante n'est pas précise.

5) M est *totale* si tout mot peut la parcourir: $L_p(M) = \Sigma^{\omega}$.

Notre système va nous permettre de construire des machines aussi bonnes que l'on veut à partir de machines de base, qui reconnaissent les opérateurs et d'opérations de compositions algébriques. Nous allons définir la machine de structure d'un opérateur.

Etant donné un opérateur n-aire op, $q_1,\ldots,q_n$ n lettres, $\bar{q}_1,\ldots,\bar{q}_n$ leurs conjuguées. Nous avons défini l'alphabet Val_n. $\mathcal{Q} = \{q_1,\ldots,q_n\}$ étant pris comme formules atomiques, une *machine de structure* pour l'opérateur op sera une machine sur Val_n qui reconnaît op $q_1 \ldots q_n$. Les macnines de la planche sont des machines de structure.

Il nous reste à parler des opérations: nous allons étendre aux mots infinis, celles des machines séquentielles dans le cas de mots finis (cf. par exemple, Eilenberg).

IV - OPERATIONS SUR LES MACHINES

i) *Produit*: si M = < N,A,P,m,D,I > est une machine sur Σ,Γ et M'= < N',A',P',m', D',I'> est une machine sur Σ',Γ', on définit une machine produit M" = < N",A",P",m", D",I">, notée M x M', sur $\Sigma \times \Sigma'$, $\Gamma \times \Gamma'$ par:

$N" = N \times N'$; $A" = A \times A'$, $P" = P \times P'$; $m" = m \times m'$; $D" = D \times D'$.

Et si π et π' sont les projections canoniques de A" sur A et A', I" est $\pi^{-1}(I) \times A' \cup A \times \pi'^{-1}(I')$: l'image réciproque par π d'un graphe instable de M est un graphe instable de M x M', de même pour π'.

Proposition 1: La relation associée à M x M' est le produit des relations associés à M et à M'. Plus précisément les parcours sur M x M' sont exactement les produits des parcours sur M et M'.

ii) *Composition*: si $\Gamma = \Sigma'$, la machine M" = < N", A", P", m", D", I" > sur Σ, Γ' déduite de M x M' en prenant comme arcs: $A" = \{(a,a')/m(a) \in P'(a')\}$ comme graphes instables la trace de ceux de M x M' sur A"; comme condition de passage $P"(a,a')=P(a)$ et $m"(a,a')=m'(a')$, est appelée la composée de M et de M', elle est notée MM'.

Proposition 2: La relation associée à MM' est la composée des relations associées à M et à M'. Les parcours sur MM' sont de la forme p x p' où p est un parcours de s sur M et p' un parcours de m(s) sur M'.

iii) *Produit restreint* : si $\Sigma = \Sigma'$ la machine M" = < N", A", P", m", D", I") sur Σ, $\Gamma \times \Gamma'$ restreinte de M x M' en prenant comme condition de passage $P"(a,a') = P(a) \cap P'(a')$, est appelée le produit restreint de M et M' et notée $M \wedge M'$.

Proposition 3: s est en relation avec (g,g') par $M \wedge M'$ ssi s est relation avec g pour M et g' pour M'. Les parcours sur $M \wedge M'$ sont les produits des parcours sur M et M'd'un m

Ces produits présentent de bonnes propriétés naturelles comme l'associativité que nous utiliserons sans justification: on notera $M_1 \wedge \ldots \wedge M_q$ le produit restreint de q machines.

Si φ est une relation alphabétique entre Σ et Γ, la relation qu'elle induit entre Σ^{ω} et Γ^{ω} est décrite simplement par la machine à un noeud noté aussi φ:

$\varphi = < \{n_o\},\Gamma,P,m,\{n_o\}, \emptyset >$ avec $P(\gamma) = \varphi^{-1}(\gamma)$; $m(\gamma) = \gamma$.

On peut se servir de ces opérations pour "éclater" les divers composants d'une machine M, on peut ainsi montrer que M est équivalent à une machine $(id_{\Sigma})M_s(id_{\Gamma} X \alpha M_n)$ où M_s a la même architecture que M mais sans graphe instable et a un message plus riche: elle signale quel arc elle emprunte; id_{Σ} et id_{Γ} sont des fonctions identités; α est la relation d'appartenance entre éléments de A et I; et M_n est une machine qui ne dépend que de n(cardinal de I) et n'a qu'un seul graphe instable: on montre ainsi que nos machines peuvent se ramener à des automates de Büchi, tout en séparant le comportement local de la machine de son comportement infini.

On trouve sur la planche l'exemple d'un petit réseau où deux machines M_1 et M_2 lisent le mot d'entrée, communiquent leur résultat à M_3 qui passe le sien à M_4 qui émet le message: la machine résultante est donc : $(M_1 \wedge M_2)M_3M_4$.

iv) Certains problèmes de logique (décidabilité, satisfaisabilité) vont se ramener à savoir si certaines machines ont un langage vide ou non. Il est d'autre part très intéressant de réduire une machine à une machine équivalente plus petite. Aussi notons les deux propositions suivantes :

Proposition 4: Il existe un algorithme (simple) qui ramène une machine M à une machine équivalente M_R telle que tout arc a une condition de passage non vide, tout noeud n est accessible d'un noeud initial et a un successeur et pour tout graphe instable G, n est coaccessible à un noeud source d'un arc qui n'est pas dans G. M_R sera dite réduite.

Proposition 5: Si M est une machine réduite et s un mot fini sur Σ, p un parcours partiel de s, on peut énumérer les mots finis d et infinis s', leurs parcours partiels q et p', tels que qpp' soit un parcours (ou un parcours partiel) de dss'. On sait décider si un parcours partiel vient d'un parcours. Et en particulier L(M) est vide si et seulement si M est vide.

v) Enfin nous aurons besoin du complémentaire $L(M)^c$ de L(M) dans $(\Sigma\times\Gamma)^\omega$. D'après le théorème de Büchi-Mac Neughton, $L(M)^c$ est un ω-langage rationnel, reconnaissable par un automate de Büchi. L'auteur a trouvé une construction de ce complémentaire, peut-être plus concise, qui se présente comme le produit d'une machine "locale" (sans graphes instables) et d'une machine qui surveille le comportement infini ([MIC]).

Nous pouvons maintenant construire les machines à formules à partir des machines d'opérateurs.

V - COMPOSITION DES MACHINES

Il est immédiat de reconnaître les formules atomiques, ce sont des fonctions alphabétiques et la lecture d'une lettre de Σ permet d'émettre sans erreur q_i ou $\sim q_i$. Si la connaissance de machines qui reconnaissent $F_1, \ldots, F_n$ et d'une machine M_{op} qui reconnaît op $q_1 \ldots q_n$ permet de reconnaître op $F_1 \ldots F_n$, on voit par induction qu'il suffit d'avoir les machines de structure pour tout calculer.

Intuitivement on fera tourner simultanément les machines qui donnent $F_1, \ldots, F_n$, $\sim F_1, \ldots, \sim F_n$; on se servira des F_i ou $\sim F_i$ émis pour faire tourner M_{op} en faisant correspondre F_i à q_i et $\sim F_i$ à $\bar{q}_i$ et là où on émettait op $q_1 \ldots q_n$ on pourra émettre op $F_1 \ldots F_n$. Seulement il va être très avantageux d'être plus précis: l'alphabet d'entrée d'une machine de structure étant Val_n il faudrait à chaque instant fournir l'un des deux: F_i, $\sim F_i$, ce qui peut être inutile et coûteux: (pour satisfaire $F_1 \vee F_2$ si F_1 est vrai, on n'a pas à se soucier de la valeur de F_2). Aussi on étend l'alphabet d'entrée de M_{op} à $Consis_n$ (ensemble des parties de $\{q_1, \ldots, q_n, \bar{q}_1, \ldots, \bar{q}_n\}$ qui ne contiennent pas simultanément q_i ou $\bar{q}_i$) en modifiant seulement la condition de passage P de M_{op} en P': si a est un arc de M_{op}, P(a) est un ensemble d'éléments de Val_n et P'(a) sera l'ensemble des éléments de $Consis_n$ dont tous les majorants dans Val_n sont dans P(a); P' peut ainsi être défini par ses plus petits éléments Q(a) ce qui donne la *condition de passage réduite* Q(a): un élément de $Consis_n$ vérifie P'(a) ssi il est plus grand qu'un élément de Q(a).

On dit alors que Q demande une lettre x (q_i ou $\bar{q}_i$) si pour un arc a, Q(a) a un élément qui contient x et que Q demande fortement x si x apparait dans Q(a) et Q(a') et que l'on peut aller de a à a'. Si x est demandé mais pas fortement on dit que x est faiblement demandé. Par exemple la machine $M_{\mathcal{D}}$ demande fortement $\bar{q}$ et faiblement q. Si une lettre n'est pas demandée, on n'a pas à savoir reconnaitre la formule correspondante, et si elle est faiblement demandée, comme, lors d'un parcours sur M_{op}, on la rencontre au plus une fois, il n'est pas nécessaire de la reconnaitre de façon réentrante.

Il nous faut définir pour des raisons techniques des critères de reconnaissance qui parle de plusieurs formules de FOR à la fois: on dit qu'une machine M est *efficace* par rapport à (FO_u, FO_r) où FO_u (u pour unique) et FO_r (r pour réentrant) sont des ensembles de formules, si pour tout mot s de Σ^ω, toute fonction partielle d de FO_u dans ω telle que s valide F en d(F) il existe un parcours de s sur M qui émet F à d(F) et chaque formule de FO_r chaque fois que s la valide (sauf peut-être si d est vide et s ne valide jamais aucune formule de FO_r). La notion de précision se généralise sans peine à un ensemble de formules FO_p.

On énonce maintenant les théorèmes qui permettent de calculer op $F_1 \ldots F_n$ à partir de op $q_1 \ldots q_n$ et de $F_1 \ldots F_n$, en définissant au passage des applications alphabétiques qui permettent d'ajuster les alphabets d'entrées des machines.

L'application d'union U_r de Γ^r dans Γ est: $U_r(\gamma_1,\ldots,\gamma_r) = \gamma_1 \cup \ldots \cup \gamma_r$.

__Théorème 1:__ Si $M_1,\ldots,M_r$ sont r machines, qui ont le même langage de parcours L_p, si M_i reconnaît efficacement (FO_u^i, FO_r^i) et précisément FO_p^i alors ($M_1 \wedge \ldots \wedge M_r$) U_r reconnaît efficacement ($FO_u^1 \cup \ldots \cup FO_u^r$, $FO_r^1 \cup \ldots \cup FO_r^r$) et précisément $FO_p^1 \cup \ldots \cup FO_p^r$. Son langage de parcours est L_p.

Soient op un opérateur n-aire, M_{op} une machine de structure pour op, Q la condition de passage réduite de M_{op}, si $F_1 \ldots F_n$ sont n formules et $q_1,\ldots,q_n$ n lettres, on fait correspondre F_i à q_i et $\sim F_i$ à $\bar{q}_i$ et, on définit la fonction de transfert T de Γ dans $Consis_n$ telle que γ a une image ssi γ ne contient pas à la fois F_i et $\sim F_i$; et alors $q_i \in T(\gamma)$ ssi $F_i \in \gamma$ et $\bar{q}_i \in T(\gamma)$ ssi $\sim F_i \in \gamma$. On appelle FO_u l'ensemble des formules correspondant aux lettres faiblement demandées par Q et FO_r à celles fortement demandées. On a enfin une petite application de retour R qui traduit op $q_1 \ldots q_n$ en op $F_1 \ldots F_n$; et on énonce le théorème 2:

__Théorème 2:__ Si M est une machine totale, efficace pour (FO_u, FO_r) la machine $MTM_{op}R$ reconnaît {op $F_1 \ldots F_n$} et sera réentrante, précise ou totale selon que M_{op} l'est.

__Remarque:__ L'hypothèse que M est totale peut être levée facilement: elle ne sert que pour des opérateurs qui émettent Vrai à des instants fixes indépendants de $q_1,\ldots,q_n$. De plus on peut rendre une machine M totale en lui rajoutant un noeud isolé muni d'un seul arc qui n'émet rien: elle reste aussi efficace (mais n'est plus aussi précise).

__Exemple:__ On se sert des théorèmes 1 et 2 en cascade: essayons de reconnaitre la formule F: $P(\sim A(q_1, q_2, q_3))$; la machine M_P reconnait précisément Pq et $\sim P_q$ et demande fortement $\sim q(\bar{q})$ et faiblement q, on a donc besoin de la machine M_A qui reconnait de façon réentrante $A(q_1, q_2, q_3)$ et de la machine $M_{\bar{A}}$ qui reconnait simplement $\sim A(q_1, q_2, q_3)$, alors la machine $(M_A \wedge M_{\bar{A}})U_2TM_PR$ reconnait précisément F et $\sim F$: la machine M_f lui est équivalente et est obtenu à la main en appliquant ces théorèmes avec quelques précautions pour éviter de garder des noeuds inutiles.

Indiquons le principe de la démonstration: soit s un mot sur Σ^ω, on lui associe le mot g de Γ^ω $\gamma_0 \ldots \gamma_n \ldots$ où γ_t est l'ensemble des formules F telles que s valide F en t; transformons g par T, ce qui nous donne un mot g' de Val_n^ω, s validera op $F_1..F_n$ en t exactement quand g' validera op $q_1..q_n$, par définition de la valeur de vérité. Alors :

1) MTM_{op} R est fidèle: si p est un parcours de s sur M, M étant fidèle le message g" émis par MT est plus petit que g', et si p" est un parcours de g" sur M_{op}, p" sera aussi un parcours de g' sur M_{op} et op $q_1..q_n$ ne sera émis que lorsque op $F_1..F_n$ est valide. (On utilise ici la forme de la condition de passage réduite de M_{op} sur $Consis_n$)

2) MTM_{op} R reconnaît op $F_1..F_n$ aussi bien que M_{op} op$q_1..q_n$. Soit p' un parcours de g' sur M_{op}: d'après la façon dont M_{op} demande les lettres, il existe pour chaque lettre x faiblement demandée correspondant à la formule F_x au plus un instant t_x où x apparaît dans la condition de passage réduite $Q(p'(t_n))$. Soit p un parcours de s sur M qui émet F_x à t_x et les formules de FO_r chaque fois que possible: le mot MT(p)

peut prendre le parcours p'.

Quand on sait reconnaître une formule F, pour pouvoir la composer avec d'autres opérateurs il faut éventuellement avoir une machine réentrante ou calculer ~F. Or:

Théorème 3: Si une machine M reconnaît un ensemble de formule FO, il existe une machine M^r qui est réentrante pour FO.

La construction est un peu technique bien qu'un peu plus facile que celle du complémentaire, l'idée est de mener de front sur M tous les calculs possibles tout en évitant les chemins sans suite (on ne se contente pas de déterminiser M) ou qui restent dans les graphes partiels instables. A nouveau, on présente cette machine comme produit d'une machine locale et d'une machine qui surveille les comportements infinis. Cette construction est chère. Une machine simple à n noeuds aura une machine associée qui pourra avoir n^n noeuds.

Théorème 4: Si M est une machine qui reconnaît une formule F, on sait construire une machine M^c qui reconnaît ~F.

On peut expliciter une construction: on déploie partiellement M pour obtenir une machine qui sur tout parcours émette F au plus une fois, on lui applique l'algorithme de réentrance du théorème 3 puis on la complémente. Ceci est très cher. Pour une machine donnée, on peut souventfaire beaucoup mieux en essayant de comprendre ce qu'elle fait.

Théorème 5: Si M est une machine qui reconnaît une formule F, on peut construire une machine M^p qui reconnaît précisément (et totalement) F (et ~F).

Il suffit de reconnaître (F,~F) de façons réentrantes par une machine M puis de ne garder que les arcs qui émettent F ou ~F et pas les deux, ce qui peut être fait en composant M' par une machine filtre φ qui prend les messages de M' et ne laisse passer que ceux qui contiennent F ou ~F et pas les deux.

En combinant les théorèmes 1 à 5, on voit que ce système permet de traiter exactement tous les opérateurs définis ainsi: on se donne une machine M sur Val_n, {$\emptyset$, Vrai}; on voit Val_n comme $\{Vrai, Faux\}^n$ (en faisant correspondre Vrai sur la i-ème composante à q_i et Faux à $\overline{q}_i$) et on définit la sémantique de op par: si s est un mot de $(2^\omega)^n$ et donc de $(Val_n)^\omega$, S(op)(s) est Vrai à t si et seulement si il existe un parcours p de s sur M qui émet Vrai à t. Notre système traite ainsi tous les opérateurs rationnels (futurs ou non).

Exemple: Les opérateurs de Wolper [WOL] sont définis par une grammaire linéaire à droite et sont purement futurs: pour les reconnaitre simplement, il suffit de traduire cette grammaire par un automate fini avec un seul noeud initial (pour la traduction, pas au sens de nos machines), de faire émettre Vrai en sortant de ce noeud et de rajouter en amont du noeud initial un noeud d'attente du moment où l'opérateur sera satisfait: la machine M_1 (cf planche) reconnait $\mathcal{U}$ et correspond à la grammaire: $\mathcal{U} \to p\mathcal{U}$ $\quad \mathcal{U} \to q$.

Nous saurons donc reconnaitre une formule construite à partir de n'importe quel opérateur rationnel; ceci permet de répondre à de nombreuses questions: en réduisant la machine, on peut savoir si la formule est satisfaisable et mieux (cf. proposition 5) on peut engendrer exactement tous les modèles qui peuvent la valider, en choisissant éventuellement l'instant: par exemple, pour générer les mots qui valident la formule à l'origine on part d'un noeud initial qui l'émet, puis on parcourt la machine en s'attachant à vérifier les conditions de passage qui se présentent.

Pour vérifier une formule F de logique temporelle sur un programme P donné comme un automate à état fini (R-structures [CES,CS]) il suffit de voir P comme une machine qui émet au départ, de construire une machine qui reconnaît ~F et de vérifier que la machine ~F∧P se réduit à la machine vide. On ramène la vérification à une décision d'insatisfaisabilité de formule. La méthode est linéaire en la taille de P et exponentielle en la profondeur temporelle de la formule.

V - AUTRES EXEMPLES D'UTILISATION EN LOGIQUE TEMPORELLE: CALCUL DE COMPLEXITE

1) Les machines $M_{\mathcal{U}}$ et M_o représentées sur la planche sont précises: seul $M_{\mathcal{U}}$ a un graphe instable, réduit à un arc, et toutes deux ont deux noeuds: on peut donc reconnaître précisément une formule de logique temporelle linéaire sur □, <>, $\mathcal{U}$, o (□F est F$\mathcal{U}$ Faux) par une machine qui a au plus 2^n noeuds si n est le nombre d'opérateurs temporels de la formule et au plus m graphes instables où m est le nombre de $\mathcal{U}$, □, <>.

2) On peut prendre un autre alphabet d'entrée pour les machines à formules (pas pour les machines de structure) pour tenir compte de cas particulier: par exemple chez Manna et Wolper [M-W] une proposition atomique correspond à une action commune de deux processus, deux actions ne peuvent avoir lieu en même temps et on est amené à ne garder que les valuations qui valident une seule proposition.

3) Dans [CS] Clarke et Sistla ont évalué la complexité de la logique linéaire propositionnelle. Il nous semble que notre méthode permet de retrouver leurs résultats à moindre effort.

Par exemple ils montrent qu'en logique temporelle linéaire réduite aux opérateurs ∧, ∨, ~, □, <> une formule a un modèle ssi elle a un modèle dont la "taille" est linéaire en la longueur de la formule, ce qui permet de trouver une procédure de décision de complexité NP. Retrouvons ce résultat sur les modèles.

Pour reconnaître une telle formule F, on a besoin seulement de deux machines de base qui sont précises: $M_{<>}$ qui sert pour <>, □, ~□, ~◇, et Bool pour les opérateurs booléens classiques, plus quelques machines de transfert qui lisent les données ou qui adaptent le message d'une machine à l'entrée d'une autre machine (Par exemple si on a besoin de □F_1 il faut pour $M_{<>}$ faire correspondre F_1 à $\bar{q}$ et ~F_1 à q). A la formule F on associe un *réseau en arbre* de machines (qui correspond à l'analyse syntaxique de la formule): en négligeant les opérations de transfert, si M_{F_1} et M_{F_2} reconnaissant précisément F_1 et F_2: ($M_{F_1} \wedge M_{F_2}$) Bool reconnaîtra précisément, par exemple $F_1 \supset F_2$ et $M_{F_1}M_{\Box}$ □F_1. Le réseau de la planche en prenant $M_{<>}$ pour M_1, M_2, M_4 et Bool pour M_3 pourra reconnaitre □(□p ⊃ ◇q).

Cette représentation en réseau revient à ne pas effectuer les opérations algébriques: aussi un parcours d'un mot sur la machine résultante revient, en suivant la caractérisation des parcours d'un produit ou d'une composition, à faire tourner le réseau sans blocage: or, la machine Bool n'a qu'un seul noeud (un seul état) et ne se bloque jamais; la machine $M_{<>}$ a deux noeuds: un en amont O et un en aval A: la seule condition pour rester dans le noeud amont est de finir par faire un q, mais, pendant un temps fini il n'y a pas de condition; une fois arrivé dans le noeud aval on est obligé de faire $\bar{q}$ à jamais; et enfin il y a une seule transition possible de O vers A; le message émis ne dépend que du noeud source: <>q pour O, □$\bar{q}$ pour A: on va caractériser l'état du réseau E par la partie de l'ensemble des machines $M_{<>}$ du réseau qui sont dans le noeud aval; au sens de l'inclusion entre parties, E croît et finit donc par être stationnaire. L'état du réseau étant connu toutes les sous-formules de F qui sont précédés d'un □ ou d'un <> peuvent être réduites pour la transition à venir à Vrai ou Faux;(et si l'état est stationnaire, cette réduction est valable à jamais)et dans ce cas une sous-formule de F se réduit à une proposition booléenne sur les propositions atomiques d'entrée. On ramène alors le problème de pouvoir prolonger un parcours fini sur le réseau à un instant successif, à ce que la formule booléenne C_A qui correspond à la conjonction des sous-formules correspondant aux $\bar{q}$ des machines dans l'état A est satisfaisable. Pour que la machine puisse rester dans le même état infiniment, il faut pouvoir prendre l'arc q du noeud O des machines restées en amont infiniment souvent, mais ce peut-être à des instants différents pour chacune de ces machines; ainsi il suffit que si C_q est la formule booléenne correspondant à q, $C_A \wedge C_q$ soit satisfaisable et ceci pour chaque machine. Trouver un état qui peut être stationnaire du réseau revient donc à pouvoir satisfaire des formules de la logique propositionnelle classique.

Un modèle pour F est un mot qui peut parcourir le réseau et qui émet F à l'origine: pour générer un tel mot, on choisit un état E_0 à l'origine valide (une certaine C_A est satisfaite) qui émet F: si E_0 est un état qui peut être stationnaire, on a gagné; sinon il va falloir effectuer des transitions $0 \to A$ sur certaines machines $M_{<>}$; ce qui revient à satisfaire des conditions C_q (et à choisir $0 \to A$ au lieu de rester en 0), en plus de la condition C_A, et ce jusqu'à atteindre un état stationnaire: il est inutile de ne pas faire de transition, car si une transition $0 \to A$ est faisable à un instant et que l'on en effectue aucune, elle reste faisable à l'instant suivant; et donc si le réseau a m machines $M_{<>}$, il faut pouvoir atteindre un état stationnaire en au plus m transitions. On en conclut que si on a m symboles <> ou □ dans F, donc m machines $M_{<>}$ dans le réseau, la formule F a un modèle si et seulement si elle a un modèle qui, passé l'instant initial, déclenche n transitions $0 \to A$ sur n machines (en au plus n instants) et tourne ensuite périodiquement (en satisfaisant succesivement la condition C_q de chacune des m-n machines restées dans l'état 0) avec une période m-n: un tel modèle a une "taille" au plus 1+n+m-n = m+1.

CONCLUSION -

Nous avons proposé une nouvelle méthode qui établit une correspondance précise entre la logique temporelle et la théorie des automates: elle permet de traiter tous les opérateurs rationnels (On peut mélanger passé et futur; en remplaçant les noeuds initiaux par des graphes instables dans le passé on peut s'occuper de mots bi-infinis). La méthode des tableaux n'était pas aussi souple: elle ne permettait pas de générer les modèles aussi systématiquement; elle n'était pas modulaire et si elle esquissait un lien entre logique temporelle et automates, elle ne montrait pas comment un opérateur de logique temporelle linéaire est déjà lui-même une machine.

Nous essayons de rendre le système plus efficace: les calculs étant de nature exponentielle, il faut développer des méthodes, qui profitent de la modularité, pour ne pas effectuer les produits: c'est ce que suggère l'exemple des réseaux ci-dessus. D'autre part il est envisagé une implémentation qui pourra traiter des exemples plus conséquents: pour cela il faut naturellement étudier des principes de calcul plus fins que l'application immédiate des théorèmes.

Ici, on a peut être donné l'impression que les problèmes tenaient plus de la logique que de la théorie des langages; cependant l'approximation d'une fonction rationnelle par une relation, notre construction (non présentée ici) du complémentaire d'un langage ou d'une machine réentrante nous semblent être des prémisses intéressants d'études dans la théorie des automates finis. Et des progrès dans la minimisation d'un automate fini qui reconnaît un langage infini, question non encore totalement éclaircie, permettraient de pouvoir réduire au mieux nos machines.

Finalement, si la logique temporelle apparaît comme pouvant spécifier des automates, il serait interessant a contrario de développer d'autres métalangages que les grammaires pour définir les opérateurs et faire la synthèse de machines (comme cela existe dans le cas fini [T-B]).

BIBLIOGRAPHIE -

[A-N] A. ARNOLD et M. NIVAT: "Comportements de processus" Rapport LITP 82-12. Université de Paris VII. 1982.

[BMP] M. BEN ARI, Z. MANNA, A. PNUELI: "The Temporal Logic of Branching Time". Proceedings of the Eighth ACM Symposium on Principles of Programming Languages, Williamsburg, VA, 1981.

[CE] E.M. CLARKE, E.A. EMERSON: "Design and Synthesis of synchronisation skeleton using branching time temporal logic". Proceedings of Workshop on Logics of Programs, Lecture Note in Computer Science n° 131.

[CES] E.M. CLARKE, E.A. EMERSON, A.P. SISTLA: "Automatic Verification of Finite State Concurrent Systems Using Temporal Logic Specifications". A practical Approach". ACM 1983.

[CS] E.M. CLARKE, A.P. SISTLA: "The complexity of propositional linear temporal logics"; ACM 1982.

[EIL] EILENBERG: "Automata, Languages and Machines". Vol. A. Academic Press (1974).

[MIC] M. MICHEL: "Machines Algebra and Temporal Logic" (A paraître).

[MP] Z. MANNA et A. PNUELI: "Verification of concurrent Programs: The temporal framework" in the Correctness Problem in Computer Science (R.S. Boyer et J.S. Moore Eds.), International Lecture Series in C.S., AP Londres 1981.

[MW] Z. MANNA et P. WOLPER: "Synthesis of communicating processes from temporal logic specifications". Proceedings of Workshop Logics of Programs, Lecture Note in Computer Science n° 131.

[NIV] M. NIVAT: "Behaviours of synchronized systems of Processes", Rapport LITP 81-64. Université de Paris VII (1981).

[PNU1] A. PNUELI: "The Temporal Logic of Programs", Proc. 18th FOCS, Providence, RI, November 1977.

[PNU2] A. PNUELI: "The Temporal Semantics of Concurrent Programs", Proc. Symposium on Semantics of Concurrent Computations. Evian, France (1979). L.N.C.S. n° 70.

[T-B] TRAKHTENBRODT et BARZDIN': "Finite Automata" North Holland - American Elsevier (1973).

[WOL] P. WOLPER: "Temporal Logic can be more expressive", Proceedings of the Twenty-Second Symposium on Foundations of Computer Science, Nashville, TN, 1981.

ALGEBRAIC AND TOPOLOGICAL THEORY OF LANGUAGES AND COMPUTATION

Part I: Theorems for Arbitrary Languages Generalizing the Theorems of Eilenberg, Kleene, Schützenberger and Straubing

John Rhodes*
Department of Mathematics
University of California
Berkeley, CA 94720

The aims of this paper are several. One is to change the concept and eventually the definition of a computation in both mathematics and computer science in a manner that is simpler mathematically and more relevant computationally speaking. Another, and much more modest aim, which is accomplished within this paper, is to generalize the central results of finite-state, or regular, or recognizable languages to a much wider class of languages, and in cases, to arbitrary languages over finite alphabets.

Specifically, in Appendix I we generalize the "Stream Theorem" of Eilenberg to arbitrary languages (see [Ei] or [L]). In section II we generalize the Kleene Theorem, [B], to (not necessarily regular) torsion languages, the Schützenberger Theorem, [Ei], to (not necessarily regular) aperiodic languages, and the Straubing Theorem on regular-solvable languages to (not necessarily regular) torsion languages. See [L].

The powerful algebraic methods of finite-state languages are very well established, but the applicability of finite-state languages is too restrained to be of great value. An aim of these papers is to extend the powerful methods of finite-state languages to much wider classes of languages of importance in mathematics and computer science.

A standard algebraic way of generalizing finite is the concept of bounded torsion or torsion. An algebraic object is finite iff it has a finite number of elements, is torsion iff each of its elements has only a finite number of distinct powers, and is bounded-torsion iff there exists an integer $n \geq 1$ such that for all elements s, the number of distinct powers of s is $\leq n$. Around 1900 Burnside conjectured that all finitely generated bounded-torsion groups were finite. The Russians about seventy years later showed this to be false. See [Bu]. We use this direction of generalizing finite state languages to torsion languages, etc. in Sections 1 and 2.

In Section 3 we present two theorems on arbitrary languages over finite alphabets of the form of 'efficient approximations' of (membership in) an arbitrary language L over a finite alphabet by finite-state or regular languages.

Sections 2 and 3 lead to surprising connections with topology, [K], via metrics on automata. There are various well established machine models, [H-U], e.g. Turing machines, Push-Down-Automata (PDA), finite or infinite state sequential machines, etc. An intuitive way to view a machine model is that "it provides the glue which ties together the finite state machines". Precisely this means the machine model gives

*This research was supported by The National Science Foundation under grant number MCS83-01306. This is the introduction of a paper submitted to Information and Control.

rise to metrics on the set of all finite-state machines for which the Cauchy-sequences (when the space of finite-state machines is completed) converge to the various realizations of the machine models. Given a machine model (e.g. Turing Machine) for each integer n we can bound the amount of time or space available, or the value of any suitable function of time and space, which we will term "stuff". In almost all models (or we can take this as an Axiom of a machine model) any realization M of the machine model restricted to using $\leq n$ stuff is a finite state machine M_n. Thus in some sense $M_n \to M$ as $n \to \infty$ or $m(M_n, M) \to 0$ as $n \to \infty$, with m a suitable metric. See Section 1 and 2 and Discussion (1.15).

A closely related concept to the following. Suppose, for example, a Turing Machine T (with a specific program) is doing a computation C for (say) finite input strings from the finite set X, denoted X^*, i.e. the machine T is computing $c(w)$ for given input $w \in X^*$. Let $f(w)$ be some suitable measure of time/space required to compute $c(w)$ on T. This leads to the following filtration on X^*, namely $\{Ij\}$ with $I_j = \{w : f(w) \geq j\} = \{w$: on computing $c(w)$, T uses $\geq f(w)$ stuff$\}$. A filtration of X^* is by definition $\{I_j\}$ such that $I^* = I_0 \supseteq I_1 \supseteq \cdots \supseteq I_j \supseteq \cdots$, $\bigcap_j I_j = \emptyset$ where $j = 0,1,2,3, \cdots$. If $\forall j \; X^* I_j X^* \subseteq I_j$ we say $\{I_j\}$ is an ideal filtration which can be achieved by defining $I_j = \{w$: if $w = \alpha\beta\gamma$ for some α, β then $f(\gamma) \geq j\}$. Two filtrations $\{I_j\}$ and $\{J_i\}$ are considered equivalent iff each one refines the other; i.e. $\forall i \exists j$ so that $I_j \subseteq J_i$ and $\forall j \exists i$ so that $J_i \subseteq I_j$.

Now any filtration gives rise to a topology on $X^* \cup \{+\infty\}$ (see Section 1), namely strings $w_1, w_2, \cdots \to +\infty$ if $\forall i \exists j$ so that $\forall n \; w_{j+n} \in I_i$ (i.e., $I_j \cup \{+\infty\}$ is a neighborhood system for $+\infty$ and $\{w\}$ is open for $w \in X^*$). It is easy to see that two filtrations are equivalent iff they give rise to the same topology on X^*.

Now we want to say two computations C_1 and C_2 have the same idea (but maybe different systems of execution) iff the filtration (C_1) is equivalent to the filtratio (C_2). From the above we see this means given $w_1, w_2, w_3, \cdots$ then $f_1(w_1), f_1(w_2), f_1(w_3), \cdots \to +\infty$ iff $f_2(w_1), f_2(w_2), f_2(w_3), \cdots \to +\infty$ where $f_i(w_j)$ is the quantity of stuff (in some space time units) required to compute $c_i(w_j)$. Thus "idea" (C_1) = "idea" (C_2) iff the same sequences of input go to $+\infty$ for both C_1 and C_2.

The emphasis on the length of a string w, and the value $C(w)$ is not so important in a computation, but the amount of time/space, $f(w)$, required to compute $C(w)$ is important. E.g. in recognizing odd primes written in reverse order (i.e. each number written from right to left), if the first digit of an input is zero, then the number is even, and has time/space usage one independent of the length of the string.

If two computations have the same idea their speed (in f[time/space]) can vary greatly. The difference in speed can be measured using a function h where given C_1, C_2 leading to filtrations $\{I_j\}$ and $\{J_i\}$ respectively, we define $h(i) = j$ where j is minimal so that $I_j \subseteq J_i$ and then take some norm from classical analysis (ℓ_1, ℓ_2, exponential). This leads to hard analysis. See discussion (1.15) of Section 1 for further elaboration.

Another way to view the results of this paper is as a generalization of the "finiteness" of finite-state machines. We have already mentioned the algebraic generalization of "finite" to "torsion". The more classical generalizations of "finite" are "compact" or "complete". Let's consider languages $L \subseteq X^*$ where X is a finite alphabet. One could first consider finite number of strings. The first generalization is to regular or recognizable languages. Here L is recognizable iff Syn(L), the syntactic monoid of L (see Appendix 0) is a finite semigroup. Equivalently there exists a homomorphism $H:X^* \to S$ with S a finite semigroup, and a subset $Z \subseteq S$ such that $H^{-1}(Z) = L$. See Appendix 0 and Appendix I.

The next generalization is to make Syn(L) compact. The way to make $S = \mathrm{Syn}(L)$ compact when S is infinite is to give an ideal filtration $\{I_j\}$ on S ($\bigcap_j I_j = \emptyset$, $S = I_0 \supseteq I_1 \supseteq I_2 \supseteq \cdots$, $S^{\bullet} I_j S^{\bullet} \subseteq I_j$ where $S^{\bullet}$ denotes $S^{\bullet}$ with an identity adjoined if S does not have one) with each I_j cofinite (i.e. $\forall j S - I_j$ is finite). Then S is made compact by adding $+\infty$ and making the $I_j \cup \{+\infty\}$ a neighborhood system of $+\infty$ and all ordinary strings open. The expansion $\hat{S}^3$ of any finitely generated semigroup S which is introduced in Appendix IV is always compact in this sense and the projection $\eta:\hat{S}^3 \twoheadrightarrow S$ is a surmorphism which shows $\hat{S}^3$ is 'close' to S. See Theorem (4.7) of Appendix IV and the entire Section 4 of Appendix IV.

Hence we generalize from L finite to Syn(L) finite, to Syn(L) compact. The Theorems for Arbitrary Languages over finite alphabets contained in Section 3 use $\hat{S}^3$ to expand $S = \mathrm{Syn}(L)$ 'slightly' to make it compact, and then approximate the expansion 'rapidly' by recognizable languages L_j with $\mathrm{Syn}(L_j) = \hat{S}^3 - I_j$.

A related theme is the following. In Section 2 we introduce a complete metric on all sequential machines (with the finite state machines being dense). Gap theorems (e.g. P vs. NP vs. P-space) are strongly related to compactness and completeness. See Section 4.

Another way to look at this is that associativity is a more inclusive and important concept that decidability. Like the very early definitions of numbers in calculus (infinitesimal), the concept of decidability is uncovering an important concept but is currently technically imperfect. The definitions at the foundations are too complex. ('There exists a Turing Machine such that ...') and unweildly to deal with mathematically. Some topologies must be introduced on all proposed computations, (e.g. Turing Machines), and on all computations, etc. Then the 'correct' definition of 'decidable' is $\overline{\mathrm{dec}}$ where 'dec' is the current definition and $\overline{\mathrm{dec}}$ denotes the closure of dec in this introduced topology. In this topology 'dec' equals 'continuous' (inverse image of open sets are open), the mathematics becomes easier, etc. The boundary points are sometimes considered "decidable" sometimes "undecidable". We are mainly interested in speedy, state of the art computations. If C is 'undecidable' in the current sense, but all values of $C(n)$ for $0 \leq n \leq 2^k$ $k = 10^{100}$ are rapidly computable, then C is (to an engineer) computable. If you tell an engineer to use 'part a' if Fermats' theorem is true and use 'part b' if Fermats' theorem is false, and if both parts are inexpensive, the engineer tries both, and so to him it is computable.

This can also be said another way. Decidable properties, functions, computations, etc. all mean that eventually some assertion can be made about the limiting process; i.e., some simplifying condition is true about passing from computation or answers or information available at level j to level $j+1$. This is an 'oracle-like' condition on what 'eventually happens'. The usual definition of decidable is that the 'transformation rules' are 'uniform' in transition (general grammars). However many such simplification rules are possible, e.g. the finite state machines given by bounding the space/time by j all satisfy a fixed equation (equation on their semigroups). We use this in Section 1. In Section 2 we use a different condition. See definitions (2.2) - (2.4) and Discussion (2.6) of Section 2 which heuristically says that the limit is obtained uniformly with respect to a given filtration.

The boundary points of $\overline{\text{dec}}$ are undoubtedly tied up with P-space, infinite parallel vs. finite unbounded computations, Burnside problems, etc. We consider this in Parts II and III. When we understand all this it may well be that both Church's thesis and the P, NP, P-space conjectures are naive and false. We don't necessarily believe Church's thesis.

Associativity is deeply related to computability in the following manner. That 'information is available when you need it' or that 'information moves maturally with the process' is the most important thing in a computation. The associativity law $(a\cdot b)\cdot c = a\cdot(b\cdot c)$ expresses these above heuristic statements in a precise form.

To make this connection clearer, we state the following amazing theorem discovered by the author. Let X be any finite alphabet. Let $\equiv$ be any congruence on X^* (X^* equals all finite strings over X under concatenation). Thus $\equiv$ is an equivalence relation on X^* such that $\forall w_1, w_2, w_3, w_4 \in X^*$, $w_1 \equiv w_2$ and $w_3 \equiv w_4$ implies $w_1w_3 \equiv w_2w_4$. Congruence is a disguised form of the associative law since the equivalence classes have a natural (associative) multiplication imposed upon them $[w_1][w_2]$ $[w_1w_2]$ and $([w_1][w_2])[w_3] = [w_1]([w_2][w_3])$.

For $\alpha, w \in X^*$ write α/w if there exists $w_1, w_2 \in X^*$ such that $w_1\alpha w_2 = w$. We say α divides w. For arbitrary $w \in X^*$ let $\|w\|_{\equiv} = |\{\alpha/\equiv : \alpha/w\}|$ = the number of $\equiv$-distinct divisors of w. Here $\alpha/\equiv\, = [\alpha]$ is the equivalence class of $\equiv$ containing α. Now $\equiv$ may not be decidable or recursive or have any pleasant computable properties or logical properties, however; the amazing theorem is that for all non-negative integers n, $I_n = \{w : \|w\|_{\equiv} \geq n\}$ is a regular (i.e. finite-state computable) language.

Thus if the finite state machine M_n, with $\sigma(n)$ states, which computes membership in I_n has a small enough number of states $\sigma(n) \leq k_0$, then M_n can be practically built by engineers if $\equiv$ is not computable, etc.

In these papers we have used the associativity law as the guiding light as to what definitions, concepts and theorems to pursue. For example, we consider formula of the form $\forall w \exists n \forall q$: $\cdots$ (torsion) with $w \in X^*$, $n \in \mathbb{N} = \{0,1,2,\cdots\}$, $q \in$ states, or $\exists n \forall w \forall q$: ··· (bounded torsion), but not $\exists q$ ···, since we want the concept to depend only on the semigroup and not just on what is happening at one state.

Mathematics and combinatorics seem to differ in the following way. Their approach to analyzing situations take opposite directions. Given the objects of study (e.g. a language L), mathematics proceeds to study associated canonical objects (e.g. Syn(L) or $\mathfrak{A}(L)$, (see Appendix 0), and then embeds those (non-canonically) in some manner e.g. $S \to \hat{S}^3 \to$ embedding S or inside in universal object). Combinatorics first makes a non-canonical move (e.g. choose a (non-unique) Turing Machine to do a computation) and then does (maybe) canonical things. Mathematics works better, but takes more years to develop.

In Section 1 we do the 'baby theorems' for bounded-torsion to set the concepts with limited technical complications. In Section 2 we state the main theorems for torsion languages and introduce the important metric on sequential (finite or infinite) machines. In Section 3 we state the theorems for arbitrary languages over finite alphabets. In Section 4 we give a quick preview of the contents of future papers.

There are five appendices. In Appendix 0 we give terminology in semi-groups, syntatic monoids, etc. In Appendix 1, we generalize Eilenberg's 'Stream Theorem' to arbitrary languages. The Bool/Trans Axiom is the key! In Appendix II we supply the missing proofs for Sections 1 and 2. In Appendix III we give the proofs for Section 3, assuming Appendix IV. In Appendix IV we state and prove (or quote) all the necessary semigroup results.

One way to look at this paper is as a generalization of the Prime Decomposition Theorem (PDT) for finite semigroups, first proved by Krohn and the author, to (finitely generated) infinite semigroups.

Using associativity as the 'guiding light' leads not to Algebra (as one would expect) but to topology, metric spaces, compactness, and hard analysis (in interpolation theory)!

We have not been careful about the distinction between recognizable and rational. We believe the importance to be overstated. However, the interested reader can reconstruct the results using these distinctions. This is not difficult.

I want to thank J-C Birget for generous help and encouragement. Also thanks to E. Spanier. A very special debt is owed to Douglas Albert whose great knowledge of computer science and whose deep insights he has so generously shared. S. Lazarus read the entire manuscript. We thank her for her comments and help.

Preliminary versions of this paper were presented at the Berkeley Logic colloquium and to the Computer Science department at Stanford. Their responses were very encouraging.

REFERENCES

[A] Algebraic theory of Machines, Languages and Semigroups, ed. M.A. Arbib, Academic Press, N.Y., 1968.

[B] Berstel, J. Transductions and Content-Free Languages, Teubner Studienbucker Informatick, 1979.

[B-R] Birget, J-C and J. Rhodes, Almost Finite Expansions of Arbitrary Semigroups, Center for Pure and Applied Mathematics, U.C. Berkeley.

[Bu] Burnside Groups, ed. J.L. Menicke, Springer-Verlag Lecture Notes in Mathematics, #806, 1980.

[C+P] Clifford, A.H. and G.B. Preston, The Algebraic Theory of Semigroups, Vol. 1 and 2, American Mathematical Society, Mathematical Surveys, 7 1961 and 1967.

[Ei] Eilenberg, S., Automata, Languages and Machines, Vol. B, Academic Press, 1976

[H+U] Hopcroft, J. and J. Ullman, Formal Languages and Their Relation to Automata, Addison-Wesley, 1969.

[Gap] Karp, R. Some Bounds on the Storage Requirements of a Sequential Machines and Turing Machinery, 478-489. Journal of the Association for Computing Machines, Vol. 14, 1967.

[K] Kelley, J., General Topology, D. Van Nostrand, N.Y., 1955.

[L] Lallement, G., Semigroups and Combinatorial Applications, Wiley, N.Y. 1979.

[Mo] Moore, E.F., Sequential Machine: Selected Papers by Arthur W. Burke and Others, Addison-Wesley, Reading, MA 1964.

[I] Rhodes, J., Infinite Iteration of Matrix Semigroups Part I: Structure Theore for Torsion Semigroups, Center for Pure and Applied Mathematics, U.C. Berkele

[II] _________, Infinite Iteration of Matrix Semigroups Part II: Structure Theor for Arbitrary Semigroups up to Aperiodic Morphisms, Center for Pure and Applied Mathematics, U.C. Berkeley.

[St. 1] Straubing, H., Families of recognizable sets corresponding to certain varieti of finite monoids, Journal of Pure and Applied Algebra, Vol. 15, 305-318, 1979.

[St. 2] ___________, Aperiodic Homomorphisms and the Concatenation Product of Recognizable Sets, Journal of Pure and Applied Algebra, Vol. 15, 319-327, 1979.

A PROPERTY OF THREE-ELEMENT CODES

Juhani Karhumäki
Department of Mathematics
University of Turku
Turku Finland

ABSTRACT

Let w be a word and A a language of a finitely generated free monoid Σ^*. We say that w is ambiguously covered by A if there exist words α and β in A, with $\alpha \neq \beta$, such that $w \in \mathrm{pref}(\alpha A^+) \cap \mathrm{pref}(\beta A^+)$. We show that if A is a three-element code then any two words which are ambiguously covered by A are comparable, i.e., one of them is a prefix of another. This property is characteristic for three-element codes.

1. INTRODUCTION

The theory of codes was initiated by Schützenberger [5] in the 1950's. Since that the study of codes has been an active research area, especially in France, and a number of important and nice results have been achieved, cf. [1].

Codes can be viewed as basis of free monoids, or equivalently, as injective morphisms of free monoids. Therefore they constitute a well-motivated and fundamental part of formal language theory.

The purpose of this note is to provide a property which is characteristic to three-element codes but does not hold for arbitrary ones. In the case of two-element codes such a property is "aperiodicity". Indeed, a language $\{x,y\}$ over any alphabet is a code if and only if it is aperiodic, i.e., there does not exist a word p such that $\{x,y\} \subseteq p^*$. Consequently, any two-element code has a bounded delay in both directions, cf. [4].

A three-element code need not have a bounded delay as shown by the code $\{a,ab,bb\}$. Namely an infinite word ab^ω can be decoded in two different ways. Clearly, ab^ω is the only such word. We shall show that this is the case in general, too: If A is a three-element code without having a bounded delay, then there exists exactly one infinite word which can be decoded in two different ways.

Our result can be stated for bounded delay morphisms as well. Let A be a three-element code having a bounded delay. We say that a word w can be ambiguously covered by A if $w \in \text{pref}(\alpha A^+) \cap \text{pref}(\beta A^+)$ for some α and β in A with $\alpha \neq \beta$. Now, our result states that any two words w and w', which can be ambiguously covered by A, are comparable, i.e., one is a prefix of another.

Combining the above two cases we can say that if A is a three-element code, then among the words which can be ambiguously covered by A there exists a unique maximal one. This word is finite or infinite depending on whether or not A has a bounded delay.

Examples show that our result is not true for all codes, or even for all four-element codes.

2. PRELIMINARIES

We shall need only very basic notions of formal languages and free monoids, cf. [2], [3] or [4]. Mainly to fix our notation we want to specify the following.

A free monoid generated by an alphabet Σ is denoted by Σ^* and its identity by 1. We set $\Sigma^+ = \Sigma^* - \{1\}$. Elements of Σ^* are words. By an ω-word we mean an infinite word (from left to right), i.e., a mapping from the set of nonnegative integers into Σ. The set of all ω-words is denoted by Σ^ω. Similarly, we may define A^ω for each $A \subseteq \Sigma^+$.

For a word x we denote $|x|$ its length and by $\text{pref}_k(x)$, for $k \geq 0$, its prefix of the length k. If $|x| < k$, we set $\text{pref}_k(x) = x$. Let x and y be two words. We write $x < y$ if x is a prefix of y, and denote by xy^{-1} (resp. $y^{-1}x$) the right (resp. left) quotient of x by y. We say that two words x and y are <u>comparable</u> if either $x < y$ or $y < x$ holds. Finally, we use the notation $x \wedge y$ for the maximal common prefix of the words x and y. Since the operation $\wedge$ is associative no parentheses are needed and we can write, e.g., $x \wedge y \wedge z = x \wedge (y \wedge z)$. All the above notions can be defined, in a natural way, for words in $\Sigma^* \cup \Sigma^\omega$ as well.

We call subsets of Σ^* languages. For a language L the notation pref(L) refers to as the set of all prefixes of words in L. For two languages L and K their quotients LK^{-1} and $K^{-1}L$ are defined in a natural way via the quotients of words.

A language $C = \{ c_i \mid i \in I\} \subseteq \Sigma^*$ is a <u>code</u> if C^* is free with

C as a basis, or equivalently, if the morphism $h: I^* \to \Sigma^*$ defined by $h(i) = c_i$ is injective. We say that a code C has a bounded delay p if the following holds: For each words u and v in C^* and each α and β in C, if $\alpha u < \beta v$ and $|u| \geq p$, then necessarily $\alpha = \beta$. In particular, bounded delay 0 means that the code is a so-called prefix. Furthermore, we say that a code has a bounded delay if it has a bounded delay p for some $p \geq 0$.

We still define few technical notions. Let A be a language and w a word or an ω-word over a finite alphabet Σ. We say that A covers w if $w \in \mathrm{pref}(A^* \cup A^\omega)$. Moreover, we say that A covers ambiguously w if there exist words α and β in A, with $\alpha \neq \beta$, such that $w \in \mathrm{pref}(\alpha(A^* \cup A^\omega)) \cap \mathrm{pref}(\beta(A^* \cup A^\omega))$. Let $Amb(A)$ denote the set of all words ambiguously covered by A.

In the case when A is a code we define for each word w in Σ^* and each α in A the set

$$Cov_\alpha(w) = \{z \in \alpha A^+ \mid w \neq z,\ w < z \text{ and whenever } z = z'\beta \text{ with } z' \text{ in } A^+ \text{ and } \beta \text{ in } A, \text{ then } z' < w\}.$$

Elements in $Cov_\alpha(w)$ are called α-covers of w (with respect to A). By definition, if A has a bounded delay, then for all sufficiently long words w at most one of the sets $Cov_\alpha(w)$, where α ranges over A, is nonempty.

3. MAIN RESULT

Before stating our main result we take an example.

EXAMPLE 1. Let $A = \{ab, aba, babb\}$. Clearly, A is a code, in fact, it is a so-called suffix code. $Amb(A)$ can be determined from the following graph:

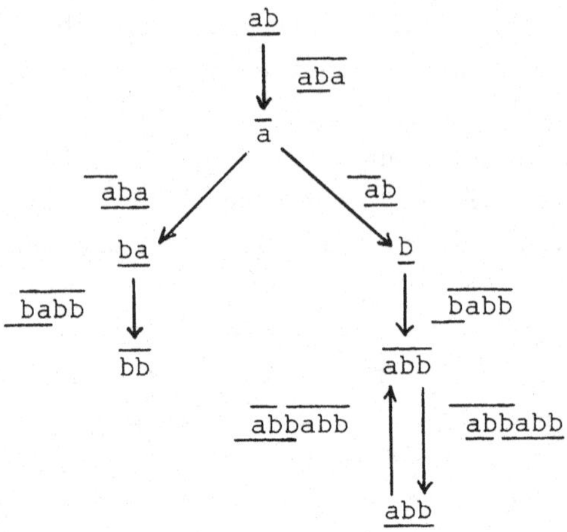

The nodes of the graph are suffixes of words in A provided with an upper or lower bar. The arrows of the graph are obtained as follows: First, from the node $\underline{ab}$ we have an arrow to $\overline{a}$ since $(ab)^{-1}aba = a$. Further, from a node $\overline{w}$ (resp. $\underline{w}$) we have an arrow to $\overline{w'}$ (resp. $\underline{w'}$) if there exists a word u in A^+ such that $w' = w^{-1}u$ and, moreover whenever $u = u'\alpha$ with α in A and u' in A^+, then $|u'| < |w|$.

We call a path in our graph nonterminal if it does not end at a node having no outcoming arrows. Then, clearly, *Amb*(A) contains all words which are obtained as products of nodes (without bars) corresponding to nonterminal paths of the graph, and it is contained in the set of all prefixes of words obtained in the same way by using all the paths of the graph. Therefore *Amb*(A) = $\text{pref}(abab(abb)^{\omega})$.

We proceed with our main result.

THEOREM 1. Let $A = \{\alpha, \beta, \gamma\}$ be a code without a bounded delay. Then there exists exactly one ω-word which can be covered ambiguously by A.

Proof. Let

$$p = \alpha^{\omega} \wedge \beta^{\omega} \wedge \gamma^{\omega} .$$

Since A is a code p is a finite word, in fact, $|p| \leq \min\{|\alpha\beta|, |\beta\gamma|, |\alpha\gamma|\} - 1$. It also follows that for each z in A^*, if $|z| \geq |p|$, then p is a prefix of z. We set

$$\overline{\alpha} = p^{-1}\alpha p$$
$$\overline{\beta} = p^{-1}\beta p$$
$$\overline{\gamma} = p^{-1}\gamma p .$$

Now, one of the words $\bar{\alpha}$, $\bar{\beta}$ and $\bar{\gamma}$ is a proper prefix of another, say $\bar{\beta} < \bar{\alpha}$ and $\bar{\alpha} \neq \bar{\beta}$. This is because A is a code without a bounded delay. Moreover, by the definition of p, we obtain

(1) $$\mathrm{pref}_1(\bar{\gamma}) \neq \mathrm{pref}_1(\bar{\alpha}) = \mathrm{pref}_1(\bar{\beta}) .$$

To prove the theorem it is enough to show that there exists at most one ω-word which has both α- and β-covers with respect to $\bar{A} = \{\bar{\alpha},\bar{\beta},\bar{\gamma}\}$, i.e., to show that

(2) $$card(\bar{\alpha}\bar{A}^{\omega} \cap \bar{\beta}\bar{A}^{\omega}) \leq 1 .$$

For simplicity we rename $\bar{x} = x$ for all $\bar{x}$ in $\bar{A}$.

We derive a contradiction from the following

Assumption. The inequality (2) does not hold.

This means that there exist two different ω-words in $\alpha A^{\omega} \cap \beta A^{\omega}$. Therefore there also exist two incomparable words u and v in Σ^+ such that both of the words

$$u \wedge v\ \mathrm{pref}_1((u \wedge v)^{-1}u) \quad \text{and}$$
$$u \wedge v\ \mathrm{pref}_1((u \wedge v)^{-1}v)$$

possess both α- and β-covers. We choose u and v in such a way that $u \wedge v$ is as short as possible. Clearly, $u \wedge v \neq 1$. Let the α- and β-covers of $u \wedge v\ \mathrm{pref}_1((u \wedge v)^{-1}u)$ (resp. $u \wedge v\ \mathrm{pref}_1((u \wedge v)^{-1}v)$)) be α_u and β_u (resp. α_v and β_v). These assumptions are illustrated in Figure 1.

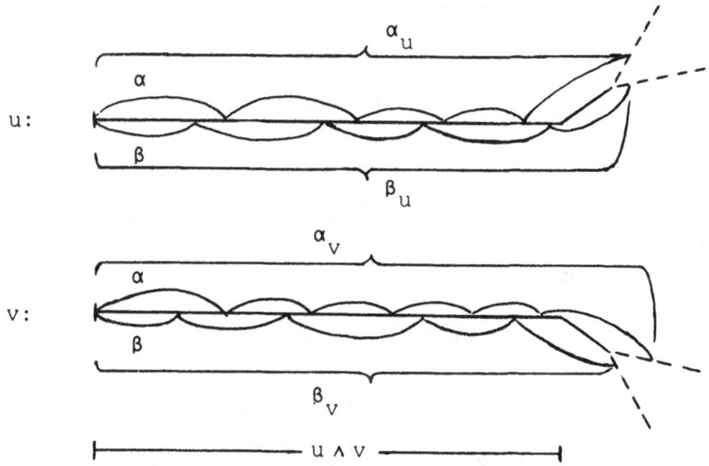

Figure 1

We identify A with the morphism $h\colon \{1,2,3\} \to \Sigma^*$ defined by $h(1) = \alpha$, $h(2) = \beta$ and $h(3) = \gamma$. By the injectivity of h we may assume that, e.g.,

$$u \wedge v \notin h(\mathrm{pref}(h^{-1}(\mathit{Cov}_{\alpha}(u \wedge v)))) \tag{3}$$

and, in particular,

$$\alpha_u \wedge \alpha_v \notin h(\mathrm{pref}(h^{-1}(\{\alpha_u,\alpha_v\}))) \; . \tag{4}$$

Observe here that although the case when α is replaced by β is not quite symmetric, since we already have $\beta < \alpha$, it can be handled in the very same way.

Next we start to work with the words α_u and α_v. We recall that

$$\begin{cases} \alpha_u \neq u \wedge v\ \mathrm{pref}_1((u \wedge v)^{-1}u) < \alpha_u \\ \alpha_v \neq u \wedge v\ \mathrm{pref}_1((u \wedge v)^{-1}v) < \alpha_v \end{cases} \tag{5}$$

and redraw the necessary parts of Figure 1:

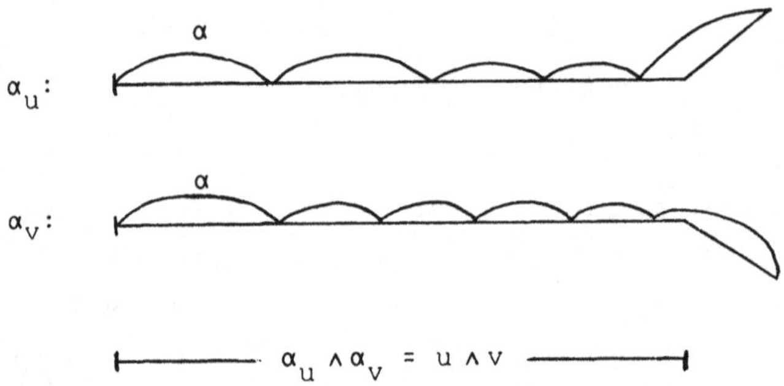

Figure 2

Let

$$\rho = h^{-1}(\alpha_u) \wedge h^{-1}(\alpha_v) \; .$$

Then it follows from (4) that

$$|\alpha| \leq |h(\rho)| < |\alpha_u \wedge \alpha_v|$$

and therefore, by (1) and the definition of ρ, we conclude that

$$h(\rho)^{-1}\alpha_u \in xA^* \quad \text{and}$$
$$h(\alpha)^{-1}\alpha_v \in yA^*$$

for some x and y in $\{\alpha,\beta\}$ with $x \neq y$. We assume that $x = \alpha$; the other possibility can be handled in the very same way. Consequently, we have the situation of the Figure 3:

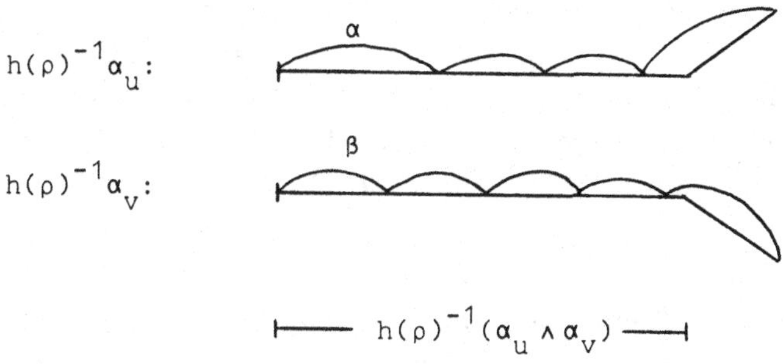

Figure 3

By the choice of u and v, i.e., by the minimality of $u \wedge v$, we conclude that $h(\rho)^{-1}(\alpha_u \wedge \alpha_v)$ is a prefix of $u \wedge v$, and therefore

(6) $$(h(\rho)^{-1}\alpha_x) \wedge (u \wedge v) = h(\rho)^{-1}(\alpha_u \wedge \alpha_v)$$

for some x in $\{u,v\}$. We assume that this holds for $x = v$; again the other possibility can be handled in the similar way.

Next we compare the prefixes of the words β_u (or β_v) and $h(\rho)^{-1}\alpha_v$, and we illustrate this in Figure 4:

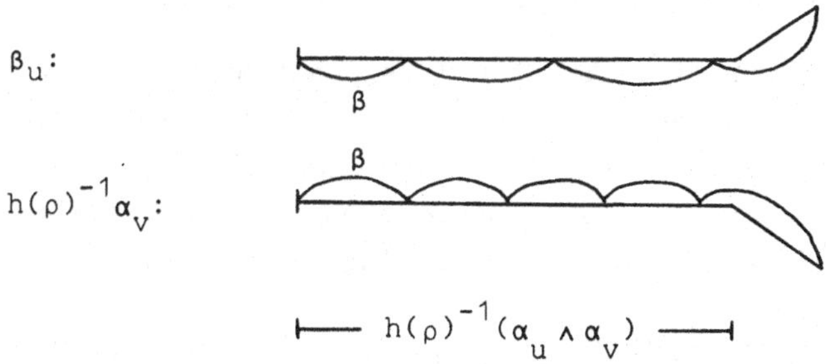

Figure 4

From (3) it follows (as drawn in Figure 4) that

(7) $$h(\rho)^{-1}(\alpha_u \wedge \alpha_v) \notin h(\mathrm{pref}(h^{-1}(\alpha_u))) \ .$$

We also have, by (4) and the choice of ρ, that

(8) $$h(\rho)^{-1}(\alpha_u \wedge \alpha_v) \notin h(\rho)^{-1}h(\mathrm{pref}(h^{-1}(\alpha_v))) .$$

Now we repeat with the pair $(\beta_u, h(\rho)^{-1}\alpha_v)$ all what we did with the pair (α_u,α_v). The situation of Figure 4 together with (7) and (8) is entirely analogous to that of Figure 2 together with (5). Consequently, we can derive a situation similar to that of Figure 2 and after that using the minimality of $u \wedge v$ we obtain a situation similar to Figure 4. Moreover, the analogies of the relations (7) and (8) remain. Indeed, if this would not be the case then we would obtain a contradiction to (3).

All in all we encounter again a situation similar to Figure 2 together with (5). After repeating the process a finite number of times we obtain, corresponding to the situation of Figure 3, that $\alpha \wedge \beta \neq \beta$, a contradiction to our Assumption.

Hence, our proof is complete.

4. CONCLUDING REMARKS

In the previous section we established a theorem for three-element codes having unbounded delay. Actually, the property of unbounded delay was not really needed so that the theorem can be reformulated as follows

THEOREM 2. For each three-element code A there exist words x and y in Σ^* such that $Amb(A) = \mathrm{pref}(xy^\omega)$. Moreover, y is empty if and only if A has a bounded delay.

Proof. The proof of Theorem 1 is applicable here without any essential changes. Indeed, what we needed in that proof was the existence of two incomparable (but not necessarily infinite) words u and v in $Amb(A)$. Beside this some obvious modification, which we leave to the reader, are needed at the beginning of the proof.

We conclude this paper with an example showing that the property of Theorem 1 (or Theorem 2) is characteristic for three-element codes and does not hold in general, or even for four-element codes.

EXAMPLE 2. We expand the code A of Example 1 to $A' = \{ab,aba,babb,bbabba\}$. Clearly, A' is still a code, in fact, it is also a suffix code. As in Example 1 $Amb(A')$ can be determined from the following graph, which shows that the structure of $Amb(A')$ is much more complicated than Theorem 2 allows.

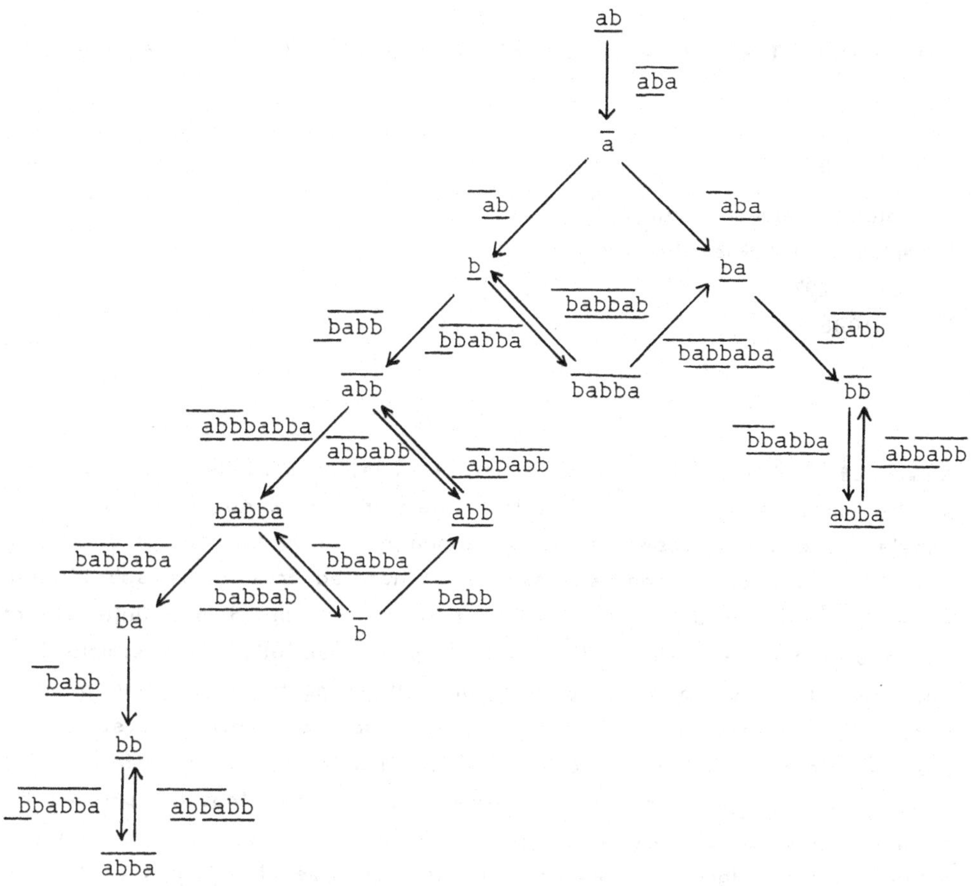

REFERENCES

[1] Berstel,J. and Perrin,D., The Theory of Codes, (to appear).

[2] Harrison,M., Introduction to Formal Language Theory, Addison-Wesley, Reading, Mass. (1978).

[3] Lothaire,M., Combinatorics on words, Addison-Wesley, Reading, Mass. (1983).

[4] Salomaa,A., Jewels of Formal Language Theory, Computer Science Press, Maryville (1981).

[5] Schützenberger,M.P., Une theorie algebraique du codage, Seminaire Dubreil-Pisot, annee 55-56, exp. n. 15 Inst. Henri Poincare, Paris (1956).

Polynomial Time Inference of General Pattern Languages

Klaus P. Jantke

Humboldt University Berlin
Department of Mathematics
P.O.Box 1297
DDD – 1086 Berlin

Abstract: Assume a finite alphabet of constant symbols and a disjoint infinite alphabet of variable symbols. A pattern p is a non-empty string of constant and variable symbols. The language L(p) is the set of all words over the alphabet of constant symbols generated from p by substituting some non-empty words for the variables in p. A sample S is a finite set of words over the same alphabet. A pattern p is descriptive of a sample S if and only if it is possible to generate all elements of S from p and, moreover, there is no other pattern q also able to generate S such that L(q) is a proper subset of L(p). The problem of finding a pattern being descriptive of a given sample is studied. It is known that the problem of finding a pattern of maximal length is NP-hard. Till now has be known a polynomial-time algorithm only for the special case of patterns containing only one variable symbol. The main result is a polynomial time algorithm constructing descriptive patterns of maximal length for the general case of patterns containing variable symbols from any finite set a priori fixed.

1. Introduction

The inductive inference of pattern languages has been introduced by D. ANGLUIN in her talk /1/ and her paper /2/. Inductive inference in general can be understood as a mathematical theory of learning processes based on incomplete information. We refer to the survey papers /3/ and /4/ in this regard. In particular, inductive inference turns out to be a well-founded basis for mathematical approaches to the automatic or interactive synthesis of programs from information which can be incomplete, in general. In the author's opinion, program synthesis is the most challenging and exciting application of inductive inference methods. The reader should consult SMITH's survey /8/ concerning the application of inductive inference ideas in the synthesis of LISP programs. SHINOHARA shows how to get theoretical results in the inductive inference of pattern languages /6/ and how to apply them to the design of a data entry system with a learning component /7/. NIX's paper /5/ is one more example of applied research in the field of inductive inference.

The objects of the inductive inference approach investigated here are so-called pattern languages. Assume a finite alphabet A of constant symbols and a disjoint finite set X of variable symbols. Without loss of generality we fix X to contain exactly the variables x_1 , x_2 , x_3 , ... Especially, X(m) denotes the set of elements x_1 , ... , x_m for an arbitrary positive integer m. A pattern is a non-empty string (or word) of constant and variable symbols. An m-variable pattern is a pattern with variables from X(m). The class of all patterns and the class of all m-variable patterns (for some positive integer m) are denoted by **P** and $\mathbf{P}_m$, respectively. Taking any pattern p from **P** we are interested in the language L(p) generated by p. A word w over the given alphabet A can be generated from p if and only if there is a certain substitution of non-empty words for all variable symbols occuring in p which yields w as a result. L(p) is the class of all words which can be generated from p. The reader is referred to /1/ and /2/ for some basic results concerning pattern languages which turn out to be quite different from formal languages in the sense of the CHOMSKY hierarchy.

Imagine that some pattern language is stepwise presented by samples exhausting the language in the limit. The inductive inference problem consists in constructing a pattern correctly generating the language which is presented step by step. Each recursive inductive inference strategy can work up only finitely many words to output a pattern as hypothesis. A pattern p is descriptive for a sample S (within a class **Q** of patterns) if and only if (1) it is consistent with S, i.e. each word of S can be generated from p, and (2) there is no other pattern q (which belongs to **Q**) being consistent with S which generates a language L(q) which is a proper subset of L(p). Obviously, a recursive method constructing descriptive patterns for arbitrary given samples forms an inductive inference strategy for pattern languages. It is conjectured that the construction of descriptive patterns is an NP-hard problem (see /2/), in general. Till now it has been found a polynomial time algorithm for constructing descriptive patterns only for the special case of one-variable patterns /2/. The task to find an inductive inference method of polynomial time complexity for m-variable pattern languages (for m = 2, 3, 4, ...) remained open. The present paper is aimed at solving this problem in general. The pattern languages investigated by SHINOHARA /6/ are quite different.

2. Basic Results in the Inductive Inference of Pattern Languages

First we recall ANGLUIN's basic results (see /2/) essential for classifying the power of our algorithm explained below.

Theorem 1 The problem of deciding whether w belongs to L(p) for an arbitrary word w over A and pattern p from **P** is NP-complete.

The next result is an immediate consequence of theorem 1.

Theorem 2 If P $\neq$ NP then there is no polynomial-time algorithm to solve the following problem: given a sample S, find a pattern p of maximum length that is descriptive of S.

Consequently, it raises the problem to characterize classes of patterns as large as possible such that for the concerning pattern languages there exists an inductive inference algorithm of polynomial time complexity. ANGLUIN constructed an inductive inference algorithm for one-variable pattern languages.

Theorem 3 There exists a polynomial time algorithm which given a sample S will output a one-variable pattern p that is descriptive of S within $\mathbf{P}_1$.

ANGLUIN introduces so-called pattern automata for proving this theorem. Each pattern automaton constructed from a given sample S accepts exactly all patterns which are consistent with S. She explains in /2/ how to generalize the concept of pattern automata. And she announces that in the case of m-variable pattern automata the bounding arguments no longer apply (see chapter 7 of /2/). We have developed a method to overcome the difficulties mentioned by ANGLUIN.
For complexity-theoretic considerations we assume any computability concept polynomially equivalent to random access machines. The reader should imagine some model of this type with a reasonable menu of operations and tests each working in unit time.
The main part of the paper presented is devoted to a detailled explanation of the inductive inference method developed. Because of the restricted space almost all proofs and related discussions must be omitted.

3. The Polynomial Time Algorithm

The pattern synthesis algorithm to be presented depends essentially on the number m of variables possibly occuring in the underlying pattern. It is called PSA_m , for short. The following figure compares ANGLUIN's results and the result (see theorem 4) presented here.

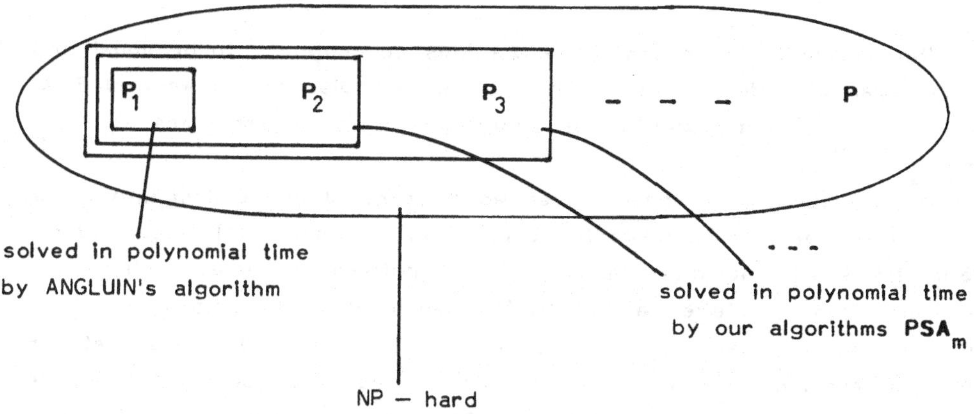

Figure 1: The pattern inference problem

The PSA_m consists of three parts which are rather different and independend.
The task of the first part called **Part1** is to take any first input word w from a given sample and to construct a data structure of polynomial size in dependence on the input w such that this data structure describes the set of exactly all patterns able to generate w. Note that the size of this set of patterns can only be bounded exponentially in dependence on w. The constructed data structure is a set of pattern automata in the sense of ANGLUIN /2/, in fact.
The second part **Part2** is an updating algorithm. It is based on any data structure defined by **Part1** or resulting from an earlier updating step. It takes a new input word w' from a given sample and deletes exactly all patterns from the data structure which are not able to generate the new word w'.
The third part named **Part3** is the output generating component of the PSA_m. It chooses a certain part of the data structure and takes it as a basis for constructing a pattern which turns out to be descriptive of the underlying sample worked up so far within P_m.
Assume m to be an arbitrary positive integer througout the rest of the

chapter 3. We give a brief description of the main ideas forming the **PSA**$_m$ The three components are explained separately.
For clearness we will mix the general explanation of the inductive inference method with the detailled discussion of a certain example. In the sequel, words will be presented with blanks between every two letters, for the sake of readability. Sometimes the presentation will be shortened by introducing exponents to abbreviate repetitions of letters in the usual way.
For the possibility to present some drawings we confine m to be equal to 2 in the example under consideration, i.e. we will discuss the work of **PSA**$_2$ in detail. The input words to be processed in the example are $w_1 = a^{21}$ and $w_2 = a^{10}\ b\ a^9\ b\ a^3$.
Part1: Assume w_1 to beany given word representing the first information on a ceratin pattern language to be identified in the limit. This part of the **PSA**$_m$ takes w_1 and constructs a set of pattern automata. Each pattern automaton can be viewed as an (m+1)-dimensional parallelepiped with some internal nodes indexed by (m+1)-tupels of non-negative integers. Between some neighbouring nodes there are directed edges possibly labelled. The parallelepipeds are defined step by step as explained in the following dependend on w_1. Throughout the following construction n denotes the length of the input word w_1. Note that n = 21 holds in the example under consideration.
For each positive integer d not greater than m and for each increasing list of positive integers $(k_1,...,k_d)$ bounded by n in each component there is performed the same construction. First the algorithm takes successively all numbers y between zero and n–d and checks all lists $(l_1,...,l_d)$ of positive integers bounded by n–d whether or not the following linear diophantine equation has positive solutions in the indeterminates $u_1,...,u_d$.

$$l_1u_1 + . . . + l_du_d = n - y$$

If this equation turns out to be unsolvable, the considered list is cancelled. Otherwise, the data are used as a basis for constructing a certain parallelepiped.
Concerning the underlying example we discuss the case characterized by the parameters d = 2 , y = 5 , $k_1 = 2$, $k_2 = 8$, $l_1 = 2$, and $l_2 = 3$. Consequently, the linear diophantine equation in this regard is

$$2u_1 + 3u_2 = 16$$

Possible solutions are (2,4) and (5,2) . We take the second solution with $u_1 = 5$ and $u_2 = 2$ as a basis for the following discussion of the example.
For each solution of the concerning diophantine equation the first

component of the $\mathbf{PSA}_m$ tries to construct a certain parallelepiped. Thus a construction of such a parallelepiped depends on positive integers d, $y = u_0$, k_1, ..., k_d, l_1, ..., l_d, u_1, ..., u_d. The intention is that d is the number of different variables occurring in a pattern (without loss of generality, we assume that these variables are x_1, ..., x_d), y is the concerning number of constant symbols. The increasing sequence $k_1,...,k_d$ denotes the points in w_1 where subwords are beginning which has been substituted for the first occurence of the variable $x_1,...,x_d$, respectively, in the underlying pattern to be described. $l_1,...,l_d$ are the corresponding lengths of subwords. Therefore, the algorithm needs these subwords.

The construction proceeds only if $n-k_d+1$ is not less than l_d and $k_{i+1}-k_i$ is not less than l_i, for $i = 1,...,d-1$. In case these conditions are satisfied the algorithm computes the subword t_i of length l_i beginning at the k_i-th letter in w_1. Otherwise, the construction will be cancelled for the data set d, y, k_1, ..., k_d, l_1, ..., l_d, u_1, ... u_d under consideration.

Now all information has been accumulated for defining a (d+1)-dimensional parallelepiped. The initial node is named by a vector $(0,...,0)$ containing $d+1$ zeros. If $k_1 = 1$ then the only successor of the initial node is the point indexed (or named, equivalently) by $(0,1,0,...,0)$. If k_1 is greater than 1, then the only successor of the initial node is the point indexed by $(1,0,...,0)$. In this case the edge between both nodes is labelled by the first letter of w_1. The induction step of this construction is as follows. Assume any point reachable by a chain of edges from the initial node and being indexed by some vector $(v_0,v_1,...,v_d)$. If each v_i is equal to u_i the construction is finished. Otherwise, if v_i is less than u_i (for some i) the construction proceeds as follows:

– Assume that $v_0 + v_1l_1 + ... + v_dl_d = k_i - 1$ holds. In this case the only edge outgrowing from $(v_0,v_1,...,v_d)$ leads to the point indexed by $(v_0,...,v_{i-1},v_i+1,v_{i+1},...,v_d)$.

Otherwise, there are two different constructions possibly performed:

– Assume v_0 to be less than u_0. The edge from $(v_0,v_1,...,v_d)$ to the node $(v_0+1,v_1,...,v_d)$ is put into the parallelepiped being constructed. It is labelled by the $(v_0+v_1l_1+...+v_dl_d+1)$-th letter of the input word w_1.

– For each i, where $v_0+v_1l_1+...+v_dl_d$ is greater than or equal to k_i, the algorithm computes the subword t of w_1 beginning at the concerning $(v_0+v_1l_1+...+v_dl_d+1)$-th letter of w_1. If and only if this subword t is identical to the word t_i computed before, the edge from $(v_0,v_1,...,v_d)$ to its i-successor is included.

The final node $(u_0, u_1, \ldots, u_d)$ has no successors. This completes the definition of the induction step.

But it may happen that some internal node $(v_0, v_1, \ldots, v_d)$ with $v_0 = u_0$ has no successor. Thus the parallelepiped would contain a death end. For understanding this difficulty the reader should study the special example with $w_1 = a\ b\ a\ a\ a\ b\ b$, $d = 1$, $k_1 = 1$, $l_1 = 2$, $u_0 = 3$, and $u_1 = 2$ shown in figure 2.

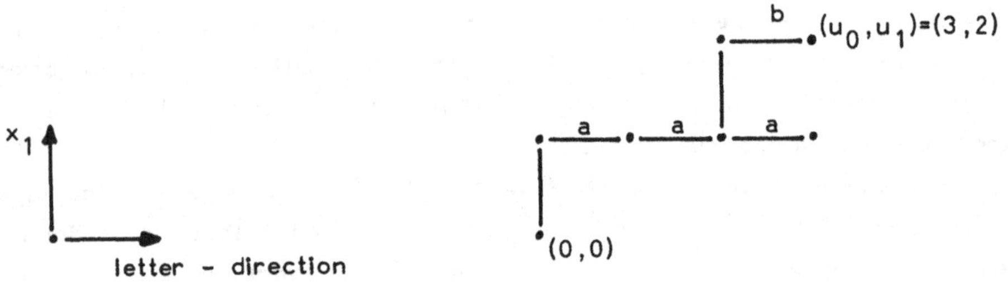

Figure 2

A special top-down procedure removes death ends by stepwise deleting all nodes having no successor. Similary, all edges being connected with an erased node are deleted.

This completes the description of **Part1**.

The resulting parallelepiped describes a pattern automaton in the sense of ANGLUIN /1/, /2/.

The concerning parallelepiped of the discussed example is presented now:

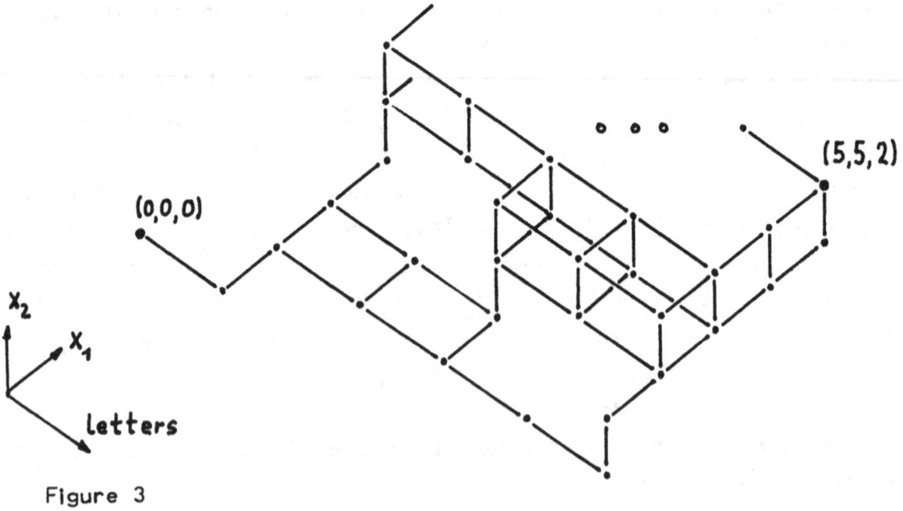

Figure 3

Figure 3 on the page before shows the result of applying **Part1** to the input word w_1 = a a a a a a a a a a a a a a a a a a a a a with the parameters $d = 2$, $y = u_0 = 5$, $k_1 = 2$, $k_2 = 8$, $l_1 = 2$, $l_2 = 3$, $u_1 = 5$, and $u_2 = 2$. The omitted part indicated by dots contains all edges and nodes up to the final node (5,5,2). All edges of the letter-direction should be labelled by the letter a in accordance with the rules above. But this is omitted for simplicity.

Lemma 1 The data structure defined by **Part1** of the **PSA**$_m$ in working up a word w of length n is size-bounded by $O(n^{4m+2})$. The time complexity of **Part1** is bounded by a function of the order $O(n^{4m+3})$.

Proof: The proof is rather simple. First we estimate the number of data sets $d, y, k_1, \ldots, k_d, l_1, \ldots, l_d, u_1, \ldots, u_d$ possibly occurring in **Part1**. Substituting d by its upper bound m and all parameters by their bound n one gets the upper bound n^{3m+1} for the number of data sets taken into account. Each parallelepiped contains at most n^{m+1} nodes. This proves the size bound above. The construction method of **Part1** consists of steps defined in dependence on single points in a parallelepipped. As all decisions and constructions are based on simple arithmetic operations and comparisons with w performable in linear time, the resulting time bound is of the order of n^{4m+3}. This completes the proof of our first lemma.

Part2: The updating component takes a set of parallelepipeds as its basis. Its actual input is a new word w_2 (note that the index does not say that there could not follow a third word and so on) taken from the sample presented. Its task is to correct all parallelepipeds in such a manner that the resulting describe only patterns which are able to generate w_2. We present a sketch of the method.

Each parallelepiped is characterized by its final node indexed by some vector $(u_0, u_1, \ldots, u_d)$ for some positive integer d not exceeding m. The intention is that such a parallelepiped describes patterns consisting of exactly u_0 letters, u_1 occurrencies of x_1 , . . . , and u_d occurrencies of x_d. Assume n' to be the length of w_2. First the algorithm checks whether there are positive solutions of the linear diophantine equation

$$u_1 z_1 + \ldots + u_d z_d = n' - u_0$$

in the indeterminates $z_1, \ldots, z_d$. If there are no solutions, then the whole parallelepiped has to be deleted from the data structure and **Part2** takes the next one (if possible) or terminates. Otherwise, all solutions of the diophantine equation above are calculated. For each non-deleted parallel-epiped and for each solution of the equation above the **Part2** algorithm starts its work to be explained below.

We take the underlying example with $w_2 = a^{10}\ b\ a^9\ b\ a^3$ to illuminate the key ideas of the main part of the $\mathbf{PSA}_m$. The equation to be solved is

$$5z_1 + 2z_2 = 19$$

Let us take the solution (3,2) as a basis for a further discussion of the example below.

Part2 as a whole consists of a first bottom-up procedure for labelling x_i-edges, defining lists associated with nodes, and deleting certain edges, of two procedures for removing death ends and of a final procedure for splitting the resulting data structure into the parallelepipeds to be stored. Assume $z_1,\dots,z_d$ to be a solution under consideration. Recall that each node $(v_0,v_1,\dots,v_d)$ refers to a certain point in the input word to be processed. This is the point before the $(v_0+v_1z_1+\dots+v_dz_d+1)$-th letter in the word.

The work of the first bottom-up procedure is guided by the following rules:

Rule 0: The list associated with the initial node is empty.

For the following rules assume a node indexed by $(v_0,v_1,\dots,v_d)$ such that the definition of the list associated with this node has been finished.

Rule 1: This rule applies if and only if there is an edge of the letter-direction outgrowing from the node under consideration and labelled by a certain letter c. c is compared with the letter following the point in w_2 where the node refers to. In case they are identical this edge remains unchanged. Otherwise, it has to be deleted.

Rule 2: Assume an x_i-edge outgrowing from $(v_0,v_1,\dots,v_d)$. t_i denotes the subword of length z_i beginning at the point indicated by the node in w_2. a) If $v_i = 0$ then this edge is lab elled by t_i. b) Otherwise, the algorithm checks whether the word t_i especially labelled by i (this is written as (t_i,i)) occurs in the list associated with the node under consideration. In case it belongs to this list the edge is labelled by t_i. Otherwise, the edge has to be deleted.

Rule 3: Assume a node reachable by an edge in accordance with rule 1 or rule 2, respectively. The list associated with this node is defined as follows: If the node is reachable from a certain predecessor by an edge of the letter-direction, the full list of this predecessor belongs to the list to be defined. If the node is reachable from some i-predecessor by an edge of the x_i-direction labelled by some t_i, then all labelled words (t,j) in the list of the predecessor (for $j\neq i$) has to be put into this new list. Finally, the labelled word (t_i,i) has to be put into this list. No other rule has to be applied.

The figure on the next page shows the initial part of the parallelepiped of figure 3 after the application of the rules above. Some data are omitted.

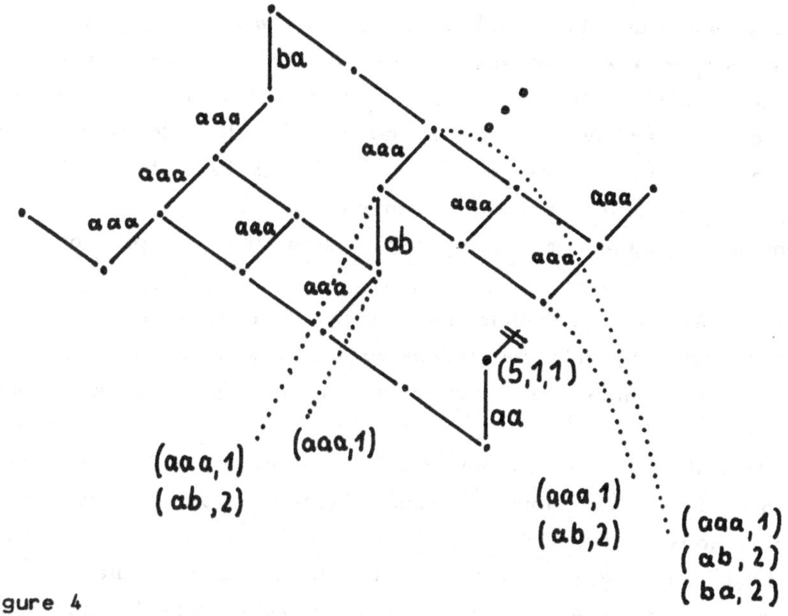

Figure 4

The parallelepiped shown in the figure above contains a death end at the node (5,1,1).

Next **Part2** removes all death ends by means of a top-down procedure (for removing upward death ends like in the figure above) and a bottom-up procedure (for removing downward death ends). Both are similar to the concerning procedure of **Part1**.

The next figure shows the resulting parallelepiped of our example under consideration. For simplicity almost all labes are omitted.

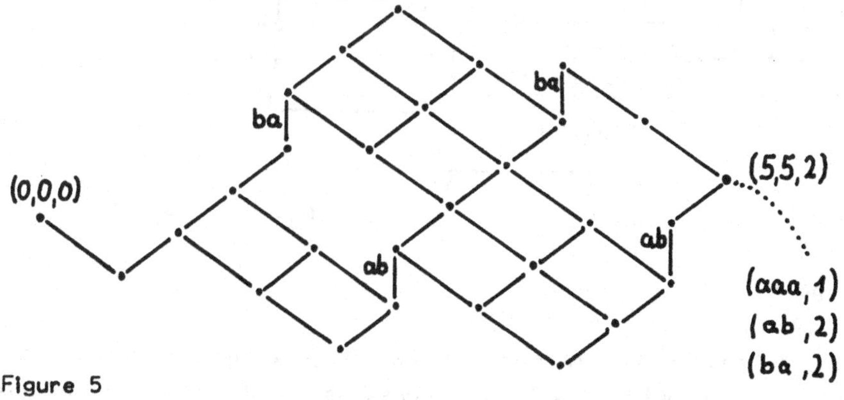

Figure 5

Not all paths through this parallelepiped from its initial to its final node are describing admissible patterns. Therefore, the splitting procedures is applied.

The splitting procedure takes all sequences of words $t_1,\ldots,t_d$ in such a way that each t_i is a word labelled by i in the list associated with the final node of the actual parallelepipeped.In a first bottom-up part it deletes all x_i-edges not labelled by the concerning t_i and all nodes with v_i greater than zero not having the concerning (t_i,i) in their list. Its second part is a top-down procedure for removing death ends.
We can only mention the summarizing result about the main part of the $\mathbf{PSA}_m$:

Lemma 2 Assume a parallelepiped and an input word w. The complexity of **Part2** for updating this parallelepiped in working up w is polynomially bounded in dependence on the size of the parallelepiped and w.

Part3: This final part takes only the parallelepipeds with a maximal index sum of their final node into account. Starting from all initial nodes in parallel it chooses the lexicographically first pattern described. This lexicographical ordering is based on the following simple rules: A letter is of the highest priority. A variable x_i is of a higher priority than x_j if and only if i is smaller than j.
The result ist that a pattern produced as output by **Part3** is descriptive of the underlying sample within P_m.

The following figure illustrates the structure of the $\mathbf{PSA}_m$ for some positive integer m.

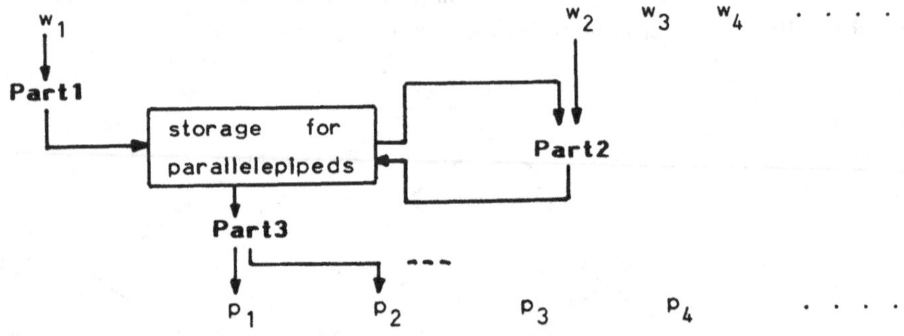

Figure 6

Now we are ready to summarize our knowledge about the algorithm $\mathbf{PSA}_m$. The proof will be omitted as it is a consequence of a suitable combination of the lemmata above.

Theorem 4 Assume any positive integer m. $\mathbf{PSA}_m$ given any sample S word by word outputs a pattern p of maximal length descriptive of S within $\mathbf{P}_m$ in polynomial time.

4. Conclusions

Besides the fact that the $\mathbf{PSA}_m$ (for any m greater than 1) solves a problem which remained open until now, this algorithm (more precisely, this family of algorithms) is interesting because of its considerably small average complexity. Unfortunately, the author has no good estimation of it so far. In his opinion, it is a central task in complexity theory to put more emphasis on average complexities instead of worst-case bounds. It seems that the $\mathbf{PSA}_m$ is a promising object for research work in this field.

The author is grateful to Dana ANGLUIN for some critical hints about an earlier version of this paper.

References

/1/ ANGLUIN, Dana Finding patterns common to a set of strings, 11th Annual ACM Symposium on theory of Computing, Atlanta, Georgia, 1979, 130-141

/2/ ANGLUIN, Dana Finding patterns common to a set of strings, Journal of Computer and Systems Science 21 (1980) 1, 46 - 62

/3/ ANGLUIN, D. / SMITH, C. A survey of inductive inference: theory and methods, Yale Univ., Dep. Comp. Sci., Techn. Rep. 250, 1982

/4/ KLETTE, R. / WIEHAGEN, R. Research in the theory of inductive inference by GDR mathematicians - a survey, Inf. Sciences 22 (1980), 149 - 169

/5/ NIX, Robert P. Editing by Example, Yale Univ., Dep. Comp. Sci., Techn. Rep. 280, 1983

/6/ SHINOHARA, Takeshi Polynomial time inference of extended regular pattern languages, RIMS Symposia on Software Science and Engineer., Kyoto, 1982, Lecture Notes in Comp. Sci. 147, 115-127

/7/ SHINOHARA, Takeshi Polynomial time inference of pattern languages and its application, Proc. 7th IBM Symp. on MFCS, 1982

/8/ SMITH, Douglas R. A survey of the synthesis of LISP programs from examples, BIERMANN/GUIHO/KODRATOFF (eds.), Automatic program construction techniques, MacMillan, 1983

ON EXTENDIBILITY OF UNAVOIDABLE SETS*

Christian CHOFFRUT

Laboratoire d'Informatique Théorique et Programmation
Université Paris VII
Paris, France

Karel CULIK II

Department of Computer Science
University of Waterloo
Waterloo, Ontario N2L 3G1
Canada

ABSTRACT

A subset X of a free monoid A^* is said to be unavoidable if all but finitely many words in A^* contain some word of X as a subword. A. Ehrenfeucht has conjectured that every unavoidable set X is extendible in the sense that there exist $x \in X$ and $a \in A$ such that $(X-\{x\}) \cup \{xa\}$ is itself unavoidable. This problem remains open, we give some partial solutions and show how to efficiently test unavoidability, extendibility and other properties of X related to the problem.

1. INTRODUCTION

A subset X of a free monoid A^* is said to be *unavoidable*, if all but finitely many words in A^* contain some word of X as a subword. Ehrenfeucht has conjectured that provided A is finite, every unavoidable set X is *extendible* in the sense that there exist $x \in X$ and $a \in A$ such that $(X\backslash\{x\}) \cup \{xa\}$ is itself unavoidable.

The purpose of this paper is, after having introduced the main notions of unavoidability and extendibility in Section 2 and having shown that we can restrict ourselves to finite sets, to present the following results.

In Section 3 we consider the computational aspect of the problem. Indeed, we associate with every finite subset X a finite deterministic automaton and we show how to use it to deduce the properties of X related to the problem.

In Section 4 we give a partial solution to the conjecture in two special cases. As a consequence of the second case, we show that Ehrenfeucht's conjecture

---

* This research was supported by the Natural Sciences and Engineering Research Council of Canada, under the grant No. A-7503.

is equivalent to the statement where the word "extendible" need not necessarily mean extendible to the right as is implied by the above definition, but rather extendible either to the right or to the left.

Section 5 presents a reduction result which shows, via an encoding, that the conjecture need only be proved for highly restricted finite subsets of $\{a,b\}^*$.

2. PRELIMINARIES

Throughout this paper, A is a fixed finite alphabet containing at least two symbols. We denote by A^* the free monoid it generates and by 1 the unit or empty word . As usual we denote by $|u|$ the length of the word $u \in A^*$ and by A^+ the set of words of nonzero length : $A^+ = A^*\backslash\{1\} = \{u \in A^* \mid |u| > 0\}$.

The partial ordering on A^* "prefix of" is denoted by $\leq$: $u \leq v$ iff there exists $w \in A^*$ such that $v = uw$. We write $u < v$ if $u \leq v$ and $u \neq v$.

Assume we have $v = w_1 u w_2$ for some words u, v, w_1, w_2. Then u is a *subword* of v. If w_1 (resp. w_2) is the empty word, then u is a *prefix* (resp. a *suffix*) of v.

For any set S, we denote by $|S|$ its cardinality.

In the sequel, $X \subseteq A^+$ is a fixed set.

2.1 Unavoidability, Extendibility

We are interested in the set of all words in A^* which have no element of X as a subword. When this set is finite, X is unavoidable.

More formally, a word $w \in A^*$ *avoids* X if no subword of w belongs to X : $w \notin A^*XA^*$. Furthermore X is *avoidable* if there exist infinitely many words in A^* avoiding it. When X is not avoidable, it is *unavoidable* which amounts to saying that there exists an integer $n > 0$ such that :

(2.1) $$A^n A^* \subseteq A^*XA^*.$$

Assume X is unavoidable. An element $x \in X$ is *extendible by the letter* $a \in A$ (or simply *extendible*) if $Y = (X\backslash\{x\}) \cup \{xa\}$ is itself unavoidable. In this case, Y is *an extension* of X. Furthermore, X is *extendible* if it possesses some extendible element.

Example 2.1 With $A = \{a,b\}$, $X = \{aaa, ab, bbb\}$ is extendible since :

$$A^*\backslash A^*XA^* = (A^*\backslash A^*abA^*)\backslash A^*\{a^3,b^3\}A^* = (b^*a^*)\backslash A^*\{a^3,b^3\}A^* = \{a^ib^j \mid 0 \leq i,j \leq 2\}.$$

The word ab is not extendible. Indeed, $Y_a = \{aaa,aba,bbb\}$ is avoidable because $(bba)^* \cap Y_a = \emptyset$ and so is $Y_b = \{aaa,abb,bbb\}$ because $(ab)^* \cup Y_b = \emptyset$. However X is extendible in different ways. For exemple, $\{aaaa,ab,bbb\}$ is unavoidable.

We recall that the problem we are dealing with is the following :

Conjecture 1 *Every unavoidable set is extendible.*

We shall now show that the conjecture needs only be proved for finite avoidable sets.

Assume $X \subseteq A^+$ is unavoidable. Then it is *minimal* if no proper subset $Y \subseteq X$ is unavoidable.

Example 2.2 With $A = \{a,b\}$, $X = A^2$ is unavoidable. However, it is not minimal since $Y = \{a^2, ab, b^2\}$ is unavoidable.

The following observation is straightforward :

(2.2) Let $Y \subseteq A^*XA^*$ be unavoidable. Then X is unavoidable.

As a consequence we have :

(2.3) The set $X \subseteq A^+$ is unavoidable iff the set $X' = X \setminus (A^*XA^+ \cup A^+XA^*)$ is unavoidable.

In particular we say that $X \subseteq A^+$ is *normal* if $X \cap (A^*XA^+ \cup A^+XA^*) = \emptyset$, that is if no word of X is a proper subword of an other word of X.

Thus we have :

(2.4) If $X \subseteq A^+$ is a minimal unavoidable set, it is normal.

Assume now that X is unavoidable and normal. Then by (2.1) all words of length n contain a subword in X. This shows that the length of the words X is bounded by n.

In view of (2.4) we obtain :

(2.5) If $X \subseteq A^+$ is a minimal unavoidable set, it is finite.

With the help of this last observation we shall restrict ourselves, from now on, to finite unavoidable sets.

2.2 Preliminary Results on Unavoidable Sets

We first recall two known estimates on the number n appearing in (2.1) and on the cardinality of unavoidable sets.

Assume n is the minimum value for which (2.1) holds. Then the maximum length of a word avoiding X is equal to $n-1$. As we shall see in the next section, this number is bounded by $|A|^m$ where m is the maximum length of the words of X. In the case of unavoidable sets consisting only of words of the same length, we have the following result (cf. [Cr et al.]) :

Theorem 2.1 *Let $m > 0$ be an integer and $X \subseteq A^m$. If there exists a word of length $|A|^{m-1}+m-1$ avoiding X, then X is avoidable.*

Furthermore, for all $m > 0$ there exists an unavoidable subset $X \subseteq A^m$ and a word of length $|A|^{m-1}+m-2$ which avoids it.

With respect to the cardinality of unavoidable subsets we have (cf. [Sch]) :

Theorem 2.2 *If $X \subseteq A^m$ is unavoidable, then*

$$|X| \geq \frac{|A|^m}{m} .$$

We now relate unavoidable sets to some conditions involving sets of infinite words. These conditions are equivalent to condition (2.1) and prove useful in the sequel.

Let A^ω, ${}^\omega A$ and ${}^\omega A^\omega$ be respectively the set of all right infinite, left infinite, and two way infinite words. Thus, typically $a_0a_1a_2\ldots, \ldots a_{-2}a_{-1}a_0$ and $\ldots a_{-1}a_0a_1\ldots$ with $a_i \in A$ are elements of A^ω, ${}^\omega A$ and ${}^\omega A^\omega$ respectively. As usual the elements of ${}^\omega A^\omega$ are defined up to a translation : $\ldots a_{-1}a_0a_1\ldots = \ldots b_{-1}b_0b_1\ldots$ if there exists an integer $t \in \mathbb{Z}$ such that $a_i = b_{i+t}$ for all $i \in \mathbb{Z}$. Given $u \in A^+$, we let $u^\omega = uu\ldots \in A^\omega$, ${}^\omega u = \ldots uu \in {}^\omega A$ and ${}^\omega u^\omega = \ldots uuu\ldots \in {}^\omega A^\omega$.

Lemma 2.3 $X \subseteq A^+$ *is unavoidable iff it satisfies any one of the following conditions :*

(i) $A^\omega = A^* X A^\omega$

(ii) ${}^\omega A^\omega = {}^\omega A X A^\omega$

(iii) *For all* $u \in A^+$, $u^\omega \in A^* X A^\omega$.

(iv) *For all* $u \in A^+$, ${}^\omega u^\omega \in {}^\omega A X A^\omega$.

Proof : The implications (2.1) ⇒ (i) and (i) ⇒ (iii) are straightforward. We shall prove (iii) ⇒ (2.1).

Assume by contradiction that X is avoidable. Since X is finite, the infinite set $A^* \backslash A^* X A^*$ is rational, and by the pumping lemma there exists two words $w \in A^*$ and $u \in A^+$ such that $wu^n \notin A^* X A^*$ for all $n \geq 0$. Thus, $u^\omega \notin A^* X A^\omega$ contradicting (iii).

The implications (2.1) ⇒ (ii), (ii) ⇒ (iv) and (iv) ⇒ (2.1) can be proven similarly. □

Using condition (i) of the previous lemma we obtain :

(2.6) Let $x \in X$. Then X is unavoidable iff $(X\backslash\{x\}) \cup xA$ is itself unavoidable.

2.3 A Reformulation of the Conjecture

In order to give some equivalent statements of the conjecture, we introduce a partial ordering over all finite subsets of A^*.

Let $X, Y \subseteq A^+$ have the same cardinality $n \geq 0$. We write $X \leq Y$ whenever there exists an ordering $X = \{x_i\}_{1 \leq i \leq n}$ and $Y = \{y_i\}_{1 \leq i \leq n}$ such that x_i is a prefix of y_i for all $1 \leq i \leq n$. We write $X < Y$ whenever $X \leq Y$ and $X \neq Y$.

The following assertions are straightforward

(2.7) $X \leq Y$ implies $Y \subseteq A^* X A^*$.

(2.8) If Y is an extension of X, then $X \leq Y$.

Now we show that minimality of unavoidable sets is preserved by extension.

Lemma 2.4 *Let* X *be a minimal unavoidable set. If* Y *is an unavoidable set such that* $X \leq Y$*, then* Y *is minimal.*

Proof : By hypothesis, for some integer $n \geq 0$ we have $X = \{x_i\}_{1 \leq i \leq n}$,

$Y = \{y_i\}_{1\le i\le n}$ and $x_i \le y_i$ for $1 \le i \le n$.

Assume the contrary, that is there exists $y_i \in Y$ such that $Y\backslash\{y_i\}$ is unavoidable. Then because $X\backslash\{x_i\} \le Y\backslash\{y_i\}$, (2.2) and (2.7) imply that $X\backslash\{x_i\}$ is unavoidable, a contradiction. □

We may now restate Ehrenfeucht's conjecture in terms of infinite extensions.

Lemma 2.5 *The following statements are equivalent :*

(i) For every unavoidable set $X \subseteq A^+$ *there exists* $x \in X$ *and* $a \in A$ *such that* $Y = (X\backslash\{x\}) \cup \{xa\}$ *is unavoidable.*

(ii) For every unavoidable set $X \subseteq A^+$ *there exists* $x \in X$ *and an infinite sequence* $a_1a_2,\ldots,a_i,\ldots$ *where* $a_i \in A$ *such that* $X_n = (X\backslash\{x\}) \cup \{xa_1a_2\ldots a_n\}$ *is unavoidable for all* $n > 0$.

(iii) For every unavoidable set $X \subseteq A^+$, *there exists* $x \in X$ *and an infinite sequence* $x_1,x_2,\ldots,x_n,\ldots$ *where* $x_i \in A^+$, *such that* $X_n = (X\backslash\{x\}) \cup \{xx_1\ldots x_n\}$ *is unavoidable for all* $n > 0$.

Proof : Because of (2.2) and (2.8), statements (ii) and (iii) are equivalent. Clearly (ii) implies (i).

Now (i) implies that there exists an infinite sequence $X < Y_1 <\ldots<Y_i<\ldots$ of unavoidable sets. Since X is finite, there exists an infinite subsequence $i_1 < i_2 <\ldots< i_n <\ldots$ and an infinite sequence $x < x_1 < x_2 <\ldots< x_n <\ldots$ such that $x \in X$ and $x_n \in Y_{i_n}$ for all $n > 0$. Define $X_n = (X\backslash\{x\}) \cup \{x_n\} \subseteq Y_{i_n}$. Because of assertion (2.2), X_n is unavoidable, thus completing the proof. □

Whenever x satisfies condition (ii) or (iii), we say that it is *infinitely extendible*.

3. AN AUTOMATON RECOGNIZING $A^*\backslash A^*XA^*$

With every normal subset X, we associate a finite deterministic (in general non-minimal) automaton recognizing the set of words avoiding X. Next we provide an efficient algorithm to decide whether or not X is unavoidable, and moreover, when it is, whether or not it is extendible and minimal.

We denote by $P(X)$ the set of all prefixes of all words in X. Let s be the partial function undefined over A^*XA^+, which to every word $w \in A^*\backslash A^*XA^+$ assigns the longest word $u \in P(X)$ which is suffix of w.

Let $\equiv$ be the equivalence relation defined on A^* by $w_1 \equiv w_2$ iff either w_1, w_2 both belong to A^*XA^* or $s(w_1) = s(w_2)$. Since X is normal, $\equiv$ is a right congruence, and we may consider a transition function $\lambda : P(X) \times A \to P(X)$ undefined on $X \times A$, and otherwise satisfying :

$$\lambda(w,a) = s(wa).$$

Taking $P(X)$ as the set of states, $\{1\}$ as the initial state, $P(X)\backslash X$ as the set of final states and λ as the transition function, we obtain a finite deterministic automaton recognizing $L = A^*\backslash A^*XA^*$. Thus X is unavoidable iff L

is finite. This again amounts to saying in terms of the state diagram of the automaton, that X is unavoidable iff there is no cycle in the state diagram.

Abusing terminology somewhat, we refer to the above automaton as the "automaton of X" and we shall denote it by A(X). If necessary, we shall write s_X and λ_X instead of λ and s, to remind ourselves to which set X the partial functions refer.

For the pictorial representations of A(X) we first draw the usual tree hanging from its root whose leaves are the elements of X and whose internal nodes are all proper prefixes P(X)\X. In order to complete the automaton, i.e. to define the transitions $\lambda(w,a)$ where $w \in P(X)\setminus X$ and $wa \notin P(X)$, it helps to observe that if $c,d \in A$ and $cw \in P(X)\setminus X$ satisfy $cwd \notin P(X)$, then $\lambda(cw,d) = \lambda(w,d)$. The transitions on the prefixes may thus be easily computed by increasing lengths.

Example 3.1 $A = \{a,b\}$, $X = \{a^4, a^2ba, bab, b^2\}$.

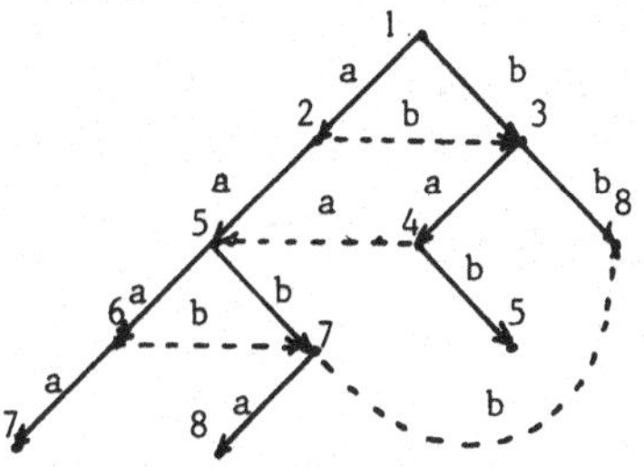

$\lambda(a,b) = \lambda(1,b) = b$

$\lambda(ba,a) = \lambda(a,a) = aa$

$\lambda(aaa,b) = \lambda(aa,b) = aab$

$\lambda(aab,b) = \lambda(ab,b) = b^2$

3.1 Unavoidability

For the previous example, the state diagram immediately shows that there is no cycle. However for more complex examples, a visual inspection is insufficient. We need a more efficient procedure.

It is standard to associate with each letter $a \in A$ a square matrix indexed by P(X), and having at position (p,p') a 1 if $\lambda(p,a) = p'$ and 0 otherwise.

The following result amounts to show how to simultaneously triangulate, if possible, the matrices associated with all $a \in A$, by a m re permutation of the columns.

Theorem 3.1 *A subset $X \subseteq A^+$ is unavoidable iff there exists a function $f : P(X) \to \mathbb{N}$ satisfying the two conditions :*

(i) $f(1) = 0$

(ii) $f(p) = 1+max\{f(p') \mid \lambda(p',a) = p$ for some $a \in A\}$ for $p \neq 1$.

Proof : Condition (ii) implies $f(\lambda(p,u)) \geq f(p) + |u|$ whenever $\lambda(p,u)$ is defined, which shows that the automaton has no cycle, that is X is unavoidable.

Conversely, if X is unavoidable, for all $p \in P(X)$ let $f(p)$ be the length of the longest word $w \in A^*$ such that $\lambda(1,w) = p$. Then f satisfies conditions (i) and (ii). □

Example 3.1 (continued)

The corresponding values of the function f are shown in the diagram as node labels.

3.2 Extendibility

By definition, in order to check whether or not a given unavoidable set X is extendible, it suffices to verify that for some $x \in X$ and some $a \in A$, $(X\backslash\{x\}) \cup \{xa\} = Y$ is unavoidable. We know from the previous subsection, how to verify whether or not Y is unavoidable. It thus suffices to know how to construct its automaton, that is to show how the automaton $A(X)$ is modified by an extension.

Proposition 3.2 *Let $X \subseteq A^+$ be a normal unavoidable set $x \in X$ and $a \in A$. Consider $Y = (X\backslash\{x\}) \cup \{xa\}$ and observe that $P(Y) = P(X) \cup \{xa\}$.*

Then the transition function λ_Y of the automaton of Y satisfies for all $p \in P(X)\backslash\{x\}$ and $b \in A$:

$$\lambda_Y(p,b) = \lambda_X(p,b).$$

Proof : Assume the contrary, that is $\lambda_Y(p,b) \neq \lambda_X(p,b)$ for some $p \in P(X)\backslash\{x\}$ and $b \in A$. Then $\lambda_Y(p,b) = xa$, i.e. $p = ux$ for some $u \in A^+$ which violates the hypothesis that X is normal. □

3.3 Minimality

The following lemma shows that if X is a minimal unavoidable set, then every word of X which can be extended, can only be extended by one letter of the alphabet.

Lemma 3.3 *Let X be a minimal unavoidable set, $x \in X$ and $a,b \in A$. If $(X\backslash\{x\}) \cup \{xa\}$ and $(X\backslash\{x\})\backslash\{xb\}$ are both unavoidable, then $a = b$.*

Proof : It suffices to prove that for every $x \in X$ there exists a letter $a \in A$ and an infinite word $s \in A^\omega$ having occurrences of x, no occurrence in $X\backslash\{x\}$ and such that all occurrences of x are followed by the same letter $a \in A$. In other words, all factorizations $s = s_1 y s_2$ with $s_1 \in A^*$, $y \in X$ and $s_2 \in A^\omega$ imply $y = x$ and $s_2 \in aA^\omega$.

Because of the minimality of X, there exists a word w $\in A^*$ having exactly two occurrences of x and no occurrence in $X\backslash\{x\}$: $w = w_1 x u w_2 = w_1 v x w_2$ for some $u,v \in A^+$. Equality $xu = vx$ implies $x = (zt)^r z$ $u = tz$ and $v = zt$ for some $z,t \in A^*$ and $r \geq 0$.

Consider the infinite word $s = (zt)^{\omega}$ and an occurrence of $y \in X$ in $s : s = s_1 y s_2$ with $s_1 \in A^*$ and $s_2 \in A^{\omega}$. Because X is normal, y must be a subword of $(zt)^{r+1}z = xu = vx$ which implies $y = x$. Now because the two occurrences of x in w are consecutive, we obtain $s_1 \in (zt)^*$ and therefore $s_2 \in (tz)^{\omega}$ which completes the proof. □

As a consequence, we obtain a characterization of minimal unavoidable sets, which via Theorem 3.1 and Proposition 3.2 provides an efficient procedure to test minimality.

Corollary 3.4 *Let X be an unavoidable set. Then it is minimal iff for each $x \in X$ there exists at most one letter $a \in A$ such that $X \backslash \{x\} \cup \{xa\}$ is unavoidable.*

4. PARTIAL SOLUTIONS

In this section we consider two different conditions under which unavoidable sets are extendible.

Among the words of an unavoidable set there is necessarily some power a^n of any letter $a \in A$. These words definitely play a special role and we are able to establish under which conditions they are extendible.

In the second case, we try to formalize the intuition that if a minimal unavoidable set possesses some word x which is very long compared with all other words in X, then this word must be extendible.

Theorem 4.1 *Let X be a minimal unavoidable set and $a^n \in X$ for some $n > 0$. Then a^n is extendible iff $X \cap A^*ba^{n-1}bA^* = \emptyset$.*

Proof : Assume first $X \cap A^*ba^{n-1}bA^* = \emptyset$. We shall show that any $s \in {}^{\omega}A^{\omega}$ contains an occurrence of a word in $Y = (X \backslash \{a^n\}) \cup \{a^{n+1}\}$. If it contains no occurrence of a^n then because X is unavoidable, s contains an occurrence of a word in $X \backslash \{a^n\} = Y \backslash \{a^{n+1}\}$. So we may assume from now on that s contains some occurrences of a^n and no occurrence of a^{n+1}.

Denote by $s' \in {}^{\omega}A^{\omega}$ the word obtained from s by substituting a^{n-1} for each occurrence of a^n in s :

$$s = \ldots w_{-1}x_{-1}w_o x_o w_1 x_1 \ldots w_p x_p \ldots$$

$$s' = \ldots w_{-1}x'_{-1}w_o x'_o w_1 x'_1 \ldots w_p x'_p \ldots$$

where for all $i \in Z$ we have $w_i \in bA^* \cap A^*b \backslash A^*a^nA^*$

$$x_i = a^n \text{ and } x'_i = a^{n-1}.$$

Since X is unavoidable, s' has some occurrence x in $X \backslash \{a^n\}$. Because of the hypothesis, x is necessarily a subword of $x'_{i-1}w_i x'_i$ for some $i \in Z$, i.e. a subword of $x_{i-1}w_i x_i$, thus proving one direction.

Conversely, assume by contradiction that X contains a word $x \in A^*ba^{n-1}bA^*$ and that a^n can be extended.

Since X is minimal there exists a two-way infinite words $s \in {}^{\omega}A^{\omega}$ which has some occurrences of x and no occurrence of any word from $X\backslash\{x\}$.

Denote by x' the word obtained from x by substituting ba^nb for the first occurrence of $ba^{n-1}b$ in x and by $s' \in {}^{\omega}A^{\omega}$ the two-way infinite word obtained from s by substituting x' for all occurrences of x in s. Formally we have :

$$s = \ldots w_{-1}x_{-1}w_ox_o\ldots w_px_p\ldots$$

$$s' = \ldots w_{-1}x'_{-1}w_ox'_o\ldots w_px'_p\ldots$$

where for all $i \in \mathbb{Z}$ we have

$$w_i \in bA^* \cap A^*b,\ x'_i = a^n,\ x_i = a^{n-1},$$

and there exist a suffix u of $\ldots w_{i-1}x_{i-1}w_i$ and a prefix v of $x_iw_{i+1}\ldots$ such that $vx_iu = x$ and $vx'_iu = x'$.

Since $Y = (X\backslash\{a^n\}) \cup \{a^{n+1}\}$ is unavoidable, s' contains some occurrence $y \in Y\backslash\{a^{n+1}\} = X\backslash\{a^n\}$. Because $Y \cap A^*a^nA^* = \{a^{n+1}\}$, y is necessarily a subword of $x_{i-1}w_ix_i$ for some $i \in \mathbb{Z}$, i.e. $y = x$. But this contradicts the fact that x'_{i-1} and x'_i are two consecutive occurrences of a^n. □

<u>Theorem 4.2</u> *Let X be a minimal unavoidable set and assume there exist an integer $n > 0$ and a word $x \in X$ such that $|x| \geq 3.2^{n+1}$ and $|y| \leq n$ for all $y \in X\backslash\{x\}$.*

Then there exist $u = u_1u_2 \in A^+$ and $r > 0$ satisfying the following conditions :

(i) ${}^{\omega}u^{\omega}$ is the only two-way infinite word avoiding $X\backslash\{x\}$.

(ii) $x = (u_1u_2)^ru_1$.

(iii) For all $p \geq 0$, $X_p = (X\backslash\{x\}) \cup \{(u_1u_2)^{r+p}u_1\}$ is unavoidable.

<u>Proof</u> : Observe first that (i) trivially implies (iii). Further, if ${}^{\omega}u^{\omega}$ is the only two-way infinite word avoiding $X\backslash\{x\}$, then x is a u word of this word. This means that there exists a word $u'u''$ such that $u = u''u'$ and $x = (u'u'')^ru'$ for some integer $r \geq 0$. But ${}^{\omega}(u'u'')^{\omega} = {}^{\omega}u^{\omega}$ which shows that (i) implies (ii).

We now turn to prove assertion (i). Given any state q of $A(X\backslash\{x\})$ we define :

$$F_q = \{w \in A^+ \mid \lambda(q,w) = q\}$$

and we denote by E_q the subset of words in F_q which define an elementary cycle in the state diagram of the automaton, i.e. the words which satisfy :

$w = w_1w_2w_3$, $\lambda(q,w_1) = p$, $\lambda(p,w_2) = p$, $\lambda(p,w_3) = q$, and $w_1w_3 \neq 1$ implies $w_2 = 1$.

Observe that all words in E_q are of length less than 2^{n+1}.

<u>Claim 1</u> There exists, up to a conjugacy class, a unique primitive word $u \in A^+$, such that $E_q \subseteq u_q^+$, where u_q is a conjugate of u depending only on q.

Let q,p be two states in the automaton $A(X\setminus\{x\})$, $v \in E_q$ and $w \in E_p$. Then ${}^\omega v^\omega$ and ${}^\omega w^\omega$ avoid $X\setminus\{x\}$. Thus these two words have x as a common subword. Since $|x| \geq |v| + |w| - 1$, by ([LeSch]Cor. 1) v and w are powers of two conjugate primitive words. Thus there exist $u_1, u_2 \in A^*$ with $u_1 \neq 1$, and $i,j > 0$ such that u_1u_2 is primitive and :

$$v = (u_1u_2)^i, \; w = (u_2u_1)^j. \tag{4.1}$$

It now suffices to prove that $p = q$ implies $u_2 = 1$. Thus, assume that $p = q$, and therefore $v,w \in E_q$. Then the words ${}^\omega(vw)^\omega$ and ${}^\omega v^\omega$ have a common subword x of length $|x| \geq |v| + |vw| - 1$ which by the same result quoted above implies that $vw = (u_1u_2)^i(u_2u_1)^j$ is a power of some conjugate of u_1u_2. We obtain $u_1u_2 = u_2u_1$, i.e., $u_2 = 1$ which proves the claim.

<u>Claim 2</u> $F_q \subseteq u_q^+$ holds for all $q \in P(X)$.

Using Claim 1, assume by contradiction that for some state q and some word of minimal length $w \in F_q$ we have $w \notin u_q^+$. Then there exists a factorization $w = w_1w_2w_3$, with $w_2 \neq 1$ and $w_1w_3 \neq 1$ and a state p such that the following holds :

$$\lambda(q,w_1) = p \;,\; \lambda(p,w_2) = p \;\text{ and }\; \lambda(p,w_3) = q.$$

By the minimality of $|w|$, and the fact that w_2 and w_3w_1 belong to F_p we have $w_2 = u_p^i$ and $w_3w_1 = u_p^j$ for some $i,j > 0$. Furthermore $w_1w_3 \in F_q$ implies $w_1w_3 = u_q^j$. Now equality $w_3u_q^j = u_p^jw_3$ implies $w_3u_q^k = u_p^kw_3$ for any $k \geq 0$. Thus :

$$w_3w_1w_2w_3 = u_p^ju_p^iw_3 = w_3u_q^{i+j}, \text{ i.e., } w \in u_q^+, \text{ a contradiction.}$$

In order to complete the proof, it suffices to observe that for any primitive word v such that ${}^\omega v^\omega$ avoids $X\setminus\{x\}$, there exists a state q and some integer $i > 0$ such that $v^i \in F_q$, which by Claim 2 shows that v is a conjugate of u. □

As a consequence of this last result, we will show that Conjecture I is equivalent to its "two-way" version where instead of extending to the right, we may extend in either direction.

<u>Conjecture II</u> : *For every finite unavoidable set* $X \subseteq A^+$ *there exist* $x \in X$ *and* $a \in A$ *such that either* $(X\setminus\{x\}) \cup \{xa\}$ *or* $(X\setminus\{x\}) \cup \{ax\}$ *is unavoidable*

<u>Theorem 3.4</u> *Conjectures I et II are equivalent.*

<u>Proof</u> : Obviously Conjecture I implies Conjecture II. We are going to prove that the reverse also holds.

Let us say that an unavoidable set $Y \subseteq A^+$ is a two-way extension of the unavoidable set $X \subseteq A^+$ if there exist $x \in X$ and $a \in A$ such that either

$$Y = (X\setminus\{x\}) \cup \{xa\} \text{ or } Y = (X\setminus\{x\}) \cup \{ax\}.$$

If Conjecture II holds, then for any unavoidable set X there exists an infinite sequence $Y_o, Y_1, \ldots, Y_k, \ldots$ of subsets such that $Y_o = X$, and Y_{k+1} is a two-way extension of Y_k for each $k \geq 0$. Since X is finite there exist $x \in X$, two sequences $s_o, s_1, \ldots, s_k, \ldots$ and $p_0, p_1, \ldots, p_k, \ldots$ and a subsequence $i_0, i_1, \ldots, i_k, \ldots$ such that the following conditions hold :

(i) $p_k \ldots p_0 x s_o \ldots s_k \in Y_{i_k}$

(ii) $|p_k \ldots p_0 s_o \ldots s_k|$ is strictly increasing.

Assume first the sequence $s_o, s_1, \ldots, s_k, \ldots$ contains infinitely many elements different from the empty word. Then, if necessary by considering a subsequence, we may assume that all elements are different from the empty word. By (2.2) all subsets $X_k = (X\setminus\{x\}) \cup \{x s_o \ldots s_k\} \subseteq Y_{i_k}$ are unavoidable, showing thus that x is infinitely extendible in the usual way.

Assume next that the sequence $p_0, p_1, \ldots, p_k, \ldots$ contains infinitely many elements different from the empty word. Then, as in the previous case, we may assume that they are all different from the empty word. By (2.2) all subsets $X_k = (X\setminus\{x\}) \cup \{p_k \ldots p_0 x\} \subseteq Y_{i_k}$ are unavoidable. Thus, the word x is infinitely left extendible, and since Theorem 4.2 dually applies to left extendibility there exist $u = u_1 u_2 \in A^+$ and $r > 0$ such that $x = u_1 (u_2 u_1)^r$ and such that all $X_p = (X\setminus\{x\}) \cup \{u_1 (u_2 u_1)^{r+p}\}$ are extendible. Now it suffices to observe that $u_1 (u_2 u_1)^{r+p} = u_1 (u_2 u_1)^r (u_2 u_1)^p = x (u_2 u_1)^p$ to show that $X < X_1 < \ldots < X_p < \ldots$ holds. □

5. A REDUCTION RESULT

Let $A = \{a_i\}_{1 \leq i \leq n}$ and $B = \{a,b\}$. Denote by $\psi : A^* \to B^*$ the morphism defined by $\psi(a_i) = a^i b$ for $1 \leq i \leq n$ and extend it in the usual way to A^ω, ${}^\omega A$, and ${}^\omega A^\omega$ (e.g. $\psi(a_o a_1 \ldots) = \psi(a_o)\psi(a_1)\ldots$). Since the image $\psi(A)$ is a comma free code, ψ maps ${}^\omega A^\omega$ bijectively onto $I = {}^\omega B^\omega \setminus {}^\omega B\{a^{n+1}, b^2\}B^\omega$.

Now with the set $X \subseteq A^+$, we associate the set $Y = \theta(X) = b\psi(X) \cup \{a^{n+1}, b^2\}$. This "encoding", preserves the main properties of X as is now shown.

Lemma 5.1 *X is unavoidable (resp. unavoidable and minimal) iff Y is unavoidable (resp. unavoidable and minimal).*

Proof : We first verify that the following holds for all X :

$$\psi({}^{\omega}AXA^{\omega}) = I \cap {}^{\omega}Bb\psi(X)B^{\omega}.$$

The inclusion $\subseteq$ is obvious. Thus it suffices to prove $I \cap {}^{\omega}Bb\psi(X)B^{\omega} \subseteq \psi({}^{\omega}AXA^{\omega})$. Indeed, if $w = zb\psi(x)t \in I$ for some $z \in {}^{\omega}B$, $x \in X$ and $t \in B^{\omega}$, then $z \in {}^{\omega}Ba\backslash{}^{\omega}B\{a^{n+1},b^2\}B^*$ and $t \in aB^{\omega}\backslash B^*\{a^{n+1},b^2\}B^{\omega}$, i.e. z and t may be factorized in elements of $\psi(A)$. Therefore there exist $w_1 \in {}^{\omega}A$ and $w_2 \in A^{\omega}$ such that $\psi(w_1) = zb$ and $\psi(w_2) = t$ which implies $w = \psi(w_1bw_2)$.

Now observe that ${}^{\omega}B^{\omega}$ is partitioned into :

$${}^{\omega}B^{\omega} = I \cup {}^{\omega}B\{a^{n+1},b^2\}B^{\omega}.$$

Thus, the set $Y = b\psi(X) \cup \{a^{n+1},b^2\}$ is unavoidable iff $I \subseteq {}^{\omega}Bb\psi(X)B^{\omega}$, i.e. because of (4.1) and the fact that ψ maps ${}^{\omega}A^{\omega}$ bijectively onto I, iff ${}^{\omega}A^{\omega} = {}^{\omega}AXA^{\omega}$. This proves the first part of the proposition.

The second part relies upon the fact that if $Y' \subseteq Y$ is unavoidable then $Y' \cap (a^+ \cup b^+) = Y \cap (a^+ \cup b^+) = \{a^{n+1},b^2\}$. Thus there exists an unavoidable proper subset $X' \subseteq X$ iff there exists an unavoidable proper subset $Y' \subseteq Y$. □

Using the same notations we have

<u>Lemma 5.2</u> *Assume X is unavoidable. Then an element $x \in X$ is infinitely extendible iff the element $b\psi(x) \in Y$ is infinitely extendible.*

<u>Proof</u> : If x is infinitely extendible, then there exists an infinite sequence $a_1,a_2,\dots,a_k,\dots$ where $a_k \in A$ for all $k > 0$, such that $X_k = (X\backslash\{x\}) \cup \{xa_1\dots a_k\}$ is unavoidable. By the previous lemma, this shows that $Y_k = (Y\backslash\{b\psi(x)\}) \cup \{b\psi(xa_1\dots a_k)\}$ is unavoidable, which proves one direction.

Now if $b\psi(x)$ is infinitely extendible, there exists an infinite sequence $u_1,u_2,\dots,u_k,\dots$ where $u_k = a^{i_k}b$ for some $1 \le i_k \le n$, such that $Y_k = (Y\backslash\{b\psi(x)\}) \cup \{b\psi(x)u_1 \dots u_k\}$ is unavoidable. Because of the preceding lemma, $X_k = (X\backslash\{x\}) \cup \{x\psi^{-1}(u_1) \dots \psi^{-1}(u_k)\}$ is unavoidable, which completes the proof. □

<u>Example 5.1</u> Consider $A = \{a,b\}$ and $X = \{a^2,abab,b^2\}$. Then X is unavoidable (basically for the same reasons as in Example 2.1) and $abab$ is the only infinitely extendible element of X. Then by Theorem 4.1 and the two previous lemmas, the subsets $\theta^k(X) = \theta(\theta^{k-1}(X))$ are unavoidable for all $k > 0$ and have a unique infinitely extendible word $\psi^k(x)$. Furthermore the cardinality of $\theta^k(X)$ is equal to $2k+3$. In other words this shows that there are unavoidable sets of arbitrary cardinality having a unique infinitely extendible word.

The following surprising result shows that Conjecture I need only be proven in the case $B = \{a,b\}$ and $X \cap (a^+ \cup b^+) = \{a^3,b^2\}$.

Theorem 5.3 *Ehrenfeucht's conjecture holds iff it holds for all unavoidable sets X over a binary alphabet $B = \{a,b\}$ such that $a^3, b^2 \in X$.*

Proof : Consider an unavoidable set $X \subseteq A^+$ where $|A| = n \geq 2$. If $X = A$, then every element of X is infinitely extendible. Therefore assume $X \neq A$.

Let $A = \{a_i\}_{1 \leq i \leq n}$ be an enumeration of the alphabet and consider $Y = b\psi(X) \cup \{a^3, b^2\}$.

Because of Lemma 5.1, Y is unavoidable. By Theorem 4.1 a^{n+1} and b^2 are not extendible. Thus, by hypothesis there exists some $x \in X$ such that $b\psi(x)$ is infinitely extendible. By Lemma 5.2, $x \in X$ is itself infinitely extendible.

If $n = 2$, then we are done. Otherwise we repeat the same argument with $Y \subseteq B^+$. □

REFERENCES

[Cr et al] M. Crochemore, M. Le Rest, and P. Wender, An optimal test on unavoidable sets of words. Information Proc. Letters, 16, 1983, 179-18

[Le Sch] A. Lentin and M.P. Schützenberger, A Combinatorial Problem in the Theory of Free Monoids, Proceedings of the Conference held at the University of North Carolina at Chapel Hill, Box & Bowling (ed.), Chapell Hill (1967), 128-144.

[Sch] M.P. Schützenberger, On the Synchronizing Properties of Certain Prefix Codes, Information and Control 7, (1964), 23-36.

Vol. 117: Fundamentals of Computation Theory. Proceedings, 1981. Edited by F. Gécseg. XI, 471 pages. 1981.

Vol. 118: Mathematical Foundations of Computer Science 1981. Proceedings, 1981. Edited by J. Gruska and M. Chytil. XI, 589 pages. 1981.

Vol. 119: G. Hirst, Anaphora in Natural Language Understanding: A Survey. XIII, 128 pages. 1981.

Vol. 120: L. B. Rall, Automatic Differentiation: Techniques and Applications. VIII, 165 pages. 1981.

Vol. 121: Z. Zlatev, J. Wasniewski, and K. Schaumburg, Y12M Solution of Large and Sparse Systems of Linear Algebraic Equations. IX, 128 pages. 1981.

Vol. 122: Algorithms in Modern Mathematics and Computer Science. Proceedings, 1979. Edited by A. P. Ershov and D. E. Knuth. XI, 487 pages. 1981.

Vol. 123: Trends in Information Processing Systems. Proceedings, 1981. Edited by A. J. W. Duijvestijn and P. C. Lockemann. XI, 349 pages. 1981.

Vol. 124: W. Polak, Compiler Specification and Verification. XIII, 269 pages. 1981.

Vol. 125: Logic of Programs. Proceedings, 1979. Edited by E. Engeler. V, 245 pages. 1981.

Vol. 126: Microcomputer System Design. Proceedings, 1981. Edited by M. J. Flynn, N. R. Harris, and D. P. McCarthy. VII, 397 pages. 1982.

Voll. 127: Y.Wallach, Alternating Sequential/Parallel Processing. X, 329 pages. 1982.

Vol. 128: P. Branquart, G. Louis, P. Wodon, An Analytical Description of CHILL, the CCITT High Level Language. VI, 277 pages. 1982.

Vol. 129: B. T. Hailpern, Verifying Concurrent Processes Using Temporal Logic. VIII, 208 pages. 1982.

Vol. 130: R. Goldblatt, Axiomatising the Logic of Computer Programming. XI, 304 pages. 1982.

Vol. 131: Logics of Programs. Proceedings, 1981. Edited by D. Kozen. VI, 429 pages. 1982.

Vol. 132: Data Base Design Techniques I: Requirements and Logical Structures. Proceedings, 1978. Edited by S.B. Yao, S.B. Navathe, J.L. Weldon, and T.L. Kunii. V, 227 pages. 1982.

Vol. 133: Data Base Design Techniques II: Proceedings, 1979. Edited by S.B. Yao and T.L. Kunii. V, 229–399 pages. 1982.

Vol. 134: Program Specification. Proceedings, 1981. Edited by J. Staunstrup. IV, 426 pages. 1982.

Vol. 135: R.L. Constable, S.D. Johnson, and C.D. Eichenlaub, An Introduction to the PL/CV2 Programming Logic. X, 292 pages. 1982.

Vol. 136: Ch. M. Hoffmann, Group-Theoretic Algorithms and Graph Isomorphism. VIII, 311 pages. 1982.

Vol. 137: International Symposium on Programming. Proceedings, 1982. Edited by M. Dezani-Ciancaglini and M. Montanari. VI, 406 pages. 1982.

Vol. 138: 6th Conference on Automated Deduction. Proceedings, 1982. Edited by D.W. Loveland. VII, 389 pages. 1982.

Vol. 139: J. Uhl, S. Drossopoulou, G. Persch, G. Goos, M. Dausmann, G. Winterstein, W. Kirchgässner, An Attribute Grammar for the Semantic Analysis of Ada. IX, 511 pages. 1982.

Vol. 140: Automata, Languages and programming. Edited by M. Nielsen and E.M. Schmidt. VII, 614 pages. 1982.

Vol. 141: U. Kastens, B. Hutt, E. Zimmermann, GAG: A Practical Compiler Generator. IV, 156 pages. 1982.

Vol. 142: Problems and Methodologies in Mathematical Software Production. Proceedings, 1980. Edited by P.C. Messina and A. Murli. VII, 271 pages. 1982.

Vol. 143: Operating Systems Engineering. Proceedings, 1980. Edited by M. Maekawa and L.A. Belady. VII, 465 pages. 1982.

Vol. 144: Computer Algebra. Proceedings, 1982. Edited by J. Calmet. XIV, 301 pages. 1982.

Vol. 145: Theoretical Computer Science. Proceedings, 1983. Edited by A.B. Cremers and H.P. Kriegel. X, 367 pages. 1982.

Vol. 146: Research and Development in Information Retrieval. Proceedings, 1982. Edited by G. Salton and H.-J. Schneider. IX, 311 pages. 1983.

Vol. 147: RIMS Symposia on Software Science and Engineering. Proceedings, 1982. Edited by E. Goto, I. Nakata, K. Furukawa, R. Nakajima, and A. Yonezawa. V. 232 pages. 1983.

Vol. 148: Logics of Programs and Their Applications. Proceedings, 1980. Edited by A. Salwicki. VI, 324 pages. 1983.

Vol. 149: Cryptography. Proceedings, 1982. Edited by T. Beth. VIII, 402 pages. 1983.

Vol. 150: Enduser Systems and Their Human Factors. Proceedings, 1983. Edited by A. Blaser and M. Zoeppritz. III, 138 pages. 1983.

Vol. 151: R. Piloty, M. Barbacci, D. Borrione, D. Dietmeyer, F. Hill, and P. Skelly, CONLAN Report. XII, 174 pages. 1983.

Vol. 152: Specification and Design of Software Systems. Proceedings, 1982. Edited by E. Knuth and E. J. Neuhold. V, 152 pages. 1983.

Vol. 153: Graph-Grammars and Their Application to Computer Science. Proceedings, 1982. Edited by H. Ehrig, M. Nagl, and G. Rozenberg. VII, 452 pages. 1983.

Vol. 154: Automata, Languages and Programming. Proceedings, 1983. Edited by J. Díaz. VIII, 734 pages. 1983.

Vol. 155: The Programming Language Ada. Reference Manual. Approved 17 February 1983. American National Standards Institute, Inc. ANSI/MIL-STD-1815A-1983. IX, 331 pages. 1983.

Vol. 156: M.H. Overmars, The Design of Dynamic Data Structures. VII, 181 pages. 1983.

Vol. 157: O. Østerby, Z. Zlatev, Direct Methods for Sparse Matrices. VIII, 127 pages. 1983.

Vol. 158: Foundations of Computation Theory. Proceedings, 1983. Edited by M. Karpinski, XI, 517 pages. 1983.

Vol. 159: CAAP'83. Proceedings, 1983. Edited by G. Ausiello and M. Protasi. VI, 416 pages. 1983.

Vol. 160: The IOTA Programming System. Edited by R. Nakajima and T. Yuasa. VII, 217 pages. 1983.

Vol. 161: DIANA, An Intermediate Language for Ada. Edited by G. Goos, W.A. Wulf, A. Evans, Jr. and K.J. Butler. VII, 201 pages. 1983.

Vol. 162: Computer Algebra. Proceedings, 1983. Edited by J.A. van Hulzen. XIII, 305 pages. 1983.

Vol. 163: VLSI Engineering. Proceedings. Edited by T.L. Kunii. VIII, 308 pages. 1984.

Vol. 164: Logics of Programs. Proceedings, 1983. Edited by E. Clarke and D. Kozen. VI, 528 pages. 1984.

Vol. 165: T.F. Coleman, Large Sparse Numerical Optimization. V, 105 pages. 1984.

Vol. 166: STACS 84. Symposium of Theoretical Aspects of Computer Science. Proceedings, 1984. Edited by M. Fontet and K. Mehlhorn. VI, 338 pages. 1984.